COMPREHENSIVE CLASSROOM MANAGEMENT

Creating Communities of Support and Solving Problems

Eleventh Edition

Vern Jones
Lewis & Clark College

Louise Jones
Retired from Beaverton School District and Lewis & Clark College

PEARSON

Boston   Columbus   Indianapolis   New York   San Francisco   Hoboken
Amsterdam   Cape Town   Dubai   London   Madrid   Milan   Munich   Paris   Montreal   Toronto
Delhi   Mexico City   Sao Paulo   Sydney   Hong Kong   Seoul   Singapore   Taipei   Tokyo

Vice President and Editorial Director: Jeffery W. Johnston
Vice President and Publisher: Kevin Davis
Editorial Assistant: Caitlin Griscom
Executive Field Marketing Manager: Krista Clark
Senior Product Marketing Manager: Christopher Barry
Project Manager: Lauren Carlson
Procurement Specialist: Carol Melville
Cover Designer: Jennifer Hart

Cover Art: ©Shutterstock/Marko Poplasen (top); ©Shutterstock/Jerry Portelli (bottom)
Full Service Project Management: Mohinder Singh/ Aptara®, Inc.
Printer/Binder: LSC Communications
Cover Printer: LSC Communications
Text Font: Janson Text

Credits and acknowledgments for materials borrowed from other sources and reproduced, with permission, in this textbook appear on appropriate page within text.

Every effort has been made to provide accurate and current Internet information in this book. However, the Internet and information posted on it are constantly changing, so it is inevitable that some of the Internet addresses listed in this textbook will change.

Library of Congress Cataloging-in-Publication Data
Jones, Vernon F.
  Comprehensive classroom management : creating communities of support and solving problems / Vern Jones, Lewis & Clark College, Louise Jones, Lewis & Clark College.—Eleventh edition.
      pages cm
  ISBN 0-13-414354-X
1. Classroom management.   2. Interaction analysis in education.   3. Motivation in education.   4. School discipline.
I. Jones, Louise S., 1949-   II. Title.
  LB3013.J66 2014
    371.102'4—dc23   2014028721

PEARSON

ISBN-10:   0-13-414354-X
ISBN-13: 978-0-13-414354-5

To the thousands of teachers and students whose ideas and responses to the materials in the book have enriched its content and have been a source of professional and personal satisfaction; to our children, Sarah, a wonderful mother and teacher; and Garrett, a gifted vegan/gluten-free baker and a compassionate and creative man; and to Vern's first mentor, Jere Brophy, who helped define the field of classroom management and was a model of a dedicated and gifted scholar.

About the Authors

Vern Jones, Ph.D., has been a junior high school teacher, a junior high school vice principal, and a district coordinator for students with emotional and behavioral disorders. He is Professor of Teacher Education in the Graduate School of Education and Counseling at Lewis & Clark College in Portland, Oregon. He received his Ph.D. in Counseling Psychology from the University of Texas.

Dr. Jones's other books include *Adolescents with Behavior Problems* (1980), *Responsible School Discipline* (1991), *Creating Effective Programs for Students with Emotional and Behavior Disorders* (2004), *Practical Classroom Management* (2011) and Prevention and Intervention for Students with Emotional and Behavioral Problems (2016)". He has written chapters in *Helping Teachers Manage Classrooms* (1982), *Management of Disruptive Pupil Behaviour in Schools* (1986), and *Severe Behavior Disorders of Children and Youth* (1987). He was selected by the National Association of Colleges of Teacher Education to write the chapter on classroom management for the *Handbook of Research on Teacher Education* (1996). He also wrote the chapter "How Do Teachers Learn to Be Effective Classroom Managers?" for the *Handbook of Classroom Management: Research, Practice, and Contemporary Issues* (2006). Dr. Jones is coauthor of the *State of Oregon Technical Assistance Paper on the Identification and Treatment of Seriously Emotionally Disturbed Students. Comprehensive Classroom Management* has been translated into Korean, Chinese, and Taiwanese.

From 1986 to 1989, Dr. Jones was cochair of the American Educational Research Association Special Interest Group on Classroom Management. Dr. Jones has served as Scholar in Residence at several universities. He won the Burlington Northern Award as Graduate School Teacher of the Year at Lewis & Clark College. He has given keynote addresses at state conferences in more than ten states and has consulted with school districts and staff in more than 25 states.

Louise Jones was a teacher in grades three through six for thirty-two years. She earned her master's degree from Lewis & Clark College, where, after retiring from teaching, for three years, she coordinated cohorts of twenty graduate students simultaneously earning their master's degrees and initial teaching licenses. Her graduate school teaching included courses on elementary school social studies methods, classroom management, and student teaching seminar. She has presented at regional and national workshops on creating positive classroom climates and has worked with school staff to develop schoolwide student management plans.

PREFACE

Purpose

Research clearly indicates that teachers are the single most important factor affecting student achievement (Haycock, 1998; Marzano, 2003). Research also supports the fact that classroom management skills are perhaps the most important set of teacher skills influencing student learning.

Faced with large class sizes, an increasing number of students who arrive at school experiencing considerable emotional stress, and classes in which students' academic and behavior skills vary widely, teachers are experiencing a heightened need for improving effectiveness in motivating and managing students. The movement toward increased inclusion of students with various disabilities and the growing number of students whose first language is not English have increased the complexity of teaching and effectively managing classrooms. Regardless of changes that may be made in the education system, schooling in the United States will not improve significantly unless teachers develop skills in the widely varied teaching methods generally described as classroom management.

Fortunately, technology in classroom management has kept pace with the increasing demands placed on teachers. Research in classroom management has grown explosively in the past forty years. Most teachers trained in the 1960s learned only such simple prescriptions as "don't smile until Christmas" and "don't grin until Thanksgiving." In recent years, however, thousands of articles and hundreds of thoughtful research projects have focused on student behavior and learning. The concept of school discipline, which had concentrated on dealing with inevitable student misbehavior, was replaced by the concept of classroom management, which emphasized methods of creating positive learning environments that facilitate responsible student behavior and achievement.

Our purpose is to provide the reader with specific strategies for creating positive, supportive, respectful environments that encourage all students to view themselves and learning in a positive light. Our heartfelt desire is that this book will increase each reader's ability to empower students to believe in themselves, understand the learning environment, and view the school as a place where their dignity is enhanced and where they can direct and take credit for their own learning. We agree with Mary McCaslin and Thomas Good (1992), who wrote:

> We believe that the intended modern school curriculum, which is designed to produce self-motivated, active learners, is seriously undermined by classroom management policies that encourage, if not demand, simple obedience. We advocate that a curriculum that seeks to promote problem solving and meaningful learning must be aligned with an authoritative management system that increasingly allows students to operate as self-regulated and risk-taking learners. (p. 4)

Although authors can provide research-proven methods and the theory that supports these methods, we realize that the teacher is the decision maker. We strongly believe (and the best current educational research supports) that in order to create schools that will help an increasing number of students succeed in life, educators must implement many of the methods presented throughout this book. We acknowledge and respect that teachers must consider each new approach in light of their personal styles and teaching situations; we also know that the methods in this book have proven effective for thousands of teachers. Engaging in thoughtful, reflective decision making before implementing a new approach is the sign of a competent professional; failing to incorporate methods proven effective with a wide range of students is irresponsible behavior.

Research Basis for the Materials Presented in This Book

Extensive research and experience went into the development of this book. The junior author taught elementary school for thirty-two years and then for five years taught classroom management and supervised student teachers at the college level. Over the past forty years, the senior author has been a middle school teacher, assistant principal, district-level special education coordinator, consultant in more than twenty-five states, and teacher educator teaching classroom management. He has chaired the American Educational Research Association's Special Interest Group on Classroom Management, written the chapter "Classroom Management" for the *Handbook of Research on Teacher Education* and the chapter "How Do Teachers Learn to Be Effective Classroom Managers?" in the *Handbook of Classroom Management: Research, Practice, and Contemporary Issues*—a 1,445-page compilation of classroom management research edited by Carolyn Evertson and Carol Weinstein (2006). The senior author has also written the books *Creating Effective Programs for Students with Emotional and Behavior Disorders* (2004) and *Practical Classroom Management* (2015) as well as numerous chapters and articles on classroom management. Each year, the senior author continues to teach classroom management to between sixty-five and seventy-five graduate school students who are completing a year-long school internship while earning their master's degree in a fourteen-month full-time program. The questions, concerns, and implementation of best practices by these bright young educators, and the questions and feedback during their first years of teaching, have significantly enriched the content in this book. In preparing for this book, the authors reviewed the 300 most recent articles as well as dissertations completed over the past five years on classroom management. In writing this eleventh edition, the authors also drew on the dozens of other studies conducted during the past forty years, ranging from the foundational work of Jere Brophy, the meta-analysis by Robert Marzano (2003), the aforementioned *Handbook of Classroom Management* (Evertson & Weinstein, 2006), the summary of research-supported practices for *Reducing Behavior Problems in the Elementary School Classroom* (Epstein, Atkins, Cullinan, Kutash, & Weaver, 2008), a summary of "Evidence-Based Practices in Classroom Management" (Simonsen, Gairbanks, Briesch, Myers, & Sugai, 2008), and dozens of other key research studies and summaries of these studies. The most important research, however, will be that which the reader conducts as he or she implements the methods described in this book. Effective classroom management is influenced by the context in which one teaches—including the unique needs and styles of the teacher and his or her students. Educators must conduct their own action research by implementing research-based methods and determining how these methods work most effectively within the context of their own classrooms and schools.

Throughout this edition of the book, we refer to brain-based research and its implications for effective classroom management and instruction. While great strides have been made in developing theoretical connections between current knowledge of the human brain and methods that support positive student behavior and learning, "The idea that applying this knowledge base to educational psychology to yield positive outcomes in the teaching and learning process sounds promising, however, there is a lack of empirical research conducted in K–12 classrooms to support the positive results of applying brain research to teaching practices" (Erbes, Folkerts, Gergis, Pederson, & Stivers, 2010, p. 120). It is therefore imperative that teachers and school district personnel conduct sound action research as they implement methods that have brain-based research as a primary support for their implementation.

New to This Edition

Updated material on the relationship between effective classroom management and PBIS

- New material on the how classroom management methods can support the creation of classrooms that are sensitive to students who have experienced trauma
- Updated discussion of brain-based research that supports classroom management methods
- Material on effectively using behavior specific feedback (praise)
- New material on the importance of creating positive, supportive peer relationships within the classroom and additional methods for creating these positive relationships
- Updated material on bullying and preventing bullying
- Methods for teaching students how to effectively respond to stress and frustration they experience in the classroom
- Methods for dealing with students' use of electronic devices in the classroom
- New methods on using student choice to enhance motivation and academic success
- Methods for implementing peer tutoring
- New methods for preventing and responding to student behavior that disrupts the learning environment
- New ideas and methods on using reinforcement in the classroom
- Updated material on the use of zero tolerance and suspensions
- New methods for classroom teachers conducting a functional behavior assessment
- Updated materials on using the "check-in-check-out" procedure and other forms of contracts
- Ten interactive reviews that enable the reader to test their knowledge of the content by applying it to classroom scenarios

Audience

This book is for preservice and in-service teachers, counselors, administrators, school psychologists, and special educators. Its comprehensive and research-based presentation offers practical ideas for creating positive classroom and school climates, organizing and managing classrooms, improving instruction, dealing with classroom discipline problems, developing individualized plans for students experiencing persistent or serious behavioral problems, and developing schoolwide student management programs. These ideas enable educators in their various roles to understand the broad issues and specific skills involved in effective classroom and schoolwide student management and to work collegially in responding to unproductive student behavior.

The concepts and strategies presented in this book will assist educators who work with a wide range of students. They stem from research and have been field-tested by thousands of teachers who work with students who are African American, Hispanic, Native American, Asian, Caucasian, poor, rich, learning disabled, emotionally disturbed, and talented and gifted. Educators who work with students at risk for school failure will find these methods essential to their students' success.

Approach

Materials used to educate teachers and administrators have too often focused on isolated aspects of effective instruction and management. To develop a realistic, workable approach to classroom management, educators have had to seek out and integrate information from literally dozens of sources—many of which have claimed to provide "the answer." This eleventh edition of *Comprehensive Classroom Management* offers a thorough research-based synthesis of current knowledge in effective classroom management. Extensive review of the research and our own experiences in classrooms highlight five major factors or skill areas involved in effective classroom management:

1. Developing a solid understanding of students' personal/psychological and learning needs
2. Establishing positive teacher–student and peer relationships that help meet students' basic psychological needs, building a community of support within the classroom, and extending this to involve students' caregivers
3. Using organizational and group management methods that maximize on-task student behavior that supports learning
4. Implementing instructional methods that facilitate optimal learning by responding to the academic needs of individual students and the classroom group
5. Using a wide range of counseling and behavioral methods that involve students in examining and correcting behavior that negatively affects their own learning or that of other students

This emphasis on providing a variety of specific methods to consider does not, however, imply that teachers should implement these methods by rote. We believe that teachers should (and will) implement recommendations selectively, attending to their own teaching styles, learning goals, students' needs, and other context variables. As Brophy and Evertson (1976) stated:

> Effective teaching requires the ability to implement a very large number of diagnostic, instructional, managerial, and therapeutic skills, tailoring behavior in specific contexts and situations to the specific needs of the moment. Effective teachers not only must be able to do a large number of things; they also must be able to recognize which of the many things they know how to do applies at a given moment and be able to follow through by performing the behavior effectively. (p. 139)

We have stayed away from providing a cookbook of what to do if Johnny cheats or steals because we agree with Allen Mendler (1992), who wrote:

> It will never be possible to compile a list of all possible techniques to be used when problem behaviors occur. Formulas fail to fit all situations. It is therefore more important that educators be guided by a sound set of principles and guidelines from which they can use existing strategies or develop new ones. (p. 26)

Unlike several classroom management texts, this text does more than merely summarize the work of leading classroom management theorists and suggest that educators examine their own behavior in light of someone's theory. We believe teachers need to examine and integrate specific, research-based methods into their approach to creating supportive learning environments that maximize the learning gains for all students. Because we strongly believe all educators should have access to this basis for their decision making, throughout the text we have listed references to support our statements and recommendations. While most readers will choose not to examine these while reading the text, they provide important support for the methods recommended throughout the text.

As mentioned earlier, our approach places a major emphasis on creating positive learning environments and empowering students to understand and be actively involved in classroom management and instruction. We strongly believe that a significant number of serious management problems are responses to the manner in which students are treated as human beings and the types of instructional tasks they are asked to perform.

The methods presented in this book have been used by us and by numerous teachers whom we have taught and with whom we have worked during the past forty years. The methods have been field-tested by teachers in thousands of classrooms evenly divided among primary, intermediate, middle, and high school settings. These settings include classrooms in inner-city, rural, and suburban schools.

The first edition of this book was published more than thirty years ago. We are delighted and rewarded by the fact that most of the current "best accepted practice" in classroom management is consistent with the model we presented then and have continued to present. The Positive Behavior Support model presented by George Sugai and his colleagues (Sugai, Horner, & Gresham, 2002) includes most of the components found in our text since its first edition in 1981. Similarly, Jerome Freiberg's (1996) "Consistency Management" and Cooperative Discipline model, which has proved so successful, emphasizes creating a caring community of support; having students develop classroom norms; giving students responsibility for running the classroom and school; implementing interactive, meaningful learning experiences; and reinforcing students. Evelyn Schneider's (1996) "Educational Responsibility" involves building a community, giving students choices, and increasing student academic success. William Glasser's (1990) *The Quality School: Managing Students without Coercion* and Curwin and Mendler's (1988) *Discipline with Dignity* focus on creating schools and responding to misbehavior in ways that enhance students' sense of personal value and efficacy. The kind of teacher behavior and learning environments Gloria Ladson-Billings (1994) speaks of in *The Dreamkeepers* and Crystal Kuykendall (2004) writes about in *From Rage to Hope* that help African American and Latino children succeed are similar to the methods presented in this book. Deborah Meier's (1995) work at the Central Park East Schools in New York, Anne Ratzki's (1988) work with German schools, Barbara Ries Wager's (1993) work at James P. B. Duffy School No. 12 in New York, and the schooling Linda Darling-Hammond (1997) describes in *The Right to Learn* all have much in common with the vision we have shared over the past thirty years.

We celebrate the fact that there is increasing agreement among writers, researchers, teachers, administrators, and parents regarding the factors that are associated with creating classroom and school communities that enable virtually all children to experience a community of support that enhances their academic and personal lives. We believe this book will enrich you on your journey to integrate these methods into your classroom and school.

It is our heartfelt wish and prayer that the materials in this book will assist you and your colleagues in creating positive, nurturing environments for students from all ability levels; socioeconomic classes; ethnic groups; and with varied personal, social, developmental, and intellectual backgrounds. In addition, we hope this book will increase the enjoyment and rewards you experience in the incredibly important job of educating children and adolescents.

How to Use This Text

Compared to many texts on classroom management, this text is quite long and detailed. Our goal is to provide readers with a truly comprehensive, research-based, and practical source for implementing effective classroom management methods in their classroom. Since we wrote one of the first classroom management books in 1981, many authors have followed suit with much shorter and less comprehensive books that may be easier to read for students who have limited time to study this topic. We have continued, however, to present a more detailed, practical approach, trusting the professors who use this book will select activities that highlight key concepts they believe can be mastered within the time limitations they and their students experience.

Sadly, teaching is perhaps the only profession many people believe one can practice without extensive training. We have all heard and read many statements to the effect that if someone knows the content, he or she should be able to teach it in public schools. We would not want to be operated on, have dental work completed by, be defended in court by, or drive across a bridge designed by someone without extensive and detailed knowledge of the skills those in their profession deem essential for effectively practicing the profession. However, we often provide teachers with extremely limited knowledge and skills in critical areas of the profession and then wonder why students are too often failing in our public schools.

In order to provide students with an opportunity to select when and how to apply the material in this text, we have inserted numerous "Pause & Consider" activities throughout the book. We certainly do not expect every reader to complete all of these. Our hope is that professors and readers who use this text will select those they believe will meet their immediate instructional goals and will return to others as they continue their professional journey.

In short, we trust professors and students to use this book in a manner that will provide teachers and future teachers with key knowledge and skills, while also returning to this text as a resource as they continue to implement best practices in classroom management.

Acknowledgments

We wish to acknowledge the many teachers whose application of the methods presented in *Comprehensive Classroom Management* have validated their effectiveness. We thank Susan Foster, Peter Grauff, Heather Lilley, Dean Long, Lisa Stevens, Marjorie Miller Tonole, and Terri Vann for allowing us to use student behavior change projects they completed in our graduate classes. We also thank our daughter, Sarah Rudzek, for her editing and many suggestions in Chapter 5.

We want to thank Lynn Reer, who shared her ideas for working with second language learners. She has committed decades of passionate work to creating better school environments for these students. Finally, we would like to thank our daughter, Sarah, who shared ideas she generated to help her diverse first grade and fourth/fifth blend classes during her first six years of teaching.

We would also like to thank the reviewers of this edition for their helpful comments: Susan Edington, Murray State University; Joan S. Lawson, Hudson Valley Community College; Doug MacIsaac, Stetson University; and Bettie Willingham, Barton College.

Brief Contents

CONTENTS

xii

FOUNDATIONS OF COMPREHENSIVE CLASSROOM MANAGEMENT

It is very likely you considered teaching as a profession because you envisioned yourself as creating a supportive community of learners, helping students better understand themselves and the world around them, and facilitating students' developing knowledge and skills to be sensitive, thoughtful, productive members of a diverse and changing society. While these are demanding times for public school personnel—funding problems create obstacles to reaching these goals—the good news is the manner in which you approach classroom management can be a significant factor in enabling you to overcome these obstacles and reach these important goals.

Part 1 is directed toward alleviating the confusion associated with the topic of classroom management and helping you develop an understanding of classroom management that can serve as a foundation for your efforts to ensure that all students successfully master key social and academic skills. Chapter 1 places the concept of classroom management in perspective by examining the extent of the problem, considering the reasons for an increase in problems associated with student behavior, describing historical and recent trends in classroom management, defining comprehensive classroom management, and discussing the relationship between classroom management and teachers' professional needs. Chapter 2 examines personal needs that must be met for students to become productively involved in the learning process. Classroom management strategies have too often overemphasized controlling unproductive student behavior and, more recently, teaching students appropriate behavior and reinforcing them for displaying this behavior rather than creating environments that meet students' personal/psychological/learning needs and therefore encourage productive behavior. The concepts in Chapter 2 provide a foundation for refocusing attention on creating learning environments that support positive student behavior.

After completing Part 1, you should understand why discipline problems arise and the factors that can be examined and implemented in order to reduce these problems. This perspective provides a foundation for assisting you in analyzing your own classroom or school environment creatively and evaluating how you might implement the ideas presented in this book or create new solutions for dealing with the behavior problems that occur in your classroom or school. Understanding the theoretical and research base associated with the field of classroom management will also help you be a better consumer of the various classroom and schoolwide behavior management methods presented to you during your professional career.

CHAPTER 1

CLASSROOM MANAGEMENT IN PERSPECTIVE

The findings show that teachers who approach classroom management as a process of establishing and maintaining effective learning environments tend to be more successful than teachers who place more emphasis on their roles as authority figures or disciplinarians.

—Thomas L. Good and Jere Brophy (2008)

Classroom management can and should do more than elicit predictable obedience; indeed, it can and should be one vehicle for the enhancement of student self-understanding, self-evaluation, and the internalization of self-control.

—Mary McCaslin and Thomas L. Good (1992)

No other topic in education receives greater attention or causes more concerns for teachers and parents and students than classroom discipline. . . . The lack of effective classroom discipline or behavior management skills is the major stumbling block to a successful career in teaching.

—Nicholas Long, Ruth Newman, and William Morse (1996)

Management must be presented in an intellectual framework for understanding classroom events and consequences rather than simply as a collection of tricks and specific reactions to behavior.

—Walter Doyle (1986)

The ways we organize classroom life should seek to make children feel significant and cared about—by the teacher and by each other. Unless students feel emotionally and physically safe, they won't share real thoughts and feelings. Discussions will be tinny and dishonest. We need to design activities where students learn to trust and care for each other. Classroom life should, to the greatest extent possible, pre-figure the kind of democratic and just society we envision, and thus contribute to building that society. Together students and teachers can create a "community of conscience," as educators Asa Hilliard and George Pine call it.

—Bill Bigelow, Stan Karp, and Wayne Au (2007)

Classroom management is an enterprise of creating conditions for student involvement in curricular events. . . . The emphasis is on cooperation, engagement, and motivation, and on students learning to be part of a dynamic system, rather than on compliance, control and coercion.

—David Osher, George Bear, Jeffrey Sprague, and Walter Doyle (2010)

At every level of prevention, effective instructional and classroom management practices provide the foundation for youth engagement and learning, which in return is associated with decreases in problem behaviors.

—Gregory Benner, Krista Kutash, J. Ron Nelson, and Marie Fisher (2013)

Teaching is a profession. Effective teachers are reflective practitioners who constantly seek to analyze the impact their behavior has on the success of those they serve. While we may wish that the conditions under which we work were ideal or the students with whom we work experienced less trauma in their lives, our focus must remain on how our decisions and behaviors can positively impact our students. It is also our responsibility as professional educators to move beyond simply implementing prefabricated methods to truly understanding, analyzing, reflecting on, and constantly improving our decisions in order to assist all students to find joy in learning and to maximize their potential. In the area of classroom management, this includes having a deep understanding of the field and the reasons we choose the methods we use.

LEARNING GOALS

After reading this chapter, you will know:

1. Why teachers are concerned about student behavior and the need for effective classroom management
2. The factors involved in effective classroom management
3. The historical trends in classroom management
4. The significant impact school variables have on student behavior and learning
5. The factors that influence teachers' decisions regarding classroom management

Why Are These Goals Important?

Research indicates that teachers' skills in creating safe, supportive classrooms are a major factor influencing students' motivation, achievement, and behavior. In March 1984, a ten-member Panel on the Preparation of Beginning Teachers, chaired by Ernest L. Boyer, the president of the Carnegie Foundation for the Advancement of Teaching, issued a report listing three major areas of expertise needed by beginning teachers:

1. Knowledge of how to manage a classroom
2. Knowledge of subject matter
3. Understanding of their students' sociological backgrounds

Ten years later, Wang, Haertel, and Walberg (1993) conducted a sophisticated data analysis of factors influencing student learning and identified classroom management as being the most important factor. Another decade later, issues of effective classroom management were highlighted by research studies as a key to effective student learning (Marzano, 2003; Shinn, Stoner, & Walker, 2002). In a *Los Angeles Times* article, Randi Weingarten, the president of the American Federation of Teachers, stated that the management of student behavior was one of the most complex aspects of teaching and the most difficult skill for many teachers to master. In this same article, U.S. Education Secretary Arne Duncan criticized U.S. teacher education programs for their failure to prepare teachers, partly because graduates of these programs lacked classroom management skills (Mehta, 2009).

Research suggests that skills in classroom management are a significant factor in enhancing student achievement in a variety of content areas (Deickmann, 2009; Frazer-Abder, 2010) and in schools serving very diverse students (National School Climate Council, 2007; Poplin et al., 2011 ; Ratcliff et al., 2010). The concept of discipline, with its emphasis on dealing with inevitable misbehavior among students, has for many years now been replaced by a more comprehensive body of knowledge that also emphasizes the importance of increasing students' positive behavior and achievement by creating classroom communities in which students' personal and academic needs are met (Brophy, 2004).

CONCERNS ABOUT STUDENT BEHAVIOR AND THE NEED FOR IMPROVED TEACHER KNOWLEDGE AND SKILLS IN CLASSROOM MANAGEMENT

PAUSE & CONSIDER 1.1

Before reading this section, stop for a minute and write a response to the questions "What is it about teaching that most interests and excites me, and what am I most concerned about?" Share your response with colleagues or fellow students in a course you are taking.

Student behavior problems have for years been a major concern of parents, teachers, and administrators. After many years of rating discipline as the second biggest concern about America's schools, the 2014 Phi Delta Kappa/Gallup Poll of Public Attitudes Toward Public Schools reported that the American public listed discipline third behind "lack of financial support" and "concerns about educational standards" (Bushaw & Calderon, 2014).

© George Abbott

"So, other than that, how was your first day as a teacher?"

The public's concerns about student behavior appear well grounded. Based on an extensive review of the literature, several leaders in the field of serving students with emotional and behavioral disorders recently indicated that at any one time at least 12 percent of students in K–12 classrooms have a relatively serious behavioral and emotional disorder, and 20 percent experience mild to serious problems in this area (Forness, Kim, & Walker, 2012). Researchers have reported that 58 percent of classroom time allocated for instruction is lost due to student behavior that disrupts their learning and that of others (Martella, Nelson, Marchand-Martella, & O'Reilly, 2012).

© Joyce Button

"I can't tell you what a relief it is to relax after a year of teaching!"

These are significant numbers that help explain why many teachers report students with ongoing and serious behavior problems are their greatest concern (Burkman, 2012), and classroom management is the area where they most need additional training (He & Cooper, 2011; Reinke, Stormont, Herman, Puri, & Goel, 2011). In one study, 34 percent of teachers agreed or strongly agreed that student behavior problems interfered with their teaching (National Center for Education Statistics, 2010). An anonymous survey of 3,000 teachers in 48 states conducted by the American Psychological Association Task Force on Violence Directed Against Teachers found that 80 percent of teachers reported some form of victimization during the previous year, and 94 percent of these were caused by students. Of these experiences, 44 percent of teachers experienced physical attacks, 50 percent reported property loss or damage, and 72 percent reported some form of verbal harassment (Espelage et al., 2013).

Perhaps not surprising given these numbers, a study reported that more than one-third of teachers indicate they know a colleague who quit teaching because of discipline issues (Goodman, 2007). In a 2006 poll of teachers and administrators conducted for MetLife, one in five teachers indicated they were not prepared to maintain order in their classrooms, and teachers who were leaving the field were significantly more likely to state they felt unprepared in classroom management. Beginning teachers continue to indicate they received little effective training in classroom management (Brevik, 2009; Kuster, Bain, Newton, & Milbrandt, 2010). This is understandable given that, based on a survey of ten large universities with nationally recognized teacher preparation programs in elementary education, only three had a specific course on classroom management (Shook, 2012). Until initial teacher preparation in classroom management is improved and ongoing in-service work in this area becomes more common and better grounded in best practices, issues of student behavior will continue to be a major factor in teacher burnout (Durr, 2008), and principals will continue to identify classroom management as a major area of weakness for new teachers (Merkel, 2009; Smolnisky, 2009).

Concerns about student behavior and classroom management do more than create stress for teachers and very likely limit the number of teachers who enter teaching or remain in teaching for an extended period of time. In addition, these concerns often cause teachers to limit their use of instructional methods that actively engage students in the learning process (Lotan, 2006). If teachers are to implement engaging, meaningful instructional activities that enhance student motivation and higher-level thinking skills, teachers must become comfortable with their classroom management skills.

While much progress has been made in providing teachers with skills and systems for preventing and responding effectively to student behavior that disrupts the learning environment, many teachers continue to believe factors beyond their control are keys to student behavior.

Participants in our study attributed student behavior to unalterable variables such as internal student characteristics and family dynamics. These attributions of student behavior appeared to affect teachers' decision-making processes and thereby their daily practices. (Feuerborn & Chinn, 2012, p. 227)

Even though social factors have made the teacher's job more challenging, studies indicate that teachers and schools make a dramatic difference in the lives of many children. Schools and teachers working with similar student populations differ dramatically in their ability to help students develop desirable behaviors and increase students' achievements. A U.S. Department of Education publication (2000) stated: "Studies indicate that approximately four of every five disruptive students can be traced to some dysfunction in the way schools are organized, staff members are trained, or schools are run" (p. 10). Research also indicates teachers who are involved in in-service classroom management work can dramatically improve their classroom management skills. In one study of fourteen teachers who received support in improving classroom management, thirteen of these teachers reduced student misbehavior in their classrooms by an average of 71 percent (Nard, 2007).

This text was written with the express intent of providing the kind of research-based, practical support that will help both preservice and in-service teachers significantly improve their classroom management skills and thus reduce disruptive student behavior and improve student learning. These types of improvements are best supported by learning communities in which teachers are actively involved in analyzing their practices, discussing developments with other educators, and collecting data on the outcomes associated with incorporating the methods they develop to improve their classroom management skills (Casey, 2009). The Pause & Consider sections interspersed throughout this book are intended to increase your active engagement with the content and to encourage you to support this by interacting with your colleagues.

UNDERSTANDING CLASSROOM MANAGEMENT

After reading the next section, you should have a better understanding of past and future trends in the field of classroom management and the multiple methods you will need to consider as you plan to develop a safe, supportive learning community.

PAUSE & CONSIDER 1.2

Take a few minutes to write your own definition of effective classroom management. What classroom management skills do you believe effective teachers demonstrate? What attitudes and behaviors characterize educators who are effective at helping students develop and commit to using responsible, caring behavior in classroom and school settings? You might think about teachers you had who were very effective at creating this type of environment. What was it about them and what they did that helped to create this supportive environment where almost all students made good choices? If possible, share these ideas with a group of fellow students or colleagues. After completing this text or course, revisit what you wrote and discussed in this activity and write a new definition that incorporates your new ideas and understandings.

The Authors' Basic Assumptions about Classroom Management

Based on our extensive review of the research and our experience in the field, six basic assumptions organize our beliefs and practices related to classroom management.

1. Effective classroom management is first and foremost about creating classroom environments in which *all* students feel safe and valued. Only in this type of environment are students able to maximize their learning of important social and academic skills. When teachers and students create these types of classroom settings, students make a high percentage of good choices and their learning is enhanced.

2. Effective classroom management is closely connected to effective instruction. Students will tend to act responsibly and their learning will be enhanced when they are successfully and actively engaged in constructing meaningful, culturally relevant knowledge and skills.

3. Effective classroom management methods should enhance students' sense of ownership, responsibility, and personal efficacy. This includes teachers incorporating into their decision making regarding instruction and behavior management an understanding and respect for their students' cultural backgrounds and their families' and communities' beliefs, norms, values, and traditions.

4. Effective classroom management involves methods for helping students develop new behavioral skills that can assist them in working collaboratively and successfully with others.

5. Effective classroom management requires teachers to thoughtfully consider their goals for students as well as their own values and beliefs about working with students.

6. Effective classroom management involves thoughtful planning and focused professional growth. It is both a very personal and a very professional activity that requires that teachers integrate their own professional knowledge and skills with careful attention to their own personal beliefs and values and students' wants and needs—including students' developmental and learning needs and cultural values.

THE COMPONENTS OF COMPREHENSIVE CLASSROOM MANAGEMENT

Jere Brophy (1988) provided a thoughtful, general definition of classroom management when he wrote:

> Good classroom management implies not only that the teacher has elicited the cooperation of the students in minimizing misconduct and can intervene effectively when misconduct occurs, but also that worthwhile academic activities are occurring more or less continuously and that the classroom management system as a whole (which includes, but is not limited to, the teacher's disciplinary interventions) is designed to maximize student engagement in those activities, not merely to minimize misconduct. (p. 3)

More recently, Osher et al. (2010) have indicated, "There are at least four social and emotional conditions for learning—emotional and physical safety, connectedness, authentic challenges, and a responsible peer climate" (p. 55). Adkins-Coleman (2010) adds that "culturally responsible classroom management requires that teachers set high expectations for students, ensure that students meet their expectations, and maintain a caring, structured, cooperative classroom environment that addresses students' lived experiences and cultural backgrounds" (p. 41). We believe effective classroom management must ensure that all these conditions are met, and in order to do so, suggest that comprehensive classroom management includes five areas of knowledge and skill:

1. *Classroom management will be most effective when it is based on a solid understanding of current research and theory in classroom management and students' personal and psychological needs (Chapters 1 and 2).*

    Just as physicians must understand a great deal about the human body in order to effectively implement the many specific skills necessary to help their patients, teachers will be more effective when they understand the theoretical and research support for the classroom management methods they implement.

2. *Classroom management requires that teachers create positive personal relationships and a community of support in the classroom by establishing positive teacher–student and peer relationships and having positive involvement with students' caregivers* (Chapters 3, 4, and 5).

   The value of establishing positive, supportive classroom environments is based on a concept presented by numerous psychologists, neuroscientists, and educators: Individuals learn effectively in environments where they experience a sense of being known, valued, and cared for and where they, therefore, feel safe and supported.

3. *Classroom management involves helping students develop and commit to behavior standards that support a physically and psychologically safe classroom learning environment. It also involves teachers' using organizational and group management methods that facilitate a safe, calm, smooth-flowing classroom structure* (Chapter 6).

   This is perhaps the most well researched aspect of effective classroom management, and the development of behavior standards is the most commonly implemented approach to classroom management.

4. *Classroom management includes teachers' using instructional methods that facilitate optimal learning by responding to the academic needs of individual students and the classroom group* (Chapter 7).

   Active student engagement in meaningful work at which the student is successful plays a major role in increasing students' motivation to learn, on-task behavior, and learning.

5. *Classroom management requires that teachers have the ability to respond effectively when students behave in ways that detract from their own learning and that of others* (Chapters 8, 9, and 10).

   Given that disruptions will occur even in the most supportive, well-organized, and academically engaging classrooms, it is imperative that teachers possess methods for responding in ways that respectfully refocus the student while maintaining a smooth flow to classroom instruction. Comprehensive classroom management involves a commitment to and skills in responding to an individual student's ongoing classroom behavior problems by analyzing the classroom environment, making changes to support the student, and helping the student develop skills for making responsible behavior choices within the classroom.

   While combining all components of effective classroom management will enhance the learning and behavior of all students, it seems particularly important when working with students who have historically struggled academically and behaviorally (Kennedy, 2011). It also appears that these components of effective management interact so that to some extent they are dependent on each other.

   Another way to conceptualize a comprehensive approach to classroom management is to consider various levels or a sequence for classroom management interventions. Hill Walker and his colleagues (Walker et al., 1996) developed a three-staged model for serving students with emotional and behavior problems. This model, initially developed by the Office of Juvenile Justice and Delinquency Prevention (OJJDP) (1995) as a recommended approach for addressing the problems of youth offenders has also been used as a model for preventing mental disorders in school-age children (Greenberg, Domitrovich, & Bumbarger, 2001) and is a key component in the Positive Behavioral Interventions and Supports approach. Figure 1.1 presents this type of sequential approach as it relates to classroom management.

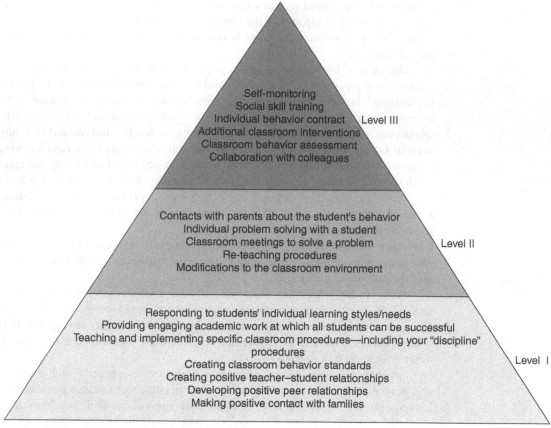

FIGURE 1.1
CLASSROOM DISCIPLINE PROCEDURE

Pause & Consider 1.3

Take a moment to review the six key factors in comprehensive classroom management. Where are you most comfortable in your skills regarding comprehensive classroom management? What areas most concern you or do you view as important for your professional growth?

Just as teachers must be able to effectively differentiate instruction, they must be able to use multiple methods to help all students behave in ways that support their own learning and that of their classmates. By having this type of classroom management system available for all students, when these supports are provided to students who have been or may be considered for eligibility under the Individuals with Disabilities Education Act (IDEA), the teacher may implement these methods because they are no different than what is used with any child needing behavioral instruction within the general education classroom. Many relatively simple yet effective approaches are available for helping students examine and change their behaviors. Because teachers are increasingly faced with the task of teaching students who require special assistance in consistently behaving in ways that support the learning of all students in the classroom, it has become necessary that teachers acquire skills in implementing all aspects associated with comprehensive classroom management.

When faced with problems concerning students' classroom behaviors, teachers too often intervene using disciplinary responses without carefully considering interpersonal relationships or the organizational and instructional changes that could be made in the classroom to increase positive student behavior and learning. A U.S. Department of Education publication (2000) stated: "Studies indicate that approximately four of every five disruptive students can be traced to some dysfunction in the way schools are organized, staff members are trained, or schools are run" (p. 10). Ennis and McCauley (2002) examined the methods eighteen teachers in urban classrooms used to successfully assist struggling students. These authors reported that the methods included "creating a curriculum and class environment that permitted many opportunities for engagement, provided positive interactions, encouraged the development of shared curriculum, and fostered student ownership" (p. 149). The teachers in this study also involved students in developing classroom behavior standards and had positive, supportive relationships with their students. In a study of effective classroom management in urban schools, Ullucci (2009) reported similar findings.

THE HISTORY OF CLASSROOM MANAGEMENT RESEARCH AND PRACTICE

Teacher–Student Relationships and Counseling Approaches

Because the emphasis in psychology during the late 1960s and early 1970s was on personal growth and awareness, often termed *humanistic psychology*, most methods focused on understanding students' problems and helping them better understand themselves and work cooperatively with adults to develop more productive behaviors.

Emphasis on humanistic psychology was most obvious in the models of self-concept theorists. This research was first widely reported in the late 1960s and early 1970s in books such as LaBenne and Green's *Educational Implications of Self-Concept Theory* (1969) and William Purkey's *Self-Concept and School Achievement* (1970). This work was extended to a more practical program for teachers by Tom Gordon (1974), whose *Teacher Effectiveness Training* provided them with techniques for responding to students' behavioral errors with open communication and problem solving.

One of the earliest and most widely used problem-solving models was William Glasser's reality therapy (1965). Glasser's model derived from the belief that young people need caring professionals willing to help them take responsibility for their behavior and develop plans aimed at altering unproductive conduct. Rudolf Dreikurs and his associates (Dreikurs, Grunwald, & Pepper, 1971) developed a model based on the belief that acting-out children made poor choices because of inappropriate notions of how to meet their basic need to be accepted. Dreikurs proposed a variety of methods for responding to children's misconduct, depending on the goal of the behavior. His model provided teachers and parents with strategies for identifying the causes of students' misbehavior, responding to misbehavior with logical consequences, and running family and classroom meetings. In the early to mid-1990s, the focus on students' needs and problem solving continued with books such as Glasser's *Quality School* (1990), Brendtro, Brokenleg, and Van Bockem's *Reclaiming Youth at Risk* (1990), Curwin and Mendler's *Discipline with Dignity* (1988), Mendler's *What Do I Do When . . . ? How to Achieve Discipline with Dignity in the Classroom* (1992), and Fay and Funk's *Teaching with Love and Logic* (1995).

The third major research area within the teacher–student relationship and counseling approach was the more data-based analysis of how the frequency and quality of teacher–student interactions affected student achievement. Robert Rosenthal and Lenore Jacobson's *Pygmalion in the Classroom* (1968) reported that teachers' expectations for students' performance became self-fulfilling prophecies. In other words, students seem to perform as teachers expect them to. The important question

© Martha F. Campbell

"I've tried various forms of discipline, and I find that radio control works best."

became what, specifically, teachers do to communicate high or low expectations to students. This question was initially studied by Brophy and Good (1971, 1974) at the University of Texas and led to recommendations and professional development on positive expectation effects (Cooper & Good, 1983), and providing students with behavior-specific praise (Brophy, 1981).

Teachers' Organizational and Management Skills

The initial study on the importance of teachers' organizational and management skills was reported in Jacob Kounin's 1970 book, *Discipline and Group Management in Classrooms.* Kounin's study involved videotaping many hours (285 videotaped lessons) in classrooms that ran smoothly with a minimum of disruptive behavior and classrooms in which students were frequently inattentive and disruptive. The videotapes were then systematically analyzed to determine what teachers in these two very different types of classrooms did differently when students misbehaved. The results showed no systematic differences. Effective classroom managers were not notably different from poor classroom managers in their ways of responding to disruptive student behavior. Further analysis, however, demonstrated how effective classroom managers used various teaching methods that prevented disruptive student behavior.

The Texas Teacher Effectiveness Study was a second landmark study dealing with organizing and managing behavior. In this study, reported in *Learning from Teaching* by Jere Brophy and Carolyn Evertson (1976), the researchers observed fifty-nine teachers over two years. Teachers were selected to provide two groups: teachers who were very effective at increasing student achievement and those whose students consistently made relatively poor academic progress. Classroom observations focused on teachers' behaviors previously suggested as being related to effective teaching. The results of the study supported Kounin's, that specific teacher behaviors were strongly related to student academic achievement and positive school behavior.

Kounin's and Brophy and Evertson's findings were expanded by Emmer, Evertson, and Anderson (1980) in the Classroom Organization and Effective Teaching Project carried out at the Research and Development Center for Teacher Education at the University of Texas at Austin. In the first of a series of studies, these researchers observed twenty-eight third-grade classrooms during the first several weeks of school. The research findings showed that the smooth functioning found throughout the school year in effective teachers' classrooms was heavily influenced by effective planning and organization during the first few weeks of school. Effective classroom managers provided students with clear instruction in desirable classroom behavior, carefully monitored students' performance, and spent time reteaching behaviors that students had not mastered. Effective teachers also made consequences for misbehavior clear and applied these consequences consistently.

This study was followed by research in junior high school classrooms (Evertson, 1985; Evertson & Emmer, 1982a), which verified the importance of early planning and effectively teaching rules and procedures to all students. Carolyn Evertson has continued this pioneer work, and her Classroom Organization and Management Program (COMP) provides instructional modules for helping teachers organize and effectively run classrooms. Studies by Jerome Freiberg (1999), Ron Nelson and others (Nelson, Martella, & Galand, 1998), and the Positive Behavioral Interventions and Supports work (Lewis & Newcomer, 2005; Lewis, Newcomer, Trussell, & Richter, 2006) have reinforced the importance of teaching desired behavior and establishing agreed-on behavior standards.

Instructional Skills

A third area of investigation on teacher behavior that prevents disruptive student behavior and enhances learning examines how teachers engage students in the learning process. Some of the earliest work on this subject was conducted by Madeline Hunter. For more than two decades, her Instructional Theory into Practice (ITIP) program attempted to translate findings in educational psychology into practical strategies that improved instruction. Though her work emphasizes some of the skills high-lighted by researchers studying classroom organization and teacher–student relationships, her major contribution was in helping teachers understand the need to develop clear instructional goals, state these to students, provide effective direct instruction, and monitor students' progress.

This research was expanded by studies that examined the relationship between various teacher instructional patterns and students' achievement. Often called process-product research because it examines correlations between instructional processes and student outcomes or products, these studies were thoughtfully reviewed by Rosenshine (1983).

Another area of study examined the relative merits of competitive, cooperative, and individualized instruction. Carried out by David Johnson and Roger Johnson (2009), this work demonstrates that cooperative learning activities are associated with many desirable learning outcomes. Students who work cooperatively on learning tasks tend to relate more positively to their peers, to view learning as more positive, and to learn more information. Additional work in cooperative team learning was carried out by Robert Slavin (1995, 1996), who developed the teams-games-tournaments approach, and by Spencer Kagan (2009), who developed a practical book entitled *Cooperative Learning: Resources for Teachers*.

Researchers have also examined factors influencing how individual students learn most effectively and how teachers can adjust instruction to respond to students' individual learning styles. Work by Rita Dunn and others (Dunn & DeBello, 1999; Dunn, Thies, & Honigsfeld, 2001) has shown that when teachers allow students to study in environments modified to respond to students' varying learning preferences, students, including those with special learning needs, learn more and behave in ways that facilitate their learning and that of others. Howard Gardner's work on multiple intelligences (1999b, 2006) has suggested there are at least eight types of intelligence. Gardner suggests that teachers should attempt to adapt instruction and assessment to respond in some ways to each child's individual strengths. He also suggests that teachers will be more effective in enhancing student achievement when they help students relate instructional activities to something valued in the students' world.

More recently, several new methods have been presented to increase teachers' ability to assist students in obtaining academic skills. Response to Intervention (RTI) is an approach where student mastery of specific learning objectives is carefully assessed and usually highly structured instructional interventions are implemented to enhance student mastery

(Northwest Education, 2008). A second approach, called Place-Based Education, enhances students' engagement in the learning process by integrating multiple content areas as students study issues and solve problems in their communities (Smith, 2002).

Behavioristic Methods/Positive Behavioral Interventions and Supports

As social uneasiness rose about disruptive behavior of youth, the focus of classroom discipline moved in the direction of teacher control. This increased attention to discipline was associated with the development and popularization of behavioristic methodology. Beginning in the mid-1970s, most courses that aimed at helping teachers cope with disruptive student behavior focused almost exclusively on behavior modification techniques. Teachers were taught to ignore inappropriate behavior while reinforcing appropriate behavior, to write contracts with recalcitrant students, and to use time-out procedures. This emphasis on control was most systematically presented to teachers in Canter and Canter's (1976) *Assertive Discipline*. Teachers learned to state clear general behavioral expectations, quietly and consistently punish disruptive students, and provide group reinforcement for on-task behavior. Behavioral control has also been emphasized in the work of Fredric Jones (1987). Jones focuses on teachers' effective use of body language, the use of incentive systems, and individual assistance for academic problems.

In recent years, the most noted approach emphasizing data collection and focused behavioral interventions with students is termed *Positive Behavioral Interventions and Supports*. This approach incorporates much of the work from earlier studies in effective classroom management.

Given the popularity of School-Wide Positive Behavioral Interventions and Supports (SWPBIS)—more than 15,000 schools are implementing the approach—it is important to describe the relationship between the materials presented in this text and the SWPBIS approach. SWPBIS is a thoughtful, systematic compilation of a variety of methods, including the seminal work on teaching students rules and procedures (Evertson, 1985; Evertson & Emmer, 1982a; Evertson & Harris, 1995), the focus on data collection (Duke, 1980), and the emphasis on ensuring that discipline interventions are focused on helping students develop new skills (Jones, 1980; Jones & Jones, 1981, 1986). Specifically, the PBIS approach emphasizes (1) using data to make decisions about serving individual students and implementing schoolwide interventions; (2) working with school staff to define, teach, and reinforce socially acceptable school behaviors; (3) implementing a reinforcement system to encourage students to demonstrate responsible behavior; (4) providing small-group and individual instruction for appropriate behavior to students who need additional assistance; (5) developing an individualized plan to assist students who continue to make poor behavior choices based on a detailed analysis of the factors influencing student behavior (functional behavior assessment); and (6) creating family, school, and community partnerships to support the academic and behavioral needs of individual students (Simonsen, Sugai, & Negron, 2008; Sugai et al., 2010). These interventions are placed within three tiers. Tier 1 focuses on teaching schoolwide behavioral expectations to all students, reinforcing appropriate use of these skills, and reteaching appropriate behavior when students fail to behave responsibly. Tier 2 is geared to assist students demonstrating a pattern of problem behavior or academic failure and to prevent these issues from becoming serious. Tier 3 typically involves the use of functional behavior assessment to devise specialized assistance for students who continue to struggle despite receiving Tier 2 support.

While the SWPBIS system includes some methods for helping teachers more effectively respond to classroom behavior that disrupts the learning environment, SWPBIS is not specifically focused on classroom management and the creation of supportive classroom learning environments. Therefore, there is limited focus on teacher–student or peer relationships, ensuring that instruction is engaging and culturally sensitive, or the importance of assessing and implementing changes in the classroom as a response to student behavior problems. Effective, culturally sensitive classroom management must thoughtfully address all of these issues (Evertson & Weinstein, 2006; Monroe, 2009; Jones, 1996, 2006; Ullucci, 2009).

While we strongly support staff implementing SWPBIS, it should also be mentioned that studies suggest more research is needed to support this approach. A meta-analysis of PBIS results reported that "SWPBIS is moderately effective in reducing problem behavior in students" (Solomon, Klein, Hintze, Cressey, & Peller, 2012, p. 116). Another assessment of the research on this approach reported that "although there is evidence pointing to its efficacy, the research behind SWPBIS is still weak" (Chitiyo, May, & Chitiyo, 2012, p. 20). Some writers suggest that further research is needed to ensure that SWPBIS is implemented in a manner that is culturally sensitive (Vincent & Tobin, 2011), while others have noted that "The majority of research on SW-PBIS has been at the school-wide level, and more research is needed to understand classroom-level characteristics associated with positive outcomes" (Reinke, Herman, & Stormont, 2013, p. 40). Other researchers suggest, The assessment of this approach would be strengthened by including a greater emphasis on observational data as opposed to office referrals and other more general indicators of behavior (Solomon et al., 2012). In addition, some researchers have raised the question of whether it is more effective and a better use of resources to reduce disruptive behavior and improve school climate by focusing on the most disruptive classrooms and individuals rather than on universal schoolwide interventions (Osher et al., 2010).

As mentioned earlier, SWPBIS Tier 1 interventions place relatively little emphasis on assessing classroom factors that are impacting student behavior. Tier 2 interventions also seldom focus on observation and modifications of the classroom environment, but rather emphasize single interventions focused solely on the student (Carter, Carter, Johnson, & Pool, 2012). As presented in this book, a comprehensive focus on classroom management incorporates all key classroom components impacting students' behavior and learning. In order to assist all students in reaching their potential, it would be ideal if all teachers were effectively educated and supported to provide the skills presented in this text and were also supported by an effectively implemented SWPBIS system.

PAUSE & CONSIDER 1.4

You have just read sections describing the key concepts and skills associated with effective classroom management as well as a brief history of classroom management methods. Look back at what you wrote in Pause and Consider 1.1. How does what you just read compare with what you wrote regarding a definition and key components associated with effective classroom management? You may want to write briefly about this or share your discoveries with a peer or small group.

SOCIAL FACTORS INFLUENCE STUDENTS' BEHAVIOR

It is beyond the scope of this text to document the extent of problems such as divorce, domestic violence, poverty, racism, the impact of television and video games, and so on that affect the anxiety and concerns students bring to school and that negatively affect students'

© Bob Vojtko

"I'll do my homework just as soon as something bad comes on TV."

learning. As anyone who works in K–12 public schools knows, many classrooms today include children living in poverty, children who have recently experienced their parents being divorced, children experiencing physical and/or psychological abuse at home, and so forth.

An organization called the Search Institute has developed a list of forty assets that assist students in reaching their potential. This organization also lists five developmental deficits: (1) drinking parties, (2) being alone at home, (3) being a victim of violence, (4) overexposure to television, and (5) physical abuse. Sadly, research indicates that "only 15 percent of young people surveyed experienced none of these deficits. One-third of youth (32%) experienced three or more" (Benson, Scales, Leffert, & Roehlkepartain, 1999, p. xiii).

PAUSE & CONSIDER 1.5

Stop for a moment and consider the home and community factors you believe have the greatest negative impact on students coming to school with the personal support and psychological energy needed to perform their best at school. Next, write a statement or share your thoughts with peers. What are the implications regarding how school staff work with students to help them make responsible decisions in a school setting?

Creating a Trauma-Sensitive Classroom

By the age of sixteen, 68 percent of children in the United States have experienced a traumatic event (Pappano, 2014). The National Survey on Children's Exposure to Violence reported that 25 percent of children had witnessed violence and 10 percent had seen a family member assault another family member (Finkelhor, Turner, Ormrod, Hamby, & Kracke, 2009). Students who have experienced trauma are at greater risk for school failure and need environments that provide them with personal support and a stable, predictable environment (Levine & Kline, 2010).

A variety of classroom factors has been recommended to support students who have experienced trauma. Blaustein and Kinniburgh (2010) identify four characteristics of a positive learning environment for children who have experienced significant adverse events that provide a foundation for learning and personal growth.

1. Adults demonstrate awareness of their own emotions and behavior and respond to students in a calm, educational manner.
2. Adults focus not on student behavior alone but rather on the function the behavior may be serving the student.

3. Adults are consistent and predictable in the way they respond in providing a safe setting for students.
4. Adults teach and consistently use predictable routines and thus provide students with a sense of structure and order rituals.

Another group of writers has suggested the key characteristics of a trauma-sensitive classroom include:

- Develolping a consistent approach to responding to disruptive behavior
- Creating predictable classroom routines and relationships
- Reducing bullying and harassment
- Teaching children skills in self-regulation and coping with stressful events
- Building on students' strengths
- Communicating high behavioral and academic expectations
- Providing opportunities for students to be meaningfully engaged in the learning process (Wisconsin Group, 2014)

Similarly, Bath (2008) suggests that trauma-informed responses to children and youth involve creating a safe setting where children feel connected to the adults and are provided with support in learning how to manage their emotions.

Creating positive and collaborative teacher–student relationships is felt by many to be the context where the regulation of emotions, trust, and self-awareness that are often lacking in children who have experienced trauma can emerge (Perry, 2006). Positive teacher–student relationships are a centerpiece of classrooms and schools focused on reducing the negative impact trauma has on students' schools success (Brinamen & Page, 2012; Dods, 2013; Wright, 2013).

A student's challenging behavior often reflects a mismatch between his or her current skill set and what the environment is asking of the student. Classrooms sensitive to trauma pay close attention to the match between the demand characteristics within the classroom and the student's capacity to respond to those demands. Ongoing assessment of the compatibility between environmental demand and student skills is necessary when working with students who have experienced adverse events. Many students who have experienced trauma have weaknesses in executive function skills and difficulty accessing these skills in novel or unpredictable situations. Teachers need to pay close attention to a student's exposure to novel as opposed to familiar expectations and events. This means teachers working with students who have experienced emotional trauma need to ensure that classroom routines are clear and mastered by students and that new events, including new types of instructional activities, are introduced by providing clear statements and demonstrations of the new behavior expectations.

Trauma-sensitive classrooms also enable students to feel safe making academic and behavior errors (Cole, Eisner, Gregory, & Ristuccia, 2013). Classrooms need to be places where students understand that effective learners take risks, make mistakes, and ask questions and that both peer and adult responses to mistakes will be respected. Trauma-sensitive classrooms also provide clear and educational responses to students' errors (Blaustein & Kinniburgh, 2010; Cole et al., 2005; Cole et al., 2013). In a trauma-sensitive classroom, "a behavior-management system should be based on an understanding of why a particular child might respond inappropriately in the classroom and on the relational and academic needs of that child" (Cole et al., 2005, p. 55).

The approach to classroom management presented in this text is consistent with the leading work on creating classrooms that support students who have experienced trauma. Indeed, this is one reason the methods presented throughout this text enable teachers to effectively support a wide range of students who may have previously demonstrated behavior that was disruptive to the learning environment.

PAUSE & CONSIDER 1.6

Write a brief statement about the key components of the trauma-sensitive classroom. How do the characteristics of this type of classroom compare to or contrast with what you have just learned about the key components of comprehensive classroom management? Generate a list of reasons a trauma-sensitive classroom might be an essential factor in facilitating both positive behavior and academic achievement for today's students.

SCHOOL FACTORS SIGNIFICANTLY INFLUENCE STUDENTS' LEARNING AND BEHAVIOR

Consider what classroom factors made your K–12 school experience positive and what factors made the classroom feel unsafe or caused you to feel a sense of frustration and failure. If you discuss these factors with fellow students or colleagues, it is likely you will realize most of these factors were influenced by the decisions and actions (or inactions) of teachers.

Even though social factors have made the teacher's job more challenging, studies indicate that teachers and schools make a dramatic difference in the lives of many children (Darling-Hammond, 1997, 2010, 2013; Jackson & Lunenburg, 2010).

Teachers have control over many factors that significantly influence the achievement and behavior of students. Schools and teachers working with similar student populations differ dramatically in their ability to help students be academically successful and develop desirable behaviors. Mortimore and Sammons (1987) summarized their extensive research on factors that influence students' academic and social gains by noting that school factors were six to ten times more influential than factors such as age, sex, social class, or race in determining students' academic progress.

Kellam and his colleagues (1998) reported that highly aggressive six-year-old boys assigned to first-grade classrooms with teachers skilled in classroom management were three times less likely to be highly aggressive when they reached eighth grade than similarly aggressive boys placed in first-grade classrooms characterized by poor classroom management. These findings are consistent with experimental studies conducted in middle school classrooms by David Hawkins and others at the University of Washington (1988). Clearly, teachers make a difference, and teachers' classroom management skills are an important aspect of teachers' being able to bring about positive gains in student achievement and behavior.

There is increasing agreement among researchers (Algozzine, Audette, Ellis, Marr, & White, 2000; Freiberg, 1999; Jones, 2006; Lewis et al., 2006; Nelson & Roberts, 2000; Simonsen, Gairbanks, et al., 2008) regarding the type of school and classroom environments needed to support positive behavior among a wide range of students. These writers indicate the importance of working with students to clearly define and accept behavior expectations; developing clearly understood and educationally sound responses to rule violations, including the reteaching of expected behaviors; and developing individualized behavior support plans for

"Hard day at school?"

© Martha F. Campbell

students who present ongoing behaviors that violate the rights of others. In addition, several of these writers (Freiberg, 1999; Jones, 2002) highlight the importance of creating an engaging curriculum and modifying curriculum and instruction for students who experience academic difficulties. These authors also emphasize the importance of ensuring that students experience a community of support within the school setting.

Unfortunately, much of the material written about methods that prevent students from experiencing behavior problems virtually ignores the aspect of students' experiencing a sense of significance or belonging and involvement in academic tasks that are meaningful to the students and in which the students can experience success (Jones, 2002). Too often we have visited schools in which staff were working to teach prosocial skills and develop plans for recalcitrant students, but the ethos of the school lacked warmth and joy, and academic tasks were relatively uninteresting and failed to actively engage students. Often a significant minority of students in these schools felt alienated, found their academic work to be tedious and unrelated to their lives and interests, and did not believe teachers cared about them. Unless the factors of creating personal connections between peers and between students and staff and implementing meaningful, engaging academic tasks are addressed, the popularized behavioral approaches to changing student behavior will be inadequate as interventions to create safe, productive learning environments.

In April 1999, two very alienated male students entered Columbine High School in Colorado and killed twelve students and one adult. Several months after this incident, one student summarized what he had learned about preventing violence when he stated, "I don't tease my friends as much as I used to. I try to be a lot nicer to everyone." A senior who was in a video class with one of the killers said that this year, "a lot of seniors have been more open to people, even to underclassmen" (Goldstein, 1999, pp. 56, 57). The principal noted, "I think where money needs to be spent is educating our students about tolerance, about respecting one another, about communication" (Goldstein, 1999, p. 57). The key to preventing school violence is ultimately not in guards and cameras but in students feeling cared for, competent, and valued.

THE ISSUES OF ORDER, CARING, AND POWER

For classrooms and schools to meet the academic and personal needs of students, schools must be safe environments characterized by a considerable degree of order. Weinstein (1998) suggests that many teachers (especially beginning teachers) mistakenly view a teacher's actions to create a caring and orderly classroom as mutually exclusive. Beginning teachers often want students to like them and view setting clear limits and responding politely yet firmly to student behavior that disrupts others' right to feel safe and learn as endangering the fragile relationship they are attempting to develop with their students. The important question related to order is not whether order needs to exist but how order is established and maintained. In his book *Constructive School Discipline*, Walter Smith (1936) wrote:

> It must be admitted, however, that the failure of the old disciplinary regime, not inaptly styled "beneficent tyranny," has left the situation somewhat chaotic. Many have discarded the authoritative type of control without developing any adequate system to take its place. . . . Discipline under the new regime cannot be made easier, but it may be made a more vital element in moral education than it ever could under any system of autocratic domination. (pp. 8, 9)

Although Smith's statement was written more than seventy-five years ago, there is an increasing body of research and literature suggesting that the issue of how order is established may be the most important factor influencing student behavior in schools. Pedro Noguera (1995) stated that schools that feel safe are characterized by teachers knowing, valuing, and caring about students.

> The urban schools that I know that feel safe to those who spend their time there don't have metal detectors or armed security guards, and their principals don't carry baseball bats. What these schools do have is a strong sense of community and collective responsibility. Such schools are seen by students as sacred territory, too special to be spoiled by crime and violence, and too important to risk one's being excluded. (p. 207)

Discussing the importance of caring in working with students experiencing serious behavior problems, H. James McLaughlin (1992) wrote:

> [A] teacher's legitimate authority has four characteristics: it derives from personal and positional relationships with students; it is both assumed and conferred; it is constrained or enabled by school and societal contexts; and it is predicated on the transformation of control by caring. (p. 4)

Bowers and Flinders (1990) have suggested that "control and caring are not opposing terms; but the form of control is transformed by the presence of caring" (p. 15). Sergiovanni (1994) stated that one's commitment to exemplary practice serves as the basis for authority. This concept is supported by comments John Holt made in the early 1970s when he noted that all teachers needed to have authority but that there were two types of authority. *Natural authority* is based on a teacher's natural skill in assisting students in the learning process, solving problems, and modeling thoughtful, caring behavior. *Arbitrary* or *role-bound authority* is the authority granted to educators by their roles as teachers, principals, counselors, and so on. This authority is based on educators' legal right to maintain order. Holt suggested that students are impressed by and respond well to natural authority, whereas they often respond to arbitrary authority with confrontation and withdrawal. He suggested that the two types of authority are difficult to blend and that the more educators use natural authority, the less they would need to call on arbitrary authority. Similarly, the more educators use arbitrary authority, the less students will be able to see educators' natural authority.

© Stan Fein

"I'm your teacher, Mrs. Gridley. Learn to read, write, and do arithmetic, and nobody will get hurt."

In their book *Conflict in the Classroom*, Nicholas Long, Ruth Newman, and William Morse (1996) provide a thoughtful statement about the choices teachers make when considering how to maintain a safe classroom environment:

> For some educators, discipline means the power of the teacher to control the behavior of their students. . . . For other educators, discipline means an opportunity to teach students a set of values about how people can live together in a democratic society. This would include the values of honesty, fair play, the rights of others to learn, respect for property, respect of multicultural differences, and so on. Discipline is perceived as the process of helping students internalize these values and to develop self-control over their drives and feelings. (p. 238)

We have all worked in classrooms and even schools in which students behave responsibly when the teacher is present but become disruptive when a substitute teacher, bus driver, or playground supervisor becomes involved. Our experiences suggest that a common characteristic of classrooms and schools in which this occurs is the focus on adult control through rewards and punishments. When adult power is used to influence student behavior, the behavior is likely to change dramatically when the power differential between adults and children changes. Interestingly, when discussing current methods in effective discipline, Lee Canter (1996), once perhaps the most noted advocate for a control/power method of discipline, wrote:

> There are teachers who believe that to have order, you just get tougher and tougher with kids— that you impose more rules and harsher consequences to get students' respect.
>   But it doesn't work. . . .
>   To be successful, a discipline plan should be built on a foundation of mutual trust and respect. That's the fundamental change in the Assertive Discipline plan for the '90s. . . . Too many kids have been let down by the adults in their lives. You have to demonstrate that you're fair, that you stick by your word, *that you care*. (p. 6)

Sleeter (1991) wrote, "For me, and for many other advocates and theorists of multicultural education, empowerment and multicultural education are interwoven, and together suggest powerful and far-reaching school reform" (p. 2). In discussing the relationship between multicultural education, empowerment, and social change, Sleeter (1991) stated:

> The multicultural education approach, or cultural democracy, attempts to redesign classrooms and schools to model an unoppressive, equal society which is also culturally diverse. Explicitly this approach does not strongly teach social criticism and social change, but implicitly it does so in that a multicultural classroom or school implementing this approach is clearly different from the existing society. Students are empowered as individuals by achieving and receiving validation for who they are, and are empowered for social change by having lived a pluralistic model. (p. 11)

In his book *Building Community in Schools*, Thomas Sergiovanni (1994) stated, "if we want to rewrite the script to enable good schools to flourish, we need to rebuild community. Community building must become the heart of any school improvement effort" (p. xi). Sergiovanni further stated:

> Compliance strategies actually make things worse. Responsibility strategies are helpful but just not powerful enough. Strategies aimed at helping classrooms become democratic communities, on the other hand, can help young people reconnect with each other and with their schoolwork. Democratic communities can help students and adults come together to construct a standard for living their school lives together. And democratic communities can help students meet their needs to belong, to be active, to have control, and to experience sense and meaning in their lives. (p. 122)

One of the most important professional decisions you will make is how you choose to create and maintain a learning environment that is comfortable and supportive for all learners. Johnson and colleagues (Johnson, Whitington, & Oswald, 1994) studied the discipline responses of more than 3,400 Australian teachers. He found that teachers' views of discipline fell into three categories: (1) *traditional*, characterized by the teacher as an authority figure who presents and follows strict rules and responds with clear and escalating responses to student misbehavior; (2) *liberal progressive*, in which teachers apply democratic principles that involve students in decision making and solving problems; and (3) *socially critical*, in which unproductive student behavior is viewed as a response to conditions in the classroom that fail to meet students' needs and where creating positive, supportive environments characterized by engaging and intellectually appropriate instructional activities is the key to preventing undesirable student behavior. Johnson reported that 98 percent of the teachers fell into the first two categories. More than 70 percent of secondary teachers rated themselves as traditional, while nearly two-thirds of elementary teachers rated themselves as liberal progressives.

While all teachers develop their own style of classroom management, as you read this text, you will discover that our reading of current research and our own experience in K–12 classrooms support a blend of the liberal progressive and socially critical approaches. We agree with the findings of Brophy (1996) that more successful teachers view classroom management as the proactive development of a safe, supportive, engaging classroom environment, whereas less successful teachers view classroom management as maintaining teacher authority and implementing discipline methods.

Some educators and writers suggest that teachers should select an approach that is consistent with their own personality and matches their own preferences. Consider for a moment situations in which you seek professional help—possibly seeing a physician or dentist. Do you want the professional to choose an approach to treating you based on what makes that person most comfortable or on the most current research related to the condition that caused you to seek assistance? We have worked with many educators whose approach to classroom management involved controlling students and attempting to have the least possible contact with parents and guardians. During their high school experiences, one of our children was sprayed in the face with water for turning his body to be comfortable in a chair, and the other was yanked out of her seat for quietly asking a question of a friend seated next to her in a study hall. These methods were defended by the educators involved as being methods they felt were most effective. Certainly there is no "one correct way" to effectively maintain a safe and calm learning environment. However, there are strong guiding principles—methods that have proven effective, methods with sound research support—and there are methods such as those used by these teachers that are not professionally defensible.

Pause & Consider 1.7

Picture yourself responsible for maintaining an orderly environment for the twenty-five to forty students you currently teach or a group of students you plan on teaching. What type of authority do you believe will be most effective for you in order to create a positive, productive learning environment? Write a brief statement about the general classroom management methods/approaches to classroom management you believe are associated with this type of authority. After completing your work with this text, you are encouraged to return to this statement, once again determining the type of authority you believe is most effective and listing, outlining, or creating a schema indicating specific classroom management methods that will support your effectively implementing this type of authority in the classroom.

FACTORS THAT INFLUENCE TEACHERS' CLASSROOM MANAGEMENT DECISIONS_____

The Teacher's Personal History

Teachers' approaches to classroom management are clearly impacted by their own life experiences. Johns and Espinoza (1996) noted that "what teachers consider to be 'discipline problems' are determined by their own culture, filtered through personal values and teaching style" (p. 9). Similarly, how we organize our classroom and how we respond to disruptions of the learning environment are also influenced by our personal histories.

Studies report significant relationships between teacher personality factors and their orientation to classroom management. In a study of 156 preservice teachers, Kaplan (1992) found that "teachers' disciplinary experiences in their families of origin are predictive of the strategies they select for classroom management" (p. 263).

As you work to create positive, supportive learning communities in which all students feel safe and respected, you must be aware of your own personal history and beliefs and ensure these do not limit your ability to incorporate methods that facilitate learning for all students. For example, you may have been raised in a setting where any form of challenge to adult authority was responded to with firm discipline with no discussion even considered. Some teachers may prefer an impersonal, even distant relationship with their students, but their students may need a more personalized relationship with their teacher. As you select methods for creating a positive, supportive learning community and responding to behavior that detracts from this productive learning environment, it is absolutely essential that you understand your students' beliefs and values about learning and personal relationships and that you incorporate them into your decision making. It is equally imperative that you understand what research suggests is most effective in preventing and responding to disruptive student behavior. This knowledge must always take precedence over what feels right to us.

Beliefs Regarding the Goals of Schooling

Another key school factor influencing teachers' decisions regarding classroom management methods is the goals teachers have for their students. We serve students best if we consistently ask ourselves, "What are my long-term goals for my students? How do I want their lives to have been impacted by the time they spent with me?" Whenever you consider what approach to use when establishing a classroom climate, motivating students, or responding to disruptive behaviors, it is influenced by your educational goals.

There is little argument that a primary goal of public education is to provide students with skills to be happy and productive members of their societies. When considering how to best assist students in reaching this goal, we may need to ask such questions as: "What type of academic skills do I believe students will need in order to live productive adult lives?" "What skills other than academic knowledge do I believe are necessary to reach this goal?" "What type of environment do I believe facilitates the attainment of my classroom instructional goals?"

In his book *The Optimistic Child*, Martin Seligman (1995) wrote:

> We want more for our children than healthy bodies. We want our children to have lives filled with friendship and love and high deeds. We want them to be eager to learn and be willing to confront challenges. We want our children to be grateful for what they receive from us, but to be proud of their own accomplishments. We want them to grow up with confidence in the future, a love of adventure, a sense of justice, and courage enough to act on that sense of justice. We want them to be resilient in the face of the setbacks and failures that growing up always brings. And when the time comes, we want them to be good parents. (p. 6)

Alfie Kohn (1991) suggested that schools will best serve students and our society most productively if they focus on producing not only good learners but good people. Kohn noted that "a dozen years of schooling often do nothing to promote generosity or a commitment to the welfare of others. To the contrary, students are graduated who think that being smart means looking out for number one" (p. 498).

Kohn further suggested that schools are ideal places to nurture children's innate sense of caring and generosity of spirit. He suggested that both students' future success and the quality of learning will be enhanced in classroom and school environments that emphasize collaboration and caring.

In his article "Discipline and Morality: Beyond Rules and Consequences," John Covaleskie (1992) suggested that "children must develop a sense of what it means to be a good person—what it means to choose to do the right thing, especially when circumstances are such that one is faced with the possibility of doing the wrong thing to one's own advantage, and getting away with it" (p. 174). He goes on to state that "the standard by which we should be judging 'discipline programs' in schools is that of moral responsibility: do our children learn to think, talk, and act morally? The goal is not compliance with rules, but making the choices to live a good life, an ethical life" (p. 176).

Nel Noddings (1992) responded to this issue when she wrote:

> To suppose, for example, that attention to affective needs necessarily implies less time for arithmetic is simply a mistake. Such tasks can be accomplished simultaneously, but the one is undertaken in light of the other. We do not ask how we must treat children in order to get them to learn arithmetic but, rather, what effect each instructional move we consider has on the development of good persons. Our guiding principles for teaching arithmetic, or any other subject, are derived from our primary concern for the persons whom we teach, the methods of teaching are chosen in consonance with these derived principles. An ethic of caring guides us to ask, What effect will this have on the person I teach? What effect will it have on the caring community we are trying to build? (p. 499)

In their examination of national and regional studies on educational requirements needed for the job market, researchers from the Sandia National Laboratories (1993) wrote that "according to business leaders polled, the most important workplace 'skills' for future employees were not academic skills. Rather, behavioral 'skills' . . . were all listed in the 'highly critical' categories" (p. 295). It would seem that using classroom management methods that focus on teaching students to interact and collaborate more effectively may not only enhance positive classroom behaviors that support academic skill development but also may help students develop important life skills.

A recruiting network recently reported that employers were finding it difficult to find the employees they wanted because many applicants lacked key skills. These skills included self-reliance, communication abilities, flexibility, self-awareness, organizational skills, self-promotion, decision making, the ability to build and work as part of a team, problem solving, action planning, leadership, negotiation, and adaptability and social confidence, including the ability to network effectively. In a similar vein, the National Association of Colleges and Employers (NACE), a nonprofit organization that connects college career placement offices to employers, reported that in 2013 employers rated the two most important skills for candidates seeking new jobs as the ability to verbally communicate with persons inside and outside the organization and the ability to work in a team structure. The next two highest-rated skills involved problem solving and organization (naceweb.org [search for "skills employers want 2013 recruits").

Along similar lines, in his book *Emotional Intelligence* Daniel Goleman (1995) suggested that how happy, fulfilled, and productive people are as adults is due only in small part to their intellectual ability as traditionally measured. He stated:

> My concern is with a key set of these "other characteristics," *emotional intelligence*: abilities such as being able to motivate oneself and persist in the face of frustrations; to control impulse and delay gratification; to regulate one's moods and keep distress from swamping the ability to think; to empathize and to hope. (p. 35)

In support of his beliefs, Goleman noted that in a follow-up study of 450 boys, results indicated that success at age forty-seven was related more to how the boys handled frustration, controlled their emotions, and got along with others than it was to intellectual ability (Felsman & Vaillant, 1987).

PAUSE & CONSIDER 1.8

We suggest you stop at this point and write a brief response to the following questions: What kind of learning and what personal skills and attitudes do I want my students to develop while they are with me, and what type of classroom environment do I believe enhances this kind of learning? We believe your responses to these questions will significantly influence how you choose to organize and manage your classroom. Keep these questions in mind as you read this text and decide which classroom management skills you will incorporate in your professional repertoire.

Students' Cultural Backgrounds

During the past several decades, there has been a significant increase in student diversity in our schools. In 2012, the U.S. Department of Education's National Center for Education Statistics reported that its most recent data indicated 20 percent of children ages five to seventeen in the United States spoke a language other than English in their home. When making decisions about classroom structure and discipline, teachers must consider students' cultural backgrounds and the associated values and beliefs that influence their students' behavior.

Ballenger (1992) provides an engaging description of a North American teacher's discovery that the perspective from which she viewed behavior management and her use of language needed to be altered to effectively engage young Haitian students. Ballenger found that, when dealing with behavior problems, Haitian parents and teachers did not talk about children's feelings or individual consequences. Instead, they focused on the fact that the behavior was "bad" and that it was disappointing to significant adults in the child's life that the child would act in this manner. Ballenger (1992) noted that:

> The North American teachers characteristically are concerned with making a connection with the individual child, with articulating his or her feelings and problems. . . . The Haitian people I spoke with and observed, emphasize the group in their control talk, articulating the values and responsibilities of group membership. (p. 204)

Ballenger commented that her observations suggested that North American teachers, particularly those in the primary grades, were reluctant to firmly correct students, while Haitian teachers seemed to see this as part of strengthening teacher–student relationships. While acknowledging the fact that "North Americans perceive Haitians as too severe, both verbally and in their use of physical punishment" (p. 206), Ballenger emphasized that creating too great a discrepancy between parental and teacher responses to disruptive student behavior may cause serious problems because it can have a negative impact on the relationships between the teacher and the child.

Macias (1987) also described concerns regarding continuity in her study of Tohono O'odham preschoolers (members of an Native American group in Arizona). She noted:

> For many children of ethnic minority origin, the transition from home to school in early childhood appears to be a critical period of discontinuity. The way in which cultural disparities—between what has been learned at home and what school teaches—are dealt with determines to some degree the efficacy of their schooling. (p. 364)

Several years ago, one of us was working in an elementary school located in a community in which approximately one-third of the students were Native American. Several teachers expressed annoyance when they discovered nice, shiny, "I'm #1" buttons in the wastebaskets. During a faculty discussion concerning the lack of respect for school property displayed by these students, a Native American staff member informed the teachers that in her culture, students were encouraged not to outshine their friends. She noted that students from her tribe would be chastised by members of the tribe for bringing home an item indicating they had outperformed their friends and focused attention on themselves. The staff assistant had provided the teachers with an important lesson in how methods used to encourage and motivate students are more effective when they are responsive to students' cultural values.

This problem of cultural incongruence clearly impacts some African American students. African American students, particularly males, are the most disproportionately disciplined student group. Data collected in 2012 by the U.S. Department of Education show that Black students comprise 18 percent of students in the United States but 35 percent of the students suspended at least once and 39 percent of the students expelled. The manner in which some Black children prefer to learn and are accustomed to act in social settings may play a significant role in this unfair treatment (Bireda, 2010). African American students are more likely to support their peers, to have a collaborative approach to learning, and have a "we" approach to defending their peers. African American students are more likely to be confrontational, intense, and more active and animated in discussions, not taking turns or asking for permission to speak. In addition, African American students may view time differently and place a higher value on social issues than timeliness (Bireda, 2010; Gay, 2000). A number of these characteristics—for example, being more field dependent; viewing time differently; and valuing supportive, collaborative relationships—are also common among Latino and Native American students. These values often differ from those of White teachers, who value punctuality and more often "rely on more dispassionate, impersonal, and emotionally restrained communication styles" and "sequential versus simultaneous patterns of interaction. . . . Repeated reprimands for expressing culturally derived communication styles may irritate African American youngsters, diminish their sense of self-worth, lead to escalating discipline problems, and impede academic progress" (Day-Vines & Day-Hairston, 2005, p. 238). The book *Cultures in Conflict: Eliminating Racial Profiling* (Bireda, 2010) presents an excellent description of cultural factors that influence the learning and behavior of African American and Latino students as well as approaches educators can take to make schools more inviting, culturally sensitive places for students from these cultural groups.

In their article "Toward a Conception of Culturally Responsive Classroom Management," Weinstein, Tomlinson-Clarke, and Curran (2004) state that culturally responsive classroom management "is a frame of mind, more than a set of strategies or practices, that guides the management decisions that teachers make" (p. 27). They suggest that developing culturally responsive classroom management requires the following:

> (a) recognition of one's own ethnocentrism and biases; (b) knowledge of students' cultural backgrounds; (c) understanding of the broader social, economic, and political context of our educational system; (d) ability and willingness to use culturally appropriate classroom management strategies; and (e) commitment to building caring classroom communities. (p. 27)

In their review of "culturally responsive" teaching, Shevalier and McKenzie (2012) noted that "classroom management arose from a family-like community defined by a shared vocabulary, with all responsible to one another to do the right thing" (p. 1099). The materials presented in this text have been carefully selected to offer multiple classroom management strategies—including the creation of caring classroom communities—that are considered best practice in working with a diverse student population (August & Hakuta, 1997; Freeman & Freeman, 2002; Garcia, 2001; Kuykendall, 2004).

DEVELOPING YOUR OWN APPROACH TO EFFECTIVE AND PROFESSIONALLY RESPONSIBLE CLASSROOM MANAGEMENT

How do you go about developing skill and a sense of confidence in the area of classroom management? As suggested throughout this chapter, your decisions about how you teach involve a delicate blend of who you are, who you want to be, what you believe about your students and student learning, and how you integrate this into the classroom. In a very real sense, the most effective classroom management will be that which you create based on being a teacher-researcher in your own classroom (Fries & Cochran-Smith, 2006). The theories, research, and strategies provided in this book can serve as an important and necessary foundation for your role as teacher-researcher. However, the most important factor will be your willingness to continually ask questions about student behavior and learning, to blend this with your considerable knowledge of research and best practice in the area of classroom management, and to think critically and deeply about the dynamics in your classroom as a basis for working with students to make changes you believe will enhance the quality of student learning in your classroom. We have attempted to help you in this process throughout the text by including Pause & Consider activities to assist you in developing the habit of asking how research can inform your practice by analyzing your teaching context in light of new information.

SUMMARY

Teachers continue to experience persistent and often serious problems stemming from students acting in ways that disrupt the learning environment. Fortunately, research in classroom management has expanded dramatically during the past forty years. Teachers no longer need to depend on simplistic advice or one-dimensional answers to the complex tasks of motivating and managing students. Teachers can increasingly draw on an expanding body of methods that will enable them to create more positive, supportive classroom environments; better organize and instruct their students; and more effectively respond to the behavior of students who act irresponsibly, even in supportive, well-managed classrooms characterized by clear, meaningful instruction. The efficacy of new methods can be enhanced if teachers have a clear philosophy of classroom management and understand their own responsibilities and those of their students and school support personnel. Finally, school systems can better assist students with serious behavior problems if all educators within the system understand the methods to be followed in responding to unproductive student behavior.

Students who create classroom management and instructional challenges are, in fact, our best staff development specialists. They let us know that even though we may be very good, we can always expand our skills. Fortunately, almost without exception, the new methods we implement to assist students who are struggling with their learning and behavior will be beneficial for all students. Effective classroom management is not a zero-sum game in that efforts to assist students in need detract from other students. When you use the methods suggested in this book, you not only enhance your ability to reach students with special academic and/or behavior needs but also simultaneously enrich the learning experience of all students.

IMPLEMENTATION ACTIVITIES

ACTIVITY 1.1

Developing a Philosophy about Student Behavior Management

Write an answer to each of the following questions regarding your beliefs about students' behavior.

- What is the most common cause of student misbehavior?
- When students misbehave, what type of teacher response or consequence is the most effective? Why?
- As a parent or someone caring for children outside of a school setting, how do I usually respond to a behavior problem?
- How does what I believe about preventing and responding to disruptive classroom behavior relate to those that were used with me when I was growing up?
- In what aspects of comprehensive classroom management do I possess the most skills?
- In what aspects of comprehensive classroom management am I least skilled, or what aspects do I use less in my approach to classroom management?

1. After reading these statements, write a brief summary describing your general belief or philosophy about managing the behavior of children and youth.
2. As you work with the material in this text, you are encouraged to return to this summary and add comments and modifications, so that it becomes a working document for your professional examination of your classroom management methods.

RECOMMENDED READING

Baker, J. (1998). Are we missing the forest for the trees? Considering the social context of school violence. *Journal of School Psychology, 36*, 29–44.

Beyer, L. (Ed.). (1996). *Creating democratic classrooms: The struggle to integrate theory & practice*. New York, NY: Teachers College Press.

Darling-Hammond, L. (1997). *The right to learn: A blueprint for creating schools that work*. San Francisco, CA: Jossey-Bass.

Elliott, D., Hamburg, B., & Williams, K. (Eds.). (1998). *Violence in American schools: A new perspective*. Cambridge, England: Cambridge University Press.

Epstein, M., Atkins, M., Cullinan, D., Kutash, K., & Weaver, R. (2008). *Reducing behavior problems in the elementary school classroom: A practice guide* (NCEE #2008–012). Washington, DC: National Center for Education Evaluation and Regional Assistance, Institute of Education Sciences, U.S. Department of Education.

Evertson, C., & Weinstein, C. (Eds.). (2006). *Handbook of classroom management: Research, practice, and contemporary issues*. Mahwah, NJ: Lawrence Erlbaum.

Freiberg, H. J. (1999). *Beyond behaviorism: Changing the classroom management paradigm*. Boston, MA: Allyn & Bacon.

Garcia, E. (2001). *Student cultural diversity: Understanding and meeting the challenge* (3rd ed.). Boston, MA: Houghton Mifflin.

Gathercoal, F. (2004). *Judicious discipline* (6th ed.). San Francisco, CA: Caddo Gap Press.

Good, T., & Brophy, J. (2008). *Looking in classrooms* (10th ed.). Boston, MA: Allyn & Bacon.

Grant, G. (2009). *Hope and despair in the American city: Why there are no bad schools in Raleigh*. Cambridge, MA: Harvard University Press.

Hammond-Darling, L. (2000). Teacher quality and student achievement: A review of state policy evidence.

Education Policy Analysis Archives, *8,* 1–44.

Hyman, A., & Perone, D. (1998). The other side of school violence: Educator policies and practices that may contribute to student misbehavior. *Journal of School Psychology, 36,* 7–27.

Kuykendall, C. (2004). *From rage to hope: Strategies for reclaiming Black and Hispanic students* (2nd ed.). Bloomington, IN: National Educational Service.

Ladson-Billings, G. (1994). *The dreamkeepers: Successful teachers of African American children.* San Francisco, CA: Jossey-Bass.

Meier, D. (1995). *The power of their ideas.* Boston, MA: Beacon Press.

Noddings, N. (1992). *The challenge to care in schools: An alternative approach to education.* New York, NY: Teachers College Press.

Sergiovanni, T. (1994). *Building community in schools.* San Francisco, CA: Jossey-Bass.

Simonsen, B., Gairbanks, S., Briesch, A., Myers, D., & Sugai, G. (2008). Evidence-based practices in classroom management: Considerations for research to practice. *Education and Treatment of Children, 31,* 351–380.

Smith, G. (Ed.). (1993). *Public schools that work: Creating community.* New York, NY: Routledge.

CHAPTER 2

UNDERSTANDING STUDENTS' BASIC PSYCHOLOGICAL NEEDS

Teaching is difficult under the best educational conditions, and this failure to take into account the needs of students or teachers makes what is already a hard job almost impossible. Any method of teaching that ignores the needs of teachers or students is bound to fail.

—William Glasser (1990)

Teachers can augment the academic self-image by identifying and developing some of the unique cultural and social strengths Black and Hispanic youth bring to the classroom. An understanding of how the social self-image can be used to bolster the academic self-image is critical.

—Crystal Kuykendall (2004)

The job of the educator is to teach students to see the vitality in themselves.

—Joseph Campbell (American mythologist, writer, and lecturer)

Students behave appropriately and learn more effectively in environments that meet their basic personal and psychological needs. All students learn best in school settings in which they are comfortable and feel safe and accepted. Students' academic failure and misbehavior can be understood—and subsequently prevented or corrected—by examining classroom and school environments to determine which student needs are not being met.

LEARNING GOALS

After reading this chapter, you will know:

1. Several key concepts regarding students' psychological needs that influence their behavior and success at school
2. Why some students may be at higher risk for having an unsuccessful school experience
3. Why the issues of power and caring are so important in a school setting

Why Are These Goals Important?

There is a tendency in any job as complex as teaching to look for simple solutions and to seek methods that adults feel most comfortable implementing. In the education profession, it is essential that we always focus on the questions "What methods most effectively help students to learn essential academic and behavior skills?" and "What student needs must be met in order to ensure that these methods are most effective?" This chapter will assist you in answering this second question and in maintaining it as an essential question you ask throughout your teaching career.

Aaron Bacall/www.CartoonStock.com
"Students are influenced by television, video games, advertising, music, fashion, and their teachers. I'm looking to hire teachers that can reverse that order."

Teachers are frequently frustrated by their inability to determine the source of disruptive student behavior that detracts from students' learning. When asked to describe why children misbehave, teachers often include in their responses such factors as poor attitude, poor home environment, lower-than-average IQ, lack of parental support for school, and medical or emotional problems. These views suggest that teachers can merely coax or bribe these students into behaving appropriately or remove or punish these children when behavior errors occur. Teachers may thus absolve themselves of responsibility for students' behavior problems. In this scheme, teachers are confronted with unpredictable forces over which they have little control.

Even though it is true that student behavior is influenced by factors outside the control of the school, studies on school and teacher effectiveness have demonstrated that teachers and schools have a major impact on how students behave and learn and on how they feel about themselves. Therefore, another approach to analyzing unproductive or irresponsible student behavior is to believe that almost all students can function productively in a classroom and to consider what classroom variables can positively affect student learning and behavior. Much of this text provides specific methods used by teachers to create such environments. However, professional educators must understand *why* these techniques are effective rather than merely using them as gimmicks that positively influence student behavior. Consider for a moment if you took a child with a stomachache to see a physician. How would you react if, without examining the child, the physician indicated that an appendectomy would be performed? When you asked why the physician intended to perform the operation, the doctor indicated that the previous summer he had taken a class on appendectomies, had been told the operation was helpful to all children, and had demonstrated skill in performing it. It is likely you would seek another opinion and would perhaps even report the incident to the appropriate authority. Allen Mendler (1992) placed this in perspective when he wrote:

> Most discipline programs incorrectly place their emphasis upon strategies and techniques. The latest gimmick is offered to get Johnny to behave. The problem is that there are a lot of Johnnys out there and not all respond according to how the text or technique says they should. Having worked with thousands of children and adults, I have concluded that it is fruitless to expect that any technique will work with all people who present the same symptom. . . . The competent teacher needs to get at the reasons or functions of a given maladaptive behavior to formulate a strategy likely to work. . . . When they [children] misbehave, they tell us that they need help learning a better way. They are telling us that there are basic needs not being met which are motivating the behavior. (pp. 25, 27)

Teachers are involved daily in creating the atmosphere in which children spend approximately one-fourth of their waking lives. Although this necessity obviously places considerable responsibility on the teacher, it simultaneously imparts a positive, creative dimension into teachers' professional lives. Teachers are not faced with the prospect of merely reacting to student behaviors over which they have no control. On the contrary, by creating environments that respond sensitively to students' needs, teachers can ensure that most student behavior will be positive and goal directed.

This chapter describes the basic psychological needs that must be met for students to behave in positive, productive manners. No attempt is made to present an in-depth description of any one theorist's work or to describe child and adolescent development. Rather, the chapter highlights needs that, when met within the school setting, enhance positive teacher and student behavior and thereby facilitate learning.

THEORETICAL PERSPECTIVES

One approach to understanding students' unproductive school behavior suggests that much of this behavior is a response to students not having their basic needs met within the environment in which the unproductive behavior occurs. This explanation suggests that teachers may significantly impact student behavior by creating classroom and school environments that meet students' basic needs.

Another way to view unproductive student behavior is as a skill deficit. This model suggests that students who act aggressively on the playground or in the hallway lack skills to make appropriate contact with peers, to handle the inevitable frustrations and conflicts that arise, and to solve problems. Similarly, students who act out during instructional time may lack skills in understanding or organizing the work, using self-talk to handle frustration, or knowing how to obtain assistance. This social-cognitive skill deficit model suggests that students need more than reinforcement for appropriate behavior and negative consequences for inappropriate behavior. Students need to be taught social and work skills in the same manner that they are taught reading and math skills. Indeed, it is interesting that when students have serious difficulties reading, they are referred to a specialist who works intensively with them for an extended period of time. Educators do not expect students to learn to read by being placed in time-out or otherwise isolated from classmates. Likewise, teachers seldom expect students with reading difficulties to be at grade level after only a few sessions with the reading specialist. However, when students experience difficulties with their behavior, educators often isolate them, provide little or no instruction in how to behave appropriately, and expect one or two visits to a counselor or principal to resolve the problem and ensure that the student has the skills necessary to function as effectively as his or her classmates. If we believe student behavior problems often represent skill deficits, this is not realistic. Instead, educators must respond to unproductive student behavior by creating multiple opportunities for students to develop needed skills.

Personal Needs Theories

Abraham Maslow

Abraham Maslow (1968) suggested that for students to have energy for learning, their basic personal needs must be met. Maslow has suggested that there is a hierarchy of basic human needs and that lower-level needs generally take precedence over higher-order needs. His hierarchy of needs, which has been divided in a variety of ways, includes these components:

Knowledge and understanding
Self-actualization

© Scott Masear

"It takes four cups of coffee just to get on their wavelength."

Self-respect
Belongingness and affection
Safety and security
Physiological needs

A good discussion of these needs can be found at xenodochy.org/ex/lists/maslow.html.

Maslow's theoretical position is that people have an innate need to be competent and accepted. Unproductive behavior is therefore not viewed as an indication of a bad child but rather as a reaction to the frustration associated with being in a situation in which one's basic needs are not being met. Maslow further suggested that these basic needs cannot be met without assistance from other people. Finally, he postulated that only when the basic needs are met can the individual become motivated by self-actualization or the need to take risks, learn, and attain one's fullest potential.

Rudolf Dreikurs

Rudolf Dreikurs centered his ideas for working with children on the belief that their basic need is to be socially accepted: "We should realize that a misbehaving child is only a discouraged child trying to find his place; he is acting on the faulty logic that his misbehaviour will give him the social acceptance which he desires" (Dreikurs & Cassel, 1972, p. 32).

Dreikurs described four goals associated with students' disruptive behavior: attention getting, power, revenge, and displays of inadequacy. He suggested that "when a child is deprived of the opportunity to gain status through his useful contributions, he usually seeks proof of his status in class through getting attention" (1972, p. 34). If adults are ineffective at responding to this attention getting, Dreikurs indicated that students will seek power. If this response is thwarted by teachers' own power methods, students become deeply discouraged and seek revenge. Finally, Dreikurs suggested that "a child who has tried passive destructive forms of attention getting in order to achieve the feeling of 'belonging' may eventually become so deeply discouraged that he gives up all hope of significance and expects only failure and defeat" (Dreikurs & Cassel, 1972, p. 39). In *Discipline without Tears* (Dreikurs & Cassel, 1972) and *Maintaining Sanity in the Classroom* (Dreikurs et al., 1971), Dreikurs suggested methods for assisting teachers in identifying which of the four mistaken goals the child is seeking and ways teachers can respond to children to help them return to positive involvement in the regular classroom.

Topper and colleagues (Topper, Williams, Leo, Hamilton, & Fox, 1994) offered a slightly modified list of needs met by students' challenging behaviors.

- **Attention**—the behavior serves the need to draw attention away from others and to oneself
- **Avoidance/Escape**—the behavior serves the need to end an event or activity that the student does not like, or to avoid an event
- **Control**—the behavior serves the need to control events
- **Revenge**—the behavior serves the need to punish others for something that was done to the student

- **Self-Regulation/Coping**—the behavior serves the need to regulate feelings (e.g., boredom, embarrassment, anger, fear, anxiety) or energy levels
- **Play**—the behavior serves the need to have fun (p. 47)

The idea that all behavior is purposeful is an important concept in working with students. Students are not "bad" or "disruptive"; they are simply attempting to meet their needs using behaviors that are not in their best interests or the best interests of others. Oftentimes these are behaviors that have provided them with much-needed attention, a sense of control, escape from work they find difficult, a method of self-regulation, or a method for having fun. It is our role as educators to help them develop behaviors that not only meet these needs but also serve them effectively throughout their lives.

William Glasser

For half a century, William Glasser (1965) crusaded for increasing the sense of efficacy and power students experience. In his book *Control Theory in the Classroom*, Glasser (1986) stated, "Our behavior is always our best attempt at the time to satisfy at least five powerful forces which, because they are built into our genetic structure, are best called basic needs" (p. 14). Glasser described the five basic needs as "(1) to survive and reproduce, (2) to belong and love, (3) to *gain power* [emphasis added], (4) to be free, and (5) to have fun" (p. 22). Glasser indicated that students will function productively only in school environments that allow them to experience a sense of control or power over their learning.

In *The Quality School: Managing Students without Coercion*, Glasser (1990) extended his ideas on enhancing students' sense of involvement and empowerment. When describing why educators see relatively high rates of off-task behavior in schools, Glasser noted:

> For workers, including students, to do quality work, they must be managed in a way that convinces them that the work they are asked to do satisfies their needs. The more it does, the harder they will work.
>
> Instead, teachers are required to stuff students with fragments of measurable knowledge as if the students had no needs—almost as if they were things. . . .
>
> Because this low-quality, standardized, fragmented approach is so unsatisfying to students (and teachers), more and more students are actively resisting and this resistance is seen as a discipline problem. (p. 22)

Stanley Coopersmith

Another useful concept of students' needs is offered by Coopersmith (1967). In his research on the factors associated with self-esteem, Coopersmith found that in order to possess high self-esteem, individuals need to experience a sense of significance, competence, and power. *Significance* can best be defined as the sense of being valued that an individual attains from involvement in a positive two-way relationship in which both parties sincerely care about each other. *Competence* is developed by being able to perform a socially valued task as well as or better than others at one's age level. For example, winning a free-throw shooting competition involving her peers would provide a fifth-grader with a sense of competence. Finally, *power* refers to an ability to understand and control one's environment.

Coopersmith's research indicates that students need to experience a sense of trust and personal involvement as well as a sense of accomplishment or competence if their needs are to be met. Coopersmith also noted that in order for individuals to feel good about themselves and their environment, they must experience a sense of power or control. Students who clearly understand classroom rules and procedures and who understand what is to be learned and why it might be useful to them will experience a sense of power. Likewise, students experience a sense of power when they are allowed to choose a topic of special interest to study, provide input into how the classroom is arranged, understand their own learning style and its relationship to their learning and teacher decision making, or study material related to their cultural heritage.

What Students Need

A number of other writers have researched and written about the major needs that dominate and influence student behavior. Figure 2.1 presents the views of four researchers/theorists regarding this topic. As noted in this figure, all four theorists share the belief that for students to have their basic needs met, and thereby function effectively in the school environment, they need to experience positive relationships with others (belonging, significance, collaboration, love). Likewise, three of the writers specifically highlight students' needs for academic accomplishment (mastery, competence, content). All four writers indicated that students need some sense of choice or ability to influence their environment (independence, power, choice). Finally, two of the writers suggest a need to share with or give to others. A third author mentioned this but did not include it in his list (Glasser, 1990).

Based on their review of the research and interviews with students, Topper et al. (1994) report that students provide a similar list regarding their needs and wants. Students mentioned, "wanting to be engaged in interesting and fun learning activities, being able to make choices, develop skills needed to be successful and independent, having friends, having an advocate and being able to make a difference in the lives of others" (p. 7).

Notice how similar these needs and wants are to those created by the theorists. Students want and need to have positive personal relationships characterized by mutual caring and support, an opportunity to demonstrate mastery and competence, a chance to learn and use their own decision-making skills and to influence their environment, and an opportunity to make a difference in the lives of others.

It is important to realize that, just as children enter school with dramatically different reading readiness, they also vary in their ability to meaningfully engage in the social life of the classroom and to be receptive to adults' attempts to provide them with significance, competence, and power. Some children have had life experiences that have led them to view relationships as less supportive and to interpret a higher range of peer and adult behaviors as negative and unsupportive. Therefore, before they can trust others, behave in a reciprocal manner, and begin to maximize their potential, some students require more time in a positive, supportive classroom environment in which their competence is validated and they are given choices and opportunities to express themselves openly.

FIGURE 2.1 STUDENTS' BASIC NEEDS	Brendtro et al. (1990)	Coopersmith (1967)	Kohn (1999)	Glasser (1990)
	belonging	significance	collaboration	love
	mastery	competence	content	fun
	independence	power	choice	power/freedom
	generosity		virtue	survival

PAUSE & CONSIDER **2.1**

Consider a classroom with which you are familiar. Label three columns on a sheet of paper: significance, competence, and power. List ways in which all students have an opportunity to achieve each of these in the classroom you are considering. If one of the lists is quite short or very few students have an opportunity to experience this factor, add several specific changes you might suggest for this class to improve this particular list. We believe you will benefit from sharing this list with others and perhaps adopting methods used in their classrooms to strengthen your list.

PAUSE & CONSIDER **2.2**

Take a few minutes to consider a student you have observed or taught or with whom you are otherwise familiar whose behavior has occasionally had a negative impact on his or her learning or the learning of classmates. Try to envision a specific instance in which this student behaved in such a manner. Hypothesize which of the six needs presented by Topper et al. the child's behavior may have served. Not only may this help you better understand the student's behavior but it also provides you with valuable information concerning how to assist the student in developing substitute behaviors. Write a statement about an activity in which you could engage this student that would provide him or her with a better way to meet the need you believe is being met by the current behavior.

Human Development Theory

Erik Erikson

According to Erikson (1963), there are eight stages of human psychosocial development. Each stage is characterized by a conflict in which the individual either attains a key psychosocial understanding or develops an emotional liability. Although he indicates that three stages are most likely to be experienced by school-age children, he poignantly highlights the concept that each stage builds on its predecessors. Therefore, if a child does not reach satisfactory resolution of an earlier stage such as trust, this will negatively affect the child's ability to successfully work through later developmental stages. Figure 2.2 presents the first five stages in Erikson's developmental theory—those that apply most directly to children and adolescents in K–12 schools.

A key concept for teachers is that not only must we assist students in developing a positive resolution of the developmental stage most characteristic of their age but we must also support students who are struggling

© George B. Abbott

"Actually, I don't know how to act my age. I just turned seven today!"

Stage	Key Developmental Tasks	Implications for Teachers
Infancy	Develop a sense of trust and hope or a sense of mistrust and despair	Help children know you are a caring adult who knows and understands them and can be trusted to provide a safe, supportive environment
Autonomy	Opportunities to test oneself in order to develop a sense of self-expression and self-control	Create opportunities for choice and self-expression and enough structure to ensure the child's behaviors are positive
Initiative	Child expands autonomy to include their own planning and increased interaction with others	Ensure that there is adequate support but numerous opportunities for creative expression, productive peer engagement, and problem solving
Industry	Child learns to do meaningful work well and develop a sense of competency	Individualize work and use goal setting and data displays so students know they are improving at their work and developing important and valued knowledge and skills
Identity	Increased sense of self-consciousness and lower self-esteem as young adolescents struggle to develop a sense of who they are as individuals. New formal operational thought is being developed and previously accepted beliefs and values are being challenged as adolescents view their world more subjectively and critically.	Create a classroom climate in which students experience support from their peers and which students view as a "safe zone" where harassment and discrimination are not allowed to exist. Students need fair, clearly articulated structures and adults who are personally strong and flexible enough to become involved in openly discussing questions adolescents have about subject matter, teaching techniques, and school rules and procedures.

FIGURE 2.2
STAGES 1–5 IN ERIKSON'S DEVELOPMENTAL THEORY

because of unsatisfactory resolution of earlier stages. The clingy third grader and the sixth grader who appears unable to work independently are examples of students who may need support in working through earlier developmental issues. In a very real sense, we are providing effective reparenting for many children. While this may occur through the coordinated efforts of a team of educators developing a special plan to assist a child, it may also happen as a natural outcome of using the effective classroom management methods presented in this text.

Social Factors Theory

David Elkind

In *The Hurried Child*, Elkind (1981) added an interesting dimension to the topic of children's psychological needs. He stated that relationships among all individuals, but especially between children and adults, involve basic patterns of dealing with each other. He described these patterns as implicit contracts and noted that they are constantly changing. He further commented that children's needs are met when contracts change in response to changing personal and cognitive skills demonstrated by children, but that contracts must not change primarily in response to adults' needs.

Elkind described three basic contracts between adults and children: (1) responsibility–freedom, (2) achievement–support, and (3) loyalty–commitment. The responsibility–freedom contract refers to adults "sensitively monitor[ing] the child's level of intellectual, social, and emotional development in order to provide the appropriate freedoms and opportunities for the exercise of responsibility" (1981, p. 124). The achievement–support contract refers to adults expecting age-appropriate achievements and providing the necessary personal and material support to help children reach expected goals. The loyalty–commitment contract emphasizes adults' expectations that children will respond with loyalty and acceptance of adults because of the time, effort, and energy adults give. Although Elkind focused on the parent–child relationship, these contractual areas apply to all adult–child relationships.

Elkind's key concept related to contracts is that they are frequently violated by adults and that this violation causes stress for youngsters. Violation of the responsibility–freedom contract occurs when adults fail to reward responsibility with freedom. For example, when students act responsibly in making a reasonable request of a teacher or administrator and this request is not taken seriously or handled respectfully, this contract has been violated. Likewise, students who have demonstrated skill in directing portions of their own learning but are not treated as independent thinkers and learners experience frustration and stress through violation of the responsibility–freedom contract. The achievement–support contract is violated when adults do not provide adequate support for students' achievement. The low-achieving student who receives few opportunities to respond in class, little assistance in answering questions, and less reinforcement for appropriate answers is not receiving support commensurate with desired and potential achievement. Difficulties in the loyalty–commitment contract occur when children, especially adolescents, fail to provide adults with indications of loyalty commensurate with the efforts or commitment that adults see themselves as having made. When adults respond with removal of commitment, giving up on or criticizing the student, rather than by understanding and discussing the problem, contract violation occurs. This condition is more likely to happen with low-achieving students who may not immediately repay teachers for what appear to be considerable amounts of time and effort. It may also occur when cultural discontinuity exists between teachers and students with teachers perceiving themselves as providing support but students not feeling respected or supported.

Joan Lipsitz

While serving as director of the Center for Early Adolescence at the University of North Carolina at Chapel Hill, Joan Lipsitz wrote extensively on the needs of early adolescence. She noted that adults often fail to understand this age group, which leads to classroom management and instructional decisions that cause a considerable amount of the unproductive behavior that so frequently frustrates teachers who work with this age group. Lipsitz emphasized the importance of developing school environments that meet young adolescents' developmental needs. These were summarized by her colleague, Gayle Dorman (1981), and include many of the methods we consider as effective classroom management and instruction, including active and meaningful participation in their learning; clear, supportive structure; experiencing a sense of competence; and positive relationships with

© Dave Carpenter/www.CartoonStock.com

"The challenge in teaching junior high is that the maturity levels can fluctuate from 12th grade to 3rd grade in a matter of seconds."

© Joyce Button

"Oh, the stress on this job doesn't bother me. I used to teach in a junior high school."

their peers and teachers. Joan Lipsitz's thoughtful book *Successful Schools for Young Adolescents* (1984) examined four schools that have successfully met these needs.

Lipsitz's work has been supported by recent work regarding the importance of matching teacher–student relationship, instructional, and discipline issues to students' developmental needs. Pianta (2006) wrote that "using control-oriented discipline and competitive academic values with early adolescents who value autonomy, exploration, and a sense of identity, tends to produce lower levels of motivation and achievement and higher levels of problem behavior in large part because of the mismatch between context and developmental forces" (p. 689). A number of researchers have echoed this concern (Roeser, Eccles, & Sameroff, 1998; Wentzel, 2003). For example, there appears to be a mismatch between the more role-bound, impersonal relationships teachers began to develop with their students in middle school and early adolescents' needs for supportive relationships (Roeser & Galloway, 2002). This may be a particularly serious problem for students who enter middle school with fewer skills and less motivation (Harter, 1996). In addition, teachers may more effectively respond to students' sensitivity about their identity and competence by emphasizing instructional methods involving mastery, effort, and improvement rather than methods emphasizing comparison between students (Roeser et al., 1998).

In order to better understand why students behave in ways that fail to support learning, we strongly encourage every public school educator or prospective teacher to spend an entire day every year being a student in their school. This should involve the educator either riding the bus to school or entering the school at the same time as the student and completing all activities as if he or she were a student (including lunch, physical education, recess, etc.). Adults who have this experience are surprised at the uncomfortable seating, the lack of breaks, and the low levels of academic involvement and positive personal contact experienced by the student they are shadowing. Activity 2.1 (on page 46) provides additional ideas for this learning activity.

Social Cognitive Development Theory

In their book *Treating Explosive Kids: The Collaborative Problem-Solving Approach*, Ross Greene and Stuart Ablon (2006) suggest that students who struggle to follow adult expectations "have lagging skills in the global domains of flexibility/adaptability, frustration tolerance, and problem solving" (p. 7). Rather than view students' acting out or withdrawal behavior as caused by needs not being met, this approach suggests skill deficits in children's cognitive skills are the cause of noncompliance and explosiveness. The authors place the cognitive skills that are the basis for effectively or ineffectively responding to setting events as follows:

1. Executive Skills
   * Working memory
   * Organization and planning
   * Shifting cognitive set

2. Language-Processing Skills
   * Labeling one's emotions
   * Communicating feelings and needs
   * Sorting through and selecting response options
   * Receiving feedback about the appropriateness of one's actions

3. Emotion Regulation Skills
   * Regulate arousal in the service of goal-directed activity
   * Regulate acute emotional response

4. Cognitive Flexibility Skills
   * Need predictable routines

5. Social Skills
   * Recognizing the impact of one's behavior on others
   * Attending to social cues and nuances

When confronted by a student whose behavior is not supporting his learning or that of others, this model emphasizes the importance of educators determining the cognitive skills that are lacking and working with children to develop these skills through involving them in problem solving that incorporates the steps of: (1) showing empathy for the student's legitimate needs/concerns, (2) helping the student define the problem, and (3) collaborating with the student to develop new understandings and skills. Notice how this approach emphasizes the support for increasing students' sense of significance, competence, and power.

Brain Research

Research on the operation of the brain and what this may mean for creating effective learning environments and presenting effective instruction has progressed dramatically in the past decade. As the recommended reading at the end of the chapter indicates, numerous books present instructional strategies that logically connect to what we know about the human brain. Researchers and writers who present educational strategies that support what we know about the brain are providing teachers with many creative, practical, and beneficial methods for helping students succeed in school. Many, if not most, of these methods are not new and are also supported by a wide range of applied educational research. We agree with the following assessment by Howard Gardner (1999a):

> To be sure, knowledge of the brain's structure and functioning might well hold interesting implications for learning and pedagogy. But the only way to know for sure whether something is possible is to try it. And should one succeed despite the predictions of neuroscience, that success becomes the determining fact. (p. 79)

In an article in *Education Week*, Sarah Sparks (2012) presents the views of a number of leading neuroscientists regarding the connection between the field of neuroscience and practical implications for education. She quotes Dr. Kenneth Kosik, a neuroscience professor at the University of California, Santa Barbara and co-director of the Neuroscience Research Institute, as saying, "We still have a paucity of real, concrete findings in neuroscience that we can say will change what goes on in the classroom" (p. 17). She goes on to quote leaders in the field of brain-education research as noting that "the neuroscience evidence in their field has been sketchy so far" and "We need to figure out how to do more practical research" (p. 17). She suggests that more laboratory schools are needed where ideas generated by scientists can be applied and researched.

Like a number of other writers in this field, Sparks suggests that a major benefit of current neuroscience as it applies to education settings involves teaching students how the brain works and how they can improve their own learning through effort and practice. She also notes that brain research has taught us to understand the role of stress in limiting effective brain functioning and the importance of teaching students how to take breaks and relax themselves in order to facilitate their learning.

These ideas have been presented by Dr. Judy Willis (2010a, 2010b). Prior to becoming a teacher, Dr. Willis practiced child neurology for fifteen years, and she discussed how she uses her knowledge of neurology to enhance student engagement, excitement for learning, and achievement. Dr. Willis talks about the positive impact on brain functioning of reducing stress and failure associated with learning, ensuring that students are successful and appreciate their successes; the importance of creating supportive, safe learning environments; the benefits of helping students understand that they have the power to positively influence their brain's development; and the benefits of instructional activities that are interactive and personally relevant.

Materials at the end of the chapter reference several books by credible authors with backgrounds in neuroscience. While we caution educators about making a simple extrapolation from neuroscience to the classroom, it is important to study this area of research and conduct action research in your own classroom to see whether ideas with face validity between neuroscience and pedagogy can be implemented to enhance your students' learning.

We can say for certain that most of the research-supported methods presented in this text are also consistent with methods being presented as supported by what we know about the human brain.

PAUSE & CONSIDER 2.3

Based on what you currently know about brain-based research and learning, write a statement indicating how you might apply this knowledge to a classroom setting. After completing this text, you may want to revisit this Pause & Consider and add new information to your answer. You may also want to meet with colleagues or fellow students to discuss this topic.

STUDENTS AT RISK FOR SCHOOL FAILURE

Concern for students at risk is a major theme in U.S. education. The term *at risk* has generally referred to students who are likely to drop out of school. The Business Advisory Commission of the Education Commission of the States (ECS) has extended this concept to include youngsters who are unlikely to make successful transitions to becoming productive adults.

Students may be at risk for a variety of reasons. In addition to the fact that a student may not have had important personal or developmental needs met prior to entering the classroom or within the school setting, he or she may also be at risk for poor academic performance because (1) the school system provides relatively few educators from the social/cultural group with which this student identifies and presents a curriculum that fails to value the student's cultural background; (2) the classroom environment and instructional approach is inconsistent with how the student learns best; (3) the student has limited English proficiency and is thus less able to understand the material being presented; (4) the student has special needs associated with an identified disability; (5) outside of school, the student has limited support for school success; (6) the student has demands outside of school that limit time and energy for school-related learning tasks; or (7) the student lacks a sense of hope that school-based learning will positively impact his or her future.

Based on the most recent data from the National Center for Education Statistics (2013), dropout and suspension rates vary dramatically by ethnicity. Dropout statistics show 12.7 percent of Hispanic, 12.4 percent of American Indian/Alaska Native, 7.5 percent of Black, 4.4 percent of White, and 4.2 percent of Asian/Pacific Islander students drop out of school. Statistics reported in 2012 indicate the percentage of male students who have been suspended at least once also shows dramatic variability by ethnicity with 49 percent of Blacks, 29 percent of Hispanics, 29 percent of those who identify themselves as being of two or more races, 18 percent of Whites, and 13 percent of Asian/Pacific Islanders having been suspended. Interestingly, 32 percent of all males had been suspended at least once compared to 17 percent of all females. While there are many factors for these discrepancies, it is interesting that Futrell, Gomez, and Bedden (2003) found that 80 percent of the classroom teachers they surveyed felt unprepared to effectively teach students from diverse backgrounds.

Writers such as James Banks, Johnella Butler, Harold Dent, James Garcia, Geneva Gay, Crystal Kuykendall, and Pedro Noguera have written extensively on the problems students of color confront in their attempt to achieve success in U.S. classrooms. Studies indicate that many African American, Hispanic American, and Native American students are more field dependent and group oriented than the average White student and that schools are structured as highly individualistic, competitive environments (Freeman & Freeman, 2002). According to Geneva Gay (1993), "the sameness of educational resources for diverse individuals and groups does not constitute comparability of quality or opportunity. Teachers, materials, and teaching environments that work well for European American students do not necessarily work equally well for ethnic minorities" (p. 182). Gay highlighted three reasons students of color may fare less well than their White counterparts in traditional classrooms:

1. Most [teachers] do not know how to understand and use the school behaviors of these students, which differ from their normative expectations, as aides to teaching. Therefore, they tend to misinterpret them as deviant and treat them punitively.
2. Most curriculum designs and instructional materials are Eurocentric. . . . They are likely to be more readily meaningful and to have a greater appeal to the life experiences and aspirations of European American students than to those of ethnic minorities. Thus, when attempting to learn academic tasks, European American students do not have the additional burden of working across irrelevant instructional materials and methods.

3. A high degree of cultural congruency exists between middle-class European American student culture and school culture. These students do not experience much cultural discontinuity, social-code incompatibility, or need for cultural style shifting to adjust to the behavioral codes expected of them in school. (pp. 182–183)

Compared to their peers from high-income living situations, students from low-income living situations are also disproportionately unsuccessful in school. High school students in low-income living situations are six times as likely to drop out of school as are their peers from high-income families (National Center for Education Statistics, 2010). Clearly, one's ethnicity, disabilities, and family income significantly impact academic access and success in U.S. public schools. One important goal of this text is to provide the knowledge and skills to more effectively serve the learning needs of a wide range of students. Consequently, the methods presented in this text have been selected because they have proven to be effective with virtually every group of students that has historically been poorly served in U.S. public schools.

Students who struggle in school are our best staff-development experts. Through their academic frustration and behavior problems, they frequently inform us that while we may be doing a fine job of teaching for some students, we need to modify our strategies for them. Interestingly, although the instructional and classroom management modifications we make in response to the demands of these students are often necessary prerequisites to their experiencing success, they also benefit virtually all other students. Many of the strategies presented in this text would be desirable but not absolutely necessary if we were teaching a senior honors class or a graduate seminar. However, when teaching a heterogeneous group of students, some of whom find the work extremely challenging or frustrating, these strategies can make the difference for both teacher and student between an exciting, enjoyable year and a year filled with anger and frustration.

Unique Needs of Immigrant Children

Although all students experience the developmental and social/personal needs described in this chapter, immigrant children experience unique needs associated with moving into a new culture.

> In 431 B.C. Euripides wrote, "There is no greater sorrow on earth than the loss of one's native land." Students who have recently moved to this country are struggling with this loss as well as numerous other specific adjustments. One very basic stressor for immigrant children is that "once an immigrant student walks into a U.S. classroom, the rules and knowledge they received from their home culture do not readily apply." (Olsen & Jaramillo, 1999, p. 205)

In her book *The Inner World of the Immigrant Child*, Cristina Igoa (1995) considers how immigrant children often believe they cannot accept their culture of origin but they also feel unaccepted and alienated from U.S. culture. She discusses the importance of validating and supporting their culture of origin. In writing about her own experiences as an immigrant student, Igoa (1995) noted that because she was bilingual, the issues she faced were not so much about language as about her feelings of confusion and inadequacy about how she should act, her loss of a cultural identity, and the difficulty of adapting to new cultural expectations when no one was trying to understand and adapt to who she was.

She talks about the loneliness and sadness experienced by many immigrant children and their desperate need to be connected to someone who they believe cares and understands. Igoa makes an important point when she notes:

> In my work with immigrant children, I have become aware that each student's response and behavior in my classroom and out in the yard are a result of the complex interaction of his or her cultural background, individual nature, and length of time that student has been in the host country. (p. 17)

A number of factors influence the experience of immigrant families (Edwards, Ellis, Ko, Saifer, & Stuczynski, 2005). These include the following:

- Background and reasons for immigrating
- Immigrant or refugee status
- Adjustment issues
- Family and cultural supports
- Cultural differences
- Language issues
- Economic status
- Marketability of skills in U.S. economy
- Acceptance by U.S. mainstream society
- Generational issues

In order to understand the needs of our immigrant students, we must go beyond understanding theories of human development and understand the journeys that have led our students to our classrooms. It is helpful for us to know what kind of instructional activities are most and least comfortable for them, what types of teacher responses are most comfortable, and the expectations or ways of behaving that make them uncomfortable.

As discussed throughout this text, this will involve meeting with families and seeking out individuals in the community and the education profession who have a deep understanding of the needs of our immigrant children.

It is important to realize that the issues facing immigrant children are not unique to children who have recently arrived from another country. Native American students who have lived in rural areas, often on reservations, and move to urban areas will experience stressors very similar to those of students from other countries. Similarly, students from families who live in poverty will often find the peer pressures and social demands of middle-class school communities to be unfamiliar and intimidating. Our role as educators is to understand all students with the goal of providing every student a safe, caring, supportive learning community.

Your views may differ from those expressed in this section. What is important is to have a solid foundation in research and theory to support your views. It is also imperative that you develop specific teaching methods that enable you to effectively implement your beliefs and goals in a manner that enhances students' dignity, academic success, and social skill development.

A Case Study: Meeting Students' Needs in a Middle School

Several years ago, one of us worked with a middle school located in an area where nearly 90 percent of the students were on free or reduced lunch and were either Hispanic or Native American. When confronted with problems of student absenteeism and failure, the staff initially looked at national research on middle schools and developed a schedule and instructional strategies that they believed were best suited to the needs of middle school students. They created a block schedule in which students spent nearly half the day in a language arts, reading, and social studies block and the other half in a science, math, and health block. In addition, to respond to problems of student tardiness and students' learning styles related to time of day, the blocks were rotated at the end of the semester. In addition, a study period was scheduled following the morning block, and students who were having difficulty with their work remained with their block teacher and an assistant while other students attended an elective. Therefore, for half the school year students had the potential for a tutorial in nearly half their academic subjects. During this time, students were guaranteed to have assistance from someone who spoke their first language.

To increase the students' sense of significance and power, the staff created a yearly fall retreat in which approximately forty students and ten adults spent several days camping and developing a vision for the following school year. This vision was used as a theme for decorating the school, for helping students set goals, and for school events. One year when one of us was working at the school, the theme was "Make all the right moves." Chess figures were used to decorate the cafeteria, and students used this motto as a lead-in to short- and long-term goal setting.

In addition, the staff created a number of clubs representing activities selected by the students. The Native American club became well known regionally for its performances, and several other cultural clubs made performances and arranged special events. Students formed a recycling club that became actively involved in the community.

The faculty became concerned, however, when they noted that despite the fact that student achievement and attendance were improving dramatically, there was still a very high rate of late arrivals to school. Rather than assign detentions or use some other form of coercive discipline, the faculty met with students and parents to discuss the issue. Cultural differences regarding time were discussed. The group, therefore, decided to place the responsibility on the students to decide how important it was to be on time. The school decided to move the club program from fourth to first period. Students who arrived late were invited to study in the cafeteria but were not allowed to participate in the club for that day. Student tardies virtually disappeared. The students simply decided that the club activities were important enough to offset their lack of concern with timeliness.

SUMMARY

Many teachers view their lack of ability to understand and effectively respond to unproductive student behavior as a major cause of job-related stress and personal frustration. Anyone who has taught has heard a colleague say in exasperation, "I just don't understand why Johnny acts that way." This chapter presented the important concept that student behavior can be understood by considering basic psychological needs students bring to the school setting. In many if not most cases when students act unproductively at school, they are responding to the fact that basic needs are not being met in the school setting. Unproductive school behavior is more frequent among students whose basic needs are not being met at home and in the community. Nevertheless, the problems outside of school are often not the major cause of the students' school difficulties, nor does their presence absolve us of our responsibility to create learning environments that meet students' basic needs.

Beginning teachers often struggle with the issues of creating order, providing care and support, and sharing power and responsibility. Understanding how these concepts interact and how they are most effectively developed in the classroom is a critical factor in developing an effective philosophy and practice of classroom management.

Educators must also be particularly sensitive to the issue of how classroom environments support or disadvantage students who have historically been less successful in public school settings in the United States. This includes African American, Hispanic, and Native American students, as well as students whose first language is not English and those who have been raised in poverty. It is essential that school settings systematically and thoughtfully support the cultural values and interests as well as the personal and learning style needs students bring to the classroom. In order to accomplish this, educators will need ongoing assistance in developing increased knowledge and skills in this area.

IMPLEMENTATION ACTIVITIES

ACTIVITY 2.1

Examining Various Perspectives of a Behavior Problem

Select an incident in which a student disrupted the learning environment to such an extent that you had to send him or her to the office. Before continuing this activity, write down the punishment or consequence you would expect the student to receive for this act.

On a separate sheet of paper, write a one-half- to one-page statement indicating how each of the following individuals would describe the incident leading to the referral: (1) yourself, (2) the student involved, (3) a student-centered counselor, and (4) the administrator who heard both your and the student's points of view. At the bottom of each paper, write a brief statement indicating what you think each individual would suggest as the solution or resolution to this situation.

Having completed this exercise, write a statement concerning how you believe the situation should be responded to or resolved.

ACTIVITY 2.2

Behavior Problems and Students' Personal Needs

Consider a situation where the data from your school indicates you are having ongoing behavior problems in a certain area of the school, for example, cafeteria, an area of the playground, specific hallway areas, a certain classroom, and so forth. Make sure to consider whether a pattern exists concerning the students who are most commonly involved in the behavior problems. Based on your reading of this chapter, what might you consider regarding how this situation relates to students' personal needs? What might these finding suggest regarding the manner in which educators responsible for students in this setting responded to create an environment that more effectively met the needs experienced by these students. After completing this course, return to this activity and add other ideas for how educators might help to alleviate this problem.

RECOMMENDED READING

Banks, J., & McGee Banks, C. (Eds.). (1993). *Multicultural education: Issues and perspective* (2nd ed.). Boston, MA: Allyn & Bacon.

Carger, C. (1996). *Of borders and dreams: A Mexican-American experience of urban education.* New York, NY: Teachers College Press.

Cozolino, L. (2013). *The social neuroscience of education: Optimizing attachment and learning in the classroom.* New York, NY: W.W. Norton & Company.

Cummins, J. (1996). *Negotiating identities: Education for empowerment in a diverse society.* Ontario, CA: California Association for Bilingual Education.

Darling-Hammond, L. (1997). *The right to learn: A blueprint for creating schools that work.* San Francisco, CA: Jossey-Bass.

Davidman, L., & Davidman, P. (1997). *Teaching with a multicultural perspective: A practical guide.* New York, NY: Longman.

Della Salla, S., & Anderson, M. (2012). *Neuroscience in education: The good, the bad, and the ugly.* Oxford, UK: Oxford University Press.

Five, C. (1992). *Special voices.* Portsmouth, NH: Heinemann.

Freeman, Y., & Freeman, D. (2002). *Closing the achievement gap: How to reach limited-formal-schooling and long-term English learners.* Portsmouth, NH: Heinemann.

Garbarino, J. (1999). *Lost boys: Why our sons turn violent and how we can save them*. New York, NY: Free Press.

Garcia, E. (2001). *Student cultural diversity: Understanding and meeting the challenge* (3rd ed.). Boston, MA: Houghton Mifflin.

Gardner, H. (1999b). *Intelligence reframed: Multiple intelligences for the 21st century*. New York, NY: Basic Books.

Garrod, A., & Larimore, C. (1997). *First person, first peoples: Native American college graduates tell their life stories*. Ithaca, NY: Cornell University Press.

Garrod, A., Ward, J., Robinson, T., & Kilkenny, R. (Eds.). (1999). *Souls looking back: Life stories of growing up Black*. New York, NY: Routledge.

Goleman, D. (1995). *Emotional intelligence*. New York, NY: Bantam Books.

Igoa, C. (1995). *The inner world of the immigrant child*. New York, NY: St. Martin's Press.

Kandel, E., Schwartz, J., Jessell, T., Siegelbaum, S., & Hudspeth, A. (Eds.). (2013). *Principles of neural science* (5th ed.). Columbus, OH: McGraw-Hill.

Karr-Morse, R., & Wiley, M. (1997). *Ghosts from the nursery: Tracing the roots of violence*. New York, NY: Atlantic Monthly Press.

Kauffman, J. (1997). *Characteristics of emotional and behavioral disorders of children and youth* (6th ed.). Upper Saddle River, NJ: Merrill/Prentice Hall.

Kuykendall, C. (2004). *From rage to hope: Strategies for reclaiming Black and Hispanic students* (2nd ed.). Bloomington, IN: National Educational Service.

Lee, S. (1996). *Unraveling the "model minority" stereotype: Listening to Asian American youth*. New York, NY: Teachers College Press.

Noguera, P. (2008). *The trouble with Black boys . . . and other reflections on race, equity, and the future of public education*. San Francisco, CA: Jossey-Bass.

Reyes, P., Scribner, J., & Scribner, A. (Eds.). (1999). *Lessons from high-performing Hispanic schools: Creating learning communities*. New York, NY: Teachers College Press.

Sousa, D. (Ed.). (2010). *Mind, brain, and education: Neuroscience implications for the classroom*. Bloomington, IN: Solution Tree Press.

Willis, J. (2010a). The current impact of neuroscience on teaching and learning. In D. Sousa (Ed.), *Mind, brain & education: Neuroscience implications for the classroom* (pp. 45–66). Bloomington, IN: Solution Tree.

Willis, J. (2010b). Using my neuroscience to treat the sickness in our classrooms. *Catalyst for Change, 36*, 46–55.

Zull, J. (2011). *From brain to mind: Using neuroscience to guide change in education*. Herndon, VA: Stylus Publishing.

CREATING A SAFE AND SUPPORTIVE LEARNING COMMUNITY

PART 2

An ounce of prevention is worth a pound of cure. This statement is the key to effective classroom management. A large percentage of classroom problems can be prevented by creating positive, safe classroom environments.

The focus on improving standardized test scores has led many school districts to push teachers to use every minute of instructional time to focus on information that will be on the tests. This has often occurred at the expense of time allocated to developing classrooms as communities of support. Efforts to help students know and work collaboratively with their peers, as well as helping students construct and understand the importance of a democratic classroom where everyone is valued and values the rights of others, have often been short-circuited so more time is available for test preparation. Research suggests this focus is shortsighted. Brain research clearly supports the concept that student learning will be enhanced when students work in calm, safe learning environments where they feel supported and valued (Connell, 2009; Rushton & Juola-Rushton, 2008; Willis, 2006). Numerous studies also clearly support the concept that student learning and positive behavior is enhanced in settings characterized by warmth and emotional support where students feel safe, cared for, respected, and encouraged (Brophy, 2004; National School Climate Council, 2007).

Most current models of classroom management focus on the important factor of developing rules and procedures as the key prerequisite to creating a safe, calm classroom environment. We strongly support this concept, and Chapter 6 provides current best practices for accomplishing this goal. However, as supported by much of the material presented in the previous chapter, we also believe the creation of positive, supportive interpersonal relationships in the classroom is a central component to creating environments in which students feel safe and are motivated to achieve. Part 2 includes methods for creating these positive relationships in your classroom.

Research (Wentzel, 2003) indicates that student motivation and positive behavior increase when students perceive their relationships with peers and teachers to be positive and supportive. McNeely, Nonnemaker, and Blum (2002) found that "When adolescents feel cared for by people at their school and feel like part of their school, they are less likely to use substances, engage in violence, or initiate sexual activity at an early age" (p. 138). Indeed, Resnick et al. (1997) reported that connectedness to school was the only school-related factor that helped protect against a wide variety of student health risks, including violence, illegal drug use, school failure, and pregnancy.

Educators should be aware of the dangers inherent in the completely unsubstantiated belief that time spent in creating classrooms in which students feel involved, safe, and happy could somehow be better spent in additional instructional time. As discussed in Part 2, students' academic performance is enhanced when teachers take time to respond to students' personal and psychological needs. Research indicates that students experiencing positive feelings about themselves and school is associated with improved student attitudes and higher-level thinking skills. Another important reason for blending academic and personal–social skill building is that if schools' goals include preparing young people to be involved citizens, activities aimed at developing a sound base of knowledge must be balanced with skills in interpersonal relations and problem solving.

Chapter 3 examines two pivotal aspects of teacher–student relationships: (1) the personal, affective quality of these relationships and (2) how teachers communicate expectations to students. Chapter 4 focuses on the quality of peer relationships within classrooms. The chapter provides numerous activities for enhancing positive, cooperative peer relationships. The significant adults in students' lives outside of school can do much to encourage positive student attitudes toward school. Chapter 5 examines methods teachers can use to create positive, supportive relationships with these adults. Chapter 6 presents numerous research-supported methods for involving students in developing and committing to positive classroom behavior standards.

CHAPTER 3

Establishing Positive Teacher–Student Relationships

Most important, students say they like classrooms where they feel they know the teacher and the other students. While students appreciate a well-organized and orderly environment, they do not like one in which the teacher is detached and treats the classroom as a whole rather than as a roomful of individuals.

—Patricia Phelan, Ann Locke Davidson, and Hanh Thanh Cao (1992)

Nowadays, to be successful in a position of authority requires an ability to connect in a caring way by inspiring hope within others and by leading one's own life in a manner that models the message.

—Allen Mendler (1992)

If a child is to live freely and creatively and acculturate to a new social environment, then the deeper part of the child must surface. We need to help the child remove his or her mask through warmth, reverence, understanding, and listening closely.

—Cristina Igoa (1995)

The heart of the professional ideal in teaching may well be . . . a commitment to the ethic of caring. Caring requires more than bringing state-of-the-art technical knowledge to bear in one's practice. It means doing everything possible to enhance the learning, developmental, and social needs of students as persons. The heart of caring in schools is relationships with others (teachers, parents, and students) characterized by nurturance, altruistic love, and kinshiplike connections.

—Thomas Sergiovanni (1994)

The most powerful restraints on violent behavior are healthy human attachments.

—Larry Brendtro and Nicholas Long (1995)

Moreover, when teachers are taught to provide students with warmth and support, clear expectations for behavior, and developmentally appropriate autonomy, their students develop a stronger sense of community, increase displays of socially competent behavior, and show academic gains.

—Kathryn Wentzel (2006)

The quality of teacher–student relationships dramatically affects whether students' personal needs are met in the classroom. Students spend nearly a quarter of their waking lives between ages six and seventeen with teachers. Because teachers are responsible for evaluating students' work and controlling the quality of life in the classroom, they are powerful adult figures in students' lives. Effective teachers understand the influence they have on students and use this influence positively.

LEARNING GOALS

After reading this chapter, you will know:

1. What characteristics students say they want in their teachers
2. How to establish positive, professional relationships with your students
3. How to create appropriate, high expectations for your students
4. How to use language to effectively reinforce student behavior
5. The basic communication skills associated with effectively listening to students
6. Some central issues related to culturally sensitive communication
7. Methods for evaluating the quality of your relationships with your students

Why Are These Goals Important?

The quality of an educator's relationships with students is an incredibly important factor influencing student learning and behavior. Perhaps no other factor will influence how effective you are at motivating students, establishing a safe, positive learning environment, and having students respond respectfully when you need to correct their work or behavior.

RESEARCH ON TEACHER–STUDENT RELATIONSHIPS

Based on their meta-analysis of more than one hundred studies, Marzano, Marzano, and Pickering (2003) reported that positive teacher–student relationships were the foundation of effective classroom management and that these positive relationships could reduce behavior problems by 31 percent. More recent research indicates a significant relationship between the quality of teachers' relationships with their students and students' behavior. Gregory and Ripski (2008) found that ". . . teachers who reported that they used a relational approach were more likely to have students who exhibited lower defiant behavior than those teachers who did not report using such an approach. This significant association between a relational approach and low defiant behavior was explained by student trust in teacher authority." This should not be surprising because most people are more likely to react positively to someone they feel likes them and whom they trust. In a study of 1,500 randomly selected adults who had recent interactions with legal authorities, the degree to which the adults were willing to voluntarily comply was affected by whether they felt they were being fairly treated and trusted the authority figure (DeCremer & Tyler, 2007). Similarly, research suggests that when adolescents perceive someone's actions as being hostile, they are more likely to respond aggressively (Dodge, Laird, Lochman, & Zelli, 2002).

Shirley & Cornell (2011) found that African American students were more likely to view adults as less supportive and thus to experience a less positive school climate. Since students who feel less supported by teachers and are less likely to ask adults for assistance are more likely to be involved in behavior that violates school norms, these authors suggest this may be a significant factor influencing the disproportionate number of discipline referrals and suspensions for African American students. In their study on why African American students are disciplined at a higher rate than other students, Gregory and Weinstein (2008) wrote:

> African American students reported uncaring treatment and low academic expectations from teachers with whom they behaved more defiantly and less cooperatively, as rated by themselves and by these teachers. In contrast, the students reported that their nominated teachers treated them with care and high expectations. Moreover, students expressed a willingness to comply with the authority of teachers who had earned trust and legitimacy. (p. 469)

An excellent example of the importance of combining acceptance with respect for students was reported by Kleinfeld (1972) in a powerful analysis of teachers' interactions with Inuit and Native American students who had recently moved to urban settings. Kleinfeld found that teachers who were effective with these children were able to combine showing a personal interest in the students with demands for solid academic achievement. Summarizing her findings, she stated:

> The essence of the instructional style which elicits a high level of intellectual performance from village Indian and Eskimo students is to create an extremely warm personal relationship and to actively demand a level of academic work which the student does not suspect he can attain. Village students thus interpret the teacher's demandingness not as bossiness or hostility, but rather as another expression of his personal concern, and meeting the teacher's academic standards becomes their reciprocal obligation in an intensely personal relationship. (p. 34)

Kleinfeld used the term *warm demanders* to describe this combination of high expectations, warm relationships, and high demands. Kleinfeld's work is consistent with research conducted twenty-five years later showing that successful adults who were raised in poverty point to the importance of a supportive adult who believed in and encouraged them to continue their education (Harrington & Boardman, 1997). Similarly, Adkins-Coleman (2010) reports the level of concern teachers demonstrate for their students, especially Black students, is directly related to the quality of teacher effectiveness in facilitating student learning. Adkins-Coleman further states,

> Students of color, in particular, acknowledge that caring teachers not only build strong relationships with them, but also assertively insist on high behavioral expectations that include completing all assignments, actively participating in the class, working hard, and treating others with respect (Bondy, Ross, Gallingane & Hambacher, 2007; Brown, 2004; Ware, 2006). (p. 47)

In a study conducted at the Center for Research on the Context of Secondary School Teaching at Stanford University, researchers examined high school students' perceptions regarding school factors that influence their school performance. The researchers reported, "A recurring theme in students' comments is the tremendous value they place on having teachers who care. . . . In fact, the number of student references to 'wanting caring teachers' is so great that we believe it speaks to the quiet desperation and loneliness of many adolescents in today's society" (Phelan et al., 1992, p. 698). Not surprisingly, research suggests strong positive relationships between a teacher and second-grade students can help reduce later aggressive behavior, and this effect was strongest for African American and Latino students (Meehan, Hughes, & Cavell, 2003).

In their extensive study of school environments that meet the needs of students at risk for school failure, Wehlage, Rutter, Smith, Lesko, and Fernandez (1989) reported the following four common impediments to students developing a sense of school community:

1. *Adjustment:* Students at risk need a more personal and supportive relationship with adults than schools typically provide.
2. *Difficulty:* "Although we found literal inability to do the work a relatively rare characteristic of at-risk students, it is the case that increased time and more intensive tutoring were required for many. . . . The educational situation students complained most about was the ubiquitous 'lecture-discussion' based on reading assignments" (p. 124).
3. *Incongruence:* This related to the lack of personal–social match between the student and the institution.
4. *Isolation:* "We found that students who had persistent conflicts with adults or who found no teacher with whom to establish a personal relationship were at risk of dropping out" (p. 131).

The authors also stated that "there are four teacher beliefs and/or values, accompanied by corresponding sets of behaviors, that together constitute a positive teacher culture facilitating membership and engagement for students" (p. 135). These beliefs are the following:

1. Teachers accept personal responsibility for student success.
2. Teachers practice an extended teacher role.
3. Teachers are persistent with students.
4. Teachers express a sense of optimism that all students can learn.

A clear relationship exists between positive teacher–student relationships and a wide variety of positive outcomes for students. Not surprisingly, elementary students who rate their school experience more positively also rate their relationships with their teacher as more positive (Murray & Greenberg, 2000). African American youth in an alternative program indicated they would work harder when teachers were caring, believed in their potential, and provided structure (Muller, Katz, & Dance, 1999). Positive relationships with teachers appear to be a factor that prevents high-risk students from being retained or referred for special services (Pianta, Steinberg, & Rollins, 1995). In discussing school programs that assist alienated students, Testerman (1996) wrote, "an adult in school who shows individualized concern for an at-risk student can have a significant positive effect on that student's attendance" (p. 364). Testerman reports a program in Lely High School in Naples, Florida, in which a group of students with a lower than 1.5 grade point average (GPA) were provided with an adult adviser who met with them for at least fifteen minutes per week. When compared to a control group, students who worked with an adviser were less likely to drop out. The experimental group also had a GPA during the experiment that was almost double that of the control group. Hamre and Pianta (2001) reported that when other factors such as students' cognitive ability and behavior were controlled for, students who had more positive relationships with their kindergarten teacher were more likely to be academically successful and to behave more responsibly in eighth grade.

Emotionally supportive teacher–student interactions are associated with higher academic achievement (Curby, Rimm-Kaufman, & Ponitz, 2009), lower rates of aggressive student behavior, students showing more emotional self-control (Merritt, Wanless, Rimm-Kaufman, Cameron, & Peugh, 2012), and lower rates of minor disruptive classroom behavior (Demanet & Houtte, 2012).

Emotionally supportive teachers were defined as listening to students' perspectives, creating a positive classroom climate, the existence of respect for students, and generally warm and supportive interactions between student and teacher.

Educators often express concern about the ability of students who struggle academically and behaviorally to self-regulate their behavior. The quality of teacher–student relationships appears to have an impact on this factor. A recent study reported that "The results of the current study support the idea that teachers who communicate appreciation for children's efforts, who show more warmth and less often disapprove, create a classroom in which internal regulation is fostered in children (Fuhs, Farran, & Nesbitt, 2013, p. 356).

In a study of more than 1,300 third graders, Mercer and DeRosier (2008) found a relationship between how much teachers reported liking a student and the student's levels of loneliness, social anxiety, and grades. Another study demonstrated that elementary school students who are less well liked and receive less support from their teachers are more likely to be rejected by their peers (Hughes, Zhang, & Hill, 2006). When teachers demonstrate personal liking for students who demonstrate behavior problems, this can increase how positively peers view and interact with the students and decrease the disruptive behavior presented by these students (Mikami, Gregory, Allen, Pianta, & Lun, 2011; Mikami, Griggs, Reuland, & Gregory, 2012). A summary of research on the impact teachers' interactions with students have on peer relationships reported:

> Collectively, the results of this study suggest that the relationships teachers develop with individual students may impact how students are viewed by classmates both academically and socially, and that this may have consequences for their adjustment in subsequent school years. These findings suggest that it may be fruitful to include teacher-student relationship quality . . . as an intervention target to enhance at-risk students' peer relations, peer academic reputations, and academic self-concept. (Farmer, Lines, & Hamm, 2011, p. 253)

What Do Students Say They Value in Teachers?

Students' statements regarding effective teachers mirror those supported by research on effective teachers. "When I have asked students in interviews what makes a particular teacher 'special' and worthy of respect, the students consistently cite three characteristics: firmness, compassion, and an interesting, engaging, and challenging teaching style" (Noguera, 1995).

Interviews conducted over a three-year period with 400 inner-city middle and high school students in Philadelphia present similar results (Corbett & Wilson, 2002). These students stated that good teachers:

- Made sure that students did their work
- Controlled the classroom
- Were willing to help students whenever and however the students wanted help
- Explained assignments and content clearly
- Varied the classroom routine
- Took time to get to know the students and their circumstances (p. 18)

This list is similar to that presented by Noguera (2008) based on interviews with 132 students in ten Boston high schools. These students stated that teachers should

- get to know students better.
- be patient and ask students if they understand the material. If they don't get the material being taught, the teacher should explain the material in a different way.

- have a strong command of the material and a passion for the subjects so that they can get students to be excited about learning it.
- show respect to students in the same way that they expect to receive respect.
- be firm and not allow students to get away with preventing other students from learning. (pp. 64, 65)

Based on an extensive review of the literature, Woolfolk Hoy and Weinstein (2006) found that students preferred and responded best to teachers who possessed three sets of skills: (1) establishing caring relationships with students; (2) setting limits and creating a safe environment without being rigid, threatening, or punitive; and (3) making learning fun. These findings are reinforced by Wentzel (2002), who reported that middle school students wanted teachers who "cared." In a later study, Wentzel (2006) described these teachers as ones "who demonstrate democratic and egalitarian communication styles designed to elicit student participation and input, who develop expectations for student behavior and performance in light of individual differences and abilities, who model a 'caring' attitude and interest in their instruction and interpersonal dealing with students, and who provide constructive rather than harsh and critical feedback" (p. 633).

In a survey of 225 seniors in an urban high school, Plank, McDill, McPartland, and Jordan (2001) reported that all students indicated they had the ability to act in a manner either supportive of or contradictory to the teacher's goals and wishes, and their decision was based on their perceptions of the teacher, particularly whether the teacher attempted to get to know them and be respectful of them. Studies involving middle school students (Bosworth, 1995), African American high school students (Cothran & Ennis, 1997), Latino middle school students (Katz, 1999), immigrant Mexican American high school students (Valenzuela, 1999), and high school students who were defined as being disruptive (Garner, 1995) all support these findings. Students clearly behave in ways more conducive to learning when they perceive that their teachers are willing to assist them with their school work; value them as individuals; treat them respectfully; care about their learning and their personal lives; and maintain an orderly, safe classroom environment. It is extremely important to note, however, that although students will tend to like teachers who demonstrate interest in and support of students, this is not synonymous with being liked or popular. Indeed, Cushman (2003) reported that "Students say that if a teacher sets a steady example of fairness and respect, they respond positively whether or not they like a teacher personally" (p. 17).

© Joyce Button

"Of course I believe that a teacher should offer a positive role model; however . . ."

Students want more from teachers than caring and personal support. They also want teachers who can set clear limits in the classroom (Weinstein, 2003) without being overly rigid or distant (Davidson, 1999) and who can be fair (Garner, 1995) and calm (Pomeroy, 1999) in responding to student behavior that disrupts the learning environment. Students prefer teachers who help create clear behavior standards; use humor and calm responses when responding to classroom disruptions; and when appropriate, allow students an opportunity to explain their side of a story. Students also prefer and act more responsibly when working with teachers who can create a variety of learning activities that actively engage students in meaningful learning (Cothran & Ennis, 1997; Davidson, 1999).

In summarizing research on motivation, Wentzel (2006) noted that "students will engage in valued social and academic activities when they perceive their involvement and relationships with their teachers . . . as being emotionally supportive and nurturing" (p. 635). Gallahar (2009) reported that students are more successful in improving their mathematics skills when they believe their teacher is fair, treats students equitably, and maintains a positive learning environment. Kawall (2009) found that teachers who were successful in raising test scores of low-income students were more often described as strict, fun, and caring. While "caring" has often been described as showing personal interest in students, a study suggests that for Latino and African American students in particular, teachers' willingness to provide academic support may be the factor students identify as the most important component of a "caring" teacher (Garrett, Barr, & Rothman, 2009). "Findings indicate that suburban and rural students have similar opinions, and the three most frequently mentioned teacher characteristics valued by students included a caring attitude, knowledge of the subject and how to teach it, and classroom management skills" (Williams, Sullivan, & Kohn, 2012, pp. 104, 105). The next most common characteristic listed by these secondary students was that teachers needed to have fun.

Teachers are increasingly aware of the importance of positive teacher–student relationships. Darling-Hammond (1997) found that 84 percent of teachers she interviewed stated that developing positive relationships with students and developing materials related to student needs were the most important ingredients of effective teaching. This teacher perception is supported by research. Based on their meta-analysis of more than 100 studies, Marzano et al. (2003) reported that positive teacher–student relationships were the foundation of effective classroom management and that these positive relationships could reduce behavior problems by 31 percent.

Although students and educators seem to agree on many of the qualities of a good teacher, students too often believe teachers do not display these characteristics, and when this occurs, the results are predictable. William Glasser (1990) noted that "By the end of the seventh grade, more than half the students believe that teachers and principals are their adversaries" (p. 29). Students often respond to this perceived sense of being devalued by misbehaving. Cusick (1994) reported that most student resistance to teacher directions occurs in classes where students report disliking their teacher. In a study of sixty-eight high school students, 84 percent indicated that discipline problems could be prevented by improved teacher–student relationships (Sheets, 1994). This is not surprising given the fact that research indicates "at least 50% to 60% of school children suffer from at least one occurrence of maltreatment by an educator which leads to some stress symptoms, including aggressive responses" (Hyman & Perone, 1998, p. 20). Another way to view students' alienation is that, "students see their misbehavior as a way to distance themselves from uncaring and disrespectful teachers, and the cycle seems to continue in spite of teachers' desire to correct student behavior" (Milner, 2006).

Although positive teacher–student relationships are an essential factor influencing the motivation, achievement, and behavior of all students, this is particularly true for students who may find school more challenging. In discussing his interviews with teachers viewed as highly effective with a culturally and linguistically diverse student population, Garcia (2001) wrote,

"Each teacher spoke of the importance of strong and caring relationships among class members and particularly between the teacher and the students" (p. 276). In his book on empowering minority students, Cummins (1996) wrote, "in classroom interactions respect and affirmation are central to motivating second language learners to engage actively and enthusiastically in academic content" (p. 74).

PAUSE & CONSIDER 3.1

Try to remember a teacher you had in elementary, middle, or high school that you felt created a safe, supportive environment and whom you admired as an educator. What were the characteristics this teacher possessed that enabled her or him to be successful and to be remembered by you as an excellent teacher? Meet with a group of three or four colleagues or classmates and share what each of you wrote.

ESTABLISHING EFFECTIVE RELATIONSHIPS WITH STUDENTS

In his classic book *Teacher Effectiveness Training*, Thomas Gordon (1974) wrote:

> The relationship between a teacher and a student is good when it has (1) *Openness* or *Transparency*, so each is able to risk directness and honesty with the other; (2) *Caring*, when each knows that he is valued by the other; (3) *Interdependence* (as opposed to dependency) of one on the other; (4) *Separateness*, to allow each to grow and to develop his uniqueness, creativity, and individuality; (5) *Mutual Needs Meeting*, so that neither's needs are met at the expense of the other's needs. (p. 24)

In a similar vein, Noddings (1984) wrote that moral education based on caring consists of four components: modeling, dialogue, practice, and confirmation. *Modeling* refers to how we as educators treat others—adults and children. *Dialogue* means an open-ended discussion in which the adult has not predetermined the decision. Dialogue allows students to ask why and to have input into decisions that affect them. *Practice* means that students must have opportunities to be involved in caring relationships. This may involve community-service activities, tutoring, or other occasions in which students learn to assist and encourage others. Finally, *confirmation* refers to finding opportunities to validate each student's growth toward being a caring member of the community. It also means seeking to understand why students would make bad choices and helping students see that we value them and want to help them find more acceptable and caring ways to meet their needs. As you read this book, you will see how many of the best-accepted practices in classroom management support Noddings's concepts of moral education based on caring.

Teachers must also ensure that these practices incorporate sensitivity to cultural differences. "It is critical that teachers deliberately model respect for diversity—by expressing admiration for a student's bilingual ability, by commenting enthusiastically about the number of different languages that are represented in the class, and by including examples and content from a variety of cultures in their teaching" (Weinstein, Curran, & Tomlinson-Clarke, 2003, p. 272). More effective teachers "discuss issues surrounding ethnicity, skin color and race directly, seemingly without tension or discomfort" (Ullucci, 2009, p. 20).

We encourage you to put the book aside for a moment and create four columns headed by the four components described by Noddings. In each column, list five specific teacher behaviors or classroom activities you use (or would like to use) to develop each of these components of moral education based on caring.

Creating Open, Professionally Appropriate Dialogue with Students

Although the specific decisions teachers make concerning their relationships with students vary depending on their students' ages, the basic themes related to teacher–student relationships are similar across grade levels. One important question involves deciding how open and involved a teacher wishes to be with students. Teachers can select from among three general types of teacher–student relationships. Although teacher–student relationships vary on numerous dimensions, a primary factor involves the level of openness chosen. We can choose a teacher–student relationship characterized by:

1. Almost complete openness, in which we share a wide range of personal concerns and values with students
2. Openness related to our reactions to and feelings about the school environment, with limited sharing of aspects reflecting our out-of-school life
3. An almost exclusive focus on a role-bound relationship; that is, we share no personal feelings or reactions but merely perform our instructional duties

Not surprisingly, beginning teachers often grapple with whether they should be involved in very open, personal relationships with their students. They may wonder about the extent to which they should join in with students, share students' interests, use student slang, and so on. Our own experiences suggest that students respond best to adults who are comfortable with themselves, their values, and their personal preferences and who, when appropriate, can share these nonjudgmentally with students. These teachers, however, also understand their role as being a professional who is thoughtful and planful regarding what aspects of their personal life are shared with their students.

The topic of one's sexual orientation presents an area where it is important to consider the best interests of students along with school district policy when determining what aspects of one's personal life to share with students. Many districts have policies regarding discussing sensitive or personal information with students, and it is essential that people working with students follow the protocols existing in their districts. If no protocols exist, it is strongly recommended that, prior to sharing any form of highly personal information or a potentially controversial topic with students, teachers—especially those new to the field or school—discuss this with their administrators. We are aware of a recent situation where a high school teacher changed gender during the summer and continued to successfully teach in the same school. Throughout the process, the teacher discussed the decision with the principal, and they worked collaboratively to create a smooth transition. As professionals, we must always consider what is best for our students, and when any doubt exists, it is imperative to seek the counsel of other educators.

These issues highlight the value of establishing the second type of teacher–student relationship— one in which we share our reactions to and feelings about occurrences within the school setting

© Douglas Blackwell

"It's great how Mr. Watson's able to communicate with kids on their own level!"

and share with students limited aspects of our out-of-school life. Teachers who choose this type of relationship will often share with students occurrences involving their children, recreational activities, or cultural events they have attended. These teachers will also show considerable openness in discussing their feelings about events in the classroom as well as topics related to issues students are studying. Regarding this latter issue, it is important that teachers allow students to speak prior to presenting their own opinions so students are not overly influenced by the teachers' views.

The importance of being open enough to allow students to know us as people was highlighted for one of the authors during his experiences teaching junior high school students who had behavioral disorders. Discussions with students indicated that a number of them were involved in shoplifting from a large chain store near the school. However, these same students frequently visited a leather shop where the proprietor kept money, tools, and leather on the outer counter while he worked in a back room. When asked why they stole from the chain store but not the leather worker, the students expressed some surprise and indicated emphatically that they knew this man and they did not steal from "real people." This incident emphasized an important issue in dealing with young people. They often react negatively to and abuse people whom they view as merely roles, but they less often create problems for individuals whom they know and understand.

In addition to letting students know us as people, we can model a degree of openness to our own students' verbal expressions of concerns and feelings in our classrooms. An excellent example of effective modeling occurred several years ago when one of us visited the classroom of an extremely effective teacher. The eighth-grade students in his class were actively involved in a science project, and the room buzzed with noise and interest. A boy called across the room to his friend, John, and requested that John throw him the scissors. John immediately obliged, and the airborne scissors narrowly missed hitting another student. Rather than shouting at John, the teacher walked over to him and put his hand on John's shoulder. He proceeded to share with John the fact that the near miss had frightened him because he cared about and felt responsible for the students in his class. He then asked John if in the future he would carry the scissors across the room. The teacher then spoke briefly with the boy who had requested the scissors and with the student who had narrowly missed being hit. At the end of the period, the teacher took time to review the importance of the classroom procedure regarding scissors and had students demonstrate the correct procedure.

After class, the teacher explained why his intervention had been so calm and personal. He stated that young adolescents are involved in so many changes that their egos are very fragile and they personalize almost everything. He went on to say that his goal was to provide the student with information in a manner that would enhance the likelihood the student would listen. Had he yelled at the student or made an example of him in front of the class, the student probably would have responded by focusing on the teacher's mean behavior rather than by examining his own behavior. The teacher stated that by admitting to his own feeling and sharing it with the student, he had provided the student with valuable information without making him defensive.

This incident is an excellent example of a skilled teacher's ability to synthesize spontaneously a working knowledge of adolescent development with practical communication skills. The result of this synthesis was that the teacher was able to respond in a way that facilitated the student's personal growth while modeling emotional control and sensitivity to the student's feelings.

While supervising an intern, one of us saw another poignant example of the benefits of openness. The intern had taken over for a very dynamic and popular teacher, and the students were behaving poorly and at times even being cruel to the intern. The author suggested that the intern openly discuss her feelings with the class while also acknowledging her appreciation for the students' feelings and sense of loss. Several educators advised the intern against this, indicating she might be opening a Pandora's box. The intern chose to have the discussion with the class and reported that students were very open in thoughtfully sharing their frustration. Indeed, one student indicated her grade had dropped from an A to a C since the intern took over and that she was very frustrated. The intern noted that this was her first experience grading high school work and that she would be glad to meet with students to discuss their grades. Many students expressed appreciation for the intern's openness, and the intern reported that the tenor of the class changed dramatically.

As educators, we must realize that the feelings and perceptions of individuals in the classroom are important, legitimate issues of concern that affect students' motivation and achievement. If we are to be successful teaching students today, we must be willing to deal with the affective component of the classroom milieu as well as with the cognitive content. A central theme of this book is that effective classroom managers are aware of classroom processes and are willing and able to engage students in assessing and adjusting classroom procedures and instructional methods. This involves not only our own awareness and self-analysis but also engaging students in open dialogue and problem solving.

We must also be aware that for some students, the fact that we are concerned about them personally and about their lives outside of school is a significant factor influencing their commitment to their schoolwork and standards of acceptable school behavior. To work effectively with all students, especially students whose cultures and lifestyles are different from their own, teachers must develop empathy. Norris (2003) noted that empathy involves listening carefully to others and understanding their "perspectives, points of view, and feelings" (p. 315). In her study of eight highly successful recently retired African American teachers, Mitchell (1998) reported that these teachers understood the importance of the affective domain in enhancing student motivation and responsible behavior. She noted that these teachers "were critically aware of the experiences of the students, both in and out of school, and of the contexts shaping their experiences" (p. 105).

Especially for beginning teachers, there often occurs some confusion between being a "friend" and being a kind, empathetic professional. Practicum students and student teachers who may initially be allocated to observing and assisting in a classroom might find themselves in situations that lead them to assist students with their work and praise student success without responsibility for redirecting student behavior. This may lend itself to being seen by students as "cool" or "fun" without any type of authority being involved. We strongly encourage individuals placed in these types of situations to work early on with the classroom teacher to determine ways the professional-in-training can effectively redirect students who are making poor behavior choices and also take small amounts of responsibility for teaching structured, routine academic activities such as morning calendar, working with small groups, and so on. This enables the practicum student to be seen as having a role in the students' learning that also requires the effective use of authority. The problem is that when an adult moves from simply being a kind support person to a person who takes responsibility for the classroom, students are confused by the change in roles, and this confusion and frustration are often associated with students' challenging the adult. Frequently, the adults' response is to respond with an authoritarian and distant approach to classroom management (Pellegrino, 2010).

As a student teacher begins to change his or her role in the classroom, it is important to discuss this with the class, perhaps providing a timeline or other representation of the change in the teacher's and student teacher's roles. This provides students in the classroom with a cognitive schema for what is occurring in terms of the adults' roles in classroom learning and behavior, and this clarity can have a calming effect on students. Furthermore, as discussed extensively in Chapter 6, if classroom behavior standards have been effectively established by the teacher of record, the most effective method is for the practicum student/student teacher/intern to review these with students and then to be firm and consistent in ensuring that students follow these expectations/agreements while also expressing appreciation/praise when students demonstrate behavior and academic effort that support their learning and that of their classmates.

Research suggests that as students move from elementary to middle school, they perceive teachers as less nurturing, more focused on students' grades and competition between students, showing less personal interest in students, and more focused on adult control (Harter, 1996). Interestingly, students who report this type of change in teacher response indicate they are less motivated than students who do not experience this change in teacher attitude. These findings are supported by research (Hargreaves, 2000) suggesting that "there seems to be a tacit emotional grammar of secondary teaching . . . where emotions are neutralized to make the pedagogical process as smooth as possible" (p. 822). While secondary teachers interact with many more students and students whose developmental tasks include developing less dependent relationships with adults, our own experiences and the extensive literature discussed earlier in this chapter clearly indicate that many students desire a more open, personal relationship with their teachers than they currently experience. Therefore, if you are teaching middle or high school students, we encourage you to consider how you can develop relationships with your students in which they see you as caring about them both as students and individuals.

Another aspect of appropriate affect with students is teachers' abilities to be comfortable with their students. Students know when we enjoy them and are comfortable with them. Likewise, they are confused and often respond negatively when working with teachers who seem uncomfortable or even fearful of them. Noguera (1995) noted, "I have generally found that teachers who lack familiarity with their students are more likely to misunderstand and fear them" (p. 202). He suggests that violence in schools is significantly influenced by teachers' being uncomfortable with and even fearing their students. This leads to teachers' ignoring inappropriate behavior, using oversimplified and impersonal discipline techniques, and referring students to administrators without first attempting to work with the situation.

Lightfoot (1983) wrote that the "fearless and empathetic regard of students" (p. 342) is a key dimension of good high schools. She means that good teachers understand and appreciate the developmental challenges facing their students. In addition to this understanding, good teachers are not self-conscious around their students and seem to be comfortable with and enjoy students.

Marva Collins (1992), the founder of Westside Preparatory School in Chicago, stated it this way:

> When I taught in a public high school for three years I always ate lunch with a different group of students whether they were in my class or not, until I got to know most of them. The teachers thought I was idiotic, but they didn't realize that it actually made it easier for me to teach, that before I could effectively discipline students, I had to earn their friendship and respect. (p. 4)

One suspects that this educator also enjoyed her time with the students and often found it to be as intellectually stimulating and personally satisfying as her time in the faculty room.

A final example of the decision we must make about openness to student feedback occurred when a student teacher being supervised by one of us was challenged by a student in his sophomore biology class. Frustrated by his inability to understand a lecture, the student stood up at the back of the class and stated loudly, "This class sucks!" Rather than sending the student to the office, the student teacher responded by stating that, though he wished the student would share his frustration in a more polite manner, he was glad that he was able to state his anger rather than not come to class. The student teacher proceeded to inform the student that he would like to discuss the student's concern but that first he needed to determine whether it was shared by a majority of the class or only by a few students. The student teacher's inquiry indicated that only three students shared this concern. Therefore, the student teacher indicated that it made more sense for him and the three students to work together to consider how to make the class better for them. The student responded positively, and several discussions led to a positive resolution.

An interesting sidelight to this story involved the mentor teacher's reaction. This teacher strongly supported the third approach to teacher–student relationships. He stated that teachers cannot afford to be open with students or to discuss classroom instructional or behavioral matters. Instead, he believed that teachers must always be in authoritarian command of the classroom and that students must be required to do what teachers expect with no questions asked. The teacher called one of us, very upset that the intern had not immediately thrown the student out of class and asked the other students whether any of them wanted to join the student in his visit to the office.

An optional manner for handling this situation within the context of the second type of teacher–student relationship was offered by a skilled middle school physical education teacher. She indicated that even though she supports the concept of teachers being open about their reactions to classroom events, she believes students can be taught that the teacher will not allow abusive language or direct confrontation of a teacher in front of a class. She believes that students should know ahead of time that when this occurs, they will be politely but firmly required

© Dave Carpenter

to leave the class, knowing also that at a later time they will have an opportunity to discuss their concerns and behaviors with the teacher.

The different reactions chosen by the teachers in this example exemplify the decisions we must make concerning the type of openness to students' input we select. Certainly, each teacher must operate at a degree of openness that is personally comfortable. Nevertheless, the second type of openness enhances students' sense of ownership in, and impact on, the classroom environment and thus can improve classroom management and student motivation.

PAUSE & CONSIDER 3.3

Write and share with a colleague a brief statement about a situation in which you believe you demonstrated (1) an appropriate amount of self-disclosure that contributed to developing a positive relationship with a student or group of students, (2) too much openness or self-disclosure, (3) a failure to share about yourself in a way that may have assisted a student, (4) an appropriate amount of interest in a student that helped the student understand that you valued and cared about him or her, and (5) too much intrusion into or involvement with a student's life.

Electronic Communication and Teacher–Student Relationships

In an age when even elementary students are using sites such as Facebook, and most secondary students have access to this type of media, it is essential that teachers be aware of the potential problems associated with interacting with students on social media or posting materials students may access on social media. Perhaps the most straightforward advice is, "educators would be wise to think of their social networking identity as an extension of who they are in the classroom" (Hamblin & Bartlett, 2013, p. 4).

The use of e-mail is another area where teachers must carefully consider the manner in which they engage students and caregivers. Research (Young, Kelsey, & Alexander, 2011) suggests e-mail communication between college professors and students may have positive impact on how students view their professors, the course, and their evaluation of the course. However, no substantial studies exist regarding this relationship in K–12 schools, and some districts, for example, New York and Los Angeles, have established guidelines regarding e-mail communication between students and teachers (Davis, 2012). One suggestion is that teachers create school-related e-mail accounts that are separate from their personal e-mail accounts.

You are strongly encouraged to find opportunities for professional growth that are available through your university or district regarding this matter and to always be aware of policies that exist within the district where you work.

PAUSE & CONSIDER 3.4

Join with three or four colleagues or classmates and discuss how teachers in your school or a school where you are observing or student teaching are using electronic communication to interact with students. Also discuss how this relates to existing school district policies. You may wish to look at Internet sites for information on policies recommended by major school districts or professional organizations.

METHODS FOR COMMUNICATING CARING AND SUPPORT

Even though using the second type of teacher–student relationship will generally enhance the rapport teachers can establish with students, it is sometimes desirable for teachers to act more systematically in developing positive teacher–student relationships. We can express our interest, concern, and respect for students by (1) getting to know them and expressing interest in them as individuals; (2) maintaining a high ratio of positive to negative statements; (3) communicating high expectations to all students; (4) giving specific, descriptive feedback; (5) listening to students; (6) using culturally sensitive communication; (7) sharing responsibility with students; and (8) responding effectively to behavior that detracts from a positive, supportive learning environment.

Getting to Know Students

Teachers can enhance their ability to be invitational with their students by understanding their students and the social factors that influence their students' lives. Peregoy and Boyle (1993) suggest that teachers can ask the following questions about students who have a cultural background different from their own:

1. *Family structure:* What constitutes a family? Who among these or others live in one house? What is the hierarchy of authority?
2. *Life cycle:* What are the criteria for defining stages, periods, or transitions in life? What rites of passage are there?
3. *Roles and interpersonal relationships:* What roles are available to whom, and how are they acquired? Is education relevant to learning these roles?
4. *Discipline:* What is discipline? What counts as discipline and what does not?
5. *Time and space:* How important is punctuality? Speed in completing a task?
6. *Religion:* What restrictions are there concerning topics that should not be discussed in school?
7. *Food:* What is eaten? In what order? How often?
8. *Health and hygiene:* How are illnesses treated and by whom? What is considered to be the cause?
9. *History, traditions, holidays:* Which events and people are a source of pride for the group? To what extent does the group in the United States identify with the history and traditions of the country of origin? What holidays and celebrations are considered appropriate for observing in school? (Peregoy & Boyle, 1993, pp. 8–10)

Teachers who are effective at serving culturally diverse classrooms find ways to make personal connections with their students through informal conversations in which teachers and students discuss personal interests and events in their lives (Bondy et al., 2007; Dunn, 2010). For three years, one of us worked with a school located on a Native American reservation. One high school teacher was particularly effective in helping his students complete high-quality assignments and do well on tests. The vast majority of his colleagues expressed extreme frustration with the lack of motivation they believed characterized their students. While one aspect of this teacher's work was clearly his use of many of the instructional methods described in Chapter 7, students also stated how well this teacher knew them and how much he respected their families. Further exploration led to the fact that this was the only teacher in the school who lived in the community and the only one who attended cultural events in which the majority of his students and their families were involved.

In their book on educating immigrant students, Olsen and Jaramillo (1999) noted that "understanding our English Language Learners is the key to responding effectively to their differing needs. . . . The most effective advocates know 'how to know' about their students" (p. 180). Similarly, in her book *The Inner World of the Immigrant Child*, Cristina Igoa (1995) suggests the importance of teachers developing positive relationships with their second-language learners and maintaining conversations with these students about their needs and interests.

Teachers can ask students questions about their interests, how they spend their time, what subjects and learning activities are most interesting or difficult, and so on. For high school teachers, it is important to know how many hours students work and the degree of their extracurricular activities. Because he was aware of his students' numerous and extensive out-of-school and extra-curricular time commitments, a high school teacher we know worked with his students in the second week of school to chart a calendar of when major tests and papers were scheduled in their other courses. He and his students then scheduled when the major work would be due in his class.

Greeting Students at the Classroom Door

A simple way to make the statement that you are glad to see students and value their presence is to stand by the door and greet students as they enter. You can make a comment to them about something you heard they did well, a positive statement about their work in your class, a comment about some interest you know they have, or merely give a high five or a handshake as they enter.

A number of years ago, a high school social studies teacher shared with his colleagues at an in-service session, facilitated by one of the authors, a situation that highlights the benefits of a simple greeting. He stated that several weeks earlier, he had arrived at school upset about an incident from home. His first-period class had gone quite poorly, and he was concerned because his second-period class was usually his most challenging. As the students left the class, he asked one of the more academically and socially capable students in that class to stay for a moment and simply help him by greeting students as they entered for second period. The two decided that, as students walked in, they would simply say hello and make a statement about what an interesting class this was going to be. The teacher reported that he wrote the student helper a quick tardy slip and then turned to see his entire class looking attentively at him. He also noticed two additional students, who were not in his second-period class. When asked, the first reported he had heard the student at the door comment that this was going to be a really interesting class and had obtained permission from his second-period teacher to join this class for the day. The other student acknowledged he had not been so responsible, but when passing by the classroom, he'd heard the class was going to be great and was willing to take his chances. The teacher reported that his positive energy level returned and he had one of the most engaging and enjoyable class sessions he had experienced all year with this second-period class.

Beginning School Surveys

One method for getting to know more about your students is to ask them to complete a survey about themselves and their goals, wants, and needs related to your class. You can ask students which subjects they like best, what types of instructional activities best facilitate their learning, what they find most helpful from teachers, any special needs they have, and so on. In their article "Building Culturally Responsive Communities," Polleck and Shabdin (2013) share a variety of ideas and forms they use to become better acquainted with their students and to help their students know them better.

Arranging Individual Conferences with Students

Teachers at all grade levels can schedule time to meet individually with students. This can be done during your preparation period, during lunch, before school, or after school. We have worked with literally hundreds of teachers who shared with us the powerful, positive impact of meeting individually with students to discuss their work and behavior or simply to get to know them better. Igoa (1995) discussed the value of individual conferences with students new to the United States as a method for "validating the child's cultural history, and establishing a trusting, respectful, and warm relationship" (p. 125).

Demonstrating Interest in Students' Activities

An important way to indicate our concern for students and to enjoy our relationships with them is to take time to attend the activities in which they are involved. Students and their guardians are extremely appreciative of and impressed with teachers' attendance at events where students are involved. This attendance often is associated with dramatic academic or behavior improvement in the students whose activities were attended.

Eating Lunch with Students

Most teacher–student contact occurs in the presence of twenty-five to thirty other children. Unless students take the initiative by staying after school, they may never have individual private time with their teachers. One way to provide this personal time is to have lunch in the classroom with individual students. This time can be arranged by providing a sign-up sheet so that students who are interested can reserve a time to eat lunch alone with you. You and the student can use the lunch period to share personal interests. You should be willing to listen to the student's concerns about personal or school problems, but the time together should not be used as a conference in which you discuss the student's schoolwork or behavior.

© Bob Vojtko

"When I approved your field trip, Ms. Harris, I assumed you'd be going along with your class."

Arranging Interviews

Anyone who has taught young children for several years has experienced an instance in which a student appeared surprised to see the teacher in a nonschool setting, such as the grocery store. Students often view the teacher solely as a teacher and are quite unaware of his or her interests and life outside the school setting. One approach for making you seem more real is to allow your students to interview you. You can expand this activity by having your spouse or older children visit the classroom to be interviewed by the class.

Sending Letters and Notes to Students

Beginning the school year with a personal letter from you is an effective technique for establishing rapport with students. A positive individualized letter placed on each student's desk informs your students that you are happy to have them in class, eager to get to know them, and excited about the upcoming school year. Notes given to students throughout the school year can enhance the personal relationship between you and the student. Appropriate times for expressing thoughts or providing information by notes or letters include when a student has been successful at a new or difficult task, when a student's behavior has improved, when a personal matter seems to be worrying a student, and on a student's birthday. Students also appreciate receiving a note or a get-well card along with their homework when they are sick and must miss school for several days.

Using a Suggestion Box

One method that indicates our interest in students' ideas is to display a suggestion box and encourage students to write ideas for making the class a better place in which to learn. This approach can be expanded to include holding class meetings in which students discuss their ideas and concerns about the classroom. When classroom meetings are used, having students place agenda items on the board can replace the suggestion box. Either way, our willingness to request, accept, and respond to students' suggestions can be an effective method for improving teacher–student rapport.

Joining in School and Community Events

Schools often organize special events such as hat days, carnivals, and bike rodeos. Similarly, communities have picnics, carnivals, and other social events. We can demonstrate our interest in students and our own enjoyment of a good time by becoming involved in these activities. Schools can also organize special events or displays that give students a chance to view teachers in a personal light and increase positive teacher–student interaction. We have both worked in buildings where a childhood picture of each staff member was displayed and students attempted to match the teachers with the childhood pictures. Similarly, we have both taught in schools where a bulletin board was arranged so that teachers and students could publicly write positive statements to other students or teachers. Involvement in activities such as these helps create a positive school atmosphere, thereby significantly reducing unproductive student behavior.

Joining in Playground Games

Students enjoy having teachers participate in their playground activities. Occasionally, sharing recess time with the children is an excellent way for us to show our humanness and to demonstrate that we enjoy our students. Not only can this activity enhance teacher–student relationships but it can also provide us with an excellent form of relaxation. The physical activity and the opportunity to interact with children in a relaxed and nonacademic setting can provide a refreshing break in the school day. One way to formalize this type of teacher–student interaction is to develop several opportunities for friendly athletic competition between students and teachers.

PAUSE & CONSIDER 3.5

Stop for a minute and create a list of what you or a teacher with whom you are working or observing has done to get to know the students. If you are not teaching, consider ways your own teachers learned about who you were. We encourage you to share these with colleagues or classmates. If you are keeping note cards, a journal, or some other record while reading this book, this would be an excellent item to place in this record.

Helping Students New to the School Meet Key Adults

One fun and productive strategy for new students to become more effectively connected to all adults in the school is a "new student greeter program." New students are given coupon books with pages for each adult who assists students in the school. Each new student takes this coupon book around and has it signed by each adult. The adults tell how they help students and then give each new student a small gift (e.g., a cookie from the cook, bookmark from the media specialist, and so forth). By the end of the day, the new students have met virtually every key adult with whom they will come into contact in an initial interaction that has been positive and informative.

Showing Support for Student Diversity

One incredibly important aspect of communicating caring and support for students is to model and insist that all students in the classroom and common areas of the school show respect for student diversity. This includes such factors as students' exceptionality or disability, gender, sexual orientation, race, ethnicity, social class, religion, immigration status, nationality, or geographic area of origin or last residence. It is absolutely imperative that teachers not allow any student to be made fun of, bullied, harassed, or in any way demeaned for any of these characteristics or any combination of these. Later sections of the text will discuss factors related to this issue, including the creation of classroom norms concerning how all students are to be respected and how to respond when students violate these agreements. In this section, it is important to note that teachers must both model appreciation and respect for student diversity as well as respond whenever they observe any violation of respect for this diversity. Only when teachers do this can students from any underrepresented group feel they are respected and supported by their teachers or experience a sense of safety at school, and therefore be able to do their best academic work. Students take their cues from teachers, and it is imperative that teachers model unconditional respect for all students and tolerate absolutely no form of disrespect being committed toward a student. This is an example of what is meant by caring *for* rather than *about* students. It is wonderful that teachers care about issues of diversity, but it is a professional imperative that they care for each student and ensure that each student feel respected, valued, cared for, and safe in the school setting.

Physical Contact with Students

Although educators want to create communities of support in which students feel cared for and valued by adults, teachers are often told to guard against physical contact with students. Some teachers respond by setting very clear boundaries regarding their physical contact with students. Others protect themselves by never letting students get too close. "Probably leave about this much space," said an experienced elementary teacher, as she held her hands about four feet apart. One Colorado elementary teacher who had been falsely accused and finally exonerated drew a red line across the front of his classroom and said, "Nobody crosses this line" (Yaffe, 1995, pp. K9–K10).

We strongly believe the professionally responsible decision is to be cautious but is far from drawing a line between ourselves and our students. Certainly, teachers must be careful not to touch students in ways that make students uncomfortable. Teachers must notice when students shy away from or appear uncomfortable with touch. In addition, teachers need to guard against situations in which students may misinterpret teacher behavior or in which the rare student may fabricate an event to obtain attention or "get back" at a teacher. One good rule of thumb is to have others around whenever you are working with a student. When working with a student during lunch or after school, find a space that is visible to others. Likewise, anytime you hug a student, it is advisable for this to be in front of other students. We strongly believe that physical contact is a natural, healthy part of positive, supportive, interpersonal relationships. Teachers need to model this with their colleagues and with students. However, we live in a society in which physical contact has been sexualized by the media and in which a significant number of students have experienced tragic physical and sexual interactions with adults. As professionals, we need to carefully monitor our behavior so that it heals and teaches but never offends, intimidates, or frightens our students.

Several years ago, the morning following the first day of school, *The Oregonian* included several articles describing the important contributions and sacrifices made by educators. One article described the work of Mary Beth Van Cleave, a principal who offered to retire but remained on the job for one year to save a teaching position. After thirty-two years as an educator, this principal gave up half her salary to help children. The article described her first day: "Van Cleave spent Tuesday doling out hugs to returning students, soothing anxious parents and helping lost students find their teachers" (*The Oregonian*, 1996, p. E7). The article was accompanied by a large picture of Mary Beth hugging a seven-year-old second grader as the child entered the school. In the same section was a picture of a teacher shaking hands with a student. The caption reads, "Pat Gonzales, a Madison High School English teacher, starts class by showing seventeen-year-old Jamicia Jackson the difference between a good and a bad handshake" (*The Oregonian*, 1996, p. E1). It appears that neither of these educators was willing to create a cold, artificial learning environment void of touch. Both, however, are handling touch in a public and professional manner to ensure safety for both their students and themselves.

While writing this book, we spoke with our dear friend and colleague Forrest Gathercoal, educator, attorney, and author of *Judicious Discipline*. Gathercoal shared his strong belief, based on numerous statements he has heard from teachers and in his legal background, that it is best if teachers refrain from hugging students but that handshakes, pats on the backs, and high fives generally are safe. He also noted his belief that teachers can create a positive, warm, and professional relationship without excessive touch. He noted that if a teacher is hugging children, one has to ask if this is necessary in a professional relationship and whether it meets the teacher's or student's needs. Although we believe that hugs, especially those initiated by elementary school students, are a healthy and natural part of adult–child relationships, we suggest that prior to making a decision regarding the type of touch you will choose to use with your students, you consider Gathercoal's argument. If you are a beginning teacher or will be teaching in a new school, we strongly recommend that you discuss the policies and expectations in your school with the counselor, administrator, and/or other teachers.

Developing Positive Teacher–Student Relationships with All Students
For an interactive review of methods for creating positive teacher–student relationships that support positive student behavior and learning, click on the link below in your Pearson etext.

ENHANCEDetext *interactive case study*

PAUSE & CONSIDER 3.6

Before moving on to the next section, stop for a minute and write down or share with a colleague your thoughts about physical contact with students. What feels comfortable and natural to you? Do your students appear to be comfortable with this? Are your decisions consistent with school, district, and community standards? Do you agree with Forrest Gathercoal's perspective, or do you believe it is important to have relationships with your students that include physical touch?

Maintaining a High Ratio of Positive to Negative Statements

Educational research and associated recommendations regarding providing feedback—both academic and behavior—to students has often used the term *praise* or *behavior-specific praise*. We strongly recommend educators use the term *feedback* or *recognition*. *Praise* seems to us to be based on judgments and subjectivity while *feedback, encouragement*, or *recognition* seems to apply more to statements that are more objective, descriptive, and less personally judgmental. When students are being judged, the locus of control is externalized as they cannot predict or control more positive judgments. If students are being encouraged and recognized for observable descriptive behaviors, they have more control and predictability to experience self-reinforcement. It seems to us that judgments, both negative and positive, are about the judger and encouragement is about the observed student. Our experience is that students experiencing ongoing or serious behavior problems feed off subjective experiences, both negative and positive, and externalize responsibility. Praising students can have the effect of reinforcing an external locus of control when what we are wanting is to encourage and promote an internal locus of control in the student. Therefore, unless the material is a direct quote or we are referencing specific concepts presented by other authors, we will use terms such as *feedback, encouragement*, and *recognition* to refer to positive feedback teachers provide students about their academic work and social behavior.

Children are sensitive to praise and criticism given by adults. Unfortunately, many teachers find that disruptive behavior is more noticeable and, therefore, respond to it more frequently than to on-task behavior. Although we often fall into the trap of believing that critical remarks will improve students' behaviors, research suggests that the opposite is true.

> In one study we took a good class and made it into a bad one for a few weeks by having the teacher no longer praise the children. When the teacher no longer praised the children, off-task behavior increased from 8.7 percent to 25.5 percent. The teacher criticized off-task behavior and did not praise on-task behavior. When the teacher was asked to increase her criticism from 5 times in 20 minutes to 16 times in 20 minutes, the children showed even more off-task behavior. Off-task behavior increased to an average of 31.2 percent, and on some days was over 50 percent. Attention to that off-task behavior increased its occurrence when no praise was given for working. Introduction of praise back into the classroom restored good working behavior. (Becker, Engelmann, & Thomas, 1975, p. 69)

An excellent example of the effect of teachers' negative or positive statements occurred a number of years ago in a school district in Oregon. Much to their credit, district administrators became worried about what they perceived as a negative attitude among a significant number of their young schoolchildren. The district subsequently sought the services of an outside agency to examine the situation. The consultants decided initially to examine the ratio of positive to negative statements made by teachers. They began their intervention by simply asking children in second-grade classrooms to answer "yes" or "no" to the question, "Do you like school?" At the beginning of the school year, most students in all classes responded "yes" to this question. The consultants discovered, however, that for students who experienced classrooms characterized by a low rate of positive teacher verbalizations, positive feelings about school changed dramatically within the first fifteen weeks of school.

More specifically, in the eight classes in which teachers provided less than 65 percent positive statements, the percentage of students responding that they liked school dropped an alarming 48 percent during the fifteen weeks. In the seven classrooms in which 70 percent or more of the teachers' statements were positive, though, students' responses to the question of whether they

© James Estes

"I'm very sorry about your teacher. All I can tell you is that she was in a good mood when I hired her."

liked school remained, on the average, exactly the same after fifteen weeks of school. These data suggest that children are much less comfortable in classroom environments characterized by a low rate of positive teacher statements. While there is no definitive research to indicate the optimum ratio of positive to corrective teacher statements, and this will vary somewhat with the setting and the age of your students, Sprick (2009) suggests a rate of three positive, reinforcing statements to every one corrective response to student behavior. This is quite striking given that research suggests in most classrooms the rate of teacher's reinforcing comments is less than corrections and reprimands (Sutherland & Wehby, 2001). One method for ensuring that students who struggle with their behavior receive positive feedback is to simply keep a tally of your positive and negative interactions with particular students. Another method is to provide a student with positive attention at designated intervals. Research (Riely, McKevitt, Shriver, & Allen, 2011) showed that student behavior could be improved simply by providing positive attention to students every five minutes and simply responding in a typical manner during all other times.

It is important to understand the dynamics behind these suggestions. It is obviously easy for teachers to have frequent positive contacts with students who are behaving in ways that help them and other students accomplish classroom tasks designed by the teacher.

> The disruptive student, however, tends to behave in ways that are punishing to the teacher. This causes the teacher to avoid interactions with the student, except when necessary to deal with inappropriate behavior. This student then receives fewer opportunities to respond in ways that are likely to elicit a positive response from the teacher. The student has learned, moreover, that resisting adult interventions often leads to peer attention, avoidance of undesirable tasks, and sometimes even to escape from punishment. This negative pattern may take some time to develop, but once established it predisposes the teacher and student to conflict. (Emmer & Gerwels, 2006, p. 428)

In their book *Inviting School Success*, Purkey and Novak (1996) set forth four types of teacher behaviors toward students:

1. Intentionally disinviting
2. Unintentionally disinviting
3. Unintentionally inviting
4. Intentionally inviting

In defining these terms, Purkey and Novak (1996) stated, "As used here, an invitation is a summary description of message—verbal and nonverbal, formal and informal—continuously transmitted to students with the intention of informing them that they are responsible, able, and valuable. Conversely, a disinvitation is intended to tell them that they are irresponsible, incapable, and worthless" (p. 3). An example of an intentionally disinviting behavior would be the teacher who, on the first day of school, privately singles out a student whose sibling had been a particular problem several years earlier and informs the child that if he is anything like his brother, this will be a very difficult year for him. Even though this teacher's statement is intentional and intended to motivate the student to behave properly, the student very likely receives it as punitive, unfair, and disinviting. An example of an unintentionally disinviting statement was provided by a high school vice principal. He stated that the day before final exam week began, he observed a student requesting assistance from a teacher. The teacher's response, "Don't worry, you haven't got a chance of passing the test anyway," was devastating but probably unintentionally disinviting.

Teachers make many inviting comments to students. For example, teachers often greet students at the door, state how glad they are to see a student, and respond positively to the quality of student work. Some of this inviting behavior occurs unintentionally because teachers are positive people who care about their students. On other occasions, teachers consciously consider the impact of positive invitations and intentionally invite students to be positively involved in their classes. An elementary school principal recently shared an outstanding example of how an administrator can use invitational relationships. During a workshop presented for a state principals' association, the principal asked one of us if he could share something he had done based on his attending a similar workshop one of us had presented the previous year. The principal told his colleagues that his background had caused him to be a very authoritarian person and that when he became a principal, he informed teachers that they could be assured of firm support from the office. He noted that his most common intervention with students sent to his office for discipline was to intimidate and threaten the students. He proceeded to note that after attending the workshop, he carefully considered his reactions and realized that they were seldom associated with positive, long-term changes in student behavior and that he had received some negative comments from parents. He decided to try an experiment in which he selected twelve students who were experiencing ongoing behavior problems. He divided these students into three groups, and each day the three groups began their day by spending approximately four minutes with the principal during which time all four students in each group shared a positive thing that had happened to them the previous day, one thing they were looking forward to in school that day, and anything adults at school could do to help them that day. At the end of each session, each student gave the principal his or her sign (high five, handshake, etc.) and went to class. The principal noted a dramatic improvement in these students' attendance, work completion, and on-task behavior. He shared with the audience that from that point on, he decided to alter the manner in which he worked with students.

One of our favorite examples of the impact of invitational teaching was shared by an elementary teacher who decided to request for her fifth-grade classroom a student who was considered the most difficult to manage in the entire grade and whose mother was viewed as extremely critical and not supportive of school personnel. Knowing that the student was quite negative about school, the first day of school the teacher spoke to the student during the morning recess and informed him that she had requested that he be in her class. She noted that she knew he had outstanding leadership skills, and she knew he could use them to be a positive leader in the classroom this year. Throughout the day, she found opportunities to reinforce him for positive involvement in the classroom. Soon after returning home from school that evening, the teacher received an unexpected call from the student's mother. She began by stating that when returning from school that afternoon, her son had broken the front screen door as he ran into the house. Her next statement was that her son had done so because he was so excited and he ran into the house shouting, "Mom, Mom, there's a teacher at school who likes me!" The student, who had been suspended numerous times the previous year, was never suspended again, made outstanding academic gains, and years later was a class officer in his high school. One can only speculate what impact his fifth-grade year had on his subsequent school and personal experiences, but it may well have been substantial.

One way we have thought about the establishment of positive relationships with students is as a "positive relationship bank account." Just as a person has to make deposits into a checking account to make a withdrawal, educators need to have positive interactions with students if they want students to respond positively to adult requests for effort or modified behavior. Some students come to school with many deposits already made through positive relationships with adults in their families and communities. Unfortunately, many students have limited positive interactions with adults. If we want these students to respond positively to the requests we make (often including the difficult task of attempting what they perceive as demanding schoolwork), we must have made deposits in the positive relationship bank account. Many of the ideas presented throughout the remainder of this chapter will help you to create these important deposits.

PAUSE & CONSIDER 3.7

We encourage you to stop for a few minutes and write one example of each of these four types of statements—intentionally disinviting, unintentionally disinviting, intentionally inviting, and unintentionally inviting—based on something you have heard a staff member (including yourself) say to a student. We recommend you share these with three or four colleagues or fellow students.

Communicating High Expectations

PAUSE & CONSIDER 3.8

Before reading this section, stop for a minute and think about your class(es). Do some students receive more attention, praise, and opportunities to respond than others? What are the characteristics of those students given these favorable responses? Write a brief statement regarding any student characteristics that might make you more or less likely to positively engage a student. Are you more comfortable with boys or girls, high or low achievers, members of your ethnic group, and so on?

As educators, we must be extremely careful about our potential biases against some types of students and any tendency to expect more or less capable academic behavior from any subset of students. This section will help you understand how expectations can impact student learning and behavior.

How teachers communicate their expectations about how well students perform in the classroom is an important and well-documented factor in teacher–student relationships. School effectiveness research has consistently pointed to teachers' high expectations of students' performances as a key factor associated with students' achievements. In a positive vein, research suggests that in schools where Hispanic students are successful, teachers consistently express high expectations for their students (Reyes et al., 1999). In a negative vein, research indicates that many teachers expect less acceptable behavior and lower levels of academic performance from minority students (Weinstein, Gregory, & Strambler, 2004). Teachers may provide less emotional support and lower instructional quality when teaching classrooms with high rates of minority students or students with high rates of free and reduced lunches (Pianta et al., 2005). Noguera (2003) noted:

> Students who get into trouble are typically not passive victims; many of them understand that the consequences for violating school rules can be severe, particularly as they grow older. However, as they internalize the labels that have been affixed to them, and as they begin to realize that the trajectory their education has placed them on is leading nowhere, many simply lose the incentive to adhere to school norms. (p. 343)

In a variety of subtle and not-so-subtle ways, we communicate to some students that they are bright, capable, and responsible, whereas other students receive the message that they are dull, incapable, and irresponsible.

Results from classroom interaction studies indicate that teachers generally respond more favorably to students they perceive as high achievers. High achievers receive more response opportunities; are given more time to answer questions; receive more positive, nonverbal feedback such as smiles, nods, and winks; and are less likely to be ignored. Cooper and Good (1983) provided the following list of common ways in which teachers respond differently to students who are high achieving versus those who are low achieving:

1. Seating low-expectation students far from the teacher and/or seating them in a group.
2. Paying less attention to lows in academic situations (smiling less often and maintaining less eye contact).
3. Calling on lows less often to answer classroom questions or to make public demonstrations.
4. Waiting less time for lows to answer questions.
5. Not staying with lows in failure situations (i.e., providing fewer clues, asking fewer follow-up questions).
6. Criticizing lows more frequently than highs for incorrect public responses.
7. Praising lows less frequently than highs after successful public responses.
8. Praising lows more frequently than highs for marginal or inadequate public responses.
9. Providing lows with less accurate and less detailed feedback than highs.
10. Failing to provide lows with feedback about their responses as often as highs.
11. Demanding less work and effort from lows than from highs.
12. Interrupting performance of lows more frequently than highs. (p. 10)

In reviewing the research on expectation effects, Brophy (1983) cited studies suggesting that "teacher expectations do have self-fulfilling-prophecy effects on student-achievement levels, but that these effects make only a 5 to 10 percent difference, on the average" (p. 635).

It is often desirable that we initiate a higher percentage of our academic contacts with students who are low achieving during individual or small-group instruction. Similarly, especially when introducing new material to younger children, we should try to maximize the percentage of correct responses so that students do not become confused by competing, inaccurate information. The critical issue is that we must become aware of ways in which we respond differently to various types of students and thoughtfully and systematically implement differential interaction patterns that support individual student and group learning. Figure 3.1 presents guidelines teachers can follow to minimize the negative effects of teacher expectations. As teachers, we need to be aware of the importance of communicating positive expectations to all students. Periodically,

- *Use information from tests, cumulative folders, and other teachers very carefully.*
    Some teachers avoid reading cumulative folders for several weeks at the beginning of the year.
    Be critical and objective about the reports you hear from other teachers, especially "horror stories"
    told in the teachers' lounge.
- *Be flexible in your use of grouping strategies.*
    Review work of students in different groups often, and experiment with new groupings.
    Use different groupings for different subjects.
    Use mixed-ability groups in cooperative exercises when all students can handle the same
    material.
- *Make sure all the students are challenged.*
    Avoid saying, "This is easy; I know you can do it."
    Offer a wide range of problems, and encourage all students to try a few of the harder ones for
    extra credit.
    Try to find something positive about these attempts.
- *Be especially careful about how you respond to low-achieving students during class discussions.*
    Give them prompts, clues, and time to answer.
    Give ample praise for good answers.
    Call on low achievers as often as high achievers.
- *Use materials that show a wide range of ethnic groups.*
    Check readers and library books. Is there ethnic diversity?
    Ask your librarian to find multiethnic stories, filmstrips, and so forth.
    If few materials are available, ask students to research and create their own, based on community
    or family resources.
- *Be fair in evaluation and disciplinary procedures.*
    Make sure equal offenses merit equal punishment. Find out from students in an anonymous
    questionnaire whether you seem to be favoring certain individuals.
    Try to grade student work without knowing the identity of the student. Ask another teacher to
    give you a "second opinion" from time to time.
- *Communicate to all students that you believe they can learn—and mean it.*
    Return papers that do not meet standards with specific suggestions for improvements.
    If students do not have the answers immediately, wait, probe, and then help them think through
    an answer.
- *Involve all students in learning tasks and in privileges.*
    Use some system for calling on or contacting students to make sure you give each student practice
    in reading, speaking, and answering questions.
    Keep track of who gets to do what job. Are some students always on the list while others seldom
    make it?
- *Monitor your nonverbal behavior.*
    Do you lean away or stand farther away from some students? Do some students get smiles when
    they approach your desk while others get only frowns?
    Do you avoid touching some students?
    Does your tone of voice vary with different students?

FIGURE 3.1
GUIDELINES FOR AVOIDING THE NEGATIVE EFFECTS OF TEACHER EXPECTATIONS
Source: From *Educational Psychology* **(7th ed.), by A. E. Woolfolk, 1998, Boston, MA: Allyn and Bacon.**
Copyright © 1998 by Pearson Education. Reprinted with permission.

we need to (1) collect data about how we interact with students in our classes, (2) analyze the data to see if we are using primarily supportive or critical statements, (3) determine whether we are responding differently (more critically or less often) to some students, and (4) ensure that we systematically and intentionally communicate high expectations to all students. There are several activities at the end of the chapter that will assist you with this. In addition, teachers can develop creative, fun ways to ensure that students receive equal opportunities. You can write each student's name on a tongue depressor, Popsicle stick, or chip and draw from a can to determine who will answer each question. (Remember to replace the name back into the can following each draw.) This keeps students alert and ensures that, over time, all students will receive an equal number of questions to answer.

PAUSE & CONSIDER 3.9

What methods will you choose to ensure you are communicating high expectations to all students? If you have an opportunity to do so, we encourage you to complete either Activity 3.3 or Activity 3.4 from the end of the chapter to practice monitoring whether a teacher is communicating consistently high expectations to all students. We also encourage you to make a list of methods you would like to add to your repertoire for increasing the likelihood that you will communicate high expectations to all students. It will be helpful to share these with a colleague or classmate and add them to your journal or set of note cards.

During discussion of teacher expectation effects, our students often ask us how they can communicate high expectations when responding to situations in which students fail to respond or are unable to provide a correct answer in response to a teacher question during large-group instruction. We have found a number of responses to be respectful of students while helping students access information they may have that will help them to answer the question:

- *Provide adequate wait time.* It may be necessary to teach all students why this is being done, for example, individuals vary dramatically in their preferred wait time, and increased wait time helps students generate more thoughtful, thorough, creative replies.
- *Rephrase the question.* Asking the question in a different way provides the student with additional time, may add cues, and also suggests that the student's failure to answer may be a response to a less-than-clear question statement.
- *Ask if another student would like to assist the student.* This is a classroom procedure that can be taught with the emphasis being that all students can help others learn.
- *Allow the student to request assistance from another student.* This can also be a procedure you use for large-group discussions.
- *Ask students to turn to a peer and discuss the question.* You might state that this is an interesting and important question and you want all students to have an opportunity to discuss possible answers. You can then call on the student who initially failed to provide an answer.
- *Offer hints or cues to assist the student in coming up with the answer.*
- *Break the question into small parts and ask the student a subset of the question.*
- *Provide some or all of the answer, and ask the student to discuss his or her thoughts about this as an answer.*
- *Allow the student to pass.* If you use this option, before the end of the lesson, try to ask this student another question—one you believe he or she will likely be able to answer.

Giving Specific, Descriptive Feedback

One of the most important communication skills teachers can use is specific, clear, descriptive feedback that helps students take responsibility for their successes. Research indicates that when teachers increase their rate of specific praise, there is a reduction in disruptive student behavior and the number of negative statements teachers make to students (Haydon & Musti-Rao, 2011) and an increase in students' on-task behavior (Allday et al., 2012).

Research on attribution theory indicates that students attribute their success or failure to ability, effort, luck, or difficulty of task. If students attribute their success or failure to effort, they are able to view their performance as influenced by factors within their control (an internal locus of control) and are, therefore, able to expect success in similar situations if they make the effort. However, when failure is attributed to ability, luck, or difficulty of task, students feel less control over results and begin to believe that making a concerted effort in the future will have little effect on the outcome. Praise that helps students focus on factors within their control that influenced performance allows students to develop an internal locus of control. By becoming skilled in providing students with useful positive feedback, teachers can help students take credit for their successes and develop an appreciation for their ability to control the school environment in positive ways.

Dweck (2008) found that students praised for their intelligence/ability were less likely to select challenging tasks and were more likely to cheat or lie about their scores. Students praised for the processes in which they were involved, "their effort, their strategies, their concentration, their perseverance, or their improvement" (p. 115) selected more challenging tasks and were concerned whether the tasks would help them learn. These students saw ability not as fixed, but as something they could change with their efforts.

O'Leary and O'Leary (1977) stated that to serve as an effective reinforcer, feedback (they use the term *praise*) to students must have three qualities:

1. *Contingency.* Praise must immediately follow desired behaviors rather than be applied simply as a general motivator. Anderson and colleagues (Anderson, Evertson, & Brophy, 1979) found that teachers failed to use praise contingently because the rate of praise following reading turns that contained mistakes was similar to the rate following correct responses.
2. *Specificity.* Praise should describe the specific behavior being reinforced. Again, Anderson et al. (1979) suggested that teachers needed improvement in this area. Their data showed that teachers were specific in only 5 percent of their praise for academic work and in 40 percent of their praise for behavior.
3. *Credibility.* Praise should be appropriate for the situation and the individual. Older, high-achieving students are aware that praise is used primarily for motivation and encouragement and may find praise unnecessary and even insulting.

Brophy's (1981) summary of research findings on the effective use of feedback (*praise*) suggested feedback is most effective when it includes several components in addition to specificity. These include:

1. Highlight for students how specific aspects of their efforts contributed to their successes. If they understand this, students are more likely to believe that their successes were not due to luck or innate ability, but rather to something that is under their control and can be replicated.

2. Emphasize the value of the accomplishment. This might involve commenting on how students might use the new learning or behavior, how they might have found the learning enjoyable, or how it might relate to their previous work or future work.
3. Help students see how they may have put in good effort on the task because they enjoyed it or wanted to obtain the knowledge or skill the task was intended to assist them in developing.

In an article on providing feedback to students with emotional and behavioral disorders (EBD), the authors (Allday et al., 2012) suggest that behavior-specific praise is defined as ". . . providing students with praise statements that explicitly describe the behavior being praised" (p. 87). Two of the three examples they provide are:

"I like how you are sitting crisscross applesauce."
"You are doing a good job of writing your letters."

We believe these are actually poor examples of feedback to students that may inadvertently have a negative impact on long-term behavior. As discussed above, feedback will ideally help students to take responsibility for their behavior and understand how their behavior impacts those around them. If an adult says, "I like the way . . ." they are suggesting the student should be performing the behavior to please the adult rather than because the behavior supports the student in his learning, helps others learn, helps others feel safe or positive, and so on, thus undermining important social cognitive learning. Instead, the teacher might say, "When you sit crisscross applesauce, you are ready to learn and helping everyone in our class learn. Thanks for showing us how an effective student is prepared to learn."

We believe enhancing the quality of feedback provided to students has the ability to help students take greater ownership for their own learning, appreciate the impact their behavior has on their own learning and that of others, and have greater motivation and appreciation related to the content.

Examples of feedback focused on specific factors within a student's control	Examples of general feedback focused on factors outside a student's control
You really worked on asking for help when you needed it and used your calming strategy very well. Nicely done!	*"Hey, you got all your positive points this morning. Congratulations! It must be your lucky day!"*
"Wow, every time you bring your book and papers to class, your contribution to our discussions is so well organized and helpful."	*"Great job. That's the best work I've seen you do this year!"*
"When you choose a topic that you're interested in, you seem to really get excited and commit time and focus to your work. This really helps you do your best work."	*"Wow, thanks for acting so responsibly this morning."*
"You looked like you were really concentrating and working hard. That helped you keep your small e under the line, and this makes it easier for people to read. Great job!"	*"You did a good job of writing your letters today. Way to go!"*

It is important to be careful how and whom we praise. Teacher praise may have different effects on students depending on their cultural background. Students from some Native American groups may not want to be singled out for attention, and students whose families and peers distrust the educational system may find public teacher praise diminishes their status with peers (Johns & Espinoza, 1996). While you need to be very careful about stereotyping students' potential responses to praise, you do need to be aware of cultural issues related to positive teacher feedback and validate your hypotheses through discussions with students, caregivers, and community members.

PAUSE & CONSIDER 3.10

Take a few minutes and consider a specific situation in which you have given or could be giving verbal or written feedback to a student regarding his or her academic work. Based on the material in the previous section, write a statement of feedback/praise you could provide this student that would help him or her understand the value of the work and take credit for the efforts in accomplishing this task. Get together with several classmates or colleagues and have each person share the feedback and situation associated with the feedback. Provide each person with both support and ideas for improving the feedback statement.

Encouraging Students to Seek Academic Help

Research shows that students who are willing to seek academic support will be more academically successful (Kessels & Steinmayr, 2013; Ryan, Shim, Lampkins-uThando, Kiefer, & Thompson, 2009). There also appear to be differences in the willingness of boys and girls to seek assistance with academic tasks. A recent study indicates that ". . . girls reported better overall attitudes towards help seeking than boys. Specifically, girls indicated a higher general intention to seek needed help and a lower intention to avoid needed help" (Kessels & Steinmayr, 2013, p. 238). When they do seek help, boys appear more likely to prefer a more private and quick type of assistance, apparently preferring not to be as obvious about their need for assistance (Butler, 1998). Boys also were more likely to seek assistance to avoid working too hard to get the answer (Freundenthaler, Spinath, & Neubauer, 2008; Kessels & Steinmayer, 2013). This suggests that teachers need to ensure that procedures are developed within the classroom to provide students with multiple ways to seek assistance and to encourage a classroom norm that obtaining assistance is a positive academic and personal skill.

Listening to Students

Listening skills are extremely important; when used effectively, they create relationships that allow students to feel significant, accepted, respected, and able to take responsibility for their own behavior. By effectively using listening skills, adults help youngsters clarify their feelings and resolve their own conflicts. Unfortunately, adults all too often provide quick answers for children rather than carefully listening in order to help the youngsters clarify the problem and then aid them in developing a solution.

Listening to students is more important now than ever before, as teachers increasingly face classrooms of students with whom they share neither a culture, nor national or ethnic background, nor community experience. Without a doubt, students can shed light on their experiences in school related to achievement and access and can help faculties understand the cultural complexities of their lives (Olsen & Jaramillo, 1999).

According to William Glasser (1988), students' attempts to have someone listen to them is the source of nearly 95 percent of discipline problems in school. Speaking of student behavior problems in schools, Glasser wrote, "I believe that frustration of the need for power, even more than the need for belonging, is at the core of today's difficulties" (p. 40). Glasser noted that there are three levels at which students can satisfy their need for power of involvement in the school environment. First, students simply need to believe that someone whom they respect will listen to them. At the second level, someone listens and accepts the validity of the student's statement or concern. The third and highest level involves an adult's stating that the student's idea may be worth implementing.

Stop for a moment and reflect on the past several times a student came to you with a problem or expressed a strong emotion. What did you do? If you are like many adults, you provided a quick answer to the problem or attempted to stop the expression of emotion by providing assurances or by suggesting that the student should not be expressing the emotion. Both of these responses are commonly used because they require a minimum of time and effort and prevent adults from having to deal with a youngster's emotions. When adults consistently provide answers, however, they subtly inform students that they do not care enough really to listen to them and do not trust students' abilities to resolve their own conflicts.

Before examining the major listening skills, we must clarify an important point. There are numerous instances (perhaps even a significant majority) during a school day when a student is merely requesting information. If a student requests permission to leave the room or asks for clarification of directions, it is appropriate simply to provide the information. However, when students share personal problems, express confusion with their work, or display emotions, it is often most effective initially to use one or more of the listening skills discussed in this section.

The primary goal of using listening skills is to help students express their real concern, need, or want. Students often initially make general, angry statements that disguise their real concerns. A student who says, "I hate this class," might be feeling frustration at his or her inability to understand the material or concern over lack of acceptance by peers. By using the methods described in the following pages, you can help the student clarify the underlying problem. Once the problem has been exposed, you must switch from merely listening to an active role in helping the student examine and solve the problem.

Empathic, Nonevaluative Listening

Empathic, nonevaluative listening involves providing the speaker with a sense that she or he has been clearly heard and that the feelings expressed are acceptable. Several major benefits can be derived from using this skill. First, students learn that their feelings are acceptable, which reduces the tension and anxiety associated with having to hide their true feelings. This act in turn makes students feel more accepted. Second, when thoughts and feelings can be expressed openly and are received nonjudgmentally, students are much less likely to express feelings through unproductive behaviors. Acting out in the classroom, vandalism, and truancy are often indirect methods of dealing with feelings that could not be expressed openly and directly. Third, when adults listen nonevaluatively, they provide young people with an opportunity to examine and clarify feelings that are often confusing and frightening. This exchange frequently enables youngsters to understand a situation and to consider approaches to coping with a situation effectively.

One of us was recently given an interesting example regarding effective listening. A special education teacher, director, and now school superintendent with whom one of us worked for more than twenty years shared his recent conversations with a student in a high school program for students with behavioral disorders. The boy approached the director (who had been the boy's special education teacher seven years earlier) and stated in a somewhat derogatory tone that the director looked older since he had lost some of his hair. The special education director noted that rather than chastise the boy for his rudeness, he acknowledged the boy's perceptive observation, shared his own feelings about losing hair, and asked the boy how he was doing. The director reported that the boy responded calmly and asked whether people still thought he was the dumbest, most cruel student in the district. This allowed the director an opportunity to discuss the boy's behavior, his abilities, and his responsibility for his behavior. He reported that the boy was very surprised by the discussion, thanked him, and left pensively. The director indicated that had he not listened carefully to the boy, the boy would not have had an opportunity to have some important misconceptions corrected.

This is an excellent example of our need to guard against our vulnerabilities. Most of us have certain key behaviors or words from children that set us off. However, most of these stem from a belief that children should not be allowed to challenge or criticize adults. Instead, we may want to consider that the issue is *how* students challenge us. If students are unskilled in providing us with important information regarding their feelings, needs, and concerns, rather than punishing their ineffectiveness, we may want to model for them and teach them how to do this in an effective, acceptable manner.

There are two basic approaches to nonevaluative listening. First, the listener can simply acknowledge the speaker's statement by looking at him or her and making oral responses such as "M-hm," "Yes," "Uh-uh," "I see," and "I understand." This form of listening encourages the speaker to continue talking by indicating that the listener is attentive and involved. Obviously, this type of response is least effective when used in isolation; most children wish to hear more than a simple acknowledgment.

The second method for using empathic, nonevaluative listening is commonly called *paraphrasing*, *active listening*, or *reflecting*. In *Learning Together and Alone*, Johnson and Johnson (1975) presented seven guidelines for using this skill.

GENERAL GUIDELINES FOR PARAPHRASING

1. Rephrase ideas and feelings made by the sender, but make sure to put these in your own words.
2. Try to rephrase the speaker's statements—both feelings and ideas—as accurately as possible.
3. Be accepting of the sender's comments. It is important not to make evaluative or critical comments.
4. Begin your statement with terms such as "It sound like you. . . .", I'm hearing you say that you . . .", etc.
5. Be sure to look interested and accepting. Make sure your verbal and non-verbal messages indicate your focus on and concern for the speaker.

Paraphrasing has the advantage of making the speaker believe he or she is being listened to while allowing the listener to be somewhat more involved than is possible when using only acknowledging responses. Furthermore, by providing a summary of the speaker's statement, the listener may help the child clarify his or her thoughts or feelings. If the paraphrased statement is not congruent with what the speaker wanted to say, the speaker has an opportunity to correct the listener's paraphrase and, thereby, clarify the initial statement.

One word of caution about the use of paraphrasing: Students may say that they do not like having someone repeat what they have just said. This response is more common among middle and high school students than among elementary children. If students frequently indicate that they view your statements as parroting their own, you will either need to reduce the amount of paraphrasing used or try to use responses that vary slightly from the student's original statement. Activity 3.6 at the end of the chapter provides several methods for helping you improve and diversify skills in empathic, nonevaluative listening.

Pause & Consider 3.11

Pause for a few minutes and think about the ways in which you listen to students. Are there times when you are accessible to students and when they believe you will really listen to them? Recall a time when listening carefully to a student provided you with information that assisted you in modifying your instruction or classroom operation in a way that helped that student (and perhaps others) have a more successful school experience. Share this situation with several colleagues or classmates.

Using Culturally Sensitive Communication

It is impossible to understand each unique aspect of communication used within the cultural group of every student you teach. We know teachers who work in schools where nearly forty languages are spoken, and there are more than 160 languages spoken in the Portland, Oregon, public schools. Therefore, although we will make several points in this section related to being sensitive to cultural differences regarding communication, any overview can only highlight the importance of learning about the culture and communication style of your own students. It is important to realize that students who have not grown up in middle-class U.S. society may misinterpret our communication and vice versa. In their engaging book *Look at Me When I Talk to You*, Helmer and Eddy (2003) provide many helpful examples of this reality. For example, they note that teachers may misinterpret signs of student attention for those of comprehension. In some Asian cultures, nodding one's head and making such statements as "uh-huh" and "yes" indicates not that the individuals understand what is being said but rather that they are attentive to the conversation, whereas in other cultures, this type of nonverbal attentive listening behavior may not even be appropriate (p. 37). These authors suggest that students new to U.S. culture may similarly misinterpret teachers' nonverbal signals. They cite the example of a teacher, trying to get a group of adolescents to come closer to her during a field trip, who used the common signal of placing her palm up and curling her fingers toward herself. This did not have the desired result, and she later learned that, for some of her students, this was a sign to move away, whereas placing her palm down and moving her fingers toward herself would have signaled those students to join her (p. 41). These authors also note that, although it is generally not possible to learn the gestures used by multiple cultural groups, there are some gestures teachers should not use:

[T]wo very common gestures in Western culture are worth avoiding with ESL students. The first is the circled thumb and forefinger to indicate approval and the second is the raised and crossed index and middle finger to indicate that we are wishing someone good luck. Both these gestures have a variety of meanings in other cultures, most of them seriously negative, slanderous or sexual. (p. 42)

Helmer and Eddy (2003) also note that students who are insecure in their place in the classroom and their mastery of a language may place negative connotations on statements about which they are uncertain. For example, they may misinterpret, "I'll help you do that another way" as "You're so stupid. You can't do anything right" (p. 39).

These authors note that students whose first language is not English or who speak differently than middle-class White teachers may often misinterpret nonverbal communication, including both gestures and voice intonations. Issues involve physical space, the meaning of eye contact, willingness to answer questions, time orientation, being competitive, physical activity while learning, and level of verbal interaction during group discussions.

As you read in Chapter 1 regarding a young teacher's work with Haitian children, by talking to other teachers, instructional assistants, other professionals, and caregivers who share the same cultural heritage, teachers can obtain helpful information about special communication patterns characteristic of specific student groups. Helpful books for assisting you in getting to know all your students better include *Turning the Tides of Exclusion: A Guide for Educators and Advocates for Immigrant Students* (Olsen & Jaramillo, 1999) and *Look at Me When I Talk to You: ESL Learners in Non-ESL Classrooms* (Helmer & Eddy, 2003).

Sharing Responsibility with Students

Many of the methods provided throughout this text are based on the concept that students' self-esteem, sense of efficacy, motivation, achievement, and school-appropriate behaviors are enhanced by actively involving students in taking responsibility for creating a positive classroom and school climate and making decisions regarding instructional activities. Later in this chapter, we will discuss the value of having students provide teachers with feedback on their teaching. In Chapter 5, we present methods for involving students in sharing their academic goals and accomplishments with their parents or guardians. In Chapter 6, we discuss ways to actively involve students in developing and committing to classroom behavior standards. Chapter 7 presents multiple ways for students to be actively involved in understanding, making choices, and evaluating their academic work.

Responding Effectively to Behavior That Detracts from a Positive, Supportive Learning Environment

In Chapters 8 and 9, we present a wide variety of methods to assist you in responding effectively to student behavior that is disrupting student learning or creating a less-than-ideal learning environment for all students. These methods emphasize responding in a respectful manner to students and also focusing on helping students learn new behavior skills that enable them to be productive members of any group. Finally, Chapter 10 offers a number of methods for assisting students who are experiencing ongoing or serious behavior problems to become actively involved in and responsible for developing and implementing successful new behaviors.

1. Do I listen to you?			
2. Do I help you enough?			
3. Do I care about you?			
4. Do I help you feel good about learning?			
5. Do I seem happy when I teach?			
6. Do I think you can do your work?			
7. Can you share your good and bad feelings with me?			
8. Am I polite?			
9. Am I fair?			
10. Do you know what I want you to do?			
11. Do I help you understand why we are doing each activity in class?			
12. Do I call on you enough in class?			
13. Do I let you know when you have done good work?			
14. Are you excited about what I teach you?			

FIGURE 3.2
ELEMENTARY SCHOOL TEACHER FEEDBACK FORM

EVALUATING THE QUALITY OF TEACHER–STUDENT RELATIONSHIPS

Before implementing any of the varied behaviors you can use to create positive teacher–student relationships, you should evaluate the current quality of your own interactions with students. This approach enables us to focus changes in areas in which students' feedback suggests that changes may be needed in order to improve teacher–student relationships. Figures 3.2 and 3.3 present forms that many teachers have found useful in assessing the quality of their relationships with their students.

In addition to or in place of the forms such as those shown in these figures, many secondary teachers with whom we work simply ask their students periodically to respond to statements such as: "Please list one or more specific things about our class you most enjoy or believe are helpful to your learning" and "Please list one or more things about our class you would like to change." Similar to the responses you receive on any teacher assessment form you ask students to complete, it is important to tally these responses, share them with students, and discuss how you will be altering the classroom experience in response to this feedback.

I believe students are knowledgeable both about how they learn best and in describing effective teaching. Therefore, I am asking you to give me some feedback on what I believe to be important aspects of my teaching. Please be serious, fair, and honest when completing this form. Also please do not put your name on the form. Place an X in the column that best describes the question.

What's the Score?	Hole in One	Birdie	Par	Bogey	Out of Bounds
1. *Are the goals and objectives for each lesson clear?*					
2. *Do you value what you are learning in this class?*					
3. *Do I use different ways to teach lessons (films, projects, discussions, guest speakers, and so on)?*					
4. *Do you get to study subjects or ideas that interest you?*					
5. *Is there a good balance for you in the amount of time spent in large- and small-group activities?*					
6. *Do you think the skills taught in this class are useful in some other areas of your life?*					
7. *Do you accomplish goals you set in this class?*					
8. *Do tests give you information about what you have learned?*					
9. *Do tests help you to see what skills still need to be practiced?*					
10. *Do you feel pressured to finish work in this class?*					
11. *Are you comfortable sharing your ideas with other students in this class?*					
12. *Are the goals of each new assignment clear?*					
13. *Are you aware of how you are doing in this class?*					
14. *Are most of the assignments challenging but not too hard for you?*					
15. *Do I allow enough time for questions and discussion?*					
16. *Does the class allow you to express yourself creatively?*					
17. *Do you think the grading is fair?*					
18. *Do you feel you have a chance to be actively involved in learning?*					

FIGURE 3.3
STUDENT'S ASSESSMENT OF TEACHER'S INSTRUCTIONAL SKILLS

SUMMARY

Positive, supportive teacher–student relationships are important for all students. However, they become critical for influencing the behavior and achievement of students who are experiencing academic and behavioral difficulties. Although our primary role as teachers is to assist students in developing academic skills, successful teachers interact with students in ways that provide encouragement, support, and a positive learning environment for their students. The methods presented in this chapter provide a basis for creating adult–student relationships that support student learning in both the academic and social and personal domains.

IMPLEMENTATION ACTIVITIES

ACTIVITY 3.1

Monitoring Courteous Remarks

1. Make a tally of the courteous remarks you make to students during a one-day period. You may want to carry a counter or a small note pad.
2. If you used fewer than twenty-five such statements (research indicates that elementary teachers have approximately 1,000 interactions with children each day and that secondary teachers have nearly 500), try to double the number next day.
3. Briefly write (or discuss with a colleague) how it felt to increase the number of courteous statements. Did your students respond any differently the second day?

ACTIVITY 3.2

Improving Your Positive-to-Negative Ratio

1. Have a student or colleague tally the positive and negative statements you make during a minimum of two hours of instructional time. Try to include several types of lessons and do not code more than thirty minutes at a time. Especially when using students to tally remarks, it is helpful to define positive and negative statements and to provide the coder with a list of commonly used positive and negative remarks. Neutral remarks, such as statements related to instruction, or comments such as "OK," "All right," or "Yes" should not be coded.
2. If your ratio of positive to negative statements was less than three to one, repeat the activity and try to focus on responding positively to productive student behavior. Following a period in which your positive-to-negative ratio was very high, ask students to evaluate the lesson.

ACTIVITY 3.3

Monitoring Students' Response Opportunities

List the four highest- and four lowest-achieving students in your class. Place these students' names in the form provided in Figure 3.4. Have a colleague tally your interactions with these students during at least two half-hour periods when the class is involved in group instruction.

This activity can also be completed by presenting the observer with a seating chart and a label for each type of teacher–student interaction on which you wish to obtain data. An observer might be asked to observe several students and to tally the number of times they were asked a question, given assistance in answering a question, criticized, praised, or volunteered an answer. Figure 3.5 shows a sample of the data you might collect using this procedure.

After examining the results, respond to these statements:

Two things I learned about my interactions with these students are . . .
Two things I will try to do differently the next time I teach a large-group lesson are . . .

ACTIVITY 3.4

Mapping a Teacher's Classroom Movement

Draw a map of your classroom, including the location of the furniture. Ask a colleague to come into your classroom during a period of at least half an hour when the class will be involved in seatwork and you will be free to assist students. Have the observer

Student's Name	Student Volunteers Answer	Teacher Asks Student a Question	Student Response			Teacher Assists Student	Teacher Praises Student	Teacher Criticizes Student	Teacher Calls on Another Student
			Correct	Partially Correct	Incorrect				

FIGURE 3.4
MONITORING TEACHER–STUDENT DYADIC INTERACTIONS

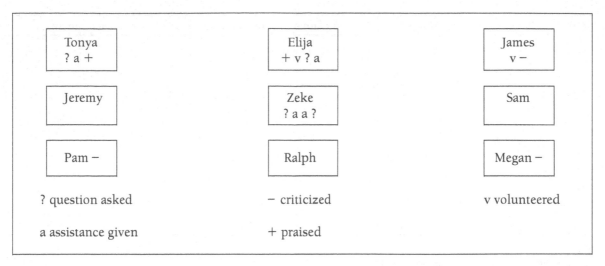

FIGURE 3.5
MONITORING TEACHER–STUDENT INTERACTIONS

mark your movement with a solid line during the entire observation. The observer should write a number by each place where you stop. To record the amount of time spent at each spot, have the observer place a tally mark next to the number for every fifteen seconds that you remain in that spot.

After examining the walking map, answer these questions:

1. Where did you spend the most time? Least time?
2. Were any students ignored? Were there specific reasons for not interacting with these students?
3. Did the classroom arrangement influence your movement? How?
4. What changes, if any, would you make in your walking pattern during this type of instruction?
5. What changes, if any, would you make in your classroom arrangement?

ACTIVITY 3.5

Balancing Positive Statements

For three days, make one inviting statement to each child in your class. In order to ensure that each child receives such a statement, make a class list and place a check by each child's name when he or she

has been given an inviting statement. After completing the activity, answer these questions:

1. Were there some students whom you had to consciously remind yourself to provide with an inviting statement? If so, did these students have anything in common?
2. Did students respond any differently during the three days? If so, how?
3. Did any students make a positive comment to you about your behavior during these three days?

A good supplement to this activity is again to list your four highest- and lowest-achieving students. Ask a colleague, an aide, or even the principal to tally the number of positive and negative statements you make to each of these students during two half-hour instructional periods. Figure 3.6 can be used to collect this data.

After completing this activity, answer these questions:

1. What do the data indicate about how you respond to high- as opposed to low-achieving students?
2. Did you find yourself behaving differently because you were being observed? If so, what did you do differently?

Student's Name	Positive Comments	Negative Comments
High achievers		
1.		
2.		
3.		
4.		
Low achievers		
1.		
2.		
3.		
4.		

FIGURE 3.6
POSITIVE AND NEGATIVE STATEMENTS

3. Did any of the eight students appear to respond differently than usual while you were observed? If so, how did their behaviors change?

ACTIVITY 3.6

Practicing Listening Skills

To examine and improve your skills in using paraphrasing, imagine that each of the following statements has just been said to you. Write two responses to each of the ten statements. In the first response, simply paraphrase the statement without mimicking the student's words. In the second response, add a feeling component.

1. Someone stole my lunch ticket!
2. This work is too hard.
3. Can we have ten extra minutes of recess?
4. Bill has had the book for two days.
5. I hate you!
6. I didn't get into trouble in music class today.
7. Nobody in the class likes me.
8. Do I have to take my report card home?
9. I never get to take the roll.
10. Mary is always picking on me.

During one school day, list five statements children make to you and five questions they ask you that could best be responded to by empathic, nonevaluative listening. When the list is complete, write a response to each of the ten student statements.

ACTIVITY 3.7

Developing a Teacher Feedback Form

Work with a group of students in your class or with several colleagues in your school to develop a format for obtaining feedback about your teaching. If you are currently student teaching or teaching, use this instrument in one of your classes, tally the results, share the results with your students, and discuss with them ways to make positive changes in the classroom based on this information.

RECOMMENDED READING

Bempechat, J. (1998). *Against the odds: How "at risk" children exceed expectations.* San Francisco, CA: Jossey-Bass.

Brendtro, L., Brokenleg, M., & Van Bockem, S. (1990). *Reclaiming youth at risk: Our hope for the future.* Bloomington, IN: National Educational Service.

Brophy, J. (Ed). (1998). *Advances in research on teaching: Expectations in the classroom.* Greenwich, CT: JAI Press.

Darling-Hammond, L. (1997). *The right to learn: A blueprint for creating schools that work.* San Francisco, CA: Jossey-Bass.

Garbarino, J. (1999). *Lost boys: Why our sons turn violent and how we can save them.* New York, NY: Free Press.

Good, T., & Brophy, J. (2008). *Looking in classrooms* (10th ed.). Boston, MA: Pearson.

Kuykendall, C. (2004). *From rage to hope: Strategies for reclaiming Black and Hispanic students* (2nd ed.). Bloomington, IN: National Educational Service.

Long, N., Newman, R., & Morse, W. (1996). *Conflict in the classroom: The education of at-risk and troubled students* (5th ed.). Austin, TX: Pro-Ed.

Mendler, A. (1992). *What do I do when . . . ? How to achieve discipline with dignity in the classroom.* Bloomington, IN: National Educational Service.

Olsen, L., & Jaramillo, A. (Eds.). (1999). *Turning the tides of exclusion: A guide for educators and advocates for immigrant students.* Oakland, CA: Coast Litho.

Paley, V. (1989). *White teacher.* Cambridge, MA: Harvard University Press.

Purkey, W., & Novak, J. (1996). *Inviting school success: A self-concept approach to teaching, learning, and democratic practice* (3rd ed.). Belmont, CA: Wadsworth.

Schmuck, R., & Schmuck, P. (2001). *Group processes in the classroom* (8th ed.). Boston, MA: McGraw-Hill.

CHAPTER 4

CREATING POSITIVE PEER RELATIONSHIPS

Our own research shows that classroom groups with supportive friendship patterns enhance academic learning. Our data indicate that student academic performances are conditioned by emotional contents associated with their self-concepts as peers and students, and these self-concepts are influenced, in part, by the students' friendships and influence relations with their classmates.

—Richard Schmuck and Patricia Schmuck (2001)

. . . feeling valued, cared for, and supported by others in a community is a positive motivating force that promotes attachment to the group and commitment to community norms and values. In the school context, students' sense of membership in a community promotes their attachment and commitment to school, motivation to engage in learning tasks, and valuing of learning.

—Thomas Good and Jere Brophy (2008)

At schools high in "community"—measured by the degree of students' agreement with statements such as "My school is like a family" and "Students really care about each other"—students show a host of positive outcomes. These include higher educational expectations and academic performance, stronger motivation to learn, greater social competence, fewer conduct problems, reduced drug use and delinquency, and greater commitment to democratic values.

—Catherine Lewis, Eric Schaps, and Marilyn Watson (1996)

An emerging body of research shows that social and emotional competencies can help students concentrate on learning through the exercise of self-control. . . . Ultimately, building social and emotional skills can contribute to students' academic success and social development.

—U.S. Department of Education (2014)

LEARNING GOALS_____

After reading this chapter, you will know:

1. The stages in the creation of a supportive group culture
2. Why knowing how to work in a group setting is so important for your students
3. How to help all students become acquainted with their classmates
4. How to establish a cohesive, supportive peer culture in your classroom
5. How to work with your colleagues to create a positive school climate

Why Are These Goals Important?

Extensive educational research as well as recent brain research has shown that students will learn more effectively and behave more responsibly in classroom and school settings where they feel safe, known, and valued. Although the recent education focus on test scores and accountability has overshadowed the work on creating classrooms and schools as communities of caring and support, unless we create classrooms and schools that meet students' basic personal and social needs, efforts to improve student achievement will never be as successful as we would like.

WHY IT IS IMPORTANT TO DEVELOP A POSITIVE CLASSROOM COMMUNITY

Peer relationships influence students' achievement in several ways. Peer attitudes toward achievement affect students' academic aspirations and school behavior (Wentzel, 2006). Noted educational psychologists Tom Good and Jere Brophy (2008) highlighted the value of positive peer relationships in classrooms when they noted the benefits.

> Feeling valued, cared for, and supported by others in a community is a positive motivating force that promotes attachment to the group and commitment to community norms and values. In the school context, students' sense of membership in a community promotes their attachment and commitment to school, motivation to engage in learning tasks, and valuing of learning. (p. 148)

The quality of peer relationships and personal support in classrooms affects the degree to which students' personal needs are met and, subsequently, their ability to be productively involved in the learning process.

> Elementary school students who are rejected by their peers not only perform more poorly on objective indicators of academic performance, like GPA and standardized test scores, but they are also more likely to have negative attitudes about school, more absenteeism from school, and lower high school graduation rates. . . . Thus, it is not surprising that peer rejection has also been found to negatively impact academic functioning not only immediately after the transition to middle school . . . but also over the middle school years. (Bellmore, 2011, p. 283)

Lack of friendships can contribute to the feelings of social alienation and can also influence patterns of social withdrawal, which in turn can influence students' behavior. Research shows that rejection by peers is a strong predictor of later serious conduct problems (McEachern & Snyder, 2012), and peer rejection has been shown to predict oppositional and aggressive behavior (Sturaro, van Lier, Cuijpers, & Koot, 2011). Recent research (Tung & Lee, 2014) has shown that peer acceptance at school can actually limit the negative impact of harsh and inconsistent parental punishment students experience at home.

Recent brain research also supports the positive impact on student learning associated with safe, supportive learning environments. This type of classroom environment increases the release of dopamine in the brain and enhances the sense of optimism and self-satisfaction students experience (Feinstein & Jensen, 2013). One reason students may struggle with academic tasks is they have less positive peer relationships, which creates more stress for them within the classroom, and this limits the brain's ability to process information (Kovalik & Olsen, 2005; Willis, 2006). Rock (2009) reported that, "When people felt excluded, we say activity in the dorsal portion of the anterior cingulate cortex—the neural region involved in the distressing component of pain . . . Those people who felt most rejected had the highest levels of activity in this region" (p. 1). By creating classroom environments where students feel valued and supported by their peers, just as they do by their teacher, educators can positively impact students' ability to learn and the likelihood they will view school as a positive place where they will make better behavioral decisions.

Being accepted by peers plays a significant factor in students' academic achievement as they transition from elementary to middle school (Kingery, Erdley, & Marshall, 2011). Substantial research exists to indicate that positive student engagement at school and academic achievement can be enhanced by creating more supportive, caring peer relationships in the classroom (Juvonen, 2007; Liem & Martin, 2011; Wentzel & Wigfield, 2007). Students who feel more accepted by their peers report lower rates of bullying or being bullied (Birchmeier, 2009; Wang, 2009).

Given the fact that research shows that being accepted and supported by one's peers significantly influences how much students say they like being in school and their academic success, it is important to implement activities within the classroom that increase students' sense of being accepted and supported by their peers (Boulton, Don, & Boulton, 2011). Research also indicates that being accepted by other ethnic groups can positively impact the behavioral and academic engagement of immigrant students (Suarez-Orozco, Pimentel, & Martin, 2009).

Another body of research suggests that how peers respond to students' academic success can impact students' motivation and persistence at future tasks (Altermatt & Ivers, 2011). Even young children are aware that discussing academic accomplishments may be negatively viewed by their peers (Watling & Banerjee, 2007). As we will discuss in Chapter 6, part of creating a positive peer community of support is helping students understand that learning is about setting and reaching goals—as opposed to outperforming others—and that we should all celebrate the success others experience.

Friendships at school can "help children to compensate for vulnerabilities acquired through stressful experiences in the home" (Schwartz, Pettit, Dodge, & Bates, 2000, p. 647) and can help children who might otherwise be victimized by peers achieve greater acceptance and success. Developing positive peer relationships helps to create a situation in which all students feel valued and respected and where bullying of any type is viewed as a violation of the family atmosphere that has been established in the classroom. An extensive summary of research on bullying concluded that ". . . it may very well be an oversimplification to analyze the roles of bully, victim, and bully/victim as fixed and static positions. A more realistic analysis must take social group dynamics into account" (Carrera, DePalma, & Lameiras, 2011, p. 484). In other words, how members of the class and school respect, value, and treat their peers is a significant factor in the extent to which bullying will exist in these settings. Not surprisingly, a key factor for students with disabilities to have successful academic and social experiences in general education courses is the degree to which classroom teachers facilitate positive and supportive peer interactions (Soodak & McCarthy, 2006; Wagner, Bos, Jascenoka, Jekeuc, & Patermann, 2012).

If schools are to prepare students for a society characterized by interdependence and cooperative effort, they must provide students with frequent and meaningful experiences in functional groups. More than three decades ago, John Dewey emphasized that life in a classroom should mirror the processes students will face in society. He wrote that the goal of schooling is to provide students with skills that will enable them to create a better living situation.

Many parents share this concern for educating the whole child. In their study of schools in which Hispanic students achieved particularly well, Reyes et al. (1999) discovered that "Parents' concerns were not only with how well children performed academically, but also with nurturing values of respect, honor, cooperation, good behavior, and responsibility of their children at school" (p. 37). These parents valued and were willing to support a school setting in which educators assisted their children in developing personal as well as cognitive skills. This is not surprising since positive peer relationships not only enhance students' school experiences but also provide a framework for the development of lifelong social skills and positive self-esteem.

Employers appear to agree with the values expressed by these parents. In a report documenting the skills and behaviors identified as essential for competence in the twenty-first-century workforce, the Employment and Training Administration in Washington, DC, listed the skills shown in Figure 4.1 (U.S. Department of Labor, 2000). Clearly, development of many skills listed under workplace competencies is facilitated by students learning how to work effectively in group settings. In an interesting analysis of this data, the Employment and Training

FIGURE 4.1
ESSENTIAL
WORKPLACE SKILLS

Source: Workplace Essential Skills, Employment and Training Administration, Office of Policy and Research, Office of Education Research and Improvement (ED): Washington, DC (2002).

Workplace Competencies	Foundation Skills
Resources	*Basic Skills*
Allocates time	Reading
Allocates money	Writing
Allocates materials and facility resources	Arithmetic
Allocates human resources	Mathematics
Information	Listening
Acquires and evaluates information	Speaking
Organizes and maintains information	*Thinking Skills*
Interprets and communicates information	Creative thinking
Uses computers to process information	Decision making
Interpersonal	Problem solving
Participates as a member of a team	Seeing things in the mind's eye
Teaches others	Knowing how to learn
Serves clients/customers	Reasoning
Exercises leadership	*Personal Qualities*
Negotiates to arrive at a decision	Responsibilities
Works with cultural diversity	Self-esteem
Systems	Social
Understands systems	Self-management
Monitors and corrects performance	Integrity/honesty
Improves and designs systems	
Technology	
Selects technology	
Applies technology to task	
Maintains and troubleshoots technology	

Administration examined the degree to which entry-level employees possessed the skills desired by employers. As seen in Figure 4.2, personal quality skills and interpersonal competencies were two of the four areas in which entry-level employees were most lacking in the skills needed for employment. It seems likely that by focusing more on interpersonal and social skills, schools could do a better job of preparing students for the workplace.

Before we discuss the theories of group development and specific methods that can help a group of students come together as a caring, supportive community, it is important to acknowledge that several factors in schools make this work more demanding. First, teachers are working with increasingly large classes. The interns we teach and supervise may be teaching classes with more thirty elementary students and more than forty secondary students. Second, the emphasis on student test scores causes teachers to be leery of taking time to build a supportive community because they are unsure whether the gains in student learning associated with this type of climate will exceed the benefits of allocating this time to instructional activities. This may be particularly true in settings where teachers are working with a high number of disenfranchised students, as research suggests that developing a supportive climate may take longer in these settings (Watson & Ecken, 2003). Increase in student mobility also makes creating a supportive classroom community more challenging. In addition, teachers are working in classrooms characterized by an increasingly diverse student population. Students may know fewer of their peers, and some may be uncomfortable or ambivalent about getting to know their classmates.

FIGURE 4.2 DIFFERENCES BETWEEN IMPORTANCE AND ACTUAL POSSESSION OF IDENTIFIED SKILLS AND COMPETENCIES

Competency or Skill	Needed for Entry-Level Employment	Entry-Level Employees Sufficiently Possess	Difference
Thinking skills	92.8%	60.0%	32.8%
Personal quality skills	96.1	66.0	30.1
Basic skills	95.9	68.4	27.5
Interpersonal competencies	91.6	65.1	26.5
Information competencies	86.5	63.1	23.4
Technology competencies	54.5	37.8	16.7
Systems competencies	52.8	41.0	11.8
Resource competencies	60.0	53.5	6.5

There are, however, numerous reasons to make the effort and allocate time to create a supportive classroom community. In addition to the desires of parents and employees, a number of factors related to school climate and student learning support the benefits of allocating time for creating positive classroom groups. Peer relationships influence students' achievement in several ways. First, peer attitudes toward achievement affect students' academic aspirations and school behavior (Wentzel, 2006). Second, the quality of peer relationships and personal support in classrooms affects the degree to which students' personal needs are met and, subsequently, their ability to be productively involved in the learning process. Third, peer relationships can directly affect achievement through cooperative learning activities. Fourth, findings suggest that a key factor in students with disabilities having successful academic and social experiences in general education courses is the degree to which classroom teachers facilitate positive and supportive peer interactions (Soodak & McCarthy, 2006). Fifth, developing positive peer relationships helps create a situation in which all students feel valued and respected and where bullying of any type is viewed as a violation of the family atmosphere that has been established in the classroom. Sixth, peer relationships can directly affect achievement by facilitating collaborative working relationships between students. Finally, creating a sense of community is an important aspect of culturally responsive classroom management.

As you read this chapter, you may ask whether it's worth the time to create positive, supportive peer relationships in the classroom. Will it reduce the amount of time allocated for instruction, or will a small but significant amount of time spent in this way minimize time and energy spent responding to problems caused by students feeling isolated, unable to obtain assistance, uninvolved, and unwanted? This chapter is intended to provide you with information about how classroom groups operate and how you can go about developing a community of support within your classroom(s).

Pause & Consider 4.1

Stop for a minute and think of a class you found particularly enjoyable, perhaps one you looked forward to attending every day. Write several sentences that describe the social aspects of this class. When considering and writing about this class, focus your attention on the relationships you had with other students in the class. We encourage you to share this with a colleague or several classmates. Did you and those with whom you shared this activity write about common factors?

UNDERSTANDING THE CLASSROOM GROUP

Classrooms are by their very nature characterized by a high level of interaction and the accompanying spontaneous interchange of feelings. By placing twenty to forty-five individuals in a thirty-foot-square room, schools create a highly interactive environment. This interaction is intensified by the competition found in many classrooms. Students compete for the highest test scores, strive to earn high grades, or run for class office. Even when we use instructional methods that deemphasize competition, students have numerous opportunities to compare their work to that of their classmates.

Although teachers often express concern and frustration about the negative aspects of peer pressure, the peer group can be a positive and supportive factor in the classroom. When students feel liked by their peers and when interactions are characterized by thoughtfulness and helpfulness, students experience a sense of safety and security, belongingness and affection, significance, respect for others, and power. Students are then able to concentrate more fully on learning and are willing to take greater risks in attempting to master new skills.

Group Development Stages

Anyone who has worked with youth groups knows that, like individuals, groups go through various developmental stages. Just like individuals, if development is skillfully facilitated, the group can become a healthful, supportive entity, but if the group development is not supported, serious problems in the life of the group may occur. Figure 4.3 presents these group stages.

Stage	Key Concepts	Strategies
Dependency	Group members look to authority figure to provide structure.	Teacher provides clarity by working with students to create classroom academic and behavior standards (Chapters 6 & 7).
Inclusion or orientation	Group members are concerned about belonging—whether other group members and the teacher will like them and whether they are as competent as other group members.	Teacher implements activities to help students know and value their peers (Chapter 4) and ensure that students know they are valued by their teacher (Chapter 3) and employs methods that help all students feel academically competent (Chapter 7).
Dissatisfaction or control	Members express concern about how the group is operating and who makes decisions. Students are comfortable enough to challenge the way things are being done.	Teacher acknowledges and responds to student concerns through obtaining student feedback about the class (Chapter 3), individual problem solving (Chapter 8), and classroom meetings (Chapter 9).
Resolution or norming	Students begin to listen more thoughtfully to one another and work more collaboratively. A greater sense of group unity is established and students make an increased number of positive statements about the classroom.	Teacher implements instructional methods that involve students in cooperative/collaborative learning (Chapter 7).
Production	Student production is high, and teacher simply needs to be attentive to social and academic needs and make the necessary adjustments.	Teacher views oneself as a reflective practitioner. (The "Pause & Consider" activities throughout this book will enhance your proficiency in this important professional skill.)
Termination or adjournment	Students need closure on the group experience. Students may experience a sense of loss and sadness.	Teacher works with students to discuss classroom events, including the end of various class projects and, eventually, the end of the class.

FIGURE 4.3
STAGES OF GROUP DEVELOPMENT

The materials in this text will help you create classroom structures that facilitate moving groups through these developmental stages in a healthful manner, and thus creating positive, supportive learning communities.

PAUSE & CONSIDER 4.2

Spend some time observing a group with which you are familiar. If you are working in a classroom, use this as your group. If not, perhaps you can observe a sports team, scouting troop, or other group. Determine the state at which you believe this group is functioning and list the factors that led you to this decision. Meet with a group of three colleagues and each discuss your observations.

Acquaintance Activities_____

You can undoubtedly recall experiencing discomfort when walking into a party or other group setting and knowing very few individuals there. Compare this feeling with those elicited when you walk into a room filled with acquaintances and friends. People usually feel more relaxed and comfortable in discussions or other activities with people they know. Students experience similar feelings. The new student who is confronted by thirty unfamiliar faces is likely to respond either by withdrawing until the environment becomes more familiar or by acting out as a means of controlling the environment by eliciting an expected response.

Several years ago, one of us was contacted by a teacher who was experiencing much frustration because the students in his sophomore English class were not becoming involved in group discussions. Furthermore, the teacher reported that absenteeism in class was relatively high and students were not handing in the number of assignments he had expected. The teacher, a hard-working, dynamic young man, indicated that the material being read and discussed seemed to be of high interest and that he had made a special effort to relate aspects of the literature to students' lives. Students were seated in a circle and open discussion was encouraged.

While discussing this situation, I asked the teacher whether students in the class knew each other. The teacher seemed surprised by the question and indicated that because the students came from only two feeder schools and had been in his class for nearly a full semester, he assumed they were well acquainted. The students' behaviors suggested, however, that they felt some discomfort, and the teacher agreed to assess how well they knew one another. He was surprised to discover that only a quarter of the students in his class knew the first names of more than half of their peers. He discussed this figure with the class and explained his decision to allocate time to activities that would help students become better acquainted. Following these activities, he again collected data on attendance, percentage of assignments handed in, and students' participation in class discussions. All three variables showed changes that were statistically significant at the 0.01 level. These results were so striking that the teacher's English department decided to incorporate a peer-acquaintance unit into the first nine weeks of the school year.

By implementing activities to enhance positive peer relationships, we increase the likelihood that a wider range of peers will be accepted and supported and we decrease the likelihood that bullying, intimidation, and isolation will be experienced by students (Schwartz et al., 2000). Friendships at school can "help children to compensate for vulnerabilities acquired through stressful experiences in the home" (Schwartz et al., 2000, p. 647) and can help children who might otherwise be victimized by peers be more accepted and successful. Because being rejected by peers tends to be associated with acting-out behavior (Laird, Jordan, Dodge, Pettit, & Bates, 2001), developing peer acceptance and support can be expected to significantly reduce disruptive classroom behavior. Students who develop a pattern of acting-out, aggressive behavior are likely to have experienced rejection from peers and not be integrated into the classroom group. Therefore, if you wish to create a classroom setting in which negative peer interactions and acting-out behavior are minimized, it is essential to incorporate methods for helping students know and interact positively with each other.

The peer-acquaintance activities presented in the following section are designed to help students get better acquainted with one another so that they will feel safe and secure and will, therefore, become more actively engaged in the learning process. As students become better acquainted, the likelihood that they will interact with and be influenced by a wider range of students increases, and cliquish behavior decreases.

The Name Chain

A name chain is an effective method for helping students learn each other's names. The following steps can make this activity run smoothly:

1. Ask the students to sit in a circle so that each one can comfortably see all the students in the group.

2. Clearly explain the reasons for being involved in the activity. You might say that one benefit of knowing everyone's name is that this increases their knowledge of the environment and thereby makes them more comfortable and more likely to become actively involved. Similarly, you may indicate that knowing other students' names will enable students to greet each other in a friendlier, more relaxed manner, which will have a tendency to make both the classroom and the school a more positive place.

3. Ask the students if they have any questions about why they are being asked to do the activity.

4. Explain to the students that each person will be asked to say his or her first name and tell the group one thing about himself or herself. They may choose to tell the group something they like to do, something interesting that happened to them recently, how they are feeling, and so on. Inform the class that they will be asked to repeat each student's name and the statement he or she made. They will begin with the person who spoke first and stop when they have given their name and have said something about themselves. The first student may say, "I'm Bob, and I went to the beach this weekend." The next would say, "That's Bob (or you're Bob), and he (or you) went to the beach last weekend. I'm Sandy, and I enjoy backpacking." Because we are faced with the difficult task of learning a large number of names and because having an adult remember their names seems particularly important to adolescents, it is best to have you be the last person to speak. You will therefore be able to list each student's name and what they have shared with the class.

5. Have everyone take a paper and pencil and change seats. Ask the students to start with a designated individual and go clockwise around the circle, writing down each person's name. It is not necessary to have them list what each student shared.

6. Ask for a volunteer who will begin with the person designated as the starting place and slowly give the name of each person in the circle. This recital serves as an opportunity for students to check the accuracy of their lists and to learn the names of any students they might have missed. (Jones, 1980, pp. 71–72)

It is important to provide follow-up for this activity. For example, for several days following the activity, you may want to attempt to go around the class listing each student's name or ask for a volunteer to do so. If you ask students to work in groups, you may suggest that they make sure they know each member's name before beginning the group activity. Teachers too often involve students in activities and then fail to follow up with behavior that reinforces the learning derived from and the values implied by the activity.

Know Your Classmates

Each student will need a copy of a page entitled Know Your Classmates (see Figure 4.4) and a pencil or pen. Ask students to find a person in the class who fits each description listed on the sheet and to obtain the person's signature on the line in front of the description. To encourage students to interact with numerous peers, inform them that they cannot have the same person sign their sheets more than twice. The descriptions can be adapted to fit the specific interests of children at different ages and in different settings.

FIGURE 4.4
KNOW YOUR
CLASSMATES

Name _____

Collect the signatures of the appropriate persons:

_____ 1. A person whose birthday is in the same month as yours.

_____ 2. A person who has red hair.

_____ 3. A person whom you don't know very well.

_____ 4. A person who has an interesting hobby. What is it? _____

_____

_____ 5. A person with freckles.

_____ 6. A person whose favorite color is yellow.

_____ 7. A person who loves to read.

_____ 8. A person who takes gymnastic lessons.

_____ 9. A person who is left-handed.

_____ 10. A person with naturally curly hair.

_____ 11. A person who has a dog. The dog's name is _____

_____ 12. A person who belongs to a scouting troop.

_____ 13. A person shorter than you.

_____ 14. A person taller than you.

_____ 15. A person with the same color shirt or dress as you are wearing.

_____ 16. A person who plays an instrument. What instrument? _____

_____

_____ 17. A person who traveled out of the state this summer. Where?

_____

_____ 18. A person who wants to play professional sports when he or she grows up. Which one?_____

_____ 19. A person with more than four children in the family. How many? _____

_____

_____ 20. A person who plays soccer.

_____ 21. A person with braces on his or her teeth.

_____ 22. A person who rides horseback.

Bingo

For upper elementary and middle school, on the first day of class, have each student complete a brief self-information sheet. You may ask them about things they did this summer, special interests, pets, hobbies, and so on. Take this information and place one interesting piece of information about each student in each square of a bingo grid. The next day, each class member is given a bingo card and the students are asked to walk around the room and obtain the signature of the person who is associated with each square. This can be continued until someone has obtained a signature for each square, has a signature on each square in two rows, or a designated period of time has elapsed.

Interviews

Interviews are an excellent means for students to become better acquainted with each other. This activity often fosters new friendships and feelings of self-importance. Lack of information about others is often a major barrier to establishing new friendships. When students do not know their peers, they tend to make assumptions and develop unrealistic fears or unfounded biases. As students interview each other, they learn new and exciting information about their peers. This knowledge, in turn, promotes diversified friendship patterns in the classroom.

We can use interviews in the classroom in many ways. One method involves introducing the interviewing process by having students list ten questions that would help them know a classmate better. Following are examples of questions that might be asked by nine-year-olds:

1. What is your favorite color?
2. What is your favorite sport to play? To watch?
3. What are you proudest of ?
4. Do you have any pets? If so, what are their names?
5. What is your favorite professional team in football? Basketball? Baseball?
6. What kinds of foods do you like to eat?
7. If you could go anyplace on a vacation, where would you go? Why?
8. Do you take any lessons?
9. Do you have any hobbies?
10. Do you like your first name? If not, what would you change it to?

Write these questions on the board and tell the students each to choose a person whom they do not know very well and, using the ten questions as a guide, learn as much as they can about their partners. The next step is to create groups of six and have each student introduce the person he or she interviewed to the group. Ideally you will be able to have students form at least a second set of groups so, in addition to the student they interviewed, all students will have learned something more about at least eight students.

A third interviewing technique has a student sit in a place of honor at the front of the classroom. The student is asked questions by the other class members. Students enjoy being in the limelight and often state that this is their favorite approach to interviewing.

A final interviewing approach has several students serve as reporters. They interview their peers and obtain such information as where students were born; the number of members in their families; a student's favorite television show, food, color, or animal; a special hobby or pet; any unusual places they have visited; and students' future goals. The teacher tabulates the information and either duplicates it and gives it to each student or makes a large chart in the hall for other classes to read.

The results of these interviewing activities can often be seen in new friendships and more open communication in the classroom. This atmosphere in turn makes the classroom a safer and more relaxed learning environment for students.

Guess Who?

An acquaintance activity used by a number of secondary teachers gives students an opportunity to discover how well they know their peers. The steps for setting up this activity are as follows:

1. Briefly describe the activity to the students and elicit their willingness to take part in the activity.
2. Ask students to write brief (two- or three-line) statements about themselves, which can include facts about their personal histories, family, hobbies, and so forth.
3. Collect all the autobiographical statements.
4. Ask each student to take out paper and pencil. Read each description and ask the students (you, too, should be involved) to write the name of the student they believe wrote the description.
5. After all the descriptions have been read, reread them and ask the authors to identify themselves. Ask the students to indicate on the list whether they made the correct choice. On completing the task, you may ask students to indicate the number of their peers whom they correctly identified. These results can be used to initiate a discussion about the degree to which class members have become acquainted.
6. An interesting alternative to this activity is to have students write their brief statements that include one false statement about themselves. Then read the student's name to the class and the statements and ask the class to decide which statement is false. This activity can be performed by the entire group or can be developed as a contest between two groups.
7. A second variation of this activity is to have students write poems or riddles about themselves. These poems are put into a box. Each student draws a poem from the box and reads it aloud to the class. Based on the information in the poem, the class tries to identify the author.

Who Are We?

In this activity, students are given a 5-by-7-inch index card and asked to complete the following information.

1. Write your student ID number on the top line of the card.
2. On the same side of the card, make three columns.
3. Label the first column "interests" and list three interests you have.
4. Label the second column "journeys" and list three journeys you have made.
5. Label the third column "facts" and list three facts about yourself others in the class might not know.
6. On the blank side of the card, create a collage containing images that represent you, your interests, things you like, things you do, and things you want to do.

Hang the cards where students can see them. During warm-ups or as part of a group activity, ask students to guess who is represented by each card.

Having students know and feel supported by their peers is valuable at all grade levels, but it may be particularly critical as young people move through early adolescence. Students in grades six through eight are experiencing rapid cognitive and physical changes. This is a time of heightened self-consciousness and decreased self-esteem. Consequently, students learn much more effectively in environments in which teacher–student and peer relationships are characterized by warmth, support, and stability. Schools for young adolescents should not only use a wide range of acquaintance activities but should also be organized so that students spend a sizable portion of the school day with students and teachers they know.

T-Shirt

Provide students with an 8½-by-11-inch sheet of paper with the outline of a T-shirt drawn on it. Ask students to design a T-shirt they could wear to school that would help others know them better. For middle and high school students, we usually indicate that the T-shirt should include materials the students could show the principal and their grandmothers. Tell students they can draw, sketch, write, or make displays—however they are most comfortable. Provide colored pencils. Once the designs are completed, have students share them in groups of four. After these groups have shared, students can form new groups of four.

Blue Ribbon Kid

This activity is appropriate in an elementary school classroom or middle school block class. On Friday, a child's name is drawn and this student is given a piece of white butcher paper. The child takes this home and has a parent, guardian, or friend trace an outline of the student's body on the paper. The "paper doll" is cut out, colored in an outfit the student selects, and brought back to school on Monday. During the weekend, the child is asked to collect artifacts that represent her or him (a table is available on which students place these items). On Monday, the student hangs the paper person on the bulletin board and the class gathers to listen to the child describe the artifacts she or he has brought. These often include pictures of family members and pets and pictures cut from magazines that depict the student's interests. Throughout the week, the class writes positive statements about the student and places these on the paper doll. On Friday, the child takes all the materials home and a new student is selected. It is important that the teacher is also part of the process of being selected and writing positive statements.

Shoe Box or Paper Bag

Students are given a shoe box covered with butcher paper or a paper bag. One approach is to provide the students with a lesson on drawing portraits and have them draw and paint self-portraits on the lids of their shoe boxes. The students take their boxes or bags home and place in them five items they select to represent them. Students are asked to be sure these items are appropriate for sharing at school; they might include pictures of their families, a golf ball indicating they like to play golf, a soccer cleat, and so on. Each day during the following several weeks, a few students share their items. If you have had students draw portraits, the boxes are kept in the room and shared with the parents at back-to-school night.

Identifying Similarities and Differences in Talents

In table groups (or any group of four you may select) students are asked to individually write about their talents and skills. These are then shared with other members of their group, and the group makes a list of those talents and skills that are shared by several members and those that are somewhat rare. These are then placed on a poster and each group shares a poster that reflects the commonalities and differences in talents that exist in their group. This can be followed by a teacher-led class discussion on how we are all different and have unique talents and how we can all share our talents to help everyone learn and make this a fun and productive school year.

Incorporating Acquaintance Activities into Course Content

Because mastery of content and preparing for state and national assessments within a limited time frame have, in many school settings, become central goals, whenever possible, it is beneficial to integrate acquaintance activities into the content. We know a high school social studies teacher who has students develop a time line of significant events in their lives and bring artifacts that help others better understand each student. He connects this to classroom work emphasizing the use of time lines and artifacts within the context of history. We also know several high school English teachers who begin the year with Sandra Cisneros's (1991) short novel *The House on Mango Street*, about a young girl growing up in a Latino neighborhood in Chicago. Early in the book, the girl talks about her name, and the teachers use this as an opportunity for students to write about and share factors related to their names.

If you are interested in incorporating additional acquaintance activities into your lesson plans, you can find numerous resources. Especially useful are Borba's *Esteem Builders* (1989); Canfield and Siccone's *One Hundred Ways to Develop Student Self-Esteem and Responsibility* (1992); Gibbs's *Tribes: A New Way of Learning and Being Together* (2000); and Duval's *Building Character and Community in the Classroom* (1997).

PAUSE & CONSIDER 4.3

As a teacher, you will make important decisions regarding the amount of time and types of activities you use to create a community of support in your classroom. Take a few minutes to write down the acquaintance activities you currently believe you would implement during the first three weeks of the school year. Highlight your favorite activity. Next, meet with a group of three or four colleagues or classmates who teach students at a grade level similar to the one you are teaching or observing and share your favorite activity. This should provide you with a wonderful array of activities for helping students become better acquainted.

ACTIVITIES FOR ESTABLISHING A COHESIVE, SUPPORTIVE GROUP

Group cohesiveness refers to the extent to which a group experiences a sense of identity, oneness, and esprit de corps. Cohesive groups are characterized by warm, friendly interactions among all members rather than by positive interchanges limited to small cliques within the group. Cohesive groups provide settings in which students feel safe, experience a sense of belonging, and view themselves as being liked and respected by others. Research indicates that students who are accepted by their classmates have more positive attitudes toward school and are more likely to achieve closer to their potential than are students who feel rejected and isolated. These findings are supported by other research indicating that students perform less effectively when they feel threatened by the environment.

Group cohesiveness and a positive group identity do not develop simply because students spend time together. Rather, positive feelings about being a group member are developed by making the group seem attractive, distinguishing it from other groups, involving the group in cooperative enterprises, and helping students view themselves as important components in the group. The activities described in this section are designed to accomplish these goals. The activities are most effective when used in association with acquaintance activities and with activities for creating diverse liking patterns.

Activities aimed at creating a cohesive classroom group will be most effective when introduced at the beginning of the school year. One important reason for developing group cohesion early in the school year is that cohesive groups are desirable only if the group's norms support your learning goals. If you can begin the year by establishing a positive group feeling while creating norms that support academic achievement and productive behavior, the school year will be more pleasant and productive.

Activities for Elementary School Classrooms

Ways of Creating a Positive Classroom

Focusing on the positive qualities of a classroom sets a tone for the entire year. In the fall, ask students to list things they can do to make the classroom a positive place to be. Encourage students to describe ways of positively interacting with each other, ideas for having fun in the classroom, and so on. Write the students' ideas on a large sheet of paper and post it in the classroom. Every month, ask students whether they are acting in accordance with the ideas expressed on the chart and to evaluate each item to see if it is still applicable. New ideas may be added at any time.

Teaching Students How to Be Positive with One Another

Students often do not realize the power positive or negative comments have on how effectively students learn in a classroom. This concept and specific methods to support it need to be taught and reinforced as important behavior goals in a classroom. One way to accomplish this is to read aloud either *Have You Filled a Bucket Today?* (McCloud, 2007) or *How Full Is Your Bucket? For Kids* (Rath, Reckmeyer, & Manning, 2009). You can then discuss how students can fill their own buckets and how they can fill or dip into the buckets of other students. Students can be assisted in generating ideas for statements and behaviors that help fill individuals' buckets. You may wish to create a bucket to place on the bulletin board with positive statements written around it and every student signing the bucket indicating they will try to always be someone who fills a bucket. During the first few weeks following this activity, every time you see a student saying or doing something kind to a peer, you might wish to place a star in another bucket you have drawn and try to completely fill the bucket with stars. Students can also be taught to thank individuals who engage in activities or make statements that make them feel good/fill up their bucket.

© George B. Abbott

"I've brought along a jury of my peers."

Classroom Arrangements

Developing a comfortable classroom environment can enhance students' motivation and provide opportunities for increasing their sense of competence and power. It can be productive to involve students in discussions about the classroom arrangement. Give them a basic floor plan of the room, including all built-ins. Then ask them to sketch in the desks and any other movable furniture in ways they think will facilitate smooth classroom operation. Display the arrangements and, along with the students, choose the floor plan with which all would be most comfortable. By giving students responsibility for a room arrangement, we indicate our respect for their judgment and they gain a sense of significance, competence, and power.

Students can also be active in decorating the room. Encourage them to take part in designing bulletin-board displays and determining the types of plants they would like in the room. Increased student involvement in organizing and decorating the room is almost always associated with an intensified group feeling, higher motivation, and reduced vandalism.

Research suggests that ". . . the classroom seating arrangement can be used as a tool to improve liking among peers and reduce peer-reported problem behaviors in the classroom" (Van den Berg, Segers, & Cillessen, 2012, p. 403). Seating students closer to peers whom they may initially not like may have a positive effect on how the less popular peer is viewed while at the same time reducing peer victimization.

While there are certainly benefits for providing students with choices regarding with whom they are seated, research indicates that by the teacher selecting where students sit, disruptive behavior during group work may be half what it was if students selected where they sit, and students selecting where they would sit during independent seatwork increased disruptive behavior threefold (Bicard, Ervin, Bicard, & Baylot-Casey, 2012).

Class Spirit

At the beginning of the school year, most students are excited and motivated. Teachers can take advantage of this excitement by establishing a class spirit that creates a bond among the students. Many activities throughout the year can revolve around this class spirit.

To create a class spirit, teacher and students discuss the kinds of group identity they would like to develop and formulate a list. The list might include a class animal, name, flower, insect, song, flag, color, cheer, game, cartoon character, sport, bird, and poem. Suggestions are welcomed, and eventually students vote to determine their choices in each category. When the class spirit is completed, it is displayed proudly in a prominent place in the room.

It is very important to reinforce this activity by using parts of the class spirit whenever possible throughout the year. For example, when sending a newsletter to parents, you might draw several of the class symbols on the letter and copy the newsletter onto paper that is the class color. Similarly, giving the class cheer before special sporting events or singing the class song at the close of each week enhances class spirit.

Class Pet

The following activity was shared with us by our daughter following her first year of teaching in a diverse fourth–fifth blend classroom.

> Each of the classes at our school has a name, and ours is Frog Bog. Since this was our class name, I found it only appropriate to have a class pet. Since we are not allowed to have live animals in our classrooms because of allergy reasons, I bought a stuffed animal frog for our room. The students voted and his name was Freddy. Every Friday I would draw a popsicle stick with a name on it out

of the bucket, and that student would get to take Freddy home. The student would also take home the black binder that went with Freddy and would be expected to write a minimum of a page about their adventures with Freddy over the weekend. I encouraged them to be creative in their writing. This was a nonthreatening way for students to become excited and interested in writing as I made it clear the only thing they would be graded on would be their participation. For the students who struggled with writing I told them instead of reading what they wrote, they could tell the class about their adventures when they reported their activities with Freddy back to the class on Monday at community jelly bean. The students loved to hear what others had done and at the end of the year they got books about all their classmates' adventures.

Class History

An effective activity that helps mold students into a cohesive group is the development of a class history or class yearbook.

Four to six students are chosen either by the teacher or by their peers to write the history, and all students are encouraged to contribute ideas. Every month, the history writers meet and decide what events, assemblies, new lessons, and so on they wish to incorporate into their class history. The historians then divide the writing assignments. At the end of the year, students have a collection of the year's events. In addition to these events, the class history can include poems written by students, a student directory of addresses and phone numbers, an autograph page, a page about students' thoughts on the year, and a letter written to the students by the teacher. The class history helps create a sense of group purposefulness and commitment and is a memorable treasure for each student.

Photo Album

Whenever a special event occurs, capture the moment in a photograph. Students can become actively involved by learning to use a camera. Pictures taken by students can be accompanied by written statements and put on the bulletin board until replaced by a picture and description of a new event. The old material can then be placed in the class photo album and some of the written material can be incorporated into the class history.

The photo album can be shown to parents during scheduled conferences or when a parent drops by the school. Parents enjoy seeing pictures of their children involved in special school activities. This sharing enhances parents' interest in their children's school experiences and increases parental support for the teacher and the school. When a particularly good picture of a child is obtained, the teacher can make a copy and send it to the parents along with a short note. Parents appreciate this thoughtful gesture, and their increased interest in their child's classroom experience helps their child develop a sense of pride and commitment.

When there are a few moments left in a day, it is enjoyable to recall several of the special events by looking at the pictures in the class photo album. This is an effective means of reinforcing a sense of identity and creating positive feelings about the class.

Opening and Closing Questions

Students arrive at school with many different feelings and needs. One student may arrive in an irritable mood because of an argument with a caregiver or sibling or lack of a proper breakfast, while another student may be happy because it is his birthday. It is often hard for students to make the transition from home to school. Therefore, it is important that students be given a few minutes at the beginning of each day to share any events that are significant to them.

Students are asked to meet in a circle. The teacher then asks whether any person needs or wants to share anything. One student who has just broken her foot may need someone to carry her lunch tray, whereas another student whose dog just died may need some care and understanding. Teachers also have days when they are tired or not feeling well and, therefore, would like the students to be particularly helpful during the day. When students are treated kindly and their needs are accepted and respected, they will respond to your needs and desires.

For students who are less comfortable sharing their needs in a group, an optional activity is to have them write down their needs and place them in a box or bag. You can check several times during the day to see whether any child has put a need in the box.

The end of the schoolday can be an important time to establish closure on any issues that occurred during the day. Questions such as "What did you learn today?" "How do you feel about the day?" or "What did you like and dislike about today?" often evoke serious discussion. It is advisable to allow at least ten minutes for this session. Taking time at the end of each day encourages students to examine what they have accomplished and also helps to ensure that the day will end on a positive note.

Special Days
Assigning special days allows students to have some influence over their environment while enhancing a sense of group identity. Special days might include a day on which everyone wears the same color, a day for wearing favorite buttons, a day for dressing as students did during the 1950s, a day when everyone wears his or her favorite hat, and so on. You can add to the special day by relating various subjects to the day's theme. Math problems to solve batting averages could be included on uniform day, music of famous singers during the early rock 'n' roll era might be discussed and listened to during music class on 1950s day, or students might read stories involving hats on hat day.

Service Projects
Students can build a sense of community by solving a common problem or sharing in assisting others. One of the first experiments in group dynamics, the classic Sherif experiment conducted in 1958, showed that groups of students who were in conflict could become unified when they experienced a common need to solve a problem. Similarly, a classroom group who mentors a group of younger students, works to beautify the school, or assists in solving a problem or providing assistance in the community will almost always develop a closer bond.

Activities for Secondary Classrooms

Because secondary school students spend considerably less time in one classroom group, most secondary teachers choose to implement fewer activities for enhancing group cohesiveness. Instead, many incorporate several structured, group-cohesiveness activities with instructional activities, such as cooperative learning and peer editing, that emphasize creating positive peer relationships and active involvement in the learning process. We have found several activities and processes particularly valuable in helping secondary students develop skills in functioning as supportive group members.

Five Square
The five-square activity involves students cooperating to reach a goal, followed by systematically discussing the behaviors that facilitated or blocked the group's efforts. As described in Figure 4.5,

FIGURE 4.5
THE FIVE-
SQUARE GAME

Preparation of Puzzle

A puzzle set consists of five envelopes containing pieces of stiff paper cut into patterns that will form 6-inch squares, as shown in the diagram. Cut the squares into parts and lightly pencil the letters *a* through *j* as shown below. Then mark the envelopes *A* through *E* and distribute the pieces thus:

Envelope A—j, h, e

B—a, a, a, c

C—a, i

D—d, f

E—g, b, f, a

Erase from the pieces the lowercase letters and write instead the envelope letters *A* through *E*, so that the pieces can easily be returned for reuse.

Several combinations of the pieces will form one or two squares, but only one combination will form five squares.

Instructions for Students

Each person should have an envelope containing pieces for forming squares. At the signal, the task of the group is to form five squares of equal size. The task is not complete until everyone has before him or her a perfect square and all the squares are of the same size. These are the rules: (1) No member may speak, (2) no member may signal in any way that he or she wants a card, and (3) members may give cards to others.

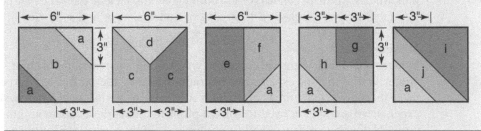

students are placed in groups of five, and each group is given the task of passing puzzle pieces until each group member has an equal-sized square in front of him or her. It is important that you write on the board and carefully monitor the "Instructions for Students" found in Figure 4.5. Tell students that groups that complete their task may quietly observe groups still at work. Finally, if one or more groups have difficulty completing the task, members of these groups can raise a hand, signaling that they would like to be replaced by a student from a group that has completed the task. This student then joins the group still working and continues to follow the rules. The addition of a new member who has seen the correct pattern will usually facilitate quick task completion.

When all groups have completed the task, you can involve students in discussing the groups' functioning. On a board or butcher paper, make columns labeled "Behaviors That Facilitated Task Completion" and "Behaviors That Hindered the Group." Then ask students to, without mentioning names, describe behaviors that helped their group complete their task. Next, students can list behaviors that blocked their group. Then lead a discussion on group behavior. Interestingly, this activity may also highlight additional factors related to establishing effective learning environments. For example, when using the activity recently, a student in one of our classes indicated that he had experienced considerable anxiety when other students began watching his group. This comment led to a productive discussion on the advantages and disadvantages of anxiety in learning and a further discussion on how anxiety could be limited in the class.

Even though this activity requires most of a class period, dozens of secondary teachers with whom we have worked have found that the benefits in terms of students' understanding how groups operate and appreciating the value of involving everyone in group activities far outweigh the time cost.

Group Contributions

A teacher of junior writing and American literature recently shared a technique for incorporating group cohesiveness activities. During the first week of school, she has the class brainstorm ways in which individuals contribute to the class as a whole. These are listed on the board and may include such statements as:

> Adding humor
> Listening carefully and quietly
> Making perceptive observations
> Contributing personal experiences
> Bringing the group back to the topic being discussed
> Asking someone to clarify a point
> Summarizing
> Asking questions
> Helping people get along

This material is used to stimulate a discussion about how there are many ways of contributing to a class and how students will differ in their contributions. About a week later, she passes out slips of paper with the name of a student on each slip. Each student in the class receives one slip and is asked to write one positive comment about a contribution the student listed on the slip has made to the class. The slips are handed in, and students volunteer to read several of them.

Another approach a high school teacher imparted for students sharing contributions they can make to the group is by having students list these on a sheet of paper, hand them in, and the teacher compiling a list and posting this on the wall or by having students share these in small groups and having the groups list at least one contribution for each student in the group and either post these or hand them in to be compiled. When using this approach, it may be helpful to initially have students brainstorm some types of contributions students can make to the group. Just as when developing classroom rules, it is helpful to have the teacher also list contributions he/she can make to the class.

Tower Building

Divide the class into groups of four or five. Give each group a deck of cards and some tape (you may also use straws and paper clips). Tell students they have ten minutes to build the highest tower. As with the five-square activity, after teams have completed the activity, ask each team (beginning with the winning team and going in order to the team with the lowest tower) to describe one factor that facilitated their work. Write these on butcher paper. Next, reverse the process and have each team, beginning with the team who built the lowest structure, list one thing that occurred in their group that blocked the group's effectiveness. Finally, have the class discuss and summarize what they have learned about group functioning and how this can apply to their work in the class.

Identifying Similarities and Differences in Talents

In table groups (or any group of four you may select) students are asked to individually write about their talents and skills. These are then shared with other members of their group and the group makes a list of those talents and skills that are shared by several members and those that are somewhat rare. These are then placed on a poster and each group shares a poster that reflects the commonalities and differences in talents that exist in their group. This can be followed by a teacher-led class discussion on how we are all unique and have different talents and how we can all share our talents to help everyone learn and make this a fun and productive school year.

Four Corners

Ask students to go and stand in the corner with the letter that best reflects their response to each prompt. Teachers with whom I have worked have, depending on the age and interests of their students, used a wide range of topics such as: My favorite vehicle is a a) truck, b) compact, c) hybrid, or d) SUV; My favorite vacation spot would be a) the beach, b) the mountains, c) the desert, e) a city; or A sport I enjoy watching is a) football, b) basketball, c) baseball/softball, d) tennis.

Shared Experiences

Ask students to briefly write about an experience they have had related to a topic. Teachers have shared with us that they have had students write about a favorite place they have gone, something that occurred associated with their teeth, a special time they have spent with a relative, and so on. Students then share these with a partner and students rotate through three or four partners.

Partner Interviews

During the first week of class, students interview a peer and then introduce the peer to the class. The prompts for these interviews can be tailored to the class, for example, related to math, science, language arts, and so forth. For example, in an English class, students might be asked to share about any of the following (tailored to reading, writing, and literature they will be exploring): (a) If I could meet any author (dead or alive), I would like to meet . . ., (b) my favorite book is . . ., (c) besides books, I like to read . . ., (d) a hobby or interest I pursue outside of school is. . . .

Paraphrasing Passport

An important component to creating a sense of cohesiveness is for all members of the group to be involved in academic learning. In many classrooms, a relatively small number of students provide a majority of the answers. In addition, while students are speaking, other students are frequently considering what they want to say rather than thoughtfully listening to what their peers are saying. One method for helping students listen effectively to their peers is to periodically implement the procedure we call "paraphrasing passport." In this procedure, prior to providing a response, an individual must first paraphrase the statement made by the previous speaker. We have found this significantly increases the degree to which students respectfully listen to their peers.

Group Decision Making

Group cohesiveness may also be enhanced by involving students in shared decision making about classroom organizational factors or problems. We will discuss in Chapter 6 how students can cooperatively develop classroom rules and procedures. In Chapter 9, we go over how teachers can work with students to resolve problems that arise. Recently, a friend reported that he had been working with his junior English class to resolve the problem of student papers being late. The teacher stated that more than half his class worked part time and several teachers were requiring that major projects be due on the same day. The teacher and his students collected data on due dates for each student's assignments and developed a series of due dates that was approved by all students in the class.

Using Base Groups

In his book *Building Community in Schools*, Thomas Sergiovanni (1994) discussed the importance of creating some form of "primary-group network of relationships" (p. 127) within school settings. Similarly, in his book *The Quality School*, William Glasser (1990) suggested that, after elementary school, more than half of all students are not friends with students doing well in school.

One method we and many teachers with whom we have worked have found particularly helpful is the formation of base groups. As defined here, a *base group* is a group of four students who support each other for either a term or a year. Like a cooperative group, a base group is usually heterogeneous with regard to gender and ethnicity, as well as how successful students are with the course content. Since the base group will stay together for an extended period of time, many teachers have found that it is worth the time to allow students some input into the makeup of their group. This can be done by asking students to list three or four students they would like to have in their group and perhaps one student with whom they would prefer not to work. Although developing groups takes longer when this information is used, the groups function much more smoothly and it appears well worth the initial investment.

The group is not intended to be a cooperative group that works together on specific course projects. Instead, the group meets several times a week for five to fifteen minutes to check on everyone's content mastery and progress. If someone is absent, a member of the base group collects assignments and is prepared to assist the absent student. If a student is absent for several days, a member of the base group might call and tell the student that she is missed and ask if any help is needed. If a member of the base group is having difficulty with content, the group can help tutor the student. This may take place during a lengthened base group session or at times arranged by the students. If a student fails to respond to this assistance or is failing to make a good effort in class, the base group can ask for the teacher's assistance.

Base groups can also be used to check homework assignments, to ensure that everyone has adequate notes or materials prior to a test or major assignment, and even to provide study groups for tests or daily assignments. At the very least, the base group provides a setting in which at least three members of the class are concerned about and support each student's learning. This helps create a sense of each student being known and valued in the class—a key prerequisite to learning for many students.

Prior to using base groups, it is important that the teacher first clearly outline the group's roles and assist the students in getting to know each other. Second, the teacher must initially provide some structure for the base groups. For example, members of a base group can be asked to go over each student's assignment sheet or to examine each student's goal sheet or portfolio to ensure that everyone understands the work or is making adequate progress. Base groups are particularly valuable for field-dependent learners and students

---

PAUSE & CONSIDER 4.4

Pause for a moment and make a list of activities you could use to increase your students' sense of group cohesiveness. Highlight your favorite activity. Next, meet with a group of three or four colleagues or classmates who teach students at a grade level similar to the one you are teaching or observing and share your favorite activity. If there are several groups completing this task, share your group's favorite activity with the larger group.

---

new to a class, but they help all students learn to work as a team and to develop empathy and communication skills.

ACTIVITIES FOR HELPING STUDENTS EXPRESS POSITIVE STATEMENTS TO THEIR PEERS

You have undoubtedly been involved in groups in which everyone was comfortable with and enjoyed every group member. Whether it was an extended family, school staff, religious group, or group of close friends, you probably looked forward to being with this group and found that the group supported personal and intellectual growth. Compare this experience with working in a group characterized by cliques and numerous isolated individuals. Anyone who has been unfortunate enough to work in such a group knows that it is much less supportive of creativity, risk taking, and productivity.

Students are similar to adults in that they are happier and more productive in environments that provide warmth and friendship. Lewis and St. John (1974) indicated that the presence of high-achieving students was not in itself enough to increase achievement among lower-achieving students. In addition to being exposed to norms that supported academic achievement, the lower-achieving students needed to be accepted as friends by their classmates. When students believe they are liked by their peers, they experience a sense of significance, belonging, safety, and respect of others. Unless these basic personal needs are met, students will have less energy to expend in learning.

The activities described in this section increase the likelihood that all students in the classroom will be liked and accepted by their peers. Though it is important to use several of these activities early in the school year, we should reinforce positive peer interactions by using activities such as these throughout the school year. As with the activities connected with helping students become better acquainted and building group cohesiveness, elementary and middle school teachers will be most likely to use the specific activities described in this section.

Good Deeds Tree

To build on the theme of helping others, place a large paper tree or branch on the bulletin board. Ask students to pay special attention to the nice things people say and do. Whenever they see something nice being done, have students write down what happened on a leaf made of green paper and pin it to the tree. The result is a tree full of leaves and a room filled with happy children.

Variations of this activity can be created by using pumpkins in a pumpkin patch at Halloween or shamrocks in a field near St. Patrick's Day. When working with children who cannot write their responses, set aside several times a day to ask children to list nice things they have seen or heard. Write these on the appropriate paper and allow the children to pin them on the bulletin board.

Compliment Chart and Books

The following related methods were shared by our daughter following her first year of teaching.

At the beginning of the year, I printed out enough class lists for each student to have one. I then hand-wrote numbers on each list. The student whose list it was would be last, so the next person down on the list would be number one. I then numbered the rest of the names accordingly until I reached the child's name whose list it was and they would always be number 27 (or however many students you have in your class). A few times a week during our writing time, I would teach a mini lesson on a particular skill and the students would be expected to use what they learned during the lesson to write a letter to the first person on their list. The next time it would be to the second person, and so forth, until everyone in the class had written a letter to everyone else in the class. This not only gave them a chance to work on specific writing skills and me a chance to assess where students were at, but the letters had to be positive and had to focus around compliments. At the end of the year, we bound each child's letters and the students took home a book of positive compliments and letters about themselves from each child in the class.

We talked a lot about respect, compliments, and manners this year. I believe it is vitally important to teach students lifelong skills as well as academic skills. The compliment chart was one way to reinforce how my students were putting into practice what they had learned in the classroom. First we talked about what a compliment looked like and sounded like, and we created several and placed them on the bulletin board to be a reminder. Anytime a staff member gave our class a compliment outside of our classroom, we put it on the chart. Anytime a staff member noticed inappropriate behavior of our class, we discussed it with that staff member and the class had to earn one additional compliment to make up for it. When we reached a designated number of compliments, I threw them a small party to celebrate their efforts in being respectful and helping our school be a positive learning environment.

Wanted Posters

Another activity that helps create an environment of warmth and friendship is construction of wanted posters. Give students a piece of parchment paper, of which an adult has burned the edges to make the paper look like a poster from the Old West. Students print the word "WANTED" on the paper. Next, a student mounts a picture of himself or herself in the center and writes the phrase "FOR A FRIEND BECAUSE . . ." underneath the picture. Around the picture each student writes words describing the qualities that make her or him a good friend. A piece of tagboard or brown construction paper can be used as a backing or support. A discussion about friendship and an opportunity to share the posters should follow this activity.

Filling Your Bucket

Students often do not realize the power positive or negative comments have upon how effectively students learn in a classroom. This concept and specific methods to support it need to be taught and reinforced as important behavior goals in a classroom. One way to accomplish this is to read aloud either *Have You Filled Your Bucket Today?* (McCloud & Messing, 2006) or *How Full Is Your Bucket? For Kids* (Rath et al., 2009). You can then discuss how students can fill their own buckets and how they can fill or dip into the buckets of other students. Students can be assisted in generating ideas for statements and behaviors that help fill individuals' buckets. You may wish to create a bucket to place on the bulletin board with positive statements written around it and every student signing the bucket indicating he or she will try to always be someone who fills a bucket. During the first few weeks following this activity, every time you see a student saying or doing something kind to a peer, you might wish to place a star in another bucket you have drawn and try to completely cover the bucket with stars. Students can also be taught to thank individuals who engage in activities or make statements that make them feel good/fill up their buckets.

Warm Fuzzies

Everyone likes to receive positive attention and recognition in the form of a warm smile, physical touch, or kind word. Unfortunately, children often receive more criticism and frowns than compliments and smiles. In response to this situation, Claude Steiner (1977) wrote a children's book entitled *The Original Warm Fuzzy Tale*. This delightful story can be read to students of all ages. After reading the story, you can lead a discussion that helps students clearly understand the concepts of warm fuzzies and cold pricklies and how they make people feel. Following this discussion, students will often initiate the idea of giving warm fuzzies to each other.

One approach to helping children learn to be more positive with their classmates is to make warm fuzzies. Warm fuzzies can be made by wrapping yarn around one's fingers several times. The wrapped yarn is then tied in the middle and the ends are cut off. The ends are then fluffed up and a warm fuzzy has been created. After students have made a warm fuzzy, they are asked to think of a reason they deserve a warm fuzzy. Students are encouraged to share their reasons. Each student then keeps his first fuzzy. The class should continue making fuzzies until each child has between five and ten fuzzies. To conclude this activity, ask students to give a fuzzy to a friend. When giving a fuzzy, students should tell the reason it is being given. Even though the teacher may choose to set time aside daily to hand out fuzzies, students should also be encouraged to give a fuzzy whenever they wish.

Another way to give warm fuzzies is to have a Fuzzy Box into which students place positive notes about their peers (students often choose to attach a warm fuzzy to their note). These notes can be read aloud during the last few minutes of the day. Students enjoy receiving compliments in front of their peers.

Valentine Booklets

Another activity that encourages sharing positive feelings is creating Valentine booklets. Give each child a Valentine's Day booklet cut in the shape of a heart with his or her name on it. The front and rear covers are red hearts, and the inside pages are white hearts. There should be as many white heart pages as there are members of the class (including the teacher). A booklet is created by punching a hole in each heart and attaching the pages with string.

Students sit in a circle with their Valentine booklets on their laps. Ask the children to pass their books to the person on their right. Students then write a nice phrase about the person whose booklet they receive. When you or the timekeeper see that each child has finished writing, speak the phrase, "Pass to the right" again. This activity continues until the students all have their own booklets again. It takes about one hour to complete this activity, but the results are worth the time spent. Students enjoy this activity and are often seen reading through their booklets when they need a lift.

This activity can be used in association with a variety of special days. Shamrock books can be used on St. Patrick's Day, with the words "I am lucky to know Scott because . . ." written on the outside. Similarly, booklets can be developed around the theme of being thankful at Thanksgiving, and special qualities each student possesses that will help that student succeed can be used as a theme on a holiday celebrating the birthday of a famous person.

Secret-Pal Books

Positive communication is vital in a classroom. The secret-pal book activity is a strategy for increasing positive communication. On Monday, each child draws the name of another student. During the week, the students observe the nice things that they see their secret pals doing and write these in their secret-pal books. These books can be made of colored construction paper covers and plain white pages. Students can be encouraged to decorate the books by drawing pictures, writing positive adjectives that describe their secret pal, or writing a word that begins with each letter of the child's name (e.g., Brian: B = brave, R = responsible, I = interesting, A = athletic, N = neat). On Friday, students reveal their secret pals and present them with their books. Students enjoy this activity very much and always look forward to finding out who their new secret pal will be.

A daily variation in the weeklong secret-pal books involves having children write their own names on a "secret-pal smiley face." These faces are placed in a basket and each child draws one, making sure that it is not his or her own name. Throughout the day, each child watches the secret pal and writes down two or three friendly or helpful things the child observes the secret pal doing. At the end of the day, the secret pals are revealed and the smiley faces may be taken home.

Student Directory

Almost all students have special interests and abilities about which they feel confident. When students feel comfortable in the classroom, they will often be excited about sharing their expertise with their peers. The creation of a student directory is an activity designed to help students identify their strengths and encourage them to use each other as resources.

Students are asked to identify the activities or skills they believe they perform effectively enough to teach another child. These topics should not be limited to school subjects. They may include skills such as basketball dribbling, downhill skiing, working with dogs, model rocketry, borrowing in subtraction, organizing desks, writing a report, or calligraphy. These lists are collected, tabulated, and placed in alphabetical order with the name(s) of the student(s) listed after each skill. The student directory is typed up and each student receives a copy. A directory is also placed in the front of the room for use by the students. The directory can be a valuable tool for a child who needs assistance with a topic. Students will often use this directory as a way to improve their skills by asking an expert to help them.

Social Skills Training Programs

Another increasingly popular approach to creating positive peer relationships and integrating isolated or aggressive children into their peer group involves implementing social skills and problem-solving training activities with the entire class. In its simplest form, social skills training can be accomplished by instructing students in many of the skills described throughout this book. For example, you could instruct children in sending I-messages (Chapter 8), giving warm fuzzies, and filling each other's buckets with positive statements. Students could practice these skills as a group and be encouraged to use them frequently in their daily classroom interactions. Similarly, we can teach students active listening (Chapter 3) and problem-solving skills (Chapter 9).

There are several advantages to using social skills training in the classroom or other school-group setting. First, youngsters generally find a group setting more attractive than individual work. Second, a group makes better use of the teacher's or counselor's time. Third, the group provides diverse models and an opportunity for students to receive feedback from peers. Fourth, the group provides an opportunity for students to teach each other, thus facilitating development of their own social competence.

The recommended reading at the end of the chapter includes several excellent resources for group social skill training. As we will discuss in Chapter 10, it is important to realize, however, that some students will require individual social skills training in response to very specific problems they are experiencing.

Pause & Consider 4.5

During your teaching career, you will undoubtedly encounter situations in which parents, fellow teachers, or administrators question your decision to use class time to develop a cohesive classroom group. Take a few minutes and write a brief statement you might write to a colleague describing why you allocate time in this manner. Share this with several colleagues or classmates. Their ideas may enrich your statement. Finally, we encourage you to save this statement and enhance and modify it as you continue your teaching career.

Creating a School Climate That Supports Students and Families from Different Cultures

In many schools, students from one or more cultural groups may be experiencing concerns about having their language and other cultural beliefs and values honored. One approach to supporting these students is to provide them with opportunities to work together. While this does not suggest these students should become isolated, it is worth considering whether students who are new to the United States or who represent a minority of students in a school who perceive themselves as culturally unique or unfairly treated might benefit from opportunities to discuss their concerns. For example, in their ethnographic study of an urban magnet school designed to support Vietnamese students, Weis and Centrie (2002) reported that school personnel created a separate homeroom for Vietnamese students. In discussing the benefits of this program, Weis and Centrie wrote:

> By establishing the homeroom for them, the school created a space within which a particular ethnic group could lay psychological and physical claim to space, time, and activities within the larger institution. It was here that the teacher and students could shape their more targeted agenda, one suited to their needs. (p. 17)

A number of years ago, one of us spent three years consulting with a school district in which approximately half of the students were Native American. One of several goals of the consultation was to increase the extremely small high school graduation rates among Native American students. One of the most successful interventions used in the high school was to have groups of Native American students meet with their Native American counselor to discuss issues of importance and concern to the students and generate solutions to problems. For example, the students expressed concern that teachers did not implement instructional methods preferred by the Native American students and that office referrals and suspensions were disproportionately high for these students. In response to these concerns, the students presented a workshop to the faculty on instructional methods they preferred, and they collected data, shared it with the vice principal, and eventually met with a group of teachers to discuss ways to reduce the referral and suspension rates for Native American students. This work was one of several factors associated with a significant increase in retention and graduation rates for Native American students at this school, and yet it did not isolate these students from their peers from other cultures.

As discussed in the next chapter, it is essential to implement activities that encourage parents from all cultural groups to feel wanted and valued at school. This may initially involve special meetings for families from various cultural/ethnic communities and the involvement of leaders in these communities. Figure 4.6 offers suggestions for creating a school climate supportive of bilingualism and multiculturalism.

1. Provide signs in the main office and elsewhere that welcome people in the different languages of the community. Provide other informational signs in the languages of the students (e.g., directions to the office; sections of the library).
2. Encourage students to use their first language around the school.
3. Provide opportunities for students from the same ethnic groups to communicate with one another in their first language when possible (e.g., in cooperative learning groups as appropriate).
4. Recruit people who can tutor students in their first language.
5. Provide books written in the various languages in both classrooms and the school library.
6. Incorporate greetings and information in the various languages in newsletters and other official school communications.
7. Display pictures and objects of the various languages in newsletters and other official school communications.
8. Display pictures and objects of the various cultures represented at the school. (Beware of stereotypes; involve people of the community to help make choices.)
9. Create units of work that incorporate other languages in addition to the school language.
10. Encourage students to write contributions in their first language for school newspapers and magazines.
11. Provide opportunities for students to study their first language, and their culture/history in elective subjects and/or in extracurricular clubs.
12. Encourage parents to help in the classroom, library, playground, and in clubs.
13. Invite second language learners to use their first language during assemblies and other official functions.
14. Invite people from ethnic minority communities to act as resource people and to speak to students in both formal and informal settings.
15. Encourage students to write about (publish) and otherwise share their stories/feelings about their home country (where applicable) and their experiences in their new country/school.
16. Directly address racism and unkindness.
17. Be sure that the curriculum includes a variety of perspectives and provides models of people of both genders and many ethnic backgrounds in all fields.
18. Recruit teachers, administrators, and counselors of diverse backgrounds.

FIGURE 4.6
CREATING A SCHOOL CLIMATE THAT ENCOURAGES BILINGUALISM AND MULTICULTURALISM
Source: Developed by Lynn Reer, retired professor, Lewis & Clark College. Adapted from Cummins, J., *Empowering Minority Students*. Sacramento, CA (1989).

In her book *From Rage to Hope: Strategies for Reclaiming Black and Hispanic Students*, Crystal Kuykendall (2004) states that to help students from historically underserved cultural and ethnic groups succeed in school, we must create school climates that reduce institutional racism and allow these students to view schools as places where adults expect them to succeed. In addition to reducing the "over-representation of Blacks and Hispanics in special education classes or lower ability groups" (p. 116), Kuykendall suggests the following changes:

- Review school policy and revise or eliminate rules that punish students for cultural habits, such as wearing African or cornrow hairstyles, signifying or playing the dozens, or being loud or expressive.
- Review institutional materials that belittle, exclude, or stereotype races and cultures. Add materials that are multicultural in all subject areas at all grade levels. If certain biased materials are kept, teachers must know how to use these materials in unbiased ways.
- Develop a basic familiarity with Black and Hispanic culture through staff development sessions or personal efforts to enhance knowledge. Such efforts might include reading, visits to art shows or museums, and participating in social events for Black and Hispanic groups.
- Eliminate the word "minorities" from the vocabulary. Schools are preparing students for a world in which people of color are not in the minority at all.
- Use flexible, heterogeneous, and cooperative grouping rather than ability groupings and tracking.
- Do all you can to ensure that schools in predominately Black and Hispanic neighborhoods are financed at least at the same level as schools in predominantly White neighborhoods.
- Incorporate provision of equal opportunity in the classroom as part of the teacher evaluation process.
- Most importantly, help Black and Hispanic students understand that school success will not require rejection of their home or family's culture. (Kuykendall, 2004, pp. 116–117)

Issues Related to Peer Harassment and Bullying

Juvonen and Graham (2001) define *peer harassment* as:

> victimization that entails face-to-face confrontation (e.g., physical aggression, verbal abuse, nonverbal gesturing) or social manipulation through a third party (e.g., social ostracism, spreading of rumors). The crucial element that distinguishes peer harassment from other types of negative encounters, such as conflict, is that there is an imbalance of power between perpetrator and target. (p. xiii)

Most definitions of bullying include three major elements: (1) involves physical, verbal, or written behavior with the intent to cause harm or distress, (2) these behaviors occur within relationships characterized by an imbalance of power, and (3) the behaviors occur over a period of time. The term *bullying* is often used interchangeably with *peer harassment*.

Reports suggest a very high rate of bullying in U.S. schools, and some student groups are more likely to be targets of bullying. The 2011 National School Climate Survey: "Key Findings on the Experiences of Lesbian, Gay, Bisexual and Transgender Youth in Our Nation's Schools" reports that 82 percent of LGBT students experienced verbal harassment, and 38 percent experienced physical harassment during the past year in the school setting. Students identified as benefitting from special education services are also more likely to experience bullying (Rose, Espelage, Aragon, & Elliot, 2011).

Not surprisingly, bullying has a strong negative effect on students' ability to feel comfortable and be successful at school. "Victimization by peers has been linked to illnesses, school avoidance, poor academic performance, increased fear and anxiety, and suicidal ideation as well as to long-term internalization difficulties, including low self-esteem, anxiety, and depression (Swearer, Espelege, Valliancourt, & Hymel, 2010, p. 38). Gay, lesbian, bisexual, and transgender students who, as indicated above, have high rates of being bullied, are five times more likely to report missing school than other students. These students are also twice as likely to report not planning to attend college, and students who indicate greater harassment have significantly lower grade averages. Students who experience bullying may suffer from anxiety about their own safety and may experience guilt about not having prevented or stopped the process (Clark, 2002). In addition, the bullies also are more likely to underachieve at school and are at risk for higher rates of criminal behavior after leaving school (Cole, Cornell, & Sheras, 2006).

More recently, students and school personnel have had to deal not only with instances where students bully peers directly, but also with cyberbullying.

> Cyberbullying is ". . . an intentional, repeated, and aggressive act or behaviour carried out by a group or individual employing information and communication technology (ICT) as an instrument. . . . Cyberbullying is bullying via the use of internet, mobile phone, or a combination of both, and the modes chosen have diversified (e.g., bullying by phone call, text messages, instant messaging, e-mails, posting or sending embarrassing photos or video clips, creating 'hate-websites')." (Marees & Petermann, 2012, p. 468)

Some studies suggest that as many as one-third of students have experienced cyberbullying (Cassidy, Brown, & Jackson, 2012). In a study of middle school and high school students across the country, 71 percent of LGBT students reported having experienced cyberbullying, 39 percent reported receiving "angry, rude, or vulgar messages" at least one to two times a week, 8 percent experienced these types of messages three or more times a week. In addition, 21 percent of LGBT students reported experiencing intimidating or threatening messages at least one or two times a week. Sadly, 56 percent of these students indicated they experienced depression as a result of this cyberbullying and 35 percent indicated they had suicidal thoughts based on the cyberbullying (Cooper & Blumenfeld, 2012).

Research suggests that a substantial amount of cyberbullying is between the same aggressors and victims as face-to-face bullying. Not surprisingly, research also shows that because the bully can remain more anonymous and because a message can be sent to many individuals at one time, cyberbullying can have a broader and perhaps more damaging impact than direct, face-to-face bullying (Snakenborg, Van Acker, & Gable, 2011).

Regardless of the type of bullying, a number of factors can influence the degree to which bullying/harassment occurs in a classroom or school.

Individual Bully Factors

Studies (Wood & Gross, 2002) suggest there are two types of bullies: *reactive bullies*, who have strong responses to what they perceive as threatening situations, and *proactive bullies*, whose behavior seems more calculated and planned. In both cases, research indicates that social/

emotional issues underlie the behavior. For example, reactive bullies are seen as students who desire but lack positive relationships with adults and may have experienced rejection from adult caregivers. Following violent behavior toward others, these students often express remorse.

> Teachers and caregivers often refer to them as having a "short fuse" because they tend to be intolerant of frustration, easily threatened, impulsive and over-reactive in response to any source of stress or fear and unpredictable in their tantrums and outbursts. (McAdams & Schmidt, 2007, p. 121)

The behavior of proactive bullies is viewed more as a component of these students' identity and is one way these students develop a sense of significance, competence, and power. These students are usually not provoked into their bullying and usually choose students who are emotionally or physically weaker and easily controlled. Proactive bullies experience little remorse and their behavior is difficult to alter because it is a fundamental aspect of their identity. These students have often lacked the supportive family relationships that help develop a sense of empathy and caring for others. What needs to occur for these students is extensive education in developing empathy for others through positive relationships with adults, while learning social skills to meet their needs for significance, competence, and power.

Bullying is more likely to take place in a social situation in which there are imbalances of power. Numerous reasons exist for students bullying others, including feelings of being offended or hurt by the other people, giving them a right to respond; the bullies enjoying the acceptance and/or attention they receive from others when they bully someone; the bully believing he or she can get something from the victim; or the aggressor simply enjoying the act of dominating someone (Rigby, 2012).

Teacher Behavior

Bullying is impacted by teachers' approach to and skill in classroom management. Teachers who are more skilled in providing engaging instruction in well-organized classrooms characterized by a positive sense of community create environments in which bullying is significantly less likely to occur (Allen, 2010; Sullivan, Cleary, & Sullivan, 2004). Research by Roland and Galloway (2002) reported that less student bullying behavior characterizes classrooms where teachers manage by emphasizing positive teacher–student and peer relationships and handle discipline issues in an educational, respectful manner. A comprehensive meta-analysis of school bullying programs included the quality of classroom management as one of the components in an effective whole-school approach to this problem (Tofi & Farrington, 2011). "A common refrain in the recent literature is that the most effective solution for bullying prevention programs lies within a holistic approach geared to foster positive school climate and classroom management skills" (Neiman, Robers, & Robers, 2012, p. 617).

Rose & Monda-Amaya (2012) suggest that one way to reduce bullying, especially against children identified as having special needs is to ensure that classroom activities allow opportunities such as tutoring and cooperative group work that require students to work collaboratively. The material on cooperative learning presented in Chapter 7 provides methods that can help reduce bullying by productively engaging students in well-structured collaborative instructional activities.

While teachers' skills in creating effectively structured classrooms and engaging students in instruction activities that allow students to work collaboratively are keys to preventing and dealing with issues of bullying, the manner in which teachers interact with students affects the amount of bullying that occurs in classrooms and schools. Students who bully have more negative views of their relationships with their teachers (Bacchini, Esposito, & Affuso, 2009). A study in seven urban elementary schools reported that 70 percent of teachers reported that teachers in their school occasionally bullied students, while 18 percent felt that such behavior occurred frequently (Twemlow, Fonagy, Sacco, & Brethour, 2006). Forty-five percent of teachers in this sample admitted to having bullied a student. The manner in which teachers model kindness and fairness and how they treat individuals who may be at risk for being bullied are key factors in reducing bullying. It is imperative that teachers provide high rates of behavior-specific praise to students who may be at risk for being bullied and interact with these students in a manner that clearly communicates they care about and respect these students.

Teacher awareness of and training in preventing and responding to bullying is another significant factor. Studies suggest that, because they believe adults cannot provide assistance, students at all ages do not report cyberbullying to either parents or teachers (Parris, Varjas, Meyers, & Cutts, 2012; Tenenbaum, Varjas, Meyers, & Parris, 2011).

"Homophobic bullying is pervasive in schools where teachers and school personnel lacked training or were uninvolved in bullying situations. . . . Conversely, sexual minority students in schools where teachers and school personnel are involved reported lower rates of victimization than those in other schools" (Hong & Garbarino, 2012, p. 275).

Responses to Bullying Incidents

While prevention is an absolute key to combating bullying, it is essential that school staff respond effectively when students are bullied. In a study, Sherer & Nickerson (2010) found school psychologists reported the three most common responses to school bullying incidents were to increase adult supervision, talk to the bullies following the incident, and provide punishment. Almost 97 percent reported their schools suspended and/or expelled those who bully, but 57 percent of these school psychologists indicated they believe these zero-tolerance methods were ineffective. The American Psychological Association Zero Tolerance Task Force (2008) also indicated an approach that depended significantly on punishment was not effective. The school psychologists reported that having a schoolwide positive behavior support system, modifying space and schedule factors, and responding immediately to incidents of bullying were the most effective responses.

When responding to an incident of bullying, the most important issue is to provide support for the student who has been bullied, to assist the student who has done the bullying in understanding why this is an unacceptable, hurtful behavior that violates the other student's rights, and to help the bully develop skills to meet his or her needs for attention or power in acceptable, healthful ways.

In their book *Early Violence Prevention: Tools for Teachers of Young Children*, Slaby, Roedell, Arezzo, and Hendrix (1995) note that when a student is aggressive toward another student, it is important for the adult to provide support for the victim and ensure that reinforcement for the aggressor is minimized. They suggest having the teacher assist the victim in assertively stating his rights to the aggressor. The teacher might say to the victim, "No one is allowed to hurt you for any reason; you can tell him to stop kicking" (p. 70). By telling this to the victim, the teacher is clarifying the rules and also providing the victim with a tool for asserting himself appropriately. Likewise, the teacher may want to assist the victim in developing skills for responding assertively when another student is being aggressive. This may involve sending a firm I-message (Chapter 8) or telling the aggressor he or she needs to talk to an adult to help solve the problem. It will often be helpful to teach such skills to all students as part of the procedures for solving conflicts nonaggressively. Mason (2008) suggests that in order to provide support for victims of bullying, staff can collaborate with families, find ways for the student to be successful in areas where he or she has talents, select high-status peers to work with the victim, and discuss bullying with the class. It is also imperative to work effectively with the bully. One important factor is to reduce the likelihood the bully is being reinforced by adult attention. Slaby and his colleagues (Slaby et al., 1995) suggest that, in order to prevent inadvertently reinforcing the offender's behavior by providing immediate teacher attention, it is best to wait at least an hour before working with this student to teach alternative skills. It is also important that the other children in the room see the teacher supporting the victim and not providing undue attention to the aggressor. If the teacher does work immediately with the aggressor, it is helpful for the other students to see and even overhear the teacher instruct the student in using new skills. For example, the teacher might say, "I understand that you wanted to use the engine. In this class, no one can hurt anyone or take anything from someone. If you wanted to play with it, how could you have asked Rolando if you could share it with him or use it?"

Bullies must learn that bullying behavior will not be accepted and that they can learn alternative ways to meet their needs for significance, competence, and power. When students are involved in bullying behavior, it is essential they are dealt with firmly and clearly and that the interventions include both sanctions and skill development. Sanctions need to clearly communicate that adults will not tolerate the behavior but care about the student. The bully needs to be removed from the setting in which the bullying occurs until he or she has had an opportunity to work with an adult to (1) understand why this behavior is unacceptable, including how it affected the victim and the school setting, and (2) practice behaviors to use in future situations to meet his or her needs without creating an unsafe classroom or school environment. It is imperative within a school that teachers, administrators, and counselors collaborate to develop a school-wide plan for ensuring that all instances of bullying are responded to in this manner.

Susanne Gervay (2009), author of *I Am Jack*, the story of an eleven-year-old boy bullied at school, suggests these additional methods: (1) counsel the bully and the bullied separately, (2) provide the victim with ongoing support from school adults, (3) support the victim in becoming more involved in school groups that will support stronger peer relationships, (4) involve the bully in activities that contribute to the good of the school or other organization, and (5) lead classroom discussions about how to create a bully-proof, safe school.

Dealing with Situations Where Students Are Being Bullied or Harassed
For an interactive review of methods for responding when students in your class are involved in bullying, click on the link below in your Pearson etext.

ENHANCEDetext *interactive case study*

As mentioned earlier, cyberbullying is an increasingly popular form of bullying that is both similar to and different from direct forms of bullying and, as such, requires both similar and different interventions. It is important to provide support to the victim and also to help the victim understand ways to prevent cyberbullying. For example, adults can discuss the dangers of placing any sensitive material into any electronic format. The victim can be asked to keep an electronic record of any form of cyberbullying and share this with an adult (Adams, 2010). The person responsible for the cyberbullying can be required to meet with an adult and the person being bullied and to provide an electronic apology.

Creating a School Climate That Supports LGBT Students

As discussed previously, students whose sexual preference is other than heterosexual are at a very high risk for being harassed and bullied at school and to subsequently experience serious mental health issues and academic struggles. Therefore, in addition to responding effectively when these students are bullied, it is imperative that school personnel work to create school environments that are safe and supportive places for these students. Russell (2010) suggests that educators can enhance the sense of well-being for LGBT students by providing school-based support groups, training teachers in how to respond when students are harassed, ensuring schools have antibullying policies that include a focus on sexual orientation and/or gender identity, and including content regarding LGBT issues in the school curriculum. Since studies suggest school staff have mixed feelings about dealing with bullying related to LGBT students (Anapnostopoulos, Buchanan, Pereira, & Lichty, 2009), it is imperative that school staff be encouraged and supported in responding any time they see any indication of physical or verbal abuse toward these students. For example, educators need to respond by correcting students whenever they hear students use terms such as "gay" being used in a derogatory manner (e.g., "That's a really gay idea"—something almost seven out of ten LGBT youth state they frequently hear in school) (Kosciw, Bartkiewicz, & Greytak, 2012). Positive attitudes and support from school staff and parents can do much to protect sexual minority students from negative experiences and multiple problems (Espelage, Aragon, Birkett, & Koenig, 2008).

Anti-Bullying Programs

Kauffman (1997) described the following features of programs that were effective in minimizing harassment and bullying in schools:

- A school climate characterized by a warm, positive, supportive school atmosphere in which adults set clear and firm limits on unacceptable behavior
- Nonhostile, nonphysical sanctions applied immediately and consistently to violation of behavioral expectations
- Continuous monitoring and surveillance of student activities in and around the school
- Adult mediation of student interactions and assumption of authority to stop bullying when it is observed
- Discussion of the issue of bullying with bullies, victims, parents, and neutral students (nonparticipants) to clarify school values, expectations, procedures, and consequences (p. 365)

Olweus, a world leader in bullying prevention, offers four key principles that support the creation of safe schools and reduced bullying:

1. Warmth, positive interest, and involvement from adults;
2. Firm limits on unacceptable behavior;
3. Consistent application of nonpunitive, nonphysical sanctions for unacceptable behavior or violation of rules; and
4. Adults who act as authorities and positive role models. (Olweus, 2003, p. 15)

These principles are completely consistent with the approach to responsible, effective classroom management you will find presented in very practical ways throughout this text. I would add the importance of providing all students with skills for being assertive when confronted with this type of behavior, the value of providing bullies with specific skills for meeting their needs without using aggressive behavior, and the importance of teaching peers who witness bullying methods for responding to express their disapproval for this behavior (Frey, Hirschstein, Edstrom, & Snell, 2009; Salmivalli, Karna, & Poskiparta, 2010).

It is beyond the scope of this text to examine the multitude of specific schoolwide programs designed to reduce bullying. Reviews of bully prevention programs present varying summaries regarding the effectiveness of these programs. One extensive analysis of bullying prevention programs reported that, "overall, school-based anti-bullying programs are effective: on average, bullying decreased by 20–23% and victimization decreased by 17–23%" (Tofi & Farrington, 2011, p. 7). This review indicated programs were more effective if they were more intensive, implemented effectively and completely, were associated with firm disciplinary responses to bullying behavior, involved parents in learning about bullying, focused on the quality of school climate by promoting positive relationships between students and between staff and students, involved the larger community in addressing the problem, and included improved playground supervision. Other elements found to be effective were good classroom management, cooperative group work in the classroom, and a whole-school antibullying policy. Other reviews (Merrell, Gueldner, Ross, & Isava, 2008; Swearer et al., 2010) report much less favorable findings. These authors suggest that, to be effective, methods for reducing bullying must focus generally on peer interactions and norms in schools and classrooms rather than on any specific program. It appears that when students view the school climate and peer relationships as positive, students most at risk for bullying are more comfortable (Espelage et al., 2008).

Therefore, the situation of bullying is an excellent example of the importance of implementing a wide range of the methods presented in this book. Virtually all of the recommendations for dealing with bullying are integrated into the implementation of Comprehensive Classroom Management:

1. creating positive teacher–student relationships (Chapter 3)
2. developing positive, supportive peer relationships (Chapter 4)
3. having students develop, understand, and honor classroom and schoolwide behavior expectations (Chapter 6)
4. having adults implement a clear, firm, and educational approach to responding when students bully (Chapter 8)
5. communicating with parents/guardians (Chapter 5)
6. conducting a functional assessment to determine the factors that may be causing the problem, responding to these issues, and teaching the bully new skills for meeting his or her needs (Chapter 10)

Excellent materials on bullying can be found at these Web sites:

- Teaching Tolerance (tolerance.org, search for "bullying")
- the U.S. Department of Health & Human Services' Stop Bullying Initiative (stopbullying.gov)
- the Gay, Lesbian & Straight Education Network (GLSEN) (glsen.org). GLSEN has developed a Safe Space Kit (safespace.glsen.org) designed to help educators create safe and supportive school environments for LGBT students.
- Embrace Civility in the Digital Age (embracecivility.org)

SUMMARY

The quality of relationships students have with their peers has a significant impact on how safe and supportive they find their classroom and school environments. Substantial research and theory supports the concept that working in a more supportive, lower stress environment enhances individuals' abilities to take risks and learn new material. Therefore, ensuring that students feel known, valued, and supported by their peers is an essential and often relatively ignored aspect of effective classroom management.

IMPLEMENTATION ACTIVITIES

ACTIVITY 4.1

Implementing Peer Relationship Activities

On a sheet of paper, create columns or areas with the following headings: (1) "Helping students become acquainted"; (2) "Creating a cohesive, supportive group"; and (3) "Helping students express positive statements to their peers." Notice that these goals relate to the second and fourth stages of group formation discussed in this chapter. For each heading, write at least three activities you can use to accomplish the goal. We strongly encourage you to share these with other teachers working with students in the same grade level. After you have selected three activities you would like to implement, write these into your long-term lesson plans. This will help you to determine how you want to space these activities and how they support one another. Keep in mind that you will want to include several of these in the first week of school. However, do not overwhelm students with these and do not ignore academic procedures and content during the first week. Also, it is important to include activities from these groups periodically throughout the year, especially when new students join the class.

RECOMMENDED READING

Allen T., & Plax, T. (1999). Group communications in the formal educational context. In F. R. Lawrence (Ed.), *The handbook of group communication theory and research* (pp. 493–515). Thousand Oaks, CA: Sage.

Borba, M. (1989). *Esteem builders: A K–8 curriculum for improving student achievement, behavior and social climate.* Rolling Hills Estates, CA: Jalmer.

Canfield, J., & Siccone, F. (1992). *One hundred ways to develop student self-esteem and responsibility.* Boston, MA: Allyn & Bacon.

Carroll, J., & Peterson, D. (1997). *Character building literature-based theme units.* Carthage, IL: Teaching and Learning.

Carson-Dellosa Publishing Company. (1998). *Character education: Ideas and activities for the classroom.* Greensboro, NC: Author.

Duke, D., & Trautvetter, S. (2001). *Reducing the negative effects of large schools.* Washington, DC: National Clearing House of Educational Facilities.

Duval, R. (1997). *Building character and community in the classroom.* Cypress, CA: Creative Teaching Press.

Education Center. (2000). *Building character (primary). The Best of Mailbox Theme Series.* Greensboro, NC: Author.

Freeman, S. (1997). *Character education: Teaching values for life.* New York, NY: McGraw-Hill.

Gibbs, J. (2000). *Tribes: A new way of learning and being together.* Sausalito, CA: Center Source.

Hall, S. (2000). *Using picture storybooks to teach character education.* Westport, CT: Oryx Press.

Huggins, P., Moen, L., & Manion, D. (1993). *Teaching friendship skills: Primary version.* Longmont, CO: Sopris West.

Johnson, R. (2009). *Reaching out* (10th ed.). Boston, MA: Allyn & Bacon.

Kerr, R. (1997). *Positively! Learning to manage negative emotions.* Portland, ME: J. Weston Walch.

Letts, N. (1997). *Creating a caring classroom: Hundreds of practical ways to make it happen.* New York, NY: Scholastic Professional Books.

Lipson, G. (1997). *Self-esteem, K–3: Concepts for activities, discussions and insights.* Carthage, IL: Teaching & Learning.

McCloud, C. (2007). *Have you filled a bucket today? A guide to daily happiness for kids.* Northville, MI: Ferne Press.

Mecca, J. (2001a). *Character education book of plays: Elementary level.* Nashville, TN: Incentive.

Mecca, J. (2001b). *Character education book of plays: Middle grade level.* Nashville, TN: Incentive.

Mumper, M. (2000). *Teaching kids to care and cooperate.* New York, NY: Scholastic.

Purkey, W., & Novak, J. (1996). *Inviting school success: A self-concept* approach to teaching, learning, and democratic practice (3rd ed.). Belmont, CA: Wadsworth.

Schmuck, R., & Schmuck, P. (2001). *Group processes in the classroom* (8th ed.). Boston, MA: McGraw-Hill.

Schwartz, L. (2001). *Taking steps towards tolerance and compassion: Creative projects to help kids make a difference.* New York, NY: Learning Works.

Wasley, P., Fine, M., Gladden, M., Holland, N., King, S., Mosak, E., & Powell, L. (2000). *Small schools: Great strides.* New York, NY: Bank Street College of Education.

Peer Harassment/Bullying

Bonds, M., & Stoker, S. (2000). *Bully proofing your school: A comprehensive approach for middle schools.* Longmont, CO: Sopris West.

Borba, M. (2005). *Nobody likes me, everybody hates me: The top 25 friendship problems and how to solve them.* San Francisco, CA: Jossey-Bass.

Caselman, T. (2007). *Teaching children empathy, the social emotion: Lessons, activities and reproducible worksheets (K–6) that teach how to "Step into others' shoes."* Chapin, SC: Youth Light.

Casto, K., & Audley, J. (2008). *In our school: Building community in elementary schools.* Turners Falls, MA: Northeast Foundations for Children.

Cohen-Posey, D. (1995). *How to handle bullies, teasers and other meanies.* Highland City, FL: Rainbow Books.

Committee for Children. (2000). *Second step to success: A violence-prevention curriculum.* 2203 Airport Way South, Suite 500, Seattle, WA 98134; (206) 343-1223.

Didax Educational Resources Inc. (2003a). *Bullying: Identify, cope, prevent! Grades 3–4.* Rowley, MA: Author. Retrieved from Didax Web site: www.worldteacherspress.com.

Didax Educational Resources Inc. (2003b). *Bullying: Identify, cope, prevent! Grades 5–6.* Rowley, MA: Author. Retrieved from Didax Web site: www.worldteacherspress.com.

Fried, S., & Fried, P. (1996). *Bullies and victims: Helping your child through the schoolyard battlefield.* New York, NY: M. Evans.

Garrity, C., Jens, K., Porter, W., Sager, N., & Short-Camilli, C. (2004). *Bully-proofing your school: Working with victims and bullies in elementary schools* (3rd ed.). Longmont, CO: Sopris West.

Hall, S. (2000). *Using picture storybooks to teach character education.* Westport, CT: Oryx Press.

Juvonen, J., & Graham, S. (2001). *Peer harassment in school: The plight of the vulnerable and victimized.* New York, NY: Guilford Press.

Kusche, C., & Greenberg, M. (2000). *PATHS: Promoting alternative thinking strategies: A comprehensive curriculum for preventing bullying and increasing critical-thinking skills in grades K–6.* South Deerfield, MA: Channing Bete.

Linn Benton Lincoln Education Service District. (2001). *Harassment prevention curriculum: Empowerment and skill-building for student safety.* Can be obtained by writing Linn Benton Lincoln ESD at 905 Fourth Avenue SE, Albany, OR 97321-3199.

Ludwig, T. (2004). *My secret bully.* Berkeley, CA: Tricycle Press.

Ludwig, T (2006a). *Just kidding.* Berkeley, CA: Tricycle Press.

Ludwig, T. (2006b). *Sorry.* Berkeley, CA: Tricycle Press.

McNamara, B., & McNamara, F. (1997). *Keys to dealing with bullies.* Hauppauge, NY: Barrons.

Northeast Foundation for Children. (2005). *Creating a safe and friendly school: Lunchrooms, hallways,* playgrounds and more *(Articles by teachers).* Turners Falls, MA: Author.

Olweus, D., & Limber, S. (1999). The bullying prevention program. In D. Elliott (Series Ed.), *Blueprints for violence prevention.* Boulder, CO: Center for the Study and Prevention of Violence, Institute of Behavioral Science, University of Colorado.

Rath, T., Reckmeyer, M., & Manning, M. (2009). *How full is your bucket? For kids.* Princeton, NJ: Gallup Press.

Romain, T. (1997). *Bullies are a pain in the brain.* Minneapolis, MN: Free Spirit.

Romain, T. (1998). *Cliques, phonies, and other baloney.* Minneapolis, MN: Free Spirit.

Ross, D. (1996). *Childhood bullying and teasing: What school personnel, other professionals and parents can do.* Alexandria, VA: American Counseling Association.

Sullivan, K. (1998). *Peacebuilders action guide.* Tucson, AZ: Heartsprings.

Sullivan, K. (2000). *The anti-bullying handbook.* Auckland, New Zealand: Oxford University Press.

Building Caring Communities among Adults Who Support the School

Bryk, A., & Schneider, B. (2002). *Trust in schools: A core resource for improvement.* New York, NY: Russell Sage.

Comer, J., Haynes, N., Joyner, E., & Ben-Avie, M. (1996). *Rallying the whole village: The Comer process for reforming education.* New York, NY: Teachers College Press.

Hagstrom, D. (2004). *From outrageous to inspired: How to build a community of leaders in our schools.* San Francisco, CA: Jossey-Bass.

CHAPTER 5

WORKING WITH PARENTS

Research has shown that parents and family are critical factors in children's education, particularly for those who are at risk of dropping out of school. Numerous studies demonstrate that the influence and support given by the family may directly affect the behavior of children in school, their grades, and the probability that they will finish high school.

—Paul Haley and Karen Berry (1988)

What are optimal conditions for a parent-teacher conference? A quiet corner, protection from interruptions and a teacher who listens. The words exchanged during the conference may be forgotten, but the mood of the meeting will linger on. It will decide the subsequent attitudes and actions of the parents.

—Haim Ginott (1972)

The way schools care about children is reflected in the way schools care about the children's families.

—Joyce Epstein (1995)

Studies indicate parental involvement in their children's educational experience plays a significant role in these students' academic successes (Carranza, You, Chhuon, & Hudley, 2009; Christenson & Sheridan, 2001; Jeynes, 2007). Teachers' understanding of and respect for the values and beliefs of their students' families is an important factor in supporting student learning (Trumbell, Rothstein-Fisch, & Hernandez, 2003). When teachers can assist parents in understanding the school culture and supporting school expectations, students' learning is enhanced (Henderson & Mapp, 2002).

In a survey of students and teachers (Binns, Steinberg, & Amorosi, 1997), 87 percent of students who earned primarily A's and B's indicated their parents were available to assist them with homework as compared to 24 percent of students who earned grades lower than C. Similarly, 84 percent of students who earned A's and B's compared to 27 percent of students who earned lower than C reported their parents encouraged them to pursue their dreams. Based on the National Longitudinal Study conducted by the National Center for Education Statistics:

> Parental involvement in school activities had a consistent effect on all three measures of school failure, even after holding constant the student's sex, race-ethnicity, and socioeconomic status. . . . The frequency of discussions between the parent and the child about school-related concerns also had a consistent impact on whether or not the student dropped out. Students were particularly at risk if their parents never talked to them about these matters. (Kaufman, Bradby, & Owings, 1992, p. 22)

One way teachers can encourage students' parents/guardians to be involved in their children's education is for teachers to find ways to communicate to parents their sincere respect for the family, their culture, and their role in their child's education. In doing so, it is imperative that teachers make every effort to be sensitive to cultural factors. For example, families may have differing beliefs regarding the roles of teacher and parents in supporting student achievement (Chrispeels & Rivero, 2001; Jackson & Remillard, 2005; Lawson, 2003). Caregivers may view involvement as supporting their children by keeping them safe, getting them to school, or encouraging academic work while teachers view involvement as attending conferences and being involved at school.

What is appropriate behavior in parents' views might not be appropriate in a school setting. And caregivers may differ dramatically in the time and energy they have available to communicate with teachers and support school functions or in the type of communication that works best for them. Teachers need to obtain information that assists them in understanding the cultural beliefs and values of their students' parents and guardians and to incorporate this information into their methods for positively engaging these family members in supporting responsible school behavior and learning.

It is also important that teachers be aware of the myriad family structures that exist and support children by showing acceptance of these varied family structures. A wonderful example of this was recently presented to us when a colleague shared an experience she had when taking her daughter to register for kindergarten. The teacher was aware that both of the girl's parents were women, and she took the girl and her mother to the classroom to show them around. On the door of the classroom were silhouettes of a variety of family structures including two parents of the same gender, single parents, grandparents, and so on. Our friend reported the powerful, positive impact this had on both her and her daughter.

Anyone working in schools today realizes that, for many students, the primary support person outside of school may not be a biological parent. Therefore, in this chapter, we interchangeably use the terms *parent*, *guardian*, *primary caregiver*, and *family* to represent the adults in the community who provide this support.

LEARNING GOALS

After reading this chapter, you will know:

1. Methods for keeping parents and caregivers informed about their student's work and behavior at school
2. How to structure a successful parent/caregiver conference
3. How to deal effectively with criticism and confrontation from adults who are responsible for your students
4. Methods for working with parents of second language learners

Why Are These Goals Important?

The support family members or other caregivers provide to our students can have a significant impact on the motivation students bring to the learning environment and their willingness to behave responsibly in school. Therefore, while a teacher's primary role is to work with students, teachers find that, for several reasons, an important and rewarding aspect of their job includes their work with parents. First, children's attitudes about school are influenced by their parents (Epstein, Coates, Salinas, Sanders, & Simon, 1997). Parent involvement in the school experience—whether supporting their child's efforts, holding high expectations, assisting their child with homework, or simply showing interest in what and how their child is doing at school—can have a positive impact on students' attitudes toward school, belief in the relationship between effort and school performance, and persistence at schoolwork. When parents feel good about their children's teacher and school, the youngsters are more likely to receive parental encouragement and reinforcement for desirable school behavior. Singh, Bickley, and Trivette (1995) reported that parents' knowledge of and discussion with their children about school events was the factor most strongly related to adolescents' school achievement. Second, parents and guardians can be valuable resources for teachers. They can volunteer time to work with students, assist teachers by putting up bulletin boards, copying materials, or sharing their expertise on special topics with students. Finally, in an increasing number of instances, the rewards and punishments available in school are not powerful enough to elicit desirable behavior from youngsters. When this occurs, school personnel may need to involve parents in developing a behavior change program for the students.

Even though teachers can derive numerous benefits from interacting with parents, many teachers indicate that parent contacts are a difficult and relatively undesirable aspect of teaching. Teachers' discomfort in working with parents is based on several factors. First, parent contacts are often time consuming and emotionally demanding. When teachers have worked with students for seven hours and usually face several hours of marking papers and planning, it is understandably difficult to be enthusiastic about additional school-related interactions. Teachers also find parent contacts difficult because the teaching profession has never been viewed with the awe or respect bestowed on such professions as medicine or law. Perhaps because all parents have been students, they believe themselves knowledgeable about what their youngsters need in order to function effectively in school. These factors cause many teachers to be somewhat intimidated by parents and, therefore, to minimize their parent contacts. In a study of teachers' interactions with families of their English language learner (ELL) students, 85 percent of the teachers indicated they made positive phone calls to less than 25 percent of their students' families; less than 25 percent indicated they asked parents to share positive information about their child; and only 15 percent said they integrated information learned from students and their families into their curriculum (Chen, Kyle, & McIntyre, 2008). Perhaps not surprising, for many years, nearly 90 percent of teachers and administrators have reported teachers need in-service education on practices for effectively involving students' caregivers (Chen et al., 2008). Research indicates teacher involvement with families decreases significantly as students become older: ". . . elementary principals reported approximately 77% of their teachers frequently communicate with parents, compared to 59% in middle school and 36% in high school" (Flynn & Nolan, 2008, p. 179). These same authors reported that:

> More than 60% of all principals ranked teachers' lack of confidence and skill as the primary reason for avoiding contact with parents. The second and third leading causes were teacher beliefs that parents are a threat and lack of understanding of the importance of parents' roles. (p. 179)

Finally, these authors report that the major concern expressed by principals in their study was that teachers primarily contact students' guardians to report problems.

Teachers can, however, develop attitudes and skills that will make parent contacts much more enjoyable and productive. This chapter provides methods for making positive contacts with parents throughout the school year, implementing effective parent conferences, and handling parent confrontations.

As with most classroom management methods, each of us must decide how much time and effort we wish to invest in working with parents. However, this is an area where a reasonable investment can be associated with significant gains. Students' achievement gains and positive behavior can be significantly increased when students' caregivers are actively involved with teachers in a

MRS. BLUE IS WOEFULLY UNACCUSTOMED
TO GOOD NEWS.

© Cartoon reprinted with permission of copyright holder.
Source: Giangreco, M.F. (2007). **Absurdities and Realities of Special Education: The Complete Digital Set [searchable CD]:** Thousand Oaks, CA: Corwin.

positive manner. Elementary school teachers are expected to maintain frequent contact with parents, and children at this age generally respond well to parents' encouragement. At the middle and high school levels, most teachers work with between 150 and 250 students and thus will choose to implement fewer of the ideas presented in this chapter. However, Walker and Hoover-Dempsey (2006) report it is worth the effort because teachers who invite parents' involvement tend to report higher levels of support from parents and tend to be perceived by parents as better teachers.

In our interactions with parents and guardians, we must ensure that we listen carefully to concerns, requests, and criticisms. Caregivers may often be able to inform us of issues at school that may need changing in order to assist their children. Regardless of social class, parents and guardians of students of color are more likely to be seen by school personnel as less supportive and to receive a less positive, less supportive response from school personnel (Lareau & Horvat, 1999). As educators committed to the success of every child, we must work to overcome our fears of receiving critical feedback as well as our biases regarding individuals who are different from us. For the sake of our students, we must maintain a supportive openness to feedback and requests from all of our students' caregivers.

KEEPING CAREGIVERS INFORMED

Being Sensitive to Caregivers

While teachers often express feeling somewhat intimidated by parents, it is important to realize that, compared to students' caregivers, in many, if not most cases, teachers have considerably more social capital than parents. When our children were in K–12 education, we were ourselves involved in education as a college professor and consultant and elementary teacher. Despite our familiarity with schools, one of the few times in our daily lives that we experienced anxiety going into a setting was when we attended our children's school conferences. Despite our familiarity with this setting, we were meeting with someone who had extensive information regarding two extremely important aspects of our children's lives—how effectively they related to others and how capable they were at processing new information. We correctly believed these two factors were critical in how effectively our children would grow to be happy, productive adults. Now consider someone who has limited understanding of schools, academic assessment, student learning styles, and so forth. In this case, the teacher becomes even more of an expert whose statements about a student's learning and behavior are, like those of a dentist, doctor, or lawyer, relatively unquestioned. Further, consider the situations of immigrant parents, who have very limited social capital in this country and limited understanding of the school system in the United States. While teachers understandably express concern about the impact parents may have through communicating with building and district administrators, the reality is that in most situations, when interacting with caregivers, teachers have substantial amounts of social capital. Instead of worrying about what parents might say or do, teachers will be more effective if they consider ways to build trusting relationships with their students' caregivers. Indeed, Adams and Forsyth (2009) suggest that the creation of trusting relationships between school personnel and parents, most specifically between teachers and parents, has a greater impact on student learning than the effects of poverty.

The key question then becomes, how do we create trust between teachers and students' family members? One answer is that when communicating with parents, as educators we focus more on listening than on telling. We can begin by asking them to provide information about how the behavioral expectations and approach to learning in our classroom relates to what the student or parents value and experience out of school. We can ask parents to share their goals and hopes for their child and to tell us what factors help their child learn and any factors that may contribute to their child's becoming unengaged or alienated at school. We can ask parents how their child learns best, what their child's interests are, what topics their child most likes to study, the academic content in which they believe their child is most skilled, and so on. We can ask caregivers when and how they prefer to receive information from school and the types of information they find most helpful. We can ask them if there are cultural, religious, or family factors we should be aware of that will help us interact more respectfully and successfully with their child.

Parents, especially those not born in the United States, often feel the relationship between the school and the family is one-way. In Dotson-Blake's (2010) study of how family–school–community relationships differed in the United States and Mexico, several parents indicated that relationships in this country are almost entirely focused on the school. The statements of three mothers reflect this perspective:

> "They call us when there is a problem with our kids."
> "They send notes home if they need us to send something for a party, like a drink or chips."
> "Parents are invited to conferences, but they do not get an opportunity to provide much feedback to the teachers, only to get instructions about how to improve their efforts to help their children with schoolwork." (p. 106)

Just as with our students, we want parents to know about and understand the academic and behavioral goals and expectations that are the driving forces behind our instructional and behavioral approaches. However, it is equally important that we understand these factors as they relate to the family and the culture in which students spend the majority of their existence. Failure to begin early on with a focus on student, family, and community factors may severely limit our ability not only to obtain important information about the student, but also to build the trusting relationship with the family that is a cornerstone to successful student achievement.

Importance of Early Contact

As suggested earlier, and as in any good relationship, the first contact should provide an opportunity for all parties to get to know each other and should focus on the family and the child. Parents who perceive themselves as being treated warmly and respectfully by us, who feel listened to and believe we understand and care about their child, and who are familiar with our instructional goals and classroom management procedures are much more likely to encourage student achievement and support us if problems arise.

During interactions with parents and guardians, especially those of students new to this country, you may want to ask parents to help you understand important factors about their child's academic background. This conversation can be facilitated by requesting school personnel who work with immigrant students to provide you with information prior to the meeting. Figure 5.1 shows a form that can provide you with helpful information about a student's academic background, which can be supported by information from the parents regarding how much schooling they have had, the areas in which they excelled or struggled, and so on. You may also request information on specific cultural factors that may influence the student's interactions in school. For example, what type of instructional practices has the student experienced, and what do adults in the student's culture expect regarding the student's interactions with peers and teachers in the school? Though you may need the assistance of an interpreter during some of these conversations, and in some cases you may have to request that the form be completed by another school professional who works with new students from different cultures, this information can prove invaluable in helping the student to feel accepted and comfortable in your classroom and to reduce dissonance that may create low motivation and behavior problems.

Research (Arunkumar, Midgley, & Urdan, 1999) suggests that when adolescents perceive the existence of major dissonance between their home and school values, student achievement is lower and students' sense of hopelessness and anger is higher. Therefore, contacts with parents and guardians that help both parties understand each other and develop agreement on academic and behavioral expectations can have a positive impact on student achievement and behavior. Contacts with parents are an excellent example of the idea that an ounce of prevention is worth a pound of cure. Several suggestions are offered here for initiating such contacts.

Methods for Obtaining Parental Support

There are many approaches to developing parental support for student achievement and positive classroom behaviors. The ideas presented here are among those we and teachers with whom we have worked have found particularly useful. We encourage you to modify these methods creatively in order to develop the approach best suited to your situation.

An Introductory Letter

Perhaps the easiest approach for making the initial contact is to send a letter to each student's parent(s) or guardian(s). Because the letter will include information that you will want to

**FIGURE 5.1
A NEW NON-
NATIVE
SPEAKER OF
ENGLISH IN
YOUR
SECONDARY
CLASSROOM**

**Source: Adapted
from a form
developed by
Carrie E. McPeak,
Madras (Jefferson
County), OR.**

Date _____

To _____

From _____

_____, a new student in your _____class,
is a non-native speaker of English.

Following is some information that we think will be helpful to you as you work with your new
student:

1. The student will receive the following ESL services:
2. Pronunciation of name: First name _____
                           Family name _____
3. Native language(s): _____
4. Age: _____   Gender: _____   Grade: _____

   Date of arrival in U.S. (if applicable): _____

5. Educational background:

Years of Education	*Grade*	*Location*
Prior to arrival in U.S. (if applicable)	_____	_____
English instruction?	_____	_____
In the U.S.	_____	_____
ESL or other services?	_____	_____
Type of service		_____

6. English language proficiency:

   _____ Profile 1—No prior experience

   _____ Profile 2—Single word/phrases

   _____ Profile 3—Emerging language

   _____ Profile 4—Intermediate proficiency (appears fluent but has big gaps)

   _____ Profile 5—Advanced proficiency

   _____ Profile 6—Proficient ELL student—no extra support needed

7. Reading and writing ability in first language:
8. Comments:

---

present personally to students, it is best to send the letter so that it arrives one or two days
after school begins. In the letter, you can introduce yourself, state your interest in developing
positive teacher–parent contacts, and invite the parents to attend a back-to-school night or a
similar event in which you and they have an opportunity to meet and discuss the school
year. Figure 5.2 is an example of an introductory letter. We strongly encourage you to provide any materials sent home in as many of the languages spoken by parents in your classroom as possible.

FIGURE 5.2
INTRODUCTORY
LETTER TO
PARENTS

[Date]

Dear Parents,

        With school under way, I'd like to take a moment of your time to welcome you and introduce myself. My name is Mrs. Louise Jones and I have taught in the Beaverton School District for thirty-two years. I completed my undergraduate work at Oregon State University and received my master's degree from Lewis and Clark College.

        I am very interested in making this a successful and happy school year for your child. To ensure this success, we must keep the lines of communication open. I respect the fact that you know your child very well, and so if your child says anything negative or expresses any concerns about school, please contact me. Likewise, if there is an activity, project, or anything else at school he or she gets very excited about and enjoys, please let me know. I am available at school until 4:00 p.m. each day and you can reach me by e-mail. I will be contacting you throughout the year about projects, upcoming events, ways you can volunteer at school, the nice things I see your child doing, and problems, if any arise.

        In a few weeks, our school will have its annual back-to-school night. At that time, I will discuss in detail what your child will be studying this year, the skills and knowledge you can expect him or her to develop, my grading methods, how I teach students to behave in school so they and other students can be successful, and my discipline procedures. There will also be a display of books and materials that your child will be using during the year. I encourage you to attend this special evening because it will give you an opportunity to understand the fourth-grade program, become better acquainted with the room and materials that your child will be using throughout the coming year, and ask me any questions you may have. I look forward to meeting you soon and am excited for a wonderful year working together to help your child have a successful school year.

Sincerely,

Mrs. Louise Jones
[e-mail address]
[School phone number with voicemail code]

Introductory Phone Calls

While introductory contacts with parents may involve a letter or a short conversation during a school-related activity, a phone call provides an opportunity for a very positive, personalized early contact. As with most parent contacts, it is best to briefly introduce yourself, express your interest in ensuring their child has a positive experience in your classroom, and ask if they have any questions or requests. The fact that you call and express your interest in their child may have surprisingly positive results.

        Our daughter, who has taught fourth, fifth, and first grades in a school with more than thirty-five languages, makes her introductory phone calls the weekend after the first week of school. She introduces herself, asks if parents have received the communications she has sent home with their children that week, makes several positive statements about their child, and asks how their child is feeling about school this year. During the first week of school, she asks students to tell her whether their parents speak English and, if not, in which language(s) they are fluent and most comfortable. If no one at home speaks a language she speaks, she will ask district translators to assist her in writing a note she will send or e-mail home. She will acknowledge that as resources are cut and she works with students whose parents speak increasingly varied languages, this form of initial communication becomes more challenging.

Several years ago, one of our students, who was an intern in a secondary social studies class in an inner-city school, expressed concern to his mentor that student behavior was disrespectful to himself and other students. This contrasted with the generally polite behavior students displayed when the mentor was teaching. Despite discussions with the class and several individual students, a number of students continued to act in ways that created a rather unproductive learning environment. Because the intern had taken over complete teaching responsibility for this class only about a week earlier, the mentor suggested the intern call every parent or guardian over the weekend and introduce himself. The mentor also suggested the intern make some positive comment about each student and indicate to the parents or guardians that he would be keeping them apprised of their student's progress. The intern acknowledged being somewhat anxious about completing this task but spent several hours during the weekend contacting each family. He indicated he spoke with members from 60 percent of the families, left messages for another 25 percent, and was unsuccessful at contacting 15 percent of the families. Despite speaking a second language common in the school where he was working, the intern noted that several of his conversations were with individuals who appeared not to speak English or Spanish.

Following these calls home, the intern reported his amazement at the change he experienced in his students' behavior. First, he noted that nearly a quarter of his students greeted him at the door and made a positive comment regarding the fact that he had spoken with their parents or guardians over the weekend. Second, he noticed a dramatic increase in students' respectful responses to his requests and instructional direction. When the intern's mentor, a twenty-year veteran teacher, shared this series of events with a group of twenty other veteran mentors, it was impressive how many of them reported having had a similar experience.

Home Visits

While home visits can be time consuming and require caution regarding personal safety and liability and sensitivity to the values and beliefs of those in the home, they can be a wonderful statement of caring and support as well as provide helpful information about the student and the family's culture. Many school districts recommend or require that during home visits, another educator such as a counselor, ELL teacher, or translator accompany the teacher. Excellent resources on home visits are available from the Parent/Teacher Home Visit Project at pthvp.org, the Center for Home Visiting at unc.edu/~uncchv/, and numerous other Web sites.

One long-standing and valuable concept associated with home visits is "Funds of Knowledge" (Ginsberg, 2007; Moll, Amanti, Neff, & Gonzalez, 1992). This concept is based on the idea that when we know more about our students, their homes, and their communities, we can integrate this knowledge into the manner in which we communicate with our students and can incorporate their stories into our curriculum. The two references in this paragraph provide excellent resources for considering both the theory and practice of incorporating home visits and the associated "Funds of Knowledge."

An Initial Event at School or in the Classroom

It is desirable to have an opportunity for parents and other caregivers to meet informally with school staff and specifically with their child's teacher(s). We have been involved in events including a schoolwide picnic, ice cream social, and meet-the-staff Popsicle night where, the day before school officially started, staff and caregivers had an opportunity to mingle informally. This has on some occasions been associated with several hours during which the school was open and teachers were in their classrooms so parents could visit the classroom(s) their children would be attending and meet the teacher(s). These events can involve culturally diverse music and even be an opportunity for students and parents to participate with staff in cooperative games. To lessen anxiety on the first day of school, students may also visit the classroom at this time and drop off school supplies.

As with any school-sponsored event, educators need to understand the importance of specific, personalized invitations to be involved in events at school. Anderson and Minke (2007) found that many parents did not view simply being informed—for example, a note or newsletter sent home— as an invitation. They viewed this as merely a statement that something was occurring but not as a request from the teacher or an indication that their involvement was important. These authors also found that resources made available to parents were not as important in determining whether parents became involved as was the parents' perception that their involvement was truly important. Apparently a personalized invitation encouraged parents to find a way to overcome resource issues and become involved.

Involving Parents in the Classroom

Parents are more likely to support us if they understand and feel a part of what goes on at school. Parents of students who are less successful in school may have had negative experiences when they were in school. Consequently, they may be more likely to respond negatively to and be intimidated by teachers. Involving these parents in a positive manner in the classroom can do a great deal to alleviate these negative feelings. Parent volunteers who are treated with respect by teachers almost always become strong supporters of the teacher.

As anyone who has worked with parent volunteers knows, you will initially need to spend time discussing the volunteer's role and helping volunteers understand and respond consistently to your instructional and discipline style. It is important to recognize situations in which a parent's style of interacting with children may contradict the teacher's methods. In such cases, the volunteers' efforts can be channeled into support activities such as working in the production room, putting up bulletin boards, or setting up workstations that involve minimal contact with students. We and teachers with whom we have worked have used the following ways to involve parents in their classrooms:

- Tutoring: With class sizes increasing in most school districts, it is difficult for teachers to provide students with the amount of support and feedback many students need. Volunteers can work individually with students or with small groups of students, helping them with daily work, preparing for tests, facilitating book groups, working on projects, practicing quick facts, working on reading skills, helping students with computer skills, frontloading materials for units, and so forth.
- Teaching special topics: Parents may be able to teach lessons based on their unique knowledge and skills.
- Providing production assistance such as preparing materials.
- Chaperoning on field trips.
- Helping the teacher find materials for units or for student projects. Many parents have excellent research skills and are very efficient at using the Internet.

Figure 5.3 presents a questionnaire parents/guardians may be given to indicate their interest in assisting in the classroom.

It is important to note that parents may not grade student work or have access to any other confidential materials related to students' personal or academic records. It is also important that, if parents will be working in the classroom, the teacher and parent are clear about the parent's role in responding to student behavior that disrupts the learning environment and the type of response (if any) the teacher would like the parent to make. In a similar manner, if parents are assisting students with academic work, it is important to instruct them on how best to give this assistance. Many parents do not know how to help students take responsibility for their own learning by asking questions rather than providing answers. If you have several parents willing to help out, you may want to conduct a parent volunteer orientation. During this time, you can introduce the volunteers to the classroom, talk with them about your academic and behavior expectations, and answer any questions they may have. You may want to keep a notebook titled

FIGURE 5.3 VOLUNTEER INFORMATION

Please fill out this form to let me know how you would like to help in our classroom this year.

_____ Facilitate a small group

_____ math

_____ reading

_____ Chaperone of field trips

_____ Work at home cutting or doing miscellaneous projects

_____ File papers as needed

_____ Art Literacy Parent

(You do not need to know how to do this yet as there will be an informational meeting. This is a once-a-month commitment and is a lot of fun. I will also be in the classroom to help you.)

_____ Organize, tally, and send book orders each month

_____ Run materials, bind books, or other such projects in the production room

_____ Party/Room Parent (there will be three parties this year)

_____ Reading or working on math skills with a child/small group

_____ Share with the students an area of interest related to life, work, culture, etc.

_____ Additional help (please describe) _____

- -

Parent Name _____

Child's Name _____

Best Days and Times _____

Best Way to Contact You _____

_____

Thank you so much for considering how you can best help out this year. It is such a blessing to have assistance as it allows me more time to focus on your child's education.

"Parent Volunteer" that facilitates communication between the volunteer and the teacher. In this notebook, you can write what you would like the parent to work on for that particular day; this allows the parent to begin working without interrupting the classroom activities. If you are teaching when the parent volunteer needs to leave, he or she can write a note in the notebook to let you know what was done during his or her volunteer time.

The Initial Meeting (Back-to-School Night)

It is very important to try to meet parents as soon as possible. The most expedient approach to meeting between 30 and 150 parents seems to be to provide an evening when parents are invited to visit their child's classroom(s) and discuss the teacher's approach to instruction and classroom management. It is helpful if the school supports this concept by arranging a formal back-to-school night. If this opportunity is not available, though, it is worth the effort to arrange such an event for ourselves and any colleagues who may be interested. It is sometimes necessary to arrange an alternative meeting time for parents who are unable to attend or uncomfortable attending an evening session. Information about the times that are most convenient for parents can be obtained by requesting this information in the initial letter sent to parents.

Prior to the initial meeting with parents, it is important for elementary teachers, or teachers in any setting where they work with few enough students to allow for individual calls home, to make a telephone contact in which something positive about the child is reported, and to obtain the parents' commitment to attend the parent orientation meeting. This telephone contact also breaks the ice and sets the stage for future telephone conversations.

First impressions are extremely important—especially when a relationship involves sporadic and somewhat role-bound interactions—and it is imperative to do everything possible to create a positive initial meeting. In addition to the obvious factors of being well groomed and personable, the teacher should be well organized and the classroom should look interesting and include a personal touch. One personal touch you might try is to learn how to greet parents and guardians in the language used in their home. As family members enter our daughter's classroom, she always has a quote on the document camera about the importance of children in our world or its future. Parents are very impressed by competence. You may start the meeting on a positive note by placing an outline of the evening's topics on the board. Figure 5.4 provides an example of an outline for a parent orientation meeting. This outline can be accompanied by a folder for each parent, which can include:

1. A description of the curriculum for the grade level
2. An introductory letter about yourself that includes professional background and a philosophy of education
3. A class schedule
4. A handout describing the emotional and social characteristics of a child at the grade level
5. A list of special projects that may require some parental assistance
6. A statement of your classroom-management procedures
7. Materials students will be reading throughout the year
8. A parent resource form eliciting information about what parents can offer to the class
9. Specific ways parents can assist their child and specific student skills and behaviors that can be positively influenced by this assistance
10. A schedule of any special events such as field trips and costs associated with any of these events

FIGURE 5.4 OUTLINE FOR PARENT ORIENTATION MEETING

I. Introducing the Teacher

   A. College training and degrees earned
   B. Professional experience:
      1. length of teaching experience
      2. type of classroom—open vs. self-contained
   C. My educational philosophy: What I believe about how students learn most effectively

II. Social and Personal Expectations for Students during the Year

   A. Students will develop responsibility:
      1. for themselves
      2. for their property
      3. for their assignments
   B. Students will learn to respect their peers' successes and weaknesses.
   C. Students will develop a feeling of pride for their accomplishments.
   D. Emphasis will be placed on maintaining and improving self-concept:
      1. focus on the positive at school
      2. encourage parents to reinforce positive behavior at home
   E. Students will learn to work harmoniously in groups: emphasis on sharing.
   F. Emphasis will be placed on teaching students the skill to communicate openly with each other and adults.

III. Academic Curriculum and Goals

   A. Students will be successful in developing a variety of new skills.
   B. Discuss the concept of a successful learner.
   C. Our classroom schedule—and the times that it is particularly important for parents to ensure that their child is in the classroom.
   D. A short discussion on the major topics covered in each academic subject:
      1. reading
      2. math
      3. language arts
      4. handwriting
      5. spelling
      6. social studies
      7. science
      8. physical education
      9. music
      10. library

IV. Emphasis Will Be Placed on Organizational Skills

   A. Notebooks will be organized by subjects and returned papers will be filed under the proper heading.
   B. Desks will remain neat and orderly.

V. Grading System

   A. Students' grades are determined by the marks: 1—outstanding; 2—satisfactory; 3—needs improvement.
   B. Report cards are given four times a year.
   C. Conferences are held in the fall and spring quarters.

(continued)

FIGURE 5.4
(CONTINUED)

VI. Issues Related to Homework

   A. Friday envelopes

   B. Weekly planner

   C. Homework is given:

      1. to reinforce a new concept (for example, short practice on a math concept or weekly spelling words)

      2. to have students read at least 15 minutes each night

      3. to provide students with additional practice on a skill they are having difficulty mastering

      4. when a student has failed to use his or her classroom academic time wisely

VII. Discipline Procedures

   A. The goal is to help students become responsible citizens in our classroom

   B. An outline of my classroom discipline system and when parents/guardians will be contacted if students continue to make poor choices after working with the teacher to develop new skills and make better decisions

VIII. Miscellaneous Comments

   A. Mark all clothing with the student's full name.

   B. Keep emergency card current.

   C. Please send a note when your child has been ill, is riding a different bus home, or is leaving before the end of the school day.

IX. Your Child's Success Is a Collaborative Team Effort

By providing parents with written information, you indicate that the information is important. A folder also creates ready-made notes and thus increases the likelihood that parents will learn and recall the information presented. By writing the student's name on each folder, you can quickly determine whose caregivers did not attend and follow up with a call to say you missed them, ask if they have questions, and inform them their child will be bringing a folder home. Once again, to the extent possible, it is important to have materials written in the language spoken by one of the parents or guardians of each student. While this might require involving several parents, older students, or a district ELL specialist, doing so will make a powerful statement about your respect for each family and will ensure that important information is effectively communicated.

You can also facilitate a positive meeting by providing a personal touch; obviously, there are many ways to do this. One activity for elementary teachers is to have each student make a silhouette of his or her head or a life-size outline of his or her body. The silhouettes are placed on the desks, or the outlines are seated in the chairs. The parent(s) are then asked to find their child's seat. Students can also write a note to their parent(s) to indicate several things they would like their parent(s) to see in the classroom. You can also have the parents write a note back to their child, perhaps stating something they enjoyed or learned about the class, excitement about something their child will be studying, and so on.

During the parent orientation, you should discuss your approach to classroom management. Parents can be provided with copies of the classroom rules, and you can discuss how both minor problems and consistent behavior problems will be handled. For example, you may wish to describe the problem-solving approach that will be used and discuss behavior contracts. You should also make a clear statement on when parents will be contacted about students' behaviors.

Similarly, you should clearly outline the instructional methods that will be used to help the students. Discuss the class schedule and indicate the types of instruction that will be used in teaching each topic. Since research indicates that parents and guardians are more likely to offer productive assistance to their children when provided with specific ideas regarding how they can help their children (Shamow & Miller, 2001; Van Voorhis, 2001), you will want to provide specific suggestions. For example, you might discuss the types of homework students will be assigned and describe how parents can best respond to the homework. You may want to state that should students ever be confused and overly concerned about a particular homework assignment, the students or parents are welcome to e-mail or call you at home for assistance. Experience indicates that although parents appreciate and are impressed by this offer, teachers receive very few evening phone calls or e-mails about assignments.

When discussing academic work, you may want to describe the various special services, such as reading or gifted programs, before or after school tutoring, and so forth, that are available for providing students with individualized instruction outside the classroom. Similarly, you should discuss how individual differences are attended to in the classroom. Along these lines, it is helpful to outline the grading system that will be used and to discuss such issues as whether grades will reflect improvement or performance measured against some external standard. You may also want to describe any special instructional methods, such as peer tutoring, individual goal setting, or group projects. Finally, parents can be informed that they will receive letters announcing any special projects or assignments that may require that they provide their children with some assistance. By clarifying the academic program and informing parents when and how they will be involved in helping their children, teachers begin to create an accepting, supportive parent response.

You should also inform parents that they can expect to receive telephone calls, e-mails, or notes when their children make a special effort, show improvement, or do something new or especially interesting. Similarly, the parents should be informed that they will also be notified when problems arise so that they are aware of what is happening and may offer assistance. Indicate that although you accept the responsibility for providing an exciting educational experience and helping the students to learn social skills and responsibility, the most effective approach to motivating student learning and dealing with any problems that arise is for the home and school to work together effectively.

For parents who may have difficulty attending meetings at school, consider holding the conferences in a site more comfortable or convenient for the parents. For example, conferences might be held at a meeting room in an apartment complex housing a number of students.

We also encourage you to ask parents for their communication preference and try to incorporate this into your pattern of communicating with them. For example, some parents or guardians cannot be contacted at work, whereas others may wish to be contacted primarily by e-mail or to meet personally at school.

Follow-Up

Do not wait too long before reinforcing the ideas presented in the orientation meeting. You may do so by arranging to involve parents in an instructional activity within a week or two following the meeting. The involvement may include an assignment in which parents are asked to help their children obtain information. You might ask the students to develop a family tree or to interview their parents for a career day. Another follow-up activity involves sending positive notes to parents about improvements or achievements their children have made in the specific areas discussed during the orientation meeting.

An additional aspect of follow-up is contacting caregivers who did not attend the orientation session. One approach is to send the parents their folder along with a letter stating that they were missed and inviting them to schedule a time to visit the classroom and discuss the material in the folder. It is helpful to call parents who do not respond and ask them whether they have any questions about the material they received. Although such contacts do require additional time, they are worth the effort because they create a foundation for increased parental support.

Since many families have DVD players, one way to provide all families access to the information in your initial meeting with parents is to videorecord the session. If you have a number of students who have interested caregivers with limited English proficiency, you might consider having the text of the presentation translated and dubbed in their first language.

Continuing Teacher–Parent Communication

Virtually all parents care about their children, and those parents want their children to be successful at school (Epstein & Sanders, 1998). Therefore, it is important to keep parents continually informed about their children's progress in your class. Teachers should also contact parents when a student consistently begins to act out in class, skips classes, falls behind in schoolwork and may need special assistance, or needs to complete some work at home. As in any relationship, it is better to deal with problems when they first arise than to wait until a crisis has occurred. Parents are justified in their annoyance when they attend a conference and discover that their child has been behind for six or eight weeks. Although it is true that some parents are less able to work with their children, it is important to hold realistic yet high expectations. It is surprising how often parents with reputations for lack of concern or for ineptness in helping their children can respond productively when contacted early and treated thoughtfully. There is an important distinction between teachers' constantly calling parents for support and calling parents to provide them with information. Parents have a right to expect teachers to handle minor problems and seek professional assistance in coping with major problems. Parents should be informed, however, when minor problems such as incomplete assignments or failure to bring supplies become frequent occurrences. Similarly, parents should be informed when major behavior or academic problems arise.

When our son was a sophomore in high school, he experienced considerable harassment, and during one semester, he skipped a number of classes. It was not until final grades were sent home that we became aware of this situation and the impact it had on our son's grades as well as his self-esteem. We believe it is imperative for school staff to communicate with parents or guardians whenever a student is making dramatic progress or experiencing significant problems. Although this requires effort for teachers who work with 180 or more students, as indicated by the response from students when the intern called all their homes, very positive benefits often occur when parents or guardians are contacted. We and hundreds of interns and teachers with whom we have worked have reported significant improvement in students' academic work and behavior following contact with parents or guardians. In addition, failure to make these contacts sends a message to students and the community that school staff do not care or are not comfortable interacting with members of the community. This can have a devastating result in terms of student achievement and behavior, just as frequent and supportive contact with families can have a dramatically positive impact on achievement and behavior (Reyes et al., 1999; Roderick, 2001).

Weekly Planner.   Especially in elementary school, parents appreciate having weekly contact regarding students' work. A weekly planner can help to accomplish this. On Monday, students are given a Weekly Planner (see Figure 5.5), which is placed in the front of their three-ring notebooks. The teacher discusses the planner with the class, explaining what the students will be doing throughout the week. Each day, students highlight any work not completed. The students are expected to take the notebook and planner home each evening. Parents are told about this at back-to-school night, through a videorecording about the classroom, or in a phone call. The planner may also include a reminder to parents about upcoming school or class events and information about long-term assignments or projects. If several parents and guardians have limited English proficiency, you may want to consider using simple language and including clip art to depict the events or activities you are describing.

If you want to increase the likelihood that caregivers receive the material you send home, it is best to ask that they sign a sheet indicating they received the material, making any comments they would like you to read, and require that this be returned. Most of us have experienced situations where younger students simply did not give the material to their parents and older students even opened their family mailbox and removed letters sent from the school. We have worked with school districts where educators send some sensitive material to parents in plain white envelopes with no return address.

Friday Envelopes.   On Friday students are given a Friday Envelope filled with the work they have completed that week, which has been responded to by their teacher, as well as school announcements. The students share the envelope with their parents and bring the envelope back the following Monday signed by their parents. Space is provided for the parents to write comments or ask for a phone call.

Newsletters.   A newsletter is an expedient way to keep large numbers of parents informed. Because most secondary teachers have three separate preparations, each for a different course, a newsletter sent every three weeks for each class requires a teacher to write one newsletter each week. The newsletter can involve less than a page, describing subjects currently being taught, projects due, films being shown, and so on. You can also use this opportunity to jot a personal note on newsletters to parents whose child is experiencing noteworthy success or problems. In third grade and beyond, students can help write the newsletter. Groups of students can volunteer to write different parts of the newsletter, and the teacher or another group of students assembles the final draft. This can help students synthesize what they have learned since the last newsletter and can provide the teacher with a form of assessment related to students' understanding of instructional activities.

Progress Reports.   Many schools require periodic progress reports; in fact, many high schools require progress reports for all students earning lower than a C grade. Most districts will have a progress report form, and you can also develop your own form to send at times other than the standard report periods. It is important to notify the parents and guardians as soon as your efforts to work with a student have not been successful in helping the student make necessary improvements in academic or behavioral areas of concern. A progress report should always present an honest description of the student's strengths and areas of concern. It is important to describe the steps you have taken and will be taking to assist the student in improving his or her academic work and/or behavior as well as what the student will need to do in order to be more successful. You should also clearly specify any support you are requesting of the parents or guardians as well as the type of contact you would like to have with them in order to discuss how best to assist their child.

FIGURE 5.5
WEEKLY
PLANNER

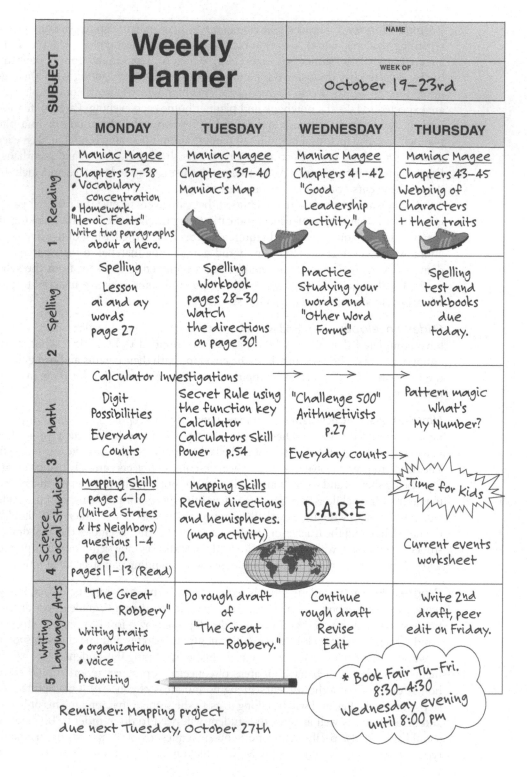

SUBJECT		MONDAY	TUESDAY	WEDNESDAY	THURSDAY
Weekly Planner	NAME			WEEK OF	October 19–23rd
Reading 1		Maniac Magee Chapters 37–38 • Vocabulary concentration • Homework. "Heroic Feats" Write two paragraphs about a hero.	Maniac Magee Chapters 39–40 Maniac's Map	Maniac Magee Chapters 41–42 "Good Leadership activity."	Maniac Magee Chapters 43–45 Webbing of Characters + their traits
Spelling 2		Spelling Lesson ai and ay words page 27	Spelling Workbook pages 28–30 Watch the directions on page 30!	Practice Studying your words and "Other Word Forms"	Spelling test and workbooks due today.
Math 3		Calculator Investigations Digit Possibilities Everyday Counts	Secret Rule using the function key Calculator Calculators Skill Power p.54	"Challenge 500" Arithmetivists p.27 Everyday counts →	Pattern magic What's My Number?
Science Social Studies 4		Mapping Skills pages 6–10 (United States & Its Neighbors) questions 1–4 page 10. pages 11–13 (Read)	Mapping Skills Review directions and hemispheres. (map activity)	D.A.R.E	Time for kids Current events worksheet
Writing Language Arts 5		"The Great ——— Robbery" Writing traits • organization • voice Prewriting	Do rough draft of "The Great ——— Robbery."	Continue rough draft Revise Edit	Write 2nd draft, peer edit on Friday.

Reminder: Mapping project
due next Tuesday, October 27th

* Book Fair Tu–Fri.
8:30–4:30
Wednesday evening
until 8:00 pm

A Classroom Web Site.   Aside from using e-mail to communicate with parents, a classroom Web site is an excellent tool. While not all families have access to the Internet, our experience indicates that many who do not have access are willing to obtain a free library pass and use the local library computers to access information online. Creating a classroom Web site is fun and easy. There are many free tutorials online which will walk you through how to set up and personalize your own site (schoolrack.com and educatorpages.com). A growing number of school districts are also offering free Web site setups for teachers. A classroom Web site might contain information about daily homework assignments, upcoming projects, special events, field trip information, book lists for that grade level, ideas for parents to be involved in their child's education at home, special recognition for a student of the week, pictures, and links to other Web sites students can use for learning and research and class newsletters. If you decide to include pictures on your classroom Web site, make sure to post only those that do not have students in them. If you post pictures that include students, you need to obtain permission from each child's parent to have his or her pictures online. Letting parents or guardians know about your Web site in your beginning-of-the-year introductory letter, and showing parents how to access it at back-to-school night will ensure that the maximum number of parents will use this important tool.

Personalized Stationery.   Another approach is to have students make personalized stationery during the first weeks of school. They can design their own patterns and decorate their stationery using pens, charcoal, paint, or any other art medium. Teachers can use this stationery to send positive notes home about the student. It is best if elementary teachers send positive notes home at least twice a term. Most teachers find it helpful to record when notes were sent as well as the content of the notes. In this way, you can send notes to all students and focus on different positive events each time a note is sent.

Recording Contacts with Caregivers.   We encourage you to keep a record of all contacts with parents, guardians, and other caregivers. It is easy to create a file folder for each student and include a sheet such as that found in Figure 5.6. This will allow you to track whether you are having positive contacts with all parents and guardians as well as provide data should caregivers report they are not being adequately informed. We encourage you to keep a notebook titled "Parent Communication." Whenever you send a note home, photocopy the note and place it under the student's tab. We also encourage you to type up notes after every home phone call and place these notes in order behind the student's tab. In fact, any form of parent contact outside of the regular materials sent home to all parents is placed in this file. This material will not only be valuable in providing you with excellent recall regarding your contact with parents; it can also be invaluable if you are asked to document efforts to assist the student or whether you have been proactive in providing parents with updated information regarding their child.

FIGURE 5.6 PARENT/ GUARDIAN/ CAREGIVER CONTACTS

Individual Contacted	Relationship to the Student	Date	Time	Summary of Conversation	Follow-Up Needed

Phone Calls.   Phone calls are another method for contacting parents. Teachers who call each child's parent(s) at least once before scheduling the initial conference and at least once a term thereafter find that parent–teacher contacts are more relaxed and enjoyable. Teachers often shy away from parents who have reputations for being difficult. These, however, are the parents whom we should make the most effort to know. Parents appreciate knowing that their child's teacher cares enough to make a phone call, and the most critical parents will frequently become supporters of the teacher who takes time to call. When making phone calls, always begin and end the conversation with a positive statement about the child. Also ask the parents how the child is reacting to school and whether the parents have any information that might assist you in making the school experience more productive for the child. Like children, parents respond more positively when given a sense of competence and power.

© Joyce Button

"Wilson sometimes has a little difficulty handling parent conferences."

Attending Activities in Which Students Are Involved.   Parents can also be contacted informally when you attend extracurricular activities in which their children are involved. This strategy is particularly effective with the parents of students who are doing poorly in school. On a number of occasions, we have made concerted efforts to attend extracurricular performances of students involved in persistent school misbehavior and have found that when the parents saw concrete evidence of our concern for their children, they became much more involved in encouraging the students to behave responsibly in school. These informal visits with caregivers also provide wonderful opportunities to learn more about students as well as to break down barriers that may exist between the parents and school.

PAUSE & CONSIDER 5.1

Take a few minutes to write down the methods you have found most effective for communicating with parents. If you are currently student teaching or observing in a classroom, ask the teacher with whom you are working and, if possible, other teachers in the building to share the methods they have found most effective. Once you have a list of specific methods, join a group of peers or classmates and share these methods.

PARENT CONFERENCES

For most teachers, parent conferences are a required form of personal contact. Parent conferences can play a vital role in eliciting parents' support for us and can help us work with students who are experiencing difficulties. Unfortunately, a poorly organized or otherwise negative conference can create or intensify parental dissatisfaction. This dissatisfaction will frequently have a negative impact on students' behaviors and academic progress. Furthermore, coping with parental criticism diverts valuable teacher time and energy. Therefore, parent conferences have a real influence on classroom discipline.

By thoughtfully preparing for and implementing a well-organized conference, we can reduce our own anxiety about conferring with parents while increasing the likelihood that parents will leave the conference feeling positive about and supportive of us. This section offers suggestions for improving skills in conferring with parents.

Preparing for a Conference

Because teacher, parent, and student all care about the outcome of a teacher–parent conference, it is important to consider how best to prepare each of these individuals for the conference. A conference will be more comfortable and productive when each person involved is prepared for the conference. It is important to remember that the student is integrally involved even if not present. At all grade levels, however, we recommend that students be present at these conferences.

Preparing Students

The first steps in preparing students are to discuss the goals of conferences and to allow students to ask questions and express their concerns. Students need to know why their parents are being given a report and what will happen at the conference. The next step is to provide students with an opportunity to evaluate their own work. Because the primary goal of periodic teacher–parent conferences is to clarify and communicate students' accomplishments, it is logical that students should be involved in this process. Providing students with an opportunity to evaluate their own work also reduces their anxiety about the type of information their parents will be receiving. Self-evaluation provides students with a sense of significance, competence, and power.

There are several approaches to involving students in self-evaluation. The most specific and valuable method is to allow students to fill out a report card on themselves. The easiest and most effective method of developing a self-evaluation report card is to ask students to rate themselves on the same items on which the district or school requires you to rate them. Figure 5.7 is an example of such a form. If you have few enough students, you can arrange an individual conference with each student. Once the student has completed a self-evaluation form (younger children or students who have difficulty with reading will require assistance in completing a form), you can schedule time to discuss the results individually with each student. Inform the students that this conference will allow them to discuss with the teacher any discrepancies between their evaluations. It is extremely important to discuss these differences. Student resentment and hostility are often the outcomes of a conference in which parents are given negative information about a student before this information has been systematically discussed with the student. One method we recommend is to have elementary or middle school students summarize their thoughts about their successes and areas for improvement using the form found in Figure 5.8. The student and then the teacher write two specific areas in which the student is doing well and one goal for improvement (in primary grades we use the terms *two stars* and *a wish*). This can be shared during a teacher–parent conference, and the parent or guardian can also be asked to complete this form. Our daughter writes notes from the conference on the back of this form, photocopies it twice, and places one copy in her file and sends one copy home the next day.

**FIGURE 5.7
SELF-
EVALUATION
REPORT
CARD**

Name _____

Reading

1. Approximately how many books have you read this term?
    _____

2. Have you reached your personal goal for outside reading?
    _____

3. Have you kept up your daily assignments in your literature book or reading text?
    _____

4. What grade do you deserve in reading?
    grade: _____ effort: _____
    reason: _____

Math

1. Have you worked hard to get all your assignments done on time?
2. Are there any of the multiplication tables that are still difficult for you?
    _____ If so, which ones? _____
3. Are there any areas of math that you are not clear about or in which you need more help?
    _____
4. What grade do you deserve this term in math?
    grade: _____ effort: _____
    reason: _____

Spelling

1. Have you studied your list words each week?
2. Have you been completing your workbook assignments each week on time?
    _____
3. Do you think you remember the words that you learn to spell each week?
    _____
4. How well do you spell your words in your writing and on daily assignments?
    superior   very good   fair   poor   (Circle one)
5. What grade should you receive for spelling this term?
    grade: _____ effort: _____
    reason: _____

Cursive Writing

1. What do you need to work on?
2. What grade do you feel you have earned this term in cursive writing?
    grade: _____ effort: _____
    reason: _____

Science, Social Studies, and Art

What grade would you give yourself in each of these areas for this term?
Please give a reason for each grade:

Science: grade: _____ effort: _____
reason: _____

Social Studies: grade: _____ effort: _____
reason: _____

(continued)

FIGURE 5.7
(CONTINUED)

Art: grade: _____ effort: _____
reason: _____
What areas are you doing well in at school? _____
What subjects would you like to improve on? _____
In what ways do you feel you have grown personally this term?

_____

Please evaluate your study habits and personal growth, using these ratings.
   + outstanding growth
   = okay or satisfactory growth
   ✓ need to improve in this area

Put the appropriate mark on each line below.

Study Habits

_____ Following directions
_____ Completing assignments on time
_____ Working well in your/a group
_____ Working well alone
_____ Listening well to whoever is speaking
_____ Showing neatness in your work and desk
_____ Taking responsibility for your work

Personal Growth Areas

_____ Considering other people's feelings
_____ Following school rules in a positive way
_____ Taking care of your personal belongings
_____ Controlling your own behavior
_____ Being able to accept responsibility for your own actions
_____ Being able to get along well with others

Is there anything that you would like to share with me about yourself or your work?

_____

Is there anything you would like me to write on your report card or share with your parents? ___

_____

Do you have any comments about my teaching this term? _____

_____

_____

Other comments that might be helpful for me to know: _____

_____

_____

_____

Thank you for your help!

Another method that can be incorporated with a self-evaluation report card is to have students examine their behavior and academic achievements compared with their stated goals. If students have been involved in writing goals for the grading period, they can be asked to write a

FIGURE 5.8
CONFERENCE
SUMMARY
FORM

TWO STARS AND A WISH Two Strengths and a Goal		
By each star, write something positive about this student (behavior or learning). By the wish, write one hope or goal for this student.		
Student's Perception	**Teacher's Perception**	**Parents' Perception**
(Doing well) ☆	(Doing well) ☆	(Doing well) ☆
(Doing well) ☆	(Doing well) ☆	(Doing well) ☆
WISH (Goal for improvement)	**WISH** (Goal for improvement)	**WISH** (Goal for improvement)

short statement about the degree to which they have met these goals. This procedure not only places their learning and subsequent grade in perspective but also reinforces the concept of students' responsibility for their own learning.

Preparing Parents

There are two basic methods for preparing parents for a teacher–parent conference. First, as discussed earlier, you should already have had several positive contacts with the parents. These contacts ideally include a back-to-school night, a phone call, and several notes home on their child's progress. Second, about one week before the conference, you should send the parents a note reminding them of the conference and providing them with an agenda for the meeting. Figure 5.9 provides an example of such a note and outline.

Teacher Preparation

Teachers are responsible for providing parents and guardians with clearly presented information in the context of a positive, comfortable interaction. There are three basic steps in accomplishing this goal: First, as discussed in the preceding paragraphs, we should adequately prepare the student and parent(s) for the conference. Second, we should acquire and clearly organize important information about the student. Third, we should create a comfortable, relaxed environment.

FIGURE 5.9
AGENDA FOR
A PARENT
CONFERENCE

Dear Mr. and Mrs. Smith:

I am looking forward to our conference on Wednesday, November 6, at 3:30 p.m. In order to help us use the time most effectively, I will try to follow the agenda listed below. I hope that this list will cover all areas you would like to discuss. If you have any special questions, it might be helpful to jot them down prior to the conference.

Conference Agenda
1. Share positive personal qualities about the student.
2. Read student's self-evaluation.
3. Discuss the report card and examine samples of the student's work.
4. Discuss the student's behavior and peer relations.
5. Parent/guardian questions or concerns.
6. Summarize the conference by discussing the student's strengths and areas that need improvement.

Sincerely,

Mrs. Johnson
Third-Grade Teacher

Parents are impressed with data. Data indicate that we have invested time and energy in preparing for a conference. Data testify directly to our professional competence and also have the obvious advantage of objectifying a discussion. The presence of data greatly diminishes the likelihood that a conference will turn into a debate over whether a student's grade is fair or whether a student's behavior really warrants concern.

Data also provide protection for the teacher by furnishing a record of a student's academic progress and behavior as well as of our attempts to make thoughtful interventions aimed at improving skills and behaviors. The availability of data prevents us from being accused of exaggerating a problem, picking on a student, or not having attempted to solve the problem ourselves. Regardless of how competent we may be, lack of specific information significantly undermines our position when working with parents. Consequently, well-organized data are a necessary component of any parent conference and are especially important when a conference focuses on dealing with inappropriate student behavior or poor student achievement. The four major types of useful data in a parent conference are the following:

1. Data on the student's and parents' feelings about the class
2. Data on the student's academic work
3. Data on the student's behavior and the results of attempts to improve the behavior
4. Data on conferences with colleagues and specialists aimed at developing a solution to any matter that is a problem

It is helpful to acquire information about how the parents perceive the school year is progressing for their child. By requesting this information, we acknowledge the importance of the parents' concerns and ideas. Information about the parents' perceptions of their child's reactions to school and the parents' own wishes can also enable us to be better prepared for the conference. Figures 5.10 and 5.11 provide examples of a cover letter and parent questionnaire used by intermediate grade teachers.

**FIGURE 5.10
COVER LETTER TO
PRECONFERENCE
PARENT
QUESTIONNAIRE**

Dear Parents,

In order to make your parent conference valuable for your child and you, I would like to have as much information as possible for the conference. You can help me by responding to the questions on the attached sheet. If there are any questions that you do not care to answer, please feel free to leave them blank. I would very much appreciate your returning this questionnaire to me at least one day before the conference. If that is not possible, please bring it to the conference with you.

I appreciate the time you are taking to help make this a rewarding conference for all of us and I look forward to seeing you next week.

Sincerely,

Ms. Wilson

Because the school's primary function is to provide each student with basic academic skills, the teacher–parent conference should heavily emphasize informing parents about their child's academic progress. You should prepare for each conference by providing a folder that includes samples of the student's work. The folder should include specific examples that will help the parents understand any areas in which the student is having particular success or difficulties. Students beyond the second grade can be involved in creating this portfolio. With younger children, the teacher can compile the work and then share it with the student.

Specific data on a student's behavior will be necessary only when conferring with parents whose child is having serious behavior problems. In such cases, the parents should be presented with specific data on the child's behavior and approaches to helping the child improve the behavior. For example, one of us recently worked with a teacher who had a parent challenge her regarding how his child was behaving in the classroom. The parent insisted his child would not disrupt other children's learning or waste time during seatwork. When the teacher met with the parent, the teacher began the discussion by highlighting some positive aspects of the student's work and behavior in the classroom. She was also prepared with specific examples of work in writing and mathematics the student had accomplished during two 20-minute segments of assigned seatwork in each subject. In addition, using a stopwatch, the teacher had collected data on the amount of time the student was on task during two 20-minute seatwork tasks in each of these subjects and compared this to two students of similar ability working on the same tasks (obviously no names were provided regarding the other two students). The teacher also had a tally of the number of times the student in question had engaged other students in nonacademic conversations during these two 20-minute segments of time. She indicated to the parent that the work was of the correct level of difficulty for the child and students had been provided with clear examples of how to complete the work and directions to work quietly on their own during these two activities. She also indicated this behavior was quite typical for the student and described two interventions she had used to assist the student in being more focused during seatwork and what her next intervention would be. The teacher concluded by stating her belief that the student could do high-quality academic work and her commitment to helping him develop skill in staying focused during short seatwork assignments. The parent's firm questioning and annoyance gradually turned to support and even admiration as he realized he was working with a

FIGURE 5.11
PRECONFERENCE
PARENT
QUESTIONNAIRE

Please complete this questionnaire and return it as soon as possible. Thank you.

Child's Name: _____

1. My child's general attitude toward school this year is _____
   _____

2. My child expresses most interest in school in _____
   _____

3. My child's greatest concern in school seems to be _____
   _____

4. Some things my child does very well are (these do not have to pertain to school)
   a. _____   d. _____
   b. _____   e. _____
   c. _____   f. _____

5. An area I would like to see my child work especially hard in is _____
   _____

6. Please list some positive qualities that your child has so that we can discuss good
   qualities at school (such as trustworthy, patient, understanding, punctual) _____
   _____

7. Something I have wondered about this year is _____
   _____

8. Some things that seem difficult for my child are (not necessarily schoolwork) (for
   example, doing small tasks with fingers) _____
   _____

9. Something my child would like to do in school is _____
   _____

10. Several subjects that my child seems to enjoy are (include interests and hobbies)
    _____
    _____

11. I would appreciate any suggestions or comments you have that would help me work
    more effectively with your child. _____
    _____
    _____
    _____

Thank you for taking time to complete this questionnaire.

skilled professional who cared about his child. Specific examples of the methods for collecting this type of data are presented in Chapter 10.

If the data on the student's academic progress indicate that the student is not functioning well, be prepared to provide the parents with examples of ways in which the student's academic program has been adjusted in order to meet the student's special needs. If you have worked with specialists in developing an individualized program, it is helpful to provide information about these conferences. This can be done by using a standard form to record the results of such conferences. Figure 5.12 is an example of a form you can use for this purpose.

There are several advantages to presenting this type of data. Data concerning professional consultation reflect the teacher's concern and resourcefulness. Furthermore, they indicate to the parents that their child's problem is not simply a personality conflict with a teacher or the result of an incompetent teacher having difficulty teaching their slightly energetic student. Another advantage to having consulted with specialists is that this procedure should present the parents with clearer and more thorough data. Especially in the area of academic difficulties, classroom teachers often have limited skills in diagnosing the specific factors that may be causing a student's problems. By consulting specialists, not only can the teacher provide the parents with more detailed information but the teacher can also simultaneously acquire information that can assist in developing a more appropriate academic program for the student.

Once we have prepared students and parents and have collected and developed the relevant data, the final preparation involves creating a comfortable conference setting. If possible, the conference should be held at a round table so that neither party is in a dominant position. The atmosphere can be made more relaxed by placing some flowers on the table and having cookies and coffee available. You can print the agenda, leaving space for notes, and give it to the parents. Provide the parents with a pen or pencil so they can take notes during the conference.

FIGURE 5.12 TEACHER–SPECIALIST CONFERENCE FORM

Source: From *Adolescents with Behavior Problems: Strategies for Teaching, Counseling, and Parent Involvement,* by V. F. Jones, 1980, p. 274, Boston, MA: Allyn and Bacon. Copyright © 1980 by Pearson Education. Reprinted with permission.

Consultant's Name _____ Date _____

Consultant's Position or Role _____

Reasons for holding the conference:

Goals for the conference:

Information obtained:

Decision(s) reached:

Additional comments:

Conducting an Effective Conference

If you have prepared effectively, the conference will usually be smooth and comfortable. After greeting the parent(s) warmly and chatting for a moment about any positive topic, begin the conference by sharing several positive personal qualities the child displays at school. The next step is to ask the parent(s) to read the student's self-evaluation report card and any other material the student has written about his or her progress during the term. Students often are so critical of their own work that this may provide sensitive preparation for any comments you may need to make. Once they have read their child's own evaluation, parents are less likely to question your statements about areas in which their child needs improvement.

Many parents are concerned about their child's report card, so the next step is usually to discuss the actual report card and examine specific examples of the student's work. When doing so, initially focus on positive aspects of the student's work. Parents respond well to the sandwich theory of feedback, in which critical comments are sandwiched between positive comments about their child. Another strategy is to introduce an area that needs improvement with the statement, "I would like to encourage your child to. . . ." By focusing on the positive, you can minimize parental defensiveness and criticism.

Once academic matters have been discussed, focus on the student's behavior and peer relationships. It is important to discuss positive aspects of the student's behavior as well as aspects that require improvement. Also, if the student has experienced serious behavior problems, provide the parents with specific data on the student's behavior and efforts to assist the student in changing behavior. During this portion of the conference, it may be appropriate to invite the principal, counselor, or any other specialists to join in the discussion.

After you have discussed the student's academic progress and behavior, the parents should be encouraged to ask questions and make comments. If the parents do not have any questions, you can help them focus on their thoughts and concerns by referring to any pertinent items on the pre-conference parent questionnaire (Figure 5.11).

"We don't have school tomorrow. It's time for parent–teacher confrontations."

© Bob Vojtko

Student-Led Conferences

Student-led conferences are a growing trend in education. They provide students with the opportunity to share their educational progress with significant adults. Students share their goals and progress toward meeting their goals with their parents or guardians. During the conference, the student shares his or her work and/or portfolio and analyzes his or her strengths and weaknesses while reflecting on the educational choices that he or she has made. Together, the student, parents, and teacher develop new goals and decide on ways to help the student achieve these goals.

The student-led conference has the advantage of promoting goal-setting skills, self-evaluation, reflection, facilitation skills, and choice awareness.

Prior to the conference, students need to be taught how to lead a conference, set an agenda, establish goals, reflect on these goals, choose what work will be shared, reflect on behaviors and attitudes, and learn facilitation skills.

Student-led conferences usually involve five steps. The first step involves an introduction to the conference. The students should outline the process so that the adults present understand the agenda. Second, the students present the report card, data that have been collected, or their portfolio. Third, the students share a reflection sheet they completed prior to the conference. Student responses to their work demonstrate their analysis of their effort and progress toward meeting their goals. Fourth, students share comments about their school behavior and the attitudes they have shown while attempting to make solid academic progress. The fifth step involves sharing new goals that have been established and possibly a plan to reach these goals.

Student preparation for the conference is an essential prerequisite to an effective student-led conference. Teachers who role-play a conference with their class and give students the opportunity to practice find the actual conferences run much more smoothly. It is particularly helpful to assist students in learning how to present academic or behavior problems to their parents or guardians. Another important aspect is to develop an outline for the conference that includes a check sheet for the students to work from as they discuss their work.

There are advantages and disadvantages to using student-led conferences. The advantages are that students feel they are part of the entire process of evaluating their work and effort. Student accountability is measured and developed. All students can produce something positive for the conference such as an essay, poem, art project, and so on that would not show up in a report card grade. Many school districts have seen parent attendance improve significantly.

One of the disadvantages is that some parents want to speak with the teacher without their child present. In some cultures, the idea of the student taking on this important role may not be deemed appropriate. To respond to this concern, many schools that implement student-led conferences offer separate appointments for parents to confer with the teacher. A second disadvantage is that if a parent fails to attend the conference, it can cause a great disappointment for the student. In addition, this approach can require more work and skill on the teacher's part as the student needs to be well prepared. Finally, this type of conference presents the opportunity for a parent to become upset with the student.

Conference Summary and Follow-Up

It is helpful to provide parents with a conference summary. Figure 5.13 is an example of an elementary grade conference summary form. For a primary grade conference summary, the teacher might choose to simply photocopy and send home the form shown in Figure 5.8 with ideas discussed at the conference and any other notes the teacher wishes to add written at the bottom or on the back of the form. Figure 5.14 presents an example of a conference summary form appropriate for a middle level or high school student.

For elementary grade and other teachers who have few enough students that it is possible to contact each parent/guardian after the conference, a follow-up has several benefits. First, it continues the relationship with the parent/guardian and reinforces the teacher's commitment to the student and the family. Second, it provides a reminder to the teacher about the commitments made to support the student. Third, it reminds the parents of any agreements they made to support their child. Finally, it provides a written record of these agreements.

In kindergarten through second grades, this may involve a letter to the parents providing them with book or other home learning ideas or reviewing a behavior strategy you discussed with them.

FIGURE 5.13
ELEMENTARY
GRADES PARENT
CONFERENCE
SUMMARY FORM

Student's Name: _____

Academic Achievement
Reading
Doing well in: _____
Needs to work on: _____

Math
Average of math scores: _____   _____
                              tests   daily work
Strong areas: _____
Needs to improve on: _____

Writing
Strength: _____
Continue to focus on: _____
Other subjects: _____
_____

Behavior and Personal Characteristics
Positive personal qualities that I see in your child: _____
_____
Improvement needed in: _____
_____
Comments about how your child is relating to his or her classmates: _____
_____

Final Comments
You could help at home by: _____
_____
Any additional comments: _____
_____
_____
_____
_____

In situations where the teacher has had to discuss rather serious academic or behavioral problems a student is experiencing, a more detailed letter provides an important summary of the teacher's concerns and interventions being implemented or planned (Figure 5.15). Another approach to clarifying specific academic or behavioral interventions is to present the caregivers with a description of the plan. Figure 5.16 provides an example of a form we have used.

PAUSE & CONSIDER 5.2

Create a list of methods you could use at your grade level for preparing parents, students, and yourself for conferences with parents or guardians. If you are currently student teaching or observing in a classroom, ask the teacher with whom you are working and, if possible, other teachers in the building to share the methods they have found most effective. Once you have a list of specific methods, join a group of peers or classmates and share these methods.

FIGURE 5.14
MIDDLE LEVEL/
HIGH SCHOOL
CONFERENCE
SUMMARY FORM

Current grade in 10th-grade social studies _____

This grade is based on the following scores:

    Test score average _____ test score grade _____

    Homework grade _____

    Classroom participation grade _____

Strengths your child has shown this year in this subject _____

_____

Areas where your child will benefit from improvement _____

_____

FIGURE 5.15
POST-
CONFERENCE
FOLLOW-UP
LETTER

Dear Mrs. Bereznity,

Thank you so much for taking time to meet with me. I very much appreciate and respect your involvement in Marat's education and I know it makes a big difference in his success in school.

As we discussed in our conference, Marat is doing an excellent job in math and science. You should be proud of how well he stays focused and how skilled he is when working on these subjects. The other students are impressed by his knowledge in these subjects and often seek him out for assistance with their work.

Like all students, Marat has a few areas where he could improve if he is to be as successful as he would like to be and you want him to be. As we discussed, I would like him to continue working on his reading comprehension. At school we will continue to ask him questions as we read, and I will begin working with him on improving his skill in asking himself questions as he reads. As you read with him at home, it will help him if every half page or so you ask him questions about what he or you have just read. I know this is an area he can improve on and he will feel better about his reading as he develops these skills. I have also included the book list you requested and I hope you and Marat will enjoy reading these.

As I mentioned, especially during times when we focus on reading or writing, Marat tends to become off task and distracts both himself and other students. As we discussed, I have been working with all of the students in our class to learn how to tell another student if that student's behavior is disrupting their learning. As I have with several other students, I have also been working with Marat to keep a record of how many times he stops working and disrupts someone else's learning. As we agreed, each day I will give you a report on how he is doing, and when he has fewer than two of these interruptions each morning and each afternoon, you will receive a call from me, and Marat will be allowed to tell Mr. Jimenez, our PE teacher, during lunch and/or after school. Please remember to tell him how well he is doing and how proud you are of him when you see him after school on the days I call.

Again, Marat is doing very well in some important subjects. I know we can work together to help him become a better student in the areas we all set as goals for him.

Warm Regards,

**FIGURE 5.16
PLAN FOR
IMPROVEMENT**

STUDENT'S NAME: _____

TEACHER'S NAME: _____

PARENT'S NAME: _____

DATE: _____

AREA TO BE IMPROVED: _____

_____

THE TEACHER WILL: _____

_____

THE STUDENT WILL: _____

_____

THE PARENT WILL: _____

_____

LONG-RANGE GOAL: _____

_____

Check-in/Review Times (when and how the teacher and parent will check in to see how
things are going):

_____
_____
_____

DEALING EFFECTIVELY WITH PARENTS' CRITICISMS AND CONFRONTATIONS

Anyone who has taught for several years has had to deal with an angry or critical parent. Many
teachers state that, along with classroom discipline, this type of confrontation is perhaps the least
desirable aspect of teaching. Although there is no foolproof method for dealing with an angry
parent, there are several strategies that can be used to cope with such situations in an effective,
professional manner.

1. Meet with the parent or guardian in a setting in which you are physically safe and
   able to obtain assistance. If you have reason to believe the guest may become confrontational, schedule the meeting to include an administrator or counselor.
2. Greet the parent in a pleasant manner. It is more difficult for parents to remain critical
   and aggressive if you seem glad to see them.
3. Use active listening to defuse the parent's emotions. Becoming defensive or initially
   arguing with the parent will usually only intensify the parent's emotions. By using
   such phrases as "I appreciate your concern" or "I can see that you are really concerned
   about this," you can help the parent feel understood. This tactic will gradually enable

© George Abbott

the parent to calm down and replace angry or frightened feelings and actions with more positive and productive responses.

4. Look genuinely interested and listen carefully. This attitude also helps the parent feel accepted and will gradually reduce negative or intense feelings.

5. Present a calm, professional manner. Stand erect, look at the parents, and remain calm. Just as students respond more effectively to teachers who remain calm and in charge during a crisis, parents need the structure provided by a calm response.

6. Ask the parents what they wish to accomplish. One method of avoiding a confrontation is by asking the parents: "I appreciate your concern. What would you like to accomplish with our discussion today?" This approach helps focus the parents' energy and moves the conference away from a gripe session into a potentially productive problem-solving conference.

7. Set a time limit if necessary. If your time is limited, it is important to inform the parent. Do so by stating, "I have twenty minutes before I have to be back with my class. Let's see how far we can get in solving the problem in that time. If we need more time, I will be glad to schedule a conference as soon as possible."

8. Ask the parent whether the student is aware of the problem. Because the student is the most important person involved, it is important to clarify how he or she feels about the issue being raised by the parent. This question also slows the parent down and creates a more productive focus for the conversation. Furthermore, the question helps introduce the issue of the student's responsibility for any problem that may exist.

9. Be honest. When confronted by parents, it is easy to understate the seriousness of a problem or to accept too much responsibility for a problem that is largely something the student must work on. Maintain your professional integrity and set the stage for future conferences by initially presenting an honest and clear statement of the problem.

10. Emphasize specific data. Data are simultaneously one of your best professional tools and your best defense. If a parent angrily states that his daughter did well in math last year but is having difficulty this year, the most logical and effective approach is to examine data on the student's math skills and associated school records.

11. Tell the parent specifically what will be done to deal with the problem. Parents have a right to know what the teacher will do to alleviate a difficulty. Furthermore, critical parents can often become strong supporters if they learn that they will be listened to, shown data, and presented with a plan. If the parents' worry was not justified, the plan may involve a follow-up conference to examine the results of the current program. If, however, the parents highlighted an area that required attention, developing a plan shows respect for the parents' concern and competence on your part.

An intern with whom we worked experienced a situation in which a student's aunt became upset because the student was required to work with the teacher and administrator regarding her physical and verbal abuse of peers. The aunt had a history of being verbally abusive to teachers but was also a strong advocate for her niece and had worked cooperatively with the intern during the first several months of school. One morning after the student's mother had been contacted concerning the student's bullying of a peer, the aunt came to the classroom and insisted on speaking with the intern. The intern agreed to meet, asked her mentor to take over the classroom, and proceeded to a small room adjacent to the main school office to meet with the aunt. The intern entered the narrow, windowless room first, seated herself near the far wall, and was followed by the aunt who shut the door and pushed her chair against the door. The aunt proceeded to shout at the intern, verbally threatened her physical safety, and on one occasion stood up and moved toward her. Fortunately, the intern had experience in deescalation methods. She listened to and paraphrased the aunt's anger and suggested the aunt might want to report this to the principal and discuss it with her. The aunt was pleased to have an opportunity to tell someone in authority how badly her niece had been treated and allowed the teacher to exit the room with her to schedule an appointment with the principal.

This incident highlights the importance of teachers' having a plan for working with angry parents or guardians and, particularly, the importance of being aware of the first point made in this section—not meeting with a potentially angry parent or guardian in a setting in which support is not available.

PAUSE & CONSIDER 5.3

We encourage you to work with three or four colleagues or classmates and select a situation in which you have been, or can imagine being, confronted by an upset parent or other adult supporting a student. After discussing the situation, have one member of the group act the part of the parent and another, the teacher. Following the role-play, have the other members of the group provide feedback. If the feedback is substantial, you may want to repeat the role-play with another student acting as the teacher.

METHODS FOR POSITIVELY ENGAGING PARENTS OF ENGLISH LANGUAGE LEARNERS

Working effectively with families whose culture is different from the teacher's is an area in which many teachers find themselves lacking knowledge and skills (Chen et al., 2008). Research suggests teachers tend to best understand overt aspects of their students' cultures such as food, art, celebrations, dress, and so on, but also realize these are the least important aspects needed to understand their students' cultural background (Eberly, Joshi, & Konzal, 2007). These authors found that issues related to child rearing were often the most discrepant between teachers and parents, and teachers had real difficulty being open-minded about parents' values in this area.

Studies suggest that teachers may also perceive the type of involvement families may have in their children's educational experiences differently than family members and guardians do. In their study of schools in which Hispanic students demonstrated high achievement,

Reyes and colleagues (1999) discovered that teachers viewed family involvement as attending school events, participating in meetings, and serving as volunteers. Family members, however, viewed the most important involvement as "checking homework assignments, reading and listening to children read, obtaining tutorial assistance, providing nurturance, instilling cultural values, talking with children, and sending them to school well fed, clean, and rested" (Reyes et al., 1999, p. 37). It is not surprising, therefore, that staff in schools in which Hispanic students were most successful focused more effectively on directly involving families in their children's education within the home environment. Similarly, based on an examination of forty-two projects, Chavkin and Gonzales (1995) reported the following strategies to be effective in fostering family involvement: (1) providing reception areas with bilingual staff, (2) communication in Spanish, and (3) visiting with family members at sites away from school.

Research suggests that schools in which Hispanic students do particularly well are characterized by the warmth of the staff and the personal relationships staff develop with families (Reyes et al., 1999). These authors found that it was important whenever staff met formally or informally with family members to acknowledge the student's accomplishments. These authors stressed the following characteristics of schools for Hispanic students to perform well:

1. Build on cultural values of Hispanic parents
2. Stress personal contact with parents
3. Foster communication with parents
4. Create a warm environment for parents
5. Facilitate structural accommodations for parent involvement

Involvement by parents of English language learners or those whose families are from cultures different than the majority of students and teachers in the school can be encouraged through special meetings for their specific ethnic or cultural group. Specific meetings can be facilitated by involving parents and guardians in setting the agenda, contacting other parents to attend the meeting, and including community leaders from the ethnic or cultural group as presenters and discussion facilitators (McKeown, 1998).

The handbook *Involving Immigrant and Refugee Families in Their Children's Schools: Barriers, Challenges, and Successful Strategies*, published by the Illinois State Board of Education (2003), suggests the following strategies for involving immigrant and refugee parents:

- Translate whenever possible
- Offer orientation sessions
- Write and distribute bilingual parent handbooks
- Develop welcome videos
- Mentor new families
- Conduct home visits
- Draw on the strengths of the minority parents
- Partner with other programs and agencies in the community
- Provide on-site adult ELL classes
- Vary the time of day or day of the week of parent activities
- Host social events

- Provide in-service training for school personnel
- Gain the principal's support

It is imperative that we realize the vast difference in power that exists between those who operate schools and the families of communities who are not members of the dominant culture. It is essential that school personnel find ways to share power and influence by supplementing traditional methods for involving parents and guardians with ways that are suggested by members of the community.

PAUSE & CONSIDER 5.4

If you work in a school with specialists who serve English language learners, meet with one or more of the specialists and discuss methods they have learned that provide assistance for family members of ELL students. Join a group of four colleagues or classmates and share the methods you have found.

ASSESSING PARENT CONTACTS

Awareness is almost always the first step in changing one's behavior. Before deciding whether to take the time and risks involved in trying new behaviors, most people choose to examine their present behavior. Activity 5.1 provides you with an opportunity to examine your current parent contacts or those used by a teacher in whose class you are working. It also offers several ideas for systematically improving these contacts.

SUMMARY

Teachers often underestimate the power parents give to teachers. Teachers provide parents with input concerning how intelligent and skilled their children are and how well they are getting along with others. These are extremely important facts to almost all parents. Indeed, the defensiveness you may experience when working with parents of children who are struggling in school is in large part because of the importance parents place on the information you are giving them and the difficulty they have accepting negative information about their children. Given the intensity of feelings that may exist as parents and teachers interact and the importance of positive interaction and support between teachers and students' caregivers, schools want to do everything possible to facilitate these positive relationships. Figure 5.17, provides an outline that Joyce Epstein, a leader in researching and developing school/family/community support, has created to highlight six areas in which school staff can positively engage families.

Because information about their children's school progress is so important to parents, it is necessary that this information be shared on a regular basis. As teachers, we can establish more positive, more supportive teacher–parent relationships when we initially inform parents about the curriculum, instruction, and classroom management to which their children will be exposed. This information needs to be followed by periodic updates about classroom activities and student progress. In addition, any time a student begins to have an academic or behavioral problem, we should contact the parents as soon as it appears that the matter cannot be quickly and smoothly resolved between us and the student.

Type 1 Parenting	Type 2 Communicating	Type 3 Volunteering	Type 4 Learning at Home	Type 5 Decision Making	Type 6 Collaborating with Community
Help all families establish home environments to support children as students.	Design effective forms of school-to-home and home-to-school communications about school programs and children's progress.	Recruit and organize parent help and support.	Provide information and ideas to families about how to help students at home with homework and other curriculum-related activities, decisions, and planning.	Include parents in school decisions, developing parent leaders and representatives.	Identify and integrate resources and services from the community to strengthen school programs, family practices, and student learning and development.
Sample Practices	**Sample Practices**	**Sample Practices**	**Sample Practices**	**Sample Practices**	**Sample Practices**
Suggestions for home conditions that support learning at each grade level	Conferences with every parent at least once a year, with follow-ups as needed	School and classroom volunteer program to help teachers, administrators, students, and other parents	Information for families on skills required for students in all subjects at each grade	Active PTA/PTO or other parent organizations, advisory councils, or committees (e.g., curriculum, safety, personnel) for parent leadership and services	Information for students and families on community health, cultural, recreational, social support, and other programs or services
Workshops, videos, computerized phone messages on parenting and child rearing at each age and grade level	Language translators to assist families as needed	Parent room or family center for volunteer work, meetings, and resources for families	Information on homework policies and how to monitor and discuss schoolwork at home	Independent advocacy groups to lobby and work for school reform and improvements	Information on community activities that link to learning skills and talents, including summer programs for students
Parent education and other courses or training for parents (e.g., GED, college credit, family literacy)	Weekly or monthly folders of student work sent home for review and comments	Annual postcard survey to identify all available talents, times, and locations of volunteers	Information on how to assist students to improve skills on various class and school assessments	District-level councils and committees for family and community involvement	Service integration through partnerships involving school; civic, counseling, cultural, health, recreational, and other agencies and organizations; and businesses
Family support programs to assist families with health, nutrition, and other services	Parent/student pickup of report card with conferences on improving grades	Class parent, telephone tree, or other structures to provide all families with needed information	Regular schedule of homework that requires students to discuss what they are learning in class	Information on school or local elections for school representatives	
Home visits at transition points to preschool and elementary, middle, and high schools	Regular schedule of useful notices, memos, phone calls, newsletters, and other communications	Parent patrols or other activities to aid safety and operation of school programs	Calendars with activities for parents and students at home	Networks to link all families with parent representatives	Service to the community by students, families, and schools (e.g., recycling, art, music, drama, and other activities for seniors or others)
Neighborhood meetings to help families understand schools and to help schools understand families	Clear information on choosing schools or courses, programs, and activities within schools		Family math, science, and reading activities at school		
	Clear information on all school policies, programs, reforms, and transitions		Summer learning packets or activities		Participation of alumni in school programs for students
			Family participation in setting student goals each year and in planning for college or work		

FIGURE 5.17
EPSTEIN'S FRAMEWORK OF SIX TYPES OF INVOLVEMENT AND SAMPLE PRACTICES
Source: From "School/family/community partnerships: Caring for the children we share," by J. L. Epstein, 1995, *Phi Delta Kappan, 76*, pp. 701–712. Reprinted with permission.

Teacher–parent contacts can be time consuming and, like all aspects of our profession, require practice before we become comfortable and adept at them. They can, however, be among the most rewarding aspects of our teaching experiences and can have a significant impact on the most important and rewarding aspect of our job—seeing improvement in the quality of student behavior and learning.

IMPLEMENTATION ACTIVITIES

ACTIVITY 5.1

Assessing and Improving Parent Contacts

Assessing Your Parent Contacts

To assess the current level of your contact with parents, answer these questions:

1. How many informational letters have you sent out to every parent so far this year? _____
2. What percentage of your students' parents has received a positive phone call about their child's work or behavior? _____
3. What percentage of your students' parents has received a positive note about their child's work or behavior? _____
4. How many students in your class are experiencing what you would define as significant academic or behavior problems? _____
5. How many parents of these students have you talked to about the problem and your approach to dealing with it? _____

6. How many parents have served as volunteers in your classroom this year? _____
7. How many hours a week is a parent present in your classroom? _____

Improving Your Parent Contacts

1. Send an informational letter to your students' parents. After two weeks, evaluate this effort by answering these questions:
   a. How many parents made a positive comment about the letter? _____
   b. How many students said something positive about the letter? _____
   c. List two advantages to sending the letter:
      1. _____
      2. _____
   d. List any disadvantages associated with sending the letter.

2. Over a two-week period, send a positive note home with each child in your class. After two weeks, evaluate this effort by answering these questions:
   a. How many parents made a positive comment about the note? _____
   b. How many students said something about the note? _____
   c. List two advantages to sending the note:
      1. _____
      2. _____
   d. List any disadvantages associated with sending the note.

RECOMMENDED READING

Christenson, S., & Sheridan, S. (2001). *Schools and families: Creating essential connections for learning.* New York, NY: Guilford Press.

Dietz, M. (Ed.). (1997). *School, family, and community: Techniques and models for successful collaboration.* Gaithersburg, MD: Aspen.

Digman, C., & Soan, S. (2008). *Working with parents: A guide for education professionals.* Thousand Oaks, CA: Sage.

Dodd, A., & Konzal, J. (1999). *Making our high schools better. How parents and teachers can work together.* New York, NY: St. Martin's Press.

Epstein, J., Coates, L., Salinas, K., Sanders, M., & Simon, B. (1997). *School, family, and community partnerships: Your handbook for action.* Thousand Oaks, CA: Sage.

Fuller, M., & Olsen, G. (2007). *Home-school relations: Working successfully with parents and families* (3rd ed.). Boston, MA: Allyn & Bacon.

Ginsberg, M. (2007). Lessons at the kitchen table. *Educational Leadership, 64,* 56–61.

Illinois State Board of Education. (2003). Involving immigrant parents and refugee families in their children's schools: Barriers, challenges and successful strategies. Retrieved from www.brycs.org/documents/upload/InvolvingFamilies.pdf.

Johnson, V. (1996). *Family center guidebook*. Baltimore, MD: Center on Families, Communities, Schools and Children's Learning, Johns Hopkins University.

Kidalgo, N., Bright, J., Siu, S., Swap, S., & Epstein, J. (1995). Research on families, schools, and communities: A multicultural perspective. In J. Banks (Ed.), *Handbook of research on multicultural education* (pp. 498–524). New York, NY: Macmillan.

Lareau, A., & Horvat, E. (1999). Moments of social inclusion and exclusion: Race, class, and cultural capital in family–school relationships. *Sociology of Education, 72*, 37–53.

Mariconda, B. (2003). *Easy and effective ways to communicate with parents: Practical techniques and tips for parent conferences, open houses, notes home, and more that work for every situation*. New York, NY: Scholastic Books.

Moll, L., Amanti, D., Neff, D., & Gonzalez, N. (1992). Funds of knowledge for teaching: Using a qualitative approach to connect homes to schools. *Theory into Practice, 31*, 132–141.

Payne, R. (2005). *Working with parents: Building relationships for student success*. Highlands, TX: aha! Process.

Reyes, P., Scribner, J., & Scribner, A. (Eds.). (1999). *Lessons from high-performing Hispanic schools: Creating learning communities*. New York, NY: Teachers College Press.

Roberts, W. (2007). *Working with parents of bullies and victims*. Thousand Oaks, CA: Corwin.

Roderick, T. (2001). *A school of our own: Parents, power, and community at the East Harlem block schools*. New York, NY: Teachers College Press.

Rudney, G. (2005). *Every teacher's guide to working with parents*. Thousand Oaks, CA: Corwin.

Turnbull, A., & Turnbull, H. (1996). *Families, professionals, and exceptionality: A special partnership*. Upper Saddle River, NJ: Merrill.

U.S. Department of Education. (1994). *Strong families, strong schools: Building community partnerships for learning*. Washington, DC: Author.

U.S. Department of Education. (1997). *Achieving the goals: Goal 8, parental involvement and participation*. Washington, DC: Author.

U.S. Office of Educational Research and Improvement. (1997). *A guide to community programs to prevent youth violence for parents/about parents*. Washington, DC: U.S. Department of Education.

Villa, R., & Thousand, J. (2000). *Restructuring for caring and effective education*. Baltimore, MD: Brookes.

CHAPTER 6

DEVELOPING STANDARDS FOR CLASSROOM BEHAVIOR AND METHODS FOR MAXIMIZING ON-TASK STUDENT BEHAVIOR

Although the rules and procedures used by effective classroom managers vary from teacher to teacher, we do not find effectively managed classrooms operating without them.

—Edmund Emmer, Carolyn Evertson, Julie Sanford, Barbara Clements,
and Murray Worsham (1981)

Until students are allowed to have and begin to feel a proprietary interest in school and classroom rules, classroom control and a good learning environment will always be at risk.

—Forrest Gathercoal (2004)

The most effective approaches to school-based prevention of antisocial behavior are proactive and instructive—planning ways to avoid failure and coercive struggles regarding both academic and social behavior and actively teaching students more adaptive, competent ways of behaving.

—James Kauffman (2001)

In their synthesis of forty classroom management studies, Evertson and Harris (1992) noted that effective classroom management included the dual functions of planning well-organized, engaging lessons and ensuring on-task student behavior by teaching students classroom procedures to facilitate smooth implementation of lessons and making management decisions that enhanced on-task behaviors. Studies indicate that the amount of time students are engaged in instructional activities varies from less than 50 percent in some classes to more than 90 percent in others. Recent research has supported this earlier research synthesis (Freiberg & Lapointe, 2006). This chapter helps you increase the time students spend actively engaged in learning. More effective teachers use their management time wisely and thereby enhance the time available for instruction and monitoring student work.

The first part of this chapter presents the methods effective teachers use at the beginning of the school year. The text emphasizes strategies for developing general rules and ensuring that all students learn such key classroom procedures as what to do during the first few minutes of class, how to request assistance with seatwork, when it is appropriate to talk, and how to request permission to leave the room. It is essential that students understand the expectations educators have regarding school behavior. Many students live in homes where behavior standards differ somewhat from those expected in most schools. Behavior standards in schools are typical of what one would find in most white-collar-job settings such as a bank, but may differ considerably from what one might expect in some work environments and in social settings among family and friends of many different cultures. Many of his colleagues would be surprised, and even upset, by the bantering and putdowns that characterized family gatherings attended by one of the authors, and would certainly not expect to see these behaviors displayed at a faculty meeting. Students need to know that the behaviors they use outside of school are not wrong or unacceptable for those situations. Likewise, students need to know and be taught the behaviors that are expected in school and to understand why these behaviors are viewed as desirable in this particular work setting.

The second major section of this chapter describes strategies that effective teachers use when presenting material to students and monitoring students' seatwork. Researchers have demonstrated that use of these strategies is associated with high rates of on-task student behavior and great academic achievement. The authors have occasionally been informed that including a section on teacher behaviors that facilitate a smooth flow to the classroom moves away from the student-centered nature of the text and presents a different focus on classroom management. Marzano's (2003) analysis of classroom management research indicated that the only factor more impactful than the teacher–student relationship was what he labeled "mind set," and the most significant factor within this category was "withitness"—one of the initial findings regarding teacher behavior that helps create a smooth-flowing classroom. Indeed, the research and associated teacher skills presented in the second half of this chapter are essential for creating a classroom environment that is safe and respectful for all students.

LEARNING GOALS

After reading this chapter, you will know:

1. How to create behavior expectations and standards in your classroom that will support a safe, positive learning environment
2. The difference between standards, rules, and key procedures that will allow your classroom to operate more smoothly
3. How to structure the beginning of a school year in order to maximize positive student behavior
4. Classroom management methods that prevent disruptive student behavior and support the smooth implementation of effective lessons

Why Are These Goals Important?

The methods teachers use to develop classroom behavior standards and the strategies they implement to maintain a smooth flow in the classroom are key factors associated with creating a positive learning community. These methods are a centerpiece of preventing classroom behavior problems.

Extensive research clearly indicates the benefits of helping students understand and accept school and classroom behavior standards. Among schools in which classroom and schoolwide behavior expectations are taught, practiced, and retaught when students fail to follow these clear guidelines, there is a significant reduction in classroom disruptions and office referrals for behaviors that violate the rights of others.

Although this book emphasizes practical methods, we believe it is important for you, as a professional, to understand the research that supports recommendations we make and methods you will implement. The initial research related to beginning the school year by creating behavior standards within the classroom occurred at the Research and Development Center for Teacher Education at the University of Texas at Austin (Emmer et al., 1980; Evertson & Emmer, 1982a). This research clearly indicates that effective classroom managers at both the elementary and junior high school levels spend time teaching students classroom rules and procedures. Emmer and colleagues (1981) described *rules* as "written rules which are either posted in the classroom, given to students on ditto or other copy, or copied by students into their notebooks" (pp. 18, 19). *Procedures* were defined as, "Procedures, like rules, are expectations for behavior. They usually apply to a *specific* activity, and they usually are directed at accomplishing, rather than forbidding some behavior" (p. 19). Effective teachers do more than post rules or present procedures. Teachers work with students to ensure that they understand and can demonstrate rules and procedures.

The initial studies involving teacher behavior at the beginning of the school year were correlational; teachers whose students made greater achievement gains were observed establishing rules and procedures, and carefully monitoring student work. Following these discoveries, however, studies were conducted to determine whether teachers trained in the materials such as those presented in this chapter were more effective in increasing student on-task behavior and learning than were teachers who did not receive this training and implement these new teacher behaviors. Results from these studies clearly demonstrate that providing training in these methods can lead to changes in teacher behaviors that are associated with improved student behavior. Carolyn Evertson has continued this pioneer work with her Classroom Organization and Management Program (COMP) (Evertson & Harris, 1999; Evertson & Smithey, 2000).

Studies by Jerome Freiberg (1999), Ron Nelson (Nelson, Crabtree, Marchand-Martella, & Martella, 1998), and the Positive Behavioral Support work (Lewis & Newcomer, 2005; Lewis, Newcomer, Trussell, & Richter, 2006) have reinforced the importance of teaching desired behavior and establishing agreed-on behavior standards. Recent proponents of the benefits of studying the human brain in order to develop and validate best practices in teaching also provide support for the benefits of classroom structures. These writers (Jensen, 2008; Sylwester, 2000; Willis, 2010b) discuss the importance of having well-organized, smooth-flowing, safe classroom settings that reduce student stress and where students can focus their energy on their academic work. Developing clear behavior expectations is one method for meeting these goals.

Several words of caution are in order before discussing approaches to establishing productive classroom rules and procedures. Rules and procedures should be developed in conjunction with teaching strategies that enhance active and meaningful student engagement in the learning process, relate to students' cultural backgrounds and interests, and help develop students' higher-level thinking skills. The educational exchange must function effectively in both directions. Students can be expected to support rules and procedures that enhance learning only if the learning process is respectful of students and their needs.

Several years ago, one of us was consulting with a middle school and sat in on the principal's initial address to the faculty. During his presentation, the principal informed the teachers that research supported that all teachers should develop their classroom rules

© Scott Masear

within the first day of class and he expected this to occur in each classroom. When the author had an opportunity to talk to the principal, he informed the principal that no research indicated the establishment of classroom rules needed to occur the first day of class. Indeed, if every teacher did this on the first day and students met with six teachers, students might become very frustrated by repeated focus on behavior. In addition, the first few days of school are often characterized by very appropriate student behavior as students "check out" their new environment. This is a good time to focus on community building (Chapter 4) and implementing methods that will help all students believe this will be an exciting and successful school year (Chapter 5). While it will be necessary to teach several key procedures that will facilitate the smooth flow of classroom or schoolwide activities, the creation of general classroom behavior standards can usually wait several days or even until there is some indication these need to be discussed and established.

Another word of caution concerns the cultural context of classroom and school behavioral expectations. As Lisa Delpit (1995) noted in her book *Other People's Children: Cultural Conflict in the Classroom*, the definition of desirable or appropriate behavior is socially constructed and determined by those who have power in the environment. Anyone who has played baseball or softball might find the expectations in the sport of cricket quite unusual and uncomfortable. Similarly, students whose backgrounds are not White, middle-class homes and communities may find the behavior standards in many classrooms to be somewhat foreign and not respectful of their cultural heritage. Delpit notes that if school staff decide on what is appropriate "workplace" behavior within a school, it is imperative for them to help students understand these standards and to work with students to make the transition to using these behaviors in the school setting. The methods presented in this chapter are not only based on the best current research, but they are also intended to be culturally sensitive by helping students understand and take part in their development and by teaching skills that provide all students with a safe and supportive classroom learning environment.

As discussed throughout this chapter and the remainder of the book, there are two primary reasons educators must establish and monitor behavior standards. First, student learning is dramatically related to the creation of a safe climate in which everyone is treated with dignity. Second, students benefit from learning about their rights as citizens and seeing that these rights and their dignity are upheld and fostered in the school environment.

Rules should provide guidelines or benchmarks that help students examine their behaviors and consider the effects on themselves and others. Consequently, behaviors that violate accepted rules should be dealt with by discussing them with students. When dealing with unproductive behavior, teachers must help students examine both their motivations and the consequences of their actions. Overemphasis on reinforcement and punishment often obscures the issue of motivation and attitude and simultaneously limits students' attention to the immediate negative consequences of the behavior. This pressure tends to limit thoughtful consideration of either the effect the behavior has on others or the long-term consequences associated with continuing the behavior. In a real sense, a reinforcement/punishment orientation reinforces a low level of moral development and does not help students develop a higher, more socially valuable level of morality.

DEVELOPING GENERAL BEHAVIOR STANDARDS OR RULES

For many students, the expectations regarding what is desirable behavior in a classroom setting may differ from what is expected in many other areas of their lives. It is important that students realize that the expectations educators hold regarding behavior at school does not mean these behaviors are necessarily better or worse than many other behaviors, only that these behaviors are necessary for effective learning within a school community. It helps students to understand these behavior expectations are what might be expected in most white-collar work environments such as a bank, medical facility, or many other businesses.

When discussing behavior standards, we have some concern about using the term *rules*. The term suggests a compliance orientation to classroom management, whereas, as presented throughout this book, we believe the goals of education and the needs of students are better served by working with students to create a sense of shared community. Therefore, it might be more effective to replace the word *rules* with words such as *behavior standards* or *norms*. Because we believe the process is far more important than the terminology, and because the term *rules* is used by many schools and better understood by younger children, throughout this chapter we variously use terms such as *rules*, *behavior standards*, *norms*, and *behavior expectations* to describe the agreements teachers and students make regarding the types of behaviors that help make a classroom a safe community of support.

It is interesting that, after years of research and a number of models emphasizing instructing students in behavior expectations, many students still attend classrooms in which behavior standards are not clearly developed. In a study of middle school students, nearly half of the students indicated their teachers had not developed clear classroom rules and did not clearly explain how the teacher would respond when a student disrupted the classroom (Wentzel, Battle, & Cusick, 2000). Similarly, many secondary teachers choose not to develop a set of behavior standards—perhaps assuming their students already know and accept these standards. However, a study involving interviews with high school students serving detention for behavior problems suggested that students needed and benefited from classroom behavior standards and that these were most effective when they involved three to five positively and clearly stated rules (Thorson, 2003).

Figure 6.1 outlines the steps in working with students to develop classroom behavior standards. The remainder of this section provides specific ideas for implementing each of these steps. Whenever significant variations are recommended for high school settings, they are included.

1. Discuss the value of having behavior standards
2. Develop a list of the standards (3–6 rules)
   a. Positively state standards
   b. Clearly differentiate/separate rules from procedures
   c. Teach the concept of "time, place, and manner"
3. Obtain a commitment to the standards
   a. Have students sign this commitment
   b. Decide if anyone else should sign and commit to supporting these standards
4. Monitor and review the standards
   a. Determine how new students will be involved in understanding and committing to these standards
   b. Review these standards when behavior problems increase or at times you expect students may need a preventive review (prior to having a substitute teacher, following major holidays, etc.)

FIGURE 6.1
STEPS IN DEVELOPING CLASSROOM BEHAVIOR STANDARDS

PAUSE & CONSIDER 6.1

Pause for a moment and think about situations you have experienced with large numbers of people. Were you ever frustrated when individuals pushed in front of you, cut you off in traffic, or otherwise failed to demonstrate thoughtful, civil behavior? At these times, did you consider that the environment would have felt safer and more healthful had all individuals followed guidelines that helped everyone meet his or her needs? Write a short statement about what you believe are the benefits and costs of having behavior standards within a group setting. Discuss this with a group of colleagues or classmates.

Discussing the Value of Behavior Standards

The first step in developing classroom rules is to discuss with students why it is important to develop standards all members of the class agree to follow. You may want to introduce or stimulate the discussion by asking students why adults have rules such as obeying traffic signals, paying taxes, and not crowding in lines. Throughout this discussion, reinforce the concept that the classroom group and the school are a society and, like larger societal groups, will function more effectively when people agree to behavior standards that help to ensure a safe, caring environment. Help students understand how rules benefit people who must work together. This topic places the focus clearly on the advantages each student derives from class members' accepting those standards. For example, students may state that rules are important because if everyone did whatever they wanted, the classroom might become too disruptive for effective studying.

In discussing behavior standards for the classroom, teachers must be aware that "definitions and expectations of appropriate behavior are culturally influenced, and conflicts are likely to occur when teachers and students come from different cultural backgrounds" (Weinstein, Tomlinson-Clarke, et al., 2004, p. 26). In addition, as Delpit (1995) notes in *Other People's Children: Cultural Conflict in the Classroom*, those who have less power often feel blindsided and manipulated by those who make the rules and wield the power. She states that it is imperative that teachers, who primarily represent White, middle-class values and styles, clearly communicate expectations to students whose own values and personal styles may be quite different than those expected in the classroom. Delpit discusses five components of power:

> (a) issues of power are enacted in classrooms; (b) there are codes or rules for participating in power; that is, there is a "culture of power"; (c) the rules of the culture of power are a reflection of the rules of the culture of those who have power; (d) if you are not already a participant in the culture of power, being told explicitly the rules of that culture makes acquiring power easier; and (e) those with power are frequently least aware of—or least willing to acknowledge—its existence. Those with less power are often most aware of its existence. (p. 24)

In his book *Judicious Discipline*, Forrest Gathercoal (2004) presents what we believe is a very thoughtful way to assist students in understanding the reason for having clear behavior expectations. His approach emphasizes the value of helping students understand their constitutional rights and the fact that rules exist to ensure that no one has these rights denied. In addition to teaching students about their constitutional rights, Gathercoal introduces students to the concept that a person's constitutional rights do not include the right to violate the rights of others. This concept, which Gathercoal calls "compelling state interests," states that students are denied their individual rights only when their actions seriously affect the welfare of others. Gathercoal notes that students cannot violate the following rights of the majority:

HEALTH AND SAFETY

Students do not have the right to act in a manner that infringes on the physical or psychological safety of others. Therefore, a student does not have the right to engage in harassment, bullying, fighting, or running in the halls.

PROPERTY LOSS AND DAMAGE

All students and staff have the right to work in an environment in which property is not stolen or damaged. One's freedom of expression, therefore, does not permit someone to write graffiti on walls or to take something from someone else.

LEGITIMATE EDUCATIONAL PURPOSE

Teachers have the right to select instructional materials, assess student learning, ask that students be on time, and so on.

SERIOUS DISRUPTION OF THE LEARNING PROCESS

Although students' freedom of speech and due process rights guarantee them the right to express frustration or disagreement with a wide range of issues related to school, they cannot express themselves in a manner that seriously disrupts the learning of others.

Gathercoal notes a major advantage of developing behavior standards based on constitutional law rather than teacher or school values:

> A shared knowledge of constitutional principles allows objectivity because educators themselves are not personally identified with the rules. When personal biases are used as the basis for rules and decisions, educators are more likely to interpret rule violations as violations against them personally. This often leads to an adversarial relationship. On the other hand, educators are far more successful with misbehaving students when those students feel they are working together with someone trying to help them understand and find ways to live within society's reasonable expectations. (F. Gathercoal, personal communication, October 1996)

Students and parents are more likely to accept the necessity for behavioral standards when they understand that these standards are derived not from the teacher's biases but from constitutional and case law. Most teachers have had a parent tell their child that in order to defend herself or himself or to retaliate, it is acceptable to hit another student. Although physical violence may be permitted in their homes, these parents and students need to know that this conduct violates another student's basic human rights and will not be allowed to occur in a school setting.

Students' statements on why it is important to develop classroom rules can be written on a large piece of butcher paper to be saved for later discussion should the group have difficulty in following its rules. A major reason Gathercoal's model is so effective is it provides a clear rationale to help students understand why behaviors that may not be expected or valued in their lives outside of school are desired and required in a school setting.

In elementary schools, the use of books that discuss the value of behavior standards is another approach to helping students understand the benefits of having these standards. Books such as *Officer Buckle and Gloria* (Rathman, 1995); *No, David!* (Shannon, 1998); *A Kingdom with No Rules, No Laws, and No King* (Stiles, n.d.); and *If Everybody Did* (Stover, 1989) can engage children in better appreciating the benefits of having classroom behavior standards.

Developing a List

The next step in developing functional behavior standards for the classroom is to have students list all standards they believe are important. Students may be asked to describe "the way we want to act in our classroom so it is a good place for everyone to learn." During this stage, encourage the students to state standards in a positive manner. If a student states, "Don't talk while others are talking," help the student rephrase this as "Listen quietly while another person is talking." Similarly, "Students should not steal from each other, the teacher, or the school" could be restated as "If you need something, ask to borrow it" or "respect property rights." Once the students and you have completed the list of standards or rules, help them cross out any that do not apply and combine as many as possible.

Gathercoal (2004) recommends having students develop a rule to cover each of the compelling state interest rights that must be protected. Figure 6.2 presents a list of rules students might develop to ensure that students' rights are protected. When developing such a list with young children, teachers can increase students' understanding by discussing, role-playing, and initially displaying (pictorially or in writing) several specific behavioral examples of following and violating each rule. Activity 6.1 (at the end of the chapter) offers you an opportunity to practice developing classroom rules that would be appropriate and effective with the students with whom you work.

Another approach to developing classroom behavior standards involves creating a circle labeled "Behaviors that respect community members' physical and psychological well-being, property, and ability to learn" and having students list behaviors that go inside and outside this circle. Yet another method involves having all students list several hopes or goals for the year. Students share these and then discuss which student behaviors will allow these hopes and goals to become a reality. This can be made into a list of behaviors of five or six positively stated general classroom norms that will support all students in reaching their goals. In an elementary or middle school homeroom, where students spend more time together, this can be expanded by putting each student's picture and goals on a bulletin board, and placing the general norms that are selected to support these goals in the center of these pictures.

Secondary teachers may not want to develop a separate list for five or six classes. Some teachers prefer to present their own behavior expectations and ask students in each class to discuss and edit them. The teacher can then combine the various classes' editorial comments and present the edited version to all classes the next day. We work with several secondary teachers who have their students generate a list of participant behaviors that must exist in order to have a productive learning environment. The teacher consolidates these into a list entitled, "Behaviors to which we commit in

FIGURE 6.2
CLASSROOM RULES
CONSISTENT WITH
ENSURING
STUDENTS'
"COMPELLING
STATE INTERESTS"

Health and safety
Treat each other politely and kindly.
Property loss and damage
Treat school and personal property respectfully.
Legitimate educational purpose
Follow reasonable teacher requests.
Be prepared for class.
Make a good effort and ask for help if you need it.
Serious disruption of the educational process
Solve problems nonviolently.

order to have a productive learning environment." The key is that students understand why these standards must exist and that students have a role in discussing these behavior expectations.

Gathercoal (2004) presents another very useful concept when he notes that all behavior needs to be evaluated by examining time, place, and manner. Most behavior is appropriate at some time, in some place, and if done in a particular manner. For example, talking with peers during cooperative learning is desirable behavior, whereas talking during the test that follows is usually inappropriate (time). Boxing is an Olympic sport but is at no time appropriate in a classroom or hallway setting (place). Likewise, although it is appropriate to politely request clarification regarding a teacher's particular instructional decision, it is not appropriate to stand up in the back of the room and announce, "This material stinks!" (manner).

Many students believe numerous adult decisions are not only arbitrary but are actually intended to frustrate and demean students. When students learn that adults are not stating that student behaviors are "bad" but rather that they must stand the test of time, place, and manner, students often have a much different reaction to limits teachers set in a school environment. When working as a junior high school vice principal, one of us happened upon two students in an embrace in a school hallway. He found it much more effective to say, "Please consider time and place," rather than confronting them with the fact that adults did not want them embracing. Almost all students accept redirection when it makes sense to them and can be stated in a manner that treats them with dignity.

Getting a Commitment

When the final list of rules has been developed, you can lead a discussion to clarify each rule and ask students to indicate whether they can accept the behavior standard. During this important stage, several students may state that they do not believe they can abide by a particular rule. You can then ask the students whether the rule seems to be one that does not help people or whether they agree that it is a good rule but do not believe they can consistently act in accordance with it. If they express the latter, you can explain that they are not expected to be able to act perfectly all the time. Just as they will improve their academic content knowledge, they will also learn how to behave in ways that are more effective. The initial question is not whether the students can already solve all their math problems or consistently behave appropriately, but whether they believe that these skills are helpful to them and if they will attempt to improve these skills. If the students state that a rule is not acceptable, you can help them clarify why they believe it to be undesirable. In most cases, students will quickly acknowledge the basic value of the rule. If one or more students persist in stating that a rule is unacceptable, however, you have the option of deleting the rule or asking to postpone further discussion of the item until you have had an opportunity to discuss it with the small group of students who disagree.

A number of teachers have their students take the list of rules home (usually with an accompanying statement about how the teacher will handle persistent rule violations) for parents to sign and return. This strategy is particularly useful when working with intermediate and middle school students or a group of students who a teacher expects may have difficulty consistently demonstrating responsible behavior. The fact that everyone responsible for the students' behaviors understands the rules and consequences can have a positive effect on their behaviors and can minimize the confusion and tension associated with instances when parents must be contacted about a student's inappropriate behavior.

When sending a list of rules and consequences home, it is important to include a general philosophy statement about your classroom management and instruction. This lets you present the issue of rules in a positive manner that indicates their relationship to effective instruction and student learning. For example, your statement might begin:

> It is my job as a teacher to work with students to create a classroom environment that helps all students learn and encourages mutual respect and cooperation among students and adults. I have worked with the students to create a list of rules and procedures that will guide our behaviors. Because I know you share my deep concern for the quality of your child's learning, I would appreciate your discussing the attached material with your child, signing it, and returning it to me by _____. I look forward to working with your child and to communicating with you concerning his or her progress, special achievements, and any concerns that may arise.

One of us worked with a talented secondary teacher who, along with her ninth-grade students, developed the student and teacher expectations shown in Figure 6.3. In addition to

---

Class Expectations

Mrs. Brown

English Department

Student Expectations

1. Treat others politely and with respect
2. Treat your school and personal property with respect
3. Follow teacher requests
4. Be prepared for class
   - Attend regularly and on time (ready to learn when music stops)
   - Have paper, pen, notebook, text, and other required materials
   - Take responsibility for any missed work
   - Turn in assignments on time
5. Make a good effort at your work and request help when you need it
   - Complete all your work *to the best of your abilities*
   - Seek out teacher assistance during Academic Support

Teacher Expectations

1. Create a fair and safe classroom atmosphere in which students will feel free to share their ideas and ask questions
2. Maintain an environment conducive to learning (limited distractions)
3. Discover and work toward improving individual students' strengths
4. Be available to students before and after school for extra help
5. Work toward making learning not only interesting but also meaningful beyond the classroom

I have read the course expectations and syllabus.

Student signature _____ Date _____

Parent signature _____ Date _____

FIGURE 6.3
CLASSROOM EXPECTATIONS
Source: Based on materials developed by mentor teacher Mary Holmes and intern Barbara Dowdell Brown. Reprinted with permission.

Name: _____
Expectations/Rules Quiz
Class Expectations
Mrs. _____
English Department

Student Expectations

1. Treat others _____ly and with _____

2. Treat your _____ and _____ _____ with respect

3. Follow _____ _____

4. Be _____ for _____
   - Attend regularly and _____ _____ (ready to ___ ___ ___ ___)
   - Have _____, _____, _____, _____, and other required materials
   - Take responsibility for _____ _____ work
   - Turn in _____ on _____

5. Make a good effort at your work and _____ _____ when you need it
   - _____ all your _____ *to the best of your abilities*
   - Seek out _____ _____ during Academic Support

FIGURE 6.4
CLASSROOM EXPECTATIONS QUIZ
Source: Based on materials developed by mentor teacher Mary Holmes and intern Barbara Dowdell Brown. Reprinted with permission.

having the students and their parents or guardians acknowledge their understanding of these guidelines by signing them, the teacher created a quiz to determine whether all students understood the expectations (Figure 6.4). Many high school teachers believe it is not necessary to involve students in this manner. Many high school students view themselves as responsible and may resent methods that remind them of elementary or middle school activities. We have found that the best policy is to discuss the matter with other teachers and students prior to determining how to work with students to develop classroom behavior expectations.

Monitoring and Reviewing Classroom Rules

Once students have developed reasonable rules and agreed to behave in accordance with them, the next step is to help them recognize and monitor their behavior. One approach helpful with primary age children is to have them take turns acting out the rules. Each child can be asked to role-play both the appropriate and inappropriate behaviors, and you can ask their peers to raise their hands whenever the student is behaving appropriately and place their hands in their laps when the student is behaving inappropriately. This activity is helpful in ensuring that every child clearly understands the rules.

Especially in elementary school classrooms, it is important to review the rules frequently for several weeks. A good approach is to review them every day for the first week, three times during the second week, and once a week thereafter. It is also helpful to display the rules in a prominent place in the classroom. During the first week, in an elementary school classroom, discuss the rules briefly at the beginning of each day, and end the day by having the class evaluate their behavior and consider whether improvement in any area is needed. If the entire class consistently displays appropriate behavior or shows considerable improvement over the previous day, you may want to send a positive note home with each student and/or invite the principal to visit and compliment the students. Significant individual improvements can be similarly rewarded.

Classroom rules need to be reviewed with each new student who enters the class. Many students who transfer during the school year come from highly mobile families. Some of these students may have had a pattern of difficulties in school. It is important that these students get off to a good start, which can be facilitated by their knowing the expectations for classroom behavior. A student who has been demonstrating responsible behavior can be assigned to help new students learn classroom rules and procedures.

Rules should also be discussed when a student or the teacher indicates that violation of one or more of the rules is detracting from learning or is infringing on a student's rights. Recently, a secondary school intern teacher met with one of us to express concern about a sophomore class he viewed as very difficult to manage. The intern noted that students talked incessantly while peers were answering questions and that there was a very high rate of put-downs. The intern, who had been skeptical of some of the materials presented in this book, decided that things were going so badly that he had nothing to lose by taking several class periods to discuss the problem with the students and attempt to establish some expectations and procedures for the class. The teacher discussed his concern with the class and allowed them to brainstorm a set of expectations they thought would be realistic. Students edited these as a whole class and signed an agreement to attempt to follow their new expectations. The teacher then asked students to give input on what should occur if students chose to violate these expectations. Students developed the procedures they believed the teacher should follow. The next day, the intern presented a typed copy of the decisions to students and everyone signed it. The expectations and procedures for responding to violations were posted on the wall. The intern commented that he simply could not believe the difference in the class. Indeed, he shared with his colleagues that on the following day, when two of his most disruptive students started to talk out, he simply nodded toward the posted lists and the students nodded their heads and returned to their work.

Creating Rules for the Teacher

After working with students to create behavior standards/expectations/rules for students, teachers may wish to work with students to create specific standards for the teacher. Clearly the teacher will follow all of the standards agreed to by the students, but the teacher plays a unique role in the classroom, and it is helpful to acknowledge this and to discuss that with this authority comes responsibilities. Teachers with whom I have worked have had students list such expectations for the teacher as the following:

- Present material so we can understand it.
- Check to make sure we understand the material before moving on.
- Get to know us and respect our differences.
- Demonstrate you believe all of us can learn.
- Don't embarrass us in class.

Teachers who implement this approach send a clear message to students regarding how much they respect their students and how sincere the teacher is in ensuring that the classroom setting meets students' needs.

Reinforcing Behavior That Supports the Classroom Behavior Norms

In general, we believe the naturally positive teacher–student interactions, high rates of specific feedback, naturally occurring positive notes to caregivers, and engaging lessons are adequate to reinforce students in engaging in behaviors they have selected as desirable and to which they have committed. There are times, however, when it is helpful to provide structured reinforcement to assist students in consistently demonstrating behaviors that support classroom behavior norms. There are many creative methods for reinforcing appropriate classroom behavior. We know teachers who have student "scouts" who are assigned for the day to observe examples of students' following classroom rules and/or being particularly helpful to other students. These examples are shared at the end of the day (or in primary grades prior to lunch and at the end of the day), and students receive a round of applause for their behavior.

We have worked with many teachers who, when they see students' tendency to follow classroom rules slipping, select a word such as *responsible* and write a letter of this word on the white board or butcher paper whenever the entire class is being particularly skilled at following all class rules. When a word or phrase is spelled out, the class celebrates with a preferred activity such as additional read-aloud time, five minutes of extra recess, and so on. We also know teachers who ask an administrator to visit the classroom and acknowledge how student behavior is supporting everyone's learning, and we have worked with teachers who send notes home or have the administrator send a note home sharing this positive information with the students' parents/caregivers. In Chapter 8, we provide more detail on methods for incorporating structured reinforcement systems to encourage students to act responsibly in the classroom.

While there are certainly times when it is helpful to implement reinforcement systems into the classroom, as Alfie Kohn (1999) highlighted in his book *Punished by Rewards: The Trouble with Gold Stars, Incentive Plans, A's, Praise, and Other Bribes*, there are disadvantages to placing too heavy an emphasis on rewarding behavior, especially behavior many students can and would demonstrate without the rewards. One disadvantage that particularly concerns us is that a behavioral approach emphasizing rewards and/or punishments may be used in place of assisting teachers in developing a wide range of the classroom management skills presented in this book. As Ullucci (2009) discovered in a study of highly effective teachers in urban settings, many effective teachers do not use structured reinforcement programs as part of their approach to classroom management.

PAUSE & CONSIDER 6.2

Consider a class you are currently teaching, one you have observed, or one in which you are working. Write a brief statement regarding how behavior standards were developed during the first week of class. Based on what you have just read, what modifications might you make in developing such standards? Share your statement with at least two other colleagues or classmates.

CLASSROOM PROCEDURES

As mentioned earlier in this chapter, research indicates that effective teachers not only work with students to develop general behavior standards (rules) but also teach the procedures they expect students to follow during specific classroom and school activities. This research also provides specific information on the types of classroom activities for which effective teachers develop procedures.

© Scott Masear

"Maybe next time you'll listen when I tell you not to lean back in your chair, Jimmy."

Effective Procedures

Figure 6.5 outlines the major classroom activities for which elementary teachers who are particularly effective managers develop and teach procedures. Appendix A presents a list of specific procedures that might be developed in an elementary school. Strout (2005) suggests creating a grid with procedures listed on the horizontal axis, key classroom areas (e.g., desk, bathroom, sink) listed on the vertical axis, and examples of what these rules would look like for various areas and routine activities listed in the chart.

For secondary school classrooms, researchers have found four key areas in

**FIGURE 6.5
ELEMENTARY
CLASSROOM
PROCEDURES**

I. *Room Areas*
   A. Student desks, tables, storage areas
   B. Learning centers, stations
   C. Shared materials
   D. Teacher's desk, storage
   E. Fountain, sink, bathroom, pencil sharpener
II. *School Areas*
   A. Bathroom, fountain, office, library
   B. Lining up
   C. Playground
   D. Lunchroom
III. *Whole-Class Activities/Seatwork*
   A. Student participation
   B. Signals for student attention
   C. Talk among students
   D. Making assignments
   E. Passing out books, supplies
   F. Turning in work
   G. Handing back assignments
   H. Makeup work
   I. Out-of-seat policies
   J. Activities after work is finished
IV. *Small-Group Activities*
   A. Student movement into and out of group
   B. Bringing materials to groups

(continued)

FIGURE 6.5
(CONTINUED)

    C. Expected behavior of students in group

    D. Expected behavior of students out of group

  V. *Other Procedures*

    A. Beginning of school day

    B. End of school day

    C. Student conduct during delays, interruptions

    D. Fire drills

    E. Housekeeping and student helpers

which effective teachers developed procedures. These are shown in Figure 6.6. Figure 6.7 outlines the areas in which effective classroom managers teach specific procedures related to student accountability for academic work.

A high school example can clarify the concept of procedures. Most high school students have only four or five minutes between classes. Therefore, they usually enter the classroom excited or agitated, having had little time to review what they learned in their previous class or to get mentally prepared for the coming class. The teacher discussed this problem with the students

FIGURE 6.6
SECONDARY
CLASSROOM
PROCEDURES

  I. *Beginning Class*

    A. Roll call, absentees

    B. Tardy students

    C. Behavior during PA

    D. Academic warm-ups or getting-ready routines

    E. Distributing materials

  II. *Instructional Activities*

    A. Teacher–student contacts

    B. Student movement in the room

    C. Signal for student attention

    D. Headings for papers

    E. Student talk during seatwork

    F. Activities to do when work is done

  III. *Ending Class*

    A. Putting away supplies, equipment

    B. Organizing materials for next class

    C. Dismissing class

  IV. *Other Procedures*

    A. Student rules about teacher's desk

    B. Fire drills

    C. Lunch procedures

    D. Bathroom, water fountains

    E. Lockers

**FIGURE 6.7
ACCOUNTABILITY
PROCEDURES**

I. *Work Requirements*
   A. Heading papers
   B. Use of pen or pencil
   C. Writing on back of paper
   D. Neatness, legibility
   E. Incomplete papers
   F. Late work
   G. Missed work
   H. Due dates
   I. Makeup work

II. *Communicating Assignments*
   A. Posting assignments
   B. Requirements/grading criteria for assignments
   C. Instructional groups
   D. Provisions for absentees
   E. Long-term assignments

III. *Monitoring Student Work*
   A. In-class oral participation
   B. Completion of in-class assignments
   C. Completion of homework assignments
   D. Completion of stages of long-term assignments

IV. *Checking Assignments in Class*
   A. Students' exchanging papers
   B. Marking and grading papers
   C. Turning in papers

V. *Grading Procedures*
   A. Determining report card grades
   B. Recording grades
   C. Grading stages of long-term assignments
   D. Extra credit

VI. *Academic Feedback*
   A. Rewards and incentives
   B. Posting student work
   C. Communication with parents
   D. Students' records of their grades

in his class and worked with them to develop procedures for making a smooth transition when entering the classroom. First, the class and the teacher listed warm-up activities for the first four minutes of class. These activities, which changed every month, included:

- An instructional warm-up activity
- Sharing something they had learned in school during the past day
- A relaxation activity

- Listening to music selected by the teacher
- Listening to music selected by the students
- A "brain teaser" activity

Students daily selected the transition activity, each activity being used once each week. The teacher also developed a procedure for tardy students to report to class, a procedure for taking roll, and a signal for gaining the students' attention at the end of the transition activity. Similar procedures were developed for summarizing the day's lesson and leaving the classroom.

Procedures can also include involving students in running the classroom. For years, one of us had her students decide on classroom jobs students could accomplish in order for the classroom to run more smoothly. In addition to such traditional classroom jobs as line leader, caring for pets, running errands, and so forth, students learned to take responsibility for such tasks as starting the school day and assisting substitute teachers. Not only does this create a greater sense of significance, competence, and power for students, but it can also dramatically assist the teacher by having students take responsibility for tasks that may take considerable time away from a teacher's availability for students. Students may need to receive some training to effectively carry out the requirements of their jobs. This can take place during lunch or recess times.

Pause & Consider 6.3

Consider a class you are currently teaching, one you have observed, or one in which you are working. Create a list of ten procedures you believe are among the most important for facilitating a smooth, calm flow in your classroom. You may want to refer to Figures 6.5 through 6.7 for ideas regarding the areas in which procedures exist in your classroom. Join with three or four colleagues and share your procedures. We are virtually certain you will find an appreciative audience and obtain several wonderful ideas for creating a more productive learning environment. In addition, you may want to complete Activity 6.2 at the end of the chapter. It will help you further clarify areas in which you may want to develop classroom procedures.

Teaching and Monitoring Classroom Procedures

A procedure is best taught by:

1. Discussing the need for the procedure
2. Possibly soliciting student ideas
3. Having students practice the procedure until it is performed correctly
4. Reinforcing the correct behavior

When introducing the procedure of developing a signal to obtain students' attention, you might work with the class to develop the signal, set a goal (everyone facing the teacher and quiet within five seconds), use the procedure while students are engaged in an activity, and reinforce them when they respond within the determined time limit. When teaching students how to work effectively in cooperative groups (discussed in detail in Chapter 7), you might discuss how these skills are essential in the workplace, elicit students' ideas for key behaviors that facilitate effective group functioning, have a group of four students demonstrate these to the whole class, and reinforce the new skills as you move around the room when students are working in groups.

Classroom procedures must be carefully monitored during their initial acquisition. Early in the school year, teachers should respond to almost every violation of a rule or procedure. When you notice that the class or an individual student is not correctly following a procedure, the best approach is to ask the student to state the correct procedure and then to demonstrate it. If a class lines up poorly after having once demonstrated the correct procedure, you should politely comment that you know the class can line up more effectively and ask them to return to their seats so that they can practice the procedure. You might then ask students to describe the behaviors associated with lining up correctly and how these benefit students. The class could then be asked to demonstrate their skill and be reinforced for their improved effort. Effectively teaching procedures to students is similar to good athletic coaching. The skilled coach first demonstrates the new procedure—often having the athlete perform the maneuver in slow motion. The athlete is then asked to perform the task and receives feedback on the performance, sometimes in the form of video replay. The coach has the athlete practice until the feat is performed satisfactorily. Later, perhaps under game conditions, if the athlete performs the task incorrectly, the coach reteaches it in a subsequent practice session.

Teaching Students How to Respond When They Experience Frustration, Anxiety, or Anger

Research indicates that teachers place a high priority on students' ability to follow teacher requests and control their emotions (Lane, Pierson, Stang, & Carter, 2010). These authors found that, "All teachers viewed four times as critical: controls temper in conflict situations with peers, controls temper in conflict situations with adults, follows/complies with directions, and attends to your instructions" (p. 171). Therefore, a key procedure that is seldom taught in classrooms is how to respond when experiencing strong emotions. Because students experiencing ongoing and/or serious behavior problems may misinterpret statements and actions as more aggressive and less supportive than they were intended or others might view them, struggle with academics, and experience lower rates of positive teacher statements and more bullying than their counterparts, they more frequently experience confusion, frustration, and anger within school settings. Therefore, while it is helpful for all students to develop strategies for dealing with strong emotions experienced within the school setting, this is particularly important for students experiencing serious behavior problems.

We have found it helpful for all students, but particularly for students experiencing serious and/or persistent classroom behavior problems, for the teacher to work with the class to develop a list of methods they can use when experiencing strong emotions. Figure 6.8 presents a list of methods the authors have taught to students in both general and special education classrooms. As with any general behavior expectation or procedure, it will be important that students practice these behaviors and for students to select specific strategies from this list they will choose to use.

Procedures for Cell Phones

Most high schools prohibit the use of cell phones during the school day (Humble-Thaden, 2011), and courts have consistently supported cell phone bans placed in school codes of conduct (Diamantes, 2010). While this will likely be a standard policy for some years to come, there is increasing interest in using cell phones as an instructional tool (Hlodan, 2010; Kolb, 2011). Students, however, find ways to subvert these rules (Ito et al., 2010). In his study of three high schools, Charles (2012) noted that, "Maria summed up the sentiment across all participants when she stated definitively, 'Everyone basically texts all the time'" (p. 7). Statements made by students involved in this study indicate that some students moderate their use of text messaging based on standards of courtesy, others because texting negatively affects their learning, and still others because the teacher may catch them and impose a sanction. Some students felt if someone was texting during class, other than when a test was in progress, they were simply harming their own learning and had to live

- Silently take three deep breaths
- Think of something that makes you happy
- Think or write down something positive that has happened to you recently
- Silently say something positive about yourself
- Use an object such as a calming rock (a smooth rock with a bend in it that you run your thumb over to calm yourself) that helps you relax
- Think of something positive that will happen if you calm yourself and continue to follow the classroom rules
- Quietly push your desk back about a foot, lower your head, and use one of the methods above
- Lock your hands behind your head and lean backward. Think of something that makes you happy
- Put your hands at your sides and think of warm energy flowing through your body and dripping slowly out of your fingertips
- In your desk/pocket/wallet/purse, keep a picture of something that makes you happy. When you begin to feel upset or angry, pull this out and take a minute to look at it and remember the good feelings you had when this picture was taken.
- Think of something you could ask the teacher to do—help you with the work, let you run an errand, modify the assignment—and raise your hand to get the teacher's attention and make this request
- Write down what is bothering you. If you need to share this with an adult, use the classroom procedure for getting the teacher's attention and share this with him or her.
- Start moving. Go to a prearranged place in the classroom where you can practice breathing, draw something, or use an approved hand exerciser or an approved fidget.
- Use a three-step frustration script.
  - Step 1: Say to yourself, "Stop. I'm getting frustrated."
  - Step 2: Move away from the situation.
  - Step 3: Take action by breathing, notifying the teacher, and writing the problem down for later discussion.

FIGURE 6.8
METHODS FOR CALMING OURSELVES IF WE BECOME FRUSTRATED OR ANGRY

Creating Classroom Behavioral Expectations
For an interactive review of methods for insuring that students will understand, accept, and consistently follow agreed-upon classroom behavior expectations, click on the link below in your Pearson etext.

ENHANCEDetext *interactive case study*

with the consequences. Several teachers in this study believed there needed to be some negotiations with students regarding a complete ban on cell phone use. For example, one teacher mentioned that if a student asked to contact a parent for an important reason, she would rather a student use a cell phone than waste class time to go to the office to make the call. A number of teachers in this study mentioned the importance of being somewhat flexible with students in this area. This is a wonderful example of the types of decisions teachers must make in terms of how they interact with their students around establishing and enforcing behavior expectations.

This issue of using electronic devices provides an opportunity for teachers and students to have an open discussion about the reasons for having policies related to cell phones, situations when exceptions might be made (e.g., a student

"Bill missed rehearsal."

© Scott Masear

needing to make an important call to a caregiver and even, if school policy allows, creating a compromise such as setting aside a brief time [five minutes] when students can either complete some schoolwork or use their cell phones prior to the end of class). As with all behavior expectations, when developing these expectations, it is also important to help students understand the consequences associated with their violating the agreed-upon policies and to be consistent in implementing these consequences. When policies have been clearly discussed, appear respectful of students' legitimate needs, and are understood by students, the acceptance of reasonable consequences in usually very high.

CREATIVE EXAMPLES OF TEACHING AND REVIEWING RULES AND PROCEDURES

Figure 6.9 lists a number of interesting and fun methods for teaching classroom rules and procedures to students.

One of us found that her classroom was becoming quite noisy during an afternoon study period. Despite several clear I-messages (Chapter 8) from the teacher as well as several students, the classroom continued to be unproductively loud during this time. Consequently, at

FIGURE 6.9
CREATIVE WAYS TO
TEACH RULES AND
ROUTINES
Source: Deborah
Johnson, Spokane
Public Schools.
Reprinted with
permission.

1. *Puppet Plays:* Use puppets to role-play responsible behaviors. Have students discuss what was appropriate. Have students identify what behaviors were not appropriate, what rules relate to the behaviors, and what behaviors should have happened instead.
2. *Storytime:* In September, read books to students that teach lessons on following rules and procedures and the rewards from self-discipline.
3. *Posters:* Have students make good behavior, good study habit, safety rules, and other posters for the classroom, school hallways, cafeteria, and so on. Hang them where appropriate to remind students of your expectations.
4. *Letters:* Teach how to write friendly letters. Have students write letters to playground aides, bus drivers, cooks, custodians, the principal, and others regarding the rules and their plans to be self-disciplined in the area of interest to whom the letter is written.
5. *Oops, I Goofed!:* Conduct a class discussion on student experiences when they broke a rule. Have students share a personal experience when they goofed in their behavior. Have students share what they should have done instead. Focus in on the idea that we all make mistakes and it is OK if you learn from the mistake and don't repeat it.

(continued)

FIGURE 6.9
(CONTINUED)

6. *Create a Play:* Have students write and produce a play on rules and procedures. Have students present the play to other classes in the school.

7. *School in Relation to Community Rules:* Have students share how school rules and the reasons for following them relate to community rules and their responsibilities as citizens.

8. *Rule Unscramble:* Have your class/school rules stated in phrases. Mix up the words in the phrase. Have students put the words in correct order so they make sense. Or mix up the letters of the words in a rule and have students put the letters of each word back in order so rules make sense.

9. *Rule Bingo:* Make bingo cards with classroom/school rules listed in each square. Have a student or the teacher act out the rule. Students cover the square if they have the rule listed that is being acted out.

10. *Wrong Way:* Have students role-play the wrong way to behave or follow procedures. Videotape the role-playing and have the whole group review and discuss not only what was done wrong but also how to do it the right way.

11. *Hug or Handshake:* When the teacher or students "catch" others following the rules, ask them if they want a hug or handshake and reward them with their wish.

12. *Contract for Success:* Have students write a letter to their parents listing the rules for the class and their plan for successful behavior and self-discipline for the school year. Have students take the letter home and review it with their parents. All persons sign the Contract for Success. Student returns the contract to school the next day.

13. *Picture Signals:* Have pictures as signals for each classroom rule. For example, ears for the rule "We listen politely" or chair for "Sit correctly in your chair." Then use these pictures to signal students if they are not following the rule. The picture signals allow silent management rather than having to stop teaching to tell students what they are doing wrong.

14. *Rules in the Sack:* Write rules on cards and put them into a paper sack. Have a student draw out a rule from the sack and explain it to the rest of the class.

15. *Hidden Rules:* Fold paper. On the inside write the class rule. On the outside of the folded paper give clues to the rule. Students read clues and guess the rule. They open the folded paper to see if they are correct, this also works well for a bulletin board display.

16. *Numbered Rules:* Give each classroom rule a number. When a student is following a rule correctly, ask students to hold up the number of fingers which related to the rule being followed. Or when teaching rules, give clues for a specific rule and have students hold up the correct number of fingers for the correct numbered rule.

17. *Discrimination:* Develop a list of correct and incorrect behaviors relating to the rules and routines of the classroom and school. Have students read through the list and separate the correct from the incorrect, thus making two lists from the one; use this discrimination activity during a reading class.

18. *Wheel of Fortune:* Adapt the *Wheel of Fortune* game, making your rules the puzzle to be solved. Students guess letters of the puzzle and try to guess the rule in the puzzle.

19. *Awards:* Design certificates or bookmarker awards for classroom rules. Give students the awards when their behaviors reflect appropriate behaviors in relation to the specific rule.

20. *Picture Posters:* Have students bring pictures of themselves to school. Use student pictures on posters to highlight a school rule. "The following students believe it is important to respect all teachers." Show their pictures listing their names and grades. Post the posters throughout the school. Use positive peer pressure for pride in school.

the beginning of the study period the next day, the teacher asked the class to discuss the procedure of maintaining a noise level that was conducive to studying. The class decided that they often became too loud and agreed to reduce their noise level. The teacher decided to provide clear instruction and a visual to assist her fourth- and fifth-grade students in developing skill in appropriate voice levels. Because she taught in a forested area with fire danger signs, she decided the students would enjoy and understand using an information sign color-coded identically to those used to inform campers of the extent of fire danger. Figure 6.10 presents the sign. For several days, prior to each activity, the teacher pointed the arrow to the area at the appropriate voice level and briefly discussed how this would help students learn more effectively. If students began to speak too loudly for the activity, the teacher simply pointed to the sign. After several days, the sign was used somewhat randomly and eventually was taken down. The students had enjoyed the sign and had learned an important procedure.

When, during her first year of teaching, this procedure did not provide enough structure for her high-needs fourth–fifth blended classroom, our daughter used the following technique:

> The Yacker Tracker is a commercially available electronic device we used to monitor the noise levels in our classroom. It was placed in the front of the room and was turned on when students were working on an assignment or project. The Yacker Tracker looks like a stoplight, and I could change the decibel level depending on how loud we as a class had agreed to be during a particular activity. If the green light was on, the students knew they were doing well. When the light started blinking yellow they would self-monitor and ask someone who was talking to please check their noise level. If the device turned red they lost five minutes of their recess and during that recess time we would practice what quiet working looked like and sounded like. Just as training wheels help a child learn how to ride a bike and once taken off the child rides the bike on his/her own, the Yacker Tracker helped my students learn to self-monitor and self-assess their work environment. By the second half of the year we no longer used the device as my students could monitor without having the visual aid. (S. Rudzek, personal communication, October 2005)

When teaching first graders, our daughter discovered that the use of finger puppets is an engaging way to help young children remember classroom and school procedures. One finger puppet is called "Loud Lion." If a child is talking softly and needs to speak up, then "Loud Lion" will pop up as a nonverbal cue to speak louder so everyone can hear what the student is sharing.

FIGURE 6.10
VOICE LEVEL METER

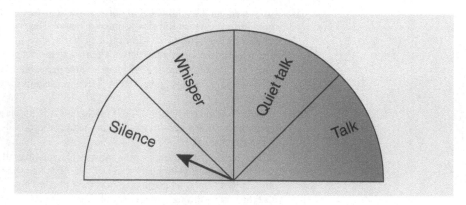

"Quiet Cricket" is used if a child is speaking too loudly. It is a clue for the student to soften his or her voice so everyone can work. "Quiet Cricket" can also be used in the hallway as a reminder for students to follow school expectations regarding quiet voices. If "Quiet Cricket" is raised three times during a walk, students know they will spend the first portion of their next recess practicing how to walk quietly in the halls. Another puppet is called "Picky Pig." If a student is seen picking his or her nose, "Picky Pig" taps the student, who then must go wash his or her hands. These examples can be expanded with any animal and procedure.

Case Study: Dealing with the Dilemma of Gum Chewing

In his thoughtful book *Judicious Discipline*, Forrest Gathercoal presents a marvelous true story about how one administrator handled the issue of gum chewing. Gathercoal (2004) wrote:

> Instead of using gum rules and punishments as a means of teaching obedience, for example, why not approach the matter as an educator would—teach students how to use gum properly. . . . [Students] are far more likely to develop good character and become accountable for their behavior when they are respected as student/citizens capable of learning personal responsibility.
>
> I remember an anecdote an elementary principal shared with me about his experience with "the gum problem." He had been a teacher in his building before being appointed principal and was familiar with the problems they had with gum damage. The custodian was constantly complaining about the wrappers on the floor and gum under the furniture. The punishments for chewing gum were harsh, but the problem continued.
>
> When he became an administrator, one of his first acts was to revise some of the rules. One change in particular reversed the ban on gum chewing. His new plan suggested that the faculty spend some time during the first day of class teaching students how to use gum properly. Teachers instructed their classes in the appropriate way to chew gum, how to wrap it in paper when out of their mouths, where to discard the gum, and how to care for the empty wrapper.
>
> Curious about the effect of this educational approach, a few weeks into the school year the principal asked the custodian if there was a problem with gum in the building. The custodian replied that he was surprised by the fact there was no gum anywhere around school, not even the wrappers on the floor. "I don't know what you did," he said, "but you are the toughest principal we ever had here."
>
> Another three weeks passed. The conversation again surfaced and still no evidence of gum damage was found. "You really are tough," the principal was told. "What did you do?" The principal explained that the old rules were replaced by a more positive educational approach to teaching responsibility. The custodian listened in disbelief and, without a word, walked away shaking his head. (pp. 80, 81)

CAFETERIA

© James Estes

"I always expect her to say 'heel.'"

PAUSE & CONSIDER 6.4

In the classroom in which you are teaching or observing, there are undoubtedly some times when student behavior and the classroom flow detract from valuable instructional time. Take a few minutes to describe a situation in the classroom in which this is the case. Next, try to determine a procedure that would allow the class to flow more smoothly. Share this with several colleagues or classmates. We believe you will discover that, when classroom management problems exist, one of the first and most important things you will learn is to examine and modify classroom procedures.

Case Study: Implementing a Developmental Recess to Reteach Playground Behavior Expectations

A number of years ago, one of us was asked to assist the staff of an elementary school in solving the problems of repeated referrals for disruptive playground behavior. The staff was concerned that their responses to continued misbehavior were not severe enough and wondered if they needed a more progressive approach to disciplining the repeat offenders. The author took two approaches to assisting the staff with their concern. First, the staff involved in playground supervision, along with the schoolwide student management committee, examined data to determine the type and frequency of disruptive playground behavior leading to a referral. This was done to determine whether there were key procedures (such as how to use a particular piece of equipment or how to play a game) that needed to be taught or retaught. The initial intervention involved reteaching (or in some cases simply teaching) the procedures for games where it was discovered a significant number of discipline referrals were occurring. Following this, a developmental recess was implemented.

Developmental recess removes students who have had a designated number of behavior problems on the playground and provides them with an opportunity to learn and practice specific behaviors they are having difficulty displaying on the playground (e.g., how to correctly participate in a particular game, what to do if they are called "out," how to react if they become frustrated with someone or some event, etc.). After demonstrating acceptable behavior for a designated number of days in the developmental recess, the student may return to the normal recess activities. Physical education teachers, parent volunteers, instructional assistants, and principals have staffed this activity.

One of us recently worked with staff who implemented a developmental lunch in which they provided students who had difficulty using acceptable cafeteria manners with an opportunity to learn and practice these behaviors. Figure 6.11 presents an outline of a developmental recess procedure developed by a state director of special education.

Case Study: Teaching Students to Respect Physical Space

One of us worked with school staff whose elementary students were frequently involved in inappropriate (violent or sexual) touch. A staff committee developed a plan for teaching students about individuals' personal space. In a large assembly followed by work in classrooms, students were shown (by a flashlight hanging over a student in a darkened room) that everyone has some physical space. Students were then asked to place yarn on the ground to delineate the physical space they needed in various situations. Students were taught that no student could cross into

FIGURE 6.11
DEVELOPMENTAL
RECESS

The Concept

Developmental recess is one technique for helping children learn the specific skills they need to behave successfully while at recess. Because successful recess experience requires skills important to success in many other areas of life, developmental recess is viewed by many as an important component of comprehensive school curriculum.

If a child is having difficulty behaving appropriately during recess, it is very likely that the child has social skill or other playground skill deficits. Although appropriate consequences for irresponsible choices can be valuable teaching tools, the application of negative consequences as a stand-alone intervention does little to remediate playground skill deficits. When a child has difficulty reading, schools teach specific reading skills. The child is not placed in time-out with the hope that reading will be better in the future. When a child has difficulty with playground behavior, it is just as essential that appropriate replacement behaviors be taught and rehearsed.

This concept may be used with activities and situations other than recess. Such structured teaching of prosocial skills may be of value in relation to cafeteria behavior, school assembly behavior, and so on.

Sample Developmental Recess Model

Developmental recess is a relatively new concept, and a number of developmental recess models are being developed. All derive from the basic concept of teaching prosocial replacement behaviors. One model gaining popularity in a number of Oregon schools involves the following:

1. Teaching prosocial skills in small groups just prior to recess
2. Monitoring student choices during recess
3. Positive debriefing with those students immediately following recess

The following specific steps may be useful to those implementing this model for the first time:

1. Identify two school adults who are skilled and willing to work with students who have behavior difficulties at recess. One of these adults might be a school counselor, school psychologist, behavior consultant, child development specialist, and so on. The other could be a classroom teacher, administrator, playground assistant, and so on.
2. Identify a small group of students who could benefit from involvement in developmental recess.
3. Inform parents of the purpose and nature of developmental recess and obtain written authorization from parents to include the selected children in the group.
4. Assess the selected students to determine skill deficits and gather appropriate instructional materials needed for teaching prosocial skills. Assessment strategies could include the use of behavior rating scales, student self-report instruments, direct observation, and the like.
5. Schedule developmental recess in consultation with the classroom teachers of the selected students. It is recommended that students participate in developmental recess at least three or four times per week for four to six weeks. Many schools have developmental recess occur during recess.
6. As children demonstrate appropriate behavior during developmental recess (usually for three to five consecutive days), they return to the regular recess.
7. For several days following their return, students check with the developmental recess facilitator prior to recess to discuss their goals and after recess to evaluate their behavior. As students experience success, they can report less frequently.

the space inside another student's yarn. This was then used during classtime and recess for several days. The staff reported that students quickly learned the procedure of not invading another person's physical space and that inappropriate touch on the playground, although still present, occurred at a much lower rate.

Case Study: Teaching Students Hallway Behavior in a Middle School

One of us worked with school staff who were concerned about student behavior in the hallways. Some teachers were concerned that students were not punished enough when caught being unsafe in the halls, and other teachers pointed to the lack of staff consistency in responding to inappropriate student hallway behavior. The author asked the staff to discuss where the problems occurred. It soon became obvious that students were having problems in two specific areas of the building. Someone suggested that the staff involve the students in examining the problem and determining a solution. The staff and students developed a series of traffic signs (such as "Yield Right," "Merge Left," etc.) that were placed in the necessary areas. Students were then given instruction in how to move in the congested areas. Results indicated that referrals for student misconduct in hallways decreased dramatically once the procedures were collaboratively developed and effectively taught.

Case Study: Changing Teachers' Procedures

Although most attention is focused on teaching students to follow selected school and classroom procedures, student behavior can often be more quickly and dramatically improved by altering the procedures adults follow. For example, one of us recently worked with an elementary school staff who expressed concern about student behavior both at the end of recess and in the hallways. After considerable discussion about how to teach students to behave more responsibly in these settings, one of the teachers noted that if teachers would develop the procedure of meeting their students outside at the end of recess and walking their students to physical education, music, and lunch, there would be much less chaos and many happier students. Data indicated that although it took approximately four minutes more each day to follow this procedure, teachers were saving at least five times that much instructional time because of the decrease in disruptive student behavior during and following transition times.

In a similar vein, one of us worked with school staff who was concerned about how rudely students responded to adults. Again, the staff was engaged in very positive discussions about how to teach students improved communication skills. After implementing this social skills training, however, the staff remained frustrated by the level of rude responses. With some outside assistance, the staff began to realize that a significant amount of this rudeness, or failure to respond positively to adult statements, occurred when adults were correcting students. The staff discovered that when, instead of criticizing or correcting students, they validated the students' feelings and asked students how else they could respond, the amount of negative student behavior was dramatically reduced.

Case Study: Teaching Rules and Procedures to New Students

When new students enter the classroom, it is imperative they understand how the classroom operates. There is a variety of methods for accomplishing this. Most teachers simply assign a student to discuss classroom behavior standards and key procedures with a new student. In an elementary school, this may be a class job. The new student may spend a recess and lunch period with the mentor learning about key classroom expectations. In a secondary school, several students may volunteer for a two-week or monthly role of teaching new students about the classroom. In both cases, this is facilitated by having the materials in writing or having the teacher or class develop a video describing these materials. The teacher may also design a quiz about classroom operation and ask all new students to earn 100 percent on this quiz.

When the new student has limited English proficiency, if at all possible, someone who speaks the student's language should work with the student to help the student understand how the classroom operates. In some cases, schools and classroom teachers have developed videos in several languages to explain these procedures. In addition, some schools have volunteers who work with new families and students to provide an orientation to the school in the family's first language.

AN OUTLINE FOR BEGINNING THE SCHOOL YEAR

The most effective way to create a safe, positive setting in which students are motivated to learn will vary with grade level, subject matter, and teacher style. However, there are some key ingredients to creating a positive learning environment. This section offers suggestions for beginning the school year in elementary, middle school, and high school classrooms.

Elementary Classrooms

Figure 6.12 presents the outline of training workshops developed by Carolyn Evertson and her colleagues (Evertson, Emmer, Sanford, & Clements, 1983) to assist teachers in improving their skills in effectively beginning the school year. Our work supports this pioneering work in beginning

FIGURE 6.12 MAJOR COMPONENTS PRESENTED IN BEGINNING-OF-YEAR TREATMENT

Source: C. Evertson, E. Emmer, J. Sanford, and B. Clements. "Improving Classroom Management: An Experiment in Elementary School Classrooms," *Elementary School Journal, 84* (1983): 173–180. Copyright © 1983 by The University of Chicago.

1. *Readying the classroom.* Be certain your classroom space and materials are ready for the beginning of the year.
2. *Planning rules and procedures.* Think about what procedures students must follow to function effectively in your classroom and in the school environment; decide what behaviors are acceptable or unacceptable; develop a list of procedures and rules.
3. *Consequences.* Decide ahead of time consequences for appropriate and inappropriate behavior in your classroom, and communicate them to your students; follow through consistently.
4. *Teaching rules and procedures.* Teach students rules and procedures systematically; include in your lesson plans for the beginning of school sequences for teaching rules and procedures, when and how they will be taught, and when practice and review will occur.
5. *Beginning-of-school activities.* Develop activities for the first few days of school that will involve students readily and maintain a whole-group focus.
6. *Strategies for potential problems.* Plan strategies to deal with potential problems that could upset your classroom organization and management.
7. *Monitoring.* Monitor student behavior closely.
8. *Stopping inappropriate behavior.* Handle inappropriate and disruptive behavior promptly and consistently.
9. *Organizing instruction.* Organize instruction to provide learning activities at suitable levels for all students in your class.
10. *Student accountability.* Develop procedures that keep the children responsible for their work.
11. *Instructional clarity.* Be clear when you present information and give directions to your students.

FIGURE 6.13
BEGINNING THE
SCHOOL YEAR IN
AN ELEMENTARY
CLASSROOM

First-Day Schedule	Second-Day Schedule
Place on the students' desks: nametags, class name word search, sacks, letter from the teacher to the student	Mystery student warm-up
	Practice morning procedures
Teacher introduces self	Bingo acquaintance activity
Take attendance using name chain	Introduce key classroom procedures
Learn the school pledge	Snack and stretch break
Practice assembly procedures	Music class
Attend all-school assembly	Paint portraits on shoe box
Overview of the year's curriculum	Practice lunch procedures
Snack from the bags placed on the students' desks (also in bag is a bookmark, pencil, sticker, and piece of candy)	Lunch and recess
	Read aloud
	Successful learner activity
Students write letters to the teacher telling about themselves, their families, summer highlights, and something they want to learn this year	Group contributions activity
	Recess
	Organize notebooks
Packets go home	Closure
Practice closure procedure	Bus dismissal
Practice bus procedure	

the school year. We have also found several additional activities that help create a positive learning community. Figure 6.13 is an outline taken from a fifth-grade classroom taught by one of us.

Secondary Classrooms

Figure 6.14 provides an outline we recommend for creating a positive, cohesive community of learners in which secondary students are motivated to learn and experience a sense of safety and personal investment in the learning process.

With the apparently ever-increasing focus on student achievement on standardized tests, many teachers express concern about spending a good portion of the first week of class building a community of support and establishing clear behavior guidelines. As stated at the beginning of this chapter, our experiences and extensive research over the past thirty-five years have supported the benefits to student achievement when teachers take the time to thoughtfully develop a safe, supportive environment.

PAUSE & CONSIDER 6.5

Consider a class you are currently teaching, one you have observed, or one in which you are working. As well as you can remember, draft an outline of the first five days this class met during the current school year. If you did not teach or observe at the beginning of this year, move immediately to the next part of this activity. Next, create an outline for how you would like to organize the first five days of your next school year. Do not include specific academic activities, but do indicate when these will occur. Once again, we encourage you to join with a group of colleagues or classmates to share your ideas and learn from each other.

**FIGURE 6.14
BEGINNING THE
SCHOOL YEAR IN A
SECONDARY
CLASSROOM**

1. *Provide a cognitive map (outline) for the year.* Describe to students the general outline of the course, content they will be working with, instructional and assessment methods you will use, and so on.
2. *Define learning.* Using the approach discussed in Chapter 7, have students work collaboratively to develop a list of characteristics they agree are found in a successful learner and create a definition of an effective learner.
3. *Ask students what they want to learn and what types of instructional activities best facilitate their learning.* Have students individually write about what they want to learn in the class. Are there special interests or knowledge they have related to the class? Ask students to describe the instructional and assessment methods that seem to work best for them and perhaps give examples of these from previous classes they have taken.
4. *Be inviting and help students know you.* Be positive and excited about your teaching. Learn students' names and something about each student. Make a positive contact with each student during the first two weeks of school. Keep your ratio of positive to negative statements at least four to one.
5. *Allow students to interview you.* Let students learn about you as a person as well as your beliefs as an educator.
6. *Help students to become better acquainted.* Involve students in at least three activities (see Chapter 4) designed to help students know each other's names and learn something about each other.
7. *Teach judicious discipline concepts and establish behavioral norms.* Inform students that one role you have is to ensure that the constitutional rights of all students will be protected in the classroom and that no class member (including the teacher) can behave in a manner that violates the rights of others. With this background, either have students develop a list of behavioral norms that ensures that all four compelling state interests are met or provide students with a list and have a discussion that may lead to modifications of this list. Have all students sign this list, indicating their understanding of it and their commitment to respect the rights of all members of the class.
8. *Teach key behavioral procedures.* Determine the key procedures you wish to teach. Teach these as they are needed in the classroom. Whenever a problem occurs, ask yourself what procedure you and your students could develop that would eliminate this problem.
9. *Develop an approach for how you and students will respond when someone's rights are violated.* Present your approach to responding to violations of classroom behavioral expectations. Allow students' input into this process. Once agreement has been reached, print this, have all students sign it, and provide a copy of this to your administrator.
10. *Carefully monitor students' work and homework and provide reteaching opportunities early.* Early in the first marking period, provide opportunities for students to present their learning in several ways—tests, projects, writing, and so on. Meet with students who have difficulty presenting a mastery of the material and discuss ways to modify the presentation of materials as well as the assessment of learning.
11. *Involve students in assessing their own efforts and learning.* Have students describe their own efforts in mastering the content. Have them list what is working for them, any assistance they might need, and methods they might use to improve their work. A success contract (Chapter 7) might be helpful.
12. *Involve students in assessing your teaching and their feelings about the class.* Have students provide you with feedback regarding the class (Chapter 3). Share this feedback with students and work with them to make some modifications in the class.

CLASSROOM MANAGEMENT SKILLS THAT HELP MAXIMIZE ON-TASK BEHAVIOR

The importance of teachers' using the skills described in this section was initially highlighted by Kounin's (1970) research on classroom discipline. Kounin began his study by collecting several thousand hours of videotapes, both from classrooms of teachers who were acknowledged to be extremely effective in managing their classes and from classrooms of teachers who had serious, continuing management problems. Kounin expected to find significant differences in how teachers from these two groups handled discipline problems that occurred in their classrooms. Surprisingly, the results indicated that the successful teachers responded to control problems in much the same manner as did the teachers whose classrooms were often disorderly.

Based on these findings, Kounin reexamined the tapes, seeking any real differences between the teaching methods of teachers who were successful and those who experienced major management problems. He discovered that the differences lay in the successful teachers' ability to prevent discipline problems. These teachers used many types of management skills to ensure that students were consistently and actively engaged in instructional activities. Successful teachers were better prepared and organized and moved smoothly from one activity to another. These teachers also maintained students' involvement in instructional activities by initially stimulating the students' interests and effectively holding their attention throughout the lesson. Similarly, successful teachers used seatwork that was individualized and interesting. Kounin also discovered that the more effective teachers had greater classroom awareness, constantly scanning the classroom so that they were aware of potential problems and could deal with these before any real difficulties arose. These teachers anticipated students' needs, organized their classrooms to minimize restlessness and boredom, and effectively coped with the multiple and often overlapping demands associated with teaching.

In research conducted to further investigate Kounin's (1970) findings, Brophy and Evertson (1976) found that the same teacher behaviors that reduce classroom disruption are also associated with increased student learning. In describing the findings of the two-year Teacher Effectiveness Project, which examined the relationship between various teacher behaviors and gains in students' learning, Brophy and Evertson (1976) stated, "Our data strongly support the findings of Kounin (1970). . . . That is, the key to successful classroom management is prevention of problems before they start, not knowing how to deal with problems after they have begun" (p. 127). Brophy and Evertson also wrote, "Of the process behaviors measured through classroom observation in our study, the group that had the strongest and most consistent relationships with student learning gains dealt with the classroom management skills of the teachers. By 'classroom management,' we mean planning and conducting activities in an orderly fashion; keeping students actively

© Scott Masear

"How do you do it, Angela?"

FIGURE 6.15
INSTRUCTIONAL
MANAGEMENT SKILLS
THAT FACILITATE ON-TASK
BEHAVIOR AND
ACADEMIC ACHIEVEMENT

1. Arranging the classroom
2. Beginning a lesson
3. Giving clear instructions
4. Maintaining attention
5. Pacing
6. Using seatwork effectively
7. Summarizing
8. Providing useful feedback and evaluation
9. Making smooth transitions
10. Planning for early childhood settings
11. Dealing with common classroom disruptions

engaged in lessons and seatwork activities; and minimizing disruptions and discipline problems" (p. 51).

The research on academic learning time (ALT) further supports the idea that teachers should incorporate teaching methods that increase on-task student behavior. "If 50 minutes of reading instruction per day is allocated to a student who pays attention about one-third of the time, and only one-fourth of the student's reading time is a high level of success, the student will experience only about four minutes of ALT-engaged reading time at a high success level" (Berliner, 1984, p. 62). Classes vary dramatically in the percentage of time students are engaged in instructional tasks, with rates ranging from consistently less than 50 percent to 90 percent.

The section is organized around the eleven general instructional management skills listed in Figure 6.15. It is critical to understand how to use the methods in this chapter. They are not offered as gimmicks for increasing students' time on task or your control. Instead, they are methods that can assist you in helping students better understand their schoolwork and enhance the quality of learning time. One mark of effective teachers is an awareness of and ability to examine and alter their own classroom behavior based on its impact on student behavior and learning. While the methods in the following pages are research based and time tested, you will want to use, adjust, or discard them based on their fit for you and your classroom. You may wish to review additional materials found in Randy Sprick's (2009) book *CHAMPS: A Proactive and Positive Approach to Classroom Management*; Denton and Kreite's (2000) book *The First Six Weeks of School*; and Good and Brophy's (2008) *Looking in Classrooms*.

Arranging the Classroom

The arrangement of the classroom can significantly impact student motivation to learn and classroom behavior as well as the teacher's ability to respond quickly and unobtrusively to student behavior that disrupts a classroom.

Methods

1. *Arrange the room to ensure maximum ability for the teacher to move about the classroom and interact with students.*
2. *Ensure that the room arrangement allows for students to move comfortably to the areas in the classroom where they will be working or obtaining materials.*

© George Abbott

"Miss Marpole, I need to talk to you about your seating arrangement."

3. *Arrange the room so students are seated in a manner that supports the type of academic work they will be completing.* For example, if students will be interacting with each other—such as in a laboratory setting or in cooperative groups, students should be arranged in table groups of the size desired for this type of work. Similarly, if class meetings are to be a central part of the class culture or if the center of the room is to be used for instructional methods, ensure that adequate space is provided for these activities.

4. *Consider placing students with low status near students with higher social status or placing students who appear to not like each other closer to each other.* Research (Van den Berg et al., 2012) suggests that this approach may improve liking patterns among peers and reduce peer conflicts.

5. *Especially early in the school year, consider assigning seats.* Research suggests disruptive behavior is between two and three times less likely to happen when the teacher assigns seats (Bicard et al., 2012).

6. *Ensure that the classroom has numerous examples of materials that represent the cultural backgrounds of the students in the classroom.* This would include not only posters and artifacts but also books that are not only available for students to read but are central aspects of the curriculum.

7. *There are a variety of Web sites dedicated to ideas for ensuring you are using classroom space to most effectively facilitate student learning and on-task behavior.* You are encouraged to review several of these and discuss them with your colleagues.

Beginning a Lesson

Teachers frequently have difficulty attracting students' attention and getting a lesson started. The reason is at least partly that students often attempt to postpone the beginning of a lesson by socializing or moving about the room. Students quite accurately realize that the best time for buying time is before the lesson begins.

Methods

1. *Develop a room arrangement that allows all students to sit comfortably and clearly see the teacher.*

2. *Select and teach a cue for getting students' attention.* Students benefit from having a consistent cue indicating that it is time to focus their attention. They hear standard phrases such as "Okay, we are ready to begin" so often that these statements are frequently ineffective for eliciting attention. One of us has her class select a new cue each month. Students enjoy being involved and choose catchy phrases. During a recent year, students chose "Boo" for October, "Gobble Gobble" for November, and "Ho Ho Ho" for December. While teaching a summer institute on classroom management, the value of using a catchy phrase was demonstrated by recording the time it took forty teachers to pay attention quietly following the phrase "May I please have your attention?" The average time for five such requests was nearly two minutes (in each instance, students were involved in group

work). The class was presented with this figure and asked to develop a less common phrase. They chose "Rain, rain, go away." This phrase was practiced until the class could attend within ten seconds. Follow-up data gathered during the next two weeks showed that the group never took more than ten seconds to become completely quiet.

3. *Do not begin until everyone is paying attention.*
4. *Begin the lesson by removing distractions.*
5. *Clearly describe the goals, activities, and evaluation procedures associated with the lesson being presented.*
6. *Stimulate interest by relating the lesson to the students' lives or a previous lesson.*
7. *Start with a highly motivating activity in order to make the students' initial contact with the subject matter as positive as possible.* One of the authors begins a unit on the Lewis and Clark expedition by dressing up as Meriwether Lewis and collaborating with a colleague to present a skit summarizing the lives of these two noteworthy explorers.
8. *Distribute an outline, definitions, or study guide to help students organize their thoughts and focus their attention.*
9. *Challenge students to minimize their transition time.* Children enjoy games and are impressed by data. Draw on this knowledge by presenting students with data indicating the amount of time it requires them to settle down and asking them to try to reduce this time. There are six basic steps to implementing this approach. First, collect baseline data (see Chapter 10) and record them on a large and easy-to-read chart. Second, the data should be discussed with the students and their assistance requested. Third, help the students choose an appropriate and reasonable goal. Fourth, define exactly what you mean by being ready for class. Fifth, the class must develop a system for collecting and recording data. Finally, it may be necessary to determine a reward for reaching the stated goal.

Giving Clear Instructions

A key step in presenting a lesson is to provide clear instructions for the activities in which students will be engaged. A significant amount of disruptive student behavior stems from students not knowing how they are to proceed or what they are to do when they require assistance or complete their work. Students are often poorly prepared for seatwork assignments.

Methods

1. *Give precise directions.* Instructions should include statements about (a) what students will be doing, (b) why they are doing it, (c) how they can obtain assistance, (d) what to do with completed work, and (e) what to do when they finish. It is also helpful to indicate how much time they will be spending on the task. This direction may include a statement about when the work can be completed if it cannot be finished within the designated time limits.
2. *Describe the desired quality of the work.* This can increase students' sense of accountability and decrease their anxiety.
3. *After giving instructions, have students paraphrase the directions, state any problems that might occur to them, and make a commitment.*
4. *Positively accept students' questions about directions.*
5. *Place directions where they can be seen and referred to by students.*
6. *Have students write out instructions before beginning an activity.*
7. *When students seem to be having difficulty following directions, consider breaking tasks down into smaller segments.*

8. *Give directions immediately prior to the activity they describe.*

9. *Model the correct behavior. If students have been asked to raise their hands before answering, you can raise your hand while asking the question.*

10. *Hand out worksheets or outlines before taking a field trip.*

11. *Create a space for placing all assignments so students who are absent or forget to write down an assignment can independently access this information.* This can be supported by having several students designated each week to provide additional information for students who are unclear about the materials found in the assignments folder.

Maintaining Attention

The amount of time students spend involved in instruction is significantly related to their achievement. Many teachers state that one of the most frustrating tasks associated with teaching is maintaining students' attention during group instruction. Although children and young adolescents do in fact have a somewhat shorter attention span than do adults, their ability to attend quietly to an interesting television program or video game suggests that the skilled teacher can stimulate more consistent attention to task than is seen in most classrooms.

Methods

1. *Arrange the classroom to facilitate the instructional activity you have selected.* When a lesson involves the teacher as the center of attention, students should be seated so that everyone is facing the teacher. This arrangement can be accomplished using rows, a circle, or a *U* shape. When students are seated in small groups, request that all students face you before beginning a lesson. Similarly, if you wish students to talk to each other, desks must be arranged in a circle, square, or *U* shape so that students can comfortably see and hear each speaker. Teachers who use a variety of instructional activities should consider teaching students a procedure for quickly and quietly moving desks. With a small amount of instruction, students in all grades can learn to rearrange desks in approximately one minute.

2. *Employ a seating arrangement that does not discriminate against some students.* Teachers tend to place higher-achieving students nearer the teacher and provide them with more contact. Research suggests that when low-ability students were moved to the front of the room, their achievements improved more than that of low-ability students who remained at the back of the room. Interestingly, the high-achieving students' achievements did not suffer when they were moved farther from the teacher. Similarly, students' involvement is more evenly distributed when high- and low-achieving students are interspersed throughout the room. Teachers can increase on-task student responses by adjusting seating arrangements and moving around the room so that all students become actively involved in meaningful classroom interaction.

3. *Use random selection in calling on students.* This can be accomplished by placing students' names on Popsicle sticks in a hat and simply drawing names to determine who will be called on.

© Martha F. Campbell

"First, you have to get their attention."

One danger in involving students randomly is that you are less likely to receive an immediate correct answer to every question. Studies indicate that, especially in the primary grades, student achievement is enhanced when teachers provide information, ask focused questions, and receive correct answers from students. Therefore, you should carefully consider when to involve lower-achieving students. For example, these students might be called on when they raise their hands during skill-acquisition lessons and might be encouraged to become actively involved during lessons that involve personal issues or opinions.

4. *Ask the question before calling on a student.* When teachers select the student before asking the question, other students may become less interested in the question. By asking the question, looking around the room, and providing students with an opportunity to consider the question, you create greater interest and anticipation, thereby increasing attending behavior. Also take this opportunity to reinforce the procedure of students raising their hands to answer questions (e.g., "Raise your hand if you can answer this question," or "John, you have your hand raised. What is the answer?").

5. *Wait at least five seconds before answering a question or calling on another student.* Most teachers are surprised to learn that research indicates that, on the average, teachers wait only one second for a student to respond before answering a question themselves or calling on another student. Consider, however, the process students must go through when asked a question. First, they must hear the question and decide whether they understand it. Second, they must search for the information. Third, they must consider whether their response will be accepted. Fourth, they must decide whether they will receive reinforcement or rebuke for their response (in some situations a correct response will be reinforced by the teacher but punished by peers). This process may occur very rapidly for bright students, but most students require considerably longer than one second to complete it.

    Rowe (1986) reported that when teachers increase their waiting time, a variety of positive things occur. Figure 6.16 summarizes her findings. In a review of studies involving wait time, Tobin (1987) found that when average teacher wait time was greater than three seconds, teacher and student discourse changed and higher cognitive level achievement occurred at all grade levels.

6. *Ask students to respond to their classmates' answers.* This will increase the likelihood they will view learning as more dynamic and interactive and, for many students, is more consistent with their cultural norms and more engaging than simply hearing a classmate or teacher.

FIGURE 6.16
ADVANTAGES OF
INCREASING
TEACHERS' WAIT
TIME

1. Length of students' responses increases
2. Number of unsolicited but appropriate answers increases
3. Failure to obtain a response decreases
4. Students' confidence increases
5. Teacher-centered teaching decreases
6. Students' questions increase
7. Lower-achieving students contribute more
8. Students' proposals increase
9. Students give more evidence to support their answers
10. The variety of students' responses increases

7. *Do not consistently repeat students' answers.* Many teachers parrot nearly every answer provided by a student. This practice is intended to ensure that all students hear the correct answer. But it also teaches students that (a) they do not need to speak loudly because the teacher is the only one who needs to hear their answer, (b) they do not need to listen to their peers because the teacher will repeat the answer, and (c) the teacher is the source of all learning in the classroom. All these negative side effects reduce students' motivation, involvement, and attention.

8. *Model listening skills by paying close attention when students speak.*

9. *Be animated.* In his classic work on classroom discipline, Kounin (1970) wrote, "Teachers who maintain a group focus by engaging in behaviors that keep children alert and on their toes are more successful in inducing work involvement and preventing deviancy than are teachers who do not" (p. 123). Studies indicate that not only do students like enthusiastic teachers but also that teacher enthusiasm facilitates student achievement. Demonstrate enthusiasm and animation by moving around the room, varying your voice level, using interested facial expressions, and maintaining a high energy level.

10. *Reinforce students' efforts and maintain a high ratio of positive to negative verbal statements.* As discussed in Chapter 2, ensure that your feedback is specific and emphasizes behaviors they may have engaged in that supported their efforts. For example, "That is an excellent example of why you believe the character has compassion for others. You read this material very carefully and connected events to character very effectively."

11. *Vary instructional media and methods.* For example, rather than simply calling on students, have students share their ideas in pairs and then write their ideas on document camera or butcher paper; have students use their personal white boards to answer a question and then share these with the group; have dyads share their ideas with another dyad and then share their favorite idea with the large group, and so on.

12. *Create anticipation.* Create a sense of interest by making statements such as "This is a tough one" or "I'm not sure we've talked about this, but maybe someone can answer it."

13. *Ask questions that relate to students' own lives.*

14. *Provide work of appropriate difficulty.* Students' misbehavior is often a response to work that is either too easy or too difficult. Students prefer work that is moderately difficult over tasks that are too easy. When work is too difficult, though, students become discouraged. Failure also causes students to lower their expectations of their own performances.

Research suggests that when the teacher is available to provide assistance (as during monitored seatwork or recitation), students should be able to answer 70 to 80 percent of questions correctly. When students must work independently (as on independent seatwork or homework), students should be able to answer 95 percent correctly (Brophy, 1982). Seatwork must not only allow for these high success rates but must also be different enough from previous work to challenge students.

Similarly, teacher questions to students should also elicit a relatively high rate of correct responses. Brophy (1986a) states that approximately three-fourths of teachers' questions should elicit correct responses and the remainder should elicit some form of incorrect or incomplete answer rather than failure to respond. Success rates can be expected to be lower when new material is being introduced but higher during reviews. Brophy noted, "Consistently low success rates (below about 65 percent), however, suggest that the teacher is 'teaching over the students' heads' or has not prepared them effectively for the questions" (p. 9).

15. *Provide variability and interest in seatwork.* Seatwork can be made more interesting by developing units that relate to current events, such as sports or students' other interests (animals, entertainment figures, etc.), or by creating seatwork that is based on some form of board game. Students can also be involved in working cooperatively with peers or presented with a competitive situation.

16. *When presenting difficult material, clearly acknowledge this fact, set a time limit for the presentation, and describe the type of follow-up activities that will clarify the lesson.*

Pacing

Methods

1. *Develop awareness of your own teaching tempo.* Students' behaviors and performances are affected by their teacher's tempo. We can learn to generate interest and enthusiasm effectively or to create a calming effect by adjusting our own personal pace in the classroom. The best method for examining your own pace is to video record yourself during large-group instruction. As you watch the replay, ask yourself questions such as the following: Did I talk too fast? Was I animated? Did I repeat myself too often? and Would I enjoy listening to my own presentations?

2. *Watch for nonverbal cues indicating that students are becoming confused, bored, or restless.*

3. *Divide activities into short segments.* The use of films as instructional aids helps demonstrate this strategy. Teachers almost always allow a film to run all the way to the end before discussing its content. There are, however, several advantages to stopping the film at important points and discussing the ideas being presented. First, major points of information can be highlighted. Second, this procedure allows students to assimilate smaller amounts of information at a time. Many students simply cannot process the material offered in a half-hour film. Third, this method differentiates viewing a film at school from watching a movie or viewing television. Students can begin to learn that movies shown in school are meant to convey specific information and ideas rather than simply to entertain.

4. *Provide structured short breaks during lessons that last longer than thirty minutes.*

5. *Vary the style as well as the content of instruction.* Students often become restless when faced with extended instructional periods using only one type of instruction. If students have completed a large-group discussion in social studies, it is best not to move directly to a large-group science presentation. Teachers with good classroom management skills learn to move smoothly among a variety of instructional approaches.

6. *Do not bury students in paperwork.*

Using Seatwork Effectively

Research in hundreds of elementary school classrooms shows that students spend more than half their time working privately at seatwork. Data from some of the classes of the Beginning Teacher Evaluation Study (Fisher et al., 1981) also show that, in some classes, students make nearly 100 percent errors during 14 percent of the time they are involved in seatwork.

FIGURE 6.17
NUMBER OF
STUDENTS WHO
HAD COMPLETED
VARIOUS AMOUNTS
OF SEATWORK AT
FIVE-MINUTE
INTERVALS

	Percentage of Work Complete			
	0–25%	*26–50%*	*51–75%*	*76–100%*
5 minutes	11	12	8	2
10 minutes	6	10	10	7
15 minutes	4	6	13	10
20 minutes	3	4	7	9

Methods

1. *Make seatwork diagnostic and prescriptive.* Seatwork should be designed to provide students with meaningful practice while enabling teacher and student to assess the student's progress. Therefore, seatwork should be checked by the teacher or student, recorded and filed by the student, monitored by the teacher, and discussed in periodic teacher–student conferences.
2. *Develop a specific procedure for obtaining assistance.*
3. *Establish clear procedures about what to do when seatwork is completed.*
4. *Add interest to seatwork.* Include cartoons, puzzles, or personalized questions on worksheets.
5. *Work through the first several seatwork problems with the students.* All students will then understand the procedure to be followed and will be able to ask questions if they do not understand the work.
6. *Monitor students' seatwork and make needed adjustments.* While observing a student teacher in a fifth-grade class, one of the authors noted that students in the class completed seatwork at varying rates, and the teacher's failure to adjust seatwork or provide optional learning activities meant that many students were free to wander and disrupt the class. To bring out this point for the teacher, the author coded at five-minute intervals the number of students who had completed one-quarter, half, three-quarters, or all their work. The results (Figure 6.17) clearly indicate the inappropriateness of giving all students the same seatwork task. In addition to monitoring the time required to complete seatwork, monitor the percentage of students who complete their work with at least 75 percent accuracy (a higher percentage should be selected if you are not available to monitor the seatwork). This information, as well as a group average score, should be recorded as a basis for determining future seatwork assignments for individual students or the class as a whole.
7. *Monitor seatwork by moving around the room systematically.*
8. *Spend considerable time in presentation and discussion before assigning seatwork.*
9. *Keep contacts with individual students relatively short.* Longer contacts minimize your ability to scan the room or to provide assistance to all students.
10. *Have students work together during seatwork.* Students can jointly develop solutions or cooperatively prepare for group competition.

Summarizing

Many children view the school day as a series of tasks to be completed and do not understand what they have learned or how the learning relates to specific learning goals or their own lives. When combined with clearly stated goals and useful feedback, the methods presented in this section provide students with a sense of accomplishment and meaning in their school experience.

Methods

1. *At the end of a lesson or a school day, ask students to state or write in a journal one thing they learned during the day.*
2. *Have students play the role of a reporter and summarize what has been learned.*
3. *Have students create a skit to act out what they have learned.*
4. *Ask students to create learning displays.* Students can develop a collage, outline, newspaper article, and so on to display their learning. They might write an article reporting on how plants grow. Students could also draw a chart that demonstrates this process.
5. *Encourage students to present their learning to others.*
6. *Display students' work.*
7. *Provide frequent review sessions.*
8. *Use tests as tools for summarizing learning.*

Providing Useful Feedback and Evaluation

Collecting and analyzing feedback regarding student learning significantly influences student motivation, learning, and behavior (Stiggins, 2001). The methods presented next reinforce these purposes and offer practical ideas for effectively using evaluation in the classroom.

Methods

1. *Help students view evaluation as part of the learning process.*
2. *Tell students the criteria by which they will be evaluated.* When working with specific skills, students should know what they are to learn and what level of performance is acceptable. Similarly, when they are assigned projects, they should be informed about the specific goals for the lesson and, if their work will be evaluated, what specific criteria will be used.
3. *Relate feedback directly to individual or teacher goals.*
4. *Record data so that students can monitor their progress.*
5. *Provide immediate and specific feedback.* Students' learning is enhanced when they are provided with specific positive and negative information about their performances. Generalized feedback, such as a grade or comments such as "Good" or "Nice work," do not tend to improve students' performances on subsequent tests.
6. *Provide honest feedback.* It is important to focus on students' successes, but students' performances are not aided by feedback that is inaccurately positive. Students resent feedback they perceive as fake. Furthermore, providing students with too much praise for work that does not meet acceptable standards only confuses them and reduces their motivation and performance.
7. *Ask students to list factors that contributed to their successes.*
8. *Deemphasize comparisons between students and their peers.*
9. *Deemphasize grades as feedback on students' work.* Instead, provide information on specific skills the student has demonstrated as well as skills the student may want to improve. While helping the student to set goals for improvement, emphasize the good decisions and important learning and improvement the student has made.
10. *Provide students with clear information regarding their progress.* This is especially helpful in high school where grades impact students' futures. This feedback should provide students with accurate, ongoing data concerning their grades.

Making Smooth Transitions

A surprisingly large amount of classroom time is spent in transition from one activity to another. The approximately thirty major transitions each day in elementary classrooms account for nearly 15 percent of classroom time (Rosenshine, 1980).

Methods

1. *Arrange the classroom for efficient movement.*
2. *Create and post a daily schedule and discuss any changes in schedule each morning prior to beginning the class.*
3. *Have material ready for the next lesson.*
4. *Do not relinquish students' attention until you have given clear instructions for the following activity.*
5. *Do not do tasks that can be done by students.*
6. *Move around the room and attend to individual needs.*
7. *Provide students with simple, step-by-step directions.*
8. *Remind students of key procedures associated with the upcoming lesson.* For elementary school teachers, this may include stopping in the hallway on the way back from lunch, recess, or special events to discuss the procedure for the academic lesson the students will begin as they enter the classroom.
9. *Use group competition to stimulate more orderly transitions.* We can involve the class in attempting to reduce the amount of time required to make a transition.
10. *Develop transition activities.* Students often find it difficult to make the transition from home to school or from lunch or physical education back to a quieter setting. Smooth transitions can be facilitated by implementing structured activities that help students make these transitions. Ask them to begin the school day by writing in their journals or by discussing the daily schedule. Transitions from active periods, such as lunch, into quieter learning activities can be facilitated by transition activities, such as reading to the students or leading students in deep muscle relaxation. When these activities are used consistently, students not only find safety and comfort in this structure but also learn how to monitor transitions for themselves. Materials in the Recommended Reading at the end of this chapter provide a wide range of fun brainteaser activities that can be added to academic content warm-ups to assist you in transitions into the beginning of class.
11. *Be sensitive to students' special needs regarding transitions.* Some students require different types of transition behaviors than others. For example, Kuykendall (2004) suggests that some African American students prefer to have what she terms "stage setting" prior to beginning individual tasks "(e.g., pencil sharpening, rearranging posture, checking paper and writing space, asking for repeat directions, and even checking perceptions with their neighbors). Many teachers are

Effectively Handling Transitions
For an interactive review of methods for increasing instructional time by limiting times when students are transitioning between activities, click on the link below in your Pearson etext.

ENHANCEDetext *interactive case study*

likely to perceive stage setting as an attempt to avoid work or disrupt class. However, this is an important activity for many Black youth" (p. 123). Similarly, some students with attention deficit hyperactivity disorder (ADHD), learning disabilities, or language-processing difficulties may need special activities and assistance in transitioning from one activity to the next. These might include written directions, checking with a partner, or having some assistance during the initial stage of an assignment. If you see a particular student identified as receiving special education services developing a pattern of difficulty with transitions, we encourage you to meet with the student's special education teacher to discuss possible learning strategies to support this student.

12. *Use teacher-directed instruction as a transition at the end of the class session.* Especially in grades six through nine, students have difficulty handling lack of structure at the end of a class period. This can be minimized by bringing students back together for teacher-directed summary time prior to releasing students to their next class. You may want to help students highlight main points from the work they have been doing, remind students of homework or test dates, have students write in their journals or log books their assignments and plans for completing them, and so on.

Planning for Early Childhood Settings

Early childhood settings provide a unique set of challenges for maximizing on-task behaviors. Wolery, Bailey, and Sugai (1998) described four environmental categories a teacher can assess when considering factors that may be influencing children's behaviors in a preschool:

1. Instructional dimension (e.g., are materials and activities too easy or difficult, or have they been used too repetitively so children have tired of them?)
2. Physical dimension (e.g., are sound, light, and movement factors influencing student behavior?)
3. Social dimension (e.g., are there too many students in one area? Is student behavior being influenced by the manner in which adults are responding to students?)
4. Environmental changes (e.g., are transitions or interruptions to the environment influencing student behavior?)

In their book *Early Violence Prevention: Tools for Teachers of Young Children*, Slaby, Roedell, Arezzo, and Hendrix (1995) suggest that teachers arrange rooms with adequate space for each activity, place materials where students can obtain them without teacher assistance, assist children in learning to play cooperatively, manage classroom transitions smoothly, and ensure adequate adult supervision of transition activities where negative peer interactions might occur. Classroom design and the type of activities presented to students can significantly affect the amount and type of negative peer interactions in a classroom. Young children are more likely to engage in negative peer interactions in play areas involving blocks, dramatic play, and woodworking centers, which are by their nature characterized by interactive play. It is important to balance the amount of structure needed to ensure positive, safe student behavior while providing enough opportunity for independent play that fosters social skill development and an internal locus of control. Our own work with early childhood and primary grade classrooms suggests a number of additional classroom organization and management issues teachers may wish to consider.

1. *When setting up learning centers, try to keep quiet area activities together and have active areas in close proximity to each other but as removed from quiet activity areas as possible.*
2. *Use dividers, tables, or something else to separate different classroom areas.* Eliminate large, open areas, which may give children too little sense of structure and encourage more outdoor-type behaviors.
3. *Limit the number of children using one area by strategies such as having tickets for each area, carpet squares to indicate the number of students who may use an area, having a number and a corresponding picture of this number of children playing in the area, or placing a limited number of chairs in an area.*
4. *Arrange materials so students have access to them in a manner the teacher deems desirable.* For example, in a preschool setting, the teacher may want to arrange some materials so students will need to use language to request the materials. Other materials that can be used for cooperative play may be placed near each other to encourage this type of play.
5. *Consider the order in which you introduce materials to students.* For example, reading to children after recess has been shown to reduce behavior problems. Similarly, having students listen to stories, having quiet music playing, or having children do calm art activities such as finger painting can be a good transition into circle time or some other more interactive and group-oriented activity.
6. *Structure transition times.* Have a set signal for transitions. Singing a particular song, playing a musical instrument, and using a rainstick are examples of effective, calm transition signals. It is also important to provide students with cues prior to transition. For example, the teacher can indicate when five minutes and one minute remain prior to terminating the activity. Transitions can also be smoothed by engaging students in games and songs as they make the transition. The teacher might read a story, play finger puppets, or have a recorded story playing as students line up and wait for their peers. A thoughtful approach to assessing your preschool environment can be found in the Preschool Assessment of the Classroom Environment Scale (PACE) (Dunst, McWilliams, & Holbert, 1986).

Dealing with Common Classroom Disruptions

1. *Students need to leave the room.* For students in grades three and up, we recommend using a sign-out/sign-in sheet where students simply sign their name, their destination, and the time they are leaving. When they return, they write the time they returned. This procedure is respectful of students and helps them take responsibility for their own behavior. The procedure also provides the teacher with a clear statement of where a student is within the building. This is critical because you are responsible for your students during the time they are assigned to you. This also provides you with data that can help determine whether a pattern exists with the student's behavior, possibly suggesting the student needs an intervention to assist in making better decisions. Finally, should someone need to contact the student or you believe it is necessary to determine if the student is where he said he would be, the sign-out sheet provides you with the necessary information. In order to ensure that students provide accurate information on the sheet and assist them in taking responsibility for their behavior, there may be times when you will want to check the sign-in sheet to determine if a student has accurately listed the times in the sign-out and sign-in columns.

2. *Student tardiness.* Use a procedure for responding to student tardiness that allows you to (a) keep accurate records, (b) limit classroom disruption, and (c) provide educational consequences when students continue such behavior. We have found it most effective to have students sign in when they are tardy. Each day simply have a sheet for students to sign in, indicate whether their tardiness is excused or unexcused, and if excused, attach (have a paper clip attached to the sheet) their excused slip. Although it may be necessary to check this for accuracy, it places the responsibility on students and limits classroom disruptions. Should a student have more tardies than you or your school policy allows, the consequence will be most effective (and deemed more fair and respectful by the student and his or her advocates) if it involves the student meeting with you or writing a statement regarding the problem and the solution. Should this tardiness continue after she or he has committed to an approach for being on time, have the student write this statement to a parent or guardian or in your presence. Calling the parent or guardian may increase the accountability.

3. *Conflicts involving homework.* If given the opportunity, some students will turn in a vast majority of their work late. This is not fair to you because it inevitably means marking large amounts of work near the end of the grading period. In addition, failure to provide students with immediate feedback on their work—especially on work that is used as the foundation for future learning, is an educationally unsound practice that reduces student learning. Therefore, it is important to develop a procedure that assists students in turning in work on time. We have found the following methods helpful.

- Provide students with a clear statement about your late paper/homework policy. This might include taking a designated percentage off for each day homework is late, accepting only a certain number of late assignments during a grading period, and accepting no work that is more than one week late.

- Provide students with a form that includes the due date, date turned in, and the grade for all assigned work—including tests. It is imperative that you maintain your own accurate records of this data. Students have busy lives and also may wish to ignore how they are doing in school. Having clear records, particularly those maintained and periodically evaluated by the students, can help students assess their own work and serve as a catalyst for helping them set and reach goals related to school performance.

Responding to Students' Failure to Follow Classroom Rules
For an interactive review of methods for responding to students' failure to follow classroom instructions, click on the link below in your Pearson etext.

ENHANCEDetext *interactive case study*

- Provide support and options for homework completion. Homework is the least educationally equitable opportunity in our schools. Students differ tremendously in the time and support available for them to complete work outside of school. Also, homework is seldom differentiated, and if all students receive similar homework assignments, this will frustrate and decrease the likelihood that work will be completed by students for whom the work is overly demanding. When assigning homework, it is important to ensure that all students have work they can complete without assistance. In addition, it is often helpful to have students complete a form (Figure 6.18) indicating when, where, and, if appropriate, with whom, they will be completing their homework. Finally, since even with structural support, completing homework may be very

FIGURE 6.18
HOMEWORK
PLANNING FORM

Homework Assignment	Where I Will Complete This	When (Exact Time) I Will Complete This	Anyone I Will Need to Ask for Assistance

difficult for some students, whenever possible, provide multiple ways for students to demonstrate competence. We work with teachers who allow students to meet with them before or after school to demonstrate their mastery of content in brief discussions, or with brief samples of work. Students may also be able to do limited demonstrations of work—for example, completing several of the more difficult math problems rather than completing an entire page of problems. The key is that students need to know you understand and will work with them when factors in their lives prevent them from being able to spend significant amounts of time completing homework.

- Allow students to have one or two assignments they do not have to turn in during a marking period. For example, you might give each student two coupons for daily homework that does not have to be submitted. This makes sense given the number of events in a student's life that might make it nearly impossible for homework to be completed on a given day.
- Use your base groups and other methods, such as having students write down assignments, and strategies for completing them.
- Ensure that work is within the ability of all students.
- Ensure that all students have someone they can call or e-mail if they become confused by their homework.

4. *Excessive student nonacademic questions.* Teachers often comment that, particularly in elementary and middle schools, some students will ask an inordinate number of questions related to procedures teachers have just presented or related to nonacademic topics (yet during instructional time). Our daughter shared the following strategy she developed during her first year of teaching in a blended fourth–fifth-grade classroom:

> I always encouraged questions as this helps in the learning process, but my students were asking far too many questions about classroom procedures that had already been explained or about matters that were completely unrelated to classroom events. In order to provide me with adequate time to help my students with their academic tasks, I implemented a card system.

Each day the students got two red cards as they walked in the classroom. The cards were one inch by one inch and had a white sticker dot on them. These were their procedural question cards. When I gave directions or explained an assignment or project [to] the students, I always provided written direction on a sheet handed out to them or on the board. This way my auditory and visual learners' needs were addressed. I also made sure to ask for any questions before the students started the assignment. After I had done all that, if they had a question, they were allowed to ask three students. If no one knew, they could give me a question card and ask me. Once they ran out of question cards for the day[,] they were not allowed to ask me any more procedural questions. A student could ask a friend to use one of their cards to ask me the question, but they were not allowed to borrow cards.

This procedure not only dramatically increased the time I had available to assist students with their work, but it also helped teach students independence as they began to figure things out on their own by thinking about the question for themselves or requesting assistance from a friend. (S. Rudzek, personal communication, October 2005)

Chapter 8 will provide numerous additional suggestions for how to respond to the minute-to-minute interruptions and disruptive behavior that occur despite teachers' best efforts to prevent them.

PAUSE & CONSIDER 6.6

We often read about strategies and either become overwhelmed by their number or complexity or simply fail to take the time to systematically consider how these could be incorporated into our teaching in a manner that will enhance student learning. For this Pause & Consider, we encourage you to complete Activity 6.4 at the end of the chapter.

SUMMARY

Teachers whose students have higher rates of on-task behavior spend time early in the school year developing and teaching classroom rules and procedures. This provides students with a much-needed sense of structure and security. More effective classroom managers also view their roles less as disciplining students and more as reteaching appropriate behaviors when students have difficulty demonstrating these behaviors. Simply stated, the teaching of appropriate behavior has become an additional curriculum in schools.

Even prior to the research on beginning the school year, the research on classroom management had focused on the noninstructional aspects of teacher behavior that prevented disruptive student behavior. Jacob Kounin discovered that what differentiated effective from less effective classroom

managers was what these teachers did before, not after, students became involved in unproductive behavior. Even though we now know that this is only one aspect of effective classroom management, you will find that by using a variety of the methods presented here, you can create a more smoothly run, efficient classroom in which student behavior is significantly more goal directed.

IMPLEMENTATION ACTIVITIES

These activities give you an opportunity to work with several of the major skills presented in this chapter. The value of these activities can be enhanced if you discuss them with a colleague. The activities may suggest changes you wish to incorporate in your classroom. If you make changes, keep a record of them. One week after implementing the change(s), take time to write about and share with a colleague the results of these changes.

ACTIVITY 6.1

Selecting Your Classroom Rules

List five classroom rules you would choose for your class. When you are satisfied with the rules, discuss them with a colleague who teaches or has recently taught at your grade level.

ACTIVITY 6.2

Deciding on Your Key Classroom Procedures

For this activity, refer to Figures 6.5 and 6.7 if you are an elementary teacher and Figures 6.6 and 6.7 if you are a middle school or high school teacher. For each area in which effective teachers teach classroom procedures, list a procedure you would feel comfortable using in your classroom. Following is an example of this activity.

General Area	Needed Procedures	Specific Procedure
Beginning the class	1. Getting students' attention	Students determine a signal
	2. Entering the class	
	3. Obtaining materials	
	4. What to do if tardy	
	5. Where to put slips that need signing	
	6.	
	7.	
Whole-class activities	1. How to leave the room	Sign your name, destination, and the time you leave and return
	2. What to do when work is completed	
	3. Voice level	
	4. How to get help on an assignment	
	5. Using the pencil sharpener	
	6. When students can leave their seats	
	7.	
	8.	
	9.	
Student assignments	1. How to find work missed while absent	Refer to the notebook on the back table
	2. How late work will be handled	
	3. Heading papers	
	4. Where to hand in work	
	5. Credit for late work	
	6.	
	7.	
Other activities	1. Dismissing	Everyone must be seated and quiet
	2. Public address system and announcements	
	3. Fire drill	
	4. Guest entering the class	
	5.	
	6.	
	7.	

ACTIVITY 6.3

Examining Your Methods of Establishing Rules and Procedures

Evaluate your use of various methods of developing classroom rules and procedures by completing the following form. If you are not currently teaching, respond by recalling a classroom in which you previously taught or observed.

	Yes	Somewhat	No
1. Do clear classroom rules apply in your class?	☐	☐	☐
2. Are the rules listed in the form of positive statements?	☐	☐	☐
3. Are there six or fewer rules?	☐	☐	☐
4. Can every student list these rules from memory?	☐	☐	☐
5. Are the rules clearly displayed in your room?	☐	☐	☐
6. Are students involved in developing the rules?	☐	☐	☐
7. Does each student make a clear commitment to follow these rules?	☐	☐	☐
8. Do you discuss these rules frequently when they are first developed?	☐	☐	☐
9. Do you review the rules every three weeks?	☐	☐	☐
10. Do students clearly understand your approach to handling rule violations?	☐	☐	☐
11. Do you teach students the important procedures related to classroom activities?	☐	☐	☐
12. Do you teach students the major procedures related to behaviors outside the classroom?	☐	☐	☐
13. When students fail to follow a procedure, do you immediately reteach the procedure?	☐	☐	☐
14. Does every parent know the classroom rules that apply in your class?	☐	☐	☐
15. Does every parent know your methods of handling discipline problems?	☐	☐	☐

Carefully examine your responses to the preceding questions and then complete the following statements:

I learned that . . .

I am pleased that I . . .

Three approaches I will implement in order to develop more productive classroom rules and procedures are:

1.

2.

3.

I will also consider the possibility that next year I could . . .

ACTIVITY 6.4

Sharing and Expanding Your Repertoire of Methods

This activity will be most effective if it can be completed with three or four colleagues.

First, select four of the eleven areas from Figure 6.15 (e.g., giving clear instruction, beginning a lesson, and so on) in which you are particularly interested in improving your skills.

Second, for each of these four areas do the following:

1. Circle the number of each of the strategies you currently use in your classroom or which you believe you are prepared to use.
2. Place a box around the number of all the strategies you would be interested in using but which you would need some assistance or practice in developing.

3. Place an X through the number preceding each of the strategies you believe do not fit your teaching style or which, given the age of your students or your teaching methods, would be inappropriate in your classroom.

Third, as a group, select three of the eleven major areas listed in Figure 6.15. This can be developed by finding out how many people in your group chose that area and selecting topics several of you chose.

Fourth, for each of the three topics on which your group chose to focus, go down the numbers, and anytime a person has a box around the number in front of a strategy, have other members of the group (perhaps someone with the strategy circled) share with you how they implement this strategy in their classroom or how they have seen it implemented.

RECOMMENDED READING

Clayton, M., & Forton, M. (2001). *Classroom spaces that work*. Greenfield, MA: Northeast Foundation for Children.

Denton, P., & Kriete, R. (2000). *The first six weeks of school*. Turners Falls, MA: Northeast Foundation for Children.

Evertson, C., & Harris, A. (1999). Support for managing learning-centered classrooms: The classroom organization and management program. In H. J. Freiberg (Ed.), *Beyond behaviorism: Changing the classroom management paradigm* (pp. 59–74). Boston, MA: Allyn & Bacon.

Freiberg, H. J. (Ed.). (1999.) *Beyond behaviorism: Changing the classroom management paradigm*. Boston, MA: Allyn & Bacon.

Gathercoal, F. (2004). *Judicious discipline* (6th ed.). San Francisco, CA: Caddo Gap Press.

Good, T., & Brophy, J. (2003). *Looking in classrooms* (7th ed.). New York, NY: Harper & Row.

Horner, R. H., & Sugai, G. (2005). School-wide positive behavior support: An alternative approach to discipline in schools. In L. Bambara & L. Kern (Eds.), *Positive behavior support* (pp. 359–390). New York, NY: Guilford Press.

Kriete, R. (2002). *The morning meeting book*. Greenfield, MA: Northeast Foundation for Children.

Landau, B. (Ed.). (1999). *Practicing judicious discipline: An educator's guide to a democratic classroom*. San Francisco, CA: Caddo Gap Press.

Lewis, T. J., Newcomer, L., Trussell, R., & Richter, M. (2006). School-wide positive behavior support: Building systems to develop and maintain appropriate social behavior. In C. S. Everston & C. M. Weinstein (Eds.), *Handbook of classroom management: Research, practice and contemporary issues* (pp. 833–854). New York, NY: Lawrence Erlbaum Associates.

Rathmann, P. (1995). *Officer Buckle and Gloria*. New York, NY: Penguin Putnam Books for Young Readers.

Scheuermann, G., & Hall, J. (2007). *Positive behavioral supports in the classroom*. Upper Saddle River, NJ: Pearson.

Shannon, P. (1998). *No, David!* New York, NY: Blue Sky Press.

Sprick, R. (2009). *CHAMPS: A proactive and positive approach to classroom management* (2nd ed.). Eugene, OR: Pacific Northwest.

Stiles, N. (n.d.). A kingdom with no rules, no laws, and no king. Retrieved from geniaconnell.com (search for "kingdom with no rules").

Stover, J. (1989). *If everybody did*. Greenville, SC: Journey Forth.

INCREASING STUDENT MOTIVATION AND LEARNING BY IMPLEMENTING INSTRUCTIONAL METHODS THAT MEET STUDENTS' ACADEMIC NEEDS

PART 3

Effective classroom management is closely related to effective classroom instruction. When students fail to attend school or classes or when they act out or fail to be productively engaged in classroom activities, teachers must carefully examine whether the curricular content and instructional methods are actively and meaningfully engaging students at an appropriate level of difficulty and in ways that respect their cultural heritage and relate to their own lives. Part 3 presents current theory and practice on student motivation and effective instruction. Chapter 7 begins with a brief examination of current research on motivation to learn and indicates the relationship between this research and classroom practice. The chapter continues with a discussion of and practical suggestions for implementing a variety of instructional methods proven effective in increasing student motivation and learning. This chapter responds to the large body of data indicating that many students find schools confusing, boring places in which to learn. Clearly, students' misbehavior, violent behavior, and leaving school are related to the degree to which they believe the academic content and the manner in which it is presented treats them with respect and engages their need for competence. In Chapter 7, methods are presented that will enable you to increase the degree to which you actively engage and show respect for your students by clarifying instruction, increasing meaningful student involvement in the learning process, and using teaching methods that respond to individual students' needs.

ENHANCING STUDENTS' MOTIVATION TO LEARN

This important work of several decades ago, as well as much of what has since been in the forefront of educational thought, stresses the importance of teachers finding ways to make subject matter relevant to students, to involve students in setting their own goals, to vary the ways of learning to use approaches that employ all of the senses, and to be sure that there are opportunities for relating the knowledge to experiences or actually using it.

—John I. Goodlad (1984)

Good instruction is now known by researchers to be the first line of defense in behavior management. That is, a good instructional program prevents many behavior problems from arising.

—James Kauffman (1997)

If school is not inviting, if the tasks are not clear, interesting, and at an appropriate level, how can we expect pupils to be on task? Adverse student reactions should be expected when classes are dull, teaching is uninspired, and failure is built in. Their oppositional behavior is a sign of personal health and integrity.

—William Morse (1987)

Teachers need to acknowledge the inseparable relationship between classroom management and instruction. Lessons that encourage students' active participation and address their interests, needs, and backgrounds are not only likely to foster academic achievement; they are much more likely to generate the good will, respect, and cooperation that is needed for the productive learning environment.

—Anita Woolfolk Hoy and Carol Weinstein (2006)

This research confirms that inclusion teachers can reach students by incorporating aspects of brain-based research, such as multiple intelligences, learning styles, and emotional intelligences, into their classroom and homework assignments.

—Diane Connell (2009)

Education is not the filling of the pail, but the lighting of the fire.

—William Butler Yeats (Irish poet and playwright)

Teaching kids to count is fine, but teaching them what counts is best.

—Bob Talbert (American journalist)

There is no more critical life support than passionate, informed teachers who resuscitate their students' joyful learning.

—Judy Willis (2010b)

Effectively planned, well-paced, relevant, and interesting instruction is a key aspect of effective classroom management. For schools to be positive, supportive communities in which students feel respected and valued, instructional methods and content must meet students' academic needs. Students' unproductive behavior and failure can often be traced to failure to create an educational environment conducive to learning. Students vary in the type of classroom structure and instruction that best facilitates their learning. Understanding the instructional needs of an individual student or group of students provides teachers with information essential for creating a positive learning environment.

Teachers currently face the dilemma of personally and meaningfully engaging students while simultaneously responding to state-mandated assessment requirements that often emphasize highly focused, standardized testing. We believe that state learning goals can be incorporated into lessons that meet students' needs as described in this chapter. Effective teaching that builds a sense of community and shows respect for students and their interests can occur while teachers help students master content that has been determined to be essential.

This chapter is not intended to replace coursework on effective instruction within a teacher education program. We have selected specific instructional methods we believe are related directly to student motivation, behavior that supports learning, and achievement of students who have historically been less successful at school.

LEARNING GOALS

After reading this chapter, you will know:

1. Key student academic needs that, when met, significantly increase student motivation and learning
2. Specific methods for ensuring these needs are met within your classroom
3. Key concepts in working with students identified under the Individuals with Disabilities Education Act (IDEA) as having special needs
4. How to incorporate cooperative learning into your lesson planning

Why Are These Goals Important?

Too often teachers implement methods for improving student behavior that fail to have the desired results because students' basic academic needs are not being met. If students do not understand what they are learning or why they are learning and do not believe they can be successful at the academic tasks they are told are important, they will be far less likely to behave responsibly and learn effectively in your classroom. As discussed previously, many teachers state their biggest concern is working with students who are experiencing ongoing and serious emotional and behavior disorders (EBD). It is important to note that research suggests that "strong academic instruction and interventions may be the first line of defense in working effectively with students with EBD" (Farley, Torres, Wailehua, & Cook, 2012, p. 37). This chapter will help you implement instructional methods that enhance students' motivation to learn and act responsibly in your classroom.

Key Issues in Student Motivation to Learn

Although meeting students' personal needs (as discussed in Chapter 2) provides a foundation for creating environments supportive of personal growth and learning, closely related and equally important needs exist within environments that are specifically designed to help children acquire academic knowledge. Many students meet their personal needs by successfully completing classroom activities and assignments. Other students find school to be an anxiety-producing, frustrating setting and look elsewhere for the significance, competence, and power they so desperately need. Understanding the research on motivation and its relationship to student academic needs enables teachers to implement instruction that results in virtually all students obtaining feelings of worth within the school setting.

When frustrated by students' failure to pay attention, complete assignments, or attend class, teachers often blame family and community factors. Our own experiences and reading of the research suggests another explanation. We have never met a student who was unmotivated to learn. We have met many students who were unmotivated in certain settings but highly motivated in others; that is, students who were motivated when their learning needs were met but appeared unmotivated when they were not. Consider how you would feel if you were placed in a third-year, second-semester medical school program and told that your future success would be influenced by how you performed. Most people would search for ways to withdraw from or deny the value of this anxiety-provoking, stressful situation. More concretely, consider how you respond in a college course, in-service workshop, or meeting in which the content seems irrelevant or boring or when you are not asked to be actively involved. In our many years of attending faculty meetings, we have seen numerous examples of teacher behavior that looked similar to the behavior of the students sent to the one of the authors' office when he was a junior high school vice principal.

Like many other writers, our view of motivation incorporates the expectation × value theory (Feather, 1982). This model suggests that the extent to which people become actively and productively involved in an activity is based on (1) whether they believe they can be successful at the task and (2) the degree to which they value the rewards associated with successful task completion. We add a third variable—climate, or the quality of relationships within the task setting during the time the people are engaged in the task. Thus, the formula becomes

$$\text{motivation} = \text{expectation} \times \text{value} \times \text{climate}$$

Because it is described as a multiplicative function, this model suggests that students will not be motivated unless all three components are present—that is, they (1) expect they can accomplish a task, (2) find value in the task, and (3) complete the task in an environment supportive of their basic personal needs.

It is important to note that this formula involves multiplication rather than addition signs, indicating that the components are related in a nonlinear fashion. For example, students might expect they can complete the work and enjoy the climate of the classroom but have virtually no motivation because they do not believe the work is interesting or valuable. Similarly, students who want to accomplish a task and are working in an emotionally supportive environment will soon lose motivation if the work is simply too difficult to accomplish with any degree of success.

Brain-based research supports this formula. First, this research emphasizes the importance of a safe, calm, healthy classroom environment (climate). Second, it clearly emphasizes the importance of students' believing they can accomplish the tasks provided them (expectation). Finally, this research suggests the necessity of value. As suggested by Kovalik and Olsen (2005), ". . . the physiology of the brain underscores the importance of defining learning as a two-step process: understanding and then using what is understood. It turns out that the brain expects to use what it understands" (p. 2.8).

PAUSE & CONSIDER 7.1

Consider a recent learning experience you found stimulating or beneficial. On a sheet of paper, create three columns or sections labeled "Expectation," "Value," and "Climate." In each section, write a brief statement describing how the learning experience met each of these criteria for motivating your learning.

In a similar vein, if you are currently teaching or observing in a classroom, try to recall a situation in which a student you and others viewed as rather unmotivated to perform in school was productively involved in the learning process. Can you list the events that allowed this student to expect he or she could be successful at that task, value the work, and feel comfortable working in the setting?

The second concept that organizes our thinking about motivation is Eccles and Wigfield's (1985) idea that three types of value may be associated with a task:

1. *Intrinsic value*—the simple interest or enjoyment associated with engaging in a task
2. *Attainment value*—the value of obtaining achievement, notoriety, or influence through accomplishing a task
3. *Utility value*—the benefits to one's career or other personal goals associated with performing a task successfully

Teachers need to ensure that at least one type of value is present if students are to be motivated by the task.

Perhaps the area in which teachers express the most concern is in the area of value or goals. Many teachers state that their students simply do not value learning, or at least not learning the content presented in their class. In his book *Motivating Humans*, Martin Ford (1992) points out that although it is desirable for students to have multiple reasons for being involved in academic activities, for some students, educators may need to be creative to find one reason for students to become productively engaged in an activity.

For example, by providing opportunities for self-determination or peer interaction, it may be possible to facilitate meaningful engagement in low-achieving students who generally focus more on fun and friendships than on learning and self-improvement. . . . Similarly, by organizing tasks so that they require teamwork and accountability to the group, students and workers who might be unenthusiastic about the substance of a task . . . will nevertheless have other reasons to commit themselves to good performance on the task. . . . In short, although high achievement may require motivational patterns strengthened by the union of multiple goals . . . one may be able to ensure at least adequate levels of performance by designing classroom and work contexts so that everyone can find at least one good reason to invest themselves in contextually appropriate activities. (p. 102)

In our experiences, this concern about students' lack of finding value in learning is disproportionately expressed by teachers working in urban and multicultural classrooms. In their article "A Framework for Culturally Responsive Teaching," Raymond Wlodkowski and Margery Ginsberg (1995) indicate that especially when teaching students who live in relatively greater poverty, a learning environment must emphasize intrinsic motivation. These authors state that their model is based on creating a learning environment that includes the following conditions:

1. Establishing inclusion—creating a learning atmosphere in which students and teachers feel respected by and connected to one another
2. Developing attitude—creating a favorable disposition toward the learning experience through personal relevance and choice
3. Enhancing meaning—creating challenging, thoughtful learning experiences that include student perspectives and values
4. Engendering competence—creating an understanding that students are effective in learning something they value (p. 19)

As with personal needs, understanding and response to students' academic needs are central factors determining whether we as educators can create communities in which learning is viewed as desirable. The remainder of this chapter presents strategies for understanding and responding to students' academic needs that will allow us to build such communities. Many, if not most, of the methods we have chosen for inclusion in this chapter as the most consistently related to positive student behavior and learning are also those recommended by individuals who research and teach about how to create productive learning environments for students whose first language is not English as well as for African American students and other student groups who have historically underachieved in our schools. These methods are supported as well by researchers who advocate for what is often called brain-based or brain-compatible learning.

As teachers continue to work in schools driven by the desire to improve student scores on standardized tests, it is imperative to consider how this pressure impacts students. In her compelling book *Cultures in Conflict: Eliminating Racial Profiling*, Martha Bireda (2010) wrote:

> With NCLB, culturally responsive instruction has been abandoned, as "teaching to the test" has become the norm. There is a general disregard for cultural learning styles or instructional approaches that would best suit students from diverse cultures. All of this makes for students whose instructional needs are not met, who become bored, alienated, disengaged from the learning process, and who in turn misbehave in class. (p. 8)

Studies suggest that on-task behavior may be enhanced when students are engaged in more cognitively challenging tasks (Amato-Zech, Off, & Doepke, 2006; Gillies, 2006). The lack of meaningful, engaging work associated with many instructional methods touted as improving students' scores on standardized tests may be a major cause of student behavior problems and alienation from school.

It must be noted that meaningful engagement can occur when students have a high rate of on-task behavior and academic success while involved in academic tasks they view as meaningful because adults they trust are clear with them that learning the content will open doors for their future. Research suggests that teacher-directed direct instructional methods, when associated with students' perceiving their teachers as supportive and believing in them, can lead to high achievement gains on standardized tests (Poplin et al., 2011). There is clearly no "one size fits all" or "one right way to teach." Teachers who are committed, believe in their students, and implement effective classroom management skills can bring about high rates of student academic success using a variety of instructional methods.

A major goal of this chapter is to provide you with both a theoretical lens and very practical methods for enhancing student achievement while simultaneously increasing students' sense of empowerment and involvement in the learning process.

STUDENTS' ACADEMIC NEEDS

Figure 7.1 provides a list of student academic needs that, when met, enhance student motivation and achievement. The list (first presented in 1990) is based on our own categorization of research and has been validated and modified by lists generated by more than a thousand teachers.

Support for these academic needs is found in the work of Eugene Garcia (2001). Based on his own research and an extensive review of existing work, Garcia presents a number of teacher characteristics and instructional methods associated with high achievement for students from diverse cultural backgrounds. These teacher behaviors include the following:

1. focusing instruction to some degree on what has meaning to students
2. using a thematic approach to instruction
3. incorporating active learning, including a workshop approach to literacy
4. implementing cooperative/collaborative learning activities
5. communicating high teacher expectations for achievement of all students
6. developing warm, caring relationships with students that often extend beyond the schoolday, including teachers learning about the students and their cultures
7. integrating aspects of all students' cultures into instructional activities
8. creating opportunities for cross-age tutoring
9. incorporating specific instructional techniques for students with limited English proficiency

The approaches presented in this chapter are consistent with and provide specific methods for incorporating all of these methods into your instructional approach.

FIGURE 7.1 STUDENTS' ACADEMIC NEEDS

1. Understand and value learning goals
2. Understand the learning process
3. Be actively involved in the learning process
4. Have learning goals related to their own interests and choices
5. Receive instruction responsive to their learning styles and strengths
6. See learning modeled by adults as an exciting and rewarding process
7. Experience success
8. Have time to integrate learning
9. Receive realistic and immediate feedback that enhances self-efficacy
10. Be involved in self-evaluating their learning and effort
11. Receive appropriate rewards for performance gains
12. Experience a supportive, safe, well-organized learning environment

The methods presented in this chapter are also consistent with recommendations from brain-based research. This research (Kovalik & Olsen, 2005) suggests that the following educational factors support student learning.

- Absence of threat/nurturing
- Movement
- Collaboration
- Meaningful content
- Choices
- Enriched environment
- Adequate time
- Immediate feedback
- Mastery

These factors are also consistent with recommendations for instructional methods that support the inclusion of students with special needs (Mastropieri & Scruggs, 2007; Soodack & McCarthy, 2006). Mastropieri and Scruggs (2007) state that in order to be successful with students needing modifications in their class work, it is essential that the work is at an appropriate level of difficulty, the tasks are meaningful, and student success is based on improvement and obtaining goals rather than on comparison to fellow students.

Academic Need 1: Understand and Value the Learning Goals

Walter Doyle (1983) wrote that "the quality of the time students spend engaged in academic work depends on the tasks they are expected to accomplish and the extent to which students understand what they are doing. It is essential, therefore, that direct instruction include explicit attention to meaning and not simply focus on engagement as an end in itself" (p. 189). Unfortunately, many students do not really understand why they are involved in a learning activity. They study to obtain good grades, please their parents or teacher, or avoid punishment. In summarizing the findings of a study on student engagement in academic tasks, Brophy (1986b) stated:

> Analysis of the teachers' presentations of assignments to the students suggested that teacher failure to call attention to the purposes and meanings of these assignments was a major reason for the students' low quality of engagement in them. Most presentations included procedural directions or special hints, such as "pay attention to the underlined words," but only 5 percent explicitly described the purpose of the assignment in terms of the content being taught. (p. 11)

Fortunately, research suggests that teachers can quite rapidly learn to give students specific explanations concerning the purpose of instructional activities. Results indicate that students taught by these teachers demonstrate significantly greater understanding of and appreciation for the purpose of the instruction.

We have worked with several colleagues who have permanently written on their whiteboards the words:

- Objective(s)
- Reason(s)
- Activity(ies)
- Assessment

They begin almost every lesson by writing a statement providing responses to these terms as they apply to the upcoming lesson. This not only provides students with an opportunity to examine and discuss the learning goals but also helps students to understand the learning process.

PAUSE & CONSIDER 7.2

We encourage you to keep a learning log of classrooms in which you are a student, observer, or teacher. Whenever a lesson is presented to a whole class, small group, or individual student, record what was said to help the students understand and value the learning goals. What percentage of the lessons or task introductions was associated with a clear statement regarding the reason for mastering the content? Were students involved in discussing and presenting their ideas regarding the benefits of mastering the learning goals? Did a pattern exist between involving students in this type of understanding and student motivation, engagement, and mastery?

Academic Need 2: Understand the Learning Process

In order to help students better understand the learning process, we have found it helpful to assist students in developing several key concepts related to learning.

Develop a Functional Definition of Learning

Attribution theory and research suggests students, particularly those who struggle with learning, see intelligence and academic skill as a fixed trait and that when they are successful, it is due to their having less difficult work or greater assistance. It is important that these students realize that effort and focus can improve the effectiveness with which their brains operate and that they can develop new capabilities just as individuals do when they put great effort into sports, music, art, dancing, or any other activity. In her engaging article "Using My Neuroscience to Treat the Sickness in Our Classrooms," Judy Willis (2010b), a neuroscientist MD who became a teacher, writes:

> I began to explain to my upper elementary and later my middle school students about the changes in their brains that take place through neuro-plasticity. I also showed them brain scans, and we drew diagrams about the construction of the connections between neurons that grow when new information is learned, and how more dendrites grow when information is reviewed. (p. 53)

She goes on to state:

> Their responses were wonderful. One ten-year-old boy said, "I didn't know that I could grow my brain. Now I know about growing dendrites when I study and get a good night sleep. I tell myself that I have the power to grow a smarter brain if I review and practice. I'd rather play video games, but I don't because I want my brain to grow smarter." (p. 53)

First, it is important to begin the school year by having students develop a functional definition of learning. The vast majority of students believe that effective learning means doing better than many of their classmates on homework assignments, in-class assessments, and standardized tests. Unfortunately, in every class and every school, 25 percent of the students are in the bottom quartile

© James Estes

"In arithmetic, we're studying 'guzintas'—three guzinta nine three times, two guzinta four two times. . . ."

on any of these tasks (statistically, they must be). If teachers continue to allow students to define learning as the process of "winning," we will continue to have a significant percentage of students acting out and dropping out in response to their perceived failure.

One technique for redefining learning involves beginning the school year by having students describe what an effective learner "looks like" and "sounds like." After students have generated this list, the class works to create several definitions of an effective learner. Figure 7.2 presents the responses generated by students in a fourth- and fifth-grade blended classroom. Once students have determined the characteristics of an effective learner, these standards can be used as criteria against which students can assess their own behavior. This allows students to redefine learning as being something concrete and obtainable rather than the elusive attempt to "be one of the best." It also creates a healthy set of behavioral norms for students.

Understand the Procedure Associated with the Learning Activity

Prior to beginning any lesson, it is important to provide students with a clear statement about how they are expected to act during this time. For example, students need to know the expectations for (1) talking (e.g., joining the group discussion, working silently or with peers, etc.), (2) obtaining assistance, (3) movement within and in and out of the room during the activity, (4) what to do when they have finished the activity (e.g., where to put their work, what additional work they can engage in, etc.), and (5) any specific procedure for the activity (e.g., how to obtain and use materials required for the activity).

© George Abbott

"You were supposed to find the hypotenuse."

Recently one of us was asked to work with a teacher who was described as struggling in the area of classroom management. The individuals responsible for supervising this teacher indicated she had limited skills in dealing with disruptive student behavior. Observations indicated her skills in responding to disruptions were actually very strong. Her major area for improvement lay in her need to improve how she clarified the academic procedures (the objective and reason for the instructional activity) and the behavioral procedures associated with each instructional activity. Students were often confused about why they were doing an activity or how they were to behave when completing the activity. This confusion led to such high rates of off-task behavior that, despite her skillful responses, created a rather chaotic classroom environment.

FIGURE 7.2
A SUCCESSFUL
LEARNER

Looks Like	Sounds Like
Eyes focused on speaker	Gives encouragement
Concentrates on one's own work	Uses appropriate voice level
Is well organized	Asks questions
Cooperates with others	Asks for help when needed
Follows classroom rules and procedures	Shares his or her ideas with others
Sets goals	Makes on-task comments
Stays calm when having a problem	Is courteous to others
Uses time wisely	Uses problem solving
Learns from mistakes	
Shares materials	
Does not give up	

A successful learner is someone who works hard, cooperates with others, takes risks, sets goals, makes a good effort and asks for help if needed, doesn't give up, and learns from his or her mistakes.

PAUSE & CONSIDER 7.3

Pause for a moment and consider what you have done or observed that helped students understand that learning is a process involving skills at which they can all be successful. You may not have your students define an effective learner, but it will be important to help them dispel the notion that effective learners are only those who find learning easy, score well on tests, or receive high grade averages. Discuss with several colleagues or classmates what you might do to help students in your class develop a healthful, functional definition of being an effective student/learner.

Learn How to Study Effectively

Many students lack skills for effectively learning new information. Interventions aimed at assisting students in developing improved learning strategies can be placed in three categories: (1) *cognitive interventions*, including skills for accomplishing specific tasks, such as underlining, highlighting, using a mnemonic, outlining, summarizing, and so on; (2) *metacognitive interventions*, including planning and monitoring one's use of strategies and determining when specific strategies are best used; and (3) *affective interventions* emphasizing attribution and attitudes (Hattie, Biggs, & Purdie, 1996). When our daughter was in eighth grade, we realized she was struggling with the speed and retention of reading academic content because she did not know how to read a novel differently from a history textbook. Therefore, we taught her to read textbooklike materials by looking at the headings and subheadings to determine what content was being covered in the chapter or section she was reading. Next, we suggested that she read the material and highlight what she believed to be the key content. As she completed each section, we taught her to write or say what she had learned from the section and how this related to the previous section or other material she was learning. We taught her to summarize by creating some form of visual schema or diagram to highlight her learning. Finally, we suggested that she write down questions she had regarding the material and develop a plan for having these questions answered. This included our teaching her how to schedule time with a teacher and ways to ask teachers questions. The process we taught our daughter and have subsequently taught our son and many students is similar to the SCROL method developed by Grant (1993) in which students are asked to (1) Survey, (2) Connect, (3) Read, (4) Outline, and (5) Look Back; and the SQ3R method of Scan, Question, Read, Reflect, and Review.

When reading a novel or other text without headings, we taught her to use a highlighter to mark key facts or concepts she thought the author was attempting to develop. We then suggested she again create some form of visual outline. Because she learns very well through interpersonal interaction, we then suggested she call or speak with someone in her class to discuss the material and the key concepts involved.

Students often have difficulty grouping or organizing material that is not in printed form. Learners construct knowledge as they build cognitive maps for organizing and interpreting new information. Effective teachers help students make such maps by drawing connections among different concepts and between new ideas and learners' prior experiences. There are several ways to help students organize their learning. First, we can provide students with a graphic organizer that provides them with an overview of key concepts and how they relate to one another. Crank and Bulgren (1993) suggest that there are three major types of graphic organizers: (1) central and hierarchical, (2) directional, and (3) comparative. Central and hierarchical organizers indicate how a key concept is divided into components. In central organizers, the topics are shown as radiating from a central theme, whereas in hierarchical organizers, key items have supporting information below them. A web is an example of a central organizer, and an outline using a format with Roman numerals, uppercase letters, numbers, and so on would be an example of a hierarchical organizer. Directional organizers show information in a time frame or cause-and-effect sequence. Comparative organizers show how two concepts compare and contrast.

We have worked with students who find spontaneous writing very difficult but who, once they create a central organizer, are freed to write rapidly and creatively. Many students simply need assistance and training in how to organize material so it is more readily accessible for retention or creative use.

Rather than present learning skills as a sequential curriculum, it is more effective to determine specific skills students may need in order to learn material within the upcoming days and to provide them with strategies for more effectively learning the material. If this learning is to generalize to other classroom settings, students will need assistance in using their new techniques and understanding that it was the use of these methods rather than your assistance, ease of task, or luck that enabled them to effectively master the content.

Study skills materials are available that provide teachers with a variety of strategies. Anita Archer and Mary Gleason (1989, 1994) have developed two programs: Skills for School Success (for grades three through six), and Advanced Skills for School Success (for middle school and high school). These programs provide a rich array of strategies. The Recommended Reading section at the end of the chapter provides other materials we have found helpful.

PAUSE & CONSIDER 7.4

Before continuing, consider a lesson or content you are currently teaching or observing someone teach. Are some students struggling to master or understand this content? Is it possible that part of their difficulty stems from their lack of skill in knowing how to study the material? Carefully observe several students who appear to be having difficulty mastering the content and consider how you might assist them in thinking about and studying the material. List one or more specific strategies you might assist them in using. Share this with at least one colleague.

FIGURE 7.3
METHODS FOR
DEMYSTIFYING
THE LEARNING
PROCESS

1. Work with students to clearly and explicitly define learning.
2. Celebrate students' successes based on this definition.
3. Write and verbally explain the goals and objectives for each lesson and why these have been chosen.
4. Relate learning to students' own lives and interests.
5. Explain to students why you chose each instructional method to reach your stated goal.
6. Have students establish learning goals.
7. Use "experts" from the community to evaluate student performance, and demonstrate and discuss its value.
8. Teach students about types of special abilities (Howard Gardner's concepts).
9. Teach students about learning disabilities (differences) and how students can work with these differences.
10. Use peer tutoring and teach students how to be tutors.
11. Involve students in teaching small lessons to the class so they can learn to appreciate the skills involved in effective teaching and the prerequisites for effective learning.
12. Have students provide ongoing feedback to the teacher regarding how the teacher is using effective instructional methods.
13. Explain to students your philosophy of assessment.
14. Be very specific in clarifying when assessment will occur, how it will be used, what to study, and how to study.
15. Have students monitor their own learning gains and grades.
16. Have students develop test questions.
17. Provide multiple methods for assessing students' knowledge.
18. Involve students in assessing their own effort in reaching learning goals.
19. Teach students a variety of study skills.
20. Provide students assistance in how to study specific types of materials.

General Methods for Demystifying Learning

There is a multitude of methods for ensuring that the learning process becomes less mysterious and better understood by students. Figure 7.3 provides a list of twenty ways to demystify the learning process by helping students develop a clear understanding of what learning is and why curriculum and instructional decisions are made.

Academic Need 3: Be Actively Involved in the Learning Process

Consider situations in which you were motivated to accomplish a task and found enjoyment in the work. It is likely that many of these tasks involved your active participation in the learning process. Although we cannot always meet this student academic need, student motivation and achievement will be enhanced by actively involving students in the learning process.

A study based on more than 1,000 observations in elementary and secondary classrooms (Scott, Alter, & Hirn, 2011) reported that teachers spent 49 percent of classroom time presenting information to students, allocated 27 percent of the time to individual seatwork, 14 percent to teacher-led small groups, 7 percent to small peer group activities, and 1 percent to one-on-one support for individual students. During teacher-led instruction, teachers provided a group opportunity to respond about every 2 minutes and an individual response opportunity to an individual student every 12.5 minutes. Positive feedback to a student was reported as occurring every 16.67 minutes and negative feedback every 14.29 minutes. In addition, ". . . students were observed to be actively engaged with the curriculum 39% of the time, passively engaged with the curriculum 42%, off task 13%, and 6% of the time was coded as 'down time,' indicating no task or expectations were apparent" (p. 631). These authors also noted that ". . . teaching was defined essentially as any teacher activity that involved interacting with, speaking to, or even passively observing students, 37.9% of time coded as not teaching is alarming" (pp. 634, 635).

These findings are very similar to those observed in ninety K–12 classrooms in California and Pennsylvania (Hayling, Cook, Gresham, State, & Kern, 2008) where 78 percent of time was allocated to whole-class instruction and independent seatwork. These authors also found that 8 percent of classroom time was spent on transitioning from one activity to the next. They noted that independent seatwork was associated with the highest rates of off-task behavior. Secondary students also spend the majority of their time in noninteractive activities such as listening to lectures and doing individual seatwork tasks (Hunter & Csikszentmihalyi, 2003). These authors indicate that when students were engaged in interactive activities about which they felt both capable and challenged, their engagement rates were 73 percent as compared to only 42 percent when involved in activities that were less stimulating. Not surprisingly, in numerous studies, students expressed their desire to have teachers incorporate more interactive strategies that involve greater student participation (Milner, 2006).

Although it is likely that almost all learners benefit from instructional activities that actively engage them, a number of writers have indicated that students of color respond more effectively to an instructional style that permits active student involvement. Kuykendall (2004) notes that "educators who are serious about enhancing the achievement and motivation of Black and Hispanic youth must be willing to use a variety of activities to stimulate interest and facilitate student growth. . . . Black and Hispanic youth are likely to respond favorably to think-pair-share activities, lively group discussions, cooperative learning, group projects, and telling of stories about personal experience" (pp. 74, 75). Writers such as Banks and McGee Banks (1993), Hale-Benson (1986), Kuykendall (2004), and Shade (1989) have noted that African American, Hispanic, and Native American students tend to be field-dependent learners who need to be more actively involved in the learning process.

Brain research also suggests that active involvement, especially when it involves choice and meaningful activity, increases the release of dopamine, which is associated with greater student motivation and focus (Willis, 2010b). As one group of authors stated, "cooperative learning and real-world applications are crucial to a successful brain-based classroom (Wilmes, Harrington, Kohler-Evans, & Sumpter, 2008). When discussing what brain research says about student engagement in the learning process, Willis (2006) wrote:

> The goal of research-based education is to structure lessons to ultimately rely less on inefficient and tedious rote memory. Helping students access and use more effective types of memory storage and retrieval will literally change their brains. (p. 6)

She goes on to state:

> The goal is for them to actively discover, interpret, analyze, process, practice, and discuss the information so it will move beyond working memory and be processed in the frontal lobe regions devoted to executive function. (p. 10)

Given these findings, it is useful for teachers to examine their daily and weekly schedules to determine the type of instructional activities in which they are engaging students. This might include the approximate percentage of time students are involved in teacher-directed activities, independent work, and cooperative group activities. This might be further broken down into active versus passive learning. For example, a week might be depicted as follows:

	Passive	Active
Teacher-directed work	20%	15%
Independent work	30%	0%
Cooperative work	0%	35%

This would suggest a blend of activities as well as a balance of passive and active learning. Of course, even the more passive learning, such as listening to a lecture or reading, will be more likely to emotionally engage students if it is related to their interests and lives. Many of the methods presented in this chapter emphasize teachers actively engaging students, both intellectually and personally, in the learning process.

A simple method for enhancing active student engagement in large-group activities while reducing the amount of disruptive behavior is to create what are often called response cards (Duchaine, Green, & Jolivette, 2011). Response cards vary from the use of white boards where students write their answers to cards with a T (True) or F (False) or letters for multiple-choice answers that students display to indicate their response to a teacher question.

Academic Need 4: Have Learning Goals Related to Their Own Interests and Choices

Incorporating Students' Interests

In addition to increasing active engagement, it is important to connect curriculum to students' lives. John Dewey (1916) wrote that academic learning "must be derived from materials which at the outset fall within the scope of ordinary life-experience" (p. 73). Dewey believed learning should help students develop lifelong skills that would assist them in being productive members of society. This value continues today. For example, the standards presented by the National Council of Teachers of Mathematics recommend a curriculum better connected to other curricular areas and to the world outside of school.

When Thomas Edison asked his teacher how water could run uphill, he was expelled from school. While we have come a long way in allowing students academic freedom, many students still find that the content of their schoolwork provides them with little opportunity to examine issues important to them or to study content related to and respectful of their cultural heritage. Studies suggest that students prefer instructional methods supportive of their special interests and needs (Davidson, 1999), and that when these are implemented, students who have a history of somewhat low achievement can be very successful. More recent work supports these findings and suggests that teenagers benefit from involvement in instructional activities that allow them to engage in processing information through authentic situations (Bartholomew, 2008). "In order for students to learn the information they have been given, teachers must plan for concrete activities that directly correlate to the knowledge that is expected to be learned" (Zarra, 2009, p. 69).

> Without lessons that are interactive, personally relevant, or experiential and without opportunities for critical thinking and creative problem solving, students lose out, not only on authentic learning and the construction of long-term memory, but they also do not have experiences that promote development of the prefrontal cortex executive functions such as judgment, analysis, resilience, tolerance, flexibility, and effective communication of their ideas. These are the qualities today's students will need to succeed in the 21st century. (Willis, 2010a, p. 49)

Several years ago, one of us was supervising a student teacher who had left a career in engineering to become a teacher. The student teacher was taking over a high school physics class and asked one of us to visit one of the first classes he would be teaching. During the class, students were quite talkative and became increasingly inattentive as the class progressed. Several critical, disgruntled comments could be heard as the bell rang and the students left the class. The student teacher, a mature and rather confident individual, was devastated. He slumped into a chair and emotionally stated that he apparently did not have what it took to be an effective teacher, that the class period had been painful, and that he did not want to face another group of students that day.

The mentor teacher (a talented teacher with many years' experience) overheard the conversation and assured the student teacher that with some minor tinkering, the lesson could be a real success. He asked the student teacher if he would be willing to teach the same lesson to a physics class two periods later with the caveat that the mentor would have five minutes to introduce the class. The mentor assured the student teacher that he had a great deal to offer the students and that his lesson needed only a little fine-tuning to be outstanding. The student teacher reluctantly agreed to teach the lesson again.

When the classroom filled, the mentor teacher began the lesson by asking how many of the students had, at the beginning of the year, listed understanding flight as an interest and learning goal for the class. Most students raised their hands, and the teacher reinforced this response by providing the data that had been generated during the first week of class. He then informed the class that the next two weeks would be spent on some difficult material that, by itself, had little meaning. He noted, however, that when combined with one additional skill, this material would allow them to figure trajectories and other factors associated with flight. He then asked how many of the students were interested in delving into this difficult but important material. All the students in the class raised their hands. The mentor then informed the class that aerospace engineering was not his strength but that the student teacher who would be teaching them had this very background and the students were in for a real treat working with him. With this introduction, the student teacher took center stage and presented a lesson identical to that which, one hour earlier, had been met with student apathy, frustration, and disruptive behavior. This time students were attentive and frequently raised their hands to ask clarifying questions. When the class ended, approximately half of the students clapped to show their appreciation of the lesson. The student teacher walked to the door, and as students left, a number of them thanked him for the lesson. In debriefing the lesson, the mentor reminded the student teacher of the importance of connecting content to students' interests. He noted that this was not always possible, but when he was able to do it, the results were usually dramatic.

Another method that has increasing interest and a solid research base is often referred to as service learning—an approach that attempts to link academic curriculum with service to and/or involvement with content based in the community. The K–12 Service-Learning Standards for Quality Practices (National Youth Leadership Council, 2008) created a list of essential elements involved in this type of learning. Studies indicate incorporating this approach can have significant positive effects on students' attitudes toward school, social skills, academic performance, and civic engagement (Celio, Durlak, & Dymnicki, 2011).

Several years ago, one of us worked with a gifted teacher of students with behavior disorders who was committed to involving students in meaningful learning. The building in which his program was located was only several feet from a highway and less than a mile from a ferry dock. Because drivers were often in a hurry to catch the ferry, speeding was a problem. In addition, only a faded white crosswalk was provided for students crossing the highway. The teacher decided to involve the seven students in his class in resolving this real-world problem. The students began the process by talking to workers at the ferry, who informed them that the road belonged to the county and they would have to work with the county commissioner's and county sheriff's office to solve the problem. The students followed a seven-step problem-solving model. The model and their description of their work in the seven stages are found in Figure 7.4.

The students initially collected their own data and then had a member of the Washington State Highway Patrol join them and use a radar gun to obtain accurate speeds. Figure 7.5 presents a chart of the actual speeds obtained in one hour and fifteen minutes during the late morning. The students then invited a county commissioner to take a bus tour of the speed zone area and observe the problem. Finally, the students developed the following eight possible solutions:

1. flashing lights to tell people to stop
2. patrol cars to stop speeders

**FIGURE 7.4
SEVEN STEPS TO
SOLVING THE
SPEEDING
PROBLEM**

Source: Reprinted
with permission of
the author.

1. **Choose a problem to work on**
   We chose the problem of the speeding cars that make it difficult for us to cross the street.

2. **Create a vision**
   Our vision is to have flashing lights or larger signs so people know this is a school area.

3. **Study the problem**
   We studied the problem by using a stopwatch to time cars going by. It takes nine seconds to go through the school zone at 20 miles per hour, which is the speed limit. Other cars were going through in four to six seconds.

4. **Accept the risks**
   We accepted the risks by knowing that if we don't stop speeders, one of us could be injured or killed. We also accept that if we do not get our plan to work, speeders will still speed.

5. **Make a commitment**
   We made a commitment to get our part of the plan done by talking to the State Police, Island County Sheriff, and the Camp Caset Manager. We are not going to back down.

6. **Plan the project**
   We planned the project by presenting our speeds for the cars to Officer Scott Wernecke of the Washington State Patrol.

7. **Move into action.**
   We moved into action by asking Officer Wernecke to come down and get the speeds of cars going by and to prepare a report.

FIGURE 7.5
DATA FROM
THE REAL-WORLD
PROBLEM-SOLVING
RADAR CHECK
Source: Reprinted with
permission of the
author.

Speed in MPH	Number of Cars
0–20	12
21–25	19
26–30	31
31–35	16
36–40	15
41–45	2

3. a radar gun to find out who is speeding
4. speed bumps by the crosswalks to slow down the cars
5. bigger school speed limit signs so they would stand out
6. brighter colored signs so people could see them
7. a traffic light
8. streamers or flags so the signs would stand out

As a result of these efforts, the County Commission requested that the County Public Works Department add flashing school speed limit signs, ripple bumps, and a crosswalk more clearly marked and located in a more visible position.

This is a wonderful example of how elementary students can make a difference in their lives and the lives of other students. It also demonstrates how real-world problem solving can be used to integrate a variety of content areas. In this case, students calculated speed times using distance and a stopwatch and graphed their results, made phone calls and had meetings with county and state officials, wrote letters, wrote a summary report and drew pictures to support their report, read ferry schedules, and learned about local governments and their decision-making processes. In addition, and perhaps more important, these students developed a sense of personal efficacy. They learned that they had important skills and influence. They learned that they could be listened to and heard, and that their voices could make a difference.

Zahorik (1996) studied how both elementary and secondary teachers made work interesting for students. Based on information from thirty secondary and thirty-five elementary teachers, the results indicated that the most frequently used and successful methods were (1) hands-on activities; (2) group work; (3) personalizing the content by connecting it to students' life experiences and interests; and (4) involving students in sharing their ideas, planning, and making choices.

Using Thematic Units

Several authors (Beane, 1997; Cummins, 1996; Garcia, 2001) suggest that in classrooms that more effectively serve students with limited English proficiency, academic content is arranged around thematic units. In many instances, students collaborate with teachers to select the themes.

One of us used this approach for more than thirty years. Working in a state that has adopted rigorous standardized testing to assess student learning, she has not abandoned this technique. Instead, much more care is taken to ensure that the academic skills learned as students become proficient are aligned with the state requirements. This creates a win–win situation for students. While remaining excited about and actively involved in meaningful learning, students continue to develop skills that will indicate to some decision makers that they have mastered key content and may progress to a higher grade. Figure 7.6 presents an outline of a thematic unit organized around the Iditarod dogsled race in Alaska. The Recommended Reading section at the end of the chapter lists books to further explore integrated curriculum as a method for enhancing students' motivation to learn.

FIGURE 7.6
IDITAROD
THEMATIC
UNIT

I. Reading
   A. Iditarod vocabulary: word search
   B. Literature novels: *Woodsong, Stone Fox, Kiana's Iditarod, Julie of the Wolves*
   C. Short stories
   D. "IditaRead" reading race

II. Social Studies
   A. Serum Run of 1925
   B. History of the Iditarod
   C. Study of Alaska
   D. Map the route
   E. Geography of Alaska
   F. Directions during the race
   G. A typical day on the trail
   H. Native peoples and cultures of Alaska

III. Math
   A. Compute the distance of the race
   B. Examine distances between checkpoints using mean, median, and mode
   C. Math problem of the day
   D. Iditarod logic problems
   E. Compare prices for groceries in Alaska with those in your own state
   F. Iditarod problem solving

IV. Writing/Language Arts
   A. Write to a musher
   B. Follow a musher and write newspaper articles
   C. Daily oral language using sentences about the race
   D. Keep a diary as if you were a musher on the trail
   E. Write a congratulatory letter to a musher for finishing the race
   F. Write a poem about some aspect of the race

V. Science
   A. Create a weather center for weather reports during the race
   B. Graph temperatures at checkpoints in Alaska
   C. Invite a rescue official to talk about hypothermia
   D. Study glaciers and volcanoes and create a model of one
   E. Study an arctic animal and write a report
   F. Pretend you are an architect. Design a home for northern Alaska. How would you guard against permafrost?
   G. Draw an ecosystem that survives and adapts to the Arctic climate
   H. Study the aurora borealis
   I. Bring a veterinarian to talk about treatment of the dogs
   J. Study the equipment needed for the race; plan to pack a sled by drawing what is needed

(continued)

FIGURE 7.6
(CONTINUED)

VI. Art
   A. Create a watercolor of the aurora borealis
   B. Design a poster for this year's Iditarod race
   C. Build a model of a musher's sled
   D. Design a picture of what clothes a musher must have on the trail
   E. Create dream catchers
   F. Make a native story mask

VII. Music
   A. Learn songs from the trail
   B. Create a song about the Iditarod using familiar tunes
   C. Listen to and make native musical instruments

Place-Based Education

Another way to create thematic units involves what has been termed *place-based education* (Smith, 2002). The key concept in place-based education is that students are actively involved in learning experiences that involve and provide benefit to the communities in which they live.

Brain-based research suggests that meaningful content is a key to student learning.

> So what makes content meaningful? For the most part, it is real-life context, richness of sensory input, and relevance to the learner that produces an emotional response of "I care." Context means that the concept to be studied is placed in real-life settings that are experienceable by students. (Kovalik & Olsen, 2005, p. 113)

Place-based education provides this opportunity. Smith (2002) suggests that there are five types of place-based education: (1) cultural studies, (2) nature studies, (3) real-world problem solving, (4) internships and entrepreneurial opportunities, and (5) induction into community processes. Individual teachers working with their students can quite readily accomplish the first three of these. In cultural studies projects, students study and write about their communities and members in the community. Nature studies may involve the study of an issue related to conservation or an endangered species. Real-world problem solving involves students in selecting a problem in their community and solving this problem. The situation for which students solved a scary traffic problem near their school is one example of this. Nancy Nagel (1996) provides numerous examples of this process being effectively implemented, including work by interns in a master's degree teaching license program. Examples include students cleaning up and refurbishing their playground in an area racked by vandalism and graffiti, and students solving a water runoff problem based on the destruction of a stand of trees at their school.

Our colleague Greg Smith provides numerous examples of secondary students working on environmental issues within their communities. The following example comes from a book he has edited.

> Responding to a request from the Colorado Department of Wildlife, middle and high school students from six schools in the Yampa Valley watershed participated in a similar regional data gathering effort in a program called Riverwatch. Students collected data from 70 miles of the river about water temperature, levels of dissolved oxygen, alkalinity, water hardness, pH, heavy metals, total dissolved solids, flow, and variety of macro invertebrates. Students then wrote 15–20 page reports including graphs, photos, and conclusions that were submitted to the Department of

Wildlife. This information was used to establish stream standards and quickly found its way into the work of the state water court, the Environmental Protection Agency, and the Colorado Department of Health. (G. Smith, personal communication, February 2010)

Results of each type of place-based education program show marked improvement in students' positive behavior and academic achievement. It is exciting to see students and entire classes that had been defined as classroom management problems viewed as responsible citizens when they are given the opportunity to serve as responsible citizens.

PAUSE & CONSIDER 7.5

Before continuing on with this chapter, take a minute to consider a unit you will be teaching within the next several months. If you are observing in a classroom, consider a unit the teacher will be teaching. Write a brief statement about how you might involve students in relating this curriculum to their lives, perhaps by developing a thematic unit around a topic the students select or developing the content within the context of a real-world problem-solving activity. Share your idea with two or three colleagues or classmates and have them provide you with feedback and suggestions.

Incorporating Academic Choice

Considerable research suggests that providing students with choices regarding their academic work can have a positive impact on students, especially those who are struggling with becoming motivated and making good behavior choices (Von Mizener & Williams, 2009). Based on a review of existing research (largely with elementary students) and their own research with secondary students in a residential facility, Ramsey and her colleagues (Ramsey, Jolivette, Patterson, & Kennedy, 2010) stated that, "Using choice-making as an antecedent intervention during academic demands can help to improve the interactions between students with EBD and teachers . . . as well as decrease inappropriate behaviors and increase task engagement" (p. 2). Research in general education settings with students at risk for developing serious behavior problems suggests that "Academic choice may have played a role in decreasing the perceived aversive nature of assignment completion, thus promoting a decrease in student escape-maintained inappropriate behavior" (Skerbetz & Kostewicz, 2013, p. 212). In addition, brain research suggests that opportunities to make choices increases the release of dopamine in the brain and enhances the sense of optimism and self-satisfaction (Black et al., 2002).

In a study of more than 200 high school students, providing students with a simple choice of two similar homework assignments was associated with students' feeling more motivated to complete the work, believing they were more competent regarding the work, and scoring higher on unit tests that incorporated content from the homework. In addition, the students who were provided with choices rated their teachers higher in terms of providing students with support (Patall, Cooper, & Wynn, 2010).

There are numerous ways teachers can provide students with choices. For example, *before the academic task*, students may select where in the classroom they will work, the length of work or the number of problems they will complete, and the method they will use for presenting the work (typed, diagrammed, outlined, etc.). *During the assignment*, students may determine how to obtain teacher attention, peers with whom to work or from whom they will seek assistance, when to take short breaks, and so on. *After the task*, students may choose with whom to share their success and how to take a short break. Figure 7.7 presents a list of methods for providing academic choice that was generated by more than 150 student teachers with whom one of the authors has worked over the past three years.

**FIGURE 7.7
ACADEMIC
CHOICE
METHODS**

- Allow students to select the spelling words they will be learning
- After completing math worksheets, allow them to choose a math game
- In daily reading, allow students to choose to read to themselves or a partner
- Allow students a choice of writing topic for writer's workshop
- In reading response journals, allow students to choose which questions they respond to
- Allow students to choose from a selection of novels during reading groups
- Allow students to select the medium for an activity (e.g., colored paper or writing tool)
- Allow students to select the order to complete a set of activities
- Use choice to redirect students' focus (e.g., in a library or cafeteria, ask students if they would like to sit at one table or two)
- Demonstrate understanding of content using different methods (e.g., writing, drawing, oral presentation). Dictate their thoughts to an adult or other student.
- Allow students to choose with whom they will complete their work
- Allow students to choose where in the classroom they will work
- Allow students to choose a quick break at a time they determine
- Allow students to select to use manipulatives for some activities
- Narrow the tasks the students get to choose in order to create necessary structure
- Allow students to continue working or choose to go to a predetermined quiet area
- Allow students to choose to tell the teacher what is going on or to write a note to the teacher
- Allow students to choose to do an activity or game prior to a worksheet
- Allow students to choose to use a computer (e.g., computer-based math game)
- Allow students to choose how to get attention
- Allow students to select consequences for behavior problems
- Have students who have been removed from the group due to their behavior select when they will rejoin the group
- Allow students to choose when to complete a classroom job
- Allow students to choose how they will redirect their own behavior
- Give students extra time to play a game if they have a high on-task rate during an activity
- Allow students to select the mode the teacher will use to gain students' attention
- Allow students to choose an event that will occur immediately following completion of an activity
- Allow students to choose from a list of topics to study
- Create a "can-do"/"must-do" list for different tasks
- Allow students to choose their own book and project associated with that book
- Allow for choice among different levels of worksheets
- Have different stations and allow students to choose the stations and order
- Provide options for solving a problem (e.g., student has a stomach complaint and teacher offers the option of getting some water, using the restroom, getting some fresh air, or taking some space)
- Allow students to select an option they can use at their desk to calm down (e.g., stress ball, water, quick break, etc.)
- Allow students to choose as a class whether to use the document camera or the white board
- If student is having difficulty sitting through a task, provide options of what he or she can get up and do (e.g., choice box with six or seven educational activities)
- For read aloud, have the group choose from two or three books that fit your objectives

Involving Students in Academic Goal Setting and Other Self-Management Methods

Individual goal setting is an effective method for enabling students to experience a sense of understanding and controlling their own learning while incorporating their own interests. Goal setting also involves a form of choice, something brain research suggests increases the release of dopamine in the brain and enhances the sense of optimism and self-satisfaction (Black et al., 2002). An academic goal statement or contract should include (1) what material the student plans to learn, (2) what activities the student will engage in to develop these skills, (3) the degree of proficiency the student will reach, and (4) how the student will demonstrate that the learning has occurred. Several approaches may be used when implementing academic goals. Each student can be involved in working toward one or more academic goals associated with a personal skill deficit or interest. This emphasis on goals can be expanded to incorporate term-length goal statements. Because most schools provide an academic report to parents (and, it is hoped, to students) following a nine-week term, students can be aided in setting several academic goals on a term basis. Nine weeks will be too long for primary children, but most intermediate grade and secondary students find nine-week goal setting provides a sense of direction and commitment. At the beginning of each term, you and the student can examine the student's current performance level and the material the student will study during the term. The student can be helped to write several goals for the term, perhaps stating that by the end of the term, she or he will be able to solve two-place multiplication problems with 80 percent accuracy. It is obviously important that you help each student choose goals that are attainable but that will require some additional effort by the student. Although students are motivated to achieve goals that require some real effort, they are also frequently intimidated by goals that seem impossible to reach. Furthermore, continued failure tends to reduce students' achievement orientation and self-concept. Figure 7.8 is an example of a form an elementary or middle school teacher could use to help students commit themselves to specific academic goals. Figure 7.9 provides a middle or high school form.

One of us recently worked with a talented high school teacher in a district serving approximately 85 percent Title I students. In order to increase student motivation, the teacher incorporated four key methods. First, he used peer-relationship activities to help create a more cohesive group. Second, he established base groups so students had peer invitations and accountability. Third, he expanded his use of cooperative learning. Fourth, he used the goal setting and monitoring form seen in Figure 7.10. He discovered that students were particularly unskilled at specifying strategies they could use to complete their work. The form provided an impetus to work with students on their planning skills and for students to hold themselves and their peers accountable. He reported that student work completion and attendance increased dramatically and that many students commented on the chance to set their own goals and evaluate their progress.

Another approach to employing academic goal setting involves designing assignments that allow students to choose the type of work they will complete and, if appropriate, the grade they will earn for completing the designated amount of work. The most common format for using this method involves listing assignments for earning each grade and having students sign a contract indicating which assignments they plan to complete. This approach is particularly effective when you wish to involve all students in an assignment on which lower-achieving students might experience considerable difficulty with more complex aspects of the assignment. A contractual approach enables each student to choose an appropriate level of difficulty, and you can ensure that the basic concepts are learned by incorporating them within each level. Students respond positively to this approach because it is a clear statement of what they will learn and what they must accomplish.

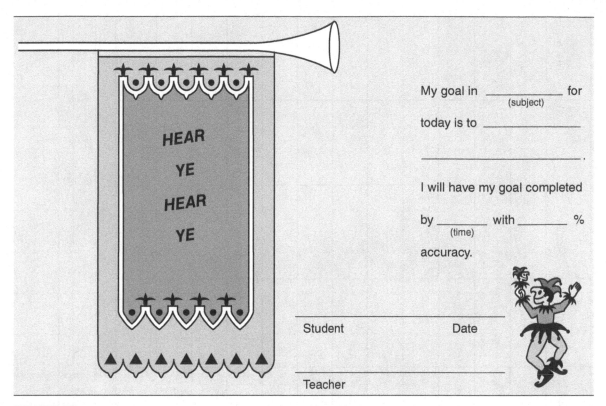

My goal in _____ for
                    (subject)

today is to _____

_____ .

I will have my goal completed

by _____ with _____ %
       (time)

accuracy.

_____
Student   Date

_____
Teacher

FIGURE 7.8
GOAL-SETTING FORM

FIGURE 7.9
SECONDARY
GOAL PLANNING
SHEET

Name _____ Date _____ Subject _____

My academic goal is to:

_____

_____

The reason I want to accomplish this academic goal is:

_____

_____

I want to have my goal accomplished by:_____

What I will need to do to accomplish this goal is:

1. _____

2. _____

3. _____

The assistance I will need from others to accomplish this goal is:

_____

_____

I will celebrate my success with: _____

Subject	Homework Assignment	Due Day/Date	Study Strategy (Where—When—How)	Target Grade	Date Completed	Strategy Grade	Grade

The study strategy that I found most helpful this week was: _____

_____

FIGURE 7.10
HOMEWORK PLAN

The benefits of academic goal setting were highlighted in a study involving adolescents with behavior problems (Maher, 1987). In this study, forty-nine high school students identified under special education classification as behavior disordered were placed in mainstream classes. Half the students and their mainstream teachers were involved in jointly setting academic goals and specifying the instructional methods that would be used to reach these goals. The remaining students were placed with teachers who were required to set instructional goals but who did not work with students in setting these goals or discussing instructional methods. Results indicated that students involved in goal setting and a discussion of instructional methods learned more, felt more positive about school, and felt that this approach would be useful with other students who have behavior problems. Teachers involved in the experimental group used a greater diversity of instructional methods, were positive about the approach, and stated that they could incorporate the approach within their normal planning.

Self-management methods are a form of goal setting, and self-monitoring has been the most frequently researched self-management method. This approach involves (1) the students understanding the work expected, (2) students selecting a goal for the amount of work they will be completing, (3) students understanding how the work will be assessed, (4) showing students an example of the self-monitoring graph that will be used to chart improvement, (5) supporting students in completing these steps, and (6) working with students to determine the type of celebration/reinforcement that will be provided when the students reach a predetermined goal.

References for teaching self-management skills to enhance academic learning can be found at nsttac.org (search for "self-management") and autismpdc.fpg.unc.edu/sites/autismpdc.fpg. unc.edu/files/SelfManagement_Steps.pdf.

As teachers, we can increase student motivation and learning by using a wide range of strategies that directly incorporate students' interests into the curriculum. The following methods suggest various approaches to incorporating students' interests.

Methods

1. *Early in the school year, have students build a list of things they would like to learn about in each major curriculum area to which they will be exposed.* This activity provides you with valuable information and stimulates students' interest by showing that some of their learning will relate directly to their interests. You may choose to create a unit on one or more topics that received widespread interest. Topics of interest can also be incorporated into the regular school curriculum. Finally, you may integrate these interests into several of the other strategies presented in this section.

2. *Prior to a unit, have students develop a K-W-L chart.* (K represents what students already know about the topic, W represents what they want to know or questions they have about the topic, and L represents what they learned about the topic.)

3. *Allow individual students or groups of students to choose topics they would like to study.* When presenting a unit, allow individual students, small groups, or the entire class to select different aspects of a topic. These might include aspects that incorporate the students' cultural backgrounds. Students might share their findings with the entire class, or the class might choose to incorporate these aspects into the content material that is culturally relevant to many or all of the students.

4. *Incorporate culturally relevant content.* It is hoped this will be thoughtfully and thoroughly presented in content-related courses you are taking or took during your teacher education program, and you will have multiple opportunities to explore this during in-service courses and workshops. While it is only one aspect of multicultural education, it is important that teachers include content that incorporates an appreciation for the history and contributions of different ethnic groups and uses interests and materials from students' lives. This can be accomplished by incorporating literature, poetry, plays, history, and biographies of individuals that represent aspects of students' cultures. Materials at the end of the chapter provide samples of culturally responsive literature. Ideas for incorporating culturally relevant curriculum into the classroom include Gregory Michie's (1999) *Holler If You Hear Me,* the story of a young teacher from the South Side of Chicago; Nancie Atwell's (1998) *In the Middle: New Understandings about Writing, Reading, and Learning;* and Keisha Edwards and her colleagues' (Edwards et al., 2005) *Classroom to Community and Back: Using Culturally Responsive Standards-Based Teaching to Strengthen Family and Community Partnerships and Increase Student Achievement.*

5. *Allow students to make choices before, during, and after the instructional activity* (Jolivette, Stichter, & McCormick, 2002). Before the activity, students may select where in the classroom they will work, the length of work or the number of problems they will complete, and the method they will use for presenting the work (typed, diagrammed, outlined, etc.). During the assignment, students may determine how to obtain teacher attention, peers with whom to work or from whom they will seek assistance, when to take short breaks, and so on. After the task, students may choose with whom to share their success and how to take a short break. Research supports that small choices such as these can be associated with improved student behavior and achievement.

© James Estes

*"That class ought to come with a warning:
'May cause drowsiness.'"*

6. *Teach students how to order films on topics that interest them.* Students can watch these films during study times when they have completed their work, in place of recess, or when you structure time for exploring individual interests. If a film is of particular interest because it relates to a topic being examined by the entire class or because many students share an interest, it can be shown to the entire class.

7. *Teach students how to invite guest speakers (including parents) to discuss a topic of interest to students.* You will, of course, always want to confirm younger students' contacts, but they can learn to take major responsibility for obtaining interesting guests.

8. *Create a unit on biographies.* Students can be asked to choose a person about whom they would like to know more and acquire information about this person. The students can then dress up like the people they have researched and make presentations to the class as those people.

9. *Create opportunities for structured sharing.* Each day of the week can be designated as a time for sharing what students have read or accomplished in a particular area. Monday might be set aside for sharing written compositions, Tuesday for newspaper articles, Wednesday for something positive students did for someone else, and so on. In a secondary classroom, this might involve students sharing material from a learning log, ending the day by having students share their new understanding with the students next to them, a small group, or their base group.

10. *Have students develop special-interest days or weeks.* Students can decide on a topic they would like to study. All subject matter for the day (or week) can be related to this topic. If they selected whales, lessons in math, reading, creative writing, science, and social studies could be constructed around whales.

11. *When involving students in creative writing, do not always assign topics.* At times, allow students to write stories related to experiences that have been meaningful to them.

12. *Use learning logs.* In their learning logs, students write in their own words what they are learning, what it means to them, and how it relates to their own lives.

13. *Allow students to develop their own spelling list.* Teachers who use this approach often find that students who have previously learned very few spelling words make dramatic gains and select words more difficult than those they had been misspelling.

14. *Develop future plans.* Many students will be more motivated when we can make important connections between their own lives and classroom content. Future plans involve students in writing about what they want to do when they grow up (e.g., when they are twenty-five years old). This includes not only the jobs they would like to have but also what they would do with their leisure time, their roles in family and community groups, and so on. As students study various content areas, they are asked to discuss how what they are learning will help them enjoy these activities or perform adult tasks more successfully. This assessment and discussion can be incorporated on a weekly basis in secondary school base groups and in middle school advisory sessions, and on a daily basis in elementary school classrooms.

PAUSE & CONSIDER 7.6

Put the book aside for a moment and create a list of methods you have used or observed a teacher use to connect learning objectives and activities to students' interests. Share this list with a group of three or four colleagues or classmates and add some of their ideas to your list.

Culturally Sensitive Teaching

Based on his three-year study of the achievement and attitudes about school among Mexican American and immigrant Mexican students in a Houston high school, Valenzuela (1999) noted that because the curriculum failed to value their culture, these students would have to participate in what he termed "cultural and linguistic eradication" (p. 62) in order for them to become committed to school. In her study of student behavior and learning in an urban, predominately African American middle school, Monroe (2009) found that student behavior was most effectively understood in the context of the type of instructional engagement provided to students.

FIGURE 7.11
CULTURAL MISMATCH
WHIRLPOOLS

Source: From "Does the way we teach
create behavior disorders in culturally
different children?" by T. McIntyre, 1996,
*Education and Treatment of Children,
19*(3), p. 358. Reprinted with permission.

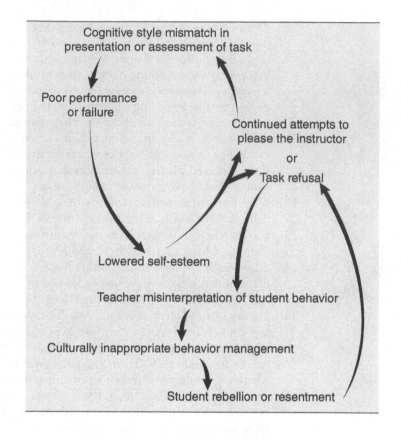

McIntyre (1996) developed a model for explaining why some students from cultures different than those of their teachers may demonstrate lower achievement and/or lower motivation for academic content and become involved in behaviors that seem to disrupt the learning environment. His *whirlpool phenomenon* model (Figure 7.11) suggests that a cognitive mismatch may lead either to students' continually attempting to please the teacher but being unable to meet academic expectations or to students' acting out or withdrawing from academic tasks. Eventually these misguided attempts may be met with disciplinary methods that fail to consider why students are expressing their frustration. In either situation, teachers' failure to understand how their students learn most effectively and what academic needs may be unique to their cultural backgrounds can have an extremely negative impact on students' academic success.

Kuykendall (2004) noted that in order to enhance students' motivation to learn and hope for the future, "curricula must be revised to foster an appreciation of all the positive components of the students' racial or cultural group as well as the most accurate portrayal of history from the perspective of that particular racial or cultural group" (p. 67).

Fortunately, as presented throughout this chapter, a wide range of strategies exists for more effectively engaging a wide range of students. Teel, Debruin-Parecki, and Covington (1998) implemented four strategies—"effort-based grading, multiple-performance opportunities, increased student responsibility and choice, and validation of cultural heritage" (p. 482)—with two seventh-grade groups of predominately African American students. The authors summarized their results by stating:

> given certain classroom conditions in which teaching strategies were used that addressed diverse student interest, talents and strengths, students at risk for school failure became just as engaged and motivated in a positive way as the more "high achieving" students. Negative motivation, observed somewhat at first, gradually decreased. (p. 492)

In reviewing research on effective instruction for students whose second language is English, Reyes and his colleagues (1999) noted that "perhaps the most powerful finding pertaining directly to classroom learning was the incorporation of students' interests and experiences" (p. 14). Work on facilitating learning for Native American students indicates that these students "thrive when taught through collaborative processes and when dialogue, open-ended questioning, and inductive reasoning are common practices" (Starnes, 2006, p. 384). This author goes on to state that Native American students "learn best when presented with the whole concept before focusing on segments and details. And, more than any other group, Native American students tend to prefer the use of visual learning strategies" (p. 385).

In their Northwest Regional Educational Laboratory document on using culturally responsive teaching, Edwards and her colleagues (Edwards et al., 2005) define culturally responsive teaching as drawing upon "the experiences, understandings, views, concepts, and ways of knowing of the students sitting in your classroom" (p. i). Their material presents a wide range of methods for using the cultural backgrounds and interests of students to enhance student motivation and learning. One very important aspect of incorporating students' cultures into the learning process is to have culturally responsive literature incorporated into the classroom and available to all students. Figure 7.12 presents a list of resources for selecting these materials.

Academic Need 5: Receive Instruction Responsive to Their Learning Styles and Strengths

Teachers can increase students' motivation and success by responding effectively to students' learning styles. Students differ in their approaches to learning. Every student has a cognitive or learning style that represents the general approach the student takes to learning and organizing material. Teachers too often examine students' failures by considering personal and social problems rather than focusing on the student's special interests or learning styles to determine the best approach to providing instruction. Teachers who use the same instructional methods with every student or who use a limited range of instructional activities will create a situation in which some students become frustrated, experience failure, and respond by misbehaving. Writers who support the concept of brain-based learning strongly support the use of instructional methods that incorporate multiple intelligences. "Simply put, teachers can begin to use brain-based learning techniques by making sure that they use all nine multiple intelligences during their instruction and assignments each day" (Connell, 2009, p. 36). In this section, we examine responding sensitively to students' learning styles related to (1) the classroom learning environment, (2) students' special abilities, and (3) various levels of abstraction.

We had this concept personally and powerfully highlighted. Our daughter, a vibrant, sensitive young woman, experienced a terrible year in tenth grade. Although she studied nearly five hours a night, she earned only a C+ grade average, experienced health problems

**FIGURE 7.12
SELECTING
CULTURALLY
RESPONSIVE
LITERATURE**

Source:
"Classroom
community and
back: Using
culturally
responsive
standards-based
teaching to
strengthen family
and community
partnerships and
increase student
achievement," by
Northwest Regional
Educational
Laboratory, 2005.
Reprinted with
permission.

For most children and youth, reading a book that they can relate to is a powerful experience. Unfortunately, it can also be difficult for students to find books in school that accurately and respectfully reflect their culture. There are many resources available online that review multicultural children's and young adult literature as well as provide tips for selecting materials—here are just a few:

Ethnic-Specific Books for Students
scholastic.com (click on Teachers then search for "choose multicultural books")
and ipl.org/div/pf/entry/48493

Cynthia Leitich Smith: Children's Literature Resources
cynthialeitichsmith.com

Oyate (Native American Resources)
oyate.org

Barahona Center for the Study of Books in Spanish for Children and Adolescents
chicanolitbib.wordpress.com/2007/12/02/barahona-center

African American Bibliography: Books for Children
http://www.lib.usm.edu/degrummond/research/bibliographies/ch-afroamericanbib

Russian Children's Books
natashascafe.com/html/book.html

The World of Arab and Muslim Children in Children's Books
lib.latrobe.edu.au/ojs/index.php/tlg/article/view/178/177

Beyond Female Protagonists—Female Voices in Picture Books
scils.rutgers.edu/~kvander/Feminist/fempic.html

Examining Multicultural Picture Books for the Early Childhood Classroom: Possibilities and
    Pitfalls
ecrp.uiuc.edu/v3n2/mendoza.html

Ten Quick Ways to Analyze Children's Books for Racism and Sexism
earlylearning.org/about-us/2013%20ELPLP%20Symposium/handouts/Govan%202%20-%
    2010%20Quick%20Ways%20to%20Analyze.pdf

The authors would add the following sites we find very helpful:
    The International Board on Books for Young People (Ibby) at facebook.com/ibby.
    international
    The International Children's Digital Library (ICDL) at en.childrenslibrary.org
    The Hennepin County Library at hclib.org

The authors would also add the following list from the blog of Dr. Ruth Shagoury:
    Toddler and young children:
        litforkids.wordpress.com/2009/05/03/many-languages-many-alphabets
        litforkids.wordpress.com/2009/03/21/a-world-of-alphabet-blocks
        litforkids.wordpress.com/2009/06/13/the-sounds-of-language-multicultural-picture-
            books-for-young-children
        litforkids.wordpress.com/2011/07/30/children-around-the-world-honoring-the-rights-
            of-children
    Tweens and teens:
        litforkids.wordpress.com/2010/02/17/celebrating-spoken-soul-in-picture-books
        homepage.isomedia.com/~jmele/joe.html

caused by tension, and seemed to find almost no joy in learning. During her years as a college undergraduate, her grades and excitement about learning steadily increased and her grades improved each year, culminating in an A– average. During her master's degree in teaching program, she was on fire for learning, and her commitment and accomplishments were impressive. The difference was clearly the fact that the content and instructional methods matched her interests and learning preferences. She is a dynamic, interpersonal learner who values relationships and warm, personal interaction in the classroom. When these factors are present, she quickly masters concepts and finds herself effortlessly putting time and energy into learning. Perhaps more than ever we understand that students' attitudes and behaviors are influenced by the instructional strategies and type of learning atmosphere they experience in the classroom.

Adjusting Environmental Factors to Meet Students' Learning Needs

Research (Dunn et al., 2001) indicates that most students' learning is significantly affected by a number of environmental factors within the classroom. Dunn suggested the following factors influenced students' ability to focus on and successfully complete academic work:

- Sound
- Light
- Temperature
- Classroom design (casual or structured)
- Perceptual input
  - Visual
  - Auditory
  - Kinesthetic
- Interpersonal (working individually, in pairs, with more frequent adult support, etc.)
- Time of day
- Need for food or drink
- Mobility

By adjusting the classroom environment and some instructional methods, teachers can easily create a learning environment more conducive to many students' learning needs. For example, some students learn material more effectively when allowed to sit on comfortable surfaces rather than at standard desks and when allowed to work in noisy environments, while some students, especially elementary children, learn more effectively and are less fidgety in lower-level lighting. In one study, half of all seventh-grade students in one junior high school learned more effectively when allowed to move about during learning activities. Student learning can also be enhanced by allowing students to eat when they need to, study material at a time of day best suited to their learning preferences, and learn through modalities they prefer. The following methods have been implemented by us and by many teachers we have taught and with whom we have worked.

Methods

1. *When presenting material, use visual displays, such as writing on an overhead projector, to assist students who are visual learners.* Dunn (1983) stated that approximately 40 percent of students learn more effectively when they can read or see something.

Interestingly, Price (1980) suggested that most children are not good visual learners until they reach third or fourth grade.

2. *Allow students to select where they will sit.* Students vary in the amount of light, sound, and heat they prefer and may, in fact, select seats that provide more productive learning environments for them. Teachers often comment, especially during junior high school, that some students may abuse this privilege. We have found that they seldom do so if they are taught the concept of learning styles and if classroom procedures, such as allowing students to select their own seats, are presented as part of a method to make learning more personalized and effective for all students.

3. *Permit students to choose where they wish to study.* Some students work most effectively at a table, others in a soft chair, and others seated at a traditional school desk. We have taught children who worked best when they could move around the room and do their work on clipboards.

4. *Be sensitive to individual students' needs to block out sound or visual distractions.* Teachers can discuss differences in learning styles with the class and allow students to select a quiet study carrel. Also, observe students to see whether they appear easily distracted during seatwork. Teachers frequently move easily distracted students nearer to the teacher's desk; however, because this is often the busiest place in the classroom, this move may aggravate the problem by creating more distractions for the student.

5. *Make healthful snacks available to students or allow them to bring their own.* Because many students fail to eat an adequate breakfast, midmorning is a key time for allowing them to have a snack. Teachers who try this tactic generally find that initially all students take a cracker, carrot, or celery stick. Soon, however, only students who are hungry or who work best when they can eat will choose to eat.

6. *Provide opportunities for students to select whether they will work alone, in pairs, or with a small group.* Students can work with peers to complete assignments, study for tests, work on long-term projects, or critique each other's work.

7. *Provide adequate structure for both short-term and long-range assignments.* Students learn more effectively when seatwork is preceded by substantial direct instruction. Likewise, students need the structure provided by periodic conferences with the teacher or an assignment checklist and timetable for longer assignments.

8. *Give students instruction in study skills.* Both reflective and impulsive learners can benefit from learning to organize material prior to writing a formal paper. Some students organize material best using an outline format. More right hemisphere–oriented students may prefer to organize by mapping—a process of making connections in nonlinear fashion. Likewise, visual and kinesthetic learners profit from learning how to take notes.

9. *Employ individual goal setting, self-monitoring, and contracts.* These devices can assist students who require structure and concrete evidence to enhance motivation.

10. *Realize that some students require more frequent breaks than do others.* Teach students how to take short breaks without disrupting the class.

11. *Consider that students doing poorly in a subject might perform better if that subject were taught at a different time of day.* It is somewhat difficult to make this adjustment, but dramatic results can be obtained by switching a student's basic-skill lesson from morning to afternoon. Secondary school schedules that rotate the periods at which classes are taught allow students to study all subjects at a time when they work best.

12. *Increase the length of time you wait before calling on a student to answer a question.* This added time assists more reflective learners. Again, it is important to explain and teach this procedure to the class before implementing it.

13. *Develop learning centers that incorporate a variety of learning modalities.* Learning centers can be created that allow students to learn visually, auditorially, and kinesthetically. Learning centers also enable students to make decisions concerning light, sound, and design preferences, whether to work independently or with other students, and to select activities that allow them to deal with the material supportive of their own cognitive learning style preference.

PAUSE & CONSIDER 7.7

Consider for a moment situations in which you have important academic demands placed upon you and also have a time crunch. In order to do your best work, what time of day would you do this work? Would you be in a formal setting like a library, or would you be at home in a comfortable chair? Would you be eating or sipping coffee or tea as you worked? Would you have music in the background? How often would you get up to stretch and move around? How bright would the lights be? Share this information with a colleague or classmate and, if you are part of a study group or class, tally the data from these questions. It is likely you find considerable variation among your colleagues. While you may be able to adjust these factors to increase your productivity, consider how little ability students have to make these adjustments at school and the possible impact this might have on their performance.

PAUSE & CONSIDER 7.8

Pause for a few minutes and consider a student who is struggling academically and behaviorally in a class you are teaching or observing. Write a list of ways you might adjust the learning environment to help this student more closely match his or her learning style to the environment. Share this with a group of two or three colleagues or classmates and provide each other with feedback and ideas.

Howard Gardner's Work on Multiple Intelligences

When examining Howard Gardner's work, it is important to realize that he has suggested that the concept of multiple intelligences is not a goal in itself but rather a way to assist students in reaching important goals selected by them and the adults with whom they work. Gardner (1999a) noted that the most important contribution multiple intelligence theory makes to education is that it "stimulates teachers and students to be imaginative in selecting curricula, deciding how the curricula are to be taught or 'delivered,' and determining how student knowledge is to be demonstrated" (p. 152).

Gardner (2006) has suggested that there are at least eight forms of intelligence or methods for understanding and learning. Figure 7.13 presents an overview of these eight types and instructional methods that enable students to interact with content to use their strengths to master the material.

FIGURE 7.13
SPECIAL
ABILITIES AND
SUPPORTIVE
INSTRUCTIONAL
METHODS

Social/Interpersonal (*Learning is enhanced by sharing and discussing ideas with others*)

Cooperative learning

Dyads (Think-Pair-Share)

Peer tutoring

Jigsaw

Drama

Debates

Verbal/Linguistic (*Learning is enhanced by messages presented through written and spoken word*)

Reading

Writing

Sharing ideas

Listen to material

Speeches

Storytelling

Visual/Spatial (*Learning is enhanced by seeing and creating images*)

Videos/films

Charts/graphs

Create posters

Draw

Paint

Bodily/Kinesthetic (*Learning is enhanced by physical movement*)

Use manipulatives

Skits/role plays

Dance

Activity-based centers

Athletic activities

Building

Logical/Mathematical (*Learning is enhanced by viewing cause and effect and the use of numbers*)

Analyze

Review, graph data

Create patterns

Prove something

Create a sequence/timeline

Critical thinking

Musical (*Learning is enhanced by sounds, rhythms, and tonal patterns*)

Sing

Create a rhythm/beat

Write a jingle/poem

Rap

Background music

Connect content being studied to songs

Intrapersonal (*Learning is enhanced by focus on self-reflection, viewing the material from their own personal perspective, and metacognition*)

Journaling

Self-talk

Independent work

Connect to learner's life

Self-assessment

Connect to personal past experiences

Naturalistic (*Learning is enhanced by connection to the learner's environment and nature*)

Create categories

Conduct an experiment

Relate to outdoors

Create labels

Environmental activities

Problem solving

Gardner points out that most of us possess each of these intelligences but in different amounts. Sadly, when schools focus primarily on verbal/linguistic and logical/mathematical intelligences, we limit the motivation, achievement, and self-esteem of many students whose gifts are ignored or underused. Instead, he suggests, we can serve all students more effectively when we create classroom environments that allow students to learn and demonstrate their knowledge using multiple forms of intelligence.

Some educators, particularly those who emphasize direct instruction as the preferred method for increasing students' learning and test scores, suggest that there is little evidence to support the use of instructional methods focused on incorporating multiple intelligences. Other educators, including those who advocate for the incorporation of research on the human brain and its impact on learning, advocate for greater use of methods that respond to varied learning styles (Chen, Chiang, & Lin, 2013; Connell, 2009).

Students can be encouraged to examine and celebrate their own skills by creating a graph indicating how strong they believe they are in each of the eight areas previously listed. Students can then set goals for improvement in each area and determine methods for reaching these goals. Figure 7.14 presents an example of one such graph developed by a fifth-grade student.

A number of books are available to assist teachers in helping students understand the concept of multiple intelligences. The one we have found most useful is *Multiple Intelligences: Helping Kids Discover the Many Ways to Be Smart* (Huggins, Manion, Shakarian, & Moen, 1997). In addition, David Lazear (1999) has developed extensive practical materials to assist teachers in implementing multiple intelligence strategies.

We have been consistently impressed with how much learning and creativity students can demonstrate when allowed to do so using multiple intelligences. A teacher in one of our in-service graduate classes shared the following story. He was teaching a sophomore history class and several weeks into the class noticed a student who was seldom involved in the class drawing cartoons during a class discussion. The teacher met privately with the student to discuss this behavior and was informed that this is how the student took notes—he drew a chronological cartoon of events and concepts being discussed. The student showed the teacher several of his daily cartoons, and

**FIGURE 7.14
TAKE A GUESS
ABOUT YOUR EIGHT
INTELLIGENCES**

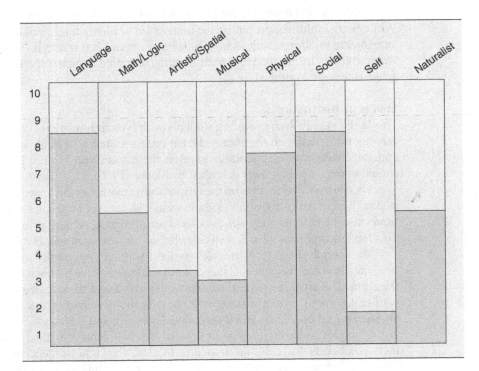

they indeed appeared to display a fine understanding of the content. The teacher expressed surprise that the student had failed the first quiz. The student informed the teacher that he was not a good writer and did not explain things well in writing. The teacher asked the student if he would be interested in using his cartoons as the class notes and having a presentation of his cartoons to the class serve as a test. The teacher suggested this might serve as a good review for the students—especially those with strong visual/spatial abilities. The student agreed. The teacher reported that, despite the fact that his school attendance had been problematic, the student did not miss a day of his class the remainder of the semester. In addition, the teacher indicated the student began to take a more active role in the class and earned a B+ for the course. Although the teacher continued to encourage the student to value and strengthen his writing skills, he honored the student's special abilities, and everyone was rewarded by the student's performance.

PAUSE & CONSIDER 7.9

We encourage you to take a few minutes to become involved in an activity with a group of your classmates or colleagues in which you consider ways in which you currently incorporate multiple intelligence concepts into your teaching and how you might more systematically implement this concept. You might form a group of four and share the methods you currently use that have proven beneficial to your students. Next, you might take a unit you will be teaching and examine ways that the curriculum, instruction, and assessment might be modified to incorporate opportunities for students to use their special abilities.

Learning Goals Emphasizing Different Levels of Abstraction

While factual information can be the foundation of higher-level thinking and meaningful problem solving, brain research (Ratey, 2001) and educational research (Smith, 2007) suggest that when students are engaged in academic work connected to higher-level thinking, motivation and achievement are improved.

Levels of Instruction

The *facts* level involves providing students with basic information. When developing a unit on ecology, information on the chemicals that are associated with pollution, what causes pollution, and the effects various pollutants have on the human body would be included. This level is similar to the *knowledge* level described by Bloom (1956).

The *concepts* level focuses on the relationships among facts and examines major themes associated with facts. An ecology unit might examine the concept of people's relationships to their environments, the benefits and costs associated with progress, or responsibility to future generations. This level incorporates what Bloom describes as *comprehension* and *analysis*.

The *generalizations* level provides students with an opportunity to use the information they have obtained and the concepts they have developed to solve problems or interpret situations. In the context of an ecology unit, students might be asked to write legislative proposals dealing with ecology or to develop a model city. The educational objectives associated with these activities are similar to those Bloom labels *application*, *synthesis*, and *evaluation*.

At the final level is *personal application*. Here, students are asked to relate their learning to their own beliefs, feelings, and behaviors. In an ecology unit, students might be asked to discuss their own behavior regarding such topics as litter, recycling, or water usage. This level relates to

FIGURE 7.15
COMPARISON OF
BLOOM'S
TAXONOMY OF
EDUCATIONAL
OBJECTIVES AND
TEACHING MORE
THAN FACTS

Teaching More Than Facts	Bloom's Taxonomy
Facts	Knowledge
Concepts	Comprehension
	Analysis
Generalizations	Application
	Synthesis Evaluation
Personal application	Affective domain

the learning objectives in the affective domain described by Krathwohl, Bloom, and Masia (1964). Because it is at this level that students relate learning directly to their own lives, teachers should, whenever possible, incorporate this level into their instruction. No other level has greater potential for stimulating students' interest and increasing on-task behavior. The relationship between these four levels and Bloom's taxonomy is shown in Figure 7.15.

It is obvious that older students will be better able to become involved in instruction associated with higher levels. Nevertheless, primary teachers should attempt to help children develop simple concepts, think creatively about generalizations and applications, and most important, view learning as something that relates to their own lives. Failure to incorporate higher levels indicates to children that learning is merely the acquisition of often unrelated facts. When this failure occurs, it is more difficult for teachers in subsequent grades to introduce higher levels of instruction.

An Example

An example of a lesson used by one of us in a fourth-grade class can help to clarify how each level can be incorporated into an instructional unit. The example, involving a unit on the Northwest Indians, begins with students learning numerous *facts* about the lives and history of these Native Americans. Individual student interests are accommodated by having each student choose a topic of special interest, obtain relevant material, and make a presentation to the class. As students learn about the beliefs Native Americans held and how their lives have changed over the years, discussions take place on *concepts* such as prejudice, progress, and might makes right. In this lesson, instruction at the *generalization* level takes two forms. First, students are asked to discuss such topics as what legislators could do to assist the Native Americans, how society should handle such current problems as salmon-fishing rights, and whether Native Americans should live their own lifestyle separately or be integrated into society. Second, students design and perform a *potlatch*. This performance involves creating costumes, learning authentic songs and dances, making dried food, and decorating the room.

One of us developed a method for incorporating the *personal application* level by providing students with an intense personal experience related to this unit. The activity has one class move out of the classroom on the pretext that the other class needs the room to complete some useful research. The displaced class is placed in a corner in the hall behind a chalkboard. When students become uncomfortable and complain, it is suggested that they petition the principal to change the situation. The principal's refusal almost inevitably provokes anger associated with a sense of impotence. Once students have been allowed to experience these feelings, they return to their classroom and are assisted in sharing their feelings with the class that displaced them. The teachers then help the students draw the analogy between their experience and that of Native Americans. The activity ends by the two classes having a small party to reduce any negative feelings that may have been created by the experience.

It is likely that students will remember this activity and the basic concept taught. Although this example provides a rather dramatic approach to incorporating students' feelings into a lesson, there are numerous less time-consuming approaches. Figure 7.16 outlines a high school unit that incorporates all four levels.

FIGURE 7.16
TEACHING
MORE THAN
FACTS:
A LESSON
DESIGN FOR
TEACHING
*ROMEO AND
JULIET*

Factual Level
Activities
1. Read the play aloud, with students taking parts and the teacher reading the more difficult parts and explaining as the students progress through the play.
2. Discuss what happens in each act, using a guide sheet.
3. Introduce students to the structure of a Shakespearean tragedy.
4. Introduce major themes and elements of a Shakespearean tragedy.
5. Give quizzes after the completion of each act and at the end of the play.

Concept Level
Activities
1. Relate the plot of *Romeo and Juliet* to movies the students have seen or books they have read. (A shortened version of *West Side Story* might be taught at the end of this unit, in which character-by-character and scene comparisons are done.)
2. Discuss the problems Romeo and Juliet had in communicating with their parents. (Relate to Romeo's tragic flaw—impetuousness.)
3. Discuss the effects of hate and prejudice.
4. Discuss the concept of fate.
5. Introduce students to Elizabethan concepts relevant to a greater understanding of the play.
6. Point out universality of themes, characters, and situations to show their relevance to students.
7. By reading the play in class, students will study it as a literary work and dramatic performance, but they also will be viewing the Franco Zeffirelli version of *Romeo and Juliet* to analyze his interpretation.
8. Discuss the plot complication of Juliet's impending marriage to Paris.

Generalization Level
Activities
1. Relate the specific problem of *Romeo and Juliet* to adolescents today.
2. Discuss alternatives to the outcome of *Romeo and Juliet*.
3. Discuss examples of hate and prejudice today.
4. Help students realize that reading Shakespeare's plays, like reading any great works of literature, is both a demanding and a rewarding experience.
5. Do environmental situations influence prejudice? Would there be more prejudice against gays in a small rural town or San Francisco?
6. Give examples of prejudice against nationalities, beliefs, appearances, and values.

Personal Application Level
Activities
1. What could Romeo and Juliet have done differently?
2. Do you think their deaths justify the ending of the feud? (Do the means justify the end?)
3. Are Juliet's parents hypocrites?
4. How do you view the nurse's relationship to Juliet, and did she betray Juliet?
5. Has the friar done the right thing for Romeo and Juliet?
6. What prejudices do you think you have?
7. How did you arrive at those prejudices? Did anyone or any situation influence you?
8. What can you and society do to help eliminate or reduce prejudice?

Academic Need 6: See Learning Modeled by Adults as an Exciting and Rewarding Process

As mentioned in Chapter 3, teachers possess many characteristics that make their behavior likely to be modeled. Research suggests that teachers who are more effective in enhancing students' motivation to learn show an interest in and excitement about learning and model task-related thinking and problem solving. When students observe you in the classroom, are they seeing someone who appears sincerely and enthusiastically interested in what he or she is doing and teaching? Many secondary teachers we know share their poetry, thoughts about social events, scientific work, and so on. Although we must be careful to not overshadow our students or provide ideas they should be generating, we will be more effective when they observe us actively and enthusiastically engaged in the learning process.

Academic Need 7: Experience Success

No one enjoys being in a setting in which he or she consistently fails. If you are like most people, you avoided getting yourself in these situations and, when required to be there, found ways to reduce your involvement in the activities or to leave the setting entirely. To a large degree, this behavior was influenced by the need to view yourself as competent. Success experiences are instrumental in developing feelings of self-worth and confidence in attempting new activities.

PAUSE & CONSIDER 7.10

Consider for a minute a situation in which you lacked the skills others around you possessed. Perhaps you were one of the last to be chosen for playground games or your artwork was met with giggles and stares of disbelief. How did you feel in these situations? Write a brief statement about a situation in which this happened to you. What was your reaction?

Both brain research and teacher effectiveness studies suggest that students' learning is increased when they experience high rates of success in completing tasks. In addition, especially as students enter the upper elementary grades, negative feedback has a greater negative impact on their motivation to engage in future tasks similar to those where they have failed (Willis, 2010a). When the teacher is available to monitor and assist students, success rates of 70 to 80 percent are desirable. When students are expected to work on their own, success rates of 90 to 100 percent are desirable. Studies suggest that when students are given inappropriate tasks, the tasks are much more likely to be too difficult than too easy. Following successful experiences, individuals tend to raise their expectations and set higher goals, whereas failure is met with lowered aspirations.

Students who are anxious about their performances divide their attention between the material being taught and their concerns about failure or being criticized or embarrassed. These students are involved in a downward spiral; they miss considerable amounts of information because of their anxiety. Indeed, many students choose a teacher's frustration and criticism about their behavior rather than risk another academic failure.

Differentiated Instruction

Students need to know that teachers will modify instruction and assessment so they can experience success. Several years ago, our daughter, who reads rather slowly, was told by her teacher that he loved to read and hoped all his students would enjoy the extensive reading they would be completing during their eighth-grade year. He also informed them that students who had difficulty completing their reading were welcome to read like he does (using audiobooks or having someone read to them)—because he is blind. This kind of creativity, compassion, and flexibility provides all students with the opportunity to feel competent and empowered in the classroom.

Differentiated instruction is a currently popular term for developing classroom instructional activities that enable all students to experience academic success (Tomlinson, Brimijoin, & Narvaez, 2008). Carol Tomlinson (2005) defines a differentiated classroom as one that "provides different avenues to acquiring content, to processing or making sense of ideas, and to developing products so that each student can learn effectively" (p. 1). She notes that the acquisition of content can be differentiated by attending to (1) students' readiness or current level of knowledge/skill, (2) students' interests, and (3) how students prefer to learn content. In listing strategies that support the process, Tomlinson notes:

> The following are among the scores of strategies educators have developed to invite more flexible and responsive sense-making: learning logs, journals, graphic organizers, creative problem solving, cubing learning centers, interest centers or interest groups, learning contracts, Literature Circles, role-playing cooperative controversy (in which students argue both sides of an issue), choice boards, Jigsaw, think-pair-share, mind-mapping, PMI (listing pluses, minuses, and interesting points about a topic under consideration), model making, and labs. (p. 80)

© George Abbott

"Of course it's wrong. That's why I go to school."

Tomlinson offers many thoughtful ways to implement the third component of a differentiated classroom—the differentiation of products or outcomes. When working with learners who are experiencing difficulty, she talks about ensuring that outcomes still require them to apply and extend the key knowledge in the unit, that students have methods other than written work to demonstrate their knowledge, that products be broken into smaller sections, and that students be given support by teachers and peers so work can be completed successfully within the school setting.

Tomlinson (2005) provides the following example of a teacher differentiating content, process, and product by attending to students' learning styles:

He might, for example, offer students four ways to explore a math concept today. One approach might ask students to use words and pictures to solve the kind of problem that's the focus of the unit. A second approach might provide multiple versions of the problem to practice, and the opportunity to check answers for accuracy as they go along. A third option might entail students investigating how the kind of math problem could be used to solve a real-life dilemma. A fourth approach might ask students to use manipulatives and words to demonstrate how the problem type works. Whatever the student's selection, they then decide whether they work more effectively alone or with a peer. (p. 65)

Authentic assessment is a term used to describe methods for providing students with multiple ways to demonstrate their mastery of content knowledge and to do so at various levels of learning. Burke (1994) presents numerous methods for incorporating authentic assessment including:

- *Portfolios:* A deliberate collection of student work designed to give a complete picture of a student's progress and skills; a portfolio may include homework, tests, learning logs, projects, rough drafts, written work, or recordings of presentations.
- *Performances and exhibitions:* Performances or exhibitions include speeches, science experiments, debates, artistic performances, mock trials, or publications.
- *Projects:* Projects allow students to investigate in depth a subject of interest to them.
- *Learning logs and journals:* Learning logs consist of brief, factual entries that may include mathematical problem solving, science experiment observations, or questions about lectures or readings. Journals can include literature responses, descriptions and reactions to events, reflections on personal experiences, and connections made to what is being studied in class.
- *Observation checklists:* Teachers, small groups, and individual students can use observation checklists to monitor specific skills or behaviors in students. A checklist may include students' names, space for four to five targeted areas, a code or rating to determine to what degree the student has or has not demonstrated the skill (such as frequently, sometimes, or not yet), and a space for comments.
- *Graphic organizers:* Venn diagrams, webs, and concept maps can be used to monitor students' thinking in the early stages of an assignment or unit.
- *Interviews and conferences:* Direct personal communication with students can elicit students' thoughts, opinions, and feelings about their work.

Because effective instruction begins with knowing your students and planning lessons based on this knowledge, Figure 7.17 presents a list of planning decisions you may want to consider in order to facilitate your modification of materials for students who need some special assistance.

Once you have determined the type of assistance a student may need, you will find many methods available for assisting students in having successful learning experiences. One approach we have found very helpful involves a model developed by Cole and colleagues (2000a) that provides a conceptual framework for adapting curriculum and instruction to ensure success for all students. The components of this model were developed by teachers at the elementary, middle, and high school levels. The process begins with the selection of the subject, lesson, curricular goal, and instructional plan for most learners. The next step is to identify the learners who will need adaptations to the curriculum or

FIGURE 7.17
DIFFERENTIATION
PLANNING

1. Define the key objectives
2. Select the methods to assess student learning
3. Determine which students may need to have the curriculum and/or instruction adjusted
4. Decide whether there needs to be different levels of objective for different learners
5. Determine any alternative curricular materials that are available to teach this content
6. Assess whether the students can access the content if provided with alternative reading materials, materials on tape, etc.
7. Involve students in selecting instructional activities and/or content. Make sure the content and activities will motivate the students to learn.
8. Determine which students may need enrichment materials
9. Assess whether some students may need support in demonstrating behavior that will be necessary to successfully complete the learning activities.
10. Determine whether any students will need the assistance of other adults
11. Decide whether any students will benefit from peer tutoring as a methods for insuring they successfully complete the learning activities
12. Consider the room arrangement(s) that will best support the instructional activities
13. If collaborative activities will be used, determine the most effective student groups
14. If collaborative work will be used, determine which student(s) will need support during this phase of instruction
15. Assess whether any IEP goals and objectives will need to be considered when planning the lesson objectives, instructional methods, and assessment
16. Plan how any adaptations will be discussed with the student and, if necessary, their parents or guardians.

instructional plan. Based on the curricular goal and instructional plan, educators can use the nine types (see Figure 7.18) to determine which adaptations will be the most appropriate for the individual child's needs. In this model, educators examine pupils' needs, interests, and abilities and the delivery of instruction as possible adaptations. Figure 7.19 shows how the process is applied. Although there are numerous ways to modify instructional factors, Figure 7.20 presents a list we have found helpful. Research supports the logical concept that when curriculum and instructional modifications are provided, student engagement in appropriate academic behavior increases and discipline issues are reduced (Lee, Wehmeyer, Soukup, & Palmer, 2010).

Another strategy we have found extremely helpful in implementing the idea that all students can succeed is a success contract (Figure 7.21). This contract is a formal, collaboratively designed agreement between the teacher and student to clarify what both parties will do to ensure the student's success. We have worked with more than 100 teachers who have reported dramatic results with this format.

Although differentiated instruction is an essential component to meeting the academic needs of all students, a section in a classroom management text can highlight only a few concepts on this topic. We encourage you to explore the readings at the end of the chapter and to consider

FIGURE 7.18
NINE TYPES OF
ADAPTATIONS
Source: From
*Adapting Curriculum
and Instruction in
Inclusive Classrooms:
Staff Development Kit*,
(2nd ed.) by S. Cole,
B. Horvath, C.
Chapman,
C. Deschenes,
D. G. Ebeling, & J.
Sprague, 2000.
Bloomington, IN:
Indiana Institute on
Disability and
Community. Reprinted
with permission.

Input
The instructional strategies used to facilitate student learning.
For example:
Use of videos, computer programs, field trips, and visual aids to support active learning.

Output
The ways learners can demonstrate understanding and knowledge.
For example:
To demonstrate understanding, students write a song, tell a story, design a poster or brochure, perform an experiment.

Size
The length or portion of an assignment, demonstration, or performance learners are expected to complete.
For example:
Reduce the length of report to be written or spoken, reduce the number of references needed, reduce the number of problems to be solved.

Time
The flexible time needed for student learning.
For example:
Individualize a time line for project completion, allow more time for test taking.

Difficulty
The varied skill levels, conceptual levels, and processes involved in learning.
For example:
Provide calculators, tier the assignment so the outcome is the same but with varying degrees of concreteness and complexity.

Level of Support
The amount of assistance to the learner.
For example:
Students work in cooperative groups or with peer buddies, mentors, cross-age tutors, or paraeducators.

Degree of Participation
The extent to which the learner is actively involved in the tasks.
For example:
In a student-written, -directed, and -acted play, a student may play a part that has more physical action rather than numerous lines to memorize.

Modified Goals
The adapted outcome expectations within the context of a general education curriculum.
For example:
In a written language activity, a student may focus more on writing some letters and copying words rather than composing whole sentences or paragraphs.

Substitute Curriculum
The significantly differentiated instruction and materials to meet a learner's identified goals.
For example:
In a foreign language class, a student may develop a play or script that uses both authentic language and cultural knowledge of a designated time period rather than reading paragraphs or directions.

**FIGURE 7.19
CREATING WAYS TO
ADAPT FAMILIAR
LESSONS—
SECONDARY**

Source: From *Adapting
Curriculum and
Instruction in Inclusive
Classrooms: Staff
Development Kit,*
(2nd ed.) by S. Cole,
B. Horvath, C. Chapman,
C. Deschenes,
D. G. Ebeling, & J.
Sprague, 2000.
Bloomington, IN: Indiana
Institute on Disability
and Community.
Reprinted with
permission.

1. Select the subject area (and grade level) to be taught: _____
   math science history literature   business P.E. fine arts health
   Grade level: _____

2. Select the lesson topic to be taught (on one day): _____

3. Briefly identify the *curricular* goal for most learners: By the end of this class, students will know
   _____

4. Briefly identify the *instructional* goals: As a teacher, I will _____
   _____
   _____

5. Now use nine types of adaptations as a means of thinking about ways you could adapt what or how you teach to accommodate this learner in the classroom for this lesson.

Input	Output	Size
Time	Difficulty	Level of Support
Degree of Participation	Modified Goals	Substitute Curriculum

taking additional coursework in this important area. Activity 7.3 at the end of the chapter will provide an opportunity for you to use Figure 7.19 to develop a specialized instructional plan for a student who is struggling to master content.

Academic Need 8: Have Time to Integrate Learning

Students need time during the school day to slow down and integrate what they have learned. All too often, students are rushed from one activity to another with no time allotted for summarizing the learning that has taken place in each activity. When this rush occurs, students begin to feel confused and often experience a sense of failure because they frequently have not understood what it was they were supposed to have learned from the preceding activity. As teachers, we are often lulled into believing that everyone has understood because several of our students who learn quickly indicate that the material has been learned and understood. Students learn at varying rates, however, and in different ways, and it is important to slow down and provide all students with an opportunity to organize the new ideas that have been presented. Effective teachers develop specific instructional activities designed to help students summarize new learning and relate this new knowledge to previous and future learning and the students' own lives.

Brain research suggests that "students should be given the opportunity to reflect on their experience, draw connections to key concepts, and share their conclusions with others" (Kaufman et al., 2008, p. 54). "To reflect, a person must use different areas of the brain and thereby give some overworked areas of the brain much-needed rest (Sprenger, 2009, p. 37). Far too often students rush to complete work in one class, experience a hectic and/or emotional experience in

FIGURE 7.20
INSTRUCTIONAL
ADJUSTMENTS FOR
STUDENTS WITH
SPECIAL ACADEMIC
NEEDS IN A
REGULAR
CLASSROOM

Time—Adjust Work Time by:
1. Giving a longer time to complete assignments.
2. Allowing the student to work at reading and writing assignments for short periods of time, perhaps only ten or fifteen minutes depending on student's ability to concentrate, followed by other types of activities for short periods of time.
3. Setting up a specific schedule for the students so that they know what to expect.
4. Alternating quiet and active time, having short periods of each.
5. Reading the test, if necessary.

Learning Environment—Adjust the Learning Setting by:
1. Permitting students to do their work in a quiet, uncrowded corner of the room, or in some school area they choose; however, do not isolate them against their will.
2. Placing the student close to the teacher for more immediate help when needed.
3. Placing the student next to another student who can help when needed.
4. Separating the student from students who are most likely to be distracting.
5. Formulating a small work group of three or four students, hold all members of the group responsible for making certain that each group member completes assignments successfully.
6. Providing a peer helper who can assist by (a) making certain the student understands directions or assignments; (b) reading important directions and essential materials to the student; (c) drilling the student orally on key material; (d) summarizing orally important textbook passages; (e) writing down answers to tests and assignments for the student; (f) working with the student on joint assignments; and (g) editing the student's work, making suggestions for improvements.

Content—Adjust Type, Difficulty, Amount, or Sequence of Material by:
1. Giving a lesser amount of work.
2. Breaking assignments down into short tasks.
3. Giving only one (or a few) question at a time during testing.
4. Including in assignments only material that is absolutely necessary.
5. Highlighting or underlining textbook passages that contain key facts or concepts.
6. Using markers to tell students where to start or stop an assignment.
7. Providing specific questions to guide their reading.
8. Establishing academic goals and strategies for reaching the goals.
9. Making sure students' desks are free from unnecessary material.
10. Picking up work as soon as it is completed.
11. Giving immediate feedback on tasks or work completed.
12. Having on hand alternate and supplementary materials.
13. Giving students several alternatives in both obtaining and reporting information—recordings, interviews, reading, experiences, projects, and so forth.
14. Having frequent (even if short) one-to-one conferences with students.
15. Helping students to restate what they are responsible for.
16. Helping students assess their progress toward completion of work.
17. Eliminating unnecessary words on tests.
18. Capitalizing and underlining words such as *always, never,* and *not* on test; avoid negatively stated questions, especially in true–false questions.

(continued)

FIGURE 7.20
(CONTINUED)

Organization—Organizational Notebook

Many students, especially students with learning disabilities, frequently have difficulty with tasks involving organization of time and materials. Success for these students may be facilitated by teaching such skills as notebook organization. Both the teacher and students may then have a system to ensure that activities such as homework assignments have been copied accurately. Include the following:

1. Three-ring binder to hold all materials
2. Paper calendar—attach the current month on the inside cover of the notebook for assignment due dates
3. Plastic pouch for pencils, erasers, pens, cards, file cards, and so on
4. Folder with pockets for each class to hold assignments and study guides
5. Spiral notebook
6. Copy of SQ3R (Scan, Question, Read, Reflect, Review) study technique taped to inside back cover

The organization notebook has proven effective for both elementary and secondary students.

the hallway, and, upon entering their next class, are confronted with a request to immediately focus on new material. There is simply no time for the brain to effectively process the information overload. This is especially true when the materials are unrelated to the students' lives or have not included active engagement by the student.

Academic Need 9: Receive Realistic and Immediate Feedback That Enhances Self-Efficacy

Closely associated with the need for success experiences is the need to receive immediate and specific feedback. Because students' sense of academic identity and motivation to learn is dramatically impacted by being successful, it is important that they receive feedback clearly designating the extent to which they have succeeded at a task. Studies suggest that students' achievements are enhanced by providing them with information about their current level of performance followed by specific learning tasks aimed at mastering the material.

In fact, students most concerned about failing are most in need of immediate feedback; without it, they tend to judge their performance as unacceptable. Supportive comments, accompanied by statements about specific strengths and weaknesses in students' work, are more effective in improving students' performances than are either grades or brief positive comments. Butler and Nisan (1986) compared student responses to papers with either substantive comments and no grade or grades with no comments. Students who received comments more frequently stated that they (1) found the task more interesting, (2) worked on the task because they were interested in the material, and (3) attributed their success on the task to their interest and effort.

The quality of feedback is important because it affects students' perceptions of themselves as learners. Stipek (1988) stressed the importance of students receiving feedback that helps them see their progress: "Unless students actually perceive themselves to be making progress in acquiring skills or new knowledge, they will not feel efficacious, even if they are rewarded for their efforts and even if their performance is better than others'" (p. 94).

Not all feedback is effective in improving students' performances. Studies show that hostile or extensive criticism creates negative attitudes and lowers achievement, creativity, and classroom control. Praise is often overused and is not a powerful reinforcer for many children. Praise can be an effective

FIGURE 7.21
SUCCESS
CONTRACT

> **Success Contract**
>
> I, _____, have decided that I want to pass Mr. Jones's class. Mr. Jones cares about my being successful and has agreed to provide the following assistance:
>
> a. _____
> b. _____
> c. _____
>
> What I will need to do in order to take advantage of these opportunities is:
>
> a. _____
> b. _____
> c. _____
>
> Mr. Jones and I will examine my progress and share it with my parent(s)/
> guardian(s) and _____ on _____.
>   (Support person)   (Date)
>
> I will know I have succeeded when _____
> _____
>
> Signed
>
>   _____   _____   _____.
>   (Student)   (Teacher)   (Support Person)

form of feedback when it provides students with specific information about the quality of their work and the effort made to complete the work. However, praise is often misused. Teachers frequently praise incorrect answers, and this false praise is more often given to lower-achieving students.

Rosenholtz and Simpson (1984) examined classroom variables that affect how students view their abilities. They categorize classrooms as unidimensional (creating a sense that ability is a stable characteristic and in which students know who has and does not have ability) and multidimensional (in which ability is not nearly as stratified). In unidimensional classrooms, feedback is provided in such a way that students can easily compare their work with others'. For example, charts indicating the level of student performance are placed on the walls, and exemplary work and the names of students whose work is missing or needs redoing are prominently displayed. Rosenholtz and Simpson suggest that to encourage students to see ability as a trait or factor that is flexible and related to effort, teachers should make feedback and evaluation a more private matter.

Effective feedback provides students with important benchmarks. It enables students to understand where they are in relation to achieving goals, the amount of progress they have made toward a goal, and what they need to do to continue or improve on their progress. Effective feedback also communicates that the teacher believes the student can reach predetermined goals, that the student's effort is a major factor influencing the outcome, and that how a student's progress compares to that of other students is not a major factor.

PAUSE & CONSIDER 7.11

Pause for a moment and consider how you, or a teacher with whom you are working, provide feedback to the students. Does the manner in which student work is responded to and displayed create a sense that student effort and improvement are valued, or that excellent performance is the most important factor? We encourage you to form groups of three or four and discuss ways teachers at the grade level and subject matter you are teaching or observing use feedback to encourage all students. You may want to share your small-group results with a larger group and develop several key concepts and a number of methods that encourage and empower students.

Academic Need 10: Be Involved in Self-Evaluating Their Learning and Effort

A sizable body of research supports the benefits of students monitoring their own academic progress (McCaslin et al., 2006). Involving students in self-evaluation provides students with opportunities to understand their academic performance better and to experience a sense of personal responsibility. When students evaluate and record their own work, they are more likely to develop an internal locus of control and view their progress as based on their own efforts. Similarly, self-evaluation enables students to acknowledge areas that need improvement.

Surprisingly, the benefits associated with monitoring progress may be particularly great for students who are progressing slowly. These students often view themselves as making no progress or actually falling behind (as indeed they may be when the basis for comparison is their peers' work). Providing these students with specific data that demonstrate their progress is perhaps the most effective and honest motivational strategy.

A number of Web pages provide thoughtful examples of ways to engage students at various grade levels in assessing their own academic work and efforts to successfully complete this work (cdl.org [search for "self-evaluation"] and google.com/search?q=Student+self-assessment&hl=en&client).

PAUSE & CONSIDER 7.12

Stop for a moment and consider a situation in which several of your students or students in a classroom where you are observing are struggling to master the material and perhaps feeling rather defeated. Write a brief statement describing a method you could use to help them collect data on the progress they are making and highlight the effective learning strategies they are using. We encourage you to share this with two or three colleagues or classmates.

Academic Need 11: Receive Appropriate Rewards for Performance Gains

We can all recall situations when our focus on a task was enhanced and extended because we were expecting a reward when we completed the task. When reading this text, you may tell yourself that the reward for completing a section is that you will have new skills to assist a struggling learner or that you will participate in an activity you enjoy as soon as your work is complete.

Rewards are more effective for increasing effort than improving quality of performance, so it is better to use them when there is a clear goal and a clear strategy to follow (e.g., arithmetic computation, musical scales, typing, spelling), as well as when students have the prerequisite skills for completing the task but are not doing so. Rewards are less effective when goals are more ambiguous or students must discover or invent new knowledge or strategies rather than merely activate existing skills. Rewards can act as motivators only for those students who believe that they have a good chance to obtain the rewards if they put forth reasonable effort.

Although we generally agree with Kohn's (1999) concerns about rewards expressed in his book *Punishment by Rewards*, the negative effects of extrinsic rewards appear to be greatest when students already value the work or when giving the reward distracts the students from their work. If, however, the individual has little motivation for engaging in an activity, providing a reward (especially if the reward is related to a student's goals, was negotiated with the student, or otherwise enhances the student's sense of efficacy and personal control) can be used to enhance motivation to learn. One way for rewards to be effectively integrated into your school or classroom is to view rewards as one aspect of a celebration. It is important to celebrate group and individual successes at the smallest possible unit (i.e., within the supportive classroom rather than at an all-school event). We will never forget our daughter's reaction on her last day of what she felt had been a successful sixth-grade year. She returned home following the school awards ceremony and announced in an uncharacteristically despondent manner that she must have had a terrible year because she sat for nearly two hours while awards were presented and never heard her name.

Academic Need 12: Experience a supportive, Safe, Well-Organized Learning Environment

As discussed in an earlier chapter, brain-based research suggests the creation of a safe learning environment is a prerequisite to helping students meet their academic potential. A classroom must be properly lit, well ventilated, aesthetically pleasing, personally supportive—including being respectful of one's cultural heritage—and feel physically and emotionally safe. Some writers also report that brain-based research suggests students' learning can be enhanced by the use of soft music; reducing the use of fluorescent lights; having classrooms painted in soft colors such as light yellow, beige, and off-white; and reducing sound through the use of carpets, tennis balls on chair legs, and even pleasant smells (Wilmes et al., 2008).

Chapters 3 through 6 present current best practices for creating this type of classroom environment, while Chapters 8 through 10 present methods for using respectful, educational responses to disruptions to a positive learning environment. By implementing the strategies presented in these chapters, you can virtually ensure your efforts at implementing the instructional strategies presented in this chapter will have the positive outcomes you desire.

STRATEGIES FOR FACILITATING THE LEARNING OF ENGLISH LANGUAGE LEARNERS

Have you ever been in a situation in which you needed to understand the directions and they were being given in a language you did not understand? This might have been a foreign language or language related to technical material such as physics, medicine, biochemistry, and so on. If you have traveled overseas and have limited proficiency in the language(s) spoken where you traveled, you may have had such an experience. Although this experience engenders feelings of boredom or mild frustration if the content of the situation is nonessential—such as watching a play—feelings of anxiety, anger, and distress arise if it is important that we understand what is being said, such as from where the train will be departing or how to find lodging.

Imagine the feelings experienced by many students who desperately want to succeed and be accepted in our classrooms but who do not understand what is being said or happening. Not only are these students often confused and anxious but they must also be exhausted and feel less than capable at the end of most school days. This section provides several key methods for helping these students feel safe, competent, and motivated.

Although you may have taken coursework or attended workshops on assisting students with limited English proficiency, a chapter on instruction that supports academic success for all students would not be responsibly written without acknowledging the importance of incorporating these methods. Figures 7.22 and 7.23 and Appendix B present strategies for working with second

FIGURE 7.22
METHODS
FOR
PRESENTING
INFORMATION
ORALLY TO
STUDENTS
WITH LIMITED
ENGLISH
PROFICIENCY

1. Speak clearly and carefully pronounce key words.
2. Face the students when you speak.
3. Repeat, clarify, paraphrase: Use simple subject–verb–object sentences.
4. Use gestures, intonation, and other nonverbal aspects of communication.
5. Use pictures, objects, graphs, maps, and charts both for presenting material and assessing mastery.
6. Use hands-on activities, mime, and pointing.
7. Preteach vocabulary—keep important words on the board or chart paper; use graphic organizers when possible.
8. Give and request examples of abstract and difficult concepts.
9. Check frequently for understanding.
10. Have students share in pairs—often with students who speak the same language.
11. Use peer tutoring and cross-age tutoring.
12. Provide preteaching whenever possible.
13. Allow students to use their first language.
14. Provide an outline for the lesson.
15. Review material frequently.
16. Provide samples of final projects.

language learners. You may wish to examine information on Sheltered Instruction Observation Protocol (SIOP) (Short, Vogt, & Echevaria, 2008; cal.org/siop/) as well as numerous materials presented in the Recommended Reading section on Teaching Students in Multicultural Classrooms.

In discussing their findings regarding effective schools and classrooms for Hispanic students, Reyes and colleagues (1999) reported that teachers who were more effective in facilitating learning among Hispanic students employed active learning methods, such as cooperative learning, and peer and cross-age tutoring. These teachers used thematic units to provide meaning and context for students' learning, and they drew on students' experiences and were able to scaffold instruction to build on students' English proficiency. The methods presented here also provide opportunities for students to observe modeling of other students and to seek affirmation regarding classroom events and academic content. In their book *Methods for Teaching Culturally and Linguistically Diverse Exceptional Learners*, Hoover and his colleagues (Hoover, Klingner, Baca, & Patton, 2008) state that teacher education programs that prepare educators to incorporate culturally sensitive instruction include:

- Creating classrooms organized as communities of learning in which dialogue and reflective learning are the hallmarks
- Using highly interactive classroom strategies such as inquiry projects, action plans, debates, simulations and games, and storytelling
- Exploring personal and family histories and issues around power and privilege
- Using case study approaches

This information supports ideas provided more than a decade ago by leading writers on effective strategies for second language learners (Cummins, 1996; Freeman & Freeman, 2002; Garcia, 2001). These authors suggest second language learners benefit from classrooms in which individual seatwork and large-group instruction are deemphasized and the type of learning activities listed above are emphasized. Educators who receive their teacher preparation in programs that emphasize this type of culturally sensitive pedagogy will be prepared to implement this type of teaching in their classes.

**FIGURE 7.23
SUGGESTIONS
FOR SUPPORTING
ESL/BILINGUAL
STUDENTS**
**Source: This mate-
rial was developed
by Allen Koshewa,
a teacher at
Fairview
Elementary School
in Fairview,
Oregon, and
adapted by Lynn
Reer, retired ESL
professor from
Lewis & Clark
College.**

In the Classroom
- Instill confidence by providing many potentially successful tasks.
- Demonstrate concepts whenever possible; show rather than tell.
- Make sure that directions are both spoken and written.
- Check students' comprehension of instructions shortly after you give them.
- Support dense text with less demanding supplementary materials.
- Audiorecord classroom texts for student use.
- Don't require a novice student to speak, especially in front of a large group.
- Modify assignments and exams to account for language proficiency level.
- Give writing assignments that have an authentic purpose and audience.
- Allow students to use their primary language with each other.
- Encourage students to use bilingual dictionaries. (Teach older children to beware of choosing words out of context.)
- If students can write in their primary language, find primary language pen pals for them.
- Encourage journal writing in the primary language and let students publish writing in the primary language.
- Spend time learning about ESL students' family backgrounds and educational histories.
- Have bilingual students share stories, books, or songs written in their primary language.
- Make sure that labels and signs are displayed in all student languages.
- Make sure that class time is spent discussing the heritage countries of ESL students.
- Establish a classroom climate that values cultural diversity and critiques ethnocentrism.

Who Can Help?
- If the students have an ESL teacher, collaborate with that teacher regularly.
- Establish a rotating buddy system, particularly if you can find buddies who speak the same primary language but are more proficient in English.
- Provide pair work and group work in the classroom.
- Communicate with parents. Make sure parents understand the importance of conversation and literacy activities *in the home language.*
- Find culturally sensitive translators who can help with home phone calls and conferences.
- Find volunteers or teacher assistants who can read literature to students in their first language.
- Find peer mentors, parents, volunteers, or assistants who can help students revise and edit writing in their primary language.

PAUSE & CONSIDER 7.13

By using the methods discussed in this chapter, you will facilitate the learning of many students whose first language is not English or whose cultural background is not White European American. We encourage you, however, to go further than this. We suggest that you interview several of your students with cultural backgrounds different than your own and ask them what classroom factors facilitate their learning. We encourage you to ask them what they want to learn and how they want to learn and to describe their educational goals. Based on this, your reading of this chapter, and your discussion with colleagues or classmates, what changes could you implement in your classroom to enhance the learning of students whose first language is not English or whose cultural background is not European American?

COOPERATIVE LEARNING

Cooperative learning is one of the most popular and effective methods for meeting students' varied learning styles and actively involving students in the learning process.

> Not only do teachers need to teach with exercising respect and dignity, they must also understand the learning styles of their students and direct the classroom in a manner that facilitates understanding and appreciation rather than rote learning. For example, cooperative learning groups engage students with varying levels of knowledge to work together on academic tasks. The cooperative learning approach improves academic achievement and race relations, and promotes positive attitudes toward school, yet this educational strategy is not universally used. (Orpinas & Horne, 2010, p. 52)

"Students develop better capacities for problem-solving and reasoning and obtain higher learning outcomes when they are able to interact with others, share ideas, challenge perspectives, and discuss alternative propositions before reaching agreement" (Gillies & Haynes, 2011, p. 350). Students who are involved in cooperative learning activities perform higher on standardized tests of mathematics, reading, and language and also do better on tasks involving higher-level thinking than when they study alone (Allen & Plax, 1999). Across grade levels, cooperative learning is associated with higher rates of student on-task behavior (Pate-Clevenger, Dusing, Houck, & Zuber, 2008). Our own work in helping teachers implement cooperative learning suggests that when teachers (1) ensure that students understand the learning goals and assessment associated with the activity, (2) take time to help students understand the reasons behind their decision to implement this method, (3) help students become better acquainted, (4) assist students in developing skills for working in groups, and (5) ensure that assessment methods help hold the group and individual students accountable for the academic goals associated with the group work, cooperative learning is very effective in increasing motivation and learning for a wide range of students.

Good and Brophy (2008) note that cooperative learning can be an effective technique for helping students be accepted into and function effectively in the classroom. Similarly, a review of research on cooperative learning (Allen & Plax, 1999) suggests that in classrooms characterized by high rates of collaborative, cooperative learning, students are more likely to indicate they like school, the classroom, and the subject matter. Students in classrooms using cooperative peer activities are also characterized by greater group cohesiveness, more diversified friendship patterns, and greater concern for peers (Schmuck & Schmuck, 2001). Not surprisingly, when cooperative learning is used in the classroom, students have been found to be more accepting of student diversity, including greater acceptance of and sensitivity to students with special needs. In addition, students who work collaboratively tend to have a greater sense of personal responsibility for their learning. A 1998 survey of elementary teachers indicated that 93 percent of the teachers surveyed used cooperative learning in their classrooms (Antil, Jenkins, Wayne, & Vadasy, 1998). The majority of these teachers indicated cooperative learning methods enhanced students' progress toward both academic and social learning goals. The following section provides materials we have found most important in effectively implementing cooperative learning in the classroom.

Simple Structure Activities

Simple structures refer to activities teachers can use periodically to stimulate discussion and review materials. In his book, Kagan (1989) presented a number of simple structure activities that can be used in any subject matter. Roundtable is one activity in which the teacher asks a question that has numerous possible answers—such as to list all the possible causes of the Civil War or all the common denominators for 24 and 42. Students then make a list on one sheet of paper, with each student adding one answer and passing the paper to the left. Numbered Heads Together is another activity. Students are again asked a question and placed in small groups to develop an answer. Each student in the group is assigned a number. The students work until the teacher signals them to stop. The teacher then calls out a number, and all students assigned that number raise their hands. These students are the groups' representatives and can be called on to present the groups' answers.

Another simple structure activity called Stars is used to review material and prepare students for a quiz or test. After the teacher has presented the material, study groups of three or four students of mixed abilities are assigned. Each group is asked to develop five questions related to the material being studied and to provide the correct answer for each question. Each member of the group makes a copy of this material. The next task (usually occurring the following day) involves creating quiz groups consisting of students from different study groups. In the quiz group, one person at a time reads a question from his or her list and the other students write down the answer they think is correct. The person who reads the question then provides the correct answer and the person to the right asks the next question. This process continues until each person has read all the questions prepared by the study group. The questions are then collected and the teacher prepares a test from these questions.

Teachers interested in developing simple structure cooperative activities can find excellent ideas by Spencer Kagan at kaganonline.com, in Johnson and Johnson's (1985) *Cooperative Learning: Warm-Ups, Grouping Strategies and Group Activities*, and at co-operation.org.

MRS. HOPE FOUND THAT SOME OF HER BEST INSTRUCTORS WERE STILL IN SECOND GRADE.

© Cartoon reprinted with permission of copyright holder. Source: Giangreco, M.F. (2007). Absurdities and Realities of Special Education: The Complete Digital Set: Thousand Oaks, CA: Corwin.

Involving Students in Peer Tutoring

"Research evidence strongly supports the use of peers for improving the academic achievement, time on task, and behavior of students with disabilities and specifically for students with EBD" (Farley et al., 2012, p. 38). A meta-analysis of the results of peer tutoring among K–12 students found that "peer tutoring is an effective intervention regardless of dosage, grade level, or disability status. Among students with disabilities, those with emotional and behavioral disorders benefitted most" (Bowman-Perrott et al., 2013, p. 39).

There are several methods to increase student engagement and achievement by more actively engaging students in the learning process through work with their peers. Perhaps the most direct method to implement involves peer tutoring (Falk & Wehby, 2001). "Peer tutoring is one of the most frequently cited instructional strategies for decreasing negative behavior and increasing positive behavior for students with EBD" (Niesyn, 2009, p. 229). A strategy known as classwide peer tutoring (CWPT) has been shown to be an effective model with a wide range of students (Maheady & Gard, 2010). Many teachers use the method of having students form dyads and having these pairs discuss or check their work. This can be added to by having each pair assigned to work with another pair to share the answer or ideas each pair has developed—a method often referred to as "pairs-check-pair."

Our experience clearly indicates that prior to implementing peer tutoring, it is important to teach students how to work collaboratively. This can be accomplished just as one would teach any classroom procedure. The class can be asked to discuss qualities of helping others learn, and this can be developed into a chart to be posted in the classroom. The teacher and a student can then model this as other students observe. Pairs of students can then be asked to practice this while members of the class observe. Finally, prior to having students work in dyads, the teacher can remind the students of the procedures and, while the students are working in pairs, can move around the room providing behavior-specific feedback to students regarding their use of these skills.

Process Approach

David and Roger Johnson have conducted numerous research studies and written extensively on cooperative learning. Their approach highlights a process, or series of steps, teachers can apply to implement cooperative learning with any subject matter. The Johnsons have stated that there are five basic elements of this process (Johnson, Johnson, & Holubec, 2008):

1. *Positive interdependence.* This element involves structuring goals and activities so that students must be concerned about the performance of all members of the group. This can be accomplished through such methods as providing only one copy of the material (materials interdependence), assigning each group member a role (role interdependence), making success dependent on all members' reaching a specified goal (goal interdependence), assigning the same grade or reward to each group member (reward interdependence), or providing each member only a portion of the information necessary to complete the task (resource interdependence). The key is that the group members know that they are in it together and that they sink or swim together.

2. *Individual accountability.* This means that every student is accountable for mastering the material. This can be accomplished through the traditional means of having each student take a quiz or otherwise demonstrate competence, or by indicating to students that any group member can be asked to demonstrate mastery of the content by being called to the overhead or by being called on in some other way.

3. *Face-to-face interaction.* Students are arranged in such a manner that they are knee to knee and eye to eye and are involved in actively sharing and discussing the content.

4. *Teaching collaborative skills.* To function effectively in groups, students must learn how to work cooperatively in a small group. Figure 7.24 lists specific group skills we have

FIGURE 7.24 GROUP COLLABORATIVE SKILLS

1. State the assignment.
2. State the group process goal(s).
3. Call attention to the time limit.
4. Assign group roles (if used).
5. Proceed with the assignment.
6. Summarize the activity.
7. Evaluate the group process skills.

**FIGURE 7.25
HELPING
STUDENTS
DEVELOP
COLLABORATIVE
SKILLS**

1. Do students believe the skill is needed and useful?
2. Do students understand what the skill is, what the behaviors are, what the sequence of behaviors is, and how it looks when it is all put together?
3. Have students had an opportunity to practice the skill?
4. Have students received feedback that is immediate, descriptive, and specific?
5. Have students persevered in practicing the skill?
6. Have students had the opportunity to use the skill successfully?
7. Have students used the skill frequently enough so that they have integrated the skill into their natural behavior?
8. Do the classroom norms support the use of the skill?

found important to teach students. Figure 7.25 presents the steps Johnson et al. (2008) have outlined for teaching students cooperative skills.

5. *Processing group skills.* Once students have been introduced to cooperative group skills, it is necessary to monitor and reinforce these skills consistently. This task will initially be accomplished by the teacher, but it can be transferred to students as they develop proficiency in the skills. When initially teaching and monitoring group skills, it is best to focus on one or two skills at a time. As students become more familiar with group skills, they can be monitored on three to five skills at a time. Research suggests that in addition to social skills associated with effective group work, students' academic achievement can be facilitated by teaching students specific strategic questioning strategies to use during cooperative learning activities. This may include "asking questions that probed and clarified issues, confronted and challenged discrepancies, and paraphrased and summarized key ideas" (Gillies & Haynes, p. 352). Figure 7.26 provides an example of a form we have found helpful for monitoring group skills.

Figure 7.27 presents the steps Johnson et al. (2008) suggested for teachers who are interested in incorporating cooperative learning into their classrooms. Teachers interested in incorporating the Johnsons' approach to cooperative learning into their classrooms can find a variety of materials available and can also attend well-designed workshops to develop the needed experience and skills. The materials we have found most helpful are found at the end of this chapter. (These materials can be ordered through Interaction Book Company, 7208 Cornelia Drive, Edina, MN 55435. Additional information can be obtained at co-operation.org.)

Tally the number of times a student demonstrates a skill.

	Group One			Group Two		
Skill	Bob	Nancy	Tariq	Rolando	Marissa	Beryl
Contributes ideas						
Encourages others						
Listens						
Participates						
Checks for understanding						
Organizes the task						

**FIGURE 7.26
TEACHER OBSERVATION SHEET**

FIGURE 7.27
THE
TEACHER'S
ROLE IN
COOPERATION
LEARNING

Source: From
*Cooperation in the
Classroom* by
D. Johnson,
R. Johnson, and
E. Holubec, 2008,
pp. 2:28–2:29.
Edina, MN:
Interaction Book
Company.
Reprinted with
permission.

Make Preinstructional Decisions

Specify Academic and Social Skill Objectives. Every lesson has both (a) academic and (b) interpersonal and small-group skills objectives.

Decide on Group Size. Learning groups should be small (groups of two or three students, four at the most).

Decide on Group Composition (Assign Students to Groups). Assign students to groups randomly or select groups yourself. Usually you will wish to maximize the heterogeneity in each group.

Assign Roles. Structure student–student interaction by assigning roles such as Reader, Recorder, Encourager of Participation, and Checker for Understanding.

Arrange the Room. Group members should be "knee to knee and eye to eye" but arranged so they all can see you at the front of the room.

Plan Materials. Arrange materials to give a "sink or swim together" message. Give only one paper to the group or give each member part of the material to be learned.

Explain Task and Cooperative Structure

Explain the Academic Task. Explain the task, the objectives of the lesson, the concepts and principles students need to know to complete the assignment, and the procedures they are to follow.

Explain the Criteria for Success. Student work should be evaluated on a criteria-referenced basis. Make clear your criteria for evaluating students' work.

Structure Positive Independence. Students must believe that they "sink or swim together." Always establish mutual goals (students are responsible for own learning and the learning of all other group members). Supplement goal interdependence with celebration/reward, resource, role, and identity interdependence.

Structure Intergroup Cooperation. Have groups check with and help other groups. Extend the benefits of cooperation to the whole class.

Structure Individual Accountability. Each student must feel responsible for doing his or her fair share of work. Ways to ensure accountability are frequent oral quizzing of group members picked at random, individual tests, and assigning a member the role of Checker for Understanding.

Specify Expected Behaviors. The more specific you are about the behaviors you want to see in the groups, the more likely students will do them. Social skills may be classified as **forming** (staying with the group, using quiet voices), **functioning** (contributing, encouraging others to participate), **formulating** (summarizing, elaborating), and **fermenting** (criticizing ideas, asking for justification). Regularly teach the interpersonal and small-group skills you wish to see used in the learning groups.

Monitor and Intervene

Arrange Face-to-Face Promotive Interaction. Conduct the lesson in ways that ensure that students promote each other's success face-to-face.

Monitor Students' Behavior. This is the fun part! While students are working, you circulate to see whether they understand the assignment and the material, give immediate feedback and reinforcement, and praise good use of group skills. Collect observation data on each group and student.

(continued)

FIGURE 7.27
(CONTINUED)

Intervene to Improve Taskwork and Teamwork. Provide task assistance (clarify, reteach) if students do not understand the assignment. Provide teamwork assistance if students are having difficulties in working together productively.

Provide Closure. To enhance student learning, have students summarize the major points in the lesson or review important facts.

Evaluate and Process

Evaluate Student Learning. Assess and evaluate the quality and quantity of student learning. Involve students in the assessment process.

Process Group Functioning. Ensure each student receives feedback, analyzes the data on group functioning, sets an improvement goal, and participates in a team celebration. Have groups routinely list three things they did well in working together and one thing they will do better tomorrow. Summarize as a whole class. Have groups celebrate their success and hard work.

Prior to using a cooperative group activity that will last for more than a few minutes, we have found it helpful to ask ourselves the following twelve questions:

1. Do the students clearly understand the task and the associated learning goals?
2. Do the students understand why I have chosen to use group work to facilitate their learning the content?
3. Do the students find intrinsic, achievement, or utility value in the material?
4. Do students understand how and why the groups have been selected as they have?
5. Do the students possess the skills necessary to complete the task; that is, do they know how to use the materials and can at least several students in each group read any written material associated with the task?
6. Are all materials readily available and has a procedure been established so they can be easily obtained?
7. Do the students know how much time they have to complete the task?
8. Do the students know what they should do if they require assistance?
9. Do the students know what to do if they finish early or what options are available if they cannot complete the task in the allotted time?
10. Have I established a method for gaining the students' attention should it be necessary to add an instruction, clarify a problem, or ask the groups to stop their work?
11. Do the students know the behaviors that will be expected of them while they work in the group, and have I taught and monitored key skills?
12. Have I developed a procedure to ensure that the students and I know how well each individual student has mastered the content?

PAUSE & CONSIDER 7.14

This section has provided a considerable number of methods you might add to your teaching repertoire. Take a few minutes to review this section. Next, make a list of three specific changes or additions you would like to make to enhance the quality of cooperative group work in your classroom or the classroom you are observing. Share this list with a small group of colleagues or classmates. If you have an opportunity to implement these changes, share the results with this same small group.

Peer Tutoring

A number of benefits can be derived from implementing peer tutoring in a classroom. First, tutoring fosters the concept that asking for and offering help are positive behaviors. This act encourages cooperation and concern for peers and thereby creates a more supportive, safe learning environment. Second, the opportunity to instruct another child can provide a student with a sense of competence and personal worth. Third, in assisting another student, the student frequently learns the material more thoroughly. The combination of increased understanding and the act of instructing another student frequently makes a student a more excited and confident learner. Finally, peer tutoring helps the teacher monitor and individualize instruction. By allowing students to serve as resources for other students, the teacher increases the availability of individual attention, thereby reducing students' frustrations and accompanying acting-out behaviors.

Although peer tutoring has many benefits, it can become a frustrating and counterproductive activity if students are not provided with skills in how to assist each other. Therefore, it is important that if you plan to implement peer tutoring, you provide your students with instruction in how to assist another student. Do so by listing and discussing the dos and don'ts of helping others with their work. You can then model appropriate behavior and then allow students to practice this behavior and receive feedback. If the equipment is available, students can be videorecorded while assisting other students, and the video can be viewed and discussed. A valuable side effect of providing students with instruction in how to teach another student is that this activity helps them better understand the learning process.

There are numerous approaches to implementing peer tutoring. Students can be provided with green and red 8½-inch-square cards attached to the front of their desks. Students who need help during seatwork can display a red card, and students who understand this material and are willing to assist other students can display a green card. This procedure can be particularly helpful when you are busy working with a small group and are not available to assist students. A similar approach involves listing on the board the names of students who are able to assist their peers on a project.

Assigning individual students to work with a student who needs assistance is another common approach to peer tutoring. This activity may involve students in the same class or students from higher grades. Another method involves arranging students' desks in groups of four and informing students that they may assist their peers as long as they follow previously learned procedures for effective teaching.

One of the authors observed a young teacher presenting an art lesson to a group of eighth-grade students. The teacher was working with a particularly difficult class; the class included several students the school had characterized as having behavior problems, as well as a boy who was very withdrawn and who had emotional problems. The teacher indicated that she was somewhat concerned about the day's lesson because she had a very limited background in the material she was presenting. She also said that the last period of the day on a particularly nice spring day was not the ideal time to be teaching eighth-graders a concept as difficult as depth perception. With this introduction, the author was prepared to have numerous opportunities for observing the teacher's skills in dealing with behavior problems.

The teacher began the lesson by briefly reviewing the material she had presented on the previous day. She appeared comfortable responding to a variety of students' questions. On one occasion, a student pointed out a major flaw in something she had presented. The teacher indicated that she did not see his point and asked the student if he would be willing to come up to the board and clarify his point for both her and the class. The student did so, and the class responded politely to his brief instruction. After perhaps ten minutes of instruction, the teacher indicated that the students should continue working on their assignments. She commented that some students were finding the tasks more difficult than others and suggested that when they had a problem, they find another student to help them. As students began working on their projects, the teacher circulated around the room answering students' questions and reinforcing students' work. It soon became apparent, however, that she could not possibly answer all the questions that were being fired at her. Her interventions then changed from direct work with students to serving as a clearing center for resources available within the classroom. As she moved around the room, she made comments such as, "Why don't you ask John? He does a good job with two-point perspective." "It might help, Bill, if you could explain to Maria why you . . ." "I really appreciate your helping, Sue. You did a really good job of teaching because you helped him to discover the answer for himself."

The author was impressed with the extremely high percentage of on-task behavior displayed by the students. In addition, the teacher's role as facilitator freed her to spend extra time with a special education student. Because she had structured students' responses to be positive and supportive, students' interactions throughout the class period were extremely positive. In addition to assisting each other, students frequently showed their work to their peers and almost always received either compliments or constructive suggestions.

An increasingly popular approach to peer tutoring involves creating support groups outside the classroom for students who have the ability to complete their work but who have experienced serious and persistent achievement problems. Sullivan (1988) reported the results of a special study groups program for middle school students whose ability levels indicated they could pass their courses but who were failing one or more courses. Students were involved in weekly study

Helping All Students Believe They Can Achieve
For an interactive review of methods for helping all students be successful at academic tasks, click on the link below in your Pearson etext.

ENHANCEDetext *interactive case study*

skills meetings with the vice principal, met with their group to work on assignments several times a week, and received a progress report every Friday. Results indicated that 50 percent of the total number of grades received by students in the study skills groups went up at least one grade, and only 10 percent of the grades went down. Results for a control group showed that only 14 percent of the grades went up.

A wide variety of programs for peer support of learning is available. These include Classwide Peer Tutoring (CWPT), Peer Assisted Learning Strategies (PALS), Cooperative Homework Teams (CHT), Cooperative Learning Groups (CLG), and Cooperative Integrated Reading and Composition (CIRC). You may wish to examine the Web sites for these programs.

SUMMARY

Most textbooks on classroom management ignore the area of instruction, perhaps believing this area is covered in other aspects of teacher preparation and in-service work. However, many specific aspects of instruction influence the creation of classroom environments where students are motivated to learn and behave in ways that support their learning and that of their peers. An essential aspect of effective classroom management involves implementing instructional methods that meet students' needs by actively engaging them in meaningful learning and assisting them in understanding the learning process and developing a sense of being a competent learner. When implemented alongside the other methods presented in this book, the instructional strategies presented in this chapter will enable you to create environments in which all students act responsibly and move forward feeling positive about themselves as learners.

IMPLEMENTATION ACTIVITIES

In addition to the Pause & Consider activities throughout this chapter, the following activities are offered to assist you in incorporating the materials presented in this chapter into your teaching repertoire.

ACTIVITY 7.1

Evaluating a Classroom Environment in Light of Students' Academic Needs

For each of the twelve student academic needs listed in Figure 7.1, list two ways in which you currently meet the need within the classroom. Be specific. For example: I use interest centers to respond to students' needs to follow their own interests. If you are not currently teaching, select a classroom you have observed recently. Next, list two specific ways in which you could alter your teaching methods in order to meet these needs more effectively.

ACTIVITY 7.2

Selecting Methods to Demystify the Learning Process

Turn to Figure 7.3. Circle the number in front of each method on this list that you currently incorporate into your teaching. Next, place a box around any method that sounds interesting and you believe would assist the students you teach. Finally, place an X through the number before any method you believe would not be appropriate or effective with your students. After completing this task, meet with a group of four or five colleagues. Have those who circled an item share how it works in their classrooms. Make sure that those who have a box around an item are provided with ideas on how they might incorporate that item into their classroom.

ACTIVITY 7.3

Modifying Instruction

Select a student who is having difficulty mastering some skill you are helping students learn. Complete Figure 7.19 and fill in at least five of the areas in which you could make a modification to assist this student in being more successful. Next, select and implement two of these methods. Then write a brief response to the following questions:

> Did the student experience greater success following the modifications?
> Did the student's behavior change in any way as he or she was working on this material?
> Have you noticed any difference in the student's attitude or behavior since you implemented the modifications?

Finally, we encourage you to interview the student and discuss how the student felt about the work completed.

RECOMMENDED READING

Teaching Students in Multicultural Classrooms

Banks, J., & McGee Banks, C. (Eds.). (2001). *Cultural diversity and education: Foundations, curriculum, and teaching.* Boston, MA: Allyn & Bacon.

Bigelow, B., Harvey, B., Karp, S., & Miller, L. (2001). *Rethinking our classrooms: Teaching for equity and justice* (Vol. 2). Milwaukee, WI: Rethinking Schools.

Boyer, J., & Baptiste, P. (1996). *Transforming the curriculum for multicultural understanding.* San Francisco, CA: Caddo Gap Press.

Charney, R. (2002). *Teaching children to care: Classroom management for ethical and academic growth, K–8* (2nd ed.). Turners Falls, MA: Northeast Foundation for Children.

Cummins, J. (1996). *Negotiating identities: Education for empowerment in a diverse society.* Ontario, CA: California Association for Bilingual Education.

Edwards, K., Ellis, D., Ko, L., Saifer, S., & Stuczynski, A. (2005). *Classroom* to community and back: Using culturally responsive standards-based teaching to strengthen family and community partnerships and increase student achievement. Portland, OR: Northwest Regional Educational Laboratory.

Faltis, C., & Hudleson, S. (1997). Bilingual education in elementary and secondary school communities: Toward understanding and caring. Boston, MA: Allyn & Bacon.

Fashola, O., Slavin, R., Calderon, M., & Duran, R. (1997). Effective programs for Latino students in elementary and middle schools (Report No. 11). Baltimore, MD: Center for Research on the Education of Students Placed at Risk.

Freeman, D., & Freeman, Y. (2001). Between worlds: Access to second language acquisition. Portsmouth, NH: Heinemann.

Freeman, Y., & Freeman, D. (2002). Closing the achievement gap: How to reach limited-formal-schooling and long-term English learners. Portsmouth, NH: Heinemann.

Garcia, E. (2001). Student cultural diversity: Understanding and meeting the challenge (3rd ed.). Boston, MA: Houghton Mifflin.

Garcia, E., & McLaughlin, B. (Eds.). (1995). Meeting the challenge of linguistic and cultural diversity in early childhood education. New York, NY: Teachers College Press.

Gay, G. (2000). Culturally responsive teaching: Theory, research, and practice. New York, NY: Teachers College Press.

Gay, G. (2007). Connections between classroom management and culturally responsive teaching. In C. Evertson & C. Weinstein (Eds.), Handbook of classroom management: Research, practice, and contemporary issues. Mahwah, NJ: Lawrence Erlbaum.

Reyes, P., Scribner, J., & Scribner, A. (Eds.). (1999). Lessons from high-performing Hispanic schools: Creating learning communities. New York, NY: Teachers College Press.

Thomas, W., & Collier, V. (1997). School effectiveness for language minority students. Washington, DC: National Clearinghouse of Bilingual Education.

Valdez, G. (2001). Learning and not learning English: Latino students in American schools. New York, NY: Teachers College Press.

Walqui, A. (2000). Strategies for success: Engaging immigrant students in secondary schools. ERIC Report EDO-FLO-OO-03. Washington, DC: Center for Applied Linguistics.

Meeting the Needs of Students in Inclusive Classrooms

Allington, R. (2000). What really matters far struggling readers. New York, NY: Longman.

Beers, K. (2003). When kids can't read: What teachers can do. Portsmouth, NH: Heinemann.

Chapman, C., & King, R. (2005). Differentiated assessment strategies. Thousand Oaks, CA: Corwin.

Daniels, H., & Bizar, M. (2005). Teaching the best practices way. Portland, ME: Stenhouse.

Denton, P. (2005). Learning through academic choice. Turners Falls, MA: Northeast Foundation for Children.

Gregory, G., & Chapman, C. (2002). Differentiated instructional strategies: One size doesn't fit all. Thousand Oaks, CA: Corwin.

Janney, R., & Snell, M. (1999). Modifying schoolwork. Pacific Grove, CA: Brooks/Cole.

Jolivette, K., Stichter, J., & McCormick, K. (2002). Making choices—improving behavior—engaging in learning. Teaching Exceptional Children, 34, 24–29.

Mastropieri, M., & Scruggs, T. (2007). The inclusive classroom: Strategies for effective instruction. Upper Saddle River, NJ: Merrill/Prentice Hall.

Salend, S. (1998). Effective mainstreaming: Creating inclusive classrooms. Upper Saddle River, NJ: Merrill/Prentice Hall.

Sprenger, M. (2008). Differentiated instruction through learning styles and memory (2nd ed.). Thousand Oaks, CA: Corwin.

Strickland, K. (2005). What's after assessment: Follow-up instruction for phonics, fluency, and comprehension. Portsmouth, NH: Heinemann.

Tomlinson, C. (2005). How to differentiate instruction in mixed-ability classrooms (2nd ed.). Upper Saddle River, NJ: Merrill/Prentice Hall.

Tomlinson, C., Brimijoin, K., & Narvaez, L. (2008). The differentiated school: Making revolutionary changes in teaching and learning. Alexandria, VA: ASCD.

Tomlinson, C., & McTighe, J. (2006). Integrating differentiated instruction and understanding by design. Alexandria, VA: ASCD.

Vaughn, S., Bos, C., & Schumm, J. (1997). Teaching mainstreamed, diverse, and at-risk students. Boston, MA: Allyn & Bacon.

Walpole, S., & McKenna, M. (2007). Differentiated reading instruction: Strategies for the primary grades. New York, NY: Guilford Press.

Brain-Based Teaching

Crawford, G. (2007). Brain-based teaching with adolescent learning in mind. Thousand Oaks, CA: Corwin.

Jensen, E. (2004). Brain compatible strategies. Thousand Oaks, CA: Corwin.

Jensen, E. (2005). Teaching with the brain in mind (2nd ed.). Alexandria, VA: ASCD.

Jensen, E. (2008). Brain-based learning: A new paradigm for teaching. Thousand Oaks, CA: Corwin.

Kovalik, S., & Olsen, K. (2005). Exceeding expectations: A user's guide to implementing brain research in the classroom (3rd ed.). Federal Way, WA: Books for Educators.

Ratey, J. (2001). A user's guide to the brain: Perception, attention, and the four theaters of the brain. New York, NY: Pantheon Books.

Slavkin, M. (2004). Authentic learning: How learning about the brain can shape the development of students. Lanham, MD: Scarecrow Education.

Sprenger, M. (2007). Becoming a "wiz" at brain-based teaching: How to make every year your best year (2nd ed.). Thousand Oaks, CA: Corwin.

Integrated Curriculum

Beane, J. (1997). Curriculum integration: Designing the core of democratic education. New York, NY: Teachers College Press.

Gruenewald, D., & Smith, G. (2008). Place-based education in the global age: Local diversity. New York, NY: Taylor and Francis.

Nagel, N. (1996). *Learning through real-world problem solving: The power of integrative teaching.* Thousand Oaks, CA: Corwin Press.

Pate, E., Homestead, E., & McGinnis, K. (1997). *Making integrated curriculum work.* New York, NY: Teachers College Press.

Smith, G. (2002). Place-based education: Learning where we are. *Phi Delta Kappan, 83,* 584–594.

Smith, G. (2007). Grounding learning in place. *World Watch Magazine, 20,* 20–24.

Sobel, D. (2004). *Place-based education: Connecting classrooms to communities.* Great Barrington, MA: Orion Society.

Umphrey, M. (2007). *The power of community-centered education. Teaching as craft of place.* Lanham, MD: Rowman & Littlefield.

Learning Styles

Dunn, R., Thies, A., & Honigsfeld, A. (2001). *Synthesis of the Dunn and Dunn learning-style model research: Analysis from a neuropsychological perspective.* Jamaica, NY: St. John's University School of Education and Human Services.

Multiple Intelligences

Armstrong, T. (2000). *Multiple intelligences in the classroom* (2nd ed.). Alexandria, VA: Association for Supervision and Curriculum Development.

Campbell, L., Campbell, B., & Dickerson, D. (1999). *Teaching and learning through multiple intelligences* (2nd ed.). Boston, MA: Allyn & Bacon.

Gardner, H. (1999a). *The disciplined mind: What all students should understand.* New York, NY: Simon & Schuster.

Gardner, H. (1999b). *Intelligence reframed: Multiple intelligences for the 21st century.* New York, NY: Basic Books.

Gardner, H. (2006). *Multiple intelligences: New horizons.* New York, NY: Basic Books.

Huggins, E. (1993). *The assist program: Multiple intelligence lessons.* Longmont, CO: Sopris West.

Lazear, D. (2003). *Eight ways of teaching: The artistry of teaching with multiple intelligences* (4th ed.). Arlington Heights, IL: SkyLight.

Nicholson-Nelson, K. (1998). *Developing students' multiple intelligences: Hundreds of practical ideas easily integrated.* New York, NY: Scholastic.

Cooperative Learning Materials

Abrami, E., Chambers, B., Poulsen, C., DeSimone, C., d'Apollonia, S., & Howden, J. (1995). *Classroom connections: Understanding and using cooperative learning.* New York, NY: Harcourt Brace.

Andrini, B. (1991). *Cooperative learning and mathematics: A multistructural approach.* San Juan Capistrano, CA: Resources for Teachers.

Bernstein, B. (1993). *Cooperative learning in math: Skill-oriented activities that encourage working together.* Carthage, IL: Good Apple.

Breeden, T., & Mosley, J. (1992). *The cooperative learning companion: Ideas, activities, and aids for middle grades.* Nashville, TN: Incentive.

Cantlon, T. (1991a). *The first four weeks of cooperative learning: Activities and materials.* Portland, OR: Prestige.

Cantlon, T. (1991b). *Structuring the classroom successfully for cooperative team learning.* Portland, OR: Prestige.

Johnson, D., Johnson, R., Bartlett, J., & Johnson, L. (1988). *Our cooperative classroom.* Edina, MN: Interaction Book.

Johnson, D., Johnson, R., & Holubec, E. (2007). *Nuts and bolts of cooperative learning* (2nd ed.). Edina, MN: Interaction Book.

Johnson, D., Johnson, R., & Holubec, E. (2008). *Cooperation in the classroom* (8th ed.). Edina, MN: Interaction Book.

Johnson, D., Johnson, R., & Holubec, E. (2009). *Circles of learning: Cooperation in the classroom* (6th ed.). Edina, MN: Interaction Book.

Johnson, R., & Johnson, D. (1985). *Cooperative learning: Warm-ups, grouping strategies and group activities.* Edina, MN: Interaction Book.

Johnson, R., & Johnson, D. (Eds.). (1987). *Structuring cooperative learning: Lesson plans for teachers.* Edina, MN: Interaction Book.

Kagan, S. (2009). *Kagan cooperative learning.* San Clemente, CA: Kagan Cooperative Learning.

Stone, J. (1991). *Cooperative learning and language arts: A multistructural approach.* San Juan Capistrano, CA: Resources for Teachers.

WHEN PREVENTION IS NOT ENOUGH: METHODS FOR ALTERING UNPRODUCTIVE STUDENT BEHAVIOR

PART 4

When sensitively and consistently used, the methods presented in Parts 2 and 3 can result in increased student achievement and the elimination of a significant amount of disruptive student behavior. A few students, however, will cause major or consistent behavior problems despite our efforts to create positive, supportive, well-organized, and stimulating learning environments. Furthermore, the pressures and inevitable frustrations of learning and working in a relatively small area with thirty or so classmates create a situation in which some students will occasionally misbehave and require assistance in controlling and improving their behavior.

Part IV presents many types of intervention strategies that teachers, counselors, and administrators can use to help students choose to act responsibly. When examining and implementing these strategies, educators should keep in mind that these methods will be more effective when used in conjunction with the methods discussed in the previous chapters. In fact, we believe adults harm youngsters by implementing behavior change strategies to ensure that young people act passively and positively in environments that do not meet their basic psychological and academic needs.

Several key concepts underlie the materials presented in Chapters 8, 9, and 10. First, teachers will be most effective in their efforts to help students develop new skills and demonstrate responsible behavior when everyone in the school understands their responsibility and works cooperatively. As discussed in Chapter 1, the term *systems approach* is used to describe this coordination of efforts.

Second, all interventions made in response to student behavior problems should be educational in nature. As educators, we will be most effective in assisting students if we view unproductive or disruptive student behavior as based on the dual factors of student responses to skill deficits and an environment in which students' personal and academic needs are not being met. Therefore, once we have made every attempt to adjust the environment, the next step is to assist students in developing new skills.

Third, a hierarchy exists for responding to unproductive student behavior. It is most beneficial to students if we first implement interventions emphasizing the creation of positive learning environments followed by interventions that focus primarily on student involvement and responsibility for resolving problems. Methods that depend on external reinforcers or that place outside restrictions on students' behaviors are used as a last resort.

Fourth, underlying the behavior change interventions presented in Part 4 is the belief that students should be actively involved in all attempts to alter their behavior. Students should be involved in solving problems, helped to collect and understand data about their own behavior, and instrumental in developing contracts aimed at altering their behavior. Although it is neither feasible nor desirable to have students present during all discussions of their behavior, they should be included in many such discussions and should always be aware of the problems being discussed and the programs being implemented.

Chapter 8 offers an overview of how to conceptualize and respond to student behavior that disrupts the learning environment. Chapter 9 presents methods for incorporating problem solving and conflict resolution into your approach for creating a supportive classroom community in which students learn nonviolent methods for resolving problems. Chapter 10 examines methods for developing individual behavior change plans for students who experience serious and ongoing behavior problems.

Throughout these chapters, our focus is on interventions that enhance students' dignity and teach them new skills. Violent student behavior will only be exacerbated by interventions emphasizing rules and punishments. In its 1983 report on how to handle adolescents' aggressive, violent behavior, the Panel on High Risk Youth of the National Research Council clearly stated that punitive approaches were unsuccessful in creating positive behavior changes. They noted that these methods only bred resentment and desire for revenge and increased the pattern of violence. Instead, students must be helped to realize that they are cared for and valued. They must also realize that when they choose to violate the rights of others, they will be asked to take responsibility for their behavior. They will, however, be asked to work with other students and staff to examine what factors in the environment may need to change for the classroom and school to feel like a personally and psychologically safe place. They will also be given assistance in developing more acceptable ways to express their pain, confusion, and frustration. Effective discipline always provides an answer to three questions: (1) What needs to be changed here to make the classroom and school a better place? (2) What needs to be done here to repair any physical or personal damage done by the student? and (3) What needs to be learned here so the student has other ways of presenting legitimate concerns without violating the rights of others? When adult responses to student behavior problems emphasize these three questions, students will generally accept discipline and will not view adults as arbitrary and uncaring.

CHAPTER 8

RESPONDING TO BEHAVIOR THAT DISRUPTS THE LEARNING PROCESS

Teachers and administrators must move away from the appearance of a teacher-imposed, "hard-line" method to an educational approach emphasizing our skills and abilities as professional educators.

—Forrest Gathercoal (2004)

For some educators, discipline means the power of the teacher to control the behavior of their students.... For other educators, discipline means an opportunity to teach students a set of values about how people can live together in a democratic society.... Discipline is perceived as the process of helping students internalize these values and to develop self-control over their drives and feelings.

—Nicholas Long, Ruth Newman, and William Morse (1996)

© Joyce Button

"Cheer up. Not everyone gets the hang of class control the first time."

Whether teaching classes to preservice teachers or presenting workshops to veteran educators, the question we are asked most frequently and with the greatest passion is, "What do I do when students disrupt the learning environment?" Most educators enter the field with an excitement about helping students learn and find the matter of responding to disruptive student behavior to be one of the most demanding and least rewarding aspects of teaching. Because many teachers lack training and skill in responding to behavior that is disruptive to students' learning, teachers all too often find themselves resorting to the authoritarian models they experienced as students. This point was highlighted recently when a young teacher told one of us, "My voice is one octave lower than it was at the beginning of the year. I really hate myself for yelling at the students, but I don't know what else to do." She continued by stating that while she wanted to use more respectful, less authoritarian methods for helping students act responsibly in her classroom, she did not have these skills and wondered if her students would respond to less authoritarian methods. In a study of preservice teachers, Shook (2012) reported that while these teachers did emphasize teaching rules and procedures in their classrooms, when confronted with behavior that disrupted the learning environment, they focused almost exclusively on reactive strategies such as reprimands, time-outs, and removal from the classroom, and did not consider altering classroom factors or more proactive classroom management methods to help students develop more responsible behaviors. Effective classroom management involves teachers understanding how to analyze classroom factors that may be contributing to a student's behavior difficulties, making adjustments that support the student, and implementing methods that teach students skills for making more effective choices.

Veteran teachers with whom we have worked have also often expressed their frustration with their students' responses to authoritarian, control-oriented methods and asked why students today fail to respond to the authoritarian methods of discipline. We believe this is largely because of the way students view authority. First, students today are much more aware of their own rights. The idea that children should be seen and not heard is much less common than it used to be. Second, the way children see authoritarian adult behavior implemented in their homes is different today than it was for the typical student twenty years ago. We, and many teachers with whom we have spoken, were raised in very authoritarian homes that were also highly stable, loving, supportive environments. Authoritarian control was, therefore, associated with stability and support. Unfortunately, many students today see authoritarian discipline associated with physical and psychological abuse and abandonment. Therefore, when confronted with authoritarian methods of student management, rather than comply, these students experience fear, anxiety, anger, and rebellion. This is exacerbated by the fact that they correctly believe that the authoritarian methods used by school personnel will not be as physically or psychologically damaging as those experienced at home.

An important point to consider when deciding whether to give up authoritarian control is that this approach becomes noticeably less effective as students become older. Authoritarian control can be effectively used in the primary grades (although the effects on children are often destructive), but it is less effective with older students, who are beginning to enter a developmental stage whose main task is developing an individual identity and sense of independence.

Another important factor to consider when determining the approach you want to implement in responding to student behavior that violates the rights of others is that, as mentioned earlier, there appears to be growing evidence that punitive methods, while at times necessary, serve only to aggravate students' sense of anger and alienation and also increase violent behavior (Reiss & Ross, 1994). Furthermore, studies suggest that schoolwide management methods that focus on problem solving (Nelson, 1996) and reteaching (Sugai, Horner, & Gresham, 2002) are the most effective in creating positive, safe school environments.

Although academic skills are extremely important to students, so are skills in making positive, productive choices regarding their behavior. One of the most important skills and greatest gifts we can give students is how to effectively and productively behave in a group setting. In addition, modeling for students skills in responding to behavior that is a concern to us and teaching students how to act responsibly can be a highly rewarding part of teaching. Therefore, when considering the question, "What can I do when students behave in ways that violate the rights of others?" you might reframe the question as, "How can I most effectively model productive responses to irresponsible behavior so I can teach my students these important skills?"

LEARNING GOALS_____

After reading this chapter, you will know:

1. How to develop an effective classroom system for responding to behavior that disrupts the learning environment
2. How to respond effectively to minor disruptive behaviors in a classroom or school setting
3. How to respond to major disruptions and defiant student behavior

Why Are These Goals Important?

Perhaps no area frustrates teachers more than student behavior that disrupts instructional activities. Similarly, perhaps no area creates more anxiety than concern about how to respond to major disruptions that might occur in the classroom. Teachers are faced with significant amounts of disruptive student behavior. Recent data indicates that at any one time, at least 12 percent of students in K–12 classrooms have a relatively serious behavioral and emotional disorder, and 20 percent experience mild to serious problems in this area (Forness et al., 2012). Research suggests that somewhere between 10 percent and 20 percent of students have behavior problems that require more structured interventions than those associated with the methods presented in Chapters 3 through 7 (Sugai, Horner, Lewis, & Cheney, 2002). Therefore, although the methods presented earlier in this book will dramatically reduce the amount of disruptive behavior within a classroom, teachers also need the skills presented in this chapter on how to respond to both minor and major disruptive student behavior.

PAUSE & CONSIDER 8.1

Before reading further, pause for a moment and consider your goals when responding to student behavior that violates the rights of others by disrupting the learning environment. Write a brief statement about what you hope to accomplish in responding to this behavior. We encourage you to share your statement with several peers. As you read about and practice the methods presented in this chapter, consider how they can help you accomplish these goals.

EFFECTIVE RESPONSES TO BEHAVIOR THAT DISRUPTS THE LEARNING PROCESS_____

Nelson and Roberts (2000) studied 99 elementary and middle school students who had demonstrated ongoing disruptive behavior and compared their reactions to brief redirective teacher responses to those of 278 control students identified as having few behavior problems. The control students complied immediately to teacher requests 93 percent of the time, while the focus students responded positively only 24 percent of the time, and the remainder of their responses were noncompliant and negative. Indeed, in all interventions observed, the focus students required an average of 4.56 interchanges before the behavior the teacher had intended to alter was stopped. It is imperative to develop skills that will assist you in increasing the frequency with which students who have a history of challenging adult requests will respond calmly and reasonably to your reasonable and professionally presented requests.

"Most disciplinary referrals originate in the classroom and more times than not, the referrals are for students of color and poor students" (Weinstein, Tomlinson-Clarke, et al., 2004, pp. 27–28). Skiba, Michael, Nardo, and Peterson (2002) reported that African American students are much more likely to receive harsher punishment in response to rule violations than are other students. A significant reason for this is that "[s]uch discrimination occurs when teachers fail to recognize that behavior is culturally influenced; when they devalue, censure, and punish the behaviors of non-mainstream groups; and when they fail to see that their management practices alienate and marginalize some students, while privileging others" (Weinstein, Tomlinson-Clarke, et al., 2004, pp. 27–28). These concerns are made more powerful by findings that there is a direct correlation between office referrals and dropping out (Skiba & Knesting, 2002).

Although teachers respond to incorrect academic behavior with prompts, cues, and instructional interventions, their responses to student behavior that disrupts the learning environment are often critical and punitive. This is understandable because, compared to academic errors, mistakes in demonstrating responsible behavior have a greater impact on teachers' abilities to do their jobs and thus evoke stronger emotions. These punitive responses are, however, generally ineffective in either bringing about the desired student behavior or teaching students alternative methods for responding (Nelson & Roberts, 2000).

Figure 8.1 presents a comparison of two ways to view problematic student behavior. School personnel have too often viewed inappropriate behavior as a student attitude problem rather than as a skill deficit and have therefore responded using the sequence suggested on the right side of Figure 8.1. We believe that current research and theory clearly support viewing and responding to student behavior problems using the paradigm suggested on the left side of Figure 8.1. By treating behavior problems similarly to academic problems, teachers are allowed to use their considerable expertise in analyzing environments and assisting students in developing alternative strategies.

In a study of Australian schools, Lewis (2001) collected questionnaires on teachers' discipline methods from more than 3,500 middle and high school students. His results suggest that relationship-based discipline involving greater use of nonembarrassing cues and discussions with students was associated with more responsible student behavior than was the use of aggressive discipline in which teachers clearly presented themselves as in charge and used prescribed, escalating methods of discipline. In a similar vein, Sheets's (2002) work with African American, Chicano, White, and Filipino American students indicated that students were willing to acknowledge when they had made poor decisions but responded poorly to coercive methods of discipline. This response may be explained by the fact that

> Students already believe they will not be treated fairly under the best of circumstances, and they expect the worst kind of treatment. When schools "get tough" with these students, their expectations are affirmed but their problematic actions may not be reduced at all. (Sheets & Gay, 1996, p. 91)

Numerous other studies have indicated that the use of immediate strong sanctions, including public reprimands, being asked to leave the class, and group consequences for the misbehavior of one or a few students, are perceived by students as unacceptable and ineffective (Woolfolk Hoy & Weinstein, 2006).

Interestingly, studies indicate that teachers who are willing to use a more personal, instructional approach to working with inappropriate student behavior are rated more highly by their principals (Brophy & McCaslin, 1992). In addition, Agne, Greenwood, and Miller (1994)

**FIGURE 8.1
A COMPARISON OF
APPROACHES TO
ACADEMIC AND
SOCIAL PROBLEMS**
Source: Reprinted with
permission from
Geoffrey Colvin.

It is a common practice among educators to approach academic problems differently from social problems. Essentially, instructional principles are used to remediate academic problems, whereas negative consequences typically are used to manage social problems. The differences are summarized here.

Kind of Error	Procedures for Academic Problem	Procedures for Social Problem
Infrequent	Assume student is trying to make correct response.	Assume student is not trying to make correct response.
	Assume error was accidental.	Assume error was deliberate.
	Provide assistance (model—lead—test).	Provide negative consequence.
	Provide more practice.	Do not require practice.
	Assume student has learned skill and will perform correctly in future.	Assume student will make right choice and behave in future.
Frequent (chronic)	Assume student has learned the wrong way.	Assume student refuses to cooperate.
	Assume student has been taught (inadvertently) the wrong way.	Assume student knows what is right and has been told often.
	Diagnose the problem.	Provide more negative consequences.
	Identify misrule or determine more effective manner in which to present the material.	Withdraw student from normal context.
	Adjust presentation. Focus on rule. Provide feedback. Provide practice and review.	Maintain student removal from normal context.
	Assume student has been taught skill and will perform correctly in future.	Assume student has "learned" lesson and will behave in future.

reported that teachers selected as Teacher of the Year were significantly more likely than a matched group of colleagues to view their role in responding to student behavior problems as an interpersonal, skill-based issue rather than a control issue. This suggests that administrators and others who assess teacher performance support teacher decision making that emphasizes helping students become more effective self-managers and responsible citizens. Administrators may also appreciate the benefits of having discipline methods be congruent with instructional methods.

The next section of the chapter will provide you with (1) key concepts and numerous specific methods for responding to minor disruptions in the classroom, (2) a clear classroom procedure for responding to disruptive behavior, and (3) methods for handling serious disruptive behavior. As you consider these methods, also consider the behaviors you define as being disruptive in the classroom. For example, some children may be exposed to family and cultural beliefs indicating that being emotional and confrontational is appropriate when discussing topics you believe are important, while a teacher may expect a more calm and orderly approach to the discussion. Methods for responding to students should always include an assessment of cultural factors and a consideration that it might be necessary to review and even modify behavior expectations rather than simply decide behaviors that do not fit the teacher's style are automatically unacceptable.

Another note of caution is required when reading the following sections and when incorporating these methods. Regardless of how skilled a teacher becomes in this area of classroom management, it is imperative that if a student is frequently failing to follow classroom behavior expectations, the teacher must consider what classroom factors may be contributing to the behavior. While it is professionally necessary and responsible to skillfully respond to disruptive behavior, it is also necessary to understand that the single most important aspect of promoting positive behavior in a classroom is ensuring that, to the greatest degree possible, the classroom setting is effectively meeting the unique personal, social, and academic needs of the student.

Responding Effectively to Inappropriate or Disruptive Behavior

Disruptive student behavior often occurs because students find acting out to be more interesting than a boring lesson or a better option than another failure experience. Similarly, unproductive student behavior often occurs because students do not understand a task, are not involved in the learning activity, or are unable to obtain assistance when it is needed. Therefore, most minor discipline problems can be alleviated by implementing the instructional methods discussed in Chapter 7 or incorporating the procedures discussed in Chapter 6. Nevertheless, when students are required to work for approximately six hours a day in a 30-by-30-foot area with thirty peers, minor problems will inevitably occur. A major factor in effective classroom management is teachers' abilities to deal with minor disruptions before they become major problems.

It is best if teachers handle as many instances of disruptive behavior as possible. When teachers immediately refer students to a counselor or administrator for situations in which students challenge a teacher or student, the teachers are indicating that they do not possess the

Responding to Mildly Disruptive Behavior
For an interactive review of methods for responding when students disrupt the classroom learning environment, click on the link below in your Pearson etext.

ENHANCEDetext *interactive case study*

natural authority to handle these situations in the classroom. The failure to deal directly with students may also be seen by the students and their peers as indicating the teacher does not care about students. This situation can be exacerbated if the teacher refers some students but deals directly with others. Students of color frequently view discipline as being differentially applied to them (Ruck & Wortley, 2002; Sheets, 2002). Low-income students also perceive teachers as disciplining them more often and for behaviors that are not responded to with punishment for more affluent students. Interestingly, students from more affluent home settings indicate they receive preferential treatment when it comes to discipline (Brantlinger, 1993). With more successful students, teachers tend to offer more choices and be less diligent about requiring compliance to classroom rules (Flowerday & Schraw, 2000).

We have asked thousands of teachers to recall their childhood and youth and to describe the manner in which they were responded to when they misbehaved. The vast majority of educators describe confrontational methods, such as threats, physical punishment, and loss of privileges. A very small percentage list calm dialogue, problem solving, or conflict resolution. Therefore, when confronted with a student who is noncompliant or who challenges their authority, most educators have at least some inclination to use some form of confrontational approach. Unfortunately, this type of response usually serves only to escalate the student's emotions, and the student either becomes more aggressive or, for younger children, becomes intimidated and withdrawn. When talking about how a teacher can effectively respond to behavioral errors from which a student needs to learn, Nel Noddings wrote:

> Hence, she is not content to enforce rules—and may even refuse occasionally to do so—but she continually refers the rules to their ground in caring. If she confronts a student who is cheating, she may begin by saying, *I know you want to do well*, or *I know you want to help your friend*. She begins by attributing the best possible motive to him, and then proceeds to explain—fully, with many of her own reservations expressed freely—why she cannot allow him to cheat. She does not need to resort to punishment, because the rules are not sacred to her. What matters is the student, the cared-for, and how he will approach ethical problems as a result of his relation to her. (Noddings, 1984, p. 178)

Envision a situation in which a high school student is talking continuously rather loudly to another student during large-group instruction, a middle school student refuses to move when asked to select another seat, or a primary grade student is pushing a peer in order to obtain a preferred toy. How would you respond?

The following ideas and strategies will enable you to respond to disruptive behavior in a manner that will generally have a positive effect on students' behavior and feelings about school.

Preventive Interventions

1. *Arrange seating patterns so that you can see and easily move to be near all students.* Try to arrange the classroom so you can see all students and can move comfortably about the classroom. As you have short interactions with individual students or small groups, make sure to position yourself so you can scan the rest of the class.
2. *Ensure that your academic and behavioral expectations for the activity are clear to all students.*
3. *Develop, practice, and reinforce classroom procedures for having students move into seating arrangements that support the instructional activity you have planned.*
4. *Scan the class frequently in order to notice and respond to potential problems or minor disruptions.* One of the most difficult tasks for beginning teachers to learn is how to attend to more than one thing at a time. Teachers frequently become so engrossed in working with a group or an individual student, they fail to notice potential problems stemming from a frustrated student or a minor argument. Although it is important to attend to those being taught, teachers must learn to frequently scan the room. Based on his study of thirty-one middle school physical education teachers, Johnston (1995) found when teachers responded immediately to disruptive behavior, students reacted positively and immediately 76 percent of the time. However, if the teachers did not see or respond immediately, their efforts were effective only 47 percent of the time. In addition, when the teachers correctly selected the student to redirect, students complied

86 percent of the time, whereas when the teachers spoke to the wrong student, not surprisingly the student who needed to be redirected responded only 46 percent of the time. Clearly, effective movement around the room while scanning the class is an important skill to develop. You may need to teach students that you will occasionally interrupt your interaction with them due to your responsibility to monitor and intervene to provide a calm, safe classroom for all students.

5. *Move around the room.* Your presence will create a sense of accountability and encourage students' engagement in the content and use of appropriate behaviors. Try to limit the amount of time you are seated.

Initial Interventions

1. *Ignore the behavior.* Ignoring is best for behaviors that cause only limited interference with your ability to teach or students' opportunities to learn. Although often effective for minor behaviors, this strategy also may suggest you are not aware of the misbehavior or that you do not care about the behavior. In addition, the behavior may be reinforced by attention from other students. Therefore, it is best to ignore only minor misbehavior and to associate this ignoring with praise for appropriate behavior.

2. *Make some form of nonverbal contact.* This may include looking quizzically at the student (as if to express surprise that such a good student would be making such a choice), pointing to the classroom rules, etc.

© James Estes

"Geez—who would ever have figured Ms. Killebrew for a tattletale?"

3. *Use proximity control.* Simply move closer to a student who is being disruptive or off-task. This can ideally be done as you continue to teach.

4. *Praise a student who is positively engaged.* Ideally select a student seated close to the student who needs redirection. Also, praise the off-task student the moment she or he begins to work on the assignment or focus on the class discussion.

5. *Involve the student by using his or her name in a story or question.* Sometimes simply hearing his or her name can reengage a student.

6. *Call on the student.* Sometimes mild inappropriate behavior is a sign of lack of engagement. Simply providing a brief involvement can reconnect the student with the lesson. When asking for a response, always ask a question the student can answer. If the situation involves someone who has obviously not been listening to the discussion, you will embarrass the student by asking for a response to a classmate's comment or something you have just said. Asking a new question or paraphrasing a statement made by another student and asking for an opinion can productively reintegrate the student into the mainstream of the classroom activity.

7. *Increase interest by using humor or connecting the lesson to some topic in which the student may be particularly interested.* For example, if the lesson involves division, you might relate it to how athletes' batting averages or shooting percentages are calculated. Similarly, a lesson on passing a law might be spiced up by commenting on impending legislation related to limiting teenage drivers' rights.

8. *Involve the class in a short interactive activity.* Especially if several other students appear somewhat distracted, you may wish to have students briefly work in dyads or triads to discuss or practice some aspect of the material they are learning. This is often referred to as a "Think-Pair-Share" or "Turn and Talk" activity. This active interaction may help the student(s) reengage in a positive way with the content being taught.

9. *Give the student a short task.* You may want to send the student on an errand, have the student assist you with a classroom task, and so forth.

10. *Place a small note (sticky notes work well) on the student's desk.* This might involve an invitation to talk with you when the lesson is over or a strategy the student might use to solve the problem.

11. *See whether the student needs some assistance, acknowledge this, and provide the assistance.* For example, if a student is acting out and you notice her difficulty involves an inability to draw a straight line, you could provide the student with a ruler. This type of quick environmental analysis can go a long way toward reducing behavior problems. This can be supplemented by a comment such as "When you have the right equipment, you really do well, Luanna. Next time you have trouble, try to think about what would help you, so you can solve the problem rather than getting upset."

Follow-Up Interventions

If a student fails to respond to these somewhat indirect interventions, it is often necessary to make direct contact with the student. When doing this, the following concepts and ideas will assist you in helping the student become productively involved in classroom activities.

1. *The disturbance of the teacher's intervention should not be greater than the disruption it is intended to reduce.* Teachers often create more disruptions with their attempts to discipline students than the students are causing themselves. As suggested previously, initially ignore such minor disruptions as a dropped book or one short comment a student makes quietly to a peer. If an individual student continually creates minor disruptions, this problem can be dealt with effectively by discussing the issue privately with the student. If many class members are involved in low-key disruptive behavior, the behavior can be discussed during a class meeting. Finally, as discussed later in this chapter, you may need to implement your classroom discipline plan that has been taught to all students.

2. *An inappropriately angry teacher response creates tension and increases disobedience and disruptive behavior.* Both Kounin (1970) and Brophy and Evertson (1976) found evidence of a "negative ripple effect" associated with harsh teacher criticism. Rather than improving student behavior, students tend to become more anxious and disruptive in classes characterized by overly harsh discipline. More recent research indicates that very firm teacher demands in response to students' behavior errors is related to higher rates of student off-task behavior (Ratcliff et al., 2010). It appears that while firmness can have a positive effect on classroom behavior, it should be associated with teacher warmth, politeness, and explanations.

© Bob Vojtko

"If the class doesn't stop talking, you're all staying after school. Pass it on."

3. *Remain calm.* Perhaps the most difficult yet important communication skill in responding to disruptive student behavior is to remain calm. When dealing with a situation in which a student's behavior is disrupting the flow of classroom events or causing discomfort to a student or adult, it is natural to experience feelings of frustration, annoyance, and even anger. However, we need to realize that as educators, our role sometimes involves using professional skills that do not necessarily come naturally. Our job includes always asking what will be best for the student and how we can help facilitate this. Clearly, when we are asking a student to stop a behavior and replace it with another way of acting, we are attempting to provide important social skill instruction. We need students to take responsibility for their own behavior with a receptive approach to this new instruction. If we become emotional or act in a manner that is not completely professional, we provide the students with an opportunity to project the problem or blame onto us and fail to take responsibility for their own behavior. Instead of encouraging the student to think, "I may need to reconsider this behavior," emotional or rude behavior allows the student to focus on the adult's inappropriate behavior—deflecting responsibility from them to us.

4. *Speak courteously.* When interacting with students, the use of such simple courtesies as "thank you," "please," and "excuse me" can both increase the likelihood a student will respond positively and simultaneously provide good modeling for students.

5. *Be aware of nonverbal messages.* According to an old saying, children often respond more to what adults do than to what they say. Because young people are so dependent on adults, they become adept at reading their nonverbal messages. It is therefore important that we attempt to make our nonverbal messages congruent with our verbal messages. Talking to a student while looking elsewhere may cause the student to doubt your expressions of positive feelings or sincere concern. Similarly, when we say in a very annoyed tone of voice that we care about students but would like them to change certain behaviors, they are unlikely to believe that our statements are truly based on concern for them. Also, be careful that your approach to and physical positioning as you engage the student is nonthreatening. Move calmly toward the student and make sure you are neither too close nor positioned directly in front of the student. Also, make sure your hands and arms are not pointing toward the student. These nonverbal decisions help ensure the student feels safe and thereby able to listen to our request or feedback.

6. *State expectations clearly.* It is important to consider how teachers present their initial request that a disruptive student select a more responsible behavior. Walker and Sylwester (1998) discuss the differences between alpha and beta requests. Teacher alpha requests provide a "clear, direct, and specific directive, without additional

verbalizations, that allows reasonable time for a response, [whereas] beta commands involve vague or multiple directives, given simultaneously, and accompanied by excess verbalization, and without a clear criterion or adequate opportunity for compliance" (p. 54). Golly (1994) reported that the first- and second-grade teachers in her study made alpha requests 59 percent of the time and that students complied with 88 percent of teachers' alpha requests but only 76 percent of beta requests. Perhaps more important is the fact that students who have more difficulty acting responsibly in school settings are much more likely than the typical student to respond poorly to beta directives (Wehby, Symons, & Shores, 1995). Therefore, it is imperative that teachers learn to give directions or requests calmly and clearly.

7. *Remind students of the classroom rule or procedure they are not demonstrating.* Rather than yelling, "Oscar, stop bothering Sophia while she is working!" simply walk over to Oscar and ask quietly, "Oscar, what classroom rule are you not following?" or "Oscar, I expect you to follow your classroom rules." You could also point to the chart you developed regarding what it looks like and sounds like to be an effective student and ask the student to please use these skills. Similarly, if an entire class is becoming disruptive or lining up without having cleared their desks, ask the class to describe their behavior and mention any classroom procedures that are being neglected.

8. *Provide the correction by incorporating a statement about positive behavior the student displays.* For example, you might say, "Ruiz, you usually listen so well and help other students, would you please focus on your work instead of grabbing Jeremy's work?"

9. *Take responsibility for statements by using I-messages.* It is difficult to overestimate the importance and value of I-messages. Students who experience consistent or serious behavior problems are often deficient in social cognition skills. Simply stated, they are not as capable as their peers of understanding and appreciating others' points of view. For example, they may not understand why a teacher is bothered by their talking out or why, despite their aggressive or rude behavior, their peers do not wish to play with them.

Just as many students learn to read before entering school, many children learn to understand others' perspectives through the use of language employed at home. Students who have not had these opportunities will, just like students who enter school unable to decode letters and sounds, need learning experiences to help them develop important social cognition skills. I-messages are one method of providing this important assistance.

In *Discovering Your Teaching Self*, Curwin and Fuhrmann (1975) provide a succinct and sensitive statement about this skill:

> Meaningful communication between people (the communication between adults and children is of special interest to us) often breaks down because one party (or both) continually tells the other what's wrong with him rather than identifying how he himself is feeling in the situation. When I tell someone what's wrong with him, I virtually take away from him all responsibility for himself. Since I know what is wrong, I also know how to "correct" it. Thus I leave him powerless and probably defensive. (p. 196)

If you say to a student, "You are being disruptive" or "You're late again!" the student is likely to feel attacked and defensive. If, however, you say, "When you talk while I am talking (or when you come in late), it distracts me and I'm concerned about whether other students can focus on learning," the student has been provided with some useful information about his or her effect on other people. Similarly, using the pronoun *we* is unfairly ganging up against a student. When confronted with statements beginning with "we feel" or "the

© George Abbott

"Johnny! Please exercise your right to remain silent."

entire class believes," the student is likely to feel attacked and defeated. Though they are flexible, students are also very sensitive and need to be confronted by one person at a time. Furthermore, because each of us is an expert on only our own feelings, it appears reasonable that each of us should share our own feelings and dispense with the pronoun *we*.

In *Teacher Effectiveness Training* (TET), Thomas Gordon (1974) wrote that when expressing a concern about students' behavior that affects the teacher, the teacher should employ an I-message consisting of three components: (1) the personal pronoun *I*, (2) the feeling the teacher is experiencing, and (3) the effect the student's behavior is having on the teacher. I believe an effective I-message should also include a polite request for the student to make a better choice. For example, a typical teacher's response to a student's interruption might be "If you can't stop interrupting me, you can leave the room." Using an I-message instead, the teacher might say, "When you interrupt me, I become concerned because I have difficulty helping the other students. Please wait until I finish helping Sam and I will be glad to help you."

Because I-messages express personal feelings and often deal with student behaviors that require change, it is best to send most of them privately. We should do so especially when we are dealing with adolescents, who, being particularly sensitive to peer pressure, will often respond to even the most thoughtful public criticism defensively. Because most adolescents value being treated as adults, they will usually respond positively to private expressions of our concern.

Another less open way to send an I-message involves politely yet firmly expressing a demand using the first-person singular. Therefore, if a student began talking to a classmate during a presentation, the teacher might say in a nonthreatening manner, "I expect students to listen quietly while someone in this class speaks." Although this type of I-message has few benefits when compared to asking the student to follow classroom behavior standards, it is a clear, straightforward way to present your expectations.

A young high school teacher in one of the author's classes shared with colleagues that she had quietly sent an I-message to one of her most disruptive students. She was amazed when the student stopped by after class to apologize to her and that during the following week his behavior dramatically improved. When asked why she thought he had apparently responded so well, she noted that he was probably used to being criticized for his behavior and was appreciative that someone would treat him courteously.

10. *Provide students with choices.* When responding to students who are upset, it is often helpful to provide them with choices (Karrie, Faggella-Luby, Bae, & Wehmeyer, 2004). This responds to students' needs for competence and power and helps to reduce their perception that someone is trying to control them or is going to do something to them. For example, if a student appears unready to leave an area, instead of saying, "I'll give you ten more seconds to leave this area or you will be in even more trouble!" we might say, "Looks like you're pretty upset right now. Would you rather wait in my room or the counseling office to chat about this and work out a solution?"

    During a workshop conducted by the author, a Nebraska teacher shared how she had used her new skills on giving choices while working on her son's tendency toward arguments and accompanying temper tantrums when asked to run errands with his mother. Instead of bribing or threatening him, she attempted sending an I-message—her need to go, her desire to have him with her—and asking him what would make the trip more enjoyable. The boy indicated he was hungry and would like a snack for the ride. The mother asked him what would be a healthful snack that would be neat enough for the car. The boy responded that he thought an apple would be healthful and not too messy. The mother then asked him if there was anything else that would make the trip more pleasant, and he said he would like to bring a new play figure his father had recently purchased for him. The mother said the boy was delighted at his involvement in the decisions and that, unlike many of their recent excursions, they had a very enjoyable time together.

11. *Remind the student of the positive consequences associated with behaving in a prosocial manner.* For example, you might say, "If you can wait in line without bumping anyone, we'll get out to recess sooner and have more time to play," or "If you work cooperatively with your group, you will be able to help them with the artwork. You're such a good artist that your group's project will be so much better if you help."

12. *When a student is being extremely disruptive, it is best to focus the other students' attention on their tasks and then talk privately with the disruptive student.* You might say, "Would you all please help me by working quietly on your essays while I help Mustafe?" By handling the situation calmly and positively, you indicate your competence, which in turn will have a calming effect on the other students.

Ratcliff et al. (2010) suggest that when dealing with disruptive student behavior in the classroom:

> . . . in order to avoid retreating, teachers should use behavior controls only when student behavior is harmful or disruptive; they should observe students to see that directives are being followed; they should remain calm and confident; and they should avoid confrontations in front of the class where threatening comments are used. Finally, in order to avoid retreating, teachers should wait for students to comply before continuing on with any activity. (p. 40)

It is essential for teachers to have a repertoire of skills to spontaneously and professionally respond to student behavior that disrupts the learning environment. It is equally important that students understand what teachers are saying when they use language or nonverbal communication to encourage behaviors the group has agreed are beneficial to help all students learn. Just as someone new to a city needs to know the unique driving regulations, students who are not used to the language teachers use to redirect students need to know the "rules of the road" in the classroom. For example, if the teacher uses the nonverbal cue of pointing to posted classroom guidelines or rules, students should know this is the teacher's way of saying, "We agreed to these, and I expect you to follow them." Similarly, when teachers politely request a student to make another choice, some students who are used to very firm, direct demands may misinterpret this as a lack of seriousness about the request. It will be helpful for students to know that this is the teacher attempting to be polite while seriously informing them a behavior must stop.

PAUSE & CONSIDER 8.2

Take a few minutes to write about a situation in which you had to engage a student to help him or her act more responsibly. For this specific situation, select two or three of the interventions listed on the previous pages. Ask a peer to role-play the behavior you have written while you implement the method(s) you have selected. How did this feel? Ask the other person to describe how he or she felt when you responded. Based on these two bits of information, do you believe the intervention was effective? If so, why? If not, how could you modify your response?

RESPONDING TO COMMON CLASSROOM DISRUPTIONS

While it is impossible to list all the potential classroom disruptions that concern teachers, the following section highlights several areas of concern both new and veteran teachers have asked us to address.

Difficulty Getting the Attention of the Entire Class

1. The most obvious method is to work with students to select a signal they agree will assist them in quickly providing you with their attention. You may provide them with several options, but the fact they select the method generally increases the likelihood they will respond as desired.
2. Use methods that are both somewhat soothing and yet are somewhat unusual—as opposed to turning off the lights or counting down from five. This might involve turning on music, using a chime or a rain stick, playing a musical instrument, and so on. You may also wish to use the overhead or wireless tablet and provide a cue about why you need student attention.
3. Create a space in the classroom where you stand when requesting students' attention. By adding a constant visual, you will increase the likelihood students will respond effectively.
4. Work with students to establish a goal for the amount of time you wait in a day, class period, or week after requesting students' attention. Keep a tally of this on a butcher paper chart and provide some form of celebration (activity the students value) when this goal is reached. We recommend you share with students that on-task time is one of the key factors (along with the time we allocate to learn the material and the percentage of correct responses made by students) in determining student learning gains. Students need to know why you are concerned about students being attentive and focused. You might also consider communicating to parents, perhaps through your

class newsletter or Web site, when the class has been particularly effective in increasing their ability to immediately focus when requested.

5. Provide students with time indicators informing them how long they have until you will need their attention. For example, if you plan on calling them back to a large group focus in two minutes, say this or write it where students can quickly see it.

6. Make sure students have all complied with your request before moving on.

7. Like any other procedure, it is best to practice giving a signal and having students quickly give you their attention.

8. Play the "Good Behavior Game." A simple way to use this method is each time the class meets the predetermined criteria for becoming focused soon after you request their attention, they receive a letter of a word. When the word has been spelled, the students earn some type of celebration. Other versions of this method will be discussed later in the book.

Too Many Students Want Attention at Once or One Student Is Constantly Seeking Assistance/Attention

1. Quickly review whether the lesson has been effectively taught. If a significant number of students need additional assistance, you may wish to pull these students aside and provide additional instruction.

2. Consider having students pair up and work on the activity. When doing this, consider developing the pairs ahead of time that include students with different ability levels that will support effective peer tutoring.

3. Ask students who believe they have mastered the material to place their names on the board so that students who are struggling can go to them for assistance.

4. Have materials prepared ahead of time that allow students to work at different levels of ability so students may select or be provided materials that more closely match their ability levels.

5. If this problem occurs during group instruction time and is caused by many students wishing to answer a question you have posed, consider using response cards to create greater involvement for all students. Response cards can be cards or small whiteboards students can write responses on or may be preprinted cards with responses such as true, false, letters to indicate which of several answers students believe are correct, and so forth. Research indicates that students who are more actively involved in the learning process will demonstrate more appropriate classroom behavior and increase their achievement. Duchaine, Green, and Jolivette (2011) provide an excellent description of this method.

6. If you have students, especially in the primary grades, who seek attention at a very high rate, meet with them and inform them that while you enjoy assisting them, there are many students who need help and you can usually provide individual attention only a few times each morning and afternoon. Inform them, however, that you know how much they like assistance from you, so they may have a designated number of times (we have usually used ten) in the morning and afternoon when you will assist them as soon as you finish what you are doing. It is best to provide them with tokens or a check sheet so they can see the number of assists they have remaining. Our

extensive use of this with many teachers indicates nearly 80 percent of students horde these tokens because what they really want is to be in control of their environment and believe they could obtain assistance when they needed it. Our informal studies also show the students most likely to need and benefit from this intervention have recently experienced or are currently experiencing loss or some form of stress at home and need to feel in control of some aspect of their lives.

A Student Who Will Not Become Engaged in An Instructional Activity

1. Consider whether there are times when the student does engage positively and enthusiastically in learning activities. Try to incorporate these into your lessons and discuss with the student that you will increase the frequency of learning activities that respond to his interest and needs but you need him to attempt to engage in activities that are not exactly what he wants.

2. Whenever possible, allow for choice within instructional activities. The use of choice is supported by brain-based research as well as traditional educational research as a method for increasing student engagement and learning. Recall that Figure 7.7 provides a list of ways to incorporate choice into an elementary or middle school classroom.

3. Whenever possible, relate material being learned to the interests of the student who is having difficulty becoming engaged in instructional activities.

4. Consider using goal setting where the student selects the amount or type of work he or she will complete and has an opportunity to discuss the work with you upon achieving the goal.

5. Determine whether the student is more likely to be engaged when working with other students. It may be helpful to engage in more instructional activities in which students are paired or in small groups.

6. Examine whether the student may work better under certain conditions described in the section on learning styles in Chapter 7. Perhaps this is a student who needs to have sound blocked out by using headphones or prefers to listen to soft music while she works.

7. Make sure the student believes he can successfully complete the work. If not, consider ways to provide assistance in a manner selected by the student. Frequently students do not attempt work because they believe if they do not try, they cannot fail. Goal setting and choice options listed earlier in the section on responding effectively to disruptive behavior can assist students in working through their concerns about failure.

8. Try to take away the competition factor in the classroom. Some students constantly compare their work to that of their peers and believe they come up short. Use methods such as defining what it means to be a successful learner (Chapter 7) and individual goal setting in order to help students understand they are simply working to improve their own skills.

9. Provide the student with the choice of taking periodic breaks. Some students feel that if they commit to working on classroom material, they must work nonstop or be in trouble because they have "misbehaved" by not being on task 100 percent of the time. Allowing the student to determine the type and frequency of breaks can go a long way toward helping some students become engaged in the learning process.

10. Find ways to have significant adults in the student's life congratulate him or her on even small amounts of successful work completion. This might involve an administrator, counselor, favorite teacher, coach, or other.

Frequent Talk-Outs

1. Make sure you have discussed why it is important for students not to call out when you have asked a question and have effectively taught a procedure for students engaging in discussions.
2. Prior to every discussion or other activity in which talk-outs occur, make sure to review this procedure.
3. If students fail to follow this procedure, make sure to practice it again.
4. Make sure to call on and praise students who follow the procedure.
5. As much as possible, ignore talk-outs.
6. Consider working with students to develop a procedure they find engaging. Some methods we have used include selecting Popsicle sticks to ensure a random calling of students; having a "speaking stick" that is passed to each individual who will be speaking, and one cannot speak without holding the "speaking stick"; or having the student who has answered the previous question call on the next student to speak.
7. Work with the class to set a goal to reduce talk-outs and have a celebration for when students have reached the goal a designated number of times.
8. Consider ways to engage a higher percentage of students during discussion; for example, have students turn to their partners and discuss an answer; if in small groups, use Numbered Heads Together (described in Chapter 7); or have students write their answers on some form of individual whiteboard and, when signaled, show their answers.
9. Be careful not to have instructional activities that involve one student speaking at a time last too long. For many students this is simply not an engaging learning activity.

RESPONDING TO DEFIANT BEHAVIOR

Perhaps the most demanding situation adults face in working with students is responding to defiant behavior. A common adult response to a strong student challenge is to use power to gain control. This often involves the adult yelling at the student, threatening, putting a name on the board, removing the student from the room, or even grabbing the student. Although removal may ultimately be necessary, there is a series of steps we can take prior to or along with removal. The importance of learning these methods was highlighted when one of us was asked by a major school district to address all district staff on the topic of responding to student confrontation. The request was based on the alarming number of teachers who had been involved in, and in some cases suspended or dismissed for, violent behavior toward students.

Prepare Students for Situations That May Be Difficult

Prepare yourself and your students for situations that might be associated with disruptive student behavior. For some students, situations such as working in cooperative groups, taking standardized tests, having a substitute teacher, attending an assembly, or interacting with others on the playground can evoke anxiety, frustration, and the disruptive behavior often associated with these feelings. In such situations, it is important to teach specific procedures that will reduce the likelihood students will experience strong emotions and be involved in disruptive behavior. For example, you can discuss that tests are simply a way of finding out how effectively material was designed and taught and provide feedback on how to improve these decisions as well as providing data on what areas specific students need to focus their learning. You can also teach students strategies for test taking as well as practicing self-talk they can use if they find themselves struggling with the material. A friend of ours teaches her fourth- and fifth-grade students language such as, "I'm smart, but I'm not going to know every answer. I'll just skip this and come back to it if I have time," and "I can look over the next few questions and decide which ones I think I know and can answer first."

Build a Positive Relationship Bank Account with Known Power Strugglers

Building a positive relationship bank account with students involves being intentionally inviting and using many of the methods described in Chapter 3. As noted earlier, students are far less likely to respond violently in the presence of adults whom they respect and who they believe care about them.

Ensure That Your Requests Have Been Made Clearly, Politely, and Firmly

The nonverbal cues and degree of courtesy associated with teacher requests are significant factors in determining how students respond. A key ingredient is that the student feel respected and not under attack when receiving directives. For example, when asking a student to stop talking and return to his seat, a teacher might shout, "Jeremiah, get back in your seat right now!" While this is clear and concise, it is rather rude and combative. Instead, a teacher might say firmly, "Jeremiah, please return to your seat and raise your hand if you would like me to come over and assist you."

There are obviously many ways to make requests that are clear, polite, and specific. Rhodes, Jenson, and Reavis (1993) present the "precision request." This involves the teacher's initially stating, "Please," followed by the request. If the student fails to comply, the teacher says, "I need you to," followed by the request. If the student does not comply, the teacher provides the student with a choice to comply or experience a mild negative consequence. The teacher might say, "Either you may choose to move to the quiet area or you are choosing to spend time at recess working on a problem-solving plan."

When cuing students regarding their behavior, it is more effective to use the word *reminder* or to refer to the agreed-on classroom rules rather than to use the word *warning*. Our experience suggests that students find the term *warning* somewhat aggressive and may take it as a challenge, in turn creating a springboard to further confrontation. Using polite language and reminding students about behavior norms or procedures to which they agreed are much less likely to evoke strong negative emotions than is giving them a warning.

Similarly, it is generally more effective to request that a student initiate an action rather than terminate an action. For example, when a student is wandering around the room agitated by an inability to complete a task, we might ask the student to check with a study partner as opposed to telling the student to stop wandering and sit down.

Model Self-Control

Self-control requires us to be smart and guard against our vulnerabilities. Like the wily trout who knows better than to strike at every imitation lure, we must be careful not to become snared by students' attempts to gain control or negative attention by making inappropriate comments.

It is important to remain calm when responding to defiant student behavior. Becoming anxious or angry creates a lack of structure and security that may intensify a student's emotional distress. In addition, our heightened emotional state may remind the student of other situations in which adults became aggressive, and this may increase the student's emotional stress. Finally, when we become angry or critical, students may blame our behavior and not assume responsibility for themselves. In order to remain calm, you may wish to take several deep breaths, tell yourself that you have the skill to work with this student, and tell yourself that if your efforts are not effective, others in the school will be glad to assist you.

Responding Effectively to Defiant Student Behavior

Situations where a student may become combative with a teacher are an important example of why, as discussed in Chapter 1, it is imperative to understand what your goals are for dealing with student behavior problems and also for you to be aware of your personal history and values. While a first reaction might be, "Students cannot talk to me like that," if this leads to a direct confrontation of the student in front of their peers, you have very likely made a choice that is not best for you or your students. In his excellent book *Managing the Cycle of Acting-Out Behavior in the Classroom*, Geoff Colvin (2004) stated,

> The very first and most important step in managing accelerated behavior is for staff to avoid providing escalating prompts.... [S]taff often pay so much attention to the objectionable behavior exhibited by the student that they are not sufficiently aware of the impact their responses may have on the student and the connection to the subsequent serious acting-out behavior. (p. 99)

If our goal is to have our students observe effective models of conflict resolution and to assist the student involved in understanding others' points of view and developing new skills, while at

© Larry/www.CartoonStock.com

the same time maintaining our positive relationship with the student, it is imperative the adult stay calm and use methods that will deescalate the student's emotions. Responding thoughtfully requires being aware of such early warning signs as students stopping work, refusing to talk, looking angry or upset, making comments under their breath, looking anxious or depressed, or disengaging from groups by turning away or looking distracted. When a student shows one of these signs or initially confronts you with statements such as, "This stuff is boring!" "Who wants to learn this?" "You don't care about me!" and so on, there are a variety of keys to responding in a manner that will deescalate the situation.

1. *Decide whether it is necessary to become engaged in the situation.* For example, if other students did not hear the student or

the statement had relatively little impact on the classroom setting, you may decide to discuss this with the student later. Be aware that your response may be what the student wants or needs in order to escalate his behavior. By not providing an immediate response, you may take away the source of fuel or reinforcement that would intensify the student's behavior.

2. *If your knowledge of the students indicates a response in front of peers might escalate the situation, ask the student if the two of you could talk about this privately, and provide the class with an academic task.*

3. *When interacting with the student, make sure your nonverbal behavior is supportive and nonthreatening.* Be sure to keep a calm voice, speak quietly and slowly, be respectful, do not get too close to the student, and do not use gestures that might intimidate the student such as pointing or extending an arm. Jim Fay and David Funk (1995) noted that a major disadvantage to teachers' responding too emotionally is that "the attention of children is easily captivated by emotion. When the teacher displays anger, the child gets caught up in the anger…the child is so busy thinking about the adult's anger, there is little thought about the mistake or new plan of behavior" (p. 36).

4. *Communicate sincere empathy for the student.* This involves sharing concern for a problem the student is experiencing. For example, you might acknowledge that the student seems stressed or tired and ask if he or she would like a little time to relax or talk with you at a later time. An extension of this is to *identify the feelings* the student may be experiencing. For example, you might say, "It sounds like you're frustrated with how easy the work is" or "I, too, would be angry if I thought I was asked to do something I didn't think had been explained very well."

5. *State the expectation in a positive manner.* If a student spoke out of turn, you might say, "Jorge, remember our agreement that during class discussions students will talk only when called on so it is easier for everyone to understand each other."

6. *Offer assistance.* You might say, "It looks like I didn't explain that so you could understand. Would you like me to go over that again?" or "It sounds like you're frustrated with the assignment. Let's see if we can work it out so it is more interesting to you."

7. *Provide options.* You might say, "If Melinda is bothering you, it might be better to work at the science center for a while" or "Can you use one of the strategies we agreed to use when we studied the Ladder of Success?"

8. *Predict a positive choice and its consequence.* For example, you might say, "I think if you tried two problems and then asked your partner for help, you would know what to ask for and you'd get help before you became too frustrated."

9. *Send an I-message* to let the student know the behavior is creating discomfort for you. This will work especially well if you have placed some deposits in your positive relationship bank account. An I-message can also include a clear, positive statement about your expectations. For example, you might say, "Reggie, I expect all students to treat classmates respectfully."

10. *Give the student an errand to run or in some other way structure a brief break for the student.*

11. *Review available options and consequences, and give the student space and time to make a choice.* For example, you might say, "Jeremy, remember our procedure for sharing ideas. I will call on you soon when your hand is raised, but if you talk out, we'll need to do some practice during recess." Make sure this is an option students are aware of and one that is used consistently in your class. One advantage of having a clear

classroom discipline system that is educationally oriented is that students know what they will be choosing should they make poor choices, but also know they will be treated respectfully and that the teacher's response has an educational focus.

12. *Clarify that the student must make a choice.* If a student continues to disrupt a discussion, you could say, "Celeste, I'd like you to stay because we have some interesting things planned, but you need to choose either to follow our procedure for talking during discussions or to go to the problem-solving center until we can solve this." Give the student space to comply and then either reinforce the student for making a good choice or indicate the response he or she has chosen.

13. *Implement a deescalation method.* Figure 8.2 presents a model we have used extensively in helping teachers develop skill in responding calmly and with purpose to deescalate students who are becoming agitated.

14. For students who display a pattern of becoming frustrated or angry, it may help them to *develop a menu of strategies* from which they can select when confronted with a frustrating situation. Recall that Figure 6.8 provides an example of a list of methods that could be developed with an individual or a class.

FIGURE 8.2
DEESCALATION
SEQUENCE

Phase I: Validating/Clarifying

Validate the underlying feeling: "It's okay to be frustrated with someone, but how else can you express that in our class?"

Help them understand the impact the behavior has on others: Send an I-message: "When you yell at someone, I get concerned because I care about this class being a safe place to study."

Help them understand that the behavior violates someone's compelling state interest or classroom rule: "When you yell at someone like that, which one of our classroom rules are you violating?"

Phase II: Choices/Options—Educative Function

"What would be a better way you could tell her you're frustrated?"

"What would be a better choice right now?"

"Would you like to take a few minutes in our quiet area, or would you rather do your relaxation at your desk?"

"If you continue to violate her rights, you would be choosing to work this problem out with the principal."

Phase III: An Invitation

"I'm sure we can work this out."

"You've been making good choices lately so I know we can come up with a way to solve this."

"I really want you to stay here and solve the problem because we would miss you if you left."

15. If a student demonstrates an ongoing pattern of failure to respond appropriately to reasonable teacher requests, it is professionally responsible to conduct a functional classroom assessment to determine the factors that may be influencing and maintaining this behavior (the antecedents and responses associated with this behavior). Chapter 10 presents an overview and examples of conducting a classroom behavior assessment.

These are all responses that help maintain the student's dignity while still indicating the teacher's expectation that all students follow the agreed-on behavior standards. Experience clearly indicates that teachers who use these responses have a very low number of situations where student misbehavior escalates to where it must be dealt with as a serious behavior problem.

If the behavior continues to be highly disruptive despite these interventions, it is advisable to send someone for assistance. In some instances, school staffs develop a terminology such as *code blue* to indicate that assistance is needed. When this occurs, the trained staff go to the crisis area and use deescalation skills to calm the students. Having other staff present also provides adults who can witness the teacher's interventions so they are not misinterpreted and inaccurately reported by the student (e.g., "She swore at me" or "She hit me" when the teacher had remained calm and had only raised her arm to protect herself from the student). Many schools have developed a procedure for notifying the office when a student becomes physically aggressive with another student or a staff member. Some schools have students take a red card with the name of the class or common area on the back and carry it to the office. This alerts those in the office that they need to immediately send adults to this site. This procedure is often used to report emergencies on the playground or to indicate a fight is taking place. As discussed previously, but of particular importance in this type of situation, "[t]eachers should guard against the use of punitive, confrontational and deprecatory methods because these have been shown to increase the possibility of violent reactions from students" (Murdick & Gartin, 1993). The teacher can continue to acknowledge a student's right to have strong feelings, offer assistance, inform the student of the consequences should the behavior continue, and state that the teacher does not want the student to choose these consequences. For example, if the situation involved two students who were fighting, you might say, "I know you are angry, but we can work this out. Would you like me to meet with the two of you?" You could add, "You know that if you throw punches in this school, you will be suspended and will have to return with your parents. I really would like you to be able to stay at school today." If two students are involved, it is usually most effective to speak directly to the student you know best and to personalize your statement. You might say, "Jeremy, I really want you to be involved in our debate tomorrow, and I hope you'll solve this peacefully so you can be in our class tomorrow."

One of us recently had a discussion with a highly regarded elementary school principal concerning the issue of breaking up fights. This principal, whose school is in a high-poverty urban setting, informed the author that she has a policy in her building that the staff will not restrain students except in an absolute emergency. Therefore, students are told that if they are fighting, they will be firmly asked to stop. If the fight continues, other students are removed from the area (or window blinds are closed) to eliminate the audience factor. While the principal or designated adult continues to encourage the students to stop their fight, the police and the students' parents are called. The principal believes students need to know that, unless it is necessary to protect students' physical safety, educators will not physically restrain them. She further believes physical restraint by educators is a violent act that compromises the positive, supportive perception students in her building need to have of adults in their school. She reported that during the past year there had only been four instances in which police had to be called and that incidents of violent student behavior had been reduced dramatically.

PAUSE & CONSIDER 8.3

Consider a situation in which a student is expressing a strong emotion and needs assistance in managing this emotion. Take a minute to write a brief statement about what the student is doing and saying. Next, using the sequence in Figure 8.2, write a statement you might make to the student. When you have finished, share this with several colleagues or fellow students. Once again, we strongly suggest you role-play several scenarios in order to further develop this type of intervention.

PAUSE & CONSIDER 8.4

Although you may never encounter a situation in which you are confronted by violent student behavior, it is important to be prepared for the possibility. We encourage you to meet with your building principal or vice principal to discuss any policies or procedures the school has for responding to violent student behavior. We suggest you take careful notes and encourage you to share your findings with colleagues or classmates.

Using Time-Out

Time-out is one of the most controversial interventions used to assist children in dealing with their behavior. Within a behavioral paradigm, time-out is the removal of reinforcement that may be contributing to the inappropriate behavior. Therefore, if a teacher believes a student is acting out for peer or teacher attention, the student may be placed in time-out to eliminate these reinforcers for a period of time. Within a cognitive behavioral approach, time-out provides an opportunity for children to calm down so they may benefit from some form of problem solving or opportunity to practice behaviors to use when again confronted with a frustrating situation. In addition, time-out can provide an opportunity for students to share their perceptions regarding the incident that led to time-out and to negotiate for changes in the classroom environment that will allow them to experience a greater sense of significance, competence, and power.

It is important to keep in mind that there is usually a continuum to the use of time-out. For years, we have assisted teachers in instructing students in a sequence of methods for taking some quiet time to calm themselves. Initially, students are asked to "take two" (i.e., to take two minutes to stop their work and relax at their desks). If students continue to disrupt or are unable to calm themselves after several

© George Abbott

"Quiet time not working out, Ms. Jones?"

brief opportunities at their desks, it is helpful to have a place in the classroom where students can go to work out a plan (see Chapter 9). On those rare occasions when this fails, students are asked to complete their problem solving in another area of the building (usually another classroom, but possibly a *problem-solving* or *solution room* staffed by a paraprofessional). When this procedure is taught to students and they understand that this is not a punishment but a way for them to gain control and solve the problem, and when students know that throughout the sequence they will be treated with dignity, very few students in any setting require interventions beyond the solution room. It is critical that students understand and role-play this process so they know how this process will be used.

School staff should strongly consider eliminating the use of the term *time-out* and replacing it with *resolution* or *problem-solving time*. If students were having academic difficulties, we would be considered unprofessional and quite possibly liable for a lawsuit if we placed students in a time-out setting to improve their work. Instead, we would be expected to provide support and alternative instructional strategies. Extrapolating this to students who experience behavior problems, best practice suggests we would assist the students in developing new skills. The use of the term *time-out* suggests we are isolating the student but not replacing ineffective ways of responding with new skills. Therefore, we represent ourselves and our work more professionally when we use terms that describe the intended purpose and the actual procedures we are using in our work with students.

A CLASSROOM PROCEDURE FOR RESPONDING TO DISRUPTIVE BEHAVIOR

Recall from Chapter 6 the importance of creating classroom procedures to enhance a smooth flow of academic work in the classroom. Perhaps the single most important procedure you develop is how you will respond when students act in a manner that disrupts the learning environment and violates the rights of others. One way to demonstrate to students that you are capable and care about them is your ability to respond effectively to student disruptions of the learning environment. In addition, research (Brophy, 1996) suggests fewer behavior problems occur in schools where teachers take care of minor behavior problems within the classroom.

PAUSE & CONSIDER 8.5

Consider for a moment your own classroom or a classroom in which you are working or observing. Take a moment to write a brief statement about what adults in the classroom do when students disrupt the learning environment. Specifically, focus on any sequence or procedure you use rather than on an individual strategy such as moving closer to the student.

After writing your statement, assess your approach by completing the quiz found in Figure 8.3. Tally your score. We encourage you to share the results with several colleagues or classmates and discuss the components of your classroom system that score high on this quiz and those that may need modification.

If you score high on the quiz in Figure 8.3, you have a system that is professionally defensible and should, if used along with the other methods in this book, be associated with students' developing positive feelings about school and responsible behavior. Figure 8.4 offers an additional series of questions for you to consider when examining how you and your colleagues respond to student behavior that violates the rights of others and limits the effectiveness of the learning environment.

FIGURE 8.3
CLASSROOM
MANAGEMENT
QUIZ

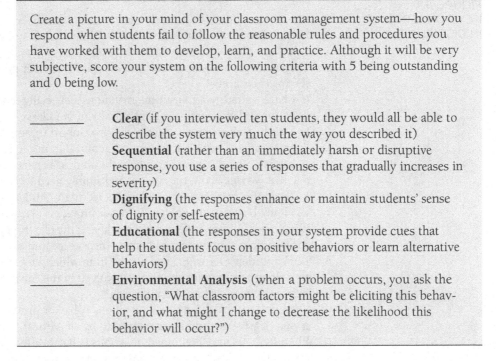

Create a picture in your mind of your classroom management system—how you respond when students fail to follow the reasonable rules and procedures you have worked with them to develop, learn, and practice. Although it will be very subjective, score your system on the following criteria with 5 being outstanding and 0 being low.

_____   **Clear** (if you interviewed ten students, they would all be able to describe the system very much the way you described it)

_____   **Sequential** (rather than an immediately harsh or disruptive response, you use a series of responses that gradually increases in severity)

_____   **Dignifying** (the responses enhance or maintain students' sense of dignity or self-esteem)

_____   **Educational** (the responses in your system provide cues that help the students focus on positive behaviors or learn alternative behaviors)

_____   **Environmental Analysis** (when a problem occurs, you ask the question, "What classroom factors might be eliciting this behavior, and what might I change to decrease the likelihood this behavior will occur?")

In the early 1980s, Lee Canter developed a system he titled "Assertive Discipline." In its initial form, this program emphasized informing students of the classroom rules and responding to rule violations by placing the student's name on the board. Any additional violation that day was met with a check placed after the student's name. Each check meant a designated time taken away from recess or lunch, and a designated number of checks (usually five) led to the student's being removed from the classroom. More recently, some teachers have changed this method to

Creating an Effective Classroom Discipline Policy
For an interactive review of methods for developing an effective classroom discipline policy, click on the link below in your Pearson etext.

ENHANCEDetext *interactive case study*

having each student's name adjacent to a cardholder. Color-coded cards are placed in the cardholder to indicate whether the student is behaving responsibly (green for responsible, yellow for warning, and red to indicate a punishment is forthcoming). Studies suggest these types of responses are ineffective (Emmer & Aussiker, 1987; Nelson, 1996; Nelson, Martella, et al., 1998), and Canter has suggested his initial model not be used in classrooms (Canter, 1996). One reason these methods have been shown to be ineffective is that although they score a strong 5 on the first two criteria listed in Figure 8.3, they score a 0 on the last three. While a batting average of .400 will likely earn one a spot in the Baseball Hall of Fame, a classroom management plan in the twenty-first century that scores .400 not only will be ineffective but also may elicit considerable student and parent criticism.

FIGURE 8.4
KEY CONCEPTS
IN DISCIPLINE

1. Do I view conflicts as a natural, neutral part of my life as a teacher?
2. Do I use conflict resolution and skill building to alter students' behavior, or do I use power-oriented methods of influence?
3. When students misbehave, do I teach them the correct procedure for meeting their needs?
4. Do I have a strategy for ensuring invitations, especially to those students who struggle behaviorally or academically in our class?
5. Do I teach students how conflicts will be resolved in our classroom?
6. When a student's behavior necessitates removal from the classroom, do I, the student, and the person to whom the student is referred all acknowledge that we care about the student and simply need to have a more effective forum for resolving the conflict that led to the student's misbehavior?
7. Are all my responses to student behavior problems oriented around providing new skills for students and modifying the classroom environment so the students can more readily meet their needs and act responsibly?
8. Prior to students returning to a setting from which they were removed, is there an opportunity for the parties involved in the "dispute" to briefly discuss any plan that has been devised?
9. When students have continued or serious behavior problems, are limits set in a clearly structured form agreed to by all parties?
10. When students have continued or serious behavior problems, is there a procedure in our school for a team to meet and work with the students to develop a plan to assist the students?

Figure 8.5 outlines a procedure for responding to rule or procedure violations. We initially wrote about this approach in 1986 (Jones & Jones, 1986), presented it in this exact form in 1995 (Jones & Jones, 1995), have used it as teachers, and have taught it to thousands of teachers. This method involves first using a signal to help students become aware of their behaviors. This might involve pointing to the classroom rules, looking at the student and calmly giving the "stop sign" of slightly raising your wrist with the palm toward the student, and so forth. If the student does not see this action or fails to respond to it, say the student's name, the word "please," and point to the classroom rules or request that the student follow the classroom rules. If the unacceptable behavior continues, inform the student that should this behavior continue, she or he will be choosing to take time to develop a solution to the problem. Ideally, this work will occur in the classroom, where the student can benefit from instruction and also realize that the problem can be resolved among those involved. Students who have adequate writing skills may be provided with an area in which to work and materials necessary for them to complete a problem-solving form. If the student is not able to calm himself and remain in the classroom, the problem solving will need to occur outside the classroom—either in another classroom or with an administrator.

It is important that teachers provide their verbal and nonverbal cues in ways they would cue a friend, family member, or colleague. As mentioned previously, teachers' use of firm demands to obtain student compliance is actually related to higher rates of off-task student behavior (Ratcliff et al., 2010).

It is essential that students clearly understand each step in this sequential process. This can be accomplished by role-playing each step in Figure 8.5 and then asking a student to violate a classroom rule (such as talking to a neighbor while you are talking). You then ask the student to

FIGURE 8.5
STEPS IN
RESPONDING TO
STUDENTS'
BEHAVIOR THAT
FAILS TO SUPPORT
THE LEARNING
PROCESS

Step	Procedure	Example
1.	Nonverbal cue	Point to the rule chart.
2.	Verbal cue	"John, please follow our classroom rules."
3.	Indicate choice student is making	"John, if you continue to talk while I am talking, you will be choosing to develop a plan."
4.	Student moves to a designated area in the room to develop a plan	"John, you have chosen to take time to develop a plan."
5.	Student is required to go somewhere else to develop a plan	"John, I really wish we could solve this here. If we cannot, you will need to see Mrs. Johnson to develop your plan."

stop the inappropriate behavior when you employ a designated step. This procedure can be continued until several students are involved in responding to each of the first three steps. You can then instruct the students in writing solutions and plans. Each student writes a plan; you check these and subsequently discuss them with the class.

Several years ago during a graduate seminar, one of us commented that it was probably not necessary to teach the problem-solving step to students in college preparatory courses for juniors and seniors. A seminar participant who had been in a course we had taught five years earlier disagreed with this statement. He said that he role-played the procedures with all his juniors and seniors in chemistry and physics. He noted that students and parents frequently commented on the value of this process. This teacher was convinced that despite needing to use the fourth step only about a dozen times each year, it was a vital aspect of an effective classroom management program.

It is essential to understand that this is not a sequence for which you keep a record, place names on a clipboard, or otherwise turn into a legalistic format. Indeed, it is not dissimilar to how we might respond at a dining room table or faculty meeting. We might try to catch the attention of the person who is behaving in a manner that is making someone feel bad or causing the environment to be less positive. Next, we might make a brief statement to the person. Finally, we might suggest that the person display the behavior somewhere else. These are natural and appropriate cues adults give each other, and they are dignifying and effective with students.

Several research studies indicate this approach is effective in responding to disruptive behavior within the classroom (Benner, Nelson, Sanders, & Ralston, 2012; Benner, Nelson, Smith, & Roberts, 2002; and Nelson, Martella, et al., 1998). In the most recent study that meets requirements for "evidence-based interventions," the authors describe the intervention as follows:

> The behavior intervention in the current study included five components: (a) a precision request from the teacher (i.e., teacher uses a short verbal statement to encourage the child to exhibit on-task social behavior and does not use threats, ultimatums, warnings, or repeated request), (b) assigning the behavior intervention, (c) a reflective period for student to gain self-control (i.e., thinking time), (d) a behavior-debriefing process, and (e) student reentry to the classroom. (Benner et al., 2012, p. 185)

The behavior intervention component of this plan involved the teacher directing the student to move to a colleague's classroom where, once calm, the student would complete a "Behavior Debriefing Form" where the students answered three questions: "(a) 'What was your behavior?' (b) 'What do you need to do differently when you go back to class?' and (c) 'Can you do it [the replacement behavior]?'" (Benner et al., 2012, p. 186). Results showed that when this method was implemented, students with externalizing classroom behavior problems had fewer problems compared to students in the control group where this method was not used. These students' on-task behaviors also improved compared to students in classrooms where this method was not implemented.

In her study of classroom management in urban schools, Ullucci (2009) found the most effective teachers to be those who, rather than depending on structured discipline procedures with points and flip cards, used natural interactions and humor while maintaining high expectations and sound classroom control. The method described in Figure 8.5 is one way to create a clear, applicable framework for responding in a natural manner to student behavior that needs to be altered in order to ensure a safe, calm, positive learning environment.

One question often asked by teachers is whether it is desirable to have students complete a problem-solving form when they have reached the point of needing quiet time to consider their behavior. A written form has the advantage of providing a record regarding the students' assessments of their behaviors and a new plan of action. It also has the advantage of providing the

FIGURE 8.6 PRIMARY GRADE PROBLEM-SOLVING FORM

Name _____   Date _____

In order to be my best self, I need to work on:

☐ Following directions of school adults.
☐ Caring for and sharing school property.
☐ Treating everyone with respect.
☐ Acting in a safe manner.
☐ Doing my personal best.

What happened: _____

Why this is a problem: _____

I will work at being responsible by: _____

This is what I look like being responsible!

Child Signature _____

Teacher Signature _____

Parent Signature _____

students with something to do while away from the group. The disadvantage of written forms is that many students who struggle to behave responsibly also struggle with academic work. Students may view completing a written form as a punishment that highlights their skill deficits. When this occurs, students often respond with frustration and anger at being asked to complete a form. Our experience in working with hundreds of school staff on this issue has shown it is best to make this decision based on your knowledge of the students with whom this program will be implemented. It is possible to create forms that require very little writing or to simply have students share their statements with the teacher or other adult involved in the process.

Figure 8.6 provides an example of a problem-solving form that a primary grade teacher might use. Figure 8.7 provides a form for an upper-elementary or secondary classroom. Once a student has completed the form, it is placed in a designated spot or shown to the teacher; the student then returns to her or his seat. It is, of course, important to have a brief discussion with the student about the responses on the form. This can be done near the end of class or at the beginning of the next class period. It is particularly important that students feel invited back to the class and that they realize that even though you could not accept the behavior that necessitated the problem solving, you care about them, respect their ability to be responsible for their behavior, and are glad they have rejoined the class. The next chapter provides an extended discussion and examples of how to implement problem solving in the classroom and presents methods for incorporating problem solving into a schoolwide student management plan.

As with all methods suggested in this book, you should carefully consider its applicability to your own teaching setting and should critically assess results when you use the new method. Should you choose to implement the preceding method for responding to behavior that disrupts the learning environment or fails to support student learning, it is critical to ensure that it is not used in a manner unduly emphasizing disruptive behavior. Studies show that teachers often attend more frequently to disruptive behavior than to on-task behavior and this action tends to increase off-task student behavior. Therefore, when implementing this method, attend to desired student behavior frequently and monitor student behavior to assess whether the new approach was indeed associated with an increase in on-task behavior.

Should a student refuse to go to the designated area or to complete the form, the teacher needs to express a belief that the problem can be resolved and that the teacher sincerely wishes the student to remain. For example, you might say, "Sam, I'm sure we can work this out, and I would like to have you remain in the class. If you will start developing a plan, I'll come over as soon as I can, and I'm sure we can work this out together." If the student continues to be defiant, the teacher needs to indicate that the student is making a choice. For example, you might say, "Sam, if you choose not to work this out here, you are choosing to do it in the office. I care about you and I would like to have you remain here."

© George Abbott

"I never use it, but I've found it to be a great deterrent."

FIGURE 8.7
PROBLEM-
SOLVING FORM

Choose to Be Responsible

Name _____ Date _____

Rules we agreed on:

1. Treat each other politely and kindly.

2. Treat school and personal property respectfully.

3. Follow teacher requests.

4. Be prepared for class.

5. Make a good effort and ask for help if you need it.

6. Solve problems nonviolently.

Please answer the following questions:

1. What rule did you violate? _____

_____

2. What did you do that violated this rule? _____

_____

3. What problem did this cause for you, your teacher, or classmates? _____

_____

4. What plan can you develop that will help you be more responsible and follow this classroom rule?

_____

_____

5. How can the teacher or other students help you?_____

_____

I, _____, will try my best to follow the plan I have written and to follow all the other rules and procedures in our classroom that we created to make the classroom a good place to learn.

The Role of Reinforcement in Encouraging Students to Act Responsibly

The term "reinforcement" refers to any event that occurs following a behavior that has the effect of maintaining, increasing, or strengthening the behavior. For example, if we want a student to raise his hand prior to responding, any event that follows hand raising and increases the percentage of time a student raises his hand prior to responding would be considered a reinforcer. A positive reinforcer involves following a desired behavior by providing students with something they value. For example, positive reinforcement would be in effect if, when he raised his hand to answer a question, a student was provided with teacher praise and/or a token/tally (and a designated number of tallies could be exchanged for something the student valued) and the amount of hand raising increased. A negative reinforcer refers to something the student finds as negative that when removed, increases the behavior in which the student was engaged. An example of effectively using negative reinforcement might involve students' work production increasing after a teacher indicated that students who completed a certain amount of seatwork would not have to take the work home to complete (this assumes most students find homework aversive). However, negative reinforcement may work in ways educators do not anticipate. For example, consider a situation where, when faced with work he finds difficult and frustrating, a student disrupts the learning of a student next to him and is removed to the hallway. If the rate of disrupting a classmate when confronted with difficult academic work increases, it is likely that being removed from the setting where he was doing difficult seatwork has served as a negative reinforcer that increased the likelihood that when faced with a frustrating academic task in the future, the student would disrupt a peer's learning.

PAUSE & CONSIDER 8.6

Write a scenario in a school setting that demonstrates a desired behavior being increased by the use of positive reinforcement. Write a second scenario where the desired behavior was reinforced through the use of negative reinforcement. Finally, write a scenario where a behavior someone wanted to reduce or eliminate was increased by the use of negative reinforcement. Share these with at least one colleague who has also completed this activity and provide each other with feedback regarding the examples.

Educators often ask whether it is wrong to use reinforcement to encourage students to behave responsibly. Teachers often indicate they have heard or read that students should not be reinforced for making positive behavior choices because this will create a dependence on external factors and minimize students' developing an internal sense of responsibility. Certainly, our goal as educators is to help students learn to make positive choices solely because these choices help them and others to feel good and learn effectively. The reality is that virtually everyone has much of their behavior impacted by outcomes other than goodwill. Many people drive more safely when they see a police car. Few teachers would work if they were not paid, and few consultants travel around the country making presentations for free. To some degree, people expect and enjoy receiving rewards for their work. This is particularly important when the work is difficult or involves risk—a situation that exists for many students whose behavior at school creates problems for others. Most of us enjoy celebrations when we perform well. One need only watch the behavior of a team who has won a championship to know that individuals are expected to celebrate after making substantial progress or reaching an important goal.

This need to have some degree of celebration associated with hard-earned success may be particularly important for individuals who have overcome significant odds or worked particularly hard to reach a goal. Therefore, students who find school more demanding but who persist and show improvement would be expected to benefit from receiving greater acknowledgment for their successes.

It must also be noted that students with certain identified disabilities benefit greatly from structured interventions that involve the clear use of rewards and consequences. For example, students identified with severe autism or fetal alcohol effect or syndrome will be much more able to function effectively when those who assist them in the educational process understand and effectively use behavior management methods based on behavior modification principles, including the effective use of reinforcement and consequences.

One of us received a call from a veteran teacher who had been a student many years ago. The teacher had taught in an inner-city school, left the profession to raise a family, and recently returned to teaching in another inner-city school with many students who were struggling academically. She called because she had classroom management concerns. She was frustrated with her students, raised her voice frequently, and believed her classroom was less safe and organized than she thought

© Randy Glasbergen

As a student teacher, the first thing you must learn is how to make your kids behave for you. My own successful disciplinary formula is based on understanding, firmness, determination, and all the bribery I can afford."

was good for her or her students. She shared that after rereading an earlier edition of our book, she had begun to reestablish a positive learning environment. She had held classroom meetings to determine students' concerns, had the students create and sign a set of behavior expectations, and began to use problem solving. She expressed concern, however, that she had also begun reinforcing students for behaving responsibly. She noted that she stamped students' cards when they made behavior choices that supported a positive, caring learning environment and that the stamps could be exchanged for school supplies and other items students valued. She reported that these combined changes had helped create a dramatically more productive learning environment, but she asked whether this was damaging to the students because it emphasized external controls.

Our response was to help her acknowledge the good work she was doing. We also shared our belief that students need to be reinforced for doing well, and we made several suggestions. First, we encouraged her to always pair the giving of the stamp with some form of verbal statement that helped the student understand how his or her behavior was helping the student and others learn. The goal is to associate the token reinforcement (the stamp) with social reinforcement so that the social reinforcement gradually replaces the need for the more concrete external reinforcement. Another important goal is to have the social reinforcement provide information that helps the student understand why the behavior is valuable in itself. Second, we encouraged her to begin to have social reinforcers replace the material reinforcement she was providing. Therefore, when students made good decisions (perhaps initially demonstrated by earning a designated number of stamps), the teacher could call home and inform the parent(s) or guardian(s) how responsibly their child was acting and how this was leading to success. The principal, counselor, or other significant adults could also be involved in providing specific social reinforcement by speaking with students, having lunch with students, and calling home. In all cases, an emphasis would be on helping the student understand how his or her behavior was leading the student to success and happiness.

The "Good Behavior Game" is one method for using reinforcement to increase on-task behavior in the classroom. The initial approach developed by Barrish, Saunders, and Wolf (1969) involved creating a game where students were divided into teams and teams were assigned a point each time a member of their team made a poor behavior choice such as talking out or leaving his or her seat when not appropriate. A designated number of points led to the loss of a privilege such as lining up first for lunch, extra recess time, and so forth. This method has been developed into a well-researched procedure in which students earn positive rewards when their team meets a criterion for limiting the number of points assigned for negative behaviors (Donaldson, Vollmer, Krous,

Downs, & Berard, 2011; Kamps et al., 2011; Lastrapes, 2014; Wright & McCurdy, 2011). This approach has proven to be effective in reducing off-task behavior in a wide range of classrooms from kindergarten through secondary school, in general and special education classrooms, and with students with ADHD and emotional and behavior disorders.

Our daughter shared another example of an activity she has implemented in both her fifth- and first-grade classrooms to use positive reinforcement to encourage desired classroom behavior. When she wants to add a little fun and incentive to encourage positive student behavior, she uses what she calls an "Effective Learner Incentive Chart." Whenever individual students or a table group are doing a good job, they are asked to put their initials in a box on the incentive chart. At the end of the week, she pulls a number and letter and whoever's initials are in the box gets to pick a prize or extra free time or another reward. The reward is constantly changed to keep students interested.

To create the chart, she writes the numbers 1–26 across the top and the letters a–z down the side. Students put their initials in any box on the chart. She has two envelopes, one containing numbers and the other with letters. She simply draws one card from the number envelope and one from the letter envelope and the person's name who is in this square gets a prize. Some weeks she pulls several letters and numbers to keep motivation high.

Several of our current preservice student teachers have used Class Dojo (classdojo.com), which can be used with a laptop, smartphone, tablet, or interactive whiteboard to collect and instantly display data that provides students immediate feedback about their positive behavior and also keeps automatic records of this behavior. Another version of this approach that is popular in a number of school districts is the PAX Good Behavior Game (goodbehaviorgame.org).

Why Focus on Problem Solving Rather Than Punishment?

No discussion of a classroom management system would be complete without a brief response to the issue of problem solving versus punishment. Over the years, one of the most frequently asked questions when we have conducted workshops for veteran teachers is, "Where is the punishment?"

First, we would return to the earlier discussion regarding the comparison between academic and behavior errors. We strongly believe that educators' responses to both types of errors need to assume the student needs support and assistance in developing new skills. Second, in addition to failing to emphasize skill development, a focus on punishment appears to inhibit learning. Students in classrooms in which teachers are judged as more punitive tend to express less value in learning, be more aggressive, and learn less. Third, research suggests that punishment is not an effective method for changing student behavior. Emmer and Aussiker (1987) examined the literature on the results of research evaluations associated with four approaches to discipline—teacher effectiveness training, reality therapy, assertive discipline, and Adlerian-based approaches. They also contacted 120 school districts in the United States and Canada to obtain evaluation studies about these programs. Their findings indicated that the most punitive-oriented approach (assertive discipline) was the least effective.

Similar findings concerning the impact of punitive responses to student misbehavior were reported more than thirty-five years ago by Becker et al. (1975). These researchers found that when teachers were asked to increase their use of punitive control methods of responding to disruptive student behavior, misbehavior in the classes actually increased from 9 to 31 percent of student behavior.

Fourth, punishment allows the student to project blame rather than to accept responsibility for the behavior. Punishment tends to create a situation in which the student becomes angry or blames the individuals responsible for the punishment rather than examining personal responsibility for the problem. Glasser (1988) stated that 95 percent of all student discipline problems in schools are caused by students' lack of power and that misbehavior is an attempt to gain some sense of power. Punitive responses to student misbehavior detract from rather than enhance students' sense of power and efficacy and often lead to withdrawal or actively destructive and confrontational responses.

Fifth, using such activities as writing sentences, assigning additional homework, and lowering a student's grade as punishment may create a negative attitude regarding these activities. Activities and settings in which one is involved when receiving punishment tend to become aversive. Teachers do not want this connection made with homework or writing.

Englander (1986) stated that even though responding to student misbehavior with punishment is both common and natural, it is nonetheless impractical. Based on his extensive background in the field and his thorough review of the research, he summarized his assessment of punishment: "If punishment works it does so only under very precise and complicated conditions, much too complicated for us to consistently use in classrooms. The controls that one must utilize to optimize the effectiveness of punishment are not possible in day-to-day operations either within families or schools" (pp. 40–41).

DISCIPLINE WITH STUDENTS IDENTIFIED WITH SPECIAL NEEDS

There are several factors to consider when applying your classroom discipline procedures with students identified under IDEA as eligible for special education. First, IDEA provides students identified as having special needs with the rights to be treated the same as their grade- and age-level peers unless specific changes to their education have been proposed and agreed to by the student's IEP team, including the parent or guardian. This is one reason it is important that you present your classroom management system, as described in Figure 1.1, to parents and administrators. By indicating that you will implement best-accepted, research-based practices as they are needed to assist any and all children in your classroom—in other words, you will differentiate behavioral instruction—you are presenting an appropriate professional stance incorporating methods that will benefit students needing a wide range of behavioral supports. Unless a student's IEP specifies conditions that would alter your discipline system, this allows you to use these best-accepted, research-based methods with any student in your class who needs assistance in behaving in a more responsible manner. It is, however, imperative that you understand and implement the academic and behavior supports listed in the student's IEP.

While it is not the responsibility of the teacher, you should be aware that students identified as having a disability are protected by law from excessive removal from the school setting. Removal for more than ten days, including in-school removals from the classroom or patterns of removals for behaviors related to the student's disability, can be considered a change of placement for that student and can occur only through the IEP process or a court order.

It is not appropriate to allow a special education–eligible student or any other student to continually behave in a manner that is not consistent with acceptable grade-level behavior. However, implementing behavior management procedures with students identified under IDEA can require the participation of the IEP team, including the parent or guardian, as well as a strong commitment to implementing the research-based best practices described in this text that best support any student's learning and behavior needs.

PAUSE & CONSIDER 8.7

You have now read our thoughts about creating a classroom procedure for responding to student behavior that disrupts the learning environment. Perhaps you have also visited several Web sites on the issue and discussed with your peers the procedures that exist in their classrooms. At this point, we recommend you put the text aside and draft an outline of the procedure you would like to use for responding to disruptive behavior in your classroom. We encourage you to write your thoughts out in enough detail that you could teach it to your students, post it in your classroom, and, if you are in an elementary or middle school, possibly communicate it to your students' caregivers. Once you have developed this procedure, we encourage you to share it with several colleagues and obtain their feedback.

The remainder of the book presents methods for responding to ongoing and increasingly serious student behavior problems. Chapter 9 examines how to incorporate problem solving into your classroom management and schoolwide discipline plans, and Chapter 10 examines how to conduct a functional behavioral assessment and develop an individual behavior change plan.

SUMMARY

Teachers who are effective classroom managers develop and teach clear methods for responding to unproductive student behavior that emphasize helping students take responsibility for their own behaviors and learn alternative ways for handling frustrating situations. As teachers are asked to work with greater numbers of students who come to school with negative emotional states and poor problem-solving skills, we will need to become more skilled at implementing the methods presented in this and the following chapters.

IMPLEMENTATION ACTIVITIES

ACTIVITY 8.1

Sending I-Messages

To test your knowledge of I-messages, change each of these five statements into an I-message:

1. Late again! What's the matter with you?
2. I don't want to hear another word out of anyone.

3. No book again? How do you expect to learn anything?
4. How can you be so inconsiderate as to stand there drinking water for so long when you know other children want a drink?
5. If you get in trouble on the playground one more time, you can miss the rest of your recesses this month!

If you have difficulty with this task, consult a colleague or refer to Thomas Gordon's (1974) *Teacher Effectiveness Training*.

ACTIVITY 8.2

Responding to Confrontation

Select two colleagues who teach or are planning to teach students similar in age to those with whom you work or want to work. Have one person agree to be an upset student, one person a teacher, and the third person an observer. Role-play a classroom situation in which the student becomes upset and confronts the teacher (possibly criticizing the assignment or refusing to complete assigned work). After the role-play, have the person who played the teacher discuss how she or he felt when confronted, why the response(s) given were selected, and how the interchange was perceived. Next, have the

student discuss how the teacher's response was perceived. Finally, have the observer discuss the response to the intervention.

Switch roles and try this several more times. You may find it productive to record the role-plays and play examples back to the class or faculty.

RECOMMENDED READING

Axelrod, S., & Mathews, S. (2003a). *How to deal with students who challenge and defy authority.* Columbia, MO: Hawthorne Educational Service.

Axelrod, S., & Mathews, S. (2003b). *How to prevent and safely manage physical aggression and property damage.* Columbia, MO: Hawthorne Educational Service.

Colvin, G. (2004). *Managing the cycle of acting-out behavior in the classroom.* Eugene, OR: Behavior Associates.

Fay, J., & Funk, D. (1995). *Teaching with love and logic.* Golden, CO: Love and Logic Press.

Garrity, C., Jens, K., Porter, W., Sager, N., & Short-Camilli, C. (2004). *Bully-proofing your school: Working with victims and bullies in elementary schools* (3rd ed.). Longmont, CO: Sopris West.

Horner, R. H., & Sugai, G. (2005). School-wide positive behavior support: An alternative approach to discipline in schools. In L. Bambara & L. Kern (Eds.), *Positive behavior support* (pp. 359–390). New York, NY: Guilford Press.

Johns, B., & Carr, V. (1995). *Techniques for managing verbally and physically aggressive students.* Denver, CO: Love.

Kauffman, J., Hallahan, D., Mostert, M., Trent, S., & Nuttycomb, D. (1993). *Managing classroom behavior.* Boston, MA: Allyn & Bacon.

Lewis, T. (2004). Classroom-level supports for students with learning

and behavioral problems. In L. M. Bullock, R. A. Gable, & K. J. Melloy (Eds.), *Effective interventions for classrooms, schools, and communities: Making a difference in the lives of students with learning and behavioral problems* (pp. 15–18). Reston, VA: Council for Exceptional Children.

Lewis, T., & Newcomer, L. L. (2005). Reducing problem behavior through school-wide systems of positive behavior support. In P. Clough, P. Garner, J. T. Pardeck, & F. Yuen (Eds.), *Handbook of emotional and behavioural difficulties in education* (pp. 261–272). London, England: Sage.

Lewis, T. J., Newcomer, L., Trussell, R., & Richter, M. (2006). School-wide positive behavior support: Building systems to develop and maintain appropriate social behavior. In C. S. Everston & C. M. Weinstein (Eds.), *Handbook of classroom management: Research, practice and contemporary issues* (pp. 833–854). New York, NY: Lawrence Erlbaum Associates.

Lewis, T. J., & Sugai, G. (1999). Effective behavior support: A systems approach to proactive school-wide management. *Focus on Exceptional Children, 31(6),* 1–24.

Long, N., Newman, R., & Morse, W. (1996). *Conflict in the classroom: The education of at-risk and troubled students* (5th ed.). Austin, TX: Pro-Ed.

Mendler, A. (1992). *What do I do when . . . ? How to achieve discipline*

with dignity in the classroom. Bloomington, IN: National Educational Services.

Murdick, N., & Gartin, B. (1993). How to handle students exhibiting violent behavior. *The Clearing House, 66,* 278–280.

Noguera, P. (1995). Preventing and producing violence: A critical analysis of responses to school violence. *Harvard Educational Review, 65,* 189–212.

Roberts, J. (2000). The bully as victim: Understanding bully behaviors to increase the effectiveness of interventions in the bully–victim dyad. *Professional School Counseling, 4,* 148–155.

Stormont, M., Lewis, T. J., & Beckner, R. (2005). Developmentally continuous positive behavior support systems: Applying key features in preschool settings. *Teaching Exceptional Children, 37(6),* 42–49.

Sugai, G., Horner, R. H., Dunlap, G., Hieneman, M., Lewis, T. J., Nelson, C. M., . . . Ruef, M. (2000). Applying positive behavior support and functional behavioral assessment in schools. *Journal of Positive Behavior Interventions, 2,* 131–143.

Walker, H., Colvin, G., & Ramsey, E. (1995). *Antisocial behavior in school: Strategies and best practices.* Pacific Grove, CA: Brooks/Cole.

Walker, H., & Walker, J. (1991). *Coping with noncompliance in the classroom: A positive approach for teachers.* Austin, TX: Pro-Ed.

CHAPTER 9

Using Problem Solving to Resolve Behavior Problems

People take time. Dealing with discipline takes time. Children are not fax machines or credit cards. When they misbehave, they tell us that they need help learning a better way. They are telling us that there are basic needs not being met which are motivating the behavior.

—Allen N. Mendler (1992)

Part of what is learned in dialogue is interpersonal reasoning—the capacity to communicate, share decision making, arrive at compromises, and support each other in solving everyday problems. The school presently puts tremendous emphasis on logical-mathematical reasoning but almost none on interpersonal reasoning. . . . Interpersonal reasoning is necessary in caring that involves associates and members of the community as well as intimate others.

—Nel Noddings (1992)

The benefits gained from learning how to manage conflict constructively far outweigh the costs of learning time lost by students being upset and angry. From a cost-analysis perspective, one of the soundest investments educators and students can make in classroom and school productivity is teaching students how to manage conflict constructively.

—David Johnson and Roger Johnson (1991)

While no one expects teachers to have sophisticated counseling skills, having the ability to skill-fully help students resolve behavior problems by understanding the impact their behavior has on others and developing new social skills is an important teacher skill. Problem solving is one method teachers can use to communicate their respect for students while at the same time teaching students an important lifelong skill.

Learning Goals

After reading this chapter, you will know:

1. How to use problem-solving methods with students in order to develop effective solutions to ongoing academic and behavior problems
2. How to conduct an effective class meeting

Why Are These Goals Important?

Although minor disruptions to classroom activities frustrate teachers, persistent behavior that disrupts the learning environment is a major cause for teacher concern and a major reason teachers leave the profession. It is imperative that all teachers have skills in working with students to solve behavior problems; effective problem-solving methods are the most basic as well as some of the least time-consuming methods of accomplishing this task.

Recall from Chapter 3 how students describe teachers whom they respected and in whose classes they were more likely to act responsibly. One characteristic is the teacher's willingness to understand students and their lives outside of school. A problem-solving approach encourages us to know our students and to take their perspective into account. Brendtro and Long (1995) offer the following example:

> A newly enrolled third grader became wild and disrespectful, resulting in almost daily removal from the class. It was several weeks before the staff discovered that he and his siblings had been abandoned by their mother shortly after they moved to a deserted farm. Fearful of being separated, the children told no one and continued riding the bus to school each day. (p. 54)

If we are to assist students, we need the clearest possible understanding of how they view a situation. We need to be willing to hear their voices but also have the knowledge to assist them in developing new skills. If we merely punish or remove students, we will be the last to find out what may be influencing their behavior, and we may be the first to incur their frustration.

Mendler (1992) provided important insight into why a problem-solving approach may be an essential component of classroom and school discipline when he wrote:

> What we must realize is that, while obedience models of discipline always had a down side, in today's world they simply no longer work. The only kids who behave as a result of "obedience" methods are those who have "respect" or fear authority. And most of them will stop obeying unless they feel respected by those in authority. . . . Nowadays to be successful in a position of authority requires an ability to connect in a caring way by inspiring hope within others and by leading one's own life in a manner that models the message. (p. xi)

Problem solving is the antithesis of the obedience model of discipline. Problem solving is a key method for showing respect for students by involving them in the process of reviewing and changing their behavior, making choices, and providing input into factors in the classroom or school environment that need to be altered to enable them to be effective learners. In addition, the manner in which educators respond to irresponsible student behavior should help students develop new skills. Figure 9.1 presents a list of skills or abilities enhanced by involving students in a problem-solving process.

FIGURE 9.1
SKILLS ENHANCED THROUGH PROBLEM SOLVING

Source: *Behavior Management: Application for Teachers* (4th ed.), by T. J. Zirpoli, 2005, p. 248. Boston, MA: Allyn & Bacon. Copyright © 2005 by Pearson Education. Reprinted with permission.

1. *Alternative solution thinking.* The ability to generate different options or potential solutions to a problem
2. *Consequential thinking.* The ability to consider consequences that a behavior might lead to, which goes beyond the consideration of alternatives to the consideration of the consequences of potential solutions
3. *Causal thinking.* The ability to relate one event to another over time with regard to why a particular event happened or will happen
4. *Interpersonal sensitivity.* The ability to perceive that an interpersonal problem exists
5. *Means–ends thinking.* The step-by-step planning done in order to reach a given goal; means–ends thinking involves insight, forethought, and the ability to consider alternative goals
6. *Perspective taking.* The ability of the individual to recognize and take into account the fact that different people have different motives and may take different actions

---

PAUSE & CONSIDER 9.1

Take a few moments to consider the types of discipline you received in your home and school. When was the discipline most helpful to you? What types of responses to your behavior that concerned others did you find the most respectful? What responses did you find the most educational?

PAUSE & CONSIDER 9.2

Take a moment to recall several recent incidents in which students in your classroom, or under your supervision in a common area such as a cafeteria, were involved in inappropriate behavior that violated the rights of other students and that caused you to speak to the students. For these situations, answer the following questions:

Did my response model effective adult communication?

Did my response assist the student in feeling valued?

Did my response tend to deescalate the situation?

Was my response dignifying to the student?

Did my response provide the student with an opportunity to express his or her thoughts or feelings?

Did my response help the student develop a new skill that could be used should a similar situation arise?

Could I recommend to the student's parents or guardians that they use a response similar to the one I used?

If my administrator needed to talk to me regarding a behavior of mine he or she thought was a concern, would I want this person to use a response similar to the ones I used in responding to my students?

Did the student leave the situation feeling positive about school and prepared to learn?

Did my response provide the student with a model he or she could use as an adult when involved in dealing with a problem in the workplace or home?

PLACING PROBLEM SOLVING IN CONTEXT

When considering when and how to implement problem solving, teachers must answer three important questions:

1. *What do I want to accomplish in responding to student behavior that is disrupting the learning environment?* Most teachers state that in addition to wanting to maintain a positive, supportive learning environment, they want to teach students to be responsible for their own behavior and they want students to develop prosocial skills. By involving students in examining their own behavior and developing alternative responses, problem solving allows students to accept greater responsibility for their behavior and develop important citizenship skills.

2. *Where does problem solving fit into my classroom management plan?* As discussed in Chapter 8, it is increasingly recommended that problem solving be used several times when a student continues to act unproductively in the classroom despite the teacher's best efforts to create a positive, well-structured learning environment. Problem solving may involve having students complete a problem-solving form while taking a brief break from involvement in the classroom, and it usually will also involve the teacher's taking time to meet with the student and verbally problem solve. In addition, effective schoolwide student management programs also involve the student in problem solving when a persistent or serious misbehavior has led to an out-of-class or office referral.

3. *How does problem solving relate to other corrective behavior management interventions?* Some students have major skill deficits or personality disorders that prevent them from responding to problem solving. Therefore, teachers may also need to incorporate other individualized intervention methods when problem solving does not have the desired results. However, if we use referrals or behavioral interventions such as time-out, travel cards, or contracts emphasizing rewards and punishments without first having problem solved with the student, we communicate our lack of interest or willingness to personally engage the student in mutual dialogue. This can only send a message that we do not care about or respect the students and wish to simply manipulate them. While it is true that teachers cannot be effective in helping students with serious behavior problems unless the school incorporates a variety of methods to provide assistance and support to teachers, teachers absolutely must be actively involved in engaging students in dialogue about classroom behavior issues prior to and along with interventions provided by counselors, administrators, special educators, and other adults.

A MODEL FOR SOLVING PROBLEMS WITH INDIVIDUAL STUDENTS

Several writers have developed methods for helping students resolve problems and take responsibility for their own behavior. In his 1965 book, *Reality Therapy*, William Glasser introduced one of the earliest and most popular approaches to problem solving. In *Teacher Effectiveness Training*, Tom Gordon (1974) offered a six-step approach to problem solving. Frank Maple's (1977) *Shared Decision Making* describes a variety of skills needed to resolve problems effectively. Richard Curwin and Allen Mendler's (1988) book *Discipline with Dignity* and Mendler's (1992) follow-up book, *What Do I Do When . . . ? How to Achieve Discipline with Dignity in the Classroom*, provide good information on helping students develop an ability to solve their own problems. Jim Fay's book *Teaching with Love and Logic* (Fay & Funk, 1995) offers another thoughtful way of viewing problem solving with students. Research by Ron Nelson (Nelson, 1996; Nelson, Crabtree, Marchand-Martella, & Martella, 1998) has demonstrated that the use of "think time"—a problem-solving approach built into the schoolwide student management plan—has been associated with significant reductions in student behavior problems and referrals. More recently Ross Greene and his colleagues have begun providing extensive training on what they call Collaborative Problem Solving (Greene, Ablon, & Martin, 2006, and at ccps.info). This process, much like Glasser's model, helps the student and adult define their concerns and brainstorm possible solutions that are acceptable to both parties. While you are encouraged to review these models and select one that best fits your style, we have found Glasser's approach to include the key components of effective problem solving that allows teachers to quickly gain skill in effectively problem solving with their students. Our research (Jones, 1991) as well as results from more than 1,500 of our student teachers and many hundreds of in-service teachers who have completed an assignment requiring the use of this intervention clearly indicate it is effective in helping students better understand and take responsibility for behavior as well as develop action plans that consistently alter their behavior in ways that enable them to be more successful in school.

Professionals who work with students experiencing serious emotional and behavioral problems may use a form of problem solving known as Life Space Crisis Intervention. This model, initially developed by Fritz Redl and later modified for school settings by William Morse, Nicholas Long, and others (Long et al. 1996), involves a more in-depth examination of the problem event. This includes determining whether the event represents a pattern of dysfunctional thinking or perceiving and providing the student with insight into the pattern as well as alternative ways of responding. Many schools use conflict resolution as an approach to help two or more individuals resolve conflicts. This process differs from problem-solving methods because it involves a third party in facilitating a dialogue to assist two parties in resolving a conflict. In addition, some students identified with special needs may benefit from a modification of a general problem-solving method such as Glasser's. O'Connor and Stichter (2011) discuss several modifications that can make problem solving more effective with students with high-functioning autism and/or Asperger's syndrome. This chapter provides a detailed examination of Glasser's approach and how it can be incorporated into a classroom management system and a schoolwide discipline system. If you are interested in exploring the Life Space Crisis Intervention or conflict resolution model, we encourage you to examine the references at the end of this chapter.

Glasser's Seven Steps to Effective Problem Solving

Four factors make Glasser's model extremely useful for school personnel. First, the problem solving can be accomplished in a short time. Most problems can be solved in less than five minutes, and frequently a solution can be developed in only a minute or two. Therefore, though it is often desirable to remove the student from the group so that the discussion can take place privately, you do not need to become involved in a lengthy discussion that diverts your attention from other instructional or supervisory duties. Second, because the model employs a step-by-step procedure, it is easy to learn. Furthermore, if a problem-solving session does not go well, you can analyze each step to discover what needs to be improved to make the session more effective. Third, by actively involving the student in the problem-solving process, the model responds to a variety of student needs. Rather than establishing a teacher-versus-student debate or a situation in which you manipulate the student by offering rewards for changed behavior, the student is meaningfully involved in examining his or her behavior, discussing his or her needs in the situation, and developing a plan for changing the behavior and improving the setting. Finally, because the model focuses on specific, observable behavior, data can be collected and this enables you and the student to realistically analyze the effectiveness of the plan. To become competent at using Glasser's approach, you need to understand each step and then frequently use the approach with students. Figure 9.2 presents an outline of Glasser's model.

FIGURE 9.2
PROBLEM-SOLVING
METHOD

Step 1:   Establish a warm, personal relationship with the student.
(Develop a "positive relationship bank account" with the student.)

Step 2:   Deal with the present behavior.
"What happened?"
(Develop a time line/functional assessment.)
"What did you do?"
(Help students take responsibility for their role in the problem. Help them develop an internal locus of control.)

Step 3:   Make a value judgment.
"Is it helping you?"
(Help students consider their own behavior and underlying assumptions.)
"Is it helping others?"
(Enhance student's social cognition.)
"Is it against a rule/does it violate a compelling state interest?"
(Help students understand their own and others' rights and responsibilities within the community.)

Step 4:   Work out a plan.
"What can you do differently?"
(Social skills training)
"What do you need me to do?"
(Empowerment/functional assessment)
"What do you need other students to do?"
(Empowerment/functional assessment)

Step 5:   Make a commitment.
"Are you going to do this?"
(Enhance student's accountability/responsibility.)

Step 6:   Follow up.
"I'll check later and see how the plan has worked."
(Supportive/caring environment)

Step 7:   No put-downs, but do not accept excuses.
"If the plan didn't work, let's analyze why and develop a new plan."
(High expectations and persistence in working with students)

Step One

The first step involves creating a positive relationship with your students. Individuals are more likely to discuss problems with and listen to ideas from someone who they believe knows, respects, and likes them. If you employ the communication skills and other strategies for improving teacher–student relationships described in Chapter 3, students will sense that you care and will almost always be willing to work with you to examine and attempt to change their behavior.

Step Two

The second step is to ask students to describe the behavior. Awareness of actions is an important component in any behavior change program. Indeed, a simple increase in students' awareness of their behavior is often accompanied by major changes in their behavior. You can help students describe their behavior by asking questions such as, "What did you do that upset Sally?" The emphasis should be placed on specific, observable behavior. If a student states that he or she was bad or didn't obey you, help the student specify what request wasn't obeyed and what was said or done when he or she rejected the request.

Students will sometimes respond to your question about what they did by saying, "Nothing" or "I don't know." You then have several options. First, you may respond by stating, "John, I'm not trying to blame you or get you in trouble. What I want to do is help solve the problem, and I need to know what you did so I understand what happened." When you focus on the problem rather than threaten the student or focus on the punishment, students are often willing to discuss their behavior.

Second, students may balk at describing what they did because in the past admitting what they did was associated with strong punishments. We have increasingly found it helpful to begin by asking the student, "What happened?" This is also important because it allows the student to describe factors in the setting that may be impacting his or her behavior. For example, students might note they are feeling embarrassed with having to do artwork because other students are teasing them about the quality of their work. Similarly, they might note that a student has been harassing them on the playground and this is not being monitored. Although a major goal of problem solving is to help students take responsibility for their own behavior and develop new skills, this must often be accompanied by the parallel goal of ensuring that the environment is conducive to the student practicing these new skills. Incorporating this important component of problem solving occurs primarily in step four, but the second step provides an opportunity for important data to be collected and for providing the student with a sense of being listened to and valued.

Another approach is to ask students if they would be willing to hear what you observed or, if you were not present, to have someone else share what was observed. It is important that this option be presented positively and not as a threat. When confronted with this option, students will normally discuss their behavior. A teacher recently solved this problem by asking students, "If I had a video camera recording what happened, what would I have seen?" She says that students find this nonthreatening because while they describe their own behavior, they are allowed to describe the entire event as they perceived it.

If a student does not respond positively to any of these options, it usually means he or she is quite emotional and may need time to calm down and think about the problem. You can deal with this situation by saying, "Dante, it seems you don't feel comfortable talking about the problem right now. Why don't we talk about it during recess?" Providing the student with time to relax often facilitates a positive resolution of the problem.

Step Three

Once the student has described the behavior, you should help the student determine whether the behavior is desirable. Students will not make meaningful, lasting changes in a behavior unless they decide that the behavior should be altered.

Glasser suggests that, when helping youngsters make a value judgment about their behavior, you ask them: "Is the behavior helping you? Is it helping me? Is it helping the other students?" When students are involved in obviously unproductive behaviors, they will almost always answer no to these questions. If they answer yes, you can ask, "How is it helping you?" or "How is it helping the others?" Finally, if the student insists that the behavior is helping the student and his or her peers, you can describe how the behavior is causing problems for you or others in the school, that it violates a school rule, or that it infringes on the rights of others (compelling state interests). If you have established a positive relationship with the student, this will usually provide the impetus for the student to acknowledge that the behavior needs to be changed.

Another approach to helping youngsters make a value judgment is to have them list the advantages and disadvantages or payoffs and costs of their behavior. When working with older students, we can ask them to put the payoffs and costs in writing. Figure 9.3 provides a form that can be used to facilitate this process. Because this procedure requires more time than simply problem solving, it is most often used by counselors, coaches, and administrators or when teachers have time to meet for an extended time with a student.

If a student continues to state that an unproductive behavior is helping him or her and that he or she wishes to continue the behavior, it is likely that the student is feeling backed into a corner or is testing your resolve. It is usually best to postpone the discussion for a short time. If a student continues to insist that an unproductive behavior is acceptable, you may need to confront the student with the logical consequences of the behavior. We should be very careful not to rush to this point without exhausting all possible approaches to helping the student decide to alter the behavior. If it is necessary to use this intervention, however, it should be discussed in a matter-of-fact, nonthreatening manner, and you should clearly explain to the student why the behavior must be altered. You might say, "I am sorry that you do not see the behavior as harmful. It is my job, though, to make sure that our classroom is a safe, comfortable place. Therefore, if you do not choose to be responsible for your behavior, I must take responsibility." If the student continues to insist that the behavior does not need to change, you should inform the student of the specific consequences that will occur if the behavior continues and why this is necessary to ensure a positive learning environment.

Step Four

After the student has decided that the behavior really does need to be changed, the next step is to help him or her develop a workable plan for making the change. This plan will be most effective when it includes both what the students will do in order to behave more responsibly

FIGURE 9.3 PAYOFF–COST MODEL OF BEHAVIORAL COUNSELING
Source: From *Adolescents with Behavior Problems: Strategies for Teaching, Counseling, and Parent Involvement,* by V. F. Jones, p. 200. Boston, MA: Allyn & Bacon. Copyright © 1980 by Pearson Education. Reprinted with permission.

	Short Term	Long Term
Payoffs		
Costs		

and what assistance or changes in the environment might be provided in order to assist the students in using the new skills. While you can decide which component of the plan you wish to discuss first, the traditional approach has been to tell the students you will first discuss what they could do differently and then discuss what they need us or other students to do in order for them to use their new skill and/or to prevent them from feeling they need to make a poor decision again.

If you begin by helping the student develop an alternative behavior, you might start by asking the student a question such as, "What do you think you can do so that you can study without bothering other students?" or "What kind of plan or strategy could you use so that you don't disrupt learning during music class?" Do not accept a superficial plan such as the statement, "I won't do it again" or "I'll try harder." You might be relieved to hear these promises, but they do not provide the student with a specific approach for dealing more effectively with the situation. You can respond to promises by saying, "I'm glad that you are going to try not to do it. That will certainly help. But what else can you do? What can you do when you start to get frustrated with your work?"

Students are refreshingly creative at devising useful plans/strategies for solving their own problems. Nevertheless, students sometimes state that they cannot think of a solution. Your first response should be to encourage them to think about the situation and report back to you at a designated time. Students have frequently become so accustomed to having adults provide answers that at first they are confused by having the burden placed on them. When given time to think about the situation, though, they often devise thoughtful plans. If the student is unable to develop a workable plan, you can offer several ideas for the student to consider. Offer several suggestions so that the student will make the final decision. This involvement in choosing the solution increases the likelihood that the student will accept and follow through on the plan.

With elementary and middle school students, it is helpful to teach several lessons on developing plans or strategies for responding to various situations in which problems frequently arise. The class can be asked to describe common situations in which students become engaged in inappropriate behavior and then list alternative behaviors for dealing with the situation. These can be posted in the classroom, and students can refer to them if they violate a school rule and become involved in problem solving. Especially when working with younger students, it can be helpful to ask them to evaluate their plan against such basic criteria as whether it is safe, fair, and kind. Will it work, and how will it make others feel?

Plans should initially be relatively simple and unstructured, such as a student's decision to work with another student in order to stay on task and complete his or her work. Plans may, however, involve a somewhat more structured approach. In fact, when less structured solutions have failed, many of the procedures described in Chapter 10 can serve as methods for implementing a plan to help a child alter his or her behavior. For example, students might be involved in writing a formal contract or self-monitoring their behavior.

The second component of the fourth step is to ask the student what assistance you might provide to help him or her be able to use the new skill or to prevent him or her from acting in ways that disrupt the learning environment. For example, with a student who fails to begin his work and instead wanders around the room disrupting others, you might ask, "Jerome, is there anything I can do that would help you get started on your work rather than wander around the room?" This stage is important for two reasons. First, as will be discussed in more detail in Chapter 10, all behavior serves a function. Students act as they do in order to meet some need. Sometimes it is necessary to alter the environment so students can meet their needs without resorting to disruptive behavior. This is an incredibly important and often missed step. Many students, especially those who come from a cultural background different than the teacher's, may question whether educators really want to hear their perspective and are willing to make adjustments to make the learning environment more supportive and culturally congruent for them. Requesting students' views and input for improving the class presents a clear statement of respect for the student and opens avenues for important dialogue about creating a culturally sensitive school and classroom community.

In the preceding example, the student may be failing to begin his work because he does not understand the material and feels he will be embarrassed by showing this or by asking for help. In this case, wandering around the room and obtaining attention from his peers helps him obtain some degree of significance and competence he feels cannot be obtained by beginning the assigned work. While we may help him develop strategies for requesting assistance, we may also be able to modify the lesson so students begin in dyads or modify the academic expectations for this student.

Step Five

The next step is to ensure that both you and the student clearly understand the plan and to ask the student to make a commitment to the plan. You can say, "All right, that seems like a good plan. Now, just to be sure that we both understand it, what are you going to do when you become frustrated with your work and what am I going to do so you are less likely to feel frustrated by the work?" After the student describes the plan, you can paraphrase the student's decision and acknowledge your role in the plan. You might say, "Okay, whenever you get frustrated, you're going to raise your hand. If I'm busy and can't help you, you're going to quietly walk over and ask Sally for help. Then it is my responsibility to come over and check your work as soon as I get a chance." Although it is often adequate simply to obtain an oral agreement, it is sometimes helpful to put the plan in writing. This is especially valuable when students are first introduced to problem solving or when the final plan is developed in the form of a contract in which both parties agree to behave in a specified manner.

Once the plan has been clarified, the student should make a commitment to try the plan. This *compact* can be accomplished by asking, "Do you believe this is a good plan? Will you give it a try?" We often conclude this step with a handshake indicating both parties have agreed to this decision.

Step Six

The sixth and seventh steps involve follow-up. In devising a workable solution to a problem, it is necessary to designate a time when the two parties will meet to discuss how the plan is working. Step six provides you with an opportunity to reinforce the student's efforts and to discuss any problems that might arise. If the plan involves a behavior that occurs frequently throughout the day, you should meet briefly with the student on the same day as the plan is made. Furthermore, if you see the student successfully implementing the plan, praise the student for his or her efforts. If the plan involves a behavior that occurs only occasionally—as during the student's music class—you can agree to meet the student as soon as possible following that class. Follow-up sessions need not take long. You can simply ask, "How did your plan work?" If the plan worked well, express your pleasure and ask the student how he or she felt about the results. If it would reinforce the student, you may choose to provide additional follow-up by asking the principal to praise the student or by sending a positive note home with the student.

Step Seven

The final step in Glasser's model deals with what to do if a plan does not work. First, do not be critical or sarcastic. A major assumption underlying the use of a problem-solving approach is that in a positive, supportive environment students will want to be responsible and behave appropriately. Therefore, the student's inability to carry out a plan should be viewed as a situation in which more work is needed to assist the student in developing responsible behavior. Simply acknowledge that it appears the plan needs some fine-tuning and begin another problem-solving conference. Because the student will already have examined the behavior and made a decision to change it, the first three steps will usually take only a minute or two to complete. The conference should then focus on asking the student to consider why the plan did not work and helping him or her develop another plan. If the behavior is one that is harmful to other students, such as pushing children on the playground, you may need to inform the student of the consequences that will be incurred should the behavior continue. Although the emphasis should always be on devising a plan rather than on punishing the student, situations in which it is necessary to incorporate a punishment into a plan do occur.

Example

The following example of an upper-elementary teacher using Glasser's model with a student indicates how effective communication skills can be combined with Glasser's step-by-step procedure to create a positive resolution to a problem.

Step 1

> **Teacher:** Darby, can I talk to you by my desk for a little bit?
>
> **Darby:** Okay.

Step 2

> **Teacher:** After we corrected math today, I went over everyone's paper. Can you tell me what I found on your paper?
>
> **Darby:** I didn't get finished.

Step 3

> **Teacher:** That's right. Is it helping you to not get your work done on time?
>
> **Darby:** I guess not.
>
> **Teacher:** What happens when you don't have your work ready?
>
> **Darby:** Jon doesn't have a paper to correct.
>
> **Teacher:** Yes, can you think of any other things that happen?
>
> **Darby:** I'll get a bad grade and have to do my work again.
>
> **Teacher:** Okay, and does it make it even harder for you to have to complete this assignment and then begin working on the one for tomorrow?
>
> **Darby:** Yeah.
>
> **Teacher:** Well, Darby, would you like to start having your work done on time so that you don't get behind and so that you can feel good about giving Jon a completed paper to correct?
>
> **Darby:** Yeah.

Step 4

Teacher: Darby, I'm glad you want to be successful. Before you develop your plan, I want to make sure the work is not too difficult or too easy for you. Is the work you're being asked to do at home something you think you can complete on your own or do you usually need help with it?

Darby: I can usually get all the problems right. I just don't have time to do the work.

Teacher: I'm glad I'm having you take the right kind of work home. Now can you think of a plan that can help you get your work done on time?

Darby: No—I'll just try to get it done.

Teacher: Well, that's super to hear, but can you think of a specific plan for getting this work completed?

Darby: Oh, I guess I could do it after I get home from school, before my mom gets home from the beauty shop each night. But I like to play, too.

Teacher: Well, let's plan it out. What time does your mother get home?

Darby: 5:30.

Teacher: And what time do you get home from school?

Darby: 3:15.

Teacher: Now, do you think you can play for a while—

Darby: Oh, I know. I'll play until 4:30 and then do my work from 4:30 to 5:30!

Step 5

Teacher: Darby, that sounds like a great idea! I'm sure that most days you won't even need a whole hour to finish your work, especially when you get into such a good habit! And won't it be nice to be all done when your mother gets home! How long do you think you could make this plan work?

Darby: Forever!

Teacher: Wow! I'm excited, too, but let's try it for a few days and talk about how it works for you.

Darby: Okay. I will do it tonight and tomorrow night.

Teacher: Great! Then Jon and I can expect to see completed assignments on Thursday and Friday!

Thursday

Step 6

Darby: It worked! I played, got my math done in thirty minutes (it was easy!), and was watching TV when Mom got home. Boy, was she surprised when I showed her my work!

Teacher: Darby, I knew you could do it! It sounds like you feel good about your plan, and I'm excited because you feel good and it will help you learn your math.

PAUSE & CONSIDER 9.3

Now that you have been introduced to the steps in problem solving with students and have read an example, it is important that you practice this approach. We have found several practice methods most effective. First, we encourage you to write a dialogue in which you implement the seven steps in helping a student solve a real or potential problem. This dialogue would look like the one you just read in that it would include your statements and those of the student. When you have completed this, we encourage you to have a colleague or classmate read your dialogue and give you feedback on how effectively you incorporated the seven steps and how you might fine-tune your use of this problem-solving model. Second, we encourage you to role-play situations with your colleagues or classmates. When doing this, it may be helpful to have a third party observe your dialogue and be the first to provide you with some feedback—the person playing the student will also have some helpful tips. Finally, we encourage you to use this method with students in your school and to discuss the results with others.

Implementing Problem Solving in the Classroom

As discussed in Chapter 8, problem solving will be most effective when it is an integral part of a teacher's classroom management plan. You must decide for yourself how this method will be incorporated into your plan. Some teachers choose to focus almost exclusively on a written form of problem solving. Other teachers prefer to have students go to a problem-solving area, think about the problem, generate a plan, and share the plan verbally when time permits. Many teachers use a combination of these methods in which written responses are the consequence for continued rule violation and verbal problem solving is used in response to behaviors that have occurred only one or two times. As mentioned earlier, several studies have shown that, when combined with teaching students classroom and school behavior expectations, the use of problem solving can have a positive effect on student behavior (Nelson, 1996; Nelson, Martella, et al., 1998).

As with any procedure used in the classroom, it will be dramatically more effective if students are taught how to use the procedure. The following ten steps are those we and many teachers with whom we work use in teaching a problem-solving method to students:

1. Provide the students with a handout and write the steps on the overhead.
2. Discuss each step and provide an example.
3. Role-play several situations in which a student misbehaves and the teacher uses this method for assisting the student in taking responsibility for his or her behavior.
4. Lead a discussion following each role-play.
5. Have the students practice by taking the role of both student and teacher and role-playing several situations.
6. Process these interactions.
7. Provide the class with an example of a violation of a classroom rule and have each student write a problem-solving plan.
8. Have students share and assist the class in evaluating and, if necessary, modifying several plans.
9. Explain how the problem-solving process relates to the classroom management plan and the difference between verbal and written plans.
10. Quiz students on the steps in the sequence and the classroom management plan.

Obviously with young students it will be necessary to modify this sequence, and with high school students, many of whom may be familiar with problem solving, it may not be necessary to teach these steps. However, in some high school settings such as alternative schools or treatment facilities, this type of detailed classroom instruction in problem solving would be appropriate.

Regardless of when and how problem solving is taught to students within the classroom setting, it will always be more effective if problem solving becomes a schoolwide approach to dealing with student behavior that violates the rights of others. A later section in this chapter discusses how to incorporate behavior problem solving into a schoolwide behavior support system.

Gender and Problem Solving

In his book *Why Gender Matters*, Leonard Sax (2005) strongly suggests boys and girls respond differently to language related to discipline. He notes that in general boys respond better to firmer, more direct disciplinary techniques, and methods that involve the student in negotiating a solution work for girls at a younger age than they do for boys. He notes that when working with boys between the ages of ten and fifteen, rather than asking them how the person they have harmed might feel, it is more effective to ask them how they would feel if someone treated them in a similar manner—and providing a specific example. He also calls for having clear consequences associated with behavior that is harmful to others as being particularly important in helping boys take responsibility for their behavior.

Our own extensive work with boys in the eight-to-fifteen age group and our many discussions with teachers working with boys in virtually all grade levels support Sax's concept that boys do respond better to more concrete discussions related to behavior. When working with boys in this age group, adults need to present themselves as being in charge with a caring but no-nonsense approach and ensure that their disciplinary response covers the two key themes of "What needs to be done here?" and "What needs to be learned here?" Our experiences also indicate that with both boys and girls, problem solving is the preferred approach to addressing behavior and addressing these two themes.

METHODS FOR GROUP PROBLEM SOLVING

Class Meetings

Class meetings allow both teacher and students to resolve problems openly and before they become major issues that negatively affect learning. Whenever people spend time in close quarters for many hours each day, it is important that time be taken to resolve minor conflicts openly. Like an automobile engine that may appear to run smoothly but will suddenly boil over unless properly lubricated, classrooms require proper maintenance checks and minor tune-ups. When implemented in a positive, supportive atmosphere, class meetings serve as the lubricant for a smoothly running classroom.

The use of class meetings will vary with grade level. The ideas presented in the following section are most appropriate for middle school block or elementary classes where teachers have major responsibility for the social and academic skill development of twenty-five to thirty-five students. Class meetings can also be an important component in other middle school and high school classrooms, although in these settings, class meetings will generally be held less often.

Nevertheless, it is important not to underestimate the value of class meetings in secondary schools. Students have numerous concerns such as the length and timing of homework assignments, the quality of classroom instruction, and relationships in the classroom, which can most effectively be dealt with as a community. In most cases, secondary teachers will simply work with students to (1) state the problem, (2) brainstorm possible solutions, and (3) select a solution. Recently, a teacher with whom we were working decided to bring to her high school class her frustration with the limited space available for group work with thirty-nine students in the class. The students decided they would select a committee to design a classroom arrangement that would facilitate group work and to develop procedures for groups working effectively in a small space. The results were thoughtful, creative, and very useful for the class. In addition, students were pleased their teacher valued and respected them enough to ask for their help, were excited about having solved their own problem, and were willing to follow the guidelines they had established.

Guidelines for Implementing a Class Meeting

The first step in implementing class meetings is to discuss the concept with students. Students should be informed that class meetings will provide them with an opportunity to discuss things they like about the class as well as things that may need to be changed in order for the class to run more smoothly. Ask students to develop their own list of reasons they think meetings are important. It is important to display enthusiasm and express interest in holding class meetings.

Once students have discussed why class meetings are helpful and are excited about holding their first meeting, present the general guidelines for class meetings. Although we encourage you to create your own guidelines, we have found the following guidelines useful for elementary and middle school class meetings:

1. If space and class size allow, class meetings will be held in a tight circle with all participants (including the teacher) seated in the circle.
2. All problems relating to the class may be discussed. Problems between two or three individuals, however, will be resolved outside the class meeting unless this problem has an effect on the class.
3. An agenda will be created prior to every class meeting. The agenda is created by students' writing the topic on a clipboard. Students must sign their names behind the agenda item. Students do not list other students' names but merely the issue to be readdressed. (If the students cannot write, they can tell you the item and you can place it on the agenda.) The items will be discussed in the order in which they appear on the board. If an agenda item no longer applies when the meeting is held, however, it will be deleted from the list.
4. Discussions during class meetings are always directed toward arriving at a solution that is not a punishment. The goal of class meetings is to find positive solutions to problems and not to criticize people or occurrences in the classroom.
5. If an individual student's behavior is listed on the agenda, the item will not be discussed without the student's permission. If the student agrees to have a behavior discussed, you should emphasize that the goal of the meeting is to help the student. Be sure that students' statements focus on the youngster's behavior and are presented as I-messages rather than as judgmental statements about the youngster or the behavior.

The focus should always be on providing the student with sensitive, thoughtful feedback and positive suggestions for altering behavior.

Students should be informed that several options are available to those who choose not to have their behavior discussed at a class meeting. First, a student may leave the room while the other students attempt to devise an approach for helping the student. You may then wish to record the discussion and share it with the student during an individual conference. Second, the student may choose to discuss the problem with you and a small group of concerned students. With the student's permission, the results of this discussion can be shared with the entire class at the next class meeting. Finally, the student can discuss the problem with you and design a plan for alleviating the problem.

6. Students' responsibilities during class meetings include (a) raising hands and being called on to speak, (b) listening to the speaker and not talking while someone else is speaking, (c) staying on the topic until it has been completed, (d) being involved by sharing ideas that will help the group, and (e) using positive, supportive words to discuss the problem and solutions.

7. The teacher will initially serve as facilitator for the class meetings.

8. You may want to end the meeting by having students compliment their peers. One way to accomplish this is to pass around a cup of Popsicle sticks with each student's name on a stick. After selecting a stick, each student gives a compliment to the student whose name is on the stick. Teachers report that students enjoy ending class meetings in this positive manner.

9. Reinforce the value of students' solutions by beginning each meeting with a discussion on the results of solutions developed at the previous meeting. Unless students believe that their solutions are useful, they will understandably soon lose interest in class meetings.

Meeting Frequency and Length

In an elementary classroom, a class meeting may be held daily for approximately fifteen minutes or weekly for about an hour. In middle and high school classes, class meeting are usually held whenever the agenda indicates that a meeting is necessary. Students should be assisted in listing only issues that are important to the smooth functioning of the classroom. Because unresolved issues will only create problems that will significantly detract from students' learning, time spent in class meetings is usually rewarded with increased on-task behavior and the associated academic gains.

© Joyce Button

"This is Wally. He's representing us in our homework negotiations."

Starting Class Meetings

Begin the first class meeting by reviewing the purpose and general guidelines for class meetings. During the initial meetings, it is very important to monitor students' behaviors carefully to ensure that general procedures and responsibilities are followed so that meetings run smoothly and students develop good habits. In order to ensure that initial meetings are viewed as positive and useful, be sure each agenda item is clearly resolved. Do so by asking several students to paraphrase the solution and ask for the group's commitment to carry out any plans that are developed. You may even initially wish to record each decision and post it in a prominent place in the room so that the class is reminded of their decisions. A positive feeling can also be enhanced by closing each meeting on a positive note. You can do this by asking each student to state one nice thing that has happened to him or her or that he or she did for someone since the last meeting. Similarly, the group can be asked to say one nice thing about each member of the group.

Reinforce the value of students' solutions by beginning each meeting with a discussion on the results of solutions developed at the previous meeting. Unless students believe that their solutions are useful, they will understandably soon lose interest in class meetings. Furthermore, because class meetings are designed to teach problem-solving skills, it is important to reinforce students' successful efforts, analyze their failures, and help them develop increasingly effective solutions.

Increasing Students' Involvement in Class Meetings

Because a major goal in implementing class meetings is to teach students skills involved in functioning effectively in a problem-solving group, it is desirable to gradually increase their responsibility for facilitating class meetings. This is difficult to do with primary grade children, but third-grade students can be taught to run their own class meetings. We have found that these four steps provide a successful approach to having students take over the class meeting:

1. After leading approximately ten class meetings, present students with a handout describing the major functions a leader serves when facilitating a group meeting (Figure 9.4). Discuss each function and behavior with the class and inform them that they will soon be asked to lead their own meetings by having students serve these important functions.
2. Introduce an agenda item or classroom problem. While the class discusses this situation, point out and define each intervention you make. Because you continue to serve all three functions shown in Figure 9.4, the discussion will be interrupted on numerous occasions. Students are usually excited about learning the new skills, however, and enjoy your instructional interventions.
3. After running three or four actual class meetings in which you consistently point out the function of each intervention, meet with and teach one student the role of discussion leader. At the next meeting, this student serves as the discussion leader while you maintain the other roles. Prior to the next meeting, you meet with another student who learns the role of task observer. At the following meeting, the student serves this function. After this meeting, you instruct a third student in the role of behavior and feeling observer, and at the following meeting, you become a group member who abides by the group responsibilities while the students run the meeting.
4. Students should function in a role for five or six meetings so that they can master the skills associated with the role and effectively model it for other students. If a student has difficulty with a role, take time between meetings to instruct the student in the skills associated with the role. Providing students with this type of experience requires a small amount of time and considerable restraint and patience, but students respond to their new skills by becoming more positive, productive class members. Behavior-problem students often respond especially well because they gain self-esteem and peer acceptance when serving as productive participants in class meetings.

**FIGURE 9.4
CLASS MEETING
JOBS**

Discussion Leader

1. Make sure everyone is comfortable and all distracting things are out of the way.
2. Make sure everyone can see all others in the circle.
3. Give the speaker time to get his or her point across.
4. Give the speaker a nod or a smile.
5. Ask clarifying questions:
   a. Are you saying that . . . ?
   b. Do you feel that . . . ?
6. Summarize:
   a. Is there anything else you would like to say?
   b. Would someone briefly summarize what has been said?

Task Observer

1. Make sure the task gets finished on time.
2. Watch the time.
3. Make suggestions of alternatives to solve the problem.
4. Point out behaviors that do not help in solving a problem.
5. Listen carefully and understand what the discussion leader is doing.
6. Understand the agenda and call out each agenda item.

Behavior and Feeling Observer

1. How did this discussion make you feel?
2. What could we do now? What might help us?
3. Was anything asked that caused you, _____ (name of person), to be concerned?
   Can you tell us what it was and how you felt about it?
4. _____ (person's name), you usually help us out. Do you have any ideas for this problem?
5. Has anyone thought of new ideas for improving our discussions?
6. How many of you feel that the discussion was of value to you? Why?

Numerous materials on class meetings are available including the following books: *The Morning Meeting Book* (Kreite & Davis, 2014), *Class Meetings* (Styles, 2001), *Class Meetings That Matter: A Year's Worth of Resources for Grades K–5* (Flerx, Limber, Mullin, & Riese, 2009); *Class Meetings That Matter 6–8: A Year's Worth of Resources* (Olweus, Limber, Snyder, & Mullin, 2009), and *Class Meetings That Matter: A Year's Worth of Resources for Grades 9–12* (Synder, Riese, Limber, & Mullin, 2012).

PAUSE & CONSIDER 9.4

Meet with a group of three or four other teachers at your grade level and have those who use class meetings discuss how they implement them in their classrooms, what they might consider adding based on reading this section, and what questions they have for members of the group regarding class meetings.

METHODS FOR RESPONDING TO SERIOUS AND CONTINUING STUDENT BEHAVIOR PROBLEMS

Studies suggest that, at least in middle schools, there is often little relationship between the behaviors for which students are referred and the consequences they receive (Skiba, Peterson, & Williams, 1997). It is, therefore, not surprising that a majority of students express anger or relief at being given a consequence by school personnel (Costenbader & Markson, 1998). Interestingly, studies suggest that students who have been suspended list numerous interventions they believe would help them more than the suspension, including, "a desire to learn alternatives to the behaviors that resulted in their suspension" (Costenbader & Markson, 1998, p. 76). It is imperative that school personnel carefully analyze how they are responding to student behavior that disrupts the learning environment.

For many years, we have written that effective responses to persistent and serious student behavior problems involve developing a schoolwide student management system that includes the following components (Jones & Jones, 1981, 1995):

1. A clear philosophy statement
2. School rules
3. Schoolwide common-area procedures
4. A clear description of the roles and responsibilities of all parties involved in managing student behavior
5. Methods for creating a positive school climate and reinforcing appropriate student behavior
6. A problem-solving model to be taught to all students
7. A format for developing positive behavior change plans for students who experience ongoing and serious behavior problems
8. Forms for communicating between teachers, administrators, and parents
9. Determining the role of the schoolwide student management committee

Many of these components have been very effectively developed into a program called Positive Behavior Support (Horner & Sugai, 2005; Lewis et al., 2006). We strongly support the work being conducted by the researchers and trainers supporting this model and encourage the reader to examine their materials online at pbis.org

For years, we have also suggested that any response to a student who demonstrates ongoing behavior that violates the rights of others include the following components:

1. Examining the environment in which the problem behavior occurred to determine what factors may be causing the undesirable behavior and what, if any, adjustments can be made to increase the likelihood that the student will behave productively in this setting
2. Meeting with the student to discuss the problem and attempt to generate a solution
3. Contacting the parent(s) or guardian(s) and informing them of the problem and the attempts being made to improve the student's behavior
4. Implementing some form of behavioral intervention to help the student improve behavior
5. Following the established schoolwide procedure for responding to behavior that violates the rights of others

6. Referring the case to a team whose responsibility is to (1) examine the student's needs, strengths, and behavior problems; (2) review previous methods used to assist the student; and (3) work with the student and significant others to design an individual behavior change plan aimed at modifying the learning environment to better meet the student's needs and providing the student with new skills to assist in benefiting from the positive learning environment

Figure 9.5 presents these components in a sequential format. Incorporating these components will (1) provide support for teachers who are implementing effective classroom management

FIGURE 9.5 BEHAVIOR INTERVENTION SEQUENCE

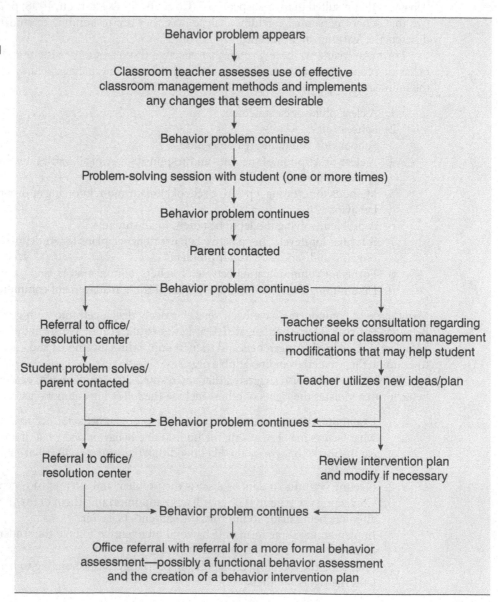

procedures but need assistance with students who display serious or persistent behavior problems, (2) reduce the ineffective use of suspensions and expulsions with almost no attention to altering classroom settings and teaching students new skills, and (3) help reduce the inequity in suspensions and expulsions of students of color.

INCORPORATING PROBLEM SOLVING INTO A SCHOOLWIDE STUDENT MANAGEMENT PLAN

It is important to note that problem solving is embedded throughout the approach outlined in Figure 9.5. In this model, educators' response to student behavior that disrupts the learning environment begins with the teacher's engaging the student in one or more problem-solving dialogues, and later includes other adults' problem solving with the student and consulting and problem solving with each other. We believe an ongoing commitment to open dialogue and creative problem solving forms the foundation for effectively assisting students in developing new skills and modifying environments so students will be supported in using these new skills.

One of the most common supports for teachers is to have another area in the building where students can go to problem solve if they are not able to successfully complete this task in their classrooms. In many elementary schools, this involves a "buddy class" in which two classrooms are paired so that students who need to take a break and problem solve somewhere else have a specified place to go. Most often this involves classrooms at different age levels, which helps to reduce students' embarrassment by being viewed as having a problem by their age-mates. It also reduces the effect of the student playing to the audience of same-age peers. In a number of schools where we have worked and consulted, the educators have established a problem-solving room staffed by an instructional assistant. This allows students to work directly with an adult trained in problem solving without having a classroom disrupted.

School staff vary on how this problem-solving time is handled. In many cases, the students take a minimum amount of time (five to ten minutes) to calm down and reflect on what happened. They may then signal their readiness to return to the classroom. On their return, they are expected to problem solve with the teacher as soon as it is convenient within the flow of classroom activities. In other cases, while in the "buddy classroom," students are asked to complete a problem-solving form such as the ones found in Figures 8.6 and 8.7. When this has been successfully completed, they return with this form to their classroom. In other schools, students complete a shorter problem-solving form in which they simply write how they plan to respond more effectively should this event occur again and how they can come to resolution of the current problem. They take this written statement back to the referring teacher. The key concepts are that students have a way to take a break from the setting in which the problem is occurring and they

PRINCIPAL
←

© James Estes

"Remember what you told us: 'If you can't say something nice, don't say anything at all'"

© James Estes

"If I had this to do over, when she asked, 'Do you boys want to go see the principal?' I would not say, 'Been there, done that.'"

have an opportunity to consider and eventually discuss with an adult how they can more effectively respond in the future.

In cases when students are not able to move to another setting or when their behavior continues to be disruptive in that setting, it is necessary to involve another educator, such as an administrator or counselor. Again, school staff committed to a problem-solving approach use this as an opportunity to have another person help students understand their behavior and develop new skills. Therefore, the counselor or administrator would problem solve with the student and find an opportunity to meet briefly with the student and teacher to reintegrate the student into the classroom. Obviously, this procedure must be modified when a student is involved in a serious behavior problem such as a fight or verbal abuse of a teacher. In these cases, the schoolwide student management system may require a suspension. It is important, however, that when the student returns from being away from school, the process is implemented prior to the student's reentering the setting in which the major problem occurred.

School staff must also decide at what point parents or guardians are informed of the student's difficulty in making responsible choices. In most schools where we have worked and consulted, the staff set a designated number of problem-solving sessions, after which the parents are informed. For example, parents will be informed when a student has more than three problem-solving events requiring leaving the classroom in any six-week period. Instances that result in the student's needing to work with a counselor or administrator usually require a contact with guardians.

Involving Students in Solving Schoolwide Problems

When considering concerns about student behavior and achievement, it is important to consider involving students in addressing the issues. Students are often aware of problems that exist in their school, the factors contributing to these problems, and ideas for improving the school experience in order to improve student behavior and achievement. By involving students in dealing with issues that concern educators in the school, we demonstrate our respect for students and also provide them with opportunities to learn how to work effectively as citizens within a community.

Day-Vines and Terriquez (2008) worked with a school experiencing very high rates of suspension and expulsion for African American and Latino students. They involved students in working with educators in the building to assess where problems were occurring and provided training for teachers on the types of teaching strategies and responses to disruptive behavior that were best accepted by students as well as having teachers share methods they felt worked best in their classrooms. In addition, the group of teachers, counselors, administrators, and students worked to develop alternatives to out-of-school suspension and to improve school climate. The result was a 75 percent reduction in suspensions the following year.

A number of years ago, I had the privilege of working with a school with a large Native American student population where a very high percentage of these students were failing to graduate and where suspension and expulsion rates for these students were much higher than for non–Native American students. The gifted Native American counselor worked with me and student teams that reviewed the discipline data and worked with teachers and administrators to develop alternative ways to respond to students who violated classroom behavior guidelines. Another group of students worked with the counselor to develop workshops for teachers on personal communication and instructional methods that were preferred by the Native American students. Implementation of these two interventions had a dramatically positive impact on the five-year graduation rates of students at this school as well as significantly reducing rates of suspension and expulsion for Native American students.

Zero-Tolerance Policies and Suspensions

As mentioned earlier, except in situations where a behavior warrants an immediate office referral—for example, a fight, sexual harassment, and so on—if behaviors occur in the classroom, the teacher should initially be responsible for dealing with the situation, often including a meeting with the student that involves a problem-solving session. This demonstrates that the teacher is competent at handling classroom matters and cares about and is willing to work collaboratively with the student. As also indicated in Figure 9.5, regardless of where and with whom a student is involved in response to a behavior that violated the rights of others, it is desirable that the adult(s) involved use some form of problem solving. While some form of consequence may be used, problem solving communicates the adult is willing to become engaged in understanding the student's point of view and assisting the student both in developing new skills and in determining factors within the classroom or school environment that can be modified to assist the student in responding more responsibly.

Zero-tolerance policies have been advocated by some as a necessary method for reducing serious school behavior problems. While we are strong advocates for having zero tolerance for such behaviors, we also believe the key is educators' commitment to and skills in assisting students in developing strategies for effectively managing their emotions and solving problems. Unfortunately, zero-tolerance policies often exclude this component of effective responses to behavior problems and instead focus on removing the student from the school environment. In addition, zero-tolerance policies often fail to incorporate a careful analysis of the classroom and school environmental issues that may significantly affect students' disruptive behavior. Furthermore, zero-tolerance policies have too frequently been implemented when the behavior did not justify such a strong response, such as for a five-year-old student who wore a firefighter Halloween costume that included a plastic axe, or for a student using a plastic knife to cut a piece of chicken in his lunch (Brownstein, 2010). In its 2014 document entitled *Guiding Principles: A Resource Guide for Improving School Climate and Discipline*, the U.S. Department of Education noted that, "Zero-tolerance policies, which generally require a specific consequence for specific action regardless of circumstances, may prevent the flexibility necessary to choose appropriate and proportional consequences" (p. 7).

While it may be necessary to remove the student from a setting while he or she is provided with new skills or the environment is modified to reduce the likelihood the student will make the

Room 210 inschool suspension

© Ortha Collins

same behavioral error, a suspension (removing the student from the school setting) has several negative results. First, the student is not able to benefit from the learning environment. Second, the suspension may communicate to the student that there is something wrong with him or her and reinforce a negative identity. Third, a focus on removal suggests the primary or sole problem resides in the student, whereas the environment always plays a factor and needs to be reviewed and modified. Fourth, a focus on suspensions may limit the emphasis placed on improving the behaviors of educators and other students that may be impacting the student's behavior.

A policy that advocates suspension for disruptive behavior will also disproportionately impact students of color. In the most recent year for which data has been collected, in grades six through twelve, 43 percent of Black students had been suspended as compared to 22 percent of Hispanic students and only 16 percent of White students (National Center for Education Statistics, 2010). In addition, recent research indicates that Black students tend to be suspended for behaviors when a subjective decision is involved (classroom disruptions, defiance of adult authority, disrespect, or excessive noise), while White students are more likely to be suspended for behaviors one would find more clearly definable such as smoking, vandalism, or skipping class (Gregory, Skiba, & Noguera, 2010). The bottom line is that little research exists to suggest zero-tolerance policies have been effective in reducing serious behavior problems in schools (LaMarche, 2011; Martinez, 2009) and considerable evidence suggests they may be damaging to various groups of students.

An appropriate response to what is perceived as a serious behavior problem involves the following:

1. ensuring the behavior had or could have had a significant impact on the safety of those involved
2. analyzing the conditions surrounding the behavior and, if possible, adjusting the environment to reduce the likelihood the student will feel the need to display the negative behavior again
3. implementing problem solving with the student to ensure both a review of the situation and the developing of new skills for the student and anyone else involved in the situation; the student may be removed from the situation where the behavior occurred until the new skill can be practiced
4. involving the caregivers in discussing the situation

Restorative resolution (Zaslaw, 2010) is one approach for creating positive solutions without excessive focus on removal from the school setting. In this approach:

The group members negotiate a settlement that addresses the harm to the victim and the school community, and a written contract is created to spell out the responsibilities of each participant and to address any legal concerns. Through this process, participants learn about one another and develop empathy by looking through a lens of respect, cooperation, and understanding. (Zaslaw, 2010, p. 59)

Yang (2009) compared two schools with virtually identical school populations. One school implemented a traditional, discipline-based, zero-tolerance policy, while the other "formed a circle of 'elders'—respected teachers who mentored suspended students academically and socially for 10 weeks and who also visited and gave feedback to the teachers of these returning students" (p. 52). The achievement data comparisons were dramatic in favor of the school that incorporated the "circle of elders" approach.

When serious behavior problems occur in school settings, students and adults in the building need to feel safe and to know the situation has been firmly and skillfully handled. The result, however, should have the least possible disruption of the involved student's opportunity to learn, must help the student develop new skills for responding in similar situations, and must involve a careful review of school factors that may have influenced the student's behavior.

Using Problem Solving on the Playground and in Other Common Areas

In elementary school settings, many of the behaviors with which students need assistance occur in common areas, such as the playground, cafeteria, hallways, and restrooms. Several methods are associated with implementing problem solving in common areas. First, staff must effectively teach all students the behaviors they expect students to display in the common areas. Second, staff must also find ways to celebrate when students make responsible choices by demonstrating these behaviors. When students make poor choices, staff must work with students to understand why the behavior was a problem and to develop alternative skills.

For example, many schools with whom we have worked set aside an area on the playground for students to move to when they are making poor choices. The staff on duty can cue a student to take time to calm down and problem solve. The student then moves to the designated area and remains there until he or she signals the staff member and is ready to share the plan. The student then joins the staff member (who continues to monitor the playground) and shares the plan. If the staff member believes the plan is productive, the staff member or the student writes the plan on a form indicating the date, time, event, and plan, and the student returns to the playground. As with problem solving in the classroom, when, within a prescribed period of time, students are involved in a designated number of instances requiring problem solving in common areas, the parents or guardians are contacted. Similarly, if the student cannot calm down or refuses to go to the problem-solving area, he or she is referred to another educator—usually a counselor or the principal.

Another type of problem solving that can occur as part of a schoolwide approach to creating more positive, safe learning communities is to involve students in solving schoolwide problems. Just as individual problem solving is intended to empower students and provide them with opportunities to solve their own problems and develop new skills, the same can occur with groups of students addressing schoolwide issues. A number of years ago, one of us was a consultant to a school district concerned about achievement and dropout rates among Native American students. At the high school level, one intervention involved having Native American students work with the counselor and vice principal to analyze the differential discipline referrals of White and Native American students and develop methods for reducing this discrepancy. In addressing the issue of academic failure, students worked with the same two individuals to design workshops in which students could teach faculty about the learning styles and preferences of Native American students. Student input also led to an extensive mentoring program where Native American adults mentored Native American students who were struggling at school. The combination of these factors had a significant positive impact on student retention and graduation rates.

The key to using a problem-solving approach is that throughout the school, students are held accountable for their behavior in a manner that emphasizes treating students with dignity and helping them develop new skills. The more broadly this approach is implemented, the more effective it will be.

PAUSE & CONSIDER 9.5

If you are observing, student teaching, or interning in a classroom, we recommend you meet with the teacher with whom you are working and separately with the principal or vice principal to discuss the procedures in your school for responding to students who are unable to quietly resolve their problems within your classroom. Write a summary of this and be prepared to share and critique it with a group of at least two other students in your program. This should allow you to understand the procedures you will be expected to follow in your classroom and also to obtain some excellent ideas from other school settings.

Case Study: The Bad, the Good, and the Ugly—A Young Teacher's Attempt to Use a Problem-Solving Approach

© Frank Cotham

"Mr. Johnson certainly makes no attempt to make this any easier."

The following example suggests why even an effectively implemented problem-solving sequence can be undermined if the staff has not decided to consistently support such an approach. This example was presented to us by a young, very skilled intern who was enrolled in a classroom management course and is intended to show how problem solving can both work effectively and be undermined by the lack of an effective schoolwide student management plan. The account is presented exactly as written except the names have been changed.

Ironically enough, I had an opportunity to utilize Glasser's problem-solving approach the day after we had our classroom discussions and role-playing concerning this procedure. On Wednesday morning, I was finishing some math preparation at school while most of the students were gone from the classroom. When the students returned from band, I watched them enter and talked with them in order to see how they were doing. Transition times can sometimes be a problem for them, so, whenever possible, I like to try and get a jump on any grievances. Suddenly Jeremy stormed into the classroom, sat down loudly in his chair, stood up again, and approached Rolando very aggressively. Rolando attempted to retreat, but Jeremy kept following him. At this point, I intercepted the two boys and asked them what the problem was. Jeremy, who has a difficult time controlling his anger, pushed me aside and punched Rolando on the shoulder. I was forced to restrain Jeremy, lest he inflict any more punches on Rolando, but I did tell him that he had chosen this action of mine as a result of his actions. I also told him repeatedly that when he had calmed down I could release him and we could talk about what had happened. A few seconds later, Jeremy was somewhat defused so I took the two boys down to the office. Using Glasser's method, I talked with Jeremy first since he had been the aggressor within the classroom. Our conversation went something like this:

> **Teacher:** I'm glad you feel able to talk about what happened and I'm sure we can figure out a plan that will help you. I like having you in class, especially since you have many special interests to share with the class, so I'd like us to try to solve this problem together.

Jeremy: (Nods)

Teacher: What happened in the classroom? What did you do that is against a school rule?

> **Jeremy:** I hit Rolando, but I was mad because . . . [Since Jeremy infrequently has a voice in these matters, I had him tell me the story of what had led up to the classroom confrontation. Jeremy said that he and Rolando had been playing around, but then Rolando pushed him away and kicked him repeatedly, even after Jeremy told him to stop.]

> **Teacher:** I'm glad you first told him to stop kicking you. That is a good, nonviolent way to deal with a problem. What happened then?

> **Jeremy:** I was really mad, so I went after Rolando. He tried to get away, but I was really mad, so I hit him.

Teacher: Yeah, I saw that part. How did hitting Rolando help you solve the problem?

Jeremy: I was mad, so I hit him.

Teacher: But did that resolve your problem? How did you feel after you hit Rolando?

Jeremy: Not very good. I feel sorry about it. I thought I might have hurt him.

Teacher: Yeah, I felt that way too. It must feel a little scary to be out of control like that too, huh?

Jeremy: (Nods and starts to cry a little.)

Teacher: Do you think that hitting Rolando helped him see your point of view?

Jeremy: No. He probably felt scared.

Teacher: And hitting is against one of our school rules, isn't it?

Jeremy: Yes.

> **Teacher:** OK. Thanks for being honest about all of that and for telling me about what happened. That helps me to see the whole picture. I also like the way you told Rolando to stop kicking you rather than just hitting him right away. We need to think of a plan for what you can do when it doesn't work to just tell someone to stop.

> **Jeremy:** I could run away and calm down. [Jeremy does this already, but he tends to run away from school, dashing out the door and into the neighborhood during the middle of the school day. I think he feels unwanted and finds the school environment so stressful that he needs to escape.]

> **Teacher:** That's a good strategy, to just walk away from the situation. But that might be a bit hard to do sometimes. Can you think of another idea, in case you find it hard to just walk away?

Jeremy: I could tell someone about it.

Teacher: That's a good idea! Who do you think you could talk to?

Jeremy: I don't know. No one really. I could talk to you but you're not always here.

Teacher: Yeah, that's a hard thing, isn't it? I would be glad to help because I enjoy working with you. Can you think of two other adults you can work with when I'm not here?

Jeremy: I guess I could talk to either the gym teacher or the science teacher.

Teacher: That sounds like a good plan. What are the strategies we've talked about so far?

Jeremy: Well, first I tell the person to stop. If that doesn't work, then I can walk away or tell you about it.

Teacher: And what if I'm not here?

Jeremy: Then I tell the science teacher or the gym teacher.

Teacher: Do you feel that you can agree to this plan?

Jeremy: Yes.

Teacher: I'm glad to hear that. Thank you very much for being so honest and for helping so much. You are really being responsible for your behavior. Is there anything you need me to do in order to help?

Jeremy: Talk to Rolando, too.

Teacher: Yes, I have planned to do that. I'll do that right now, and then I'll bring us all together and we can talk about it, okay?

Jeremy: Okay.

At this point, I had a similar discussion with Rolando, who provided me with a few more details surrounding the story. Evidently Rolando and another student were having a contest to see who could open their lockers the fastest, and this other student asked Jeremy to hold Rolando. Jeremy obliged, much to Rolando's displeasure, and Rolando told Jeremy to stop. When Jeremy did not, Rolando pushed him away and kicked him a few times. In this case, Rolando's response to the problem warranted a discussion similar to the one I had just completed with Jeremy. Rolando came up with a plan similar to Jeremy's: He would first give a verbal warning, making sure the person heard it (Rolando admitted that it had been loud in the hall, and that Jeremy may not have heard him), and then he would tell a teacher about it.

After this individual conference with Rolando, I brought the two boys together and we talked about what had happened, how they felt about it, and what plans they had developed to prevent future problems. We all agreed that it had been a productive meeting. I told them both that in a few days I would ask them how their plans were proceeding. The two boys shook hands to conclude the meeting.

Throughout this process of problem solving, I had been communicating with the principal in order to make sure I was not overstepping his jurisdiction. He told me to handle the situation as best I could, but when the meeting was over, he wanted to know exactly what I had done. Therefore, after I was finished talking with Jeremy and Rolando, I told the principal how the problem had been solved and how positive I felt about it. At this point, the principal said, "Well, you know they'll have to be punished for their actions." I felt very frustrated by this comment, because it seemed to carry the implicit message: "Well, now that you've done the 'cute' problem-solving stuff, let's get down to the *real* solution." I did not agree with this idea, because I did not feel that a

"How come when you say we have a problem, I'm always the one who has the problem?"

© George Abbott

punishment would help them to solve future problems. In talking with the boys, it was obvious to me that both of them needed appropriate strategies and skills for solving their problems, not token punishments. I was not sure how to say this to the principal, however, since his conversational tone left me feeling rather intimidated. He offered a few "acceptable" punishments and left me to choose one for the two boys. I decided to have them stay inside with me during their fifteen-minute lunch recess. Besides being on the principal's "acceptable" list, this would allow us to spend time talking about a variety of topics that would give the boys an opportunity to learn more about each other. In addition, I would have a chance to see how the two would interact together in a more informal setting.

After lunch, I noticed that something was amiss when the principal called me into his office. He stated that he had heard some "new information" pertaining to the altercation between the boys, and he asked me to restate what had happened. After he heard the story from me again, he called the boys down to his office and basically gave them a rather emotional lecture, using sarcastic language and demeaning statements. The principal then said that both boys would be getting referrals, which meant a parent contact for Rolando and an in-school suspension for Jeremy. The principal also told Jeremy, "Now you'll be just one step away from a week-long suspension. Wasn't it just two weeks ago when I had to suspend you from the bus? When are you going to get the message, Jeremy?"

At this point, the principal dismissed Rolando back to class and Jeremy to the office chair. He then told me to fill out the two referral forms. He said, "No need to be real extensive about it, just write down what basically happened." I completed the forms and asked if he at least could record that I had held a problem-solving conference with the two boys, during which they had developed thoughtful individual plans for preventing further problems. He agreed.

This example presents not only a situation in which a teacher effectively used problem solving but also an instance in which the lack of a coordinated, congruent approach to assisting students in resolving behavior problems negatively influenced the relationship and sense of empowerment experienced by two students and a teacher. This type of situation can be prevented by staff working collaboratively to develop a schoolwide student management plan.

SUMMARY

The concept of problem solving as a major focus for responding to inappropriate student behavior has existed for more than thirty years. However, experience as well as reviews of the research suggest that it has been systematically implemented into a surprisingly small percentage of teachers' classroom management plans and schoolwide student management systems. This is unfortunate because, when properly applied, problem solving responds to a number of important socioemotional needs of students and helps remediate a wide range of skill deficits experienced by many students who behave unproductively in school.

Fortunately, an increased emphasis on conflict resolution and research supporting its benefits in reducing classroom discipline problems have helped create a positive climate for the use of problem solving. This chapter describes several specific methods for incorporating problem solving into a classroom management plan and schoolwide discipline. Our experience indicates that teachers who use these approaches are impressed with the positive student attitudes they generate as well as with their students' abilities to solve problems and take responsibility for their behavior.

RECOMMENDED READING

Girard, K., & Koch, S. (1996). *Conflict resolution in the schools: A manual for educators.* San Francisco, CA: Jossey-Bass.

Glasser, W. (1986). *Control theory in the classroom.* New York, NY: Harper & Row.

Glasser, W. (1990). *The quality school: Managing students without coercion.* New York, NY: Harper and Row.

Hoover, J., & Oliver, R. (1996). *The bullying prevention handbook: A guide for principals, teachers, and counselors.* Bloomington, IN: National Educational Services.

Johnson, D., & Johnson, R. (1991). *Teaching students to be peacemakers.* Edina, MN: Interaction Book.

Johnson, D., & Johnson, R. (1995). *Reducing school violence through conflict resolution.* Alexandria, VA: Association for Supervision and Curriculum Development.

Long, N., Wood, M., & Fescer, F. (2001). *Life space crisis intervention: Talking with children and youth to improve relationships and change behavior* (2nd ed.). Austin, TX: Pro-Ed.

Mendler, A. (1992). *What do I do when...? How to achieve discipline with dignity in the classroom.* Bloomington, IN: National Educational Service.

Nelson, J. R. (1996). Designing schools to meet the needs of students who exhibit disruptive behavior. *Journal of Emotional and Behavioral Disorders, 4,* 147–161.

Nelson, J. R., & Carr, B. (1999). *Think time strategy for schools: Bringing order to the classroom.* Longmont, CO: Sopris West.

Nelson, J. R., Crabtree, M., Marchand-Martella, N., & Martella, R. (1998). Teaching good behavior in the whole school. *Teaching Exceptional Children, 30,* 4–9.

Sax, L. (2005). *Why gender matters: What parents and teachers need to know about the emerging science of sex differences.* New York, NY: Doubleday.

Schrumph, F., Crawford, D., & Usadel, H. (1991). *Peer mediation: Conflict resolution in schools.* Champaign, IL: Research Press.

CHAPTER 10

DEVELOPING INDIVIDUAL BEHAVIOR CHANGE PLANS

Strategies for managing problem behavior in the classroom are increasingly emphasizing directly teaching adaptive behavior patterns. A basic assumption underlying this trend is that many students, particularly at-risk students, have not learned the essential competencies required for school success.

—Hill Walker, Geoff Colvin, and Elizabeth Ramsey (1995)

When goals are humane, we must offer the most effective means available to reach them. In many cases, the proven effectiveness of applied behavior analysis procedures makes them the most humane choice.

—Paul Alberto and Anne Troutman (2006) *Applied Behavior Analysis for Teachers*

The classical behaviorism of the early '70s, with its emphasis on reinforcers and consequences, has given way to cognitive behaviorism with its focus on self-management and social skills training.

—Vern Jones (1996)

Students occasionally need highly structured programs to help them change specific behaviors. Research suggests that even when teachers have effectively implemented the methods described in Chapters 6, 8, and 9, approximately 5 to 7 percent of students will require some form of individualized intervention (Lewis, Sugai, & Colvin, 1998; Taylor-Greene et al., 1997). We would suggest that when the methods described in Chapters 3, 4, 5, and 7 are included within the skills and strategies teachers skillfully use, this number may be reduced considerably. Nevertheless, there are a number of students whose social and emotional problems, or whose difficulty adjusting to or working effectively in an environment significantly different from their home or community will necessitate implementing an individualized plan to help them function responsibly and successfully within even the best classroom and school environments. Classroom teachers cannot be expected to spend large amounts of time implementing behavior change programs, but to be effective, teachers must be able to incorporate behavior management methods that have proved effective in the classroom. When implemented in classroom settings characterized by supportive interpersonal relationships and instruction matched to students' needs, these methods frequently have dramatic, positive effects on students' behaviors. A student-centered approach to classroom management includes teachers having the ability to assist all students in developing the skills necessary to be academically and behaviorally successful within the general education classroom.

LEARNING GOALS

After reading this chapter, you will know:

1. The key concepts in using behavior management to positively influence students' behavior
2. How to conduct a functional behavior assessment to determine why a student is demonstrating behaviors that disrupt his or her learning and/or the learning of others
3. How to develop a behavior intervention plan to assist a student in developing specific skills that will help him or her demonstrate more responsible behavior
4. How to work with a team of colleagues to develop such a behavior plan

Why Are These Goals Important?

It is our responsibility as educators to help all students develop behaviors that will enable them to reach their fullest potential both at school and in society at large. Just as educators use differentiated instruction to help all students meet key learning goals, they can develop individualized behavior plans to assist all students in acting responsibly.

The increased emphasis on inclusion of students experiencing behavior problems and the increasing number of students living in families that are experiencing serious turmoil or adjustment problems have created a situation in which teachers are asked to work with many students who require considerable help in developing appropriate behaviors. Lundeen's (2002) study of the concerns expressed by beginning teachers found:

> The greatest concern of all new teachers was the inability to deal with the aberrant behavior and diverse needs of some students. Almost none of the voiced concerns dealt with low-level discipline issues. The issues these teachers talked about were complicated and sometimes volatile. These beginning teachers felt completely unprepared to face them. (p. 4)

Our recent work with both student teachers and veteran teachers clearly supports these findings. Teachers state their major concern regarding student behavior is dealing with students whose behavior is seriously and/or persistently disruptive to the learning community. They are almost desperate to learn methods for assisting these students to learn to function more effectively in a classroom setting.

Teachers should, however, be hesitant to use these methods unless they have first created a classroom in which all students are accepted by the teacher and their peers, classroom rules and procedures have been agreed on and are consistently monitored, students are involved in interesting work at which they can succeed, and problem solving is used. Employing behavioristic interventions to manipulate students into behaving docilely in an environment that does not meet their personal psychological and academic needs is unprofessional. Employing individualized behavior change plans to help students adjust to a positive learning environment, however, is an important aspect of being a competent teacher.

Just as we often modify academic work and provide students with special programs and tutors to assist them in the essential skills of reading, writing, and mathematics, we need to use a variety of interventions to assist students in developing the skills needed to become accepted and productive members of the classroom group. When students do not have these skills, they not only are prevented from reaching their academic potential but may also prevent the teacher and other students from doing their best work. Everyone loses when we fail to develop individual behavior change plans for students whose behavior is disrupting the learning environment.

This chapter presents the key ingredients for developing plans for students whose behavior continues to negatively influence their learning and that of other students. It begins with a discussion of behavior change interventions. Next, we discuss the concept of correctly identifying the problem behaviors and analyzing the factors that may be causing the student to use inappropriate behaviors (often termed *functional assessment*). This is followed by a discussion of several cognitive behavioral strategies that can assist students in developing important new social skills. Finally, we discuss the team planning process that can facilitate the development of individualized behavior change intervention plans.

BEHAVIOR MANAGEMENT IN PERSPECTIVE

Behavioristic interventions have, in many ways, been misunderstood by teachers. On the one hand, some teachers have viewed behavioristic methods as a complex, time-consuming approach that nevertheless held the answer to their discipline problems. On the other hand, many teachers have viewed behaviorism as a manipulative, overly repressive approach to working with students. The answer lies somewhere between these extremes. Behavioristic methods cannot and should not solve all discipline problems. There is no substitute for effective teaching in a caring environment. Behaviorism, though, is also not necessarily a mechanistic, manipulative science. Rather, it can be used to help teachers better understand students' behaviors and assist students in developing more responsible classroom behavior.

Basic Assumptions Underlying Behavioristic Interventions

Behaviorism is really more a rationale and a methodology than a specific set of procedures. It is based on examining specific data and applying experimentally validated procedures in order to alter behavior. Quite simply, behaviorism is a scientific approach to changing behavior. This approach is based on three major assumptions: (1) behavior is influenced by the antecedents and consequences associated with the behavior; (2) behavior change programs must focus on specific, observable behavior; and (3) data collection is necessary in order to alter behavior thoughtfully and systematically.

Behavior Is Influenced by the Antecedents and Consequences Associated with the Behavior

Behaviorists acknowledge the importance of both antecedents and consequences. Regarding consequences, or events following a behavior, behavioral research has developed three basic rules through careful studies of human behavior: (1) a behavior followed immediately by a reward will occur more frequently, (2) a behavior will be extinguished when it is no longer reinforced, and (3) a behavior followed closely by an undesirable consequence will occur less often. Behaviorists, however, do not ignore antecedent or stimulus conditions. Students cannot be reinforced for producing a behavior unless they possess the ability to perform the behavior. Therefore, we must create positive environments in which students will risk trying new behaviors and must systematically provide students with assistance in gradually developing new skills.

Behavior Change Programs Must Focus on Specific, Observable Behavior

If we wish to help students develop new skills or eliminate undesired behaviors thoughtfully and systematically, we must deal with specific, observable behavior. It is not helpful to either teacher or student to state that the student is disruptive and incorrigible. It is much more helpful if we state that the student will learn more and be better liked by peers if he can reduce the number of times he interrupts the teacher and other students or can decrease the number of times he hits others. Focusing on observable behavior that can be counted is the first step in developing a program for systematically altering a student's behavior.

Data Collection Is Necessary in Order to Alter Behavior Thoughtfully and Systematically

It is surprising that this basic approach is often criticized by teachers who state that data collection is too time consuming. Effective teachers base their academic instructional program on assessment activities that indicate the specific skills their students possess. This step is followed by activities specifically designed to develop new skills. Finally, assessment is used to determine how well the skill has been learned and what activities should follow. Collecting data on students' behavior serves a similar purpose. It allows us to determine whether a problem exists, how serious the problem is, and whether the interventions being used are significantly affecting the behavior. When teachers fail to collect some form of data, they often fail to assess a student's behavior accurately.

Data collection also allows us to evaluate an intervention designed to change a student's behavior. Unless we collect data, it is easy to become frustrated when a new program or intervention does not bring about an immediate change in the behavior. By collecting data, we can notice small but significant changes in a student's behavior.

The remainder of this chapter provides methods that will help you (1) determine why a student may behave in a manner that disrupts his or her learning and that of others, (2) what changes you might make in the classroom to prevent this behavior, (3) what new skills the student may need to learn in order to be successful at school, and (4) how you can work with others to implement these behavior change strategies.

UNDERSTANDING WHAT CAUSES STUDENT BEHAVIOR: CONDUCTING A CLASSROOM BEHAVIOR ASSESSMENT

Understanding Factors that Influence Student Behavior
For an interactive review of methods for better understanding factors that influence student behavior, click here in the Pearson etext.

ENHANCEDetext *interactive case study*

In his book *What Do I Do When . . . ? How to Achieve Discipline with Dignity in the Classroom*, Mendler (1992) wrote, "Most discipline programs incorrectly place their emphasis upon strategies and techniques. The latest gimmick is offered to get Johnny to behave. . . . The competent teacher needs to get at the reasons or functions of a given maladaptive behavior to formulate a strategy likely to work" (p. 25).

When a student experiences behavior problems, rather than blaming the student, educators will be more effective in helping students develop productive behaviors if they carefully examine school and classroom environments to determine factors, including instructional strategies, academic content, classroom peer interactions, and teacher–student relationships to determine what may be contributing to the student's unproductive behavior. We like to think of this way of viewing student behavior as "functional thinking." Since all behavior is functional (i.e., it serves a function for the student), a professional and effective way to consider student behavior is to think about what is happening in the classroom that is causing the student to believe he or she can get more attention or experience more success from the disruptive behavior than by being productively involved in the learning activity. Alfie Kohn (1996) highlighted this concept when he wrote:

> What matters are the reasons and feelings that lie beneath. Discipline programs can (temporarily) change behavior, but they cannot help people to grow. The latter requires a very different orientation in the classroom: looking "through" a given action in order to understand the motives that gave rise to it as well as figuring out how to have some effect on those motives. (p. 69)

In addition to ensuring the student is experiencing a supportive learning environment that is meeting his personal and academic needs, it is imperative that educators determine any social skills the student may lack that are essential to functioning effectively in the school environment. If the student has the necessary behavior skills but is not using them, educators need to incorporate methods that encourage the student to use appropriate behaviors in the school setting.

Functional behavior assessment is the term most often used for the process of determining factors that may be influencing a student's behavior and developing a plan to assist the student. Because the term *functional assessment* is most often used in connection with schoolwide procedures for assisting students who have a history of struggling to make effective behavior choices as well as in providing special education services and includes very detailed data collection methods, when discussing how a teacher can assess factors that impact a student's behavior within the classroom, we use the term *classroom behavior assessment*. This acknowledges that, much like the academic assessments teachers make in the classroom are different from those a school psychologist and team of educators might make when assessing a student to determine whether he or she is eligible for special services, a classroom behavior assessment is not a sophisticated functional assessment but is a tool to help teachers assist students in developing more responsible classroom behavior. A classroom behavior assessment process involves four components:

1. An assessment of the classroom factors impacting the student's behavior
2. The development of a behavior change plan
3. The implementation of this plan
4. The ongoing monitoring and adjustment of this plan

Furthermore, when a classroom behavior assessment has been completed, we will have answers to the following four questions:

1. What are the antecedents and the consequences that cause the behavior to exist?
2. What function(s) does the behavior serve for the student?
3. What environmental changes can be made to change the student's behavior?
4. What behaviors can we teach the student to help him or her act more responsibly and meet his or her needs without using behaviors that violate the rights of others?

We have heard educators suggest that teachers do not have the time or expertise to conduct classroom behavior assessments and develop the associated classroom behavior intervention plans. We believe, however, that this work is similar to teachers' implementing differentiated instruction. In initially dealing with a situation in which a student is having difficulty mastering new academic content, the teacher generally will not involve professionals working outside the classroom but will meet with the student, carefully examine the student's work for patterns in the academic errors, make a hypothesis about what may be causing the errors, and finally make some adjustments in the instructional methods for supporting the student's learning. This is very similar to what we might expect as a teacher conducts a classroom behavior assessment and develops a classroom behavior plan. In this case, the teacher will conduct problem-solving discussions with the student; will have collected some data regarding patterns associated with the behavior; and based on this data, will make a hypothesis about the causes of the student's disruptive behavior and determined a plan of action to assist the student.

While teachers can certainly benefit from the support of educators with different backgrounds and training, we have known for some time that teachers are capable of effectively implementing the behavior support process (Doggett, Edwards, Moore, Tingstrom, & Wilcznski, 2001; Mueller, Sterling-Turner, & Moore, 2005; Wallace, Doney, Mintz-Resudek, & Tarbox, 2004). Research also demonstrates that, within school settings, results of behavior plans based on less detailed, descriptive functional behavior assessments can be as effective as those based on experimentally based FBAs (Goh & Bambara, 2012). We believe that some training in how to conduct a classroom behavior assessment and develop an associated behavior change plan can lead to classroom plans that have a significant positive impact on a student's behavior (Maag & Larson, 2004). For many years we have taught a classroom management course to master's degree preservice teachers involved in a year-long student teaching placement. Just past halfway through the school year, these students are required to develop a classroom behavior assessment and behavior intervention plan for a student in their class who is struggling to demonstrate behavior that supports the learning of the student and his or her classmates. The quality of these behavior support plans and, in many cases, the positive impact on the students' behavior, is extremely impressive.

It is important to point out that one of the intentions in conducting a classroom behavior assessment is to provide school staff an opportunity to develop an objective view of not only the student's behavior but their own behavior as well. During the intensity of difficult exchanges with a student, this objective view of one's behavior may be unavailable to a teacher. When school staff are able to lower the emotionality that so commonly occurs in working with disruptive student behavior and examine how the adults' behaviors may support or hinder a student's prosocial behavior, this adds a powerful dimension to the teacher's effectiveness in supporting the student in developing and demonstrating desired behaviors.

Collecting information to determine why the undesirable behavior is occurring is the first step in conducting a classroom behavior assessment. Observations should initially focus on whether the teacher is implementing effective classroom instructional and classroom management methods within the classroom. As discussed throughout this book, student behavior that is deemed undesirable may be a response to a classroom setting that is not effectively designed to meet students' personal and academic needs.

A classroom behavior assessment will always involve direct observation to collect data regarding events or factors that are associated with the behavior to be changed. It may also involve indirect methods such as interviews with the student, parents, other teachers who work with or have taught the student, counselors, administrators, and instructional assistants.

Figure 10.1 is a form that has been used with hundreds of teachers to help them examine their own classroom management and instructional responsibilities as a factor in the unproductive behavior of an individual student or group of students. This form is not intended to be used as an evaluative instrument. Instead, it is to be used by a teacher or a teacher and colleague or consultant to consider whether changes may be warranted in one or more general area(s) related to

FIGURE 10.1
INTERVENTIONS
BEFORE
REMOVING A
STUDENT FROM
THE CLASSROOM
OR REFERRING
A STUDENT FOR
SPECIAL
EDUCATION
SERVICES

	Yes	*Somewhat*	*No*

Level 1: Classroom Management and Instruction

1.1 The teacher interacts positively with the student.

1.2 The teacher communicates high expectations to the student.

1.3 The student is actively involved with peers either through cooperative learning or peer tutoring.

1.4 Classroom procedures are taught to students and this student demonstrates an understanding of the procedures.

1.5 There is a consistent routine in the classroom that is understood by the student.

1.6 The student's instructional program is appropriate to his or her academic needs.

1.7 The student has been involved in some form of academic goal setting and self-recording.

1.8 Rules for managing student behavior are posted in the classroom.

1.9 Rules are appropriate, succinct, stated positively, and all-inclusive.

1.10 Consequences for inappropriate behavior are clear to all students.

1.11 Consequences are appropriate, fair, and implemented consistently.

1.12 The student demonstrates that she or he understands the rules and consequences.

1.13 The teacher has met privately with the student to discuss the problem and jointly develop a plan both parties agree to implement in order to assist the student.

Level 2: Individual Behavior Program

2.1 An academic and/or behavior program has been developed and consistently implemented and corresponding data collected for at least four weeks.

2.2 An alternative program was implemented if the original plan (2.1) proved to be ineffective.

management and instruction. Figure 10.2 presents a form one of us assisted a large K–8 school district in developing to help teachers assess their interventions prior to seeking assistance from other teachers or specialists. The purpose of this form is simply to help teachers consider the extent to which they have made reasonable and responsible classroom interventions aimed at assisting the student in having a positive learning experience and to consider additional changes that might assist the student.

**FIGURE 10.2
OBSERVATION
AND
ASSESSMENT
IN THE
LEARNING
ENVIRONMENT**
Source:
Schaumburg
School District 54,
Schaumburg, IL.
Reprinted with
permission.

	Person Responsible	Specific Interventions and Date Initiated	Outcome and Specify Duration
Circle Specific Interventions Used			

I. Classroom Environment

   A. Provide preferred seating (i.e., carrel, dividers, move with peer model/tutor).

   B. Alter location of school supplies for easy access or to minimize distractions.

   C. Assign to quiet area in classroom for short periods.

   D. Post and explain rules and consequences for inappropriate classroom behavior.

   E. Increased teacher proximity for targeted student.

   F. Other:

II. Instructional Modification

   A. Assess student's prerequisite skills.

   B. Provide small-group and/or one-on-one instruction by:

      1. Teachers

      2. Instructional assistant

      3. Peer tutor

      4. Cross-age tutor

      5. Volunteer

   C. Modify materials:

      1. Address only essential skills

      2. Simplify vocabulary of presented materials

      3. Reduce workload

      4. Alter pacing

      5. Use programmed materials (e.g., SRA, computer drill, math kits)

      6. Repeat and reinforce skills (e.g., record lesson, games, activity centers)

      7. Change basal text

      8. Provide assignments and tests in segments

      9. Use calculator/computers

      10. Provide study aids (e.g., highlight main ideas, outlines, study guides, number line, concrete materials)

STUDENT: _____ I.D.#: _____ BIRTH DATE: _____

(*continued*)

FIGURE 10.2
(CONTINUED)

Circle Specific Interventions Used	Person Responsible	Specific Interventions and Date Initiated	Outcome and Specify Duration
D. Organize materials (e.g., folder, notebook, assignment sheet).			
E. Set time expectations (e.g., use timer, set time allotment).			
F. Use cues or gestures to indicate appropriate or inappropriate behaviors.			
G. Vary student responses (e.g., writing on chalkboard, art projects, verbal response alone, recording, use manipulatives).			
H. Modify instructions:			
1. Preview questions/tests			
2. Provide rewards/reinforcers			
3. Ask student to repeat directions and then restate what he's going to do to ensure understanding			
I. Modify grades:			
1. On specific reduced workload			
2. Reflecting performance on essential skills			
3. On report cards			
J. Other:			
III. Motivation/Behavior Strategies			
A. Assess appropriateness of task.			
B. Prioritize tasks to be completed.			
C. Privately discuss and explain behavior and resulting consequences.			
D. Use behavior modification techniques (e.g., reinforce appropriate behaviors, cueing, gestures).			
E. Alter frequency of grouping changes to maximize or minimize child's movements.			
F. Change of schedule/group.			
G. Adapt assignments (e.g., reduced workload, verbal responses).			
H. Refer child to social worker/counselor/ psychologist.			
I. Provide individual assignments/behavior sheets, charts, checklists, and so forth monitored by teacher, student, and administrator.			

(continued)

FIGURE 10.2
(CONTINUED)

Circle Specific Interventions Used	Person Responsible	Specific Interventions and Date Initiated	Outcome and Specify Duration

J. Set up reward/consequence system:
  1. Goal setting—target individual behavior
  2. Set up a contract
  3. Provide reinforcers chosen from a menu (e.g., social praise, tangible/stickers, activity/free time, games, good news notes)
K. Daily/weekly progress reports.
L. Parent/teacher/principal/child conferences, weekly, bimonthly, and so on.
M. Other:			

IV. Parent Contact/Support A. Notes sent home (e.g., daily or weekly progress report, good news notes). B. Parent/teacher check-in (e.g., mutually signed assignment sheets/notebooks). C. Telephone contact (e.g., weekly, monthly, or as needed). D. Home/school learning/behavior contracts. E. Suggested in-district resources (parent group/TAP). F. Other:			

_____	_____	_____	_____
Date	Signature of Teacher	Date	Signature of Principal, CST Member, or Peer Consultant

---

PAUSE & CONSIDER 10.1

For a student in a classroom where you are teaching, observing, or consulting who is engaging in behaviors that are disrupting the learning environment and/or detracting from his or her own learning, review Figure 10.1 and determine whether there are any changes that could be made in the general classroom management methods within the environment where this student is making poor choices. Write down changes you might make, and if, possible, discuss these with a colleague or fellow student.

PAUSE & CONSIDER 10.2

Select a student who is disrupting the learning in a classroom where you teach or are observing or consulting. Examine Figure 10.2 and write down several interventions that are currently being implemented to assist this student. Next, write down several additional methods that might be incorporated in order to assist this student in following the classroom behavior guidelines. If possible, share this information with someone, and if you have responsibility for the classroom, consider whether changes in the classroom setting are desirable.

In addition to examining classroom management and instructional factors, it can be extremely valuable to analyze a student's classroom behavior systematically and specifically. Figure 10.3 presents a form designed to assist teachers in determining the factors that may be influencing a student's behavior.

PAUSE & CONSIDER 10.3

Again, consider a student with whom you are working or whom you are observing having difficulty behaving in a responsible manner—ideally the same student you considered in Pause & Consider 10.1 and 10.2. In order to better support this student, complete Figure 10.3. Again, try to discuss these results with a colleague or small group of fellow students.

If you have completed the first three Pause & Consider features, you have completed the key aspects of a classroom behavior assessment. You have information regarding classroom factors that may be influencing the student's behavior as well as interventions that have been attempted to assist this student. You have made some hypotheses regarding the function the behavior serves for the student. Figure 10.4 presents a sample Figure 10.3 completed for a third-grade student whose behavior was disrupting classroom learning.

Once you have conducted a classroom behavior assessment, it is important to observe the student and collect specific data to determine whether your hypotheses tend to hold true. For example, if you hypothesized that the student becomes overly active and noncompliant when faced with work she does not feel confident completing, to see whether your hypothesis appears valid, you could observe her in settings in which she is likely to be successful and in a situation in which the work is quite difficult. Similarly, in the same setting, you could provide her with work she can complete successfully and determine whether her behavior in this situation is quite different than when she was asked to complete work she found demanding. If your observations are validated, your next step would be to create a positive behavior change plan, often called a BIP (behavior intervention plan) or BSP (behavior support plan). This will likely include changes in classroom factors such as implementing changes in the academic work presented to the student, providing a peer tutor, ensuring other students make supportive responses to the student's behavior, teaching the student strategies for responding productively when faced with demanding academic tasks, and so on. Before you begin developing such plans, we recommend you read the remainder of the chapter. Later in the chapter, we provide a process for developing a behavior intervention plan and you will have an opportunity to develop one or more of these plans.

FIGURE 10.3
CLASSROOM
BEHAVIOR
ASSESSMENT
FORM

Student Name _____ Birth Date _____

School _____ Grade Level _____ Date _____

1. Describe the frequency, duration, and intensity of the problem behavior in specific, observable terms: How frequently does the problem behavior occur (i.e., number of times per day/week)? If the behavior occurs infrequently but lasts for a significant period of time (e.g., out-of-seat behavior), also include the duration of the behavior. If the behavior is very intense (e.g., a temper tantrum), describe the extent of the behavior.

2. What antecedent/classroom factors or events seem to precede the problem behavior (e.g., time of day, content being taught, type of instructional activity, with whom the student is seated or working, etc.)?

3. In what classroom setting(s) does the behavior not occur? Why might the behavior not be occurring in this/these setting(s)?

4. What is the specific trigger that precedes the behavior (i.e., what happens immediately before the behavior begins) (e.g., the student is asked to begin an academic task, another student says something to the student, the student receives correction or direction from an adult, etc.)?

5. What happens immediately following the behavior that may be reinforcing and maintaining it? What does the teacher or another adult do when the behavior occurs? What do other students do? What happens to the student?

6. What function(s) do you think this behavior is serving for the student (i.e., what is the student obtaining from the behavior?) (e.g., attention, removal from a difficult task, movement, etc.)?

7. What interventions have you already attempted to modify this behavior? (Be specific; attach copies of interventions used.)

8. Based on the assessment of factors influencing the student's behavior and the functions this behavior serves the student, what changes in the classroom can be made to reduce the likelihood the student will need to use the problem behavior?

9. What additional interventions do you believe would be most helpful in providing the student with an alternate behavior to serve the same function as the problem behavior?

FIGURE 10.4
SAMPLE
CLASSROOM
BEHAVIOR
ASSESSMENT
FORM

Student's Name _____ Birth Date _____

School _____ Grade Level _____ 3 _____ Date _____

1. Describe the frequency, duration, and intensity of the problem behavior in specific, observable terms: How frequently does the problem behavior occur (i.e., number of times per day/week)? If the behavior occurs infrequently but

(continued)

FIGURE 10.4
(CONTINUED)

lasts for a significant period of time (e.g., out-of-seat behavior), also include the duration of the behavior. If the behavior is very intense (e.g., a temper tantrum), describe the extent of the behavior. **Touching other students' work material and hitting or pushing the student. 4–6 times per day.**

2. What antecedent/classroom factors or events seem to precede the problem behavior (e.g., time of day, content being taught, type of instructional activity, with whom the student is seated or working, etc.)? **The behavior almost always occurs during reading or writing instructional times or in group activities that involve some form of writing.**

3. In what classroom setting(s) does the behavior not occur? Why might the behavior not be occurring in this/these setting(s)? **The behavior almost never occurs during large-group instruction or independent seatwork during math instructional times. It also does not occur during activities that involve artwork.**

4. What is the specific trigger that precedes the behavior (i.e., what happens immediately before the behavior begins) (e.g., the student is asked to begin an academic task, another student says something to the student, the student receives correction or direction from an adult, etc.)? **Being given work he believes is too difficult.**

5. What happens immediately following the behavior that may be reinforcing and maintaining it? What does the teacher or another adult do when the behavior occurs? What do other students do? What happens to the student? **The teacher tells the student to stop immediately because he is violating a class rule. If he continues, he is sent to another classroom. If he has hurt a student, he is required to immediately go to the office for 20 minutes. Students often state they do not want to work with him, and when he hits or pushes them or damages their materials, they call for teacher assistance or yell at him.**

6. What function(s) do you think this behavior is serving for the student (i.e., what is the student obtaining from the behavior?) (e.g., attention, removal from a difficult task, movement, etc.)? **The behavior may be a way for the student to deal with his frustration when he perceives the work as too difficult. The behavior often leads to the work demands being terminated.**

7. What interventions have you already attempted to modify this behavior? (Be specific; attach copies of interventions used.) **I have sent him to the office, contacted his mother, and held him in from recess.**

8. Based on the assessment of factors influencing the student's behavior and the functions this behavior serves the student, what changes in the classroom can be made to reduce the likelihood the student will need to use the problem behavior? **I could provide him with more choices when giving him work that requires reading or writing (e.g., choosing the amount or type of work he will complete). In small groups, I can put him with students who are sensitive about helping others and also try to give him group tasks at which he can feel successful (e.g., getting materials, requesting**

(continued)

FIGURE 10.4
(CONTINUED)

> my help, etc.). I can increase the amount of behavior-specific positive feedback I provide him when he is doing well dealing with difficult work. When responding to his behavior, I could ask him what would work better for him or what assistance he needs rather than simply telling him he is violating a class rule and must stop. I could also be more aware of when he appears to be getting agitated and provide this assistance earlier. Finally, I could teach students to send him an I-message rather than yell at him or call me.
>
> 9. What additional interventions do you believe would be most helpful in providing the student with an alternate behavior to serve the same function as the problem behavior? **I could work with him to develop a method for relaxing when he starts to become frustrated and upset.**

STRATEGIES FOR HELPING STUDENTS DEVELOP NEW BEHAVIOR SKILLS

In addition to the problem-solving methods discussed in Chapter 9, there are three basic, well-researched behavior management approaches for helping students monitor and alter their behavior (Eyberg, Nelson, & Boggs, 2008; Weisz & Kazdin, 2010). The first method, self-monitoring, helps students count and record their own behavior. A second approach, social skills training, involves teaching students new skills for meeting their needs. The third method involves working with students to develop some form of agreement or contract to help motivate them to use skills that are in their repertoire but which they find difficult to use. This section presents specific procedures for implementing these three general approaches.

Self-Monitoring

Students have a basic need to be viewed positively and to demonstrate their competence and power by controlling their own behavior. Often, however, students are not aware of the extent of their unproductive behavior. In addition, some youngsters have difficulty controlling their emotions and behaviors without the assistance of external cues. Self-monitoring involves assisting a student or group of students in establishing a system for monitoring and recording their own behaviors. Involving students in collecting data on their own behaviors can, in some instances, provide enough external structure to produce dramatic improvements in their behaviors. This procedure not only involves students in their own behavior change programs but also significantly reduces the amount of time spent in collecting data. Furthermore, perhaps because self-monitoring helps create an internalized locus of control, changes in behavior associated with this approach seem more likely to generalize both to other situations and to other behaviors.

Self-monitoring has been reported in the literature for more than thirty years and has been found effective in changing a wide range of specific unproductive behaviors with a diverse population of students, including students with ADHD, learning disabilities, emotional and behavior disorders, autism spectrum disorder, and in both general education and special education settings (Breire & Simonsen, 2011; Falkenberg & Barbetta, 2013; Fitzpatrick & Knowlton, 2009; Moore, Anderson, Glassenbury, Lang, & Didden, 2013; Sheffield & Waller, 2010). When developing a self-monitoring plan, we encourage teachers initially to use only social reinforcement to

FIGURE 10.5
COUNTOON

Count your hand raising   Count your talk outs

celebrate the student's success. Students can show their data to a predetermined valued other. Our experience suggests that it is seldom necessary to include additional reinforcement. Although self-monitoring can provide excellent results by itself, as noted in later sections of this chapter, it can be effectively combined with strategies for self-instruction, self-evaluation, and self-reinforcement.

Procedures

When instructing students in counting their own behavior, the first step is to ensure that the students can accurately describe the behavior. You can teach this skill by asking them to demonstrate the desirable and undesirable behaviors. The second step is to develop a method for tallying the data. In most cases, you will want to initially tally the data and show the results to the students. In some cases, simply seeing these results may be enough to encourage students to significantly reduce their behavior. In other cases, students may indicate they believe the data are incorrect. In this case, students may be particularly motivated to tally the behavior. Several years ago, one of us was working with a seventh-grade student who was talking out without being called on twenty-seven times in a class period. When the student saw these data (based on three days of teacher coding), he stated vehemently that the data were inaccurate and informed the teacher that he would prove this. He did not call out again for the next ten days. In fact, the teacher decided to meet with him and encourage him to become more involved in class discussions, but to simply raise his hand prior to responding.

Especially when working with young children, it is helpful to start by incorporating a visual display of the behavior being counted. A *countoon* can serve this purpose. A countoon includes a picture of the behavior being tallied and a place for the student to mark a tally each time the behavior occurs. Figure 10.5 is an example of a countoon used to help a student become aware of how often he talks out without raising his hand. For older students, it is often more effective to have them simply record their data on a 3-by-5-inch card or notebook paper.

The third step involves implementing the self-monitoring. We suggest you select a relatively short period of time and one that is developmentally appropriate. For example, a second-grade child might monitor talking out for two 10-minute periods, whereas a sophomore might monitor this behavior for a class period. The fourth step involves the student meeting with an adult to assess the progress the student is making. This might simply involve meeting for thirty seconds and having the student report the results. It might also include graphing the results so the student can actually see the progress he or she is making. This type of record keeping can be a significant motivator and reinforcer for many students as it provides a clear demonstration of their improvement.

The fifth step involves providing students with some form of reinforcement. In most cases, verbal praise from the teacher will be adequate because students obtain personal satisfaction from the sense of competence and empowerment associated with improving a behavior. In some cases, this verbal praise may need to be expanded to include other significant adults. In other situations, it may be necessary to provide the student with a specific activity reinforcement to increase the likelihood that the behavior at issue will improve.

Although most students will accurately monitor their own behavior after these five steps have been accomplished, some students may require more assistance. If additional support is needed, start by reinforcing the student for obtaining data that closely match those you or another adult coder obtain. As they learn to record their behavior accurately, reinforcement for accuracy can be replaced by rewarding decreases in the unproductive behavior.

Another procedure involves initially having the student receive reinforcement for improving behaviors that are being recorded by an adult. As the student's behavior improves, she can be allowed to monitor her own behavior and receive designated reinforcements for improved behavior. Finally, the reinforcement is withdrawn and the student simply receives praise for controlling and recording her behavior. Rafferty (2010) provides an engaging discussion of methods for teaching students how to effectively self-monitor.

The following case studies provide examples of how an intern and a young teacher implemented these methods in a first- and seventh-grade classroom.

Pause & Consider 10.4

Select a student who is behaving in a manner that disrupts his own learning and that of his classmates. Select a specific behavior that it would benefit the student and others to have altered. Collect baseline data on this behavior. Next, develop a format that allows the student to self-monitor this behavior. If possible, meet with the student, discuss the self-monitoring, and have the student self-monitor the behavior for a designated time frame. Meet with the student to discuss the results of the self-monitoring. We strongly encourage you to share your work with several colleagues or classmates. Even if you are not able to actually implement your plan, share your decisions and forms with your peers.

Case Study: Elementary

This study was conducted by a first-grade teacher who was confronted with a particularly difficult class in an inner-city school. Most of her students had been late registrants for kindergarten and, because of overcrowding, had spent their kindergarten experience in an isolated room in the district's administrative office building. Consequently, the students arrived in first grade having had few interactions with older schoolchildren. In addition, their kindergarten class had started nearly a month late, and they had had several teachers during the year. They were also generally a particularly immature, unskilled group, with more than half living in single-parent homes. The following material is taken directly from the teacher's report of her study.

Many distractions within my classroom were caused by students who were not attending to my instructions. My students needed to learn to sit and work without talking, opening and closing their desks, walking to someone else's desk to talk, and so on. I decided to attempt a self-management technique, or a countoon, with my class. This group wanted to please me and be viewed positively by me, but they lacked the inner skills to control their behavior on their own. This technique would let them demonstrate their competence at monitoring and controlling their own behavior. I do not think they were aware of the extent of their off-task behavior. Some children have difficulty controlling their behavior without assistance from an external cue. When children are involved in collecting data on their own behavior, sometimes this act can provide enough external structure to produce dramatic results.

I started my study by collecting baseline data on five children in my group, to determine their off-task frequency. I chose five students who varied greatly in ability, behavior, background, and so forth. I recorded their behavior during seatwork three times at ten-minute intervals, and the results [Figure 10.6] showed that during a ten-minute interval, the frequency of off-task behavior averaged eight per student. I then individually informed the students that I had collected data on them and then I informed the entire group of my results without mentioning the names of the students I had observed. I tried to emphasize to them that I did not think they realized the extent of their off-task behavior. I told them I was going to set up a program whereby they would keep track of their own off-task behavior, with the hope that it would help them to increase their time on task. We then discussed, modeled, and role-played those behaviors which would be considered off-task behaviors. This behavior included talking out loud either to oneself or to a peer; doing any other activity than what I had instructed them to do; getting up from one's desk to wander around the room; or making distracting noises, either by mouth or by opening desks, rolling pencils, and so on. They realized that if they needed assistance from me, they should raise their hand, and because I have a free bathroom-break policy, they could use the bathroom if it was necessary. Students need to be taught how to record their own behavior, and so I spent considerable time in this phase of the project. Also, with students involved in collecting their behavioral data, the time I had to spend on behavior monitoring was lessened. Self-monitoring ideally helps create an internalized source of control, and changes in behavior associated with this approach are expected to be more likely to generalize both to other situations and to other behaviors.

After we had sufficiently practiced and discussed behaviors, I gave each student a countoon. My countoon had a picture of desirable behavior on it, showing an animal deeply involved in doing a worksheet. Originally I had decided to involve only five students in the study, but after a discussion with the class, I decided to give every student a countoon. My results in this study will include only the five students described in the baseline data, but I really felt that it could not hurt to have all the students involved, making them all aware of their talking and behaviors, and keeping track of their off-task times. I then instructed the students when to keep track of their behavior. Each box on the countoon was for tallying off-task behavior. After each ten-minute interval, we circled the box with a crayon so that the children could keep track of how many intervals we had done. In that way, if a student had no off-task behavior, the box was still circled to show that we had kept track of that interval. I ran the program for six days, monitoring behavior twice each day for ten minutes each. Generally this monitoring was done during math or science, in which we were working on booklets about baby animals. Several of the children almost completely quit off-task behaviors. They were excited about the program and requested that we keep track of behaviors more often. I think they really did feel they had some control over their situation. Because the results were favorable, they also received praise and points for a class

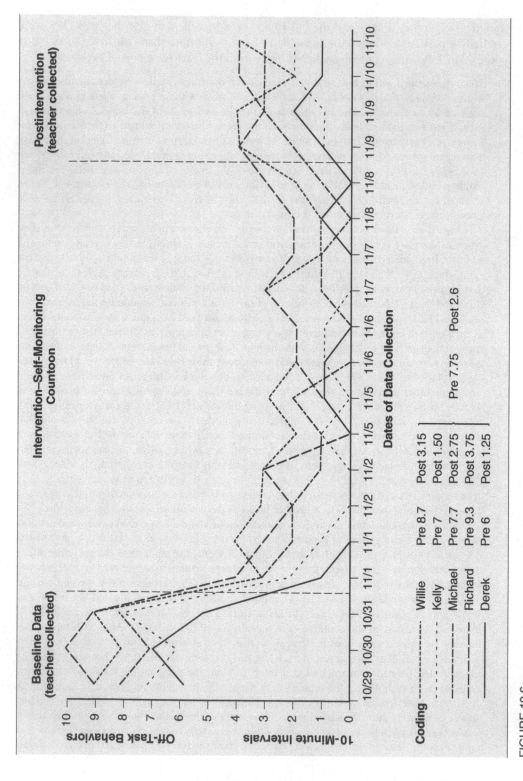

FIGURE 10.6
ELEMENTARY CLASSROOM SELF-MONITORING PROGRAM

party, and the atmosphere in the room improved significantly during use of the countoons. The five students for whom I had collected baseline data went from an average of eight off-task behaviors to less than three per ten-minute interval during data collection. When I did the follow-up data collection, without their knowledge, they did regress a little, and were a little more talkative, but overall their off-task behavior was cut in half.

Case Study: Middle School

The following study was implemented by a teacher concerned about the behavior of a student in her last-period study hall. She implemented the study with no assistance and as a project for a course in classroom management.

BACKGROUND

Samuel (not the student's real name) is a retained seventh grader who has been identified as seriously emotionally disturbed. He has been receiving special education services since the first grade and has attended the same school district since kindergarten. He is functioning in the average range on both the verbal and performance scales of the WISC. His academic achievement does not match his potential. The Woodcock-Johnson Psycho-Educational Battery shows an average knowledge score, low average reading, a mild deficiency in math, and a severe deficiency in written language.

Further testing shows that he has a weakness in visual motor tasks and in visual memory. He gains most of his knowledge auditorily as he has good hearing comprehension. Language is adequate for his age. He expresses his thoughts and ideas appropriately and has good conversational skills. He placed below the fifth percentile on the Piers-Harris Children Self-Concept Scale.

CLASSROOM PROBLEM

Samuel is in my ninth-period study hall. He has an extremely high percentage of off-task behavior, which includes talking out, drawing pictures on his assignments, distracting other students, and just generally wasting time. I have tried a variety of interventions through the quarter, including changing his seat, having him stay after school, and glaring at him. The problem continued despite these efforts.

INTERVENTION PLAN

For three days I collected baseline data on Samuel and three other students in the same study hall. The results showed that the three control students were off task an average of 6.7 percent during the 40-minute period, whereas Samuel was off task 50 percent during the same period.

I showed the graph to Samuel and told him of my concerns with his off-task behavior. We had a good informative talk, part of which was a pep talk to let him know of his cognitive and academic strengths. I told him about the class I was taking and the project I wanted to involve him in. I showed Samuel a self-monitoring form I wanted him to use for the next five days. He was to watch the clock (without having it interfere with his work) and put a plus at the end of each five-minute period that he was on task or a zero if he was off task. I would be doing the same thing, and at the end of the period we would discreetly compare our results. No one in the class would know about our project. This was extremely important to Samuel. The self-monitoring recording sheet was to be kept in his folder each day, and he would stay after school to discuss it.

RESULTS

The first day of self-monitoring Samuel was extremely aware of the clock; it really did distract him. We discussed this after class. The next day was better, and he continued to improve the third day. During the fourth and fifth days, he had only one incident each of off-task behavior. Our comparison data were very similar. A lot of verbal feedback went along with the plan, and Samuel responded well to the praise and individual attention.

The next week Samuel knew I was taking data on him but he was no longer self-monitoring. We discussed his behavior every day and looked at the data. The results [Figure 10.7] were very gratifying to us both. Samuel actually maintained an average of 5 percent of off-task behavior the third week. He was getting an incredible amount of homework done and was receiving positive feedback from his other classroom teachers as well.

AFTERTHOUGHTS

I am really excited about the results of this project. With it I was able to do in three weeks what I thought was impossible. I thought Samuel was my most difficult student and really did not think I would get dramatic results using this approach.

Self-Instruction

Although self-monitoring can provide excellent results by itself, it is often combined with strategies such as self-instruction, self-evaluation, and self-reinforcement (DiGangi & Maag, 1992). Similar to self-monitoring, self-instruction methods involve students in becoming more aware of their own behavior and learning to take responsibility for their behavior. These strategies are most commonly used to assist students who have difficulty controlling or expressing their emotions appropriately. Partially because these students have had numerous failure experiences

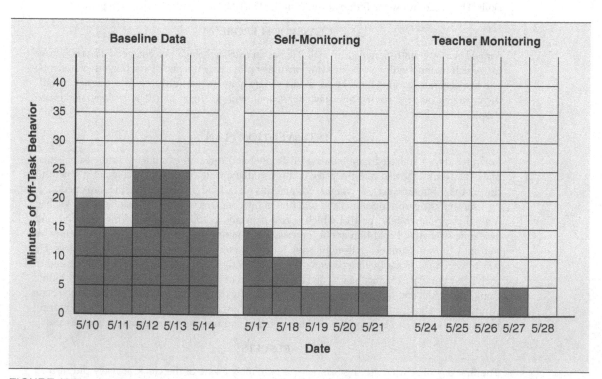

FIGURE 10.7
SELF-MONITORING PROJECT WITH SEVENTH-GRADE STUDENT WITH DISABILITIES

and lack confidence, they frequently respond with intense emotions when confronted by situations their peers handle quite comfortably.

One approach to helping students respond more effectively to frustration and stress is to teach them to give themselves verbal instructions that cue them to behave more appropriately. This approach is based on the concept that students who have attention-deficit hyperactivity disorder (ADHD) or who are labeled *impulsive* are less skilled than normal youngsters in using silent speech to monitor their behavior. When faced with a difficult problem, successful students might say to themselves, "Okay, I'll try it once more and if I can't do it, I'll ask the teacher for help." Students with behavior problems may lack the ability to monitor their behavior in this manner and, therefore, respond actively and unproductively when faced with a frustrating task. These students may also use negative silent speech. A student might say to himself, "I'm stupid and I can't do this." This internalized statement compounds the student's problem and intensifies negative emotions.

We can help students change their behavior by teaching them to make positive, thoughtful internalized statements in place of the negative, unproductive statements they often make. Research indicates that this approach can be successful in reducing students' anxiety, improving academic performance of behavior-problem students, reducing rule-breaking behavior, and responding less aggressively to oral taunts from peers.

The basic procedure involves teaching students to use silent statements to control their behavior more effectively. We can do so by providing students with specific statements they can make when confronted with specific, frustrating situations. Students who become frustrated when attempting to solve math problems can be taught to say, "I can do this if I slow down and relax. What I have to do is first add the two numbers on the right. . . ." Similarly, a student who becomes aggressive when losing a game can be taught to say, "Okay, I didn't win this time, but that's all right. The other students will like me better if I give the ball back and go to the end of the line." We can help students develop these skills by providing them with opportunities to practice self-instruction under our supervision and on tasks they can already perform. While working on fairly simple tasks, students may initially be encouraged to make statements we provide. The students can then be asked to repeat these statements on their own. Next, they can be asked to whisper the words as they complete the task. Finally, they can be encouraged to say the words to themselves. If you are interested in examining these procedures in more detail, you can find additional practical suggestions in *Behavior Management: Positive Applications for Teachers* (6th ed.) (Zirpoli, 2012), and *Behavior Management: A Practical Approach for Educators* (10th ed.) (Shea & Bauer, 2012).

A similar approach focuses both on self-talk and developing alternative methods for dealing with problem situations. Students can be asked to role-play situations in which they consistently respond in an inappropriate manner. As the role-playing unfolds, students are encouraged to replace unproductive self-talk with statements that help them control their behavior. Likewise, the teacher and other students provide alternative methods of responding. For example, a boy who consistently responds angrily to not being chosen immediately at recess may be asked to replace self-talk such as "Nobody likes me" or "I'm no good" with statements such as "I'll be chosen soon. I guess some students are a little better at this game than I am." The student may also be taught how to send an I-message in a class meeting to express his hurt over not being chosen or given help in learning positive social skills that make it more likely that peers will choose him to be on their team.

Another approach to self-instruction involves teaching students skills in self-relaxation. This can be accomplished by the teacher or counselor initially providing direct instruction in how to relax. Students can learn to relax by relaxing and tensing different muscle groups. More simple and less obvious methods involve teaching youngsters yogalike breathing skills or asking them to let their bodies go limp and imagine a warm, relaxing substance flowing through their bodies. After students have learned relaxation methods, they can be encouraged to use these methods when they experience feelings of tension or anxiety. We can assist acting-out students by providing them with cues when it is necessary for them to use relaxation procedures. We can reinforce use of these skills by using them with the entire class before or following tension-producing or exciting activities, such as tests, recesses, or assemblies.

Relaxation can also be used in association with cognitive rehearsal (a strategy similar to self-talk). Before beginning an activity that might evoke anxiety or inappropriate student behavior, we can have students close their eyes and go into a relaxed state. We then describe the upcoming situation and the desired student behavior. Before an assembly, we might have the students envision themselves walking quietly to the gymnasium, sitting quietly during the performance, and applauding at appropriate times. When students visually practice behavior in a relaxed state before performing the activity, their behavior can be significantly improved.

A final approach to self-instruction is positive affirmations. During her first year of teaching, our daughter shared the following approach she used with a very diverse fourth–fifth blended classroom. She wrote:

> At the beginning of each day I had 24 strips in the basket that had one of two compliments on them. The students would take the strips and tape them to their desk for the day. Throughout the day as a stretch break, I would have them stand up and I would say one of the two compliments out loud. Whoever had chosen that compliment strip would then say it out loud. I made sure to put an equal number of compliments so half the class would say one and half would say another. On occasion, if I did not have time to type and print the slips before the students arrived in the morning, I would write them on the board, and the students would get to choose which one they wanted to use for that day.
>
> As an extension to this daily activity, we frequently discussed self-esteem and compliments. We talked about the importance of loving and caring for yourself and not letting what others say bother you. It was my hope to instill enough positive self-reinforcement into the students that when they are faced with challenges, they will feel comfortable and confident in what they do.
>
> Before any major test, but especially the state tests, we would gather on the carpet and get in a big huddle. I would say a phrase and they would repeat it after me. For example, I would make a statement such as, "I am good at taking tests," "I know how to do my best on tests," etc., and the class would repeat that saying. (S. Rudzek, personal correspondence, November 2005)

Social Skills Training

Any student who has persistent or serious behavior problems (including such nonaggressive behaviors as infrequent contact with peers and infrequent participation in class discussions) is demonstrating a lack of certain social skills. Therefore, a responsible reaction to serious and persistent unproductive student behavior will almost always include efforts to assist the student in developing behaviors to replace those that have been the cause of concern. Like self-monitoring, social skills training has been shown effective in assisting students with a wide range of special needs, including anxiety disorders (Kearny, Pawlukewicz, & Guardino, 2014), emotional and behavior disorders (Luczynski & Hanley, 2013; van Vugt, Dekovic, Prinzie, Stams, & Asscher, 2013), and autism spectrum disorder (Wang, Parrila, & Cui, 2013).

Social skills training is currently being used in many formats. First, school staff may implement social skills training in all classrooms as part of a schoolwide plan to provide students with prosocial skills. Second, some schools have grade-level teams develop social skills specifically needed by their students. Third, many schools provide small-group social skills instruction for students who appear to be lacking specific social skills. Finally, many school staffs use social skills training to provide individual children with one-on-one assistance in developing skills they will need to more effectively respond to specific situations in which they have experienced serious or persistent behavior problems. Materials at the end of the chapter offer suggestions for the first three types of social skills training. This section provides the reader with information on effectively developing an individualized approach to teaching social skills. We are focusing on this area because we have found it to be the most effective and because it is almost always needed for students who are having serious behavior problems.

Implementing a Social Skills Lesson

The first step in implementing a social skills lesson is to determine what skills the student(s) need to develop. This is best determined by completing a classroom behavior assessment. As discussed earlier, this involves carefully examining the actual situation in which the behavior problems are occurring and determining the specific skills the student(s) failed to demonstrate that led to the problem. For example, a student who becomes angry and hits others when rejected at joining a game may be lacking skill in how to ask to be involved in the game or how to play the game in a way that does not alienate her peers. Similarly, a student who fails to obey reasonable adult requests may lack skills in accepting corrections or directions. As discussed earlier in this chapter, it is imperative to select specific behaviors that can be observed. It is not possible to use social skills training to change a student's bad attitude. The student may, however, be taught more positive and productive methods for responding to corrections from adults.

The remainder of this section presents a generic lesson outline (Figure 10.8) that can be used with either an individual student or group of students at any age level. As seen in Figure 10.8, the process begins with helping the student to identify the ineffective behavior. This is similar to the second step in problem solving (Figure 9.2). Next, the student is helped to identify the reason for changing the behavior. This is similar to the third step in problem solving, in which the student evaluates the behavior. This is critical because if the student cannot present and accept a reason for changing the behavior, there is almost no possibility that the behavior change will have any long-lasting effect.

The next step is similar to the problem-solving step of making a plan. The difference is that in social skills training, an effort is made to specify in detail the components of the new behavior. For example, if the student is going to use positive self-talk or relaxation when confronted by a negative peer comment, the specific steps of these behaviors will need to be described.

© Scott Masear

"The apples are from my best students, and the stress ball is from the class clown."

**FIGURE 10.8
SOCIAL SKILLS
LESSON DESIGN**

Describe the inappropriate behavior _____
_____
_____

Rationale for a new behavior _____
_____

Describe the appropriate behavior _____
_____

Skill components of the new behavior _____
1. _____
2. _____
3. _____
4. _____
5. _____
6. _____

Model demonstration example _____
_____
_____
_____
_____

Student practice example _____
_____
_____
_____

Natural setting practice (if different than initial practice) _____
_____
_____

Independent practice assignment _____
_____
_____

Individual or group reinforcement strategy _____
_____
_____

After the positive alternative behavior has been identified and broken into its component parts, the next step is for the adult to demonstrate or model the behavior. This can often involve the student playing the role of the other person involved (a teacher, peer, etc.) while the person assisting the student in developing the new skill will role-play the student using the new skill.

The obvious next step is to have the student practice the behavior. This will initially be done in the classroom, office, or wherever the training is taking place. The next step is crucial and is often left out. It is absolutely essential to ensure that the student has an opportunity to practice the new behavior in a setting similar to that in which she will have to use it. For example, if the problem occurs on the playground with peers, the new behavior would need to be practiced on the playground with peers.

The next step is to assign the student the task of attempting the new skill and reporting back to the group or individual adult regarding what happened when he used the new skills. Often, this will involve the student determining a specific situation in which he will attempt to use the new skill.

The final step involves determining whether the student will earn a reward for using the new skills. We once worked with a teacher who taught a developmentally delayed first grader a series of new behaviors and had the class mark on the board each time they saw the student using his skill of the week. Initially, when five incidents of use were reported, the entire class was provided with a brief activity reinforcement. Later, this was changed to require ten reports of his using the skill before the class earned its reward.

In many ways, social skills training is simply a more detailed, specific form of implementing problem solving with students. There will be many instances in which you use the problem-solving approach presented in the previous chapter and decide to expand it by actually demonstrating the new behavior (developed as the plan) for the student, having the student role-play the behavior, and giving the student an assignment to use the new behavior and report the results. We have found that many students need this additional structure and teaching in order to understand and feel comfortable attempting the behaviors in their plans.

Case Study: A Sixth-Grade Boy Involved in Aggressive Behavior

Several years ago, one of us was asked to work with a student named Warren (a fictitious name), who was experiencing rather violent behavior. As part of a functional assessment, the author and Warren's counselor were standing near the edge of the playground observing Warren involved in a game of tag in which players were *safe* as long as they were touching a piece of playground equipment. Warren had cleverly trapped one of the players hanging on the monkey bars and was simply waiting for the student to fall so he could be tagged out. As Warren waited, a student playing another game called Warren's name, and he turned to respond. Unfortunately, it was at this moment that the trapped student's arms gave out and he came crashing down, inadvertently hitting Warren on the side of the head. Warren went into a rage. He pushed the much smaller student to the ground and was preparing to kick him in the stomach when he appeared to suddenly realize what he was doing and tried to stop. He fell backward, barely grazing the student who was crouched on the ground.

At this point, the counselor and author intervened. We checked on the student who had been pushed and then asked Warren to join us in the counselor's office. The author initially helped Warren analyze what had occurred and his involvement in the incident. When asked how else he might have responded when he had become angry, Warren's only response was, "I should not kick him." At this point, the author decided to complete a social skills lesson following the outline in Figure 10.8. Warren was assisted in understanding why the behavior was a problem and was involved in generating alternative methods for handling his anger. Then he was asked to role-play the behavior with the author taking Warren's role. Following this, the situation was repeated with Warren using his new strategies. The next step involved practicing the strategy on the playground and finally practicing it with the student who was pushed and the several other students involved. At this point, the principal, who had contacted Warren's mother for permission to have the author work with him, decided not to suspend Warren. Her rationale was that no student had been hurt and the work that would need to be accomplished prior to Warren's returning to school had been accomplished.

As discussed in Chapters 8 and 9, we strongly believe it is critical, following any violent outburst or major interpersonal conflict, that the parties involved work on developing alternative strategies for responding in the situation and negotiate and practice this strategy together. This type of reentry is essential for developing social and emotional skills and building bridges back to the school community of support in which the problem occurred.

Case Study: A Fifth Grader Who Was Running Away from School

One of us recently worked with a girl named Acasia (a fictitious name) who had a history of becoming upset and leaving the school grounds. School personnel had written several contracts to encourage her to remain at school, but the behavior continued at the same rate. While observing Acasia as part of a classroom behavior assessment, the author noticed that when she became upset, two girls in her classroom were quite adept at helping her to calm herself. They provided assistance, made supportive comments, and in one instance even stroked her back. When asked about this, the teacher reported that Acasia frequently responded well to these interventions but that she had more difficulty when not seated by one of these students. When asked why Acasia was not consistently placed by one of these students, the teacher noted that she rotated her cooperative groups. Further assessment indicated that no clear pattern regarding events was associated with Acasia's becoming so distraught that she left the classroom. It was, therefore, decided to make the environmental modification of having Acasia placed in a group with one of the two students who provided such caring support.

The next step involved providing Acasia with alternative strategies for responding to her anxieties and frustrations. Because Acasia played soccer, it was determined that she and her counselor would develop a yellow and a red card. The yellow card would include a series of strategies Acasia could use if she needed to calm herself and remain in the room. The red card included four options for Acasia on those occasions when she felt she could not remain in the room. These cards were laminated so Acasia could place a check in the box in front of the strategy she was planning to use and later erase it and reuse the card. Acasia was then provided with opportunities to practice each of the strategies and to visit and develop a plan for what she would do in those areas listed on her red card.

The results indicated that while Acasia continued to become upset in class, she frequently used her strategy and did not leave the school grounds for the remainder of the year. Observations and discussions continued in order to determine any causative classroom factors associated with her anxiety and frustration.

PAUSE & CONSIDER 10.5

Select a student you are teaching or observing who displays difficulties in being successful in a specific social setting. In order to practice how you might work with this student, complete Figure 10.8 for a situation in which you might need to assist this student. Share this with several colleagues or classmates. If you are currently working with this student, meet with him or her and carry out this social skills training lesson. Again, share the results of this work with your colleagues.

Developing Contracts

Behavior contracts are considered another evidence-based intervention with a wide range of applications across student age groups and disabilities (Akin-Little, Little, Bray, & Kehle, 2009; Volpe & Fabriano, 2013). A behavior contract is an agreement between two or more parties indicating the manner in which one or more of the parties will behave in a given situation. Behavior contracts provide a specific, often written, agreement designating the exact behavior(s) each individual will display. Furthermore, behavior contracts frequently indicate the specific reinforcement or consequence associated with performing or failing to perform the behaviors listed in the contract. Behavior contracting provides students with a structure that encourages them to perform behaviors they have been unable to display consistently without some form of external, concrete payoff or negative consequences.

Because behavior contracts help a student commit to demonstrating a specific behavior, it is important to realize that this behavior must already exist in the student's repertoire. For example, a contract would be unfair and unsuccessful if it asked a student to, when being taunted, walk away or send an I-message when the student has not demonstrated skill in these methods. In this case, it would first be necessary to assist the student in developing specific skills for responding in these situations before developing a contract to encourage him or her to use these new skills.

Negotiating a Contract

Unless a contract is sensitively and concisely negotiated, you may find that it fails regardless of how effectively it is written. Contracts should ideally result from a teacher–student discussion in which you help the student describe a behavior, decide that it needs to be changed, and suggest a plan for making the change. When students are unable to devise a plan or when previous plans have failed to bring about the desired change, you can help them develop a more structured behavior contract.

An effective behavior contract includes a statement about each of these variables:

1. What is the contract's goal? Why has the contract been developed?
2. What specific behaviors must the student perform in order to receive the rewards or incur the agreed-on consequences?
3. What reinforcers or consequences will be employed?
4. What are the time dimensions?
5. Who will monitor the behavior and how will it be monitored?
6. How often and with whom will the contract be evaluated?

Behavior contracts can be presented to students in many forms. Short-term contracts with elementary school students need not include each of these six components. The important factor is that the student clearly understands the contract. Figure 10.9 is an example of a form you can use to present a contract to a primary grade student, and Figure 10.10 is a form for intermediate grade students. Figure 10.11 is a format we have used successfully with high school students. Though it is not necessary to develop a written contract, putting an agreement in writing tends to clarify each party's responsibilities. Whenever possible, students should be involved in determining the terms of a contract. Teachers should also help students express their feelings about a contract. Finally, once the contract has been negotiated, the student should be able to paraphrase clearly the conditions outlined in the contract.

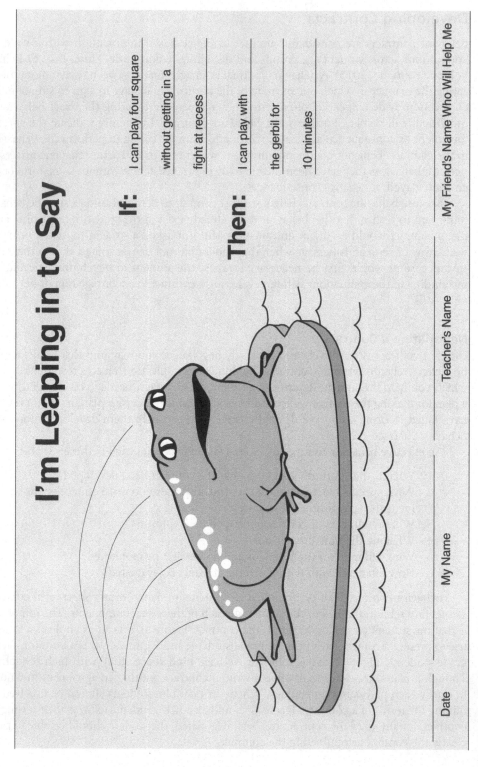

I'm Leaping in to Say

If:
I can play four square

without getting in a

fight at recess

Then:
I can play with

the gerbil for

10 minutes

_____   _____   _____   _____
Date   My Name   Teacher's Name   My Friend's Name Who Will Help Me

FIGURE 10.9
PRIMARY GRADE CONTRACT

FIGURE 10.10
UPPER
ELEMENTARY
OR MIDDLE
SCHOOL
CONTRACT

I've got the POWER!

Matt

IS GREAT!
NOT LATE!

I WILL be on time to P.E. class, 11:00 a.m. sharp FOR 5 consecutive days. Allan
HAS OFFERED TO HELP BY walking to class with Matt. MY TEACHER WILL HELP
BY telling me how well I did each day I am on time.
TO CELEBRATE I WILL BE ABLE TO be a student helper in P.E. and referee/umpire
activities for 2 days.

_____   _____
DATE   GREAT PERSON

                                              _____
                                              HELPER

                                              _____
                                              TEACHER

FIGURE 10.11
HIGH
SCHOOL
CONTRACT

Reason for contract _____

_____

Responsible behavior _____

_____

If I _____ for _____ ,
                 (responsible behavior)   (amount of time)

I will _____
                              (positive consequence)

If I do not _____ , I will _____
                 (responsible behavior)   (negative consequence)

                              Teacher signature _____

                              Student signature _____

                              Date _____

Case Study: Elementary School

One of us was asked to provide a school staff with assistance in working with a third-grade student who was highly disruptive and was viewed as having both an attention deficit disorder (ADD) and possible serious emotional problems. The boy frequently wandered around the class, disrupted other students, made quacking sounds, and banged his head on the desk. When asked when these behaviors occurred most frequently, the teacher indicated that the wandering and bothering of others occurred primarily in the morning, whereas the more unusual sounds and head banging occurred immediately following lunch. When asked in what activities the student was engaged when these behaviors occurred, the teacher indicated that it was most often during math in the morning and language arts after lunch. The teacher noted that the student, who believed he was very gifted in all academic areas, was very skilled in math but almost equally unskilled in language arts.

The author ate lunch with the student and, given the statement about the boy's potential behavior and possible mental health problems, was somewhat surprised to observe that he demonstrated at least average social skills. Following lunch, the author visited the boy's classroom and observed a language arts lesson lasting approximately forty minutes. The student was seated in a row of three students near the back right of the classroom. The students had been given several worksheets with alphabetizing activities, and the student began to complete the task. After less than five minutes, the student became agitated and began to make a quacking sound. The author moved over and commented that this seemed like an unusual behavior, especially coming from someone as intelligent as the student had indicated he was. The boy stated that he was bored with the work. It appeared, however, that the student was finding the work rather challenging. He had completed only several lines, whereas most of his classmates had completed a section involving nearly five times the amount of work he had finished. The author noted that it appeared the work was difficult for the student, who responded by emphatically repeating that he was smart. The author informed the student that even smart people found some types of work more difficult than others. For example, the author noted, even though he was probably considered by some people to be quite intelligent, he found drawing very difficult. The student asked the author to draw an elephant. The student found the attempt quite amusing and affirmed that the author was indeed not very good at drawing. The author then noted that even smart people needed to improve on some things and asked the student why it might be useful to improve on alphabetizing. The student responded by providing a number of activities that could be enhanced by rapid alphabetizing. The author noted that because this was a useful tool, perhaps the student could improve on it even if he was not one of students who found the work quite easy. The student agreed to attempt five problems and signal the author when he was done. In only a few minutes, the student signaled. After reinforcing the student's efforts, the author suggested the student set another goal. The student selected two sections and worked until the teacher signaled for attention. As the teacher worked with the class to correct the worksheets, the student raised his hand to answer nine consecutive questions (something the teacher later stated she had not seen all year). When he was not called on to answer the ninth question, the student became agitated and began to make a quacking sound. At this point, the author suggested that he and the student be allowed to meet briefly in the counselor's office. During the initial stages of the conference, the student indicated that he found all his schoolwork boring and that this was the reason for the behavior that got him in trouble. As the discussion continued, the student was able to distinguish between academic work that was too difficult and that which was not challenging. He acknowledged that his disruptive behaviors were used to remove him from the work and agreed to use several new strategies.

Figure 10.12 presents the plan or contract developed with this student. Interestingly, it was initially suggested that the student focus on having one morning or afternoon without using one of his disruptive behaviors to respond to his frustration. The student continued to argue that because he was so smart, he would go for two weeks. The author finally gave in and allowed what he knew was much too long a time frame to be written into the agreement. The student went eight days without emitting a quacking sound or disturbing another student during math. When he failed to meet his goal the ninth day, the student stated that he would go an additional

**FIGURE 10.12
A CONTRACT
TO MODIFY
THE
ENVIRONMENT**

PLAN FOR _____ DEVELOPED BY _____ AND
                    VERN JONES ON _____

Problem: Sounds and Silly Behavior during Class

Reason for Sounds and Silly Behavior

1) too easy
2) too hard
3) had to sit too long
4) attention from peers

	If work is too easy/boring	If work is too hard	If the student is restless
Plan	1) Finish your work and then get free time	1) Set a goal and then take a break when goal is reached	1) Squeeze your body
	2) Ask for harder work	2) Stretch, walk to a designated spot	2) Stretch your legs but don't bother others
		3) Solution Desk	3) Walk to Solution Desk

Why it is a good idea to do the above plan:
1) So I don't bother others or break rules
2) To stay out of trouble
3) So I can learn more and act more mature

Reward:

_____ agrees that if this plan is followed for two weeks, a mechanical pencil and a letter from Vern Jones will be the rewards.

Signatures:

_____   _____
            Student   Teacher

_____   _____
          Vern Jones   Parent

Remember, _____, even smart people need to learn skills! We all have strengths and weaknesses.

Plan beginning date: _____   Plan ending date: _____

ten days. Even though he was encouraged to go two days to complete his ten, the student insisted on the higher standard. The student reached his goal and continued for several more weeks.

In most cases, a classroom behavior assessment will suggest not only social skills needed by the student but also significant modifications in the classroom setting. In this case, an important aspect of the intervention involved providing the student with alternative math work and using goal setting and a computer in language arts. Although the student's behavior was not always what the teacher would have preferred, he did virtually eliminate the two behaviors that were of most concern. As the year progressed, further interventions were needed to assist this student in monitoring other inappropriate behaviors and replacing them with more acceptable options. This involved self-monitoring and social skills training.

Travel Cards (Check-In/Check-Out Interventions) as a Form of Contract

Travel cards, often called daily behavior report cards, have been used for more than thirty years (Jones, 1980). This form of behavior contract, now often referred to as Check, Connect, and Expect (CCE) or Check-In/Check-Out, is frequently used as a Tier 2 intervention in schools implementing the PBIS program. Implementing this approach involves determining specific behaviors you wish students to display and providing students with periodic feedback (e.g., every half hour, class period, etc.) regarding their use of these behaviors. The results are often shared with an adult mentor within the building and with parents. Student scores on this form are sometimes associated with a reinforcement or loss of privilege. Vannest, Burke, Sauber, Davis, and Davis (2011) have written a very thoughtful and useful article on the use of this method, and a recent book presents even more detailed information on this intervention (Volpe & Fabriano, 2013). Figure 10.13 presents an example of a travel card that might be used with a middle school student.

One obvious concern related to the use of the approach is there is no assurance the classroom environment has been assessed to determine whether changes need to be made in order to assist the student in experiencing academic and behavioral success. If this step is missed, it is analogous to having a student who is struggling in a subject being told he or she must work harder and will receive increased feedback, will be more clearly reinforced or punished for his or her work, but will not receive any individualized instructional support. This approach, as commonly used, assumes the student has the skills to behave as desired by the teacher and is involved in a classroom environment that supports the student using these skills. Therefore, a daily behavior report card should be used only after some form of classroom behavior assessment (see Figures 7.1 and 7.2) has been completed and necessary adjustments have been made.

One additional benefit to the Check-In/Check-Out intervention is that it may be used to involve the student and other adults in a collaborative skill development process. Sebag (2010) outlines the self-advocacy behavior management (SABM) model where the student is involved in identifying areas of his or her behavior that need to be improved, works with an adult to develop strategies for behaving more responsibly, receives ongoing feedback on his or her behavior, and meets with an adult to discuss this feedback. Even here, however, we would recommend that the student and others be involved in providing insight on how the classroom environment might be changed to better ensure it is culturally sensitive and meets the student's academic and personal/social needs.

Selecting Reinforcement Procedures and Consequences

Just as problem-solving approaches should be implemented before using behavioristic methods, you should begin your contractual interventions with the least restrictive and most natural types

FIGURE 10.13
TRAVEL CARD

Student _____   Grade _____   Date _____

Desired Behaviors

Period	On Time to Class	Brought Necessary Materials	Handed in Assignment	Obeyed Class Rules	Participated in Class	Teacher's Signature
1						
2						
3						
4						
5						
6						
7						

of reinforcers and consequences. Figure 10.14 presents a hierarchic approach to reinforcements and consequences used in behavior contracts. You should start by trying to use contractual agreements based on the types of reinforcers at the bottom of the hierarchy. Only if these fail should you develop a contract based on higher-level reinforcers.

Teachers should initially use social and activity reinforcers that are a normal part of the school day and are available to all students. Token reinforcers are also very much a part of school life since we frequently provide token reinforcers in the form of grades, points earned on tests, or

FIGURE 10.14
BEHAVIOR
CONTRACT
HIERARCHY

Tangible reinforcement
Social, token, and activity reinforcement and response cost
Curtailment of activity
Social, token, and activity reinforcement
Activity reinforcement
Social reinforcement

promises to provide a reward if students behave appropriately for a designated period. Furthermore, since research supports the benefits of focusing on positive behavior whenever possible, consequences in the form of curtailments of activities should be used only after natural reinforcers have proved ineffective in helping a student change a behavior. Curtailment of activity is listed as more desirable than implementing a response cost (the procedure of taking away points or other rewards when a student misbehaves) primarily because response cost is a complex intervention that unless very effectively implemented can evoke negative emotions and behaviors. It should not be used unless simpler interventions fail. Curtailment of activity is placed before tangible reinforcers because restricting a student's behavior by requiring the student to stay in from recess in order to practice a behavior is a more logical intervention than is providing the student with candy for completing a task. Furthermore, the use of tangible reinforcements suggests that the desired behavior is not valuable enough to warrant being displayed without a tangible payoff. This statement has subtle but potentially powerful negative consequences for long-term improvement in the student's behavior.

In the next section, procedures for implementing the first four lower-level types of consequences listed in Figure 10.14 are presented. Because few teachers use response cost or tangible reinforcers, these consequences are not discussed. If you are interested in these, refer to the references at the end of this chapter.

Social Reinforcement.   Social reinforcement refers to behaviors of other people that tend to increase the frequency with which a student emits a behavior. If a smile from you is followed by a student's continuing to work on an assignment, the smile may have served as a social reinforcer. Similarly, if a child consistently returns to a group after having been chased away, the attention inherent in being chased may be viewed as a social reinforcer. Social reinforcement can be used either as a spontaneous teaching strategy for influencing students' behaviors or as a reinforcement in a contract.

When systematically using social reinforcement as a method for improving students' behaviors, you should develop skill in employing a wide range of reinforcers, learn how to give reinforcement, and learn when to use it. Among the many types of social reinforcement, the most obvious involves saying positive things to students. When giving social reinforcement, be careful not to use the same word or phrase constantly. Students appreciate different, creative expressions of encouragement and appreciation. Figure 10.15 lists social reinforcers that can be used at a variety of grade levels.

When using social reinforcement, be especially careful to reinforce specific behaviors. Teachers often use words such as *great, good, nice,* and *super* when referring to students' work or behavior. Unfortunately, this form of reinforcement does not provide the student with specific information on which aspect of behavior is being reinforced. Therefore, it is important to describe the behavior being praised. Rather than saying, "That's nice, Bill," when Bill listens attentively, you might say, "Bill, I appreciate the way you are listening to the discussion. It should help you do well on the assignment."

Although teachers must develop an extensive repertoire of social reinforcers and learn to praise specific behavior, it is perhaps even more important to learn when to reinforce students. The reason social reinforcement is frequently ineffective in changing students' behavior is that it is so often ineffectively used by teachers. Several studies have demonstrated that teachers often dispense social reinforcement at the wrong time. Walker, Hops, and Fiegenbaum (1976) observed the interactions between five acting-out children and their teachers. The results showed that though the five teachers praised the acting-out child's appropriate behavior about once every

FIGURE 10.15
SOCIAL
REINFORCERS

Praising Words and Phrases	
Good	That's really nice
That's right	Wow
Excellent	Keep up the good work
That's clever	Terrific
Good job	Beautiful
Good thinking	I appreciate your help
That shows a great deal of work	Now you've got the hang of it
You really pay attention	Now you've figured it out
You should show this to your father	Very interesting
Show Grandma your picture	That's an interesting point
That was very kind of you	Nice going
Thank you; I'm pleased with that	You make it look easy
Great	What neat work
I like that	I like the way you got started on your
Exactly	homework
That's interesting	
Expressions	*Social Contact*
Smiling	Walking together
Winking	Sitting together
Nodding head up and down	Eating lunch together
Looking interested	Playing games together
Laughing	Shaking hands
	Working after school together

hour, they attended to inappropriate behavior nine times each hour. Similarly, Walker and Buckley (1973) observed an elementary classroom teacher and found that although 82 percent of the teacher's interactions with successful students followed appropriate behavior, 89 percent of the responses to students with behavior problems followed inappropriate behavior. Taken together, these and other studies suggest that we should attempt to increase our use of positive social reinforcement and make this reinforcement contingent on acceptable student behavior. When a student who demonstrates a high rate of irresponsible behavior demonstrates a positive behavior, we should try to reinforce this behavior immediately.

Social reinforcement is usually viewed as a spontaneous approach to changing students' behaviors, but it can also be incorporated into behavior contracts. Because social reinforcement is inexpensive, readily available, and easy to give, we should attempt to incorporate this type of reinforcement into our initial contracts with a student. There are several approaches to take when using social reinforcement in this manner. A contract can be developed in which a student receives social reinforcement from peers, the teacher, an administrator, or a custodian as a consequence for making a desirable behavior change. We can also involve parents in providing social reinforcement when their child behaves appropriately at school. A contract might indicate that if a student reaches a specified behavioral or academic goal, we will send a note home to the parent and the parents will respond by providing the student with a designated number of specific positive statements.

FIGURE 10.16
ACTIVITY
REINFORCERS

Being group leader	Performing for parents
Going first	Taking a class pet home for the
Running errands	weekend
Collecting materials	Leading the songs
Helping clean up	Being team captain
Getting to sit where he or she wants to	Reading to the principal
Taking care of class pets	Seeing a video
Leading the flag salute	Getting to read a new book
Telling a joke to the class	Seeing a movie
Being in a skit	Listening to music
Having a party	Playing games in class
Making puppets and a puppet show	Writing on chalkboard: white or
Doing artwork related to studies	colored chalk
Spending special time with the teacher	Playing with magnets or other science
Choosing the game for recess	equipment
Earning an extra or longer recess	Solving codes and other puzzles
Choosing songs to sing	Performing before a group: sing a
Working a puzzle	song; tell a poem or riddle; do a
Drawing, painting, coloring, working	dance, stunt, or trick
with clay, and so on	Choosing a book to review for class
Choosing group activity	Selecting topic for group to discuss
Taking a good note home to a parent	Reading to a friend
(arrange a reward with the	Reading with a friend
parent)	Receiving the right to tutor a classmate
Visiting another class	who needs help
Helping the teacher	Getting free time in the library
Taking a ten-minute break to choose	Being asked what he or she would like
a game and play with a friend,	to do
quietly	Listening to audio recording or radio
Building with construction materials	with earphones
Getting time to read aloud	Planning a class trip or project
Playing a short game: Tic-Tac-Toe, easy	Working in the school office
puzzles, connect the dots	Working in the school library

Activity Reinforcement. Because social reinforcement is not a powerful enough reinforcer to bring about prompt or significant change for all students, we need to use other forms of reinforcers. Involvement in various preferred activities is another natural and easily dispensable reward for desirable behavior.

The first step in activity reinforcement is to list activities that students find reinforcing. Students enjoy being involved in this process and often offer creative and surprising ideas. Figure 10.16 lists classroom activity reinforcers. The second step is to develop a contract stipulating what the student must do to obtain the activity reinforcer. Whenever activity reinforcers are used, they should be paired with social reinforcement so that the social reinforcement may gradually acquire some of the reinforcing properties associated with the activity reinforcer.

The problem of delayed gratification (the student becomes frustrated while waiting for the reinforcement) that is frequently associated with activity reinforcers can be dealt with by gradually extending the time a student must wait in order to receive the award. When first implementing a contract, the student can be informed that she can be involved in the activity immediately after performing the desired behavior. As the student's behavior improves, she can be informed that she will have to demonstrate increasingly appropriate behavior as well as wait longer before the reinforcement is provided.

An interesting approach to using activity reinforcers involves allowing students to take home school equipment they find particularly interesting. A student's contract might indicate that he can take an audio recording or video home for two days if he meets the conditions of the contract. Although this type of reinforcement may at first glance appear to be a tangible reinforcer, the student uses the borrowed item but neither consumes nor acquires permanent possession of the reinforcer. The reinforcer provides the student with an opportunity to reinforce himself by participation in an activity involving school property. In essence, the student is involved in the reinforcing event at home rather than at school. Another way to involve the home is to allow the student to select as an activity reinforcer spending time with someone at home in an activity selected by the student.

Social, Token, and Activity Reinforcement.   Token reinforcement refers to a system in which students receive immediate reinforcement in the form of a checkmark, chip, or other tangible item that can be traded in for reinforcement at a future time.

There are five basic steps to implementing a token reinforcement system in the classroom. Before introducing a token system, you should determine specifically how each step will be accomplished.

1. Determine when and with whom the program should be implemented. You might choose to employ a token system with two students whose behavior during seatwork continues to be extremely disruptive despite your attempts at instigating other types of interventions.
2. Select the specific behaviors to be reinforced. When working with an individual student, you might state that the student will receive a token for every two minutes she is in her seat, not talking to peers, and working on the assignment. When working with several students or the entire class, it is desirable to generate a list of behaviors (the classroom rules may be suitable) that will be reinforced.
3. Decide when tokens will be dispensed. When working with a seriously acting-out student, you will usually have to dispense the tokens whenever the desired behavior occurs. As the student begins to gain control of his behavior, you and the student can tally the occurrence of the desired behaviors (the tallies serve as tokens), and this total can be recorded or actual tokens can be given to the student at the end of a designated time. When employing a token system with an entire class, you may choose to use either a random or a set time frame for reinforcement. In using a random reinforcement system, you move around the room or work with a group, and present tokens to students who are behaving appropriately. Though you must be careful not to overlook students or unfairly focus on some students, a random reinforcement schedule is easy to administer and maintains acceptable behavior at a high rate. If you use a set time frame reinforcement, you simply tell the class that every time they meet the behavior criteria for a designated number of minutes, they will receive a tally. When they reach a certain number of tallies, they will earn a group reinforcement such as five minutes to chat quietly, extra recess time, and so on.

4. Determine how to dispense tokens. There are numerous methods for dispensing tokens. Each student involved in the program can have a card taped on the corner of her or his desk, and you can make a mark on the card each time the student displays the desired behavior. When working with young children, teachers occasionally choose to place a can or box on each participant's desk so that tokens can be dropped into the container when the student behaves appropriately. When working with students who change classes or teachers during the day, a travel card (Figure 10.13) can be used. The desired behaviors are written on the card, and at the end of each period, the student receives a check for each desired behavior displayed throughout the period. As discussed earlier, travel cards tend not to be effective unless (1) they are paired with other interventions, including careful analysis of the classroom environments to determine what changes can be made to support the student following classroom behavior standards, (2) there is close attention paid to the accuracy of the feedback, and (3) ongoing discussions with an adult are associated with the student's behavior as recorded on the form.

5. Select a procedure for recording tokens earned. Because most token systems involve earning tokens over a specified period, it is necessary to devise a system for recording the number of tokens each student has accumulated. Likewise, because students can trade tokens in for preferred activities, a record of tokens spent and remaining must be kept.

Curtailment of Activity.   Activity curtailment refers to any situation in which inappropriate student behavior is followed by removal of a desired activity.

1 Students should understand the behaviors that will lead to curtailment of activity, what activities will be curtailed, and how long the restriction will be effective.

2 Rules on curtailment of activity should be used consistently and fairly. If fighting on the playground is followed by sitting out the next recess or having a suspension, this restriction should be applied to all students in every instance. You should also consider, however, whether playground facilities and activities support positive play, whether rules are clearly understood, and whether students have been taught methods for resolving inevitable playground conflicts.

3 Be aware of cases in which curtailment of activity provides a more desirable alternative than the activity itself. Students may behave inappropriately in order to receive what appears to you to be a punishment but the student views as a relatively positive consequence. A student may dawdle at work in order to stay in from recess, either because recess is perceived as undesirable or the time in the room is viewed as pleasant. Continuing to use a curtailment of activity in this situation might prevent the student from dealing with important social skills deficits that are causing problems on the playground.

4 Present the negative consequences in a nonpunitive, interested manner. Communicate sincere regret that the student must miss an activity. This attitude helps students accept responsibility for their behavior rather than project the blame onto you. Punishment should never be presented in anger, which only encourages the student to feel persecuted and to transfer the blame to you.

5 When presenting a curtailment of activity to a student, always inform the student which specific behavior(s) were responsible for bringing about the undesirable consequence. The student should also be reminded of the desirable behaviors that could prevent the consequences.

6   When limiting an activity, inform the student what must be done to be able to participate again. For example, you might inform a student that she can return to the class
activity after quietly completing a problem-solving form.

7   Whenever possible, a curtailment of activity should logically relate to the behavior that
necessitated the punishment. If a child could not play on the playground without fighting, it is logical that she should miss recess until she can develop a plan for interacting
more appropriately with peers. It is not logical, though, to have students stay after
school and write sentences because they fought on the playground.

8   Activity curtailment should, whenever possible, be consolidated with activities
aimed at helping the student develop new skills that will prevent repeated performance of the undesirable behavior. Therefore, when being excluded from a desired
activity, the student should be involved in examining the problem and developing a
plan for solving it.

9   Collect data to help determine whether the curtailment of activity is effective in reducing the undesirable behavior or increasing the desired behavior. Because punishment in
any form may have numerous negative side effects, it should be discontinued if data
indicate that it is ineffective.

Group Contracts

A group contract involves a situation in which the entire group earns a reward or loses previously awarded points or privileges contingent on the entire group's behaving in a desired manner. Some writers define group contracts as including programs in which an individual
student's behavior is reinforced by a desired activity for the entire group, but this technique is
more accurately labeled an activity reinforcer. The Good Behavior Game discussed earlier is
perhaps the best-known and most effectively researched example of a group contract. As you
recall, this involves keeping a record of the group's behavior—often by letters to a publicly
displayed word when students work quietly or demonstrate other behaviors that enhance the
learning environment.

   A high school band teacher who wished to reduce talking during class presented us with an
excellent example of a group contract in a high school setting. In this situation, the students
decided that a consequence and reward would help them change their behavior. They agreed to
give up one minute of the break following band class for every minute they were off task. They
also decided that if they could meet the goal of less than thirty minutes off task in eight days they
would have a potluck lunch as a reward. Data indicated that off-task behavior reduced from 17.2
minutes to 2.88 minutes per class period.

Pause & Consider 10.6

Select a student or class with whom you have worked in developing more responsible behavior but you are not satisfied with the results. For this individual or group, develop a contract
to assist them in behaving in a manner that more consistently enhances their learning and
that of others. Share this contract with a colleague or classmate and incorporate the feedback
prior to implementing it. If you are able to implement the contract, record the data and share
the data with your colleague(s) or classmate(s).

Developing Behavior Change Plans for Students who Demonstrate Serious or Persistent Disruptive Behaviors
For an interactive review of methods for developing an individual plan for a student who is struggling to behave responsibly in class, click here in the Pearson etext.

ENHANCEDetext *interactive case study*

Developing a Classroom Behavior Change Plan

Increasingly schools have teams whose responsibility is to design behavior change plans for students who continue to struggle with their behavior. With an increasing number of schools (more than 15,000) implementing Schoolwide Positive Behavior Support (SWPBS) programs, these teams are designed to support a teacher when a student reaches Tier 2 (Carter et al., 2012) or Tier 3 (Debman, Pas, & Bradshaw, 2012) in this model. Tier 2 interventions are often only minimally individualized and include such programs as a Check-In/Check-Out intervention (Campbell & Anderson, 2012; Mitchell, Stormont, & Gage, 2011), some form of social skills group (Gresham, Sugai, & Horner, 2001; Lane et al., 2003), or the Behavior Education Program (Crone, Hawken, & Horner, 2010). Excellent materials such as Randy Sprick's book *Behavioral Response to Intervention: Creating a Continuum of Problem Solving and Support* (Sprick, Booher, & Garrison, 2009) have been developed to support school staff in establishing effective intervention teams associated with the SWPBS approach.

Based on our experience, it may take some time for a student to move to the level where he is staffed by a team involved in developing a Tier 3 intervention. In addition, our experience and that of many educators and consultants with whom we work indicate that Tier 2 and 3 interventions usually do not focus primarily on classroom factors. Therefore, we believe it is helpful for individual teachers, sometimes supported by teams of teachers, and perhaps a counselor or school psychologist, to conduct a classroom behavior assessment and develop a classroom behavior intervention plan. When other educators are supporting a teacher, these groups of educators would function in much the same way that Teacher Assistance Teams (Chalfant & Pysh, 1989) or Intervention Assistance Teams (Burns, 1999) functioned when they were popular in the 1980s and 1990s. These teams, composed primarily of teachers, focus on providing the classroom teacher with methods to implement in the classroom in order to assist the student in meeting his or her needs without using the behaviors that have been violating others' rights and harming the student's ability to learn. The development of such plans can be expedited by using a structured approach to staffing. An effective process includes these six steps:

1. Conduct a classroom behavior assessment.
2. Determine changes that need to be made in the classroom environment in order to support the student.
3. Determine the strategies to be used to assist the student in developing new behavioral skills.
4. Assign responsibility to staff for implementing each intervention.
5. Determine the data to be collected for the purpose of assessing the effectiveness of interventions.
6. Set a date to review the program.

It is suggested that you focus on no more than two behaviors and develop no more than three interventions for each behavior.

Figure 10.17 presents the form we use to record a classroom behavior intervention plan. This form can be used by an individual teacher to summarize the behavior change plan developed based on a classroom behavior assessment or by a team supporting a teacher in developing a plan. The column labeled "Is Community Intervention Needed?" is the team's prompt to determine whether they believe interventions outside of the school setting may need to be an important component of this plan. If this is the case, rather than allocate time to discuss this matter, someone is assigned to develop this portion of the intervention. This prevents a long discussion of events over which the school staff has limited control while still acknowledging the importance of out-of-school factors and ensuring someone with skills in this area is assigned to consider these factors. The numbers in parentheses near the top of the form indicate the number of minutes allocated to that task. In Figure 10.17, the items followed by an "e" refer to a classroom environment modification that can be made to assist the student in demonstrating the desired behavior (e.g., replacing the behavior you wish to change with a behavior that is more helpful for the student and other students in the classroom). The "b" notation refers to the behavior change intervention (e.g., self-monitoring) you will use to assist the student in demonstrating this improved behavior. The bottom of the sheet lists those individuals who have agreed to be involved in implementing one or more of the interventions, and the mentor is the person who agrees to monitor both the implementation of and the progress achieved in using the plan. Figure 10.18 presents a behavior intervention plan developed for the third-grade boy whose behavior was discussed earlier in the chapter (Figure 10.4). Figure 10.19 presents a plan a team developed to support a fifth-grade boy. In this case, the trigger for the student's failure to follow adult requests was being asked to do something the student did not wish to do, and the trigger event for aggressive verbal or nonverbal playground behavior was being called out or otherwise not obtaining the result he desired during a playground game.

Monitor agrees to check within seven days to determine how the program is progressing.

FIGURE 10.17 DEVELOPING A BEHAVIOR INTERVENTION PLAN

(3) Is Community Intervention Needed?	(7) Behavior to Change	(12) Intervention Plan	(5) Person Responsible	(3) Evaluation Data
	1.	1e		
	2.	1b		
		2e		
		2b		
Teacher	Teacher		Teacher (Monitor)	
Dated	Counselor		Principal	

Roles: Presenter
Recorder
Facilitator
Timer

Signed

Monitor agrees to check within seven days to determine how the program is working.

PAUSE & CONSIDER 10.7

If you are currently teaching, we encourage you to select a student who needs assistance in behaving responsibly. Work with several teachers, and possibly one other staff member such as a counselor, and, using the format from Figure 10.17, develop a behavior intervention plan. Implement this plan and meet to review the results.

If you are not able to work with a building team, we encourage you to form a group with your classmates. Select a student one of your group members is observing or working with who engages in a high rate of behaviors that are having a negative influence on his or her learning or that of others. Complete a classroom behavior assessment on this student (Figure 10.3) to determine what factors may be influencing behavior. Next, using the format in Figure 10.16, develop a behavior intervention plan that could help this student develop and choose to use more responsible behaviors.

---

(3) Is Community Intervention Needed?	(7) Behavior to Change	(12) Intervention Plan	(5) Person Responsible	(3) Evaluation Data
NA	1. Touching other students' material and hitting or pushing them	1e Provide more behavior-specific positive reinforcement for the desired behavior	Teacher	Counting the number of times the behavior(s) occur
		2e Provide academic choices related to content the student finds difficult	Teacher	
		3e Select positive peer helpers/ models for group work	Teacher	
		4e Provide group tasks at which the student can be successful	Teacher	
		5e Teach peers to give I-messages	Teacher	
		6e Provide early support when frustration appears	Teacher	
		7e Use a solution desk rather than removal from class	Teacher	
		1b Help student develop a strategy for coping with frustration (implement a social skill lesson to teach this)	Teacher	
		2b Use self-monitoring and reinforce improvement	Teacher	

FIGURE 10.18   (*continued*)
CLASSROOM BEHAVIOR PLAN FOR A THIRD-GRADE BOY

Teacher	Teacher	Teacher (Monitor)
Dated	Counselor	Principal

Roles: Presenter

Recorder
Facilitator
Timer

Signed

FIGURE 10.18
(CONTINUED)

Behavior to Change	Intervention	Person Responsible	Data
Failure to follow adult requests	1e Ensure that Jason is prepared to hear the directions prior to presenting them. This might involve adults providing a nonverbal cue when they are about to make a request.	Teacher	Tally of following or failing to follow adult requests
	2e Work with Jason to determine the manner in which he is most comfortable having adults provide requests.	Teacher and/or counselor	
	3e Have Jason select one or more peers from whom he can seek assistance if he needs help understanding directions given by an adult.	Teacher and/or counselor	
	4e Teach students to ignore Jason when he responds to teacher requests in a disruptive manner.	Teacher and/or counselor	
	5e Provide Jason with frequent private verbal reinforcement for using his new skills.	Teacher and other selected adults	
	6e Provide a space for Jason to remove himself when he feels he is becoming upset and cannot follow reasonable adult requests. Teach him methods for relaxing himself in these situations.	Teacher and counselor	
	1b Work with Jason to develop methods for responding quickly and appropriately to adult requests. This will involve social skills training on statements he could make and/or his nonverbal behavior in responding.	Counselor	
	2b Have Jason keep a record of the times he is asked to follow an adult request and his response.	Teacher and/or counselor	

(continued)

FIGURE 10.19
BEHAVIOR INTERVENTION PLAN FOR JASON

Behavior to Change	Intervention	Person Responsible	Data
Negative verbal and nonverbal interactions with peers during recess	1e Select students who can be taught how to invite Jason to join them in playground games.	Teacher and/or counselor	Record of days when Jason has a serious peer conflict at recess
	2e Help other students learn how to reinforce Jason for positive participation in playground activities.	Teacher and/or counselor	
	3e Have Jason inform a designated playground assistant each time he selects a playground activity.	Counselor or principal	
	4e Meet with Jason to select an adult to whom he will report how well he does each day during recess.	Counselor or principal	
	1b Have Jason select two or three games he may choose to join during recess and teach him skills for playing these games—including understanding the rules.	Counselor	
	2b Provide Jason with skills for requesting to join a game during recess.	Counselor	
	3b Teach Jason methods for responding verbally and nonverbally (e.g., walking away, moving to play another game, taking some quiet time) when he becomes frustrated with what is happening during a game.	Counselor	

FIGURE 10.19
(CONTINUED)

Case Study: High School

Several years ago, one of us was asked to work with a sophomore who had been referred to the office fifty-one times during the first semester. Late in the semester, he had been withdrawn from his first- and second-period classes and assigned to sit in the office. Interestingly, the student was allowed to sit in the most comfortable chair available in the main school office. In addition, this chair provided him with a wonderful view of the school commons and availability to a wide range of interesting conversations.

When the author asked to see data regarding behavioral patterns, he was informed that the vice principal simply had a list of the number of referrals. No record indicated the time of day, antecedent events, or even a clear statement regarding the type of misbehavior. After interviewing the student and his counselor, it became apparent that the student had considerable difficulty early in the school day. Interestingly, his two most difficult classes were during those periods, and the student frequently arrived at school somewhat agitated by conflicts with his mother. In addition, it became clear that most of the student's discipline referrals were associated with his aggressive responses to teachers correcting his behavior. The pattern that emerged was a student who, when he experienced academic frustration, became active and off-task, was given commands by teachers, and responded to these in what would be termed a rude and sometimes aggressive manner.

The first decision was to modify the student's schedule so that he began the day with a teacher he liked and trusted and in whose subject he experienced moderate success. This was followed by a reading lab and then a subject with which the student had experienced some difficulty. This was followed by a physical education course in which the student was very successful. This pattern continued throughout the day. Next, the student was asked how he would like teachers to make requests that he modify his behavior. He agreed that teachers needed to do this and provided the counselor with several written statements that he felt represented respectful ways of requesting that he alter his behavior. All of the student's teachers attended a brief meeting to practice these less confrontational requests and agreed to use them when addressing the student. Finally, the student was provided with individual social skills training in responding to comments or requests made by teachers.

The results were rewarding. The student had only three office referrals during his spring semester. Although his work continued to be slightly below what appeared to be his potential, he did pass all second-semester courses.

SUMMARY

Even though teachers are not responsible for developing a series of sophisticated behavior change interventions, there are a variety of effective, efficient methods teachers can implement that can dramatically influence a student's behavior. As teachers work with an increasing number of students who struggle to act in ways that support their learning and that of their classmates, teachers will benefit from being able to implement a variety of these methods.

Teachers will increasingly be asked to document both student behavior problems and their interventions aimed at altering student behavior. This chapter provides methods for accomplishing this important task. The chapter describes methods for helping students become involved in data collection and become more aware of and responsible for their own behaviors through self-monitoring and the development of important school-related social skills. Methods for involving students in setting goals and becoming more aware of the consequences associated with their behavior through the use of contracts have also been explored.

Experience and research with teachers (Jones, 1991) who have implemented these methods show that nearly 80 percent find they can use them in their classrooms and that the methods

are effective approximately 80 percent of the time. Although these teachers realize that the quality of their proactive classroom management and instruction are their major responsibilities, they find that using the methods discussed in Chapters 8 through 10 can have a major positive impact on individual students' behaviors. Furthermore, they find that their ability to help these students is professionally rewarding and has a positive impact on the behavior and learning of all students.

IMPLEMENTATION ACTIVITIES

ACTIVITY 10.1

Assessing Your Classroom Management Behavior

Think of a student whose behavior has created a problem for himself or for the class. With this student in mind, complete the interventions form in Figure 10.1 and then answer the following questions:

1. What changes could you make in your classroom that would create a more clearly structured, inviting environment for this student?
2. What interventions have you already attempted to assist this student in behaving more responsibly?

3. Based on the data you have collected, how effective do you believe you have been in assisting this student?

ACTIVITY 10.2

Assessing Your Prereferral Interventions

For the student whose behavior is detrimental to himself or herself or the class, complete the form in Figure 10.2 by (1) circling the interventions you have implemented (or, if you are observing in a class, the interventions you have seen implemented), (2) placing a box around those that you believe would assist the student and you would like to try, and (3) placing an X through the number in front of those interventions that do not seem appropriate or feasible given your teaching situation. After you have completed this, sit down with one or more teachers or students in your college class and share what you have done and the items you selected as possible new interventions.

ACTIVITY 10.3

Completing a Classroom Behavior Assessment

Think of a student whose behavior has created a problem for himself or herself or for the class. With this student in mind, complete the form in Figure 10.3 and then respond to the following items:

1. List as many specific things as possible that you learned about this student's unproductive behavior.
2. Based on these discoveries, what changes could you make in the classroom to assist this student in behaving more responsibly?

The following activities can help you improve your skills in data collection and the use of behavioral interventions.

ACTIVITY 10.4

Clearly Defining Students' Behavior

For each of the five adjectives listed in the left column, write three specific observable student behaviors that might be displayed by a student described by the adjective.

General Descriptor	Specific Behavioral Descriptor
Angry	1. 2. 3.
Unmotivated	1. 2. 3.
Hyperactive	1. 2. 3.
Uncooperative	1. 2. 3.
Inept	1. 2. 3.

ACTIVITY 10.5

Developing a Social Skills Lesson

Think of a student who appears to lack skill in one or more social skills such as accepting critical feedback, following directions, or responding to comments from peers. Use Figure 10.8 to develop a social skills lesson for this student.

ACTIVITY 10.6

Using Self-Monitoring

Think of a student who exhibits a specific behavior that is negatively impacting his or her learning or the learning of others, such as talking out or making unusual sounds. Develop a self-monitoring form that would help this student count his or her own behavior. Also determine a format for recording the results. Present these to a colleague and have this person provide you with feedback.

ACTIVITY 10.7

Implementing and Assessing a Behavioristic Intervention

Select an individual student's behavior that is detrimental to the student as well as the class. Describe the behavior in behavioral terms, collect baseline data for at least two 30-minute periods, and graph the results.

Next, select one of the procedures for developing a contract described in this chapter and develop a written contract with the student.

Implement the contract for five days. Collect and record data during all times when the contract is in effect.

At the end of five days, discuss the results with the student and determine whether to (1) continue the contract, (2) alter the contract by requiring improved behavior while reducing the reinforcement or employing a reinforcer lower on the hierarchy, or (3) discontinue the contract.

Finally, complete these statements:

The student's behavior . . .
At the end of the five days, the student said . . .
I was surprised that . . .
I was pleased that . . .

ACTIVITY 10.8

Developing a Positive Behavior Change Plan

For the student for whom you completed Figure 10.3, develop a behavior intervention plan and present it using Figure 10.16.

RECOMMENDED READING

Alberto, P., & Troutman, A. (2006). *Applied behavior analysis for teachers* (7th ed.). Upper Saddle River, NJ: Merrill/Prentice Hall.

Cartledge, G., & Fellows Milburn, J. (1995). *Teaching social skills to children and youth: Innovative approaches.* Boston, MA: Allyn & Bacon.

Chandler, L., & Dahlquist, C. (2006). *Functional assessment: Strategies to prevent and remediate challenging behavior in school settings.* Upper Saddle River, NJ: Merrill/Prentice Hall.

Clark, O., & Hull, W. (1999). *Good thinking: Helping students to reframe their thinking patterns.* Longmont, CO: Sopris West.

Fister, S., & Kemp, K. (1995). *The one-minute skill builder: Improving student social skills.* Longmont, CO: Sopris West.

Gable, R., Sugai, G., Lewis, T., Nelson, J., Cheney, D., Safran, S., & Safran, J. (1998). *Individual and systemic approaches to collaboration and consultation.* Reston, VA: Council for Children with Behavioral Disorders.

Goldstein, A., Harootunian, B., & Conoley, J. (1994). *Student aggression: Prevention, management, and replacement.* New York, NY: Guilford Press.

House, S. (2003). *Behavior intervention manual.* Columbia, MO: Hawthorne Educational Services.

Jones, V., Dohrn, E., & Dunn, C. (2004). *Creating effective programs for students with emotional and behavior disorders: Interdisciplinary approaches for adding meaning and hope to behavior change interventions.* Boston, MA: Allyn & Bacon.

Jones, V., Greenwood, S., & Dunn, C. (in press). *Prevention & intervention for students with emotional and behavior problems: A continuum of services.* Boston, MA: Pearson.

Kaplan, J., & Carter, J. (1995). *Beyond behavior modification: A cognitive-behavioral approach to behavior management in schools.* Austin, TX: Pro-Ed.

Kauffman, J. (2001). *Characteristics of emotional and behavioral disorders of children and youth* (7th ed.). Upper Saddle River, NJ: Merrill/Prentice Hall.

Kennedy, C. (2000). When reinforcers for problem behavior are not readily apparent: Extending functional assessments to complex problem behaviors. *Journal of Positive Behavior Interventions, 2,* 195–201.

Kerr, M., & Nelson, M. (2002). *Strategies for addressing behavior problems in the classroom.* Upper Saddle River, NJ: Merrill/Prentice Hall.

Lane, K., & Beebe-Frankenberger, M. (2004). *School-based interventions.* Columbia, MO: Hawthorne Educational Services.

Martin, G., & Pear, J. (1996). *Behavior modification: What it is and how to do it.* Upper Saddle River, NJ: Prentice Hall.

McConnell, K., Patton, J., & Polloway, E. (2000). *Behavioral intervention planning: Completing a functional behavioral assessment and developing a behavioral intervention plan.* Austin, TX: Pro-Ed.

Nichols, P. (1999). *Clear thinking: Talking back to whispering shadows.* Iowa City, IA: River Lights.

Nichols, P., & Shaw, M. (1999). *Whispering shadows: Think clearly and claim your personal power.* Iowa City, IA: River Lights.

O'Connor, K., & Stichter, J. (2011). Using problem solving frameworks to address challenging behavior of students with high-functioning autism and/or Asperger Syndrome. *Beyond Behavior, 20,* 11–24.

O'Neill, R., Horner, R., Albin, R., Sprague, J., Storey, K., & Newton, S. (1997). *Functional assessment and program development for problem behavior: A practical handbook* (2nd ed.). Grove, CA: Brooks/Cole.

Sheridan, S. (1995). *The tough kid social skills book.* Longmont, CO: Sopris West.

Smith, B., & Sugai, G. (2000). A self-management functional assessment-based behavior support plan for a middle school student with EBD. *Journal of Positive Behavioral Support, 2,* 208–217.

Sprick, R., & Howard, L. (1995). *The teacher's encyclopedia of behavior management: 100 problems/500 plans, for grades K–9.* Longmont, CO: Sopris West.

Todd, A., Horner, R., & Sugai, G. (1999). Effects of self-monitoring and self-recruited praise on problem behavior, academic engagement and work completion in a typical classroom. *Journal of Positive Behavior Intervention, 1,* 66–76.

Walker, H., Ramsey, E., & Gresham, F. (2003). *Antisocial behavior in schools: Evidence-based practices.* Pacific Grove, CA: Brooks/Cole.

Walker, H., & Sprague, J. (1999). Longitudinal research and functional behavioral assessment issues. *Behavioral Disorders, 24,* 335–337.

Walker, J., Shea, T., & Bauer, A. (2007). *Behavior management: A practical approach for educators* (9th ed.). Upper Saddle River, NJ: Merrill/Prentice Hall.

Watson, S., & Steege, M. (2003). *Conducting school-based functional behavior assessments.* Columbia, MO: Hawthorne Educational Services.

Workman, E. (1995). *Teaching behavioral self-control to students* (2nd ed.). Austin, TX: Pro-Ed.

POSSIBLE PROCEDURES FOR COMMON AREAS IN AN ELEMENTARY SCHOOL

PLAYGROUND

GOAL: Students will play safely in all games and on all equipment.

Responsible Playground Behavior

**1. Rough play is not allowed on the playground.
**2. When the bell rings, students are to stop what they are doing and should line up quickly.
**3. Students will settle differences peacefully using "Stop/Think/Plan" (STP).
4. Students will show respect for others and follow instructions given by staff.
5. Students will stay outside in the morning before school, and during all recesses, unless they have a "pass."
6. Students will stay out of ditches, off hills, and away from puddles and mud.
7. Students will leave rocks, bark, sticks, and other dangerous objects alone.
8. Students will play only on playground areas, not in courtyard, grassy areas, or bushes.
9. Students will show pride in their school by keeping the building and grounds free of litter.
10. Students will take turns on equipment (e.g., twenty-five swings on swings).
11. Students will not chew gum or candy on playground.
12. Students will leave knives and other unsafe objects at home along with radios, audio players, hard balls, and toys.
13. Students in grades K–3 will stay off monkey bars until the first bell during the lunch hour.
14. Students will leave the playground immediately after school and not return until after 3:00 p.m.
15. During school, students will not leave the playground for any reason without a note signed by their parent and/or their teacher and the principal. The note must be shown to the person on duty.

RESTROOMS

GOAL: The restrooms at Lincoln Elementary will be clean and safe.

Responsible Restroom Behavior

**1. Use restrooms during recess, before the last bell rings.
**2. If restrooms must be used during class, students must have a restroom pass.
**3. Use restrooms appropriately and leave them clean.
4. Put toilet paper in the toilet. Put all other paper in the garbage can.
5. Flush the toilet.
6. Leave stalls unlocked after use.
7. Wash your hands.

HALLS

GOAL: The halls and breezeways will be a safe and quiet environment where people interact with courtesy and respect.

Responsible Hallway Behavior

**1.   Students will move safely through the hallways.

**2.   Normal speaking voices will be used in the hallway. (If someone is too far away to hear, move close enough to speak in a normal voice.)

3.   During class time, students must have a signed pass to be in the halls.

4.   Everyone will be treated with respect.

5.   If an adult asks to speak with you, stop and talk with that person.

6.   If an adult requests that you correct a behavior, do what the adult asks you to do.

7.   No student should be in the halls prior to 8:15 a.m. unless escorted by an adult.

8.   Students should go directly home after dismissal from class.

LUNCHROOM

GOAL: The lunch line and lunch area will be a safe and clean environment where people interact with courtesy and respect.

Responsible Cafeteria Behavior

Coming to Lunch and Lunch Line

**1.   While in line, students will keep hands, feet, and objects to themselves.

**2.   Students will use quiet voices in the lunch line.

3.   Students are to be escorted to the lunch area in two lines: "buyers and bringers." Buyers' line is closest to the learning center. Bringers' line is closest to the lunch tables.

4.   Monitors will walk quietly and stand in the lunch monitor line.

5.   Students will buy lunch, milk, or snacks before they sit down.

Lunch Area Procedures

**1.   Students will use quiet voices when talking.

**2.   Students will keep hands, feet, and objects to themselves.

3.   Students will stay in their seats and raise their hands to get help.

4.   Students will eat quietly and use good manners.

5.   Students will walk in the lunch area.

6.   Everyone will treat others with respect.

Dismissal

**1.   Students will clean up their own area.

**2.   When the bell rings, the supervisor will check each table and dismiss students if the table and floor are reasonably clean.

3.   Slow eaters will be reassigned to overflow tables.

4.   When dismissed, students will walk quietly to the north door of the cafeteria.

5.   Lunch boxes will be left in the playground area where classes line up.

6.   Students are to remain on the playground unless they are given a pass to enter the building.

ASSEMBLIES

GOAL: Lincoln students will demonstrate respectful behavior during assemblies by listening, participating, and following directions.

Responsible Assembly Behavior

**1. When the leader goes to the microphone and says, "May I have your attention please," stop talking and look at the person at the microphone.

**2. Listen carefully.

3. Students will follow their teacher's directions regarding where to sit.

4. Everyone will wait quietly for the program to begin. Quiet talking will be allowed until the program is ready to begin.

5. Communicate with the performers with your eyes and ears.

6. Never boo, whistle, yell, or put someone down.

7. At the end of the program, the leader will conclude the assembly by thanking the performers.

8. Students will remain seated until the teacher gives them the signal to stand and follow the teacher from the assembly area.

Note: Items marked with ** indicate expectations that students must understand fully and immediately.

Source: Responsibility and Discipline Manual: Elementary Sample, by R. Sprick. Eugene, OR: Safe & Civil Schools, Inc. Reprinted with permission.

RECOMMENDATIONS FOR SECONDARY-LEVEL TEACHERS REGARDING THE TEACHING OF LIMITED-ENGLISH-PROFICIENT STUDENTS

1. **Reading:** Spend some time early in class showing students how to approach material. Go through the books, explaining how they are organized, how glossaries and indexes and chapters work. Point out things that seem obvious like chapter headings, summaries, and introductions. Talk to students about how to read a textbook versus a newspaper article versus a novel. Explain that different reading methods are appropriate to different needs as well as texts and that one needn't understand or even read every word all the time. [Note: It is a good idea to find out what a student already knows. Some students, who have had education in their first language/home country, may not need this assistance. Others may need a great deal of support in this area.]

2. **Assignments:** Explain things both orally and, as much as possible, in writing. Ask students for feedback to make sure they understood what was explained or asked of them. This could be a quick check-in such as "So what was the assignment for tomorrow, Nguyen?" a one-minute check at the end of class with the LEP students individually about the homework or the day's lesson, or having students turn to a partner or their cooperative learning group to check their understanding of assignments.

3. **Lectures:** Providing written handouts, charts, or other graphic organizers to accompany lecture or other oral input.

4. **Cooperative Learning:** If ever there was a time for cooperative learning, having ESL students in your class would be it. Encouraging group inquiry is important and very helpful to ESL students. Whether it is best for students who speak the same language to work together or to mix them with native English speakers will vary depending on the level of proficiency of ESL students or purpose of activity. Processing newly learned concepts may best be done in the first language, while discussions of concepts that have been mastered and reviewing for an exam may be best done in English. It is imperative that students get to know one another early on. Too often ESL students are isolated from their native English-speaking peers and uncomfortable asking for help. Partners can be assigned and encouraged to call one another at night to clarify assignments or to catch up on a missed class. (The effectiveness of this will depend on how well the teacher has promoted friendship and trust among the students.)

5. **Vary assessment/performance methods:** Use a variety of methods for allowing students to demonstrate their knowledge. Have students make oral presentations, draw (with or without labels), write brief summaries, and so on. Teach through graphic organizers (grids, mind maps, Venn diagrams) and encourage students to use them.

6. **Intervene early:** Don't let students fall too far behind or they may never catch up. In my experience, an ESL student who is lost in the first month will be lost all year. I know an ESL teacher who reported that one of her students confessed to her in April that her science class had been too hard all year. When asked if she was in biology, the student looked puzzled. "I don't know what it is called," she said. When asked what they were

learning about, she had no idea. It turned out she was in chemistry. Teachers need to be aware of just how incredibly lost ESL students can be.

7. **English proficiency; first language education:** Take the time to know your student's level of English. Check in with her to see how much she knows, how well she can converse. Ask an ESL teacher for a writing sample and input on the student—particularly as to whether the student is literate and how much education she has had. If the student has been placed inappropriately, raise the issue with the ESL department and try to have the student placed in the most beneficial setting. Don't resort to giving the student credit for "trying," and be sure you know whether the writing she turns in is hers. Sometimes students seek help from others—in good faith. This can be helpful in their learning, but you need to know what they themselves are capable of. Be aware that a student can develop apparent "fluency" (social fluency) within two years of entering American schools, but may still—after many years—not have enough true academic proficiency to be able to understand a teacher's speech—the more abstract or unfamiliar, the more difficult.

8. **Vocabulary:** Explain vocabulary before a reading and before or during a lecture. This is an obvious but often overlooked step. Early work with suffixes and prefixes is very helpful, especially in science.

9. **Prior to reading:** Be sure there has been discussion about some of the concepts and terms prior to reading assignments. Examples are prediction activities, discussion about students' experiences, reading and summarizing short articles or summaries in advance—even a brief "sheltered" lecture prior to the reading, with comprehension checks, of course.

10. **Syllabus:** If possible, provide a syllabus. Let students know ahead of time where you are going in the class—the big things you want them to know by the end. Make big-picture organizing principles (such as major questions considered at the beginning of class and again at the end) known to ESL aides or other assistants, so that they have a tool for keeping students on track.

11. **Agenda/Outline:** Write an agenda or outline for the day, the week, or the unit and refer to it as you change topics or activities.

12. **Prior experience:** Be aware that ESL students may not have the previous academic knowledge (e.g., the American Civil War) or the previous life experience (e.g., American medical view of illness) that one can assume for many middle-class American students. Find ways to fill in the information, such as allowing for small-group discussion, asking the ESL teacher or aide to explain background, or discussing the student's own perspective and explicitly comparing the two. Sometimes a brief discussion with the student is all that is necessary.

13. **Review:** Take the time to have students review learning. This can be an enjoyable activity. This may serve the purposes of ensuring understanding of a lecture or reading, reminding students of important points from a past lesson, or to review for an exam. Examples of techniques for reviewing are:

    1. Quick-write and share. Write for two minutes something you have learned. Share your writing with the other members of your group or with a partner. Use Whole-Class Share (WCS)—each group shares a major learning with the whole class and the teacher can add points that were not mentioned.

2. Turn-to-a-partner. Agree on the important points. (WCS afterward)

3. Think-pair-share. Jot down important points. Share with a partner. Now share with your group and agree on the important points. (WCS afterward)

4. Each group prepares a brief quiz of the important points then passes the quiz on to another group who must agree on the answers to the quiz. (WCS afterward)

14. **Expectations:** Have high expectations of all students (no excuses!), and be aware of the support many students need in order to reach those expectations.

Source: This set of recommendations written by Dr. Lynn Reer, a retired ESL professor, Lewis & Clark College. Used with permission.

References

Abrami, E., Chambers, B., Poulsen, C., DeSimone, C., d'Apollonia, S., & Howden, J. (1995). *Classroom connections: Understanding and using cooperative learning.* New York, NY: Harcourt Brace.

Adams, C. (2010). Cyberbullying: How to make it stop. *Instructor, 120,* 44–49.

Adams, C., & Forsyth, P. (2009). The nature and function of trust in schools. *Journal of School Leadership, 19,* 126–152.

Adkins-Coleman, T. (2010). "I'm not afraid to come into your world": Case studies of teachers facilitating engagement in urban high school English classrooms. *The Journal of Negro Education, 79,* 41–53.

Agne, K., Greenwood, G., & Miller, L. (1994). Relationships between teacher belief systems and teacher effectiveness. *The Journal of Research and Development in Education, 27,* 141–152.

Akin-Little, A., Little, S., Bray, M., & Kehle, T. (2009). *Behavioral interventions in schools: Evidence-based positive strategies.* Washington, DC: American Psychological Association.

Alberto, P., & Troutman, A. (2006). *Applied behavior analysis for teachers* (8th ed.). Upper Saddle River, NJ: Merrill/Prentice Hall.

Algozzine, B., Audette, B., Ellis, E., Marr, M., & White, R. (2000). Supporting teachers, principals, and students through unified discipline. *Teaching Exceptional Children, 33,* 42–47.

Allday, A., Hinkson-Lee, K., Hudson, T., Neilsen-Gatti, S., Kleinke, A., & Russel, C. (2012). Training general educators to increase behavior-specific praise: Effects on students with EBD. *Behavioral Disorders, 37,* 87–98.

Allen, K. (2010). Classroom management, bullying, and teacher practices. *Professional Educator, 34,* 1–15.

Allen, T., & Plax, T. (1999). Group communications in the formal educational context. In F. R. Lawrence (Ed.), *The handbook of group communication theory and research* (pp. 493–515). Thousand Oaks, CA: Sage.

Allington, R. (2000). *What really matters for struggling readers.* New York, NY: Longman.

Altermatt, E., & Ivers, I. (2011). Friends' responses to children's disclosure of an achievement-related success: An observational study. *Merrill-Palmer Quarterly, 57,* 429–454.

Amato-Zech, N., Off, K., & Doepke, K. (2006). Increasing on-task behavior in the classroom: Extension of self-monitoring strategies. *Psychology in the Schools, 42,* 211–221.

American Psychological Association Zero Tolerance Task Force. (2008). Are zero tolerance policies effective in the schools? An evidentiary review and recommendations. *American Psychologist, 63,* 852–862.

Anapnostopoulos, D., Buchanan, N., Pereira, C., & Lichty, L. (2009). School staff responses to gender-based bullying as moral interpretation: An exploration study. *Educational Policy, 23,* 519–553.

Anderson, K., & Minke, K. (2007). Parent involvement in education: Toward an understanding of parents' decision making. *Journal of Educational Research, 100,* 311–323.

Anderson, L., Evertson, C., & Brophy, J. (1979). An experimental study of effective teaching in first grade reading groups. *Elementary School Journal, 79,* 193–223.

Andrini, B. (1991). *Cooperative learning and mathematics: A multistructural approach.* San Juan Capistrano, CA: Resources for Teachers.

Antil, L., Jenkins, J., Wayne, S., & Vadasy, P. (1998). Cooperative learning: Prevalence, conceptualizations, and the relation between research and practice. *American Educational Research Journal, 35,* 419–454.

Archer, A., & Gleason, M. (1989). *Skills for school success.* North Billerica, MA: Curriculum Associates.

Archer, A., & Gleason, M. (1994). *Advanced skills for school success.* North Billerica, MA: Curriculum Associates.

Armstrong, T. (2000). *Multiple intelligences in the classroom* (2nd ed.). Alexandria, VA: Association for Supervision and Curriculum Development.

Arunkumar, R., Midgley, C., & Urdan, T. (1999). Perceiving high or low home-school dissonance: Longitudinal effects on adolescent emotional and academic well-being. *Journal of Research on Adolescence, 9,* 441–466.

Atwell, N. (1998). *In the middle: New understandings about writing, reading, and learning.* Portsmouth, NH: Boynton/Cook.

August, D., & Hakuta, K. (1997). *Improving schooling for language-minority children: A research agenda.* Washington, DC: National Research Council.

Axelrod, S., & Mathews, S. (2003a). *How to deal with students who challenge and defy authority.* Columbia, MO: Hawthorne Educational Services.

Axelrod, S., & Mathews, S. (2003b). *How to prevent and safely manage physical aggression and property damage.* Columbia, MO: Hawthorne Educational Services.

Bacchini, D., Esposito, G., & Affuso, G. (2009). Social experience and school bullying. *Journal of Community & Applied Social Psychology, 19,* 17–32.

Baker, J. (1998). Are we missing the forest for the trees? Considering the social context of school violence. *Journal of School Psychology, 36,* 29–44.

Ballenger, C. (1992). Because you like us: The language of control. *Harvard Educational Review, 62*(2), 199–208.

Banks, J., & McGee Banks, C. (Eds.). (1993). *Multicultural education: Issues and perspectives* (2nd ed.). Boston, MA: Allyn & Bacon.

Banks, J., & McGee Banks, C. (Eds.). (2001). *Cultural diversity and education: Foundations, curriculum, and teaching.* Boston, MA: Allyn & Bacon.

Barrish, H., Saunders, M., & Wolf, M. (1969). Good behavior game: Effects of individual contingencies for group consequences on disruptive behavior in a classroom. *Journal of Applied Behavior Analysis, 2,* 119–124.

Bartholomew, B. (2008). Sustaining the fire. *Educational Leadership, 65,* 55–60.

Bath, H. (2008). The three pillars of trauma-informed care. *Reclaiming children and youth, 17,* 17–21.

Beane, J. (1997). *Curriculum integration: Designing the core of democratic education.* New York, NY: Teachers College Press.

Becker, W., Engelmann, S., & Thomas, D. (1975). *Teaching 1: Classroom management.* Champaign, IL: Research Press.

Beers, K. (2003). *When kids can't read: What teachers can do.* Portsmouth, NH: Heinemenn.

Bellmore, A. (2011). Peer rejection and unpopularity: Associations with GPAs across the transition to middle school. *Journal of Educational Psychology, 103,* 282–295.

Bempechat, J. (1998). *Against the odds: How "at risk" children exceed expectations.* San Francisco, CA: Jossey-Bass.

Benner, G., Kutash, K., Nelson, R., & Fisher, M. (2013). Closing the achievement gap of youth with emotional and behavioral disorders through multi-tiered systems of support. *Education and Treatment of Children, 36,* 15–29.

Benner, G., Nelson, J., Sanders, E., & Ralston, N. (2012). Behavior intervention for students with externalizing behavior problems: Elementary-level standard protocol. *Exceptional Children, 78,* 181–198.

Benner, G., Nelson, J., Smith, D., & Roberts, M. (2002). The effects of a strategy to reduce the problem behaviors of students with emotional and behavioral disorders. *Academic Exchange Quarterly, 11,* 144–148.

Benson, P., Scales, P., Leffert, N., & Roehlkepartain, E. (1999). *A fragile foundation: The state of developmental assets among American youth.* Minneapolis, MN: Search Institute.

Berliner, D. (1984). The half-full glass: A review of research on teaching. In P. Hosford (Ed.), *Using what we know about teaching.* Alexandria, VA: Association for Supervision and Curriculum Development.

Bernstein, B. (1993). *Cooperative learning in math: Skill-oriented activities that encourage working together*. Carthage, IL: Good Apple.

Beyer, L. (Ed.). (1996). *Creating democratic classrooms: The struggle to integrate theory & practice*. New York, NY: Teachers College Press.

Bicard, D., Ervin, A., Bicard, S., & Baylot-Casey, L. (2012). Differential effects of seating arrangements on disruptive behavior of fifth grade students during independent seatwork. *Journal of Applied Behavior Analysis, 45*, 407–411.

Bigelow, B., Harvey, B., Karp, S., & Miller, L. (2001). *Rethinking our classrooms: Teaching for equity and justice* (Vol. 2). Milwaukee, WI: Rethinking Schools.

Bigelow, B., Karp, S., & Au, W. (2007). *Rethinking our classrooms: Teaching for equity and justice* (Vol. 1). Milwaukee, WI: Rethinking Schools.

Binns, K., Steinberg, A., & Amorosi, S. (1997). *The Metropolitan Life Survey of the American Teacher 1998: Building family–school partnerships: Views of teachers and students*. New York, NY: Louis Harris & Associates.

Birchmeier, Z. (2009). Stand by me: The effects of peer and teacher support in mitigating the impact of bullying on quality of life. *Psychology in the Schools, 47*, 636–649.

Bireda, M. (2010). *Cultures in conflict: Eliminating racial profiling* (2nd ed.). Lanham, MD: Rowman & Littlefield.

Black, K., Hershey, T., Koller, J., Videen, T., Mintun, M., Price, J., & Perlmutter, J. (2002). A possible substrate for dopamine-related changes in mood and behavior: Prefrontal and limbic effects of a D-3 preferring dopamine agonist. *Proceedings of the National Academy of Science, 99*(26), 17113–17118.

Blaustein, M., & Kinniburgh, K. (2010). *Treating traumatic stress in children and adolescents: How to foster resilience through attachment, self-regulation, and competency*. New York, NY: Guilford Press.

Bloom, B. (Ed.). (1956). *Taxonomy of educational objectives, handbook I: Cognitive domain*. New York, NY: David McKay.

Bonds, M., & Stoker, S. (2000). *Bully proofing your school: A comprehensive approach for middle schools*. Longmont, CO: Sopris West.

Bondy, E., Ross, D., Gallingane, C., & Hambacher, E. (2007). Creating environments of success and resilience: Culturally responsive classroom management and more. *Urban Education, 42*, 326–328.

Borba, M. (1989). *Esteem builders: A K–8 curriculum for improving student achievement, behavior and school climate*. Rolling Hills Estates, CA: Jalmer.

Borba, M. (2005). *Nobody likes me, everybody hates me: The top 25 friendship problems and how to solve them*. San Francisco, CA: Jossey-Bass.

Bosworth, K. (1995). Caring for others and being cared for. *Phi Delta Kappan, 76*, 686–693.

Boulton, M., Don, J., & Boulton, L. (2011). Predicting children's liking of school from their peer relationships. *Social Psychology Education, 14*, 489–501.

Bowers, C., & Flinders, D. (1990). *Responsive teaching*. New York, NY: Teachers College Press.

Bowman-Perrott, L., Davis, H., Vannest, K., Williams, L., Greenwood, C., & Parker, R. (2013). Academic benefits of peer tutoring: A meta-analytic review of single-case research. *School Psychology Review, 42*, 39–55.

Boyer, J., & Baptiste, P. (1996). *Transforming the curriculum for multicultural understanding*. San Francisco, CA: Caddo Gap Press.

Brantlinger, E. (1993). *The politics of social class in secondary school: Views of affluent and impoverished youth*. New York, NY: Teachers College Press.

Breeden, T., & Mosley, J. (1992). *The cooperative learning companion: Ideas, activities, and aids for middle grades*. Nashville, TN: Incentive.

Brendtro, L., Brokenleg, M., & Van Bockem, S. (1990). *Reclaiming youth at risk: Our hope for the future*. Bloomington, IN: National Educational Service.

Brendtro, L., & Long, N. (1995). Breaking the cycle of conflict. *Educational Leadership, 52*, 52–56.

Brevik, L. (2009). *Effectiveness of teacher preparation programs as perceived by first year teachers*. (Doctoral dissertation). Retrieved from *Dissertation Abstracts International, 70*(07A), 2310.

Briere III, D., & Simonsen, B. (2011). Self-monitoring interventions for at-risk middle school students: The importance of considering function. *Behavioral Disorders, 36*, 129–140.

Brinamen, C., & Page, F. (2012). Reflective practice creates a therapeutic preschool: Using relationships to heal trauma: I. *Young Children, 67*, 40–48.

Brophy, J. (1981). Teacher praise: A functional analysis. *Review of Educational Research, 51*, 5–32.

Brophy, J. (1982). Classroom management and learning. *American Education, 18*, 20–23.

Brophy, J. (1983). Research on the self-fulfilling prophecy and teacher expectations. *Journal of Educational Psychology, 75*, 631–661.

Brophy, J. (1986a, April). *Socializing students' motivation to learn*. Paper presented at the annual meeting of the American Educational Research Association, San Francisco, CA.

Brophy, J. (1986b, April). *Teacher effects research and teacher quality*. Paper presented at the annual meeting of the American Educational Research Association, San Francisco, CA.

Brophy, J. (1988). Educating teachers about managing classrooms and students. *Teaching and Teacher Education, 4*(1), 1–18.

Brophy, J. (1996). *Teaching problem students*. New York, NY: Guilford Press.

Brophy, J. (Ed.). (1998). *Advances in research on teaching: Expectations in the classroom*. Greenwich, CT: JAI Press.

Brophy, J. (2004). *Educational Practice Series: Vol. 1 Teaching*. Lausanne, Switzerland: International Academy of Education, International Bureau of Education.

Brophy, J., & Evertson, C. (1976). *Learning from teaching: A developmental perspective*. Boston, MA: Allyn & Bacon.

Brophy, J., & Good, T. (1971). Teacher's communication of differential expectations for children's classroom performance: Some behavior data. *Journal of Educational Psychology, 61*, 365–374.

Brophy, J., & Good, T. (1974). *Teacher–student relationships: Causes and consequences*. New York, NY: Holt, Rinehart and Winston.

Brophy, J., & McCaslin, M. (1992). Teachers' reports of how they perceive and cope with problem students. *The Elementary School Journal, 93*, 3–68.

Brown, D. (2004). Urban teachers' professed classroom management strategies: Reflections of culturally responsive teaching. *Urban Education, 39*, 266–289.

Brownstein, R. (2010). Pushed out. *Education Digest, 75*, 23–27.

Bryk, A., & Schneider, B. (2002). *Trust in schools: A core resource for improvement*. New York, NY: Russell Sage.

Burke, K. (1994). *The mindful school: How to assess authentic learning*. Arlington Heights, IL: IRI/Skylight Training.

Burkman, A. (2012). Preparing novice teachers for success in elementary classrooms through professional development. *The Delta Kappa Gamma Bulletin, 78*, 23–33.

Burns, M. (1999). Effectiveness of special education personnel in the intervention assistance team model. *The Journal of Educational Research, 92*, 354–356.

Bushaw, W., & Calderon, V. (2014). Try it again Uncle Sam: The 46th annual PDK/Gallup Poll of the public's attitudes toward the public schools. *Phi Delta Kappan, 96*, 8–20.

Bushaw, W., & Lopez, S. (2013). The 45th annual Phi Delta Kappa/Gallup poll of the public's attitudes toward the public schools. *Phi Delta Kappan, 95*, 8–25.

Butler, R. (1998). Determinants of help seeking: Relations between perceived reasons for classroom help-avoidance and help-seeking behaviors in an experimental context. *Journal of Educational Psychology, 90*, 630–643.

Butler, R., & Nisan, M. (1986). Effects of no feedback, task-related comments, and grades on intrinsic motivation and performance. *Journal of Educational Psychology, 78*, 210–216.

Campbell, A., & Anderson, C. (2012). Check-in/check-out: A systematic evaluation and component analysis. *Journal of Applied Behavior Analysis, 44*, 315–326.

Campbell, L., Campbell, B., & Dickerson, D. (1999). *Teaching and learning through multiple intelligences* (2nd ed.). Boston, MA: Allyn & Bacon.

Canfield, J., & Siccone, F. (1992). *One hundred ways to develop student self-esteem and responsibility*. Boston, MA: Allyn & Bacon.

Canter, L. (1996). First, the rapport—then, the rules. *Learning, 24*, 12–14.

Canter, L., & Canter, M. (1976). *Assertive discipline*. Los Angeles, CA: Lee Canter Associates.

Cantlon, T. (1991a). *The first four weeks of cooperative learning: Activities and materials*. Portland, OR: Prestige.

Cantlon, T. (1991b). *Structuring the classroom successfully for cooperative team learning*. Portland, OR: Prestige.

Carger, C. (1996). *Of borders and dreams: A Mexican-American experience of urban education*. New York, NY: Teachers College Press.

Carranza, F., You, S., Chhuon, V., & Hudley, C. (2009). Mexican American adolescents' academic achievement and aspirations: The role of perceived parental educational involvement, acculturation, and self-esteem. *Adolescence, 44*, 313–333.

Carrera, M., DePalma, R., & Lameiras, M. (2011). Toward a more comprehensive understanding of bullying in school settings. *Educational Psychology Review, 23,* 479–499.

Carroll, J., & Peterson, D. (1997). *Character building literature-based theme units.* Carthage, IL: Teaching and Learning.

Carson-Dellosa Publishing Company. (1998). *Character education: Ideas and activities for the classroom.* Greensboro, NC: Author.

Carter, D., Carter, G., Johnson, E., & Pool, J. (2012). Systematic implementation of a Tier 2 behavior intervention. *Intervention in School and Clinic, 48,* 223–231.

Cartledge, G., & Fellows Milburn, J. (1995). *Teaching social skills to children and youth: Innovative approaches.* Boston, MA: Allyn & Bacon.

Caselman, T. (2007). *Teaching children empathy, the social emotion: Lesson, activities and reproducible worksheets (K–6) that teach how to "Step into others' shoes."* Chapin, SC: Youth Light.

Casey, D. (2009). *The effect of classroom management training and active or information-based follow-up on inexperienced teachers' perceived classroom behavior management effectiveness.* (Doctoral dissertation). Retrieved from *Dissertation Abstracts International, 70(03A),* 844.

Cassidy, W., Brown, D., & Jackson, M. (2012). "Under the radar": Educators and cyberbullying in schools. *School Psychology International, 33,* 520–532.

Casto, K., & Audley, J. (2008). *In our school: Building community in elementary schools.* Turners Falls, MA: Northeast Foundations for Children.

Celio, C., Durlak, J., & Dymnicki, A. (2011). A meta-analysis of the impact of service learning on students. *Journal of Experiential Education, 34,* 164–181.

Chalfant, J., & Pysh, V. (1989). Teacher assistance teams: Five descriptive studies on 96 teams. *Remedial and Special Education, 10,* 49–58.

Chandler, L., & Dahlquist, C. (2006). *Functional assessment: Strategies to prevent and remediate challenging behavior in school settings.* Upper Saddle River, NJ: Merrill/Prentice Hall.

Chapman, C., & King, R. (2005). *Differentiated assessment strategies.* Thousand Oaks, CA: Corwin.

Charles, A. (2012). Cell phones: Rule-setting, rule-breaking, and relationships in the classroom. *American Secondary Education, 40,* 4–16.

Charney, R. (2002). *Teaching children to care: Classroom management for ethical and academic growth, K–8* (2nd ed.). Turners Falls, MA: Northeast Foundation for Children.

Chavkin, N., & Gonzales, D. (1995). *Forging partnerships between Mexican-American parents and the schools.* ERIC Digest (ED388489). Charleston, WV: ERIC Clearinghouse on Rural Education and Small Schools.

Chen, C., Kyle, D., & McIntyre, E. (2008). Helping teachers work effectively with English language learners and their families. *The School Community Journal, 18,* 7–20.

Chen, H., Chiang, C., & Lin, W. (2013). Learning effects of interactive white board pedagogy for students in Taiwan from the perspective of multiple intelligences. *Journal of Educational Computing Research, 49,* 173–187.

Chitiyo, M., May, M., & Chitiyo, G. (2012). An assessment of the evidence-base for school-wide positive behavior support. *Education and Treatment of Children, 35,* 1–24.

Chrispeels, J., & Rivero, E. (2001). Engaging Latino families for student success: How parent education can reshape parents' sense of place in the education of their children. *Peabody Journal of Education, 76,* 119–169.

Christenson, S., & Sheridan, S. (2001). *Schools and families: Creating essential connections for learning.* New York, NY: Guilford Press.

Cisneros, S. (1991). *The house on Mango Street.* New York, NY: Vintage Books.

Clark, M. (2002). Reaching potentially violent youth in schools: A guide to collaborative assessment, alertness, atmosphere, and accountability. In G. McAuliffe (Ed.), *Working with troubled youth in schools: A guide for all school staff* (pp. 19–30). Westport, CT: Bergin & Garvey.

Clark, O., & Hull, W. (1999). *Good thinking: Helping students to reframe their thinking patterns.* Longmont, CO: Sopris West.

Clayton, M., & Forton, M. (2001). *Classroom spaces that work.* Greenfield, MA: Northeast Foundation for Children.

Cohen-Posey, D. (1995). *How to handle bullies, teasers and other meanies.* Highland City, FL: Rainbow Books.

Cole, J., Cornell, D., & Sheras, P. (2006). Identification of school bullies by survey methods. *Professional School Counseling, 9,* 305–313.

Cole, S., Eisner, A., Gregory, M., & Ristuccia, J. (2013). *Creating and advocating for trauma-sensitive schools.* Boston, MA: Massachusetts Advocates for Children.

Cole, S., Horvath, B., Chapman, C., Deschenes, C., Ebeling, D., & Sprague, J. (2000a). *Adapting curriculum and instruction in inclusive classrooms: Staff development kit* (2nd ed.). Bloomington, IN: Indiana Institute on Disability and Community.

Cole, S., O'Brien, J., Gadd, M., Ristuccia, J., Wallace, D., & Gregory, M. (2005). *Helping traumatized children learn: Supportive school environments for children traumatized by family violence.* Boston, MA: Massachusetts Advocates for Children.

Collins, M. (1992). Making a difference in the classroom. *Special Report, 65.* Grove City, PA: Public Policy Education Fund.

Colvin, G. (2004). *Managing the cycle of acting-out behavior in the classroom.* Eugene, OR: Behavior Associates.

Comer, J., Haynes, N., Joyner, E., & Ben-Avie, M. (1996). *Rallying the whole village: The Comer process for reforming education.* New York, NY: Teachers College Press.

Committee for Children. (2000). *Second step to success: A violence-prevention curriculum.* 2203 Airport Way South, Suite 500, Seattle, WA 98134; (206) 343–1223.

Connell, D. (2009). The global aspects of brain-based learning. *Educational Horizons, 88,* 28–39.

Cooper, H., & Good, T. (1983). *Pygmalion grows up.* New York, NY: Longman.

Cooper, R., & Blumenfeld, W. (2012). Responses to cyberbullying: A descriptive analysis of the frequency of and impact on LGBT and allied youth. *Journal of LGBT Youth, 9,* 153–177.

Coopersmith, S. (1967). *The antecedents of self-esteem.* San Francisco, CA: Freeman.

Corbett, D., & Wilson, B. (2002). What urban students say about good teaching. *Educational Leadership, 60,* 18–22.

Costenbader, V., & Markson, S. (1998). School suspension: A study with secondary school students. *Journal of School Psychology, 36,* 59–82.

Cothran, D., & Ennis, C. (1997). Students' and teachers' perceptions of conflict and power. *Teaching and Teacher Education, 13,* 541–553.

Covaleskie, J. (1992). Discipline and morality: Beyond rules and consequences. *Educational Reform, 56,* 173–183.

Cozolino, L. (2013). *The social neuroscience of education: Optimizing attachment and learning in the classroom.* New York, NY: W. W. Norton & Company.

Crank, J., & Bulgren, J. (1993). Visual depictions as information organizers for enhancing achievement of students with learning disabilities. *Learning Disabilities Research and Practice, 8,* 140–147.

Crawford, G. (2007). *Brain-based teaching with adolescent learning in mind.* Thousand Oaks, CA: Corwin.

Crone, D., Hawken, L., & Horner, R. (2010). *Responding to problem behavior in schools: The behavior education program* (2nd ed.). New York, NY: Guilford Press.

Cummins, J. (1989). *Empowering minority students.* Sacramento, CA: California Association for Bilingual Education.

Cummins, J. (1996). *Negotiating identities: Education for empowerment in a diverse society.* Ontario, CA: California Association for Bilingual Education.

Curby, T., Rimm-Kaufman, S., & Ponitz, C. (2009). Teacher-child interactions and children's achievement trajectories across kindergarten and first grade. *Journal of Educational Psychology, 101,* 912–925.

Curwin, R., & Fuhrmann, B. (1975). *Discovering your teaching self: Humanistic approaches to effective teaching.* Englewood Cliffs, NJ: Prentice Hall.

Curwin, R., & Mendler, A. (1988). *Discipline with dignity.* Reston, VA: Association for Supervision and Curriculum Development.

Cushman, K. (2003). *Fires in the bathroom: Advice for teachers from high school students.* New York, NY: New Press.

Cusick, P. (1994). *The educational system: Its nature and logic.* New York, NY: McGraw-Hill.

Daniels, H., & Bizar, M. (2005). *Teaching the best practices way.* Portland, ME: Stenhouse.

Darling-Hammond, L. (1997). *The right to learn: A blueprint for creating schools that work.* San Francisco, CA: Jossey-Bass.

Darling-Hammond, L. (2010). *The flat world of education: How America's commitment to equity will determine our future.* New York, NY: Teachers College Press.

Darling-Hammond, L. (2013). *Getting teacher evaluation right: What really matters for effectiveness and improvement.* New York, NY: Teachers College Press.

Davidman, L., & Davidman, P. (1997). *Teaching with a multicultural perspective: A practical guide.* New York, NY: Longman.

Davidson, A. (1999). Negotiating social differences: Youths' assessments of educators' strategies. *Urban Education, 34,* 338–369.

Davis, M. (2012). N.Y.C. outlines social media guidelines for educators. *Education Week, 31,* 11.

Day-Vines, N., & Day-Hairston, B. (2005). Culturally congruent strategies for addressing the behavioral needs of urban, African American male adolescents. *Professional School Counseling, 8,* 236–243.

Day-Vines, N., & Terriquez, V. (2008). A strengths-based approach to promoting prosocial behavior among African American and Latino students. *Professional School Counseling, 12,* 170–175.

Debman, K., Pas, E., & Bradshaw, C. (2012). Secondary and tertiary support systems in schools implementing school-wide positive behavioral interventions and supports: A preliminary descriptive analysis. *Journal of Positive Behavior Interventions, 14,* 142–152.

DeCremer, D., & Tyler, T. (2007). The effects of trust in authority and procedural fairness on cooperation. *Journal of Applied Psychology, 92,* 639–649.

Deickmann, J. (2009). Teaching practices of highly and less effective math teachers. (Doctoral dissertation). Retrieved from *Dissertation Abstracts International, 70*(10A), 3744.

Della Salla, S., & Anderson, M. (2012). *Neuroscience in education: The good, the bad, and the ugly.* Oxford, UK: Oxford University Press.

Delpit, L. (1995). *Other people's children: Cultural conflict in the classroom.* New York, NY: New Press.

Demanet, J., & Houtte, M. (2012). School belonging and school misconduct: The differing role of teacher and peer attachment. *Journal of Youth and Adolescence, 41,* 499–514.

Denton, P. (2005). *Learning through academic choice.* Turners Falls, MA: Northeast Foundation for Children.

Denton, P., & Kriete, R. (2000). *The first six weeks of school.* Turners Falls, MA: Northeast Foundation for Children.

Dewey, J. (1916). *Democracy and education: An introduction to the philosophy of education.* New York, NY: Macmillan.

Diamantes, T. (2010). Recent court rulings regarding student use of cell phones in today's schools. *Education, 131,* 404–406.

Didax Educational Resources Inc. (2003a). *Bullying: Identify, cope, prevent! Grades 3–4.* Rowley, MA: Author. Retrieved from Didax Web site: www.worldteacherspress.com.

Didax Educational Resources Inc. (2003b). *Bullying: Identify, cope, prevent! Grades 5–6.*

Rowley, MA: Author. Retrieved from Didax Web site: www.worldteacherspress.com.

Dietz, M. (Ed.). (1997). *School, family, and community: Techniques and models for successful collaboration.* Gaithersburg, MD: Aspen.

DiGangi, S., & Maag, J. (1992). A component analysis of self-management training with behaviorally disordered youth. *Behavioral Disorders, 17,* 281–290.

Digman, C., & Soan, S. (2008). *Working with parents: A guide for education professionals.* Thousand Oaks, CA: Sage.

Dodd, A., & Konzal, J. (1999). *Making our high schools better. How parents and teachers can work together.* New York, NY: St. Martin's Press.

Dodge, K., Laird, R., Lochman, J., & Zelli, A. (2002). Multidimensional latent construct analysis of children's social information processing patterns: Correlations with aggressive behavior problems. *Psychological Assessment, 14,* 60–73.

Dods, J. (2013). Enhancing understanding of the nature and supportive school-based relationships for youth who have experienced trauma. *Canadian Journal of Education, 36,* 71–95.

Doggett, A., Edwards, R., Moore, J., Tingstrom, D., & Wilcznski, S. (2001). An approach to functional assessment in general education settings. *School Psychology Review, 30,* 313–328.

Donaldson, J., Vollmer, T., Krous, T., Downs, S., & Berard, K. (2011). An evaluation of the good behavior game in kindergarten classrooms. *Journal of Applied Behavior Analysis, 44,* 605–609.

Dorman, G. (1981). *Middle grades assessment program.* Chapel Hill, NC: Center for Early Adolescence.

Dotson-Blake, K. (2010). Learning from each other: A portrait of family-school-community partnerships in the United States and Mexico. *Professional School Counseling, 14,* 101–114.

Doyle, W. (1983). Academic work. *Review of Educational Research, 53,* 159–199.

Doyle, W. (1986). Classroom organization and management. In M. C. Wittrock (Ed.), *Handbook of research on teaching* (3rd ed.). New York, NY: Macmillan.

Dreikurs, R., & Cassel, P. (1972). *Discipline without tears: What to do with children who misbehave.* New York, NY: Hawthorn.

Dreikurs, R., Grunwald, B., & Pepper, F. (1971). *Maintaining sanity in the classroom: Illustrated teaching techniques.* New York, NY: Harper and Row.

Duchaine, E., Green, K., & Jolivette, K. (2011). Using response cards as a class-wide intervention to decrease challenging behavior. *Beyond Behavior, 20,* 3–10.

Duke, D. (1980). *Managing behavior problems.* New York, NY: Columbia University Teachers College Press.

Duke, D., & Trautvetter, S. (2001). *Reducing the negative effects of large schools.* Washington, DC: National Clearing House of Educational Facilities.

Dunn, A. (2010). We know you're Black at heart: A self-study of a White, urban high school teacher. In A. J. Stairs & K. A. Donnell (Eds.),

Research on urban teacher learning: Examining conceptual factors over time (pp. 29–40). Charlotte, NC: Information Age.

Dunn, R. (1983). Learning style and its relation to exceptionality at both ends of the spectrum. *Exceptional Children, 49,* 496–506.

Dunn, R., & DeBello, T. (Eds.). (1999). *Improved test scores, attitudes, and behaviors in America's schools: Supervisors' success stories.* Westport, CT: Bergin & Garvey.

Dunn, R., Thies, A., & Honigsfeld, A. (2001). *Synthesis of the Dunn and Dunn learning-style model research: Analysis from a neuropsychological perspective.* Jamaica, NY: St. John's University School of Education and Human Services.

Dunst, C., McWilliams, R., & Holbert, K. (1986). Assessment of preschool classroom environments. *Diagnostique, 11,* 212–232.

Durr, A. (2008). *Identifying teacher capacities that may buffer against teacher burnout.* (Doctoral dissertation). Retrieved from *Dissertation Abstracts International, 69*(12A), 4577.

Duval, R. (1997). *Building character and community in the classroom.* Cypress, CA: Creative Teaching Press.

Dweck, C. (2008). Brainology: Transforming students' motivation to learn. *Independent School, 67,* 110–119.

Eberly, J., Joshi, A., & Konzal, J. (2007). Communicating with families across cultures: An investigation of teacher perceptions and practices. *The School Community Journal, 17,* 7–26.

Eccles, J., & Wigfield, A. (1985). Teacher expectations and student motivation. In J. Dusek, V. Hall, & W. Meyer (Eds.), *Teacher expectancies.* Hillsdale, NJ: Erlbaum.

Education Center. (2000). *Building character (primary). The Best of Mailbox Theme Series.* Greensboro, NC: Author.

Edwards, K., Ellis, D., Ko, L., Saifer, S., & Stuczynski, A. (2005). *Classroom to community and back: Using culturally responsive standards-based teaching to strengthen family and community partnerships and increase student achievement.* Portland, OR: Northwest Regional Educational Laboratory.

Elkind, D. (1981). *The hurried child: Growing up too fast too soon.* Reading, MA: Addison-Wesley.

Elliott, D., Hamburg, B., & Williams, K. (Eds.). (1998). *Violence in American schools: A new perspective.* Cambridge, England: Cambridge University Press.

Emmer, E., & Aussiker, A. (1987, April). *School and classroom discipline programs: How well do they work?* Paper presented at the annual meeting of the American Educational Research Association, Washington, DC.

Emmer, E., Evertson, C., & Anderson, L. (1980). Effective management at the beginning of the school year. *Elementary School Journal, 80,* 219–231.

Emmer, E., Evertson, C., Sanford, J., Clements, B., & Worsham, M. (1981). *Organizing and managing the junior high school classroom.* Austin, TX: Research and Development Center for Teacher Education.

Emmer, E., & Gerwels, M. (2006). Classroom management in middle school and high school. In C. Evertson & C. Weinstein (Eds.), *Handbook of classroom management: Research, practice, and contemporary issues*. Mahwah, NJ: Lawrence Erlbaum.

Englander, M. (1986). *Strategies for classroom discipline*. New York, NY: Praeger.

Ennis, C., & McCauley, M. (2002). Creating urban classroom communities worthy of trust. *Journal of Curriculum Studies*, 34(2), 149–172.

Epstein, J. (1995). School/family/community partnerships: Caring for the children we share. *Phi Delta Kappan*, 76, 701–712.

Epstein, J., Coates, L., Salinas, K., Sanders, M., & Simon, B. (1997). *School, family, and community partnerships: Your handbook for action*. Thousand Oaks, CA: Sage.

Epstein, J., & Sanders, M. (1998). What we learn from international studies of school-family-community partnerships. *Childhood Education*, 74, 392–394.

Epstein, M., Atkins, M., Cullinan, D., Kutash, K., & Weaver, R. (2008). *Reducing behavior problems in the elementary school classroom: A practice guide* (NCEE #2008-012). Washington, DC: National Center for Education Evaluation and Regional Assistance, Institute of Education Sciences, U.S. Department of Education.

Erbes, S., Folkerts, M., Gergis, C., Pederson, S., & Stivers, H. (2010). Understanding how cognitive psychology can inform and improve Spanish vocabulary acquisition in high school classrooms. *Journal of Instructional Psychology*, 37, 120–132.

Erikson, E. (1963). *Childhood and society* (2nd ed.). New York, NY: Norton.

Espelage, D., Anderman, E., Brown, V., Jones, A., Lane, K., McMahon, S., . . . Reynolds, C. (2013). Understanding and preventing violence directed against teachers: Recommendations for a national research, practice, and policy agenda. *American Psychologist*, 68, 75–87.

Espelage, D. L., Aragon, S. R., Birkett, M., & Koenig, B. W. (2008). Homophobic teasing, psychological outcomes, and sexual orientation among high school students: What influence do parents and schools have? *School Psychology Review*, 37, 202–216.

Evertson, C. (1985). Training teachers in classroom management: An experimental study in secondary school classrooms. *Journal of Educational Research*, 79, 51–58.

Evertson, C., & Emmer, E. (1982a). Effective management at the beginning of the school year in junior high school classes. *Journal of Educational Psychology*, 74, 485–498.

Evertson, C., Emmer, E., Sanford, J., & Clements, B. (1983). Improving classroom management: An experiment in elementary school classrooms. *Elementary School Journal*, 84, 173–188.

Evertson, C., & Harris, A. (1992). Synthesis of research: What we know about managing classrooms. *Educational Leadership*, 49, 74–78.

Evertson, C., & Harris, A. (1995, September). Classroom organization and management program: Revalidation submissions to the Program Effectiveness Panel (PEP). U.S. Department of Education. Nashville, TN: Peabody College, Vanderbilt University. (ERIC Document Reproduction Service No. 403-247).

Evertson, C., & Harris, A. (1999). Support for managing learner-centered classrooms: The classroom organization and management program. In H. J. Freiberg (Ed.), *Beyond behaviorism: Changing the classroom management paradigm* (pp. 59–74). Boston, MA: Allyn & Bacon.

Evertson, C., & Smithey, M. (2000). Mentoring effects on protégés classroom practice: An experimental study. *Journal of Educational Research*, 93, 294–304.

Evertson, C., & Weinstein, C. (Eds.). (2006). *Handbook of classroom management: Research, practice, and contemporary issues*. Mahwah, NJ: Lawrence Erlbaum.

Eyberg, S. M., Nelson, M. M., & Boggs, S. R. (2008). Evidence-based psychosocial treatments for child and adolescent with disruptive behavior. *Journal of Clinical Child & Adolescent Psychology*, 37, 215–237.

Falk, K., & Wehby, J. (2001). The effects of peer-assisted learning strategies on the beginning reading skills of young children with emotional or behavioral disorders. *Behavioral Disorders*, 26, 344–359.

Falkenberg, C., & Barbetta, P. (2013). The effects of a self-monitoring package on homework completion and accuracy of students with disabilities in an inclusive general education classroom. *Journal of Behavioral Education*, 22, 190–210.

Faltis, C., & Hudleson, S. (1997). *Bilingual education in elementary and secondary school communities: Toward understanding and caring*. Boston, MA: Allyn & Bacon.

Farley, C., Torres, C., Wailehua, C., & Cook, L. (2012). Evidence-based practices for students with emotional and behavioral disorders: Improving academic achievement. *Beyond Behavior*, 21, 37–43.

Farmer, T., Lines, M., & Hamm, J. (2011). Revealing the invisible hand: The role of teachers in children's peer experiences. *Journal of Applied Developmental Psychology*, 32, 247–256.

Fashola, O., Slavin, R., Calderon, M., & Duran, R. (1997). *Effective programs for Latino students in elementary and middle schools* (Report No. 11). Baltimore, MD: Center for Research on the Education of Students Placed at Risk.

Fay, J., & Funk, D. (1995). *Teaching with love and logic*. Golden, CO: Love and Logic Press.

Feather, N. (Ed.). (1982). *Expectations and actions*. Hillsdale, NJ: Lawrence Erlbaum.

Feinstein, S., & Jensen, E. (2013). *Secrets to the teenage brain: Research-based strategies for reaching and teaching today's adolescents*. New York, NY: Skyhorse Publishing.

Felsman, J., & Vaillant, G. (1987). Resilient children as adults: A 40-year study. In E. J. Anderson & B. J. Cohler (Eds.), *The invulnerable child*. New York, NY: Guilford Press.

Feuerborn, L., & Chinn, D. (2012). Teacher perceptions of student needs and implications for positive behavior supports. *Behavioral Disorders*, 37, 219–231.

Finkelhor, D., Turner, H., Ormrod, R., Hamby, S., & Kracke, K. (2009). *Children's exposure to violence: A comprehensive national survey*. Washington, D.C.: Office of Juvenile Justice and Delinquency Prevention: U.S. Department of Justice.

Fisher, C., Berliner, D., Filby, N., Marliane, R., Cahen, L., & Disha, M. (1981). Teaching behaviors, academic learning time, and student achievement: An overview. *Journal of Classroom Interaction*, 17, 2–15.

Fister, S., & Kemp, K. (1995). *The one-minute skill builder: Improving student social skills*. Longmont, CO: Sopris West.

Fitzpatrick, M., & Knowlton, E. (2009). Bringing evidence-based self-directed intervention practices to the trenches for students with emotional and behavioural disorders. *Preventing School Failure*, 53, 253–266.

Five, C. (1992). *Special voices*. Portsmouth, NH: Heinemann.

Flerx, V., Limber, S., Mullin, N., & Riese, J. (2009). *Class meetings that matter: A year's worth of resources for grades K–5*. Center City, MN: Hazelden.

Flowerday, T., & Schraw, G. (2000). Teachers' beliefs about instructional choice: A phenomenological study. *Journal of Educational Psychology*, 92, 634–635.

Flynn, G., & Nolan, B. (2008). What do principals think about current school-family relationships? *NASSP Bulletin*, 92, 173–190.

Ford, M. (1992). *Motivating humans: Goals, emotions, and personal agency beliefs*. Newbury Park, CA: Sage.

Forness, S., Kim, J., & Walker, H. (2012). Prevalence of students with EBD: Impact for general education. *Beyond Behavior*, 21, 3–10.

Frazer-Abder, P. (2010). Reflections on success and retention in urban science education: Voices of five African-American science teachers who stayed. *School Science and Mathematics*, 110, 238–246.

Freeman, D., & Freeman, Y. (2001). *Between worlds: Access to second language acquisition*. Portsmouth, NH: Heinemann.

Freeman, S. (1997). *Character education: Teaching values for life*. New York, NY: McGraw-Hill.

Freeman, Y., & Freeman, D. (2002). *Closing the achievement gap: How to reach limited-formal-schooling and long-term English learners*. Portsmouth, NH: Heinemann.

Freiberg, H. J. (Ed.). (1999). *Beyond behaviorism: Changing the classroom management paradigm*. Boston, MA: Allyn & Bacon.

Freiberg, J. (1996). From tourists to citizens in the classroom. *Educational Leadership*, 54, 32–36.

Freiberg, J., & LaPointe, M. (2006). Research-based programs for preventing and solving discipline problems. In C. S. Evertson & C. M. Weinstein (Eds.), *Handbook of classroom management: Research, practice and contemporary issues* (pp. 735–786). Mahwah, NJ: Lawrence Erlbaum.

Freundenthaler, H., Spinath, B., & Neubauer, A. (2008). Predicting school achievement in boys and girls. *European Journal of Personality*, 22, 231–245.

Frey, K. S., Hirschstein, M. K., Edstrom, L. V., & Snell, J. L. (2009). Observed reductions in school bullying, nonbullying aggression and destructive bystander behavior: A longitudinal evaluation. *Journal of Educational Psychology, 101*, 466–481.

Fried, S., & Fried, P. (1996). *Bullies and victims: Helping your child through the schoolyard battlefield.* New York, NY: M. Evans.

Fries, K., & Cochran-Smith, M. (2006). Teacher research and classroom management: What questions do teachers ask? In C. Evertson & C. Weinstein (Eds.), *Handbook of classroom management: Research, practice, and contemporary issues.* Mahwah, NJ: Lawrence Erlbaum.

Fuhs, M., Farran, D., & Nesbitt, K. (2013). Preschool classroom processes as predictors of children's cognitive self-regulation skills development. *School Psychology Quarterly, 28*, 347–359.

Fuller, M., & Olsen, G. (2007). *Home-school relations: Working successfully with parents and families* (3rd ed.). Boston, MA: Allyn & Bacon.

Futrell, M., Gomez, J., & Bedden, D. (2003). Teaching the children of a new America. *Phi Delta Kappan, 84*, 381–385.

Gable, R., Sugai, G., Lewis, T., Nelson, J., Cheney, D., Safran, S., & Safran, J. (1998). *Individual and systemic approaches to collaboration and consultation.* Reston, VA: Council for Children with Behavioral Disorders.

Gallahar, T. (2009). *Students' perceptions of teachers' expectations as predictors of academic achievement in mathematics.* (Doctoral dissertation). Retrieved from *Dissertation Abstracts International, 70*(11A), 4133.

Garbarino, J. (1999). *Lost boys: Why our sons turn violent and how we can save them.* New York, NY: Free Press.

Garcia, E. (2001). *Student cultural diversity: Understanding and meeting the challenge* (3rd ed.). Boston, MA: Houghton Mifflin.

Garcia, E., & McLaughlin, B. (Eds.). (1995). *Meeting the challenge of linguistic and cultural diversity in early childhood education.* New York, NY: Teachers College Press.

Gardner, H. (1999a). *The disciplined mind: What all students should understand.* New York, NY: Simon & Schuster.

Gardner, H. (1999b). *Intelligence reframed: Multiple intelligences for the 21st century.* New York, NY: Basic Books.

Gardner, H. (2006). *Multiple intelligences: New horizons.* New York, NY: Basic Books.

Garner, P. (1995). Schools by scoundrels: The views of disruptive pupils in mainstream schools in England and the United States. In M. Lloyd-Smith & J. D. Davies (Eds.), *On the margins: The educational experience of "problem" students* (pp. 17–30). Staffordshire, England: Trentham Books.

Garrett, T., Barr, J., & Rothman, T. (2009). Perspectives on caring in the classroom: Do they vary according to ethnicity or grade level? *Adolescence, 44*, 505–521.

Garrity, C., Jens, K., Porter, W., Sager, N., & Short-Camilli, C. (2004). *Bully-proofing your school: Working with victims and bullies in elementary schools* (3rd ed.). Longmont, CO: Sopris West.

Garrod, A., & Larimore, C. (1997). *First person, first peoples: Native American college graduates tell their life stories.* Ithaca, NY: Cornell University Press.

Garrod, A., Ward, J., Robinson, T., & Kilkenny, R. (Eds.). (1999). *Souls looking back: Life stories of growing up Black.* New York, NY: Routledge.

Gathercoal, F. (1996). *Judicious Discipline.* Personal Correspondence.

Gathercoal, F. (2004). *Judicious discipline* (6th ed.). San Francisco, CA: Caddo Gap Press.

Gay, G. (1993). Ethnic minorities and educational equality. In J. Banks & C. Banks (Eds.), *Multicultural education.* Boston, MA: Allyn & Bacon.

Gay, G. (2000). *Culturally responsive teaching: Theory, research, and practice.* New York, NY: Teachers College Press.

Gay, G. (2007). Connections between classroom management and culturally responsive teaching. In C. Evertson & C. Weinstein (Eds.), *Handbook of classroom management: Research, practice, and contemporary issues.* Mahwah, NJ: Lawrence Erlbaum.

Gervay, S. (2009). *I am Jack.* New York, NY: Random House.

Gibbs, J. (2000). *Tribes: A new way of learning and being together.* Sausalito, CA: Center Source.

Gillies, R. (2006). Teachers' and students' verbal behaviours during cooperative and small group learning. *British Journal of Educational Psychology, 76*, 271–287.

Gillies, R., & Haynes, M. (2011). Increasing explanatory behaviour, problem solving, and reasoning within classes using cooperative learning. *Instructional Science, 39*, 349–366.

Ginott, H. (1972). *Teacher and child: A book for parents and teachers.* New York, NY: Macmillan.

Ginsberg, M. (2007). Lessons at the kitchen table. *Educational Leadership, 64*, 56–61.

Girard, K., & Koch, S. (1996). *Conflict resolution in the schools: A manual for educators.* San Francisco, CA: Jossey-Bass.

Glasser, W. (1965). *Reality therapy.* New York, NY: Harper and Row.

Glasser, W. (1986). *Control theory in the classroom.* New York, NY: Harper and Row.

Glasser, W. (1988). On students' needs and team learning: A conversation with William Glasser. *Educational Leadership, 45*, 38–45.

Glasser, W. (1990). *The quality school: Managing students without coercion.* New York, NY: Harper and Row.

Goh, A., & Bambara, L. (2012). Individualized positive behavior support in school settings: A meta-analysis. *Remedial and Special Education, 33*, 271–286.

Goldstein, A. (1999). The victims: Never again. *Time, 154*, 53–57.

Goldstein, A., Harootunian, B., & Conoley, J. (1994). *Student aggression: Prevention, management, and replacement.* New York, NY: Guilford Press.

Goleman, D. (1995). *Emotional intelligence.* New York, NY: Bantam Books.

Golly, A. (1994). The use and effects of alpha and beta commands in elementary classroom settings. (Unpublished doctoral dissertation). University of Oregon, Eugene, OR.

Good, T., & Brophy, J. (2003). *Looking in classrooms* (7th ed.). New York, NY: Harper & Row.

Good, T., & Brophy, J. (2008). *Looking in classrooms* (10th ed.). Boston, MA: Pearson.

Goodlad, J. (1984). *A place called school: Prospects for the future.* New York, NY: McGraw-Hill.

Goodman, J. (2007). School discipline: Buy in and belief. *Ethics and Education, 2*, 3–23.

Gordon, T. (1974). *Teacher effectiveness training.* New York, NY: Wyden.

Grant, G. (2009). *Hope and despair in the American city: Why there are no bad schools in Raleigh.* Cambridge, MA: Harvard University Press.

Grant, R. (1993). Strategic training using text headings to improve students' processing of content. *Journal of Reading, 36*, 382–388.

Greenberg, M., Domitrovich, C., & Bumbarger, B. (2001). The prevention of mental disorders in school-aged children: Current state of the field. *Prevention & Treatment, 4*, 1–62.

Greene, R. W., & Ablon, J. S. (2006). *Treating explosive kids: The collaborative problem-solving approach.* New York, NY: Guilford Press.

Greene, R. W., Ablon, S. A., & Martin, A. (2006). Innovations: Child psychiatry: Use of collaborative problem solving to reduce seclusion and restraint in child and adolescent inpatient units. *Psychiatric Services, 57*(5), 610–616.

Gregory, A., & Ripski, M. (2008). Adolescent trust in teachers: Implications for behavior in the high school classroom. *The School Psychology Review, 37*, 337–53.

Gregory, A., Skiba, R., & Noguera, P. (2010). The achievement gap and the discipline gap: Two sides of the same coin? *Educational Researcher, 39*(59), 59–68.

Gregory, A., & Weinstein, R. (2008). The discipline gap and African Americans: Defiance or cooperation in the high school classroom. *Journal of School Psychology, 46*, 455–475.

Gregory, G., & Chapman, C. (2002). *Differentiated instructional strategies: One size doesn't fit all.* Thousand Oaks, CA: Corwin.

Gresham, F., Sugai, G., & Horner, R. (2001). Interpreting outcomes of social skills training for students with high incidence disabilities. *Exceptional Children, 67*, 331–334.

Gruenewald, D., & Smith, G. (2008). *Place-based education in the global age: Local diversity.* New York, NY: Taylor and Francis.

Hagstrom, D. (2004). *From outrageous to inspired: How to build a community of leaders in our schools.* San Francisco. CA: Jossey-Bass.

Hale-Benson, J. (1986). *Black children: Their roots, culture and learning styles* (Rev. ed.). Baltimore, MD: Johns Hopkins University Press.

Haley, P., & Berry, K. (1988). *Home and school as partners: Helping parents help their children.* Andover, MA: Regional Laboratory for Educational Improvement of the Northeast and Islands.

Hall, S. (2000). *Using picture storybooks to teach character education.* Westport, CT: Oryx Press.

Hamblin, D., & Bartlett, M. (2013). Navigating social networks. *Educational Leadership, 70*, 44–47.

Hammond-Darling, L. (2000). Teacher quality and student achievement: A review of state policy evidence. *Education Policy Analysis Archives*, 8, 1–44.

Hamre, B., & Pianta, R. (2001). Early teacher–child relationships and the trajectory of children's school outcomes through eighth grade. *Child Development*, 72, 625–638.

Hargreaves, A. (2000). Mixed emotions: Teachers' perceptions of their interactions with students. *Teaching and Teacher Education*, 16, 811–826.

Harrington, C., & Boardman, S. (1997). *Paths to success: Beating the odds in American society*. Cambridge, MA: Harvard University Press.

Harter, S. (1996). Teacher and classmate influences on scholastic motivation, self-esteem, and level of voice in adolescents. In J. Juvonen & K. Wentzel (Eds.), *Social motivation: Understanding children's school adjustment* (pp. 11–42). New York, NY: Cambridge.

Hattie, J., Biggs, J., & Purdie, N. (1996). Effects of learning skills interventions on student learning: A meta-analysis. *Review of Educational Research*, 66, 99–136.

Hawkins, D., Doueck, H., & Lishner, D. (1988). Changing teaching practices in mainstream classrooms to improve bonding and behavior of low achievers. *American Educational Research Journal*, 25, 31–50.

Haycock, K. (1998). Good teaching matters . . . a lot. *Thinking K–16*, 3, 1–14.

Haydon, T., & Musti-Rao, S. (2011). Effective use of behavior-specific praise: A middle school case study. *Beyond Behavior*, 20, 31–39.

Hayling, C., Cook, C., Gresham, G., State, T., & Kern, L. (2008). An analysis of the status and stability of the behaviors of students with emotional and behavioral difficulties. *Journal of Behavioral Education*, 17, 24–42.

He, Y., & Cooper, J. (2011). Struggles and strategies in teaching: Voices of five novice secondary teachers. *Teacher Education Quarterly*, 38, 97–116.

Helmer, S., & Eddy, C. (2003). *Look at me when I talk to you: ESL learners in non-ESL classrooms*. Toronto, Ontario: Pippin.

Henderson, A., & Mapp, K. (2002). *A new wave of evidence: The impact of school, family, and community connections on student achievement*. Annual Synthesis, 2002. Austin, TX: Southwest Education Development Lab.

Hlodan, O. (2010). Mobile learning anytime, anywhere. *American Institute of Biological Sciences*, 60, 682–689.

Hong, J., & Garbarino, J. (2012). Risk and protective factors for homophobic bullying in schools. An application of the social-ecological framework. *Educational Psychology Review*, 24, 271–285.

Hoover, J., Klingner, J., Baca, L., & Patton, J. (2008). *Methods for teaching culturally and linguistically diverse exceptional learners*. Upper Saddle River, NJ: Pearson.

Hoover, J., & Oliver, R. (1996). *The bullying prevention handbook: A guide for principals, teachers, and counselors*. Bloomington, IN: National Educational Service.

Horner, R. H., & Sugai, G. (2005). School-wide positive behavior support: An alternative approach to discipline in schools. In L. Bambara & L. Kern (Eds.), *Positive behavior support* (pp. 359–390). New York, NY: Guilford Press.

House, S. (2003). *Behavior intervention manual*. Columbia, MO: Hawthorne Educational Services.

Huggins, E. (1993). *The assist program: Multiple intelligence lessons*. Longmont, CO: Sopris West.

Huggins, P., Manion, D., Shakarian, L., & Moen, L. (1997). *Multiple intelligences: Helping kids discover the many ways to be smart*. Longmont, CO: Sopris West.

Huggins, P., Moen, L., & Manion, D. (1993). *Teaching friendship skills: Primary version*. Longmont, CO: Sopris West.

Hughes, J., Zhang, D., & Hill, C. (2006). Peer assessments of normative and individual teacher-student support on elementary students' peer acceptance: A prospective analysis. *Journal of School Psychology*, 43, 447–463.

Humble-Thaden, M. (2011). Student reflective perceptions of high school educational cell phone technology usage. *The Journal of Technology Studies*, 37, 10–16.

Hunter, J., & Csikszentmihalyi, M. (2003). The positive psychology of interested adolescents. *Journal of Adolescence and Youth*, 32, 27–35.

Hyman, I., & Perone, D. (1998). The other side of school violence: Educator policies and practices that may contribute to student misbehavior. *Journal of School Psychology*, 36, 7–27.

Igoa, C. (1995). *The inner world of the immigrant child*. New York, NY: St. Martin's Press.

Illinois State Board of Education. (2003). Involving immigrant parents and refugee families in their children's schools: Barriers, challenges and successful strategies. Retrieved from www.brycs.org/documents/upload/InvolvingFamilies.pdf.

Ito, M., Baumer, S., Bittani, M., Boyd, D., Herr-Stephenson, B., Horst, H., . . . Tripp, L. (2010). *Hanging out, messing around, and geeking out*. Cambridge, MA: MIT Press.

Jackson, K., & Remillard, J. (2005). Rethinking parent involvement: African American mothers construct their roles in the mathematics education of their children. *School Community Journal*, 15, 1–73.

Jackson, S., & Lunenburg, F. (2010). School performance indicators, accountability ratings, and student achievement. *American Secondary Education*, 39, 27–44.

Janney, R., & Snell, M. (1999). *Modifying schoolwork*. Pacific Grove, CA: Brooks/Cole.

Jensen, E. (2004). *Brain compatible strategies*. Thousand Oaks, CA: Corwin Press.

Jensen, E. (2005). *Teaching with the brain in mind* (2nd ed.). Alexandria, VA: ASCD.

Jensen, E. (2008). *Brain-based learning: The new paradigm of teaching*. Thousand Oaks, CA: Corwin.

Jeynes, W. (2007). The relationship between parental involvement and urban secondary school student academic achievement: A meta-analysis. *Urban Education*, 42, 82–110.

Johns, B., & Carr, V. (1995). *Techniques for managing verbally and physically aggressive students*. Denver, CO: Love.

Johns, K., & Espinoza, C. (1996). *Management strategies for culturally diverse classrooms*. Bloomington, IN: Phi Delta Kappa Educational Foundation.

Johnson, B., Whitington, V., & Oswald, M. (1994). Teacher's views of school discipline: A theoretical framework. *Cambridge Journal of Education*, 24, 262–278.

Johnson, D., & Johnson, R. (1975). *Learning together and alone: Group theory and group skills*. Englewood Cliffs, NJ: Prentice Hall.

Johnson, D., & Johnson, R. (1991). *Teaching students to be peacemakers*. Edina, MN: Interaction Book.

Johnson, D., & Johnson, R. (1995). *Reducing school violence through conflict resolution*. Alexandria, VA: Association for Supervision and Curriculum Development.

Johnson, D., & Johnson, R. (2009). *Joining together: Group theory and group skills*. Edina, MN: Interaction Book.

Johnson, D., Johnson, R., Bartlett, J., & Johnson, L. (1988). *Our cooperative classroom*. Edina, MN: Interaction Book.

Johnson, D., Johnson, R., & Holubec, E. (2007). *Nuts and bolts of cooperative learning* (2nd ed.). Edina, MN: Interaction Book.

Johnson, D., Johnson, R., & Holubec, E. (2008). *Cooperation in the classroom* (8th ed.). Edina, MN: Interaction Book.

Johnson, D., Johnson, R., & Holubec, E. (2009). *Circles of learning: Cooperation in the classroom* (6th ed.). Edina, MN: Interaction Book.

Johnson, R. (2009). *Reaching out* (10th ed.). Boston, MA: Allyn & Bacon.

Johnson, R., & Johnson, D. (1985). *Cooperative learning: Warm-ups, grouping strategies and group activities*. Edina, MN: Interaction Book.

Johnson, R., & Johnson, D. (Eds.). (1987). *Structuring cooperative learning: Lesson plans for teachers*. Edina, MN: Interaction Book.

Johnson, V. (1996). *Family center guidebook*. Baltimore, MD: Center on Families, Communities, Schools and Children's Learning, Johns Hopkins University.

Johnston, B. (1995). "Withitness": Real or fictional? *The Physical Educator*, 51, 22–28.

Jolivette, K., Stichter, J., & McCormick, K. (2002). Making choices—improving behavior—engaging in learning. *Teaching Exceptional Children*, 34, 24–29.

Jones, F. (1987). *Positive classroom discipline*. New York, NY: McGraw-Hill.

Jones, V. (1980). *Adolescents with behavior problems: Strategies for teaching, counseling, and parent involvement*. Boston, MA: Allyn & Bacon.

Jones, V. (1991). Experienced teachers' assessment of classroom management skills presented in a summer course. *Journal of Instructional Psychology*, 18, 103–109.

Jones, V. (1996). Classroom management. In J. Silula (Ed.), *Handbook of research on teacher education* (2nd ed., pp. 503–521). New York, NY: Macmillan.

Jones, V. (2002). Creating communities of support: The missing link in dealing with student behavior problems and reducing violence in schools. *Beyond Behavior, 11,* 16–19.

Jones, V. (2006). How do teachers learn to be effective classroom managers? In C. Evertson & C. Weinstein (Eds.), *Handbook for classroom management: Research, practice, and contemporary issues.* Mahwah, NJ: Lawrence Erlbaum.

Jones, V. (2015). *Practical classroom management* (2nd ed.). Boston, MA: Pearson.

Jones, V., Dohrn, E., & Dunn, C. (2004). *Creating effective programs for students with emotional and behavior disorders: Interdisciplinary approaches for adding meaning and hope to behavior change interventions.* Boston, MA: Allyn & Bacon.

Jones, V., Greenwood, S., & Dunn, C. (in press). *Prevention & intervention for students with emotional and behavior problems: A continuum of services.* Boston, MA: Pearson.

Jones, V., & Jones, L. (1981). *Responsible school discipline.* Boston, MA: Allyn & Bacon.

Jones, V., & Jones, L. (1986). *Comprehensive classroom management: Creating positive learning environments.* Boston, MA: Allyn & Bacon.

Jones, V., & Jones, L. (1995). *Comprehensive classroom management: Creating communities of support and solving problems* (6th ed.). Boston, MA: Allyn & Bacon.

Juvonen, J. (2007). Reforming middle schools: Focus on continuity, social connectedness, and engagement. *Educational Psychologist, 42,* 197–208.

Juvonen, J., & Graham, S. (2001). *Peer harassment in school: The plight of the vulnerable and victimized.* New York, NY: Guilford Press.

Kagan, S. (2009). *Kagan cooperative learning.* San Clemente, CA: Kagan Cooperative Learning.

Kamps, D., Wills, H., Heitzman-Powell, L., Laylin, J., Szoke, C., Petrillo, T., & Culey, A. (2011). Class-wide function-related intervention teams: Effects of group contingency programs in urban classroom. *Journal of Positive Behavior Interventions, 13,* 154–167.

Kandel, E., Schwartz, J., Jessell, T., Siegelbaum, S., & Hudspeth, A. (Eds.). (2013). *Principles of neural science* (5th ed.). New York, NY: McGraw-Hill.

Kaplan, C. (1992). Teachers' punishment histories and their selection of disciplinary strategies. *Contemporary Psychology, 17*(3), 258–265.

Kaplan, J., & Carter, J. (1995). *Beyond behavior modification: A cognitive-behavioral approach to behavior management in schools.* Austin, TX: Pro-Ed.

Karr-Morse, R., & Wiley, M. (1997). *Ghosts from the nursery: Tracing the roots of violence.* New York, NY: Atlantic Monthly Press.

Karrie, A., Faggella-Luby, M., Bae, S., & Wehmeyer, M. (2004). The effect of choice-making as an intervention for problem behavior: A meta-analysis. *Journal of Positive Behavior Interventions, 6,* 228–237.

Katz, S. (1999). Teaching in tensions: Latino immigrant youth, their teachers, and the structures of schooling. *Teachers College Record, 100,* 809–840.

Kauffman, J. (1997). *Characteristics of emotional and behavioral disorders of children and youth* (6th ed.). Upper Saddle River, NJ: Merrill/Prentice Hall.

Kauffman, J. (2001). *Characteristics of emotional and behavioral disorders of children and youth* (7th ed.). Upper Saddle River, NJ: Merrill/Prentice Hall.

Kauffman, J., Hallahan, D., Mostert, M., Trent, S., & Nuttycomb, D. (1993). *Managing classroom behavior.* Boston, MA: Allyn & Bacon.

Kaufman, E., Robinson, S., Bellah, K., Akers, C., Haase-Wittler, P., & Martindale, L. (2008). Engaging students with brain-based learning. *Techniques, 83,* 50–55.

Kaufman, P., Bradby, D., & Owings, J. (1992). *National longitudinal study of 1988: Characteristics of at-risk students in NELS: 88.* Washington, DC: U.S. Office of Education, Office of Educational Research and Improvement.

Kawall, S. (2009). *Successful teachers: What it takes to raise academic achievement of urban minority students.* (Doctoral dissertation). Retrieved from *Dissertation Abstracts International, 70*(03A), 844.

Kearny, R., Pawlukewicz, J., & Guardino, M. (2014). Children with anxiety disorders: Use of cognitive behavioral therapy model within a social milieu. *Journal of Research in Childhood Education, 28,* 59–68.

Kellam, S., Ling, X., Merisca, R., Brown, C., & Ialongo, N. (1998). The effect of level of aggression in the first grade classroom on the course and malleability of aggressive behavior in middle school. *Development and Psychopathology, 10,* 165–185.

Kennedy, B. (2011). Teaching disaffected middle school students: How classroom dynamics shape students' experiences. *Middle School Journal, 42,* 32–42.

Kennedy, C. (2000). When reinforcers for problem behavior are not readily apparent: Extending functional assessments to complex problem behaviors. *Journal of Positive Behavior Interventions, 2,* 195–201.

Kerr, M., & Nelson, M. (2002). *Strategies for addressing behavior problems in the classroom.* Upper Saddle River, NJ: Merrill/Prentice Hall.

Kerr, R. (1997). *Positively! Learning to manage negative emotions.* Portland, ME: J. Weston Walch.

Kessels, U., & Steinmayr, R. (2013). Macho-man in school: Toward the role of gender role self-concepts and help seeking in school performance. *Learning and Individual Differences, 23,* 234–240.

Kidalgo, N., Bright, J., Siu, S., Swap, S., & Epstein, J. (1995). Research on families, schools, and communities: A multicultural perspective. In J. Banks (Ed.), *Handbook of research on multicultural education* (pp. 498–524). New York, NY: Macmillan.

Kingery, J., Erdley, C., & Marshall, K. (2011). Acceptance and friendship as predictors of early adolescents' adjustment across the middle school transition. *Merrill-Palmer Quarterly, 57,* 215–243.

Kleinfeld, J. (1972). *Instructional style and the intellectual performance of Indian and Eskimo students.* Project No. 1-J-027 (Final Report). Washington, DC: Office of Education, U.S. Department of Health, Education, and Welfare.

Kohn, A. (1991). Caring kids: The role of the schools. *Phi Delta Kappan, 72,* 496–506.

Kohn, A. (1996). *Beyond discipline: From compliance to community.* Alexandria, VA: Association for Supervision and Curriculum Development.

Kohn, A. (1999). *Punished by rewards: The trouble with gold stars, incentive plans, A's, praise, and other bribes.* Boston, MA: Houghton Mifflin.

Kolb, L. (2011). Adventures with cell phones. *Educational Leadership, 68,* 39–43.

Kosciw, J., Bartkiewicz, M., & Greytak, E. (2012). Promising strategies for prevention of the bullying of lesbian, gay, bisexual, and transgender youth. *The Prevention Researcher, 19,* 10–13.

Kounin, J. (1970). *Discipline and group management in classrooms.* New York, NY: Holt, Rinehart and Winston.

Kovalik, S., & Olsen, K. (2005). *Exceeding expectations: A user's guide to implementing brain research in the classroom* (3rd ed.). Federal Way, WA: Books for Educators.

Krathwohl, D., Bloom, B., & Masia, B. (1964). *Taxonomy of educational objectives, handbook II: Affective domain.* New York, NY: David McKay.

Kriete, R. (2002). *The morning meeting book.* Greenfield, MA: Northeast Foundation for Children.

Kriete, R., & Davis, C. (2014). *The morning meeting book.* Turners Fall, MA: Northeast Foundation for Children.

Kusche, C., & Greenberg, M. (2000). *PATHS: Promoting alternative thinking strategies: A comprehensive curriculum for preventing bullying and increasing critical-thinking skills in grades K–6.* South Deerfield, MA: Channing Bete.

Kuster, D., Bain, C., Newton, C., & Milbrandt, M. (2010). Novice art teachers: Navigating through the first year. *Visual Arts Research, 36,* 44–54.

Kuykendall, C. (2004). *From rage to hope: Strategies for reclaiming Black and Hispanic students* (2nd ed.). Bloomington, IN: National Educational Service.

LaBenne, W., & Green, B. (1969). *Educational implications of self-concept theory.* Pacific Palisades, CA: Goodyear.

Ladson-Billings, G. (1994). *The dreamkeepers: Successful teachers of African American children.* San Francisco, CA: Jossey-Bass.

Laird, R., Jordan, K., Dodge, K., Pettit, G., & Bates, J. (2001). Peer rejection in childhood, involvement with antisocial peers in early adolescence, and the development of externalizing behavior problems. *Development and Psychopathology, 13,* 337–354.

LaMarche, G. (2011). The time is right to end "zero tolerance." *Education Week, 30,* 35, 37.

Landau, B. (Ed.). (1999). *Practicing judicious discipline: An educator's guide to a democratic classroom.* San Francisco, CA: Caddo Gap Press.

Lane, K., & Beebe-Frankenberger, M. (2004). *School-based interventions.* Columbia, MO: Hawthorne Educational Service.

Lane, K., Pierson, M., Stang, K., & Carter, E. (2010). Teacher expectations of students' classroom behavior: Do expectations vary as a function of school risk? *Remedial and Special Education, 31*, 163–174.

Lane, K., Wehby, J., Menzies, H., Doukas, G., Muntonm, S., & Gregg, R. (2003). Social skills instruction for students at risk for antisocial behavior: The effects of small group instruction. *Behavioral Disorders, 28*, 229–248.

Lareau, A., & Horvat, E. (1999). Moments of social inclusion and exclusion: Race, class, and cultural capital in family–school relationships. *Sociology of Education, 72*, 37–53.

Lastrapes, R. (2014). Using the Good Behavior Game in an inclusive classroom. *Interventions in School and Clinic, 49*, 225–229.

Lawson, M. (2003). School-family relations in context. Parent and teacher perceptions of parent involvement. *Urban Education, 38*, 77–133.

Lazear, D. (1999). *Eight ways of knowing: Teaching for multiple intelligences* (3rd ed.). Arlington Heights, IL: SkyLight Training.

Lazear, D. (2003). *Eight ways of teaching: The artistry of teaching with multiple intelligences* (4th ed.). Arlington Heights, IL: SkyLight.

Lee, S. (1996). *Unraveling the "model minority" stereotype: Listening to Asian American youth.* New York, NY: Teachers College Press.

Lee, S., Wehmeyer, M., Soukup, J., & Palmer, S. (2010). Impact of curriculum modifications on access to the general education curriculum for students with disabilities. *Exceptional Children, 76*, 213–233.

Letts, N. (1997). *Creating a caring classroom: Hundreds of practical ways to make it happen.* New York, NY: Scholastic.

Levine, P., & Kline, M. (2010). *Trauma through a child's eyes: Awakening the ordinary miracle of healing, infancy through adolescence.* Berkeley, CA: North Atlantic Books.

Lewis, C., Schaps, E., & Watson, M. (1996). The caring classroom's academic edge. *Educational Leadership, 54*, 16–21.

Lewis, R. (2001). Classroom discipline and student responsibility: The students' view. *Teacher and Teacher Education, 17*, 307–319.

Lewis, R., & St. John, N. (1974). Contribution of cross-racial friendship to minority group achievement in desegregated classrooms. *Sociometry, 37*, 79–91.

Lewis, T. (2004). Classroom-level supports for students with learning and behavioral problems. In L. M. Bullock, R. A. Gable, & K. J. Melloy (Eds.), *Effective interventions for classrooms, schools, and communities: Making a difference in the lives of students with learning and behavioral problems* (pp. 15–18). Reston, VA: Council for Exceptional Children.

Lewis, T., Sugai, G., & Colvin, G. (1998). Reducing problem behavior through a school-wide system of effective behavioral support: Investigation of a school-wide social skills training program and contextual interventions. *School Psychology Review, 27*, 446–459.

Lewis, T. J., & Newcomer, L. L. (2005). Reducing problem behavior through school-wide systems of positive behavior support. In P. Clough, P. Garner, J. T. Pardeck, & F. Yuen (Eds.), *Handbook of emotional and behavioural difficulties in education* (pp. 261–272). London, England: Sage.

Lewis, T. J., Newcomer, L., Trussell, R., & Richter, M. (2006). School-wide positive behavior support: Building systems to develop and maintain appropriate social behavior. In C. S. Everston & C. M. Weinstein (Eds.), *Handbook of classroom management: Research, practice and contemporary issues* (pp. 833–854). New York, NY: Lawrence Erlbaum Associates.

Lewis, T. J., & Sugai, G. (1999). Effective behavior support: A systems approach to proactive school-wide management. *Focus on Exceptional Children, 31*(6), 1–24.

Liem, G., & Martin, A. (2011). Peer relationships and adolescents' academic and non-academic outcomes: Same-sex and opposite-sex peer effects and the mediating role of school engagement. *British Journal of Educational Psychology, 81*, 183–206.

Lightfoot, S. L. (1983). *The good high school.* New York, NY: Basic Books.

Linn Benton Lincoln Education Service District. (2001). *Harassment prevention curriculum: Empowerment and skill-building for student safety.* Can be obtained by writing Linn Benton Lincoln ESD at 905 Fourth Avenue SE, Albany, OR 97321-3199.

Lipsitz, J. (1984). *Successful schools for young adolescents.* New Brunswick, NJ: Transaction Books.

Lipson, G. (1997). *Self-esteem, K–3: Concepts for activities, discussions and insights.* Carthage, IL: Teaching & Learning.

Long, N., Newman, R., & Morse, W. (1996). *Conflict in the classroom: The education of at-risk and troubled students* (5th ed.). Austin, TX: Pro-Ed.

Long, N., Wood, M., & Fescer, F. (2001). *Life space crisis intervention: Talking with children and youth to improve relationships and change behavior* (2nd ed.). Austin, TX: Pro-Ed.

Lotan, R. (2006). Managing groupwork in the heterogeneous classroom. In C. Evertson & C. Weinstein (Eds.), *Handbook of classroom management: Research, practice, and contemporary issues.* Mahwah, NJ: Lawrence Erlbaum.

Luczynski, C., & Hanley, G. (2013). Prevention of problem behavior by teaching functional communication and self-control skills to preschoolers. *Journal of Applied Behavior Analysis, 46*, 355–368.

Ludwig, T. (2004). *My secret bully.* Berkeley, CA: Tricycle Press.

Ludwig, T. (2006a). *Just kidding.* Berkeley, CA: Tricycle Press.

Ludwig, T. (2006b). *Sorry.* Berkeley, CA: Tricycle Press.

Lundeen, C. (2002). The study of beginning teachers' perceived problems with classroom management and adult relationships throughout the first year of teaching. (Unpublished doctoral dissertation). University of North Carolina at Chapel Hill.

Maag, J., & Larson, P. (2004). Training a general education teacher to apply functional assessment. *Education and Treatment of Children, 27*, 26–36.

Macias, J. (1987). The hidden curriculum of Papago teachers: American Indian strategies for mitigating cultural discontinuity in early school. In G. Spindler & L. Spindler (Eds.), *Interpretive ethnography of education: At home and abroad* (pp. 363–380). Hillsdale, NJ: Lawrence Erlbaum.

Maheady, L., & Gard, J. (2010). Classwide peer tutoring: Practice, theory, research, and personal narrative. *Intervention in School & Clinic, 46*, 71–78.

Maher, C. (1987). Involving behaviorally disordered adolescents in instructional planning: Effectiveness of the GOAL procedures. *Journal of Child and Adolescent Psychotherapy, 4*, 204–210.

Maple, F. (1977). *Shared decision making.* Beverly Hills, CA: Sage.

Marees, N., & Petermann, F. (2012). Cyberbullying: An increased challenge for schools. *School Psychology International, 33*, 467–476.

Mariconda, B. (2003). *Easy and effective ways to communicate with parents: Practical techniques and tips for parent conferences, open houses, notes home, and more that work for every situation.* New York, NY: Scholastic.

Martella, R., Nelson, J., Marchand-Martella, N., & O'Reilly, M. (2012). *Comprehensive behavior management: Individualized, classroom, and school-wide approaches.* Newbury Park, CA: Sage.

Martin, G., & Pear, J. (1996). *Behavior modification: What it is and how to do it.* Upper Saddle River, NJ: Prentice Hall.

Martinez, S. (2009). A system gone berserk: How are zero-tolerance policies really affecting schools? *Preventing School Failure, 53*, 153–157.

Marzano, R. (2003). *What works in schools: Translating research into action.* Alexandria, VA: Association for Supervision and Curriculum Development.

Marzano, R., Marzano, J., & Pickering, D. (2003). *Classroom management that works.* Alexandria, VA: Association for Supervision and Curriculum Development.

Maslow, A. (1968). *Toward a psychology of being.* New York, NY: D. Van Nostrand.

Mason, K. (2008). Cyberbullying: A preliminary assessment for school personnel. *Psychology in the Schools, 45*, 323–348.

Mastropieri, M., & Scruggs, T. (2007). *The inclusive classroom: Strategies for effective instruction.* Upper Saddle River, NJ: Merrill/Prentice Hall.

McAdams, C., & Schmidt, C. (2007). How to help a bully: Recommendations for counseling the proactive aggressor. *Professional School Counseling, 11*, 120–128.

McCaslin, M., Bozack, A., Napoleon, L., Thomas, A., Vasquez, V., Wayman, V., & Zhang, J. (2006). Self-regulated learning and classroom management: Theory, research, and considerations for classroom practice. In C. Evertson & C. Weinstein (Eds.), *Handbook of classroom management: Research, practice, and contemporary issues.* Mahwah, NJ: Lawrence Erlbaum.

McCaslin, M., & Good, T. (1992). Compliant cognition: The misalliance of management and instructional goals in current school reform. *Educational Researcher, 21*(3), 4–17.

McCloud, C. (2007). *Have you filled a bucket today? A guide to daily happiness for kids.* Northville, MI: Ferne Press.

McCloud, C., & Messing, D. (2006). *Have you filled a bucket today?* Northville, MI: Ferne Press.

McConnell, K., Patton, J., & Polloway, E. (2000). *Behavioral intervention planning: Completing a functional behavioral assessment and developing a behavioral intervention plan.* Austin, TX: Pro-Ed.

McEachern, A., & Snyder, J. (2012). Gender differences in predicting antisocial behaviors: Developmental consequences of physical and relational aggression. *Journal of Abnormal Child Psycholoiy, 40,* 501–512.

McIntyre, T. (1996). Does the way we teach create behavior disorders in culturally different children? *Education and Treatment of Children, 19,* 354–370.

McKeown, H. (1998). Do you know where the parents of your children are? In E. Lee, D. Menkart, & M. Okazawa-Rey (Eds.), *Beyond heroes and holidays: A practical guide to K–12 antiracist, multicultural education and staff development* (pp. 88–91). Washington, DC: Network of Educators on the Americas.

McLaughlin, H. (1992, April). *Seeking solidarity and responsibility: The classroom contexts of control and negotiation.* Paper presented at the annual meeting of the American Educational Research Association, San Francisco, CA. (ERIC Document Reproduction Service No. ED 349 644).

McNamara, B., & McNamara, F. (1997). *Keys to dealing with bullies.* Hauppauge, NY: Barrons.

McNeely, C., Nonnemaker, J., & Blum, R. (2002). Promoting school connectedness: Evidence from the National Longitudinal Study of Adolescent Health, *Journal of School Health, 72,* 138–146.

Mecca, J. (2001a). *Character education book of plays: Elementary level.* Nashville, TN: Incentive.

Mecca, J. (2001b). *Character education book of plays: Middle grade level.* Nashville, TN: Incentive.

Meehan, G., Hughes, J., & Cavell, T. (2003). Teacher-student relationships as compensatory resources for aggressive children. *Child Development, 74,* 1145–1157.

Mehta, S. (2009, December 14). Controlling a classroom isn't as easy as ABC. *Los Angeles Times.* Retrieved from www.latimes.com/news/local/la-me-classroom-control142009dec14,0,5354521.story.

Meier, D. (1995). *The power of their ideas.* Boston, MA: Beacon Press.

Mendler, A. (1992). *What do I do when . . . ? How to achieve discipline with dignity in the classroom.* Bloomington, IN: National Educational Service.

Mercer, S., & DeRosier, M. (2008). Teacher preference, peer rejection, and student aggression: A prospective study of transactional influence

and independent contributions to emotional adjustment and grades. *Journal of School Psychology, 46,* 661–685.

Merkel, S. (2009). *A look at the beginning: Strengths, weaknesses, and the support structures for new teachers from the perspective of elementary principals.* (Doctoral dissertation). Retrieved from *Dissertation Abstracts International, 70*(04A), 1243.

Merrell, K. W., Gueldner, B. A., Ross, S. W., & Isava, D. M. (2008). How effective are school bullying intervention programs? A meta-analysis of intervention research. *School Psychology Quarterly, 23,* 26–42.

Merritt, E., Wanless, S., Rimm-Kaufman, S., Cameron, C., & Peugh, J. (2012). The contribution of teachers' emotional support to children's social behaviors and self-regulatory skills in first grade. *School Psychology Review, 41,* 141–159.

Michie, G. (1999). *Holler if you hear me: The education of a teacher and his students.* New York, NY: Teachers College Press.

Mikami, A., Gregory, A., Allen, J., Pianta, R., & Lun, J. (2011). Effects of a teacher development intervention on peer relationships in secondary classrooms. *School Psychology Review, 40,* 367–385.

Mikami, A., Griggs, M., Reuland, M., Gregory, A. (2012). Teacher practices as predictors of children's classroom social preference. *Journal of School Psychology, 50,* 95–111.

Milner, R. (2006). Classroom management in urban classrooms. In C. Evertson & C. Weinstein (Eds.), *Handbook of classroom management: Research, practice, and contemporary issues.* Mahwah, NJ: Lawrence Erlbaum.

Mitchell, A. (1998). African-American teachers: Unique roles and universal lessons. *Education and Urban Society, 31,* 104–122.

Mitchell, B., Stormont, M., & Gage, N. (2011). Tier two interventions implemented within the context of a tiered prevention framework. *Behavioral Disorders, 36,* 241–261.

Moll, L., Amanti, D., Neff, D., & Gonzalez, N. (1992). Funds of knowledge for teaching: Using a qualitative approach to connect homes to schools. *Theory into Practice, 31,* 132–141.

Monroe, C. (2009). Teachers closing the discipline gap in an urban middle school. *Urban Education, 44,* 322–347.

Moore, D., Anderson, A., Glassenbury, M., Lang, R., & Didden, R. (2013). Increasing on-task behavior in students in a regular classroom: Effectiveness of a self-management procedure using a tactile prompt. *Journal of Behavioral Education, 22,* 302–311.

Morse, W. (1987). Introduction to the special issue. *Teaching Exceptional Children, 4,* 4–6.

Mortimore, P., & Sammons, P. (1987). New evidence on effective elementary schools. *Educational Leadership, 45,* 4–8.

Mueller, M., Sterling-Turner, H., & Moore, J. (2005). Towards developing a classroom-based functional analysis condition to assess escape-to-attention as a variable maintaining problem behavior. *School Psychology Review, 34,* 425–431.

Muller, C., Katz, S., & Dance, L. (1999). Investing in teaching and learning: Dynamics of the teacher–student relationship from each actor's perspective. *Urban Education, 34,* 292–337.

Mumper, M. (2000). *Teaching kids to care and cooperate.* New York, NY: Scholastic.

Murdick, N., & Gartin, B. (1993). How to handle students exhibiting violent behavior. *The Clearing House, 66,* 278–280.

Murray, C., & Greenberg, M. (2000). Children's relationship with teachers and bonds with school: An investigation of patterns and correlates in middle childhood. *Psychology in the Schools, 38,* 425–446.

Nagel, N. (1996). *Learning through real-world problem solving: The power of integrative teaching.* Thousand Oaks, CA: Corwin.

Nard, P. (2007). *The effects of induction training on beginning teachers' classroom management.* (Doctoral dissertation). Retrieved from *Dissertation Abstracts International, 69*(08A).

National Center for Education Statistics. (2010). *Indicators of school crime and safety: Elementary and secondary schools: Fast facts.* Washington, DC: U.S. Department of Education: Institute of Education Sciences for Educational Statistics.

National Center for Education Statistics. (2013). *Fast facts: Elementary and secondary.* Washington, DC: U.S. Department of Education, Institute of Education Sciences.

National School Climate Council. (2007). The school climate challenge: Narrowing the gap between school climate research and school climate policy, practice guidelines and teacher education policy. Retrieved from schoolclimate.org/climate/documents/school-climate.

National Youth Leadership Council. (2008). *K–12 service-learning standards for quality practice.* St. Paul, MN: Author.

Neiman, S., Robers, B., & Robers, S. (2012). Bullying: A state of affairs. *Journal of Law & Education, 41,* 603–648.

Nelson, J. R. (1996). Designing schools to meet the needs of students who exhibit disruptive behavior. *Journal of Emotional and Behavioral Disorders, 4,* 147–161.

Nelson, J. R., & Carr, B. (1999). *Think time strategy for schools: Bringing order to the classroom.* Longmont, CO: Sopris West.

Nelson, J. R., Crabtree, M., Marchand-Martella, N., & Martella, R. (1998). Teaching good behavior in the whole school. *Teaching Exceptional Children, 30,* 4–9.

Nelson, J. R., & Roberts, M. (2000). Ongoing reciprocal teacher–student interactions involving disruptive behaviors in general education classrooms. *Journal of Emotional and Behavioral Disorders, 8,* 27–37, 48.

Nelson, R., Martella, R., & Galand, B. (1998). The effects of teaching school expectations and establishing a consistent consequence on formal office disciplinary actions. *Journal of Emotional and Behavioral Disorders, 6,* 153–161.

Nichols, P. (1999). *Clear thinking: Talking back to whispering shadows.* Iowa City, IA: River Lights.

Nichols, P., & Shaw, M. (1999). *Whispering shadows: Think clearly and claim your personal power.* Iowa City, IA: River Lights.

Nicholson-Nelson, K. (1998). *Developing students' multiple intelligences: Hundreds of practical ideas easily integrated.* New York, NY: Scholastic.

Niesyn, M. (2009). Strategies for success: Evidence-based instructional interventions for students with emotional and behavioral disorders. *Preventing School Failure, 53,* 227–233.

Noddings, N. (1984). *Caring: A feminine approach to ethics and moral education.* Berkeley, CA: University of California Press.

Noddings, N. (1992). *The challenge to care in schools: An alternative approach to education.* New York, NY: Teachers College Press.

Noguera, P. (1995). Preventing and producing violence: A critical analysis of responses to school violence. *Harvard Educational Review, 65,* 189–212.

Noguera, P. (2003). Schools, prisons, and social implications of punishment: Rethinking disciplinary practices. *Theory into Practice, 42,* 341–350.

Noguera, P. (2008). *The trouble with Black boys . . . and other reflections on race, equity, and the future of public education.* San Francisco, CA: Jossey-Bass.

Norris, J. (2003). Looking at classroom management from a social and emotional learning lens. *Theory into Practice, 42,* 313–318.

Northeast Foundation for Children. (2005). *Creating a safe and friendly school: Lunchrooms, hallways, playgrounds and more (Articles by teachers).* Turners Falls, MA: Author.

Northwest Education. (2008, fall). *Northwest Education, 8*(1). The journal of the Northwest Regional Education Laboratory.

O'Connor, K., & Stichter, J. (2011). Using problem solving frameworks to address challenging behavior of students with high-functioning autism and/or Asperger Syndrome. *Beyond Behavior, 20,* 11–24.

Office of Juvenile Justice and Delinquency Prevention. (1995). *Guide for implementing the comprehensive strategy for serious, violent and chronic juvenile offenders.* Washington, DC: U.S. Department of Justice, Office of Justice Programs NCJ 153681.

O'Leary, D., & O'Leary, S. (Eds.). (1977). *Classroom management: The successful use of behavior modification* (2nd ed.). New York, NY: Pergamon Press.

Olsen, L., & Jaramillo, A. (Eds.). (1999). *Turning the tides of exclusion: A guide for educators and advocates for immigrant students.* Oakland, CA: Coast Litho.

Olweus, D. (2003). A profile of bullying. *Educational Leadership, 60,* 12–17.

Olweus, D., & Limber, S. (1999). The bullying prevention program. In D. Elliott (Series Ed.), *Blueprints for violence prevention.* Boulder, CO: Center for the Study and Prevention of Violence, Institute of Behavioral Science, University of Colorado.

Olweus, D., Limber, S., Snyder, M., & Mullin, N. (2009). *Class meetings that matter: A year's worth of resources for grades 6–8.* Center City, MN: Hazelden.

O'Neill, R., Horner, R., Albin, R., Sprague, J., Storey, K., & Newton, S. (1997). *Functional assessment and program development for problem behavior: A practical handbook* (2nd ed.). Grove, CA: Brooks/Cole.

The Oregonian. (1996, September 4). Back to School. *The Oregonian,* p. E1.

Orpinas, P., & Horne, A. (2010). Creating a positive school climate and developing social competence. In S. Jimersen, S. Swearer, & D. Espelage (Eds.), *Handbook of bullying in schools: An international perspective* (pp. 49–59). New York, NY: Routledge.

Osher, D., Bear, G., Sprague, J., & Doyle, W. (2010). How can we improve school discipline? *Educational Researcher, 39,* 48–58.

Paley, V. (1989). *White teacher.* Cambridge, MA: Harvard University Press.

Pappano, L., (2014). "Trauma-sensitive" schools: A new framework for reaching troubled students. *Harvard Education Letter, 30,* 1–7.

Parris, L., Varjas, K., Meyers, J., & Cutts, H. (2012). High school students' perceptions of coping with cyberbullying. *Youth and Society, 44,* 284–306.

Patall, E., Cooper, H., & Wynn, S. (2010). The effectiveness and relative importance of choice in the classroom. *Journal of Educational Psychology, 102,* 896–915.

Pate, E., Homestead, E., & McGinnis, K. (1997). *Making integrated curriculum work.* New York, NY: Teachers College Press.

Pate-Clevenger, R., Dusing, J., Houck, P., & Zuber, J. (2008). *Improvement of off-task behavior of elementary and high school students through the use of cooperative learning strategies.* Retrieved from ERIC database (ED500839).

Payne, R. (2005). *Working with parents: Building relationships for student success.* Highlands, TX: Aha Process, Inc.

Pellegrino, A. (2010). Pre-service teachers and classroom authority. *American Secondary Education, 38,* 62–78.

Peregoy, S., & Boyle, O. (1993). *Reading, writing, and learning in ESL.* New York, NY: Academic Press.

Perry, B. (2006). *Working with traumatized youth in child welfare.* New York, NY: Guilford Press.

Phelan, P., Davidson, A., & Cao, H. (1992). Speaking up: Students' perspectives on school. *Phi Delta Kappan, 73,* 695–704.

Pianta, R. (2006). Classroom management and relationships between children and teachers: Implications for research and practice. In C. Evertson & C. Weinstein (Eds.), *Handbook of classroom management: Research, practice, and contemporary issues.* Mahwah, NJ: Lawrence Erlbaum.

Pianta, R., Howes, C., Burchinal, M., Bryant, D., Clifford, R. M., Early, D. M., & Barbarin, O. (2005). Features of pre-kindergarten programs, classrooms, and teachers: Prediction of observed classroom quality and teacher–child interactions. *Applied Developmental Science, 9*(3), 144–159.

Pianta, R., Steinberg, M., & Rollins, K. (1995). The first two years of school: Teacher–child relationships and deflections in children's classroom adjustment. *Development and Psychopathology, 7,* 295–312.

Plank, S., McDill, E., McPartland, J., & Jordan, W. (2001). Situation and repertoire: Civility, incivility, cursing and politeness in an urban high school. *Teachers College Record, 103,* 504–525.

Polleck, J., & Shabdin, S. (2013). Building culturally responsive communities. *The Clearing House, 86,* 142–149.

Pomeroy, E. (1999). The teacher–student relationship in secondary school: Insights from excluded students. *British Journal of Sociology of Education, 20,* 465–482.

Poplin, M., Rivera, J., Durish, D., Hoff, L., Kawell, S., Pawlak P., . . . Veney, C. (2011). She's strict for a good reason: Highly effective teachers in low-performing schools. *Phi Delta Kappan, 92,* 39–43.

Price, G. (1980). Which learning style elements are stable and which tend to change? *Learning Styles Network Newsletter, 1,* 1.

Purkey, W. (1970). *Self-concept and school achievement.* Englewood Cliffs, NJ: Prentice Hall.

Purkey, W., & Novak, J. (1996). *Inviting school success: A self-concept approach to teaching, learning, and democratic practice* (3rd ed.). Belmont, CA: Wadsworth.

Rafferty, L. (2010). Step-by-step: Teaching students to self-monitor. *Teaching Exceptional Children, 43,* 50–58.

Ramsey, M., Jolivette, K., Patterson, D., & Kennedy, C. (2010). Using choice to increase time on-task task-completion, and accuracy for students with emotional/behavior disorders in a residential facility. *Education and Treatment of Children, 33,* 1–21.

Ratcliff, N., Jones, C., Costner, R., Savage-Davis, E., Sheehan, H., & Hunt, G. (2010). Teacher classroom management behaviors and student time-on-task: Implications for teacher education. *Action in Teacher Education, 32,* 38–51.

Ratey, J. (2001). *A user's guide to the brain: Perception, attention, and the four theaters of the brain.* New York, NY: Pantheon Books.

Rath, T., Reckmeyer, M., & Manning, M. (2009). *How full is your bucket? For kids.* Princeton, NJ: Gallup Press.

Rathmann, P. (1995). *Officer Buckle and Gloria.* New York, NY: Penguin Putnam Books for Young Readers.

Ratzki, A. (1988). The remarkable impact of creating a school community. *American Educator, 12,* 10–43.

Reinke, W., Herman, K., & Stormont, M. (2013). Classroom-level positive behavior supports in schools implementing SW-PBIS: Identifying areas for enhancement. *Journal of Positive Behavior Interventions, 15,* 39–50.

Reinke, W., Stormont, M., Herman, K., Puri, R., & Goel, N. (2011). Supporting children's mental health in schools: Teacher perceptions of needs, roles, and barriers. *School Psychology Quarterly, 26,* 1–13.

Reiss, A., & Ross, J. (Eds.). (1994). *Understanding and preventing violence, volume 3: Social influences.* Washington, DC: National Academies Press.

Resnick, M., Bearman, P., Blum, R., Bauman, K., Harris, K., Jones, J., . . . Udry, R. (1997). Protecting adolescents from harm: Findings from the National Longitudinal Study on Adolescent Health. *JAMA, 278,* 823–832.

Reyes, P., Scribner, J., & Scribner, A. (Eds.). (1999). *Lessons from high-performing Hispanic schools: Creating learning communities.* New York, NY: Teachers College Press.

Rhodes, G., Jenson, W., & Reavis, H. (1993). *The tough kid book.* Longmont, CO: Sopris West.

Riely, J., McKevitt, B., Shriver, M., & Allen, K. (2011). Increasing on-task behavior using teacher attention delivered on a fixed-time schedule. *Journal of Behavioral Education, 20,* 149–162.

Rigby, K. (2012). Bullying in schools: Addressing desires, not only behaviors. *Educational Psychology Review, 24,* 339–348.

Roberts, J. (2000). The bully as victim: Understanding bully behaviors to increase the effectiveness of interventions in the bully–victim dyad. *Professional School Counseling, 4,* 148–155.

Roberts, W. (2007). *Working with parents of bullies and victims.* Thousand Oaks, CA: Corwin.

Rock, D. (2009). Managing with the brain in mind. *Oxford Leadership Journal, 1,* 1–10.

Roderick, T. (2001). *A school of our own: Parents, power, and community at the East Harlem block schools.* New York, NY: Teachers College Press.

Roeser, R., Eccles, J., & Sameroff, A. (1998). Academic and emotional functioning in early adolescence: Longitudinal relations, patterns, and prediction by experience in middle school. *Development and Psychopathology, 10,* 321–352.

Roeser, R., & Galloway, K. (2002). Studying motivation to learn during early adolescence: A holistic perspective. In F. Pajares & T. Urban (Eds.), *Academic motivation of adolescents* (pp. 331–372). Greenwich, CT: LAP Information Age.

Roland, R., & Galloway, D. (2002). Classroom influences on bullying. *Educational Research, 44,* 299–312.

Romain, T. (1997). *Bullies are a pain in the brain.* Minneapolis, MN: Free Spirit.

Romain, T. (1998). *Cliques, phonies, and other baloney.* Minneapolis, MN: Free Spirit.

Rose, C., Espelage, D., Aragon, S., & Elliot, J. (2011). Bullying and victimization among students in special education and general education curricula. *Exceptionality Education International, 21,* 2–14.

Rose, C., & Monda-Amaya, L. (2012). Bullying and victimization among students with disabilities: Effective strategies for classroom teachers. *Intervention in School and Clinic, 48,* 99–107.

Rosenholtz, S., & Simpson, C. (1984). Classroom organization and student stratification. *Elementary School Journal, 85,* 21–37.

Rosenshine, B. (1980). How time is spent in elementary classrooms. In C. Denham & A. Lieberman (Eds.), *Time to learn.* Washington, DC: National Institute of Education.

Rosenshine, B. (1983). Teaching functions in instructional programs. *Elementary School Journal, 83,* 335–351.

Rosenthal, R., & Jacobson, L. (1968). *Pygmalion in the classroom: Teacher expectation and pupils' intellectual development.* New York, NY: Holt, Rinehart and Winston.

Ross, D. (1996). *Childhood bullying and teasing: What school personnel, other professionals and parents can do.* Alexandria, VA: American Counseling Association.

Rowe, M. (1986). Wait time: Slowing down may be a way of speeding up! *Journal of Teacher Education, 37,* 43–50.

Ruck, M., & Wortley, S. (2002). Racial and ethnic minority high school students' perceptions of school disciplinary practices: A look at some Canadian findings. *Journal of Youth and Adolescence, 3,* 185–195.

Rudney, G. (2005). *Every teacher's guide to working with parents.* Thousand Oaks, CA: Corwin.

Rudzek, S. (2005). Interview conducted on October 15, 2005. Lake Oswego, OR.

Rushton, S., & Juola-Rushton, A. (2008). Classroom learning environment, brain research and the No Child Left Behind Initiative: 6 years later. *Early Childhood Education Journal, 36,* 87–92.

Russell, S. (2010). Supportive social services for LGBT students: Lessons from the safe schools movement. *The Prevention Researcher, 17,* 14–16.

Ryan, A., Shim, S., Lampkins-uThando, S., Kiefer, S., & Thompson, G. (2009). Do gender differences in help avoidance vary by ethnicity? An examination of African American and European American students during early adolescence. *Developmental Psychology, 45,* 1152–1163.

Salend, S. (1998). *Effective mainstreaming: Creating inclusive classrooms.* Upper Saddle River, NJ: Merrill/Prentice Hall.

Salmivalli, C., Karna, A., & Poskiparta, E. (2010). Development, evaluation, and diffusion of a national anti-bullying program (KiVa). In B. Doll, W. Pfohl, & J. Yoon (Eds.), *Handbook of youth prevention science.* New York, NY: Routledge.

Sandia National Laboratories. (1993). Future requirements: Workforce skills. *Journal of Educational Research, 86*(5), 293–297.

Sax, L. (2005). *Why gender matters: What parents and teachers need to know about the emerging science of sex differences.* New York, NY: Doubleday.

Scheuermann, G., & Hall, J. (2007). *Positive behavioral supports in the classroom.* Upper Saddle River, NJ: Pearson.

Schmuck, R., & Schmuck, P. (2001). *Group processes in the classroom* (8th ed.). Boston, MA: McGraw-Hill.

Schneider, E. (1996). Giving students a voice in the classroom. *Educational Leadership, 54,* 22–26.

Schrumph, F., Crawford, D., & Usadel, H. (1991). *Peer mediation: Conflict resolution in schools.* Champaign, IL: Research Press.

Schwartz, D., Pettit, G., Dodge, K., & Bates, J. (2000). Friendship as a moderating factor in the pathway between early harsh home environment and later victimization in the peer group. *Developmental Psychology, 36,* 646–662.

Schwartz, L. (2001). *Taking steps towards tolerance and compassion: Creative projects to help kids make a difference.* New York, NY: Learning Works.

Scott, T., Alter, P., & Hirn, R. (2011). An examination of typical classroom context and instruction for students with and without behavioral disorders. *Education and Treatment of Children, 34,* 619–641.

Sebag, R. (2010). Behavior management through self-advocacy: A strategy for secondary students with learning disabilities. *Teaching Exceptional Children, 42,* 22–29.

Seligman, M. (1995). *The optimistic child.* Boston, MA: Houghton Mifflin.

Sergiovanni, T. (1994). *Building community in schools.* San Francisco, CA: Jossey-Bass.

Shade, B. (1989). Afro-American cognitive patterns: A review of the research. In B. Shade (Ed.), *Culture, style, and the educative process.* Springfield, IL: Charles C. Thomas.

Shamow, L., & Miller, J. (2001). Parents' at-home and at-school academic involvement with young adolescents. *Journal of Early Adolescence, 21,* 68–91.

Shannon, P. (1998). *No, David!* New York, NY: Blue Sky Press.

Shea, T., & Bauer, A. (2012). *Behavior management: A practical approach for educators* (10th ed.). Boston, MA: Pearson.

Sheets, R. (1994, February). *Student voice: Factors that cause teacher/student confrontations in a pluralistic classroom.* Paper presented at the annual conference of the National Association of Minority Education, Seattle, WA. ERIC Document Reproduction Service (ED371089).

Sheets, R. (2002). "You're just a kid that's there": Chicano perception of disciplinary events. *Journal of Latinos and Education, 1,* 105–122.

Sheets, R., & Gay, G. (1996). Student perceptions of disciplinary conflict in ethnically diverse classrooms. *NASSP Bulletin, 80,* 84–94.

Sheffield, K., & Waller, R. (2010). A review of single-case studies utilizing self-monitoring interventions to reduce problem classroom behaviors. *Beyond Behavior, 19,* 7–13.

Sherer, Y., & Nickerson, A. (2010). Anti-bullying practices in American schools: Perspectives of school psychologists. *Psychology in the Schools, 47,* 217–229.

Sheridan, S. (1995). *The tough kid social skills book.* Longmont, CO: Sopris West.

Shevalier, R., & McKenzie, B. (2012). Culturally responsive teaching as an ethics- and care-based approach to urban education. *Urban Education, 47,* 1086–1105.

Shinn, M., Stoner, G., & Walker, H. (Eds.). (2002). *Interventions for academic and behavior problems: Preventive and remedial approaches.* Silver Springs, MD: National Association of School Psychologists.

Shirley, E., & Cornell, D. (2011). The contribution of student perceptions of school climate to understanding the disproportionate punishment of African American students in middle school. *School Psychology International, 33,* 115–134.

Shook, A. (2012). A study of preservice educators' dispositions to change behavior management strategies. *Preventing School Failure, 56,* 129–136.

Short, D., Vogt, M., & Echevaria, J. (2008). *Implementing the SIOP model through effective professional development and coaching.* New York, NY: Pearson.

Simonsen, B., Gairbanks, S., Briesch, A., Myers, D., & Sugai, G. (2008). Evidence-based practices in classroom management: Considerations for research to practice. *Education and Treatment of Children, 31,* 351–380.

Simonsen, B., Sugai, G., & Negron, M. (2008). Schoolwide positive behavior supports: Primary systems and practices. *Teaching Exceptional Children, 40,* 32–40.

Singh, K., Bickley, P., & Trivette, P. (1995). The effects of four components of parental involvement on eighth-grade student achievement. *School Psychology Review, 24,* 299–317.

Skerbetz, M., & Kostewicz, K. (2013). Academic choice for included students with emotional and behavioral disorders. *Preventing School Failure, 57,* 212–222.

Skiba, R., & Knesting, K. (2002). Zero tolerance, zero evidence: An analysis of school disciplinary practice. In R. Skiba & G. Noam (Eds.), *Zero tolerance: Can suspension and expulsion keep school safe? New directions for youth development* (pp. 17–43). San Francisco, CA: Jossey-Bass.

Skiba, R., Michael, R., Nardo, A., & Peterson, R. (2002). The color of discipline: Sources of racial and gender disproportionality in school punishment. *The Urban Review, 34,* 317–342.

Skiba, R., Peterson, R., & Williams, T. (1997). Office referrals and suspension: Disciplinary intervention in middle schools. *Education and Treatment of Children, 20,* 295–315.

Slaby, R., Roedell, W., Arezzo, D., & Hendrix, K. (1995). *Early violence prevention: Tools for teachers of young children.* Washington, DC: National Association for the Education of Young Children.

Slavin, R. (1995). *Cooperative learning: Theory, research, and practice.* Boston, MA: Allyn & Bacon.

Slavin, R. (1996). Cooperative learning in middle and secondary schools. *Clearing House, 69,* 200–204.

Slavkin, M. (2004). *Authentic learning: How learning about the brain can shape the development of students.* Lanham, MD: Scarecrow Education.

Sleeter, C. (Ed.). (1991). *Empowerment through multicultural education.* Albany, NY: State University of New York Press.

Smith, B., & Sugai, G. (2000). A self-management functional assessment-based behavior support plan for a middle school student with EBD. *Journal of Positive Behavioral Support, 2,* 208–217.

Smith, G. (Ed.). (1993). *Public schools that work: Creating community.* New York, NY: Routledge.

Smith, G. (2002). Place-based education: Learning where we are. *Phi Delta Kappan, 83,* 584–594.

Smith, G. (2007). Grounding learning in place. *World Watch Magazine, 20,* 20–24.

Smith, W. (1936). *Constructive school discipline.* New York, NY: American Book.

Smolnisky, S. (2009). Are we doing enough: A look at teachers struggling in the classroom. Retrieved from *Dissertation Abstracts International, 70*(12A), 4642: ISBN 978-1-109-52573-1.

Snakenborg, J., Van Acker, R., & Gable, R. (2011). Cyberbullying: Prevention to protect our children and youth. *Preventing School Failure, 55,* 88–95.

Snyder, M., Riese, J., Limber, S., & Mullin, N. (2012). *Class meetings that matter: A year's worth of resources for grades 9–12.* Center City, MN: Hazelden.

Sobel, D. (2004). *Place-based education: Connecting classrooms to communities.* Great Barrington, MA: Orion Society.

Solomon, B., Klein, S., Hintze, J., Cressey, J., & Peller, S. (2012). A meta-analysis of schoolwide positive behavior support: An exploratory study using single-case synthesis. *Psychology in the Schools, 49,* 105–121.

Soodak, L., & McCarthy, M. (2006). Classroom management in inclusive classrooms. In C. Evertson & C. Weinstein (Eds.), *Handbook of classroom management: Research, practice, and contemporary issues* (pp. 461–489). Mahwah, NJ: Lawrence Erlbaum.

Sousa, D. (Ed.). (2010). *Mind, brain, and education: Neuroscience implications for the classroom.* Bloomington, IN: Solution Tree Press.

Sparks, S. (2012). Neuroscientists find learning is not "hard-wired." *Education Week, 31,* 1–17.

Sprenger, M. (2007). *Becoming a "wiz" at brain-based research: How to make every year your best year* (2nd ed.). Thousand Oaks, CA: Corwin Press.

Sprenger, M. (2008). *Differentiated instruction through learning styles and memory* (2nd ed.). Thousand Oaks, CA: Corwin.

Sprenger, M. (2009). Focusing the digital brain. *Educational Leadership, 67,* 34–39.

Sprick, R. (2009). *CHAMPS: A proactive and positive approach to classroom management* (2nd ed.). Eugene, OR: Pacific Northwest Publishing, Inc.

Sprick, R., Booher, M., & Garrison, G. (2009). *Behavioral response to interventions: Creating a continuum of problem solving and support.* Eugene, OR: Pacific Northwest Publishing.

Sprick, R., & Howard, L. (1995). *The teacher's encyclopedia of behavior management: 100 problems/500 plans, for grades K–9.* Longmont, CO: Sopris West.

Starnes, B. (2006). What we don't know can hurt them: White teachers, Indian children. *Phi Delta Kappan, 87,* 384–392.

Steiner, C. (1977). *The original warm fuzzy tale.* Sacramento, CA: Jalmar Press.

Stiggins, R. (2001). *Student-involved classroom assessment* (3rd ed.). Upper Saddle River, NJ: Merrill/Prentice Hall.

Stiles, N. (n.d.). A kingdom with no rules, no laws, and no king. www.geniaconnell.com (search for "kingdom with no rules").

Stipek, D. (1988). *Motivation to learn: From theory to practice.* Englewood Cliffs, NJ: Prentice Hall.

Stone, J. (1991). *Cooperative learning and language arts: A multistructural approach.* San Juan Capistrano, CA: Resources for Teachers.

Stormont, M., Lewis, T. J., & Beckner, R. (2005). Developmentally continuous positive behavior support systems: Applying key features in preschool settings. *Teaching Exceptional Children, 37*(6), 42–49.

Stover, J. (1989). *If everybody did.* Greenville, SC: Journey Forth.

Strickland, K. (2005). *What's after assessment: Follow-up instruction for phonics, fluency, and comprehension.* Portsmouth, NH: Heinemann.

Strout, M. (2005). Positive behavioral support on the classroom level: Considerations and strategies. *Beyond Behavior, 14,* 3–8.

Sturaro, C., van Lier, P., Cuijpers, P., & Koot, H. (2011). The role of peer relationships in the development of early school-age externalizing problems. *Child Development, 8,* 758–765.

Styles, D. (2001). *Class meetings: Building leadership, problem solving, and decision-making skills in the respectful classroom.* Ontario, Canada: Pembroke Publishers.

Suarez-Orozco, C., Pimentel, A., & Martin, M. (2009). The significance of relationships: Academic engagement and achievement among newcomer immigrant youth. *Teachers College Record, 111,* 712–749.

Sugai, G., Horner, R., Algozzine, R., Barrett, S., Lewis, T., Anderson, C., . . . Simonsen, B. (2010). *School-wide positive behavior support: Implementor's blueprint and self-assessment.* Eugene, OR: University of Oregon.

Sugai, G., Horner, R. H., Dunlap, G., Hieneman, M., Lewis, T. J., Nelson, C. M., . . . Ruef, M. (2000). Applying positive behavior support and functional behavioral assessment in schools. *Journal of Positive Behavior Interventions, 2,* 131–143.

Sugai, G., Horner, R., & Gresham, F. (2002). Behaviorally effective school environments. In M. R. Shinn, G. Stoner, & H. M. Walker (Eds.), *Interventions for academic and behavior problems: Preventive and remedial approaches* (pp. 315–350). Silver Springs, MD: National Association of School Psychologists.

Sugai, G., Horner, R., Lewis, T., & Cheney, D. (2002, July). *Positive behavior supports.* Paper presented at the OSEP Research Project Directors' Conference, Washington, DC.

Sullivan, K. (1998). *Peacebuilders action guide.* Tucson, AZ: Heartsprings.

Sullivan, K. (2000). *The anti-bullying handbook.* Auckland, New Zealand: Oxford University Press.

Sullivan, K., Cleary, M., & Sullivan, G. (2004). *Bullying in secondary schools: What it looks like and how to manage it.* Thousand Oaks, CA: Corwin.

Sullivan, L. (1988). Special study groups: Motivating underachievers. *Middle School Journal, 19,* 20–21.

Sutherland, K., & Wehby, J. (2001). Exploring the relationship between increased opportunities to respond to academic requests and the academic and behavioral outcomes of students with EBD. *Remedial and Special Education, 22,* 113–121.

Swearer, S., Espelage, D., Valliancourt, T., & Hymel, S. (2010). What can be done about bullying in schools? *Educational Researcher, 39,* 38–47.

Sylwester, R. (2000). *A biological brain in a cultural classroom.* Thousand Oaks, CA: Corwin Press.

Taylor-Greene, S., Brown, D., Nelson, L., Longton, J., Gassman, T., Cohen, J., . . . Hall, S. (1997). School-wide behavioral support: Starting the year off right. *Journal of Behavioral Education, 7,* 99–112.

Teel, K., Debruin-Parecki, A., & Covington, M. (1998). Teaching strategies that honor and motivate inner-city African American students: A school/university collaboration. *Teaching and Teacher Education, 145,* 479–495.

Tenenbaum, L., Varjas, K., Meyers, J., & Parris, L. (2011). Coping strategies and perceived effectiveness in fourth through eighth grade victims of bullying. *School Psychology International, 32,* 263–287.

Testerman, J. (1996). Holding at-risk students: The secret is one-one-one. *Phi Delta Kappan, 77,* 364–366.

Thomas, W., & Collier, V. (1997). *School effectiveness for language minority students.* Washington, DC: National Clearinghouse of Bilingual Education.

Thorson, S. (2003). *Listening to students: Reflections on secondary classroom management.* Boston, MA: Allyn & Bacon.

Tobin, K. (1987). The role of wait time in higher cognitive level learning. Review of Educational Research, 57, 69–95.

Todd, A., Horner, R., & Sugai, G. (1999). Effects of self-monitoring and self-recruited praise on problem behavior, academic engagement and work completion in a typical classroom. *Journal of Positive Behavior Intervention, 1,* 66–76.

Tofi, M., & Farrington, D. (2011). Effectiveness of school-based programs to reduce bullying: A systemic and meta-analytic review. *Journal of Experimental Criminology, 7,* 27–56.

Tomlinson, C. (2005). *How to differentiate instruction in mixed ability classrooms* (2nd ed.). Upper Saddle River, NJ: Merrill/Prentice Hall.

Tomlinson, C., Brimijoin, K., & Narvaez, L. (2008). *The differentiated school: Making revolutionary changes in teaching and learning.* Alexandria, VA: ASCD.

Tomlinson, C., & McTighe, J. (2006). *Integrating differentiated instruction and understanding by design.* Alexandria, VA: ASCD.

Topper, K., Williams, W., Leo, K., Hamilton, R., & Fox, T. (1994). *A positive approach to understanding and addressing challenging behaviors: Supporting educators and families to include students with emotional and behavioral difficulties in regular education.* Burlington, VT: Center for Developmental Disabilities, University of Vermont.

Trumbell, E., Rothstein-Fisch, C., & Hernandez, E. (2003). Parent involvement in schools: According to whose values? *The Community School Journal, 13,* 45–72.

Tung, I., & Lee, S. (2014). Negative parenting behavior and childhood oppositional defiant disorder: Differential moderation by positive and negative peer regard. *Aggressive Behavior, 40,* 79–90.

Turnbull, A., & Turnbull, H. (1996). *Families, professionals, and exceptionality: A special partnership.* Upper Saddle River, NJ: Merrill.

Twemlow, S., Fonagy, P., Sacco, F., & Brethour, J. (2006). Teachers who bully students: Hidden trauma. *International Journal of Social Psychiatry, 52,* 187–198.

Ullucci, K. (2009). This has to be family: Humanizing classroom management in urban schools. *Journal of Classroom Interaction, 33,* 13–48.

Umphrey, M. (2007). *The power of community-centered education. Teaching as craft of place.* Lanham, MD: Rowman & Littlefield.

U.S. Department of Education. (1994). *Strong families, strong schools: Building community partnerships for learning.* Washington, DC: Author.

U.S. Department of Education. (1997). *Achieving the goals: Goal 8, parental involvement and participation.* Washington, DC: Author.

U.S. Department of Education. (2000). *Effective alternative strategies. Grant competition to reduce student suspensions and expulsions and ensure educational progress of suspended and expelled students.* Washington, DC: Safe and Drug Free Schools Programs (OMB#1818-0551).

U.S. Department of Education. (2014). *Guiding principles: A resource guide for improving school climate and discipline.* Washington, DC: Author.

U.S. Department of Labor. (2000). *Workplace essential skills.* Washington, DC: U.S. Department of Labor, Employment and Training Administration.

U.S. Office of Educational Research and Improvement. (1997). *A guide to community programs to prevent youth violence for parents/about parents.* Washington, DC: U.S. Department of Education.

Valdez, G. (2001). *Learning and not learning English: Latino students in American schools.* New York, NY: Teachers College Press.

Valenzuela, A. (1999). *Subtractive schooling: U.S.-Mexican youth and the politics of caring.* Albany, NY: State University of New York Press.

Van den Berg, Y., Segers, E., & Cillessen, A. (2012). Changing peer perceptions and victimization through classroom arrangements: A field experiment. *Journal of Abnormal Child Psychology, 40,* 403–412.

Van Voorhis, F. (2001). Interactive science homework: An experiment in home and school connection. *National Association of Secondary School Principals' Bulletin, 85,* 20–32.

Van Vugt, E., Dekovic, M., Prinzie, P., Stams, G., & Asscher, J. (2013). Evaluation of a group-based social skills training for children with problem behavior. *Children & Youth Services Review, 35,* 162–167.

Vannest, K., Burke, M., Sauber, S., Davis, J., & Davis, C. (2011). Daily behavior report cards as evidence-based practice for teachers. *Beyond Behavior, 20,* 13–21.

Vaughn, S., Bos, C., & Schumm, J. (1997). *Teaching mainstreamed, diverse, and at-risk students.* Boston, MA: Allyn & Bacon.

Villa, R., & Thousand, J. (2000). *Restructuring for caring and effective education.* Baltimore, MD: Brookes.

Vincent, C., & Tobin, T. (2011). The relationship between implementation of school-wide positive behavior support (SWPBS) and disciplinary exclusion of students from various ethnic backgrounds with and without disabilities. *Journal of Emotional and Behavioral Disorders, 19,* 217–232.

Volpe, R., & Fabriano, G. (2013). *Daily behavior report cards: An evidence-based system of assessment and intervention.* New York, NY: Guilford Press.

Von Mizener, R., & Williams, R. (2009). The effects of student choices on academic performance. *Journal of Positive Behavior Interventions, 11,* 110–128.

Wager, B. R. (1993). No more suspensions: Creating a shared ethical community. *Educational Leadership, 50*(4), 34–37.

Wagner, M., Bos, K., Jascenoka, J., Jekeuc, D., & Patermann, F. (2012). Peer problems mediate the relationship between developmental coordination disorders and behavior problems in school-aged children. *Research in Developmental Disabilities, 33,* 2072–2079.

Walker, H., & Buckley, N. (1973). Teacher attention to appropriate and inappropriate classroom behavior: An individual case study. *Focus on Exceptional Children, 5,* 5–11.

Walker, H., Colvin, G., & Ramsey, E. (1995). *Antisocial behavior in school: Strategies and best practices.* Pacific Grove, CA: Brooks/Cole.

Walker, H., Hops, H., & Fiegenbaum, E. (1976). Deviant classroom behavior as a function of combinations of social and token reinforcement and cost contingency. *Behavior Therapy, 7,* 76–88.

Walker, H., Horner, R., Sugai, G., Bullis, M., Sprague, J., & Bricker, D. (1996). Integrated approaches to preventing antisocial behavior patterns among school-age children and youth. *Journal of Emotional and Behavioral Disorders, 4,* 194–209.

Walker, H., Ramsey, E., & Gresham, F. (2003). *Antisocial behavior in schools: Evidence-based practices.* Pacific Grove, CA: Brooks/Cole.

Walker, H., & Sprague, J. (1999). Longitudinal research and functional behavioral assessment issues. *Behavioral Disorders, 24,* 335–337.

Walker, H., & Sylwester, R. (1998). Reducing students' refusal and resistance. *Teaching Exceptional Children, 30,* 52–58.

Walker, H., & Walker, J. (1991). *Coping with noncompliance in the classroom: A positive approach for teachers.* Austin, TX: Pro-Ed.

Walker, J., & Hoover-Dempsey, K. (2006). Why research on parental involvement is important to classroom management. In C. Evertson & C. Weinstein (Eds.), *Handbook of classroom management: Research, practice, and contemporary issues.* Mahwah, NJ: Lawrence Erlbaum.

Walker, J., Shea, T., & Bauer, A. (2007). *Behavior management: A practical approach for educators* (9th ed.). Upper Saddle River, NJ: Merrill/Prentice Hall.

Wallace, M., Doney, J., Mintz-Resudek, C., & Tarbox, R. (2004). Training educators to implement the functional behavioral assessment process. *Journal of Applied Behavior Analysis, 37,* 89–92.

Walpole, S., & McKenna, M. (2007). *Differentiated reading instruction: Strategies for the primary grades.* New York, NY: Guilford Press.

Walqui, A. (2000). Strategies for success: Engaging immigrant students in secondary schools. ERIC Report (EDO-FLO-OO-03). Washington, DC: Center for Applied Linguistics.

Wang, M. (2009). School climate support for behavioral and psychological adjustment: Testing the mediating effect of social competence. *School Psychology Quarterly, 24,* 240–251.

Wang, M., Haertel, G., & Walberg, H. (1993). Toward a knowledge base for school learning. *Review of Educational Research, 63,* 249–294.

Wang, S., Parrila, R., & Cui, Y. (2013). Meta-analysis of social skills interventions of single-case research for individuals with autism spectrum disorders: Results from three-level HLM. *Journal of Autism and Developmental Disorders, 43,* 1701–1716.

Ware, F. (2006). Warm demander pedagogy: Culturally responsive teaching that supports a culture of achievement for African American students. *Urban Education, 41,* 427–456.

Wasley, P., Fine, M., Gladden, M., Holland, N., King, S., Mosak, E., & Powell, L. (2000). *Small schools: Great strides.* New York, NY: Bank Street College of Education.

Watling, D., & Banerjee, R. (2007). Children's understanding of modesty in front of peer and adult audiences. *Infant and Child Development, 16,* 227–236.

Watson, M., & Ecken, L. (2003). *Learning to trust: Transforming difficult elementary classrooms through developmental discipline.* San Francisco, CA: Jossey-Bass.

Watson, S., & Steege, M. (2003). *Conducting school-based functional behavior assessments.* Columbia, MO: Hawthorne Educational Service.

Wehby, J., Symons, F., & Shores, R. (1995). A descriptive analysis of aggressive behavior in classrooms for children with emotional and behavioral disorders. *Behavioral Disorders, 20,* 87–105.

Wehlage, G., Rutter, R., Smith, G., Lesko, N., & Fernandez, R. (1989). *Reducing the risk: Schools as communities of support.* Philadelphia, PA: Falmer Press.

Weinstein, C. (1998). "I want to be nice, but I have to be mean": Exploring prospective teachers' conceptions of caring and order. *Teaching and Teacher Education, 14,* 153–163.

Weinstein, C. (2003). *Elementary classroom management: Lessons from research and practice.* Boston, MA: McGraw-Hill.

Weinstein, C., Curran, M., & Tomlinson-Clarke, S. (2003). Culturally responsive classroom management: Awareness into action. *Theory into Practice, 42,* 269–277.

Weinstein, C., Tomlinson-Clarke, S., & Curran, M. (2004). Toward a conception of culturally responsive classroom management. *Journal of Teacher Education, 55,* 25–38.

Weinstein, R., Gregory, A., & Strambler, M. (2004). Intractable self-fulfilling prophecies: Brown v. Board of Education. *American Psychologist, 59,* 511–520.

Weis, L., & Centrie, C. (2002). On the power of separate spaces: Teachers and students righting selves and future. *American Educational Research Journal, 39,* 7–36.

Weisz, J., & Kazdin, A. (Eds.). (2010). *Evidence-based psychotherapies for children and adolescents* (2nd ed.). New York, NY: Guilford Press.

Wentzel, K. (2002). Are effective teachers like good parents? Interpersonal predictors of school adjustment in early adolescence. *Child Development, 73,* 287–301.

Wentzel, K. (2003). School adjustment. In W. Reynolds & G. Miller (Eds.), *Handbook of psychology, Vol. 7: Educational psychology* (pp. 235–258). New York, NY: Wiley.

Wentzel, K. (2006). A social motivation perspective for classroom management. In C. Evertson & C. Weinstein (Eds.), *Handbook of classroom management: Research, practice, and contemporary issues.* Mahwah, NJ: Lawrence Erlbaum.

Wentzel, K., Battle, A., & Cusick, L. (2000, March). *Teacher and peer contributions to classroom climate in middle school: Relations to school adjustment.* Paper presented at the annual meeting of the American Educational Association, Seattle, WA.

Wentzel, K., & Wigfield, A. (2007). Motivational interventions that work: Themes and remaining issues. *Educational Psychologist, 42,* 261–271.

Williams, P., Sullivan, S., & Kohn, L. (2012). Out of the mouths of babes: What do secondary students believe about outstanding teachers? *American Secondary Education, 40,* 104–119.

Willis, J. (2006). *Research-based strategies to ignite student learning: Insights from a neurologist and classroom teacher.* Alexandria, VA: Association for Supervision and Curriculum Development.

Willis, J. (2010a). The current impact of neuroscience on teaching and learning. In D. Sousa (Ed.), *Mind, brain & education: Neuroscience implications for the classroom* (pp. 45–66). Bloomington, IN: Solution Tree.

Willis, J. (2010b). Using my neuroscience to treat the sickness in our classrooms. *Catalyst for Change, 36,* 46–55.

Wilmes, B., Harrington, L., Kohler-Evans, P., & Sumpter, D. (2008). Coming to our senses: Incorporating brain research findings into classroom instruction. *Education Digest, 74,* 24–28.

Wisconsin Group. (2014). "Creating trauma sensitive schools." Wisconsin Department of Public Instruction. sspw.dpi.wi.gov.

Wlodkowski, R., & Ginsberg, M. (1995). A framework for culturally responsive teaching. *Educational Leadership, 53,* 17–21.

Wolery, M., Bailey, D., & Sugai, G. (1998). *Effective teaching: Principles and procedures of applied behavior analysis with exceptional students.* Boston, MA: Allyn & Bacon.

Wood, C., & Gross, A. (2002). Behavioral response generation and selection of rejected reactive-aggressive, rejected non-aggressive, and average status children. *Child and Family Behavior Therapy, 24,* 1–19.

Woolfolk, A. E. (1998). *Educational psychology* (7th ed.). Boston, MA: Allyn & Bacon.

Woolfolk Hoy, A., & Weinstein, C. (2006). Students' and teachers' perspectives about classroom management. In C. Evertson & C. Weinstein (Eds.), *Handbook of classroom management: Research, practice, and contemporary issues.* Mahwah, NJ: Lawrence Erlbaum.

Workman, E. (1995). *Teaching behavioral self-control to students* (2nd ed.). Austin, TX: Pro-Ed.

Workplace Essential Skills. (2002). Washington, DC: Employment and Training Administration, Office of Policy and Research, Office of Education Research and Improvement (ED).

Wright, R., & McCurdy, B. (2011). Class-wide positive behavior support and group contingencies: Examining a positive variation of the Good Behavior Game. *Journal of Positive Behavior Interventions, 14,* 173–180.

Wright, T. (2013). "I keep me safe." Risk and resilience in children with messy lives. *Kappan, 95,* 39–43.

Yaffe, E. (1995). Expensive, illegal, and wrong: Sexual harassment in our schools. *Phi Delta Kappan, 77*(3), K1–K15.

Yang, W. (2009). Discipline or punishment? Some suggestions for school policy and teacher practice. *Language Arts, 87,* 49–61.

Young, S., Kelsey, D., & Alexander, L. (2011). Predicted outcome value of e-mail communication: Factors that foster professional relational development between students and teachers. *Communication Education, 60,* 371–388.

Zahorik, J. (1996). Elementary and secondary teachers' reports of how they make learning interesting. *Elementary School Journal, 96,* 551–565.

Zarra, E. (2009). Wired up and fired up: Secondary social studies and the teenage brain. *Social Studies Review, 48,* 68–70.

Zaslaw, J. (2010). Restorative resolution. *Principal Leadership, 10,* 58–62.

Zirpoli, T. (2012). *Behavior management: Positive applications for teachers.* Boston, MA: Pearson.

Zull, J. (2011). *From brain to mind: Using neuroscience to guide change in education.* Herndon, VA: Stylus Publishing.

Name Index

Subject Index